THE ENCYCLOPEDIA OF
Civil War Medicine

THE ENCYCLOPEDIA OF
Civil War
Medicine

GLENNA R. SCHROEDER-LEIN

Routledge
Taylor & Francis Group

LONDON AND NEW YORK

First published 2008 by M.E. Sharpe

Published 2015 by Routledge
2 Park Square, Milton Park, Abingdon, Oxon OX14 4RN
711 Third Avenue, New York, NY 10017, USA

Routledge is an imprint of the Taylor & Francis Group, an informa business

Library of Congress Cataloging-in-Publication Data

Schroeder-Lein, Glenna R., 1951–
  The encyclopedia of Civil War medicine / Glenna R. Schroeder-Lein.
    p. cm.
  Includes bibliographical references and index.
  ISBN 978-0-7656-1171-0 (cloth : alk. paper)
  1. United States—History—Civil War, 1861–1865—Medical care—Encyclopedias.
  2. Medicine, Military—United States—History—19th century—Encyclopedias. I. Title.

E621.S347 2008
973.7'7503—dc22   2007011423

ISBN 13: 9780765621306 (pbk)
ISBN 13: 9780765611710 (hbk)

For

Rhonda B. Schroeder

and

Michael S. Hiranuma

CONTENTS

❦ ACKNOWLEDGMENTS ❦

One of the best parts of writing a book is finishing it and being able to thank those who were so important in the process. Steve Woodworth invited me to do this project after a conference session in February 2002. Andrew Gyory, then acquisitions editor for M.E. Sharpe, saw the proposal through the acceptance process. Years later, Steve Drummond assumed that position and enthusiastically urged the encyclopedia on to completion. Nicole Cirino oversaw the manuscript submission phase, while Angela Piliouras and Henrietta Toth saw it through production. Laurie Lieb copyedited the manuscript.

My colleagues and the resources at the Abraham Lincoln Presidential Library (formerly the Illinois State Historical Library) in Springfield, Illinois, have been absolutely vital to my completion of this project. Kathryn Harris, director of library services, and Jane Ehrenhardt, supervisor of reference and technical services, provided a carrel with a cupboard where I could keep the whole *Medical and Surgical History* and other library books for convenient study and reference on my lunch hour. If someone else needed a Civil War medicine book, they knew where to look! Other members of the reference staff, Gwen Podeschi, Donna Dougherty, Dennis Suttles, and the late Linda Oelheim, rescued me at times when I could not find the books that I knew were downstairs "somewhere." Interlibrary loan librarians Mary Ann Pohl and, more recently, Bob Cavanagh found other material for me that the ALPL did not have. Jim Helm and Mark Johnson helped with illustrations. Thanks to all of them, and also to those on the staff who asked about and expressed interest in my project.

Friends, acquaintances, and fellow researchers provided me with strategic articles and other information. Thanks to Marjorie Baier, Kim Bauer, Pete D'Onofrio, John H. Fahey, Bob Fox, F. Terry Hambrecht, Christopher Losson, Jim Ogden, Gwen Podeschi, Terry Reimer, and Jack Welsh for their generosity. Thanks for answers to specialized questions go to Linda Blakley (on pneumonia), Tom Schwartz (on Lincoln), and Jack Welsh (on many medical issues).

Moral support, a listening ear, and an occasional prod were provided by Debbie Hamm, Cheryl Pence, Cheryl Schnirring, Mabel Lein, Joyce Ashby, Linda Blakley, Carol McKemie, Dave and Martha Reynolds, and Rich and Kathy Thompson. Thank you!

Special thanks go to three people in particular without whom I simply could not have completed this book. Michael "Miguel" Hiranuma, who was my boss years ago and became my friend, read all the articles soon after I finished them, beginning in 2003. He served as the test case for the intelligent general reader to see if my presentations made sense. He also noticed many ways in which the Civil War era was not so different from the U.S. Air Force and the Peace Corps in the 1960s and 1970s. Since I am a historian, not a doctor, I needed a medical reader as well, a task ably performed by Dr. Jack Welsh, who read all the articles in a year and a half and gave me much useful advice. Thank you both!

Spouses are generally left until last, I am convinced, because they deserve the most credit for putting up with all the messes made by a person writing a book. My husband, Lonnie Lein, is no exception. Always our chief bottle-washer, he often became the chief cook too, giving me time to research and write. He filed papers for me, attended to computer tantrums, and generally provided encouragement, for all of which I am most grateful.

This book is dedicated to my sister Rhonda Schroeder and my friend Michael Hiranuma. Both of them have suffered serious medical conditions that could not have been treated at the time of the Civil War.

❧ INTRODUCTION ❧

The American Civil War remains one of the most-studied wars in history. Scholars investigate new perspectives on the conflict, students write term papers about famous battles or generals, and legions of families visit battlefields and museums. Each year a surprising number of people still discover their great-great-grandfather's Civil War diary or letters stashed away in an attic or closet.

The Civil War, like all wars, produced disease, wounds, and death. Approximately two-thirds of the estimated 620,000 soldiers who lost their lives during the war were victims of disease. These medical aspects of the conflict form a greater or lesser part of all accounts, primary or secondary. Explanations may be full of medical terminology. Yet most students of the war are not medical professionals. In addition, medical terminology, perspectives, and treatments have changed since the 1860s. Many researchers therefore simply ignore medical issues or are frustrated by an inability to clarify the problem.

As an example, during my own research for my dissertation, and ultimately first book, on Samuel Hollingsworth Stout and the Confederate Army of Tennessee hospitals behind the lines, I encountered the puzzling term *v.s.* as a cause of admission to the hospital. I eventually discovered that *v.s.* was an abbreviation for *vulnus sclopeticum*, a Latinate term for "gunshot wound."

This need for basic, accurate, and understandable information about Civil War medicine has colored every aspect of my preparation of *The Encyclopedia of Civil War Medicine*. I have tried to make this the book that I wish I had had—handy information, written in lay language. While it is impossible to cover every aspect of Civil War medicine in one volume, I have attempted to be extensive and representative. I present information in many categories, including terms, diseases, wounds, treatments, notable medical personalities, medical offices, generals with notorious wounds, soldiers' aid figures and societies, medical department structure, hospital design and function, the battles with the greatest medical significance, sanitation issues, and other medically related topics. I have attempted to treat both Northern and Southern concerns in a balanced way. Southern information simply is not as complete in many cases, but I have endeavored to include what is known. Although this encyclopedia is aimed at the medical layperson, I trust that even medical professionals will find it a useful reference guide to the Union and Confederate medical departments.

The tendency in the late twentieth and early twenty-first centuries has been to label medicine at the time of the Civil War as primitive. As George Worthington Adams so famously, and perhaps unfortunately, put it in his May 1940 *Journal of Southern History* article, "Confederate Medicine," "The Civil War was fought in the very last years of the medical middle ages."

While no reader of this encyclopedia would wish to be treated by a doctor who had only the knowledge and equipment available in the 1860s, it is important to put the Civil War medical situation in its own context. Medicine has always been a developing, experimental profession. There are always new disease challenges to be met. Medical school provides only a part of the training—all physicians learn on the job. In all eras there are good doctors and bad doctors, the skilled and the unskilled, the perceptive and the clueless, based on the medical knowledge of the period. At the time of the Civil War, doctors no more saw themselves as benighted than doctors do now. It was only with hindsight, after the germ theory had been widely promulgated and accepted, that doctors began to lament the state of medical knowledge during the Civil War.

Of course doctors realized at the time that there were problems they could not solve and that people died as a result. The same situation is still true today, even if sometimes the causes of death have changed. Many Civil War physicians were very skilled for their era and knew much more than modern readers give them credit for. At least some of them did the "right" thing, even if for the "wrong" reason. Some treatments that they used, such as quinine as a preventive and a medication for malaria, still work.

A humble attitude and a sense of context are very helpful when studying Civil War medicine. Most of the people at that time were seeking to do the best they could with what they had, striving to learn from their experiences in order to improve treatments and conditions whenever possible.

In a work of this nature, it is important to explain the sources that I have used. I am not primarily presenting "new" material, but a summary of what is known. That is the definition of an encyclopedia. I have used a variety of published sources, especially primary and secondary sources, because these are materials that an interested researcher could easily find in pursuing a topic further. I have also used censuses, newspapers, and unpublished sources to supply what was lacking for some of the more obscure persons, such as David C. DeLeon, who was briefly Confederate surgeon general. For other people, such as Confederate dentist James Baxter Bean, a single article or book provided all the information available or necessary.

In many instances, however, there is the proverbial "embarrassment of riches"—either many books and articles to choose from or nuggets of information taken from wide reading in many different sources. In these entries the bibliographies do not function as footnotes citing every source that I used. Instead, they list the sources where the researcher will be able to find the most, or the most important, information. While my research is extensive, I make no claims that it is exhaustive. For some topics there is far more material available than is necessary for a summary article.

Of course, not all sources are equal. Some have important tidbits not found anywhere else. Others are readily available, but only mediocre in quality. Still other books and articles present controversial viewpoints, which may provide a valuable perspective.

It is also important to clarify that this is an encyclopedia of Civil War *medicine,* not Civil War generals or the Civil War generally. As a result, I give brief summaries of battles but focus on the medical reasons for which those battles are important. When discussing persons, I concentrate on the medically related reasons for their inclusion. Readers looking for accounts of the presidential careers of Abraham Lincoln and Jefferson Davis will need to find them elsewhere. However, anyone wanting to know about the health of the opposing presidents should find valuable information here.

Because this is an encyclopedia, material is arranged topically. For those who want a narrative overview of Civil War medicine, the best introductions to the Union and Confederate side individually are still George Worthington Adams's *Doctors in Blue* and H.H. Cunningham's *Doctors in Gray.* The best overview of both sides for students and researchers is unquestionably *Civil War Medicine: Challenges and Triumphs* by Alfred Jay Bollet, because it includes much helpful material distilled from *The Medical and Surgical History of the War of the Rebellion,* the massive collection of Union primary sources published between 1870 and 1888.

THE ENCYCLOPEDIA OF
Civil War
Medicine

A

ALCOHOL, ABUSE OF

Alcoholic beverages were very important to many of the soldiers on both sides during the Civil War. The beverage of choice, because it was most readily available, was usually whiskey, although soldiers who imbibed would drink any liquor on hand.

The soldiers' ration sometimes included a certain amount of whiskey on an irregular basis. Men were most likely to receive the ration as a reward for some particularly hard task or to ward off a chill after a long march in the rain. Some officers prohibited alcohol in their camps, and a number of soldiers espoused temperance views, even forming temperance societies. However, the average soldier, of whatever rank, appreciated a drink, and some soldiers drank to excess.

Even when it was difficult to get any or much whiskey in camp or on the march, the determined, crafty soldier was often able to find liquor. Unless restricted for some reason, soldiers in camp for a length of time could often get passes to go to the nearest town or city to buy a few supplies or treats, sightsee, visit friends or relatives, or attend entertainments of various sorts. A substantial number of these soldiers found establishments that sold liquor, and some ended up drunk and disorderly, leading to confinement in the guardhouse or possibly a court-martial. Some enterprising citizens found ways to smuggle alcohol to the troops in camp as well. One woman used false breasts that held a quart of liquor each.

Soldiers also found whiskey at farmhouses near their camp. They might purchase, steal, or, if the neighbors were on the side of the enemy, confiscate the alcohol. Foraging for supplies in enemy country meant raiding stashed liquor, as well as food.

Temptation was often closer to home. Alcoholic beverages were believed to have medicinal value as tonics and stimulants for the sick and wounded. Alcohol also served as a base to which various powdered medications, such as quinine, were added. As a result, regimental doctors and hospitals, whether field or general, had supplies of whiskey. Several doctors, including Charles T. Quintard, reported tricks played on them, even by officers. These shameless fellows swiped and consumed the contents of the canteen of whiskey that the physician took on the march and to the field to treat the sick and wounded.

Getting barrels of alcohol from the medical purveyor to the field or hospital was often a problem as well since soldiers, who knew what the casks contained, had no compunction about tapping all or part of the liquor in transit and refilling the barrel with water. Union assistant surgeon John H. Brinton found a way to combat the problem when he discovered that the barrels of alcohol that he sent to the front to be used to preserve specimens of wounds for the Army Medical Museum were being tampered with. Brinton put some tartar emetic, which causes vomiting, in the whiskey. No one disturbed his alcohol supplies after that.

It was also difficult to keep whiskey in the hospital for the needs of the patients. Attendants, from the surgeons down to the nurses and laundresses, could misappropriate it for their own use. While some did become drunk, others simply took an occasional nip. A dishonest steward might sell the medicinal alcohol for his own profit. Attempts to keep control of the whiskey supply by giving the key to the whiskey storage to a female matron led to a constant battle of will between one matron, Phoebe Pember, and the male staff members at Chimborazo Hospital in Richmond, Virginia.

Various punishments were administered to those who abused or stole alcohol. Illicit alcohol could be confiscated and either poured out or appropriated to other use. In the Washington, DC, area, confiscated alcohol was redistilled for use in shipping specimens to the Army Medical Museum. A drunken private might spend some time in the guardhouse or receive other punishment. An officer with alcohol problems could face a court-martial. Samuel H. Stout, medical director of general hospitals for the Confederate Army of Tennessee, reported that when he found out that a medical officer had been drunk, he gave the man a choice between resigning his commission and being court-martialed.

Although there are no exact figures, alcohol abuse created many problems for both the Union and Confederate armies. From May 1861 to June 30, 1865, 124 white Union soldiers were discharged from the army on a surgeon's certificate of disability for alcoholism. At least seventeen Federal and ten Confederate generals were dismissed or permanently injured their careers because of alcohol problems. These figures are surely only a small indication of a much larger problem.

See also: Alcohol, Medicinal Uses of; Army Medical Museum; Brinton, John Hill; Chimborazo Hospital; Hospitals, Field; Hospitals, General; Matrons; Medical Purveyors; Pember, Phoebe Yates Levy; Quinine; Quintard, Charles Todd; Stout, Samuel Hollingsworth; Tartar Emetic.

Bibliography

Brinton, John H. *Personal Memoirs of John H. Brinton, Civil War Surgeon, 1861–1865.* New York: Neale, 1914; reprint, Carbondale: Southern Illinois University Press, 1996.

Henry, Robert S. *The Armed Forces Institute of Pathology: Its First Century, 1862–1962.* Washington, DC: Government Printing Office, 1964.

Lowry, Thomas P., and Jack D. Welsh. *Tarnished Scalpels: The Court-Martials of Fifty Union Surgeons.* Mechanicsburg, PA: Stackpole, 2000.

Pember, Phoebe Yates. *A Southern Woman's Story: Life in Confederate Richmond*. 1879; reprint, ed. Bell Irvin Wiley. Jackson, TN: McCowat-Mercer Press, 1959; reprint, Covington, GA: Mockingbird, 1974.

Quintard, Charles Todd. *Doctor Quintard, Chaplain C.S.A. and Second Bishop of Tennessee: The Memoir and Civil War Diary of Charles Todd Quintard*. Sewanee, TN: University Press of Sewanee, 1905; reprint, ed. Sam Davis Elliott. Baton Rouge: Louisiana State University Press, 2003.

Schroeder-Lein, Glenna R. *Confederate Hospitals on the Move: Samuel H. Stout and the Army of Tennessee*. Columbia: University of South Carolina Press, 1994.

Street, James, Jr. "Under the Influence: Did Civil War Soldiers Depend on Drugs and Alcohol?" *Civil War Times Illustrated* 27 (May 1988): 30–35.

Wiley, Bell Irvin. *The Life of Billy Yank: The Common Soldier of the Union*. Garden City, NY: Doubleday, 1952, 1971.

ALCOHOL, MEDICINAL USES OF

Alcohol was a key ingredient of Civil War medicine, both North and South. In its straight beverage form, such as whiskey, alcohol was considered, both by doctors and civilians, to be an important stimulant, in a positive sense. Whiskey, brandy, sherry, wine, cordials, or whatever other liquor happened to be available was used in small doses to strengthen patients suffering from debility, fever, shock after being wounded or operated on, scurvy, depression, and other weakened conditions. Alcoholic beverages were seen as a tonic. Even soldiers in the field, who were not sick, were supposed to receive an occasional whiskey ration to keep them in good health.

Alcohol was also used as a base for liquid medicines. Powders such as quinine or opium were dissolved in whiskey or another form of alcohol. Alcohol also had external medicinal uses. It was diluted for use in lotions, gargles, and eyewashes. Unfortunately, it was not commonly used to wipe or clean any surface where, as is now known, its germ-killing abilities would have been most helpful. Alcohol was also used in the North as a preserving liquid in which to transport specimens of wounded and diseased anatomy to the Army Medical Museum.

At times it was difficult for doctors on both sides to get enough alcohol in any form. It was supposed to be procured through the medical purveyors, who often did not have enough on hand to ship. Theft was a big problem because whiskey, particularly, was stolen, and often diluted, in transit or in the storeroom. Especially in the Confederacy, not enough whiskey was manufactured, even though the government established several distilleries in an attempt to provide adequate supplies of alcohol of proper quality. Without enough alcohol, patient care suffered.

See also: Alcohol, Abuse of; Antiseptics and Disinfectants; Army Medical Museum; Debilitas; Diet, of Hospital Patients; Gunshot Wounds, Treatment of; Laboratories, Medical; Laudanum; Medical Purveyors; Medication, Administration of; Morphine; Opiate Use and Addiction; Quinine; Scurvy.

Bibliography

Bollet, Alfred Jay. *Civil War Medicine: Challenges and Triumphs.* Tucson, AZ: Galen, 2002.

Flannery, Michael A. *Civil War Pharmacy: A History of Drugs, Drug Supply and Provision, and Therapeutics for the Union and Confederacy.* New York: Pharmaceutical Products Press, 2004.

ALCOTT, LOUISA MAY (1832–1888)

Louisa May Alcott, popular author and, briefly, Civil War nurse, was born in Germantown, Pennsylvania, on November 29, 1832, the second of the four daughters of Bronson and Abigail May Alcott. She was an active, observant, tomboyish child, educated by her father, his friends, and sometimes local schools. Bronson Alcott was an impractical dreamer and philosopher whose inability to retain a paying job kept the family in genteel poverty, moving frequently, and relying on the charity of friends in the Boston and Concord, Massachusetts, areas. Nevertheless, Louisa and her sisters had a happy childhood, providing the basis for many of the scenes of Alcott's most famous work, *Little Women*. The sisters counted Ralph Waldo Emerson, Henry David Thoreau, and other literary notables as friends and important influences in their lives.

To help the family finances, Alcott worked as a servant, taught school, and sewed. She also wrote in a variety of formats—poetry, plays, sketches, short stories, and sensational tales—many of which were published, usually under a pseudonym.

With the outbreak of the Civil War, Alcott wanted to serve the Union cause by doing more than sewing jackets and picking lint for bandages. In the fall of 1862 she applied for work as a nurse. Assigned to the Union Hotel Hospital in Georgetown, DC, she began work on December 13, just a couple of days before the wounded arrived from the Battle of Fredericksburg. As a nurse, she bathed patients' faces and hands, helped doctors change dressings, gave medicine, fed patients, supervised the convalescent soldiers working as nurses, made rounds at night, and comforted the sick and dying. After less than one month, she contracted typhoid fever and became so ill that she had to be taken home to Concord, where she remained quite sick until March 1863. Alcott was fortunate; her supervisor, Hannah Ropes, also contracted typhoid or pneumonia and died on January 20, 1863.

During her convalescence, Alcott used her letters and memory to write a series of "Hospital Sketches," which were published in *The Commonwealth* beginning May 22, 1863. They were issued in book form in August 1863 and proved to be quite popular. This was Alcott's first experience with writing stories based on fact rather than her imagination. She disguised names, calling herself "Tribulation Periwinkle," and omitted a few disreputable nurses, but otherwise recounted her personal experiences.

Alcott continued to write a variety of fiction, including sensational stories published under pseudonyms, in order to support her parents and youngest sister. With the publication of *Little Women* in two parts in 1868 and 1869, Alcott became a famous, popular author. Her writings were soon in much demand, both by periodical editors desiring sketches and stories and by publishers requesting novels. She never had to hunt for a publisher or worry about money again. Always observing characters, locations, and incidents that could find a place in her stories, Alcott wrote other novels, such as *Eight Cousins* and *Little Men,* as well as many short stories, published first in magazines and later in collections.

Her last years were saddened by the death of her mother (1877) and her sister May (1879), whose infant daughter Louisa, known as Lulu, Alcott raised for several years. As a result of the constant care for her family and overwork at her writing, Alcott suffered from increasingly poor health and restricted activities for several years. She died, probably of a stroke, on March 6, 1888, in Roxbury, Massachusetts.

See also: Fredericksburg, Battle of; Hospitals, General; Nurses; Typhoid Fever; Women, as Hospital Workers.

Bibliography

Alcott, Louisa May. *Hospital Sketches.* 1863; reprint, Boston: Applewood, 1986.
Brumgardt, John R., ed. *Civil War Nurse: The Diary and Letters of Hannah Ropes.* Knoxville: University of Tennessee Press, 1980.
Stern, Madeleine B. *Louisa May Alcott: A Biography.* Norman: University of Oklahoma Press, 1950, 1978; reprint, New York: Random, 1996.

ALTERNATIVE MEDICINES

During the mid-nineteenth century there were a number of competing medical theories whose partisans were struggling to gain predominance and whose conflicts affected medical care for Civil War soldiers.

The mainstream physicians were the allopaths, also known as regular or orthodox physicians. Most of the leading medical schools in the United States were "regular." Physicians of all types believed that improper liver function caused many diseases because of an imbalance of bile secretion. This problem could be fixed, according to the allopaths, by the administration of medications in large doses, particularly such mercury-based remedies as calomel. Unfortunately, such remedies actually could cause more problems than the original disease. The allopaths believed in purging the digestive system with medicines that caused vomiting and loose bowels. Fevers called for depleting the system through drawing blood. It never occurred to the doctors that patients needed fluids when they were dehydrated. Many of the allopathic principles were based on the teachings of the noted Philadelphia physician Benjamin Rush in the 1790s. Although they did not see themselves as such, the allopaths were as much a medical sect as other groups, because allopathic principles were not based on scientific observation, which had just recently begun to be promoted as the foundation of medical knowledge, especially in France, in the 1840s. In 1847 the allopaths formed the American Medical Association as part of their effort to control and standardize medical practice on regular principles. However, for a number of years the association did not have very much influence.

All the other medical sects were opposed to the allopaths because they saw the harmful effects of "heroic" doses of medicine, believing (correctly) that many patients had actually been killed by bleeding and purging. These other sects were all some variation of botanical physicians, using only medicines made from plants, rather than minerals. (Allopathic physicians also used some plant medicines.) One historian has estimated that in 1860 there was about one sectarian physician for every ten regulars, but the proportions depended upon the region of the country.

Samuel Thomson (1769–1843) originated the earliest of the American botanic sects. Although he opposed the use of calomel and similar medicines, he did advocate cleaning out the digestive system with emetics and purgatives made from plant products. Thomsonians criticized regular doctors and their practices, but did not set up competing medical schools. Instead, Thomsonianism flourished in rural and frontier areas, practiced by self-trained doctors or simply by family members who had read Thomson's book *New Guide to Health; or the Botanic Family Physician* (1822). By the time of the Civil War, Thomsonian ideas heavily influenced other medical groups, but Thomsonians were no longer a competing medical sect.

Homeopathy was a medical system devised by a German physician, Samuel Christian Hahnemann (1755–1843). He opposed bloodletting and heroic drug doses while espousing good hygiene, exercise, a healthy diet, and fresh air as preventive measures. His system was based on two principles. The idea that "like cures like" meant that if a medicine caused a symptom in a healthy person, it would cure that symptom in a sick one. The other principle was the "law of infinitesimals"—the smaller the dose, the better the cure. The tiny, diluted drug doses administered by homeopaths essentially left healing to nature and were better for patients than the dangerous heroic doses of the regulars. Homeopathy was introduced to the United States in 1825; the first American homeopathic college opened in 1835. Homeopathy, particularly popular with the middle and upper classes, was the largest of the medical sects at the time of the Civil War.

The eclectics, a medical sect founded by Wooster Beach (1794–1859), tended to be better educated than the other sectarians, either at allopathic schools or at eclectic medical colleges, founded in the 1830s and 1840s. Eclectics borrowed whatever elements of other medical systems were practical or seemed to work, such as botanical remedies. Eclectic schools admitted students with limited financial resources and also accepted women students. Civil War physician Mary Walker, for example, was a graduate of an eclectic institute. Eclectic physicians often practiced in rural areas, especially in the Midwest. The Eclectic Medical Institute in Cincinnati, founded in 1845, was the main eclectic college. By the 1850s about one-quarter of the physicians in Ohio were eclectics.

Any of the medical sects might also advocate hydropathy, the water cure. The administration of large amounts of water, both inside and outside the patient, is an ancient remedy, but it was first introduced to the United States as a medical treatment in 1843. Hydropathy soon became very popular; more than 200 water cure institutes were established between 1843 and 1870. These water cure institutes also promoted other general health practices such as mild exercise, fresh air, and diets, including that advocated by Sylvester Graham, focusing on whole grains and fresh fruits and vegetables.

Although the allopaths regarded the members of all these alternative medical sects as quacks, other medical practitioners actually *were* charlatans. These included dispensers of heavily alcoholic patent medicines, which were usually claimed to cure an impossible variety of ailments, and phrenologists, who made their prognostications based on the types of bumps on the patient's head.

By the time of the Civil War, the regulars were engaged in a war of medical politics, especially against the homeopaths and the eclectics, their nearest competitors. Regulars had already kept homeopaths from getting hospital posts in the 1850s, and during the war the allopaths wanted to make sure that the sectarians were not selected to treat soldiers in hospitals or on the field.

Although medical sects existed in the South as well as the North, the controversies and power struggles during the Civil War seemed to be problems only in the North. To receive military medical commissions, Southern doctors had to be medical school graduates, but the type of school was not specified. All the leading medical officers had graduated from allopathic schools. However, in the period before the war, many Southerners had accepted the idea that Southerners were different from Northerners and thus had distinctive medical needs to be treated in particularly Southern ways. Southerners were also more attuned to botanical resources as substitutes for imported medicines that were no longer available because of the Union's blockade of Southern ports.

In the North, the allopaths controlled the officials and boards making medical appointments during the Civil War, leading to policies that refused appointments to sectarian physicians. Besides issues of power, control, and income, the allopaths were concerned about standardization of medicines and avoided stocking those botanicals that were prescribed only by the sectarians.

One of the problems at the time of the war was the lack of objective standards to distinguish "good" doctors from "bad" ones. Many of the homeopaths and eclectics were at least as well if not better educated than their regular counterparts. Some had even graduated from allopathic colleges before espousing sectarian medical ideas. The conflict was really about medical politics rather than scientific knowledge or skills. Standards were not evenly applied during medical board examinations, and at least fifty sectarians gained Union commissions by stressing their regular qualifications and not mentioning their sectarian background. Others served as stewards or ward masters, while some, like Mary Walker, served temporarily as acting assistant (contract) surgeons. Walker's case was complicated because she was a woman as well as an eclectic.

Several legislators attempted to make it possible for sectarians to gain official positions during the Civil War. James W. Grimes of Iowa introduced a bill in the U.S. Senate to put homeopaths in charge of several military hospitals, but the allopaths protested and prevented its passage. In May 1862 allopaths also protested a bill in the Ohio state senate that permitted any medical school graduate, not just allopathic graduates, to be eligible for a military medical commission. Also in 1862 a woman named Lavinia Payne received permission from Secretary of War Edwin M. Stanton to open a homeopathic hospital for Union soldiers in Virginia. However, Surgeon General William A. Hammond promptly shut it down because it would allegedly cause confusion by forcing the Union medical department to include other medical "isms."

These restrictions contributed to a shortage of doctors in the Union army during the war. In that sense the soldiers suffered because sectarians were not given commissions. The sectarians studied and practiced surgery and amputation in the same way as regulars, although they may have amputated less frequently. Sectarians would have used the same medicines in the standard supply table as the other physicians, although they might have prescribed less and let nature take its course more often.

The biggest sectarian medical conflict of the war was provoked by Surgeon General Hammond when he, a regular physician, issued an order that pleased sectarians and outraged regulars. Circular No. 6, issued on May 4, 1863, removed calomel and antimony from the medical supply table because Hammond believed these remedies were being overused, to the detriment of the patients. While sectarians of all sorts heartily commended the circular, allopaths howled with rage, accusing Hammond of betraying the medical profession because the use of calomel was an important distinctive of the regulars. This perceived insult to the regular physicians, both military and civilian, and the uproar it caused, helped lead to Hammond's removal from the post of surgeon general.

The homeopathic and eclectic sects survived the war and flourished until the late nineteenth century, when many of them merged with the regular physicians. By this time all three groups were basing their practices on the findings of scientific research so there was little difference among them. In the twenty-first century, osteopaths, chiropractors, and some homeopaths remain of the irregular groups of the nineteenth century.

See also: Amputation; Blockade; Calomel; Education, Medical; Examining Boards, Medical; Hammond, William Alexander; Materia Medica; *Resources of the Southern Fields and Forests;* Stewards, Hospital; Substitutes, for Supplies; Supply Table; Surgeons, Acting Assistant (Contract); Tartar Emetic; Walker, Mary Edwards; Ward Masters.

Bibliography

Duffy, John. *From Humors to Medical Science: A History of American Medicine.* 2nd ed. Urbana: University of Illinois Press, 1993.

Flannery, Michael A. "Another House Divided: Union Medical Service and Sectarians During the Civil War." *Journal of the History of Medicine* 54 (October 1999): 478–510.

Haller, John S., Jr. *Medical Protestants: The Eclectics in American Medicine, 1825–1939.* Carbondale: Southern Illinois University Press, 1994.

AMBULANCE CORPS

Neither side had an organized system of removing the wounded from the field when the Civil War began. Although some ambulances were available through the army's quartermaster department, those that accompanied the Union forces to the First Battle of Bull Run (Manassas) on July 21, 1861, were driven by civilians, many of whom became drunk and deserted their posts without taking the wounded back to Washington, DC. A wagon train had to be improvised and sent for the wounded several days later.

Union Army of the Potomac medical director Charles S. Tripler proposed the establishment of an ambulance corps in the fall of 1861, but nothing was done to set one up. As a result, Union troops suffered agonies in the poorly coordinated evacuations of the sick and wounded during the Peninsula Campaign in Virginia in May and June 1862. A wounded soldier was most likely to receive treatment in time if some of his comrades took him to a medical station or field hospital. This practice, however, removed not only the wounded man, but also one to four other soldiers from the fighting for at least a time, if not for the rest of the battle.

When Jonathan Letterman became medical director for the Army of the Potomac in July 1862, he immediately devised an ambulance corps. General George B. McClellan ordered this corps established on August 2, 1862, by General Orders No. 147. The ambulance service was organized on the basis of each army corps and headed by a captain. First lieutenants directed the ambulances at the division level, a second lieutenant managed each brigade's ambulances, and sergeants were in charge of the regimental ambulances. Each regiment was to have one medical supply transportation cart, one four-horse ambulance, and two two-horse ambulances. Each ambulance was supposed to contain two litters and be served by a driver and two stretcher-bearers with the rank of private. These men were to be trained for their duties rather than being regimental musicians doing medical service, hospital attendants taken from other work, or unwounded soldiers who happened to be on the scene. The system would also keep the unwounded soldiers in battle because someone would be caring for their wounded comrades.

The ambulances of each division were to stay together, to be used solely for medical purposes, and to be under the control of the medical director. These rules would eliminate the problem of quartermasters commandeering ambulances for nonmedical uses, such as hauling officers' baggage, making the vehicles unavailable for the sick and wounded.

The Battle of Antietam on September 17, 1862, provided the first test for the new ambulance corps. Although the corps was not yet fully organized, 300 ambulances managed to clear the wounded from the field in two days. The service was much better organized by the time of the Battle of Fredericksburg in December 1862. Nearly 1,000 ambulances and their attendants removed all the wounded from the field in twelve hours.

Surgeon General William A. Hammond recommended that an ambulance corps should be established in the western armies also. Secretary of War Edwin M. Stanton and Union army commander Henry W. Halleck rejected the idea. Nevertheless, General Ulysses S. Grant issued General Orders No. 22 on March 30, 1863, setting up an ambulance corps for the Army of the Tennessee. On March 11, 1864, the U.S. Congress passed legislation making the ambulance corps official. Stanton issued General Orders No. 106 five days later, standardizing the army ambulance corps. By this time, however, the armies had already established ambulance services of their own.

As of April 1864, the ambulance corps of the Union army's Fifth Corps consisted of 17 commissioned officers, 550 enlisted men, 171 two-horse ambulances, 62 supply wagons, 11 medicine wagons, 528 horses, and 348 mules.

In the Confederacy, the Richmond Ambulance Committee, organized in the spring of 1862, seems to have been the first concerted effort to bring order to the transportation chaos on either side. About 100 prominent Richmond men, exempted from military duty, volunteered for ambulance service at their own expense. They had thirty-nine ambulances at the Battle of Williamsburg (Virginia) on May 5, 1862, and continued to provide vital aid to the Army of Northern Virginia during the other battles of the Peninsula Campaign.

The official Confederate ambulance corps was supposed to be made up of twenty men per regiment, or two drawn from each company. Technically, the Confederates assigned two ambulances to a regiment, but more often had to use ordinary wagons. Ambulances were hard to get and the Confederates used those captured from the Union. In addition, there was usually a shortage of horses and mules to pull the vehicles. The Confederates improvised as well as they could, despite severe shortages that made medical transportation difficult.

See also: Ambulances; Antietam, Battle of; Bull Run (Manassas), First Battle of; Bull Run (Manassas), Second Battle of; Fredericksburg, Battle of; Hammond, William Alexander; Hospitals, Field; Letterman, Jonathan; Peninsula Campaign; Quartermasters; Stretchers; Tripler, Charles Stuart.

Bibliography

Bollet, Alfred Jay. *Civil War Medicine: Challenges and Triumphs.* Tucson, AZ: Galen, 2002.

Cunningham, H.H. *Doctors in Gray: The Confederate Medical Service.* Baton Rouge: Louisiana State University Press, 1958; reprint, Gloucester, MA: Peter Smith, 1970.

Duncan, Louis C. *The Medical Department of the United States Army in the Civil War.* Washington, DC: Author, 1914; reprint, Gaithersburg, MD: Butternut, 1985.

Haller, John S., Jr. *Farmcarts to Fords: A History of the Military Ambulance, 1790–1925.* Carbondale: Southern Illinois University Press, 1992.

Wood, Thomas Fanning. *Doctor to the Front: The Recollections of Confederate Surgeon Thomas Fanning Wood, 1861–1865*, ed. Donald B. Koonce. Knoxville: University of Tennessee Press, 2000.

AMBULANCE TRAINS

Railroads were extremely important during the Civil War for shipping food, supplies, ammunition, and troops. They were also used to remove sick and wounded soldiers from the field to general hospitals behind the lines.

Shipping conditions varied depending upon the number of patients to be sent, the number of cars available, the supplies used, and the season of the year. Some patients were simply placed on the bare floorboards of regular boxcars or flatcars, without food, water, or attendants, and sent away. Extreme crowding, lack of stoves and blankets in winter, and filthy cars that had not been cleaned after hauling cows or other livestock made journeys nearly unbearable for some soldiers. Railroad engineers and conductors often contributed to the misery by stopping the trains in inconvenient places, stopping and starting with a jerk, failing to allow enough time to load the patients properly, or delaying a train full of the wounded. In other instances, however, soldiers were transported with all possible care in cars padded with pine tops or several feet of straw covered with blankets.

Both the North and the South designed special ambulance cars that were used with some success. The first known ambulance cars were developed in Missouri in September 1861 by order of General John C. Frémont. Two freight cars with berths, cooking facilities, and nurses transported patients from the army to St. Louis daily. In other locations, stretchers were hung from the car ceiling by ropes, an arrangement that tended to make the soldiers occupying them feel uneasy. In another Northern design, two or three stretchers, one above the other, were lashed to upright posts. The Army of the Cumberland (Union) operated three hospital trains of ten to twelve cars each during the Atlanta campaign in Georgia in 1864. Each car held thirty patients reclining. Instead of boxcars, the army used day coaches, turning two seats to face each other and covering the space with slats and a bed sack for a mattress. For upper bunks, stretchers were suspended from rods in the walls and roof. The army made these trains distinctive externally as well by painting the engines red and using three red lights at night. Apparently Confederate raiders did not attack them.

The Confederate Army of Tennessee had already used its own ambulance train on the Western and Atlantic Railroad between Chattanooga and Atlanta, beginning in January 1863. These cars had berths, evidently more permanent than the stretchers used by the North. Unfortunately, soldiers in the top bunks could find themselves jostled out of their beds by rough tracks or jerky stops and starts. The Confederate hospital train had several assistant surgeons permanently assigned to the train service, assisted as necessary by contract surgeons and hospital stewards. Their duties were to care for the patients en route, supervise the nurses, make sure everything was clean, and keep records and make reports about each trip. One of the assistant surgeons died in an ambulance train accident in 1864.

While train travel could be extremely uncomfortable for wounded patients, it was usually preferable to a trip by a horse-drawn ambulance.

See also: Ambulances; Hospital Relocations; Hospital Ships; Hospitals, General; Mortality, of Surgeons; Stretchers; Surgeons, Assistant.

Bibliography

Duncan, Louis C. *The Medical Department of the United States Army in the Civil War.* Washington, DC: Author, 1914; reprint, Gaithersburg, MD: Butternut, 1985.

Hawk, Alan. "An Ambulating Hospital: or, How the Hospital Train Transformed Army Medicine." *Civil War History* 48 (September 2002): 197–219.

Parrish, William E. "The Western Sanitary Commission." *Civil War History* 36 (March 1990): 17–35.

Schroeder-Lein, Glenna R. *Confederate Hospitals on the Move: Samuel H. Stout and the Army of Tennessee.* Columbia: University of South Carolina Press, 1994.

AMBULANCES

The Union medical department began the Civil War with almost no ambulances, but during the conflict developed an organized ambulance system with specialized vehicles and trained personnel. In previous American wars the wounded were transported in ordinary wagons or farmcarts. The army had no ambulances at all until 1859. In that year an army board selected several designs, based on ambulances used by European armies during the Crimean War, for testing by troops in the West.

When the Civil War began, ambulances were in short supply. General Irvin McDowell had only fifty for his Union army of 35,000 at First Bull Run (Manassas) in July 1861. Most of these ambulances were of a two-wheeled type, pulled by one or two horses or mules. These vehicles held three patients at the most and were sheer torture for those who had to ride in them. They jarred the patients unmercifully going over rutted or corduroy (log) roads. The ambulances frequently broke down or overturned, further injuring the wounded. Soldiers who had ridden in them nicknamed them "avalanches" or "gutbusters."

By the second year of the war, two-wheeled ambulances had been almost entirely replaced by four-wheeled vehicles. These came in two basic types: a light, two-horse variety and a heavier, four-horse type, modeled on an army wagon, which could carry more patients. Within these basic types were a number of variations. Most of these ambulances had springs. The largest could carry four to six men lying on stretchers, including two suspended on straps from the roof, as well as a number of patients who were able to sit up. Army boards developed new designs and modifications throughout the war, but thanks to the poor roads, ambulance travel was never very comfortable. It was always desirable to take the patients the shortest distance possible to a railroad or boat for further transportation.

With the establishment of an organized ambulance corps in the Army of the Potomac in August 1862, followed by the other armies the next year, the Union medical department developed a standard number of ambulances per regiment and had less need to rely on general-purpose wagons. The ambulances were also reserved for medical needs rather than subject to impressment for other uses, such as carrying an officer's baggage. However, when dignitaries visited an army, they were usually provided with an ambulance for transportation.

In the Confederacy, the plan was to have two ambulances for each regiment. However, this standard was rarely, if ever, met. Richmond, Virginia, did have an ambulance factory, but it could not meet the need. Confederates used ambulances captured from the Union forces, but mainly relied on army wagons, farm wagons, carriages, or whatever wheeled vehicles could be rented or impressed. After the battle of Chickamauga in September 1863, Confederate wounded were removed from the battlefield in wagons padded with pine branches. Members of the Confederate medical department frequently had trouble getting any vehicles to transport the sick and wounded, and they often saw their prize appropriated by a quartermaster for hauling other supplies. The Confederacy always had a transportation shortage, which only worsened as the war continued.

See also: Ambulance Corps; Ambulance Trains; Antietam, Battle of; Bull Run (Manassas), First Battle of; Chickamauga, Battle of; Hospital Ships; Letterman, Jonathan; Quartermasters.

Bibliography

Bollet, Alfred Jay. *Civil War Medicine: Challenges and Triumphs.* Tucson, AZ: Galen, 2002.
Haller, John S. *Farmcarts to Fords: A History of the Military Ambulance, 1790–1925.* Carbondale: Southern Illinois University Press, 1992.
Schroeder-Lein, Glenna R. *Confederate Hospitals on the Move: Samuel H. Stout and the Army of Tennessee.* Columbia: University of South Carolina Press, 1994.

AMPUTATION

Amputation was the most radical treatment for gunshot wounds of the extremities used by both sides during the Civil War. The standard impression of Civil War amputation features a blood-covered doctor, a heartless butcher unnecessarily lopping off an arm or leg and tossing it onto a pile of severed limbs. Unquestionably such scenes occurred after battles when thousands of wounded needed urgent care. However, except after the early battles when some novice doctors evidently amputated simply to gain experience, senior surgeons performed most of these operations. The majority of Civil War surgeries involved bullet removal and wound cleaning rather than amputations.

Doctors established certain criteria for determining whether a patient required an amputation. Because minié balls, the bullets most commonly used during the war, were made of soft lead and tended to distort on contact, they created larger entrance and exit wounds, tore and mangled tissue, and shattered bones, rather than simply breaking them. These conditions, along with severe damage to major nerves and blood vessels, made the soldier a candidate for amputation.

Because of the vast number of wounded after a battle, doctors often had to make very quick treatment choices for the patients, based only on a visual and probe (often with fingers) analysis of the wound. Doctors had to consider whether a soldier might be able to function better with an artificial limb rather than a useless natural one. Furthermore, the risks of severe bleeding and infection in the wound might be so great that it was better to sacrifice the arm or leg in order to save the patient's life. Wounded men who had "primary" amputations (within the first forty-eight hours) usually had a better survival rate than those who suffered "intermediate" amputation (three days to a month) or "secondary" amputation (more than a month after being wounded). Therefore, if a patient would probably need an amputation, doctors generally performed it at once, if possible, rather than waiting to see if the wound might heal on its own and then operating during a higher risk period if it did not. As a result, most amputations were performed in field hospitals. Doctors in general hospitals were more likely to perform secondary operations for patients with serious infections, such as hospital gangrene, hemorrhages, or stumps that were not healing properly. The higher risk rate for intermediate amputations probably resulted from blood loss, poor nutrition, and infections that involved the whole body, not just the wound.

Another factor that affected patient risk and survival was the location of the wound and the amputation. Generally, the further the amputation was from the trunk of the body, the better the patient's chance for survival. Arm amputees had a better survival rate than leg amputees. However, amputations at a joint caused increased risk. Amputations at the hip had the highest mortality rate of all.

There were two types of amputation: circular and flap. Neither was performed by the surgeon alone. He always had several helpers. Preferably, an assistant administered anesthesia (chloroform, if possible), another held the main artery closed, while a third supported the limb as the doctor cut the tissue and bone. The first assistant tied the arteries closed while the surgeon sewed the stump. Some surgeons could perform an amputation in two minutes.

The two varieties of amputation differed in the treatment of the tissues and skin. In a circular amputation the tissue and skin were rolled up like a sleeve or cuff. After the muscle and bone were cut, the cuff was rolled down and sewn closed to form the stump. The flap amputation involved cutting the skin and tissue in such a way as to leave two long flaps that would be folded and sewn back over the end of the bone.

Each method had its advocates and its advantages. The circular operation was generally preferred by the Confederates, who saw it as more efficient. It left less

16

tissue to become infected, cut fewer blood vessels, resulted in less pain from scar tissue, and healed more quickly, and patients with circular amputations generally were easier to transport. Union surgeons more often preferred the flap method, which could be performed faster and left more soft tissue to cover the stump. In many cases, however, the nature and location of the wound affected the choice of amputation method. Either could produce a useful stump. However, a poorly done surgery could cause the bone end eventually to protrude through the stump, so that a second, higher amputation might be necessary to solve the problem.

After the amputation, the doctor covered the stump with a dressing, although some left the wound open to drain. Sometimes the stump was supported by starch or plaster splints to keep the bone still and promote healing. Opiates and whiskey were administered to control pain.

In the later period of the war, more lower arm wounds were permitted to heal in splints instead of being amputated, after surgeons saw that splints worked better than they had supposed. Surgeons also performed more excisions and resections, removing bone fragments and damaged sections, leaving a shortened limb, usually with limited function.

The Medical and Surgical History of the War of the Rebellion, a postwar compilation of Union medical sources, reported 29,980 amputations performed by Union doctors, resulting in 21,753 patients who survived, or approximately a 27 percent mortality rate. Although incomplete, these statistics are the best available, indicating the minimum number of amputations. Extant Confederate records, for a portion of the war, show a similar mortality rate (27 percent). Historians estimate that Confederate surgeons performed about 25,000 amputations. Notable Civil War generals who underwent amputations include Confederates Thomas J. "Stonewall" Jackson (arm), John Bell Hood (leg), and Richard S. Ewell (leg), and Federals Daniel E. Sickles (leg) and Oliver O. Howard (arm).

See also: Alcohol, Medicinal Uses of; Anesthesia; Artificial Limbs; Bandages; Ewell, Richard Stoddert; Gangrene, Hospital; Gunshot Wounds, Treatment of; Hood, John Bell; Hospitals, Field; Infections, of Wounds; Jackson, Thomas Jonathan ("Stonewall"); *The Medical and Surgical History of the War of the Rebellion;* Minié Balls; Mortality, of Soldiers; Opiate Use and Addiction; Resection; Sickles, Daniel Edgar; Splints.

Bibliography

Barnes, Joseph K., ed. *The Medical and Surgical History of the War of the Rebellion (1861–65).* Washington, DC: Government Printing Office, 1870–1888; reprint, Wilmington, NC: Broadfoot, 1990.

Chisolm, John Julian. *A Manual of Military Surgery.* Richmond, VA: West and Johnston, 1861; reprint, San Francisco: Norman, 1989.

Figg, Laurann, and Jane Farrell-Beck. "Amputation in the Civil War: Physical and Social Dimensions." *Journal of the History of Medicine and Allied Sciences* 48 (October 1993): 454–475.

Kuz, Julian E., and Bradley P. Bengston. *Orthopaedic Injuries and Treatments During the Civil War.* Kennesaw, GA: Kennesaw Mountain Press, 1996.

Wegner, Ansley Herring. *Phantom Pain: North Carolina's Artificial Limbs Program for Confederate Veterans*. Raleigh: Office of Archives and History, North Carolina Department of Cultural Resources, 2004.

ANDERSONVILLE PRISON

Andersonville, officially named Camp Sumter, was a prisoner of war camp for Union soldiers in Anderson, Georgia. It has, justifiably, the reputation of being the worst prison camp, North or South, during the Civil War.

By late 1863 Confederate authorities recognized the need for more prisoner of war camps. Because the prisoners were no longer being exchanged, thousands of them crowded sites in Richmond, straining scarce food supplies and creating a risk should Union forces actually capture the city. Anderson seemed an ideal site because it was isolated, far from potential Yankee incursions, but on a railroad line. It supposedly had plenty of timber, water, and local agricultural supplies. In fact, Samuel H. Stout, medical director of hospitals for the Confederate Army of Tennessee, had selected the site for a hospital. However, a location that could have maintained a hospital or prison for 500 to 1,000 men was totally inadequate for the 41,000 who ultimately spent some time there.

Although Confederates attempted to begin construction of the stockade walls in December 1863, they had great difficulty getting workmen and supplies from the neighbors, who did not want a prison there. When the military threatened to impress resources, enough became available so that construction finally began about January 10, 1864. However, Quartermaster Richard B. Winder, who was in charge of preparing the prison camp, had completed only half of the stockade fence and the skeleton of the cookhouse when, in mid-February, he received word that 10,000 prisoners would soon be on their way. No barracks had been built for them yet, and none ever were. The prisoners were supposed to be housed temporarily in tents, but Governor Joseph Brown refused to sell any that belonged to the state of Georgia. There was no prison hospital, very little food was available, and the guards were few and poorly trained, mostly from militia regiments. In addition, the secretary of war and the adjutant general had set up a very confusing, inefficient command structure with one officer to command the local area outside the prison, another to command the guards, and a third to command the actual camp.

Throughout its existence Andersonville was plagued by shortages when commissaries and quartermasters refused to fill or only partially filled requisitions, railroads did not give priority to prison shipments, and the state of Georgia refused assistance. Requisitions for supplies of all kinds had to be sent to officers in Atlanta or other distant towns for approval, where the forms became delayed in a bureaucratic web. The prisoners of war at Andersonville simply had no status in a country already strapped for resources, and therefore they suffered severely.

The first prisoners arrived on February 27, 1864, after six days on the train from

Richmond. They received a little uncooked food and a few cooking utensils, but nothing else. Those who were physically able constructed makeshift shelters out of small lumber scraps and any blankets they might have brought with them. As more prisoners arrived, the rations became even smaller. Many prisoners were sick when they reached the prison, but there was no hospital to begin with, and few surgeons. By early April 1864, 7,500 prisoners had arrived and 283 of them had died.

The stream that crossed the prison camp was the sole water source. It was supposed to provide drinking and washing water and to flush the sewage from the latrine area at the lower end of the stockade. However, there was never enough water to remove the waste unless it rained, flooding parts of the camp with filth. The entire stream area quickly became and remained a stinking, muddy morass. Upstream, outside the stockade, a guard camp and the prison bakery polluted the water before it even got to the prisoners. Those who were careless about sanitation or were too ill to reach the latrines contributed to fouling other areas of the camp. Sanitation-related diseases, evidenced by diarrhea and dysentery, were common and further weakened the health of the prisoners.

Captain Henry Wirz was appointed prison commander at Andersonville at the end of March. He tried to improve sanitation and rations at the camp, but was handicapped throughout his tenure by shortages of everything, including the most basic tools, such as shovels and buckets. The authorities in Richmond continued to ship prisoners to Andersonville at a rapid rate, but would not authorize railroad space for lumber, nails, or rations to improve conditions there. By May 5 there were about 12,000 prisoners confined in about eighteen acres.

The first hospital at Andersonville was located inside the prison along the north wall. Isaiah White, the chief surgeon, had no buildings or complete tents, only a few dozen tent flies as shelter for hundreds of sick patients. Many other ill prisoners could not even be admitted to the hospital because there was no room for them. White and his subordinates provided medicine for these prisoners when possible. However, as one hospital steward among the prisoners who worked as a pharmacist in the hospital later reported, medicines, too, were limited. The physicians mostly worked with indigenous plants and some quinine, opium, and mercurial preparations that had come through the blockade. The patients admitted to the hospital were lucky if they had straw or pine needles to lie on instead of bare ground. Smoke from the prison campfires clouded the air, and when it rained, waste from the latrines washed through the hospital. Nurses, recruited from among the prisoners, did little to care for the patients. In fact, some of the nurses and other prisoners preyed on the weak patients, stealing whatever minimal possessions they had. A sick soldier might actually do better outside the hospital if nursed by caring messmates.

After numerous complaints from White, Wirz, and an inspector from Richmond, paroled prisoners built a hospital outside the prison walls in a smaller stockade. Although the hospital was situated on a tributary creek, it, and its well, were very near the polluted stream exiting the prison camp. The patients were moved to the new hospital on May 22, 1864. However, conditions there were no better because the number of patients overwhelmed the surgeons and the space available. There were never enough doctors at Andersonville. Many of the surgeons assigned to the camp protested that assignment and found ways to avoid going there, such as pleading their own illness.

Dr. Joseph Jones and his clerk Louis Manigault, who visited Andersonville to do research in September 1864, were appalled by the conditions of filth and disease in the hospital as well as in the entire stockade, where many more sick prisoners remained. Jones determined that intestinal diseases and scurvy were the primary causes of death, although many deaths from hospital gangrene were attributed to other causes. Because the prisoners' diet was based on unsifted cornmeal and some meat, with little variety of fruits or vegetables to provide what is now known as vitamin C, scurvy soon became a serious problem. Many of the patients who might otherwise have survived ultimately died because of neglect by incompetent, uncaring, or simply overwhelmed surgeons and nurses.

The guards at the prison suffered the same diseases as the prisoners because their own water supply was polluted and their diet contained little variety. The guards, however, were more likely to get typhoid fever than the prisoners, who had developed immunity by having the disease before they reached Andersonville.

The number of prisoners at Andersonville peaked at 33,000 in early August. After Union general William T. Sherman's capture of Atlanta on September 2, 1864, Confederate authorities feared that he might raid Andersonville. Many of the prisoners were moved to Millen, Georgia, and Florence, South Carolina, by October 1, leaving fewer than 6,000 prisoners at Andersonville, with 2,000 of those in the hospital. The total population had declined to less than 2,000 when, in November, prisoners from Millen and other places were returned to Andersonville to get them out of the way of Sherman's march to the sea.

Beginning on March 18, 1865, prisoners from Andersonville were shipped to Vicksburg, and later other points, for exchange. Many of them were sick and a large number died on the way. Many of the survivors were severely emaciated. Their condition and other reports of prisoner mistreatment fed Northern hostility toward the South.

Approximately 15,000 prisoners of war died at Andersonville before the prison officially closed on May 4, 1865. Wirz was arrested for alleged mistreatment of the Union prisoners, held in Washington, DC, and tried by a military commission, beginning on August 23. Sentenced to death after a rigged trial, Wirz was hanged on November 10, 1865, essentially a scapegoat for the conditions at Andersonville, most of which were beyond his control.

See also: Barton, Clara; Diarrhea and Dysentery; Gangrene, Hospital; Jones, Joseph; Malnutrition; Prisoners of War; Sanitation; Scurvy; Stout, Samuel Hollingsworth; Typhoid Fever.

Bibliography

Marvel, William. *Andersonville: The Last Depot.* Chapel Hill: University of North Carolina Press, 1994.

Sanders, Charles J. *While in the Hands of the Enemy: Military Prisons of the Civil War.* Baton Rouge: Louisiana State University Press, 2005.

Schroeder-Lein, Glenna R. *Confederate Hospitals on the Move: Samuel H. Stout and the Army of Tennessee.* Columbia: University of South Carolina Press, 1994.

ANESTHESIA

Although undoubtedly some Civil War soldiers endured surgery while biting a bullet or under the influence of whiskey, as many accounts have related, the great majority of patients, both Union and Confederate, were anesthetized during their operations. There were two anesthetics available during the Civil War—ether and chloroform—and both were used, although chloroform was preferred.

Ether was first used in a surgical operation by Dr. Crawford W. Long in Georgia in 1842. However, he did not publicize his discovery, and credit for the first public demonstration of the use of ether as an anesthetic is given to Dr. William T.G. Morton, a dentist, who anesthetized a patient for an operation performed by Dr. John C. Warren at Massachusetts General Hospital in Boston on October 16, 1846. In 1847 a British doctor, James Young Simpson, introduced chloroform, which became more popular because it was easier to use. Yet the use of anesthesia spread slowly because some doctors thought that pain was ordained by God and had moral objections to its relief. Other doctors opposed any innovations. Some doctors with rural practices did not read medical journals and did not know anesthesia was available, and some doctors wanted to see it more fully tested before using it. Anesthesia was brand-new at the time of the Mexican War and was rarely used. During the Crimean War in the 1850s, anesthesia was utilized occasionally, but many of the British doctors were opposed to it. However, by the time of the Civil War, nearly all physicians who served the military believed that anesthesia should be used for any surgery or painful wound treatment.

Chloroform was used for almost all field surgery, while ether, or a mixture of two parts ether and one part chloroform, was used in hospitals. Although ether was somewhat safer for patients, it was very flammable. One of its manufacturers, Dr. Edward R. Squibb of New York, was severely injured by an ether explosion and fire in 1858. Chloroform was easier to use, safer around the open flames of candles and lanterns lighting the field hospitals during surgery, and took up less space to transport. The major risk for chloroform was that if a patient suddenly breathed in too deeply, an overdose of chloroform could cause the heart to stop, killing the patient. Given the fact that Union surgeons performed more than 80,000 operations using anesthetics (and recorded only 254 without) and the Confederates performed more than 28,000 with chloroform, the death rate from anesthesia was very low. A section in the postwar book, *The Medical and Surgical History of the War of the*

Rebellion analyzed 8,900 Union cases of anesthesia use and tabulated the results. Chloroform was used in 6,784 operations with thirty-seven deaths (0.5 percent), ether was used in 1,305 cases with four deaths (0.3 percent), and a mixture of ether and chloroform was used in 811 surgeries with five deaths (0.6 percent).

The low fatality rate has surprised many observers because there were no trained anesthesiologists. A medically untrained soldier might be pressed into service. Anesthesia was administered by dropping the liquid chloroform or ether onto a sponge, towel, handkerchief, or napkin held near or folded like a cone over the patient's nose. Several doctors used an inverted funnel with a sponge in the tip.

Despite the often haphazard administration of anesthesia, historians have suggested that military patients benefited from good air circulation, since most surgeries were performed outdoors or in well-ventilated buildings. This kept the chloroform from becoming too concentrated. Fatalities during the civilian use of chloroform had all occurred in stuffy rooms. A second factor accounting for the low fatality rate was that anesthesia was administered only until patients felt no pain, not until their muscles relaxed, and consequently they were less likely to get an overdose. One result of this light use of anesthesia was that patients fell into a sort of delirium, thrashing around and groaning, and had to be held down by several strong men. Observers of this process believed, and erroneously reported, that the surgery was being performed without anesthesia. Actually, the patients felt no pain and remembered nothing about the operation.

Historians have reported that the Confederates often operated without anesthesia because they were unable to get it, due to the Union blockade of Southern ports. This is not true. Blockade-runners brought in some supplies of anesthesia. The Confederates also established laboratories in North Carolina, South Carolina, Georgia, Alabama, Tennessee, Texas, and Arkansas to manufacture anesthetics and research medicinal plants. A third source of anesthetics was capture from the enemy. Whenever Confederates captured a Union supply depot or train, they focused on procuring food and medical supplies. For example, when Stonewall Jackson's cavalry captured a Union supply train on May 24, 1862, near Winchester, Virginia, they gained 1,500 cases of chloroform. Confederates captured numerous other medical supplies after the Battle of Chancellorsville in May 1863.

Union and Confederate surgeons used anesthetics in several other situations besides surgery. Some wound cleanings and treatments, such as the use of bromine solution to treat hospital gangrene, were extremely painful, so the patient was anesthetized. Anesthesia was also used at times to relax the painful muscle spasms of tetanus. It alleviated these symptoms although it did not treat the disease itself. Some doctors occasionally used anesthesia to diagnose persistent suspected cases of malingering, because a soldier under anesthesia would be unable to continue faking many kinds of injuries and ailments but would respond with normal limb motions.

During and after the war, the use of chloroform was a favorite topic of discussion by medical officers. At one of its early meetings in 1863, the Association of Army and Navy Surgeons of the Confederate States discussed battlefield reports about the use of chloroform and the best way to administer it. In the late 1890s and early 1900s, the elderly medical veterans who joined the Association of Medical Officers of the Army and Navy of the Confederacy seemed to like nothing better than to discuss the wartime use and merits of chloroform, perhaps because this anesthetic was less favored after the war. When the group gathered for its annual meeting, if someone failed to prepare a paper or the floor was opened for discussion, some doctor almost always brought up the topic of chloroform.

See also: Alcohol, Medicinal Uses of; Amputation; Association of Army and Navy Surgeons of the Confederate States; Association of Medical Officers of the Army and Navy of the Confederacy; Blockade; Gangrene, Hospital; Gunshot Wounds, Treatment of; Hospitals, Field; Hospitals, General; Infections, of Wounds; Malingerers; *The Medical and Surgical History of the War of the Rebellion;* Mortality, of Soldiers; Opiate Use and Addiction; Ventilation.

Bibliography

"Association of Army and Navy Surgeons." *Confederate States Medical and Surgical Journal* 1 (January 1864): 13–16.

Bollet, Alfred Jay. *Civil War Medicine: Challenges and Triumphs.* Tucson, AZ: Galen, 2002.

Cunningham, H.H. *Doctors in Gray: The Confederate Medical Service.* Baton Rouge: Louisiana State University Press, 1958; reprint, Gloucester, MA: Peter Smith, 1970.

Duffy, John. *From Humors to Medical Science: A History of American Medicine.* 2nd ed. Urbana: University of Illinois Press, 1993.

Schroeder-Lein, Glenna R. "'While the Participants Are Yet Alive': The Association of Medical Officers of the Army and Navy of the Confederacy." In *Inside the Confederate Nation: Essays in Honor of Emory M. Thomas,* ed. Lesley J. Gordon and John C. Inscoe, pp. 335–348. Baton Rouge: Louisiana State University Press, 2005.

Southern Practitioner 22–39 (1900–1917).

Wood, Thomas Fanning. *Doctor to the Front: The Recollections of Confederate Surgeon Thomas Fanning Wood, 1861–1865,* ed. Donald B. Koonce. Knoxville: University of Tennessee Press, 2000.

ANTIETAM, BATTLE OF (1862)

The Battle of Antietam (or Sharpsburg), the bloodiest single day of the Civil War, as well as in American history generally, took place near Sharpsburg, Maryland, on September 17, 1862. The Confederate Army of Northern Virginia, under General Robert E. Lee, marched north into Maryland and met the Union Army of the Potomac, commanded by General George B. McClellan. Terrible fighting took place all over the battlefield but especially at the Cornfield, where witnesses said that the dead were lying so thick that a person could walk across the field on the bodies without stepping on the ground. Enormous casualties also resulted from the Union attack on the Confederates at Bloody Lane, a sunken road, which always meant an advantage for the defenders.

Casualty figures vary, but some reasonable numbers are: Union—2,108 dead, 9,540 wounded, and 753 missing; Confederate—1,546 to 2,700 dead, 7,752 to 9,024 wounded, and 1,108 missing. The Confederates' casualty figures are less precise because many of their dead and wounded remained in Union hands. In addition, at least 2,000 soldiers later died of their wounds and many of the missing probably died as well. It is reasonable to estimate that between 6,300 and 6,500 soldiers were killed or mortally wounded at Antietam.

During previous battles, especially Second Bull Run (Manassas) on August 29–30, 1862, the Union medical department had had tremendous difficulties removing its wounded from the field in a timely manner. The Battle of Antietam was the first time Jonathan Letterman, medical director for the Army of the Potomac, used the new ambulance corps he had developed. Every regiment had one to three ambulances, each with a driver and two men who were trained to move and care for the wounded. Although the ambulance corps was inexperienced, it performed creditably, and all the wounded were removed from the field within twenty-four hours.

The Union forces had at least seventy-one field hospitals set up in all available houses, barns, and other outbuildings on and near the battlefield. Many of the buildings were so crowded that some of the wounded had to lie outside on the ground under whatever trees or sheds could be found. The Confederates had similar field hospitals, but little is known about them because so many Confederate records were destroyed with the fall of Richmond. The Union field hospitals suffered from a severe shortage of supplies for several days. Most field hospitals had only the supplies the doctors had brought with them and whatever could be found on the farm where the hospital was located. In one case, attendants bandaged the stumps left by fresh amputations with corn leaves. Surgeons used doors as operating tables and continued performing amputations by candlelight, leaving gruesome piles of amputated limbs.

Many of the supply problems resulted from the fact that the quartermaster's department had to be trusted with these shipments. However, that department tended to give medical supplies a low priority. Furthermore, when the supplies did get near Frederick, Maryland, the closest supply depot, they piled up because the bridge over the Monocacy River had been destroyed and there was no one with the authority to expedite the shipment of the supplies. Clara Barton, acting independently of any organization, brought four wagonloads of supplies to the Poffenberger farm, where there were about 1,500 wounded. The U.S. Sanitary Commission also sent a number of wagonloads of supplies of all sorts, which arrived the day after the battle because the commission had its own transportation. These supplies provided critical assistance until the medical department supplies began to arrive on the evening of September 20, three days after the battle.

With the repair of the bridge, the wounded could also begin to be transported from the field hospitals to Frederick, about twenty miles away. Several hundred patients with arm injuries and other slight wounds were able to walk to Frederick. The rest were transported in ambulances by way of Middletown, where the patients were given food and a chance to rest before the ambulances moved on. All the wounded had been sent to Frederick by September 25 except for about 600 severely wounded soldiers who could not be moved that far. They were consolidated in two tent hospitals on the battlefield.

Frederick had already received more than 2,000 wounded soldiers after the Battle of South Mountain on September 14. The town had had a hospital since 1861, located in Revolutionary War–era barracks, but doctors quickly opened six more hospitals in churches and other available buildings around the town. Many of the hospitals were also expanded by the use of tents. The medical officers discovered that the patients in the tents tended to recover more quickly with fewer complications than patients in the buildings. Even with expanded facilities and assistance provided by the town's citizens, not all patients could be cared for in Frederick, and more than half of the wounded were shipped to hospitals in Philadelphia, Baltimore, and Washington, DC. On November 1, there were still more than 2,500 patients in Frederick, but the hospitals gradually closed as the number of patients decreased, until on April 1, 1863, only the original barracks hospital remained.

The Confederates withdrew from the battlefield on the night of September 18, leaving about 2,000 of their wounded on the field. They had already taken some injured soldiers to hospitals set up in assorted buildings in Shepherdstown, Virginia. The Confederates were able to evacuate some of these patients to Winchester, Virginia, but the most severely wounded had to be left behind. In some cases, Confederate surgeons remained with the patients. The Confederate wounded tended to have a higher death rate than the Union wounded, not because of any lack of medical care, but because they were the most seriously wounded. When Confederate patients were sufficiently well, they were sent to Baltimore or Fortress Monroe, Virginia, to be exchanged for Union prisoners of war in Confederate hands.

The Battle of Antietam showed the usefulness of an ambulance corps but also the need for better supply arrangements. As the Confederates withdrew from Maryland, their hopes of recognition and aid from France and England dwindled, and President Abraham Lincoln announced his preliminary Emancipation Proclamation on September 22. In addition, the bloodiest day of the war provided the first opportunity for civilians at home to actually see the true horrors of war. On September 19, Alexander Gardner and James Gibson photographed the battlefield, the wounded, and the dead for Matthew Brady, who exhibited the pictures and sold copies at his store in New York.

See also: Ambulance Corps; Amputation; Barton, Clara; Bull Run (Manassas), Second Battle of; Gunshot Wounds, Treatment of; Hospital Buildings; Hospitals, Field; Hospitals, General; Letterman, Jonathan; Mortality, of Soldiers; Quartermasters; Tents, Hospital; United States Sanitary Commission; Women's Hospital Auxiliaries and Relief Societies.

Bibliography

Adams, George Worthington. *Doctors in Blue: The Medical History of the Union Army in the Civil War.* New York: Schuman, 1952; reprint, Dayton, OH: Morningside, 1985.

Duncan, Louis C. *The Medical Department of the United States Army in the Civil War.* Washington, DC: Author, 1914; reprint, Gaithersburg, MD: Butternut, 1985.

Gordon, Paul, and Rita Gordon. *Frederick County, Maryland: A Playground of the Civil War.* Frederick, MD: Heritage Partnership, 1994.

McPherson, James M. *Crossroads of Freedom: Antietam: The Battle That Changed the Course of the Civil War.* New York: Oxford University Press, 2002.

Oates, Stephen B. *A Woman of Valor: Clara Barton and the Civil War.* New York: Free Press, 1994.

Pryor, Elizabeth Brown. *Clara Barton, Professional Angel.* Philadelphia: University of Pennsylvania Press, 1987.

Sears, Stephen W. *Landscape Turned Red: The Battle of Antietam.* New Haven, CT: Ticknor and Fields, 1983.

ANTISEPTICS AND DISINFECTANTS

During the Civil War, doctors in both the North and the South used antiseptics and disinfectants. Although technically antiseptics were used to treat wound infections (*sepsis* is Greek for putrefaction or decay) and disinfectants were used for cleaning, in practice many of the same substances served both purposes.

Because Civil War doctors did not know about bacteria, they sometimes used their antiseptics and disinfectants less effectively than they could have. For example, physicians often waited until a wound infection developed before treating it with antiseptics, rather than cleaning the wound with antiseptics to prevent the infection. They also did not clean surgical instruments with disinfectants. In other cases, they used the right thing for the wrong reason. Medical officers ordered latrines and bedpans cleaned with disinfectants to reduce odors because they believed that these odors, or "miasms," spread disease. While the disinfectant might reduce the smell, it actually prevented the spread of disease by killing germs.

In Europe, Dr. Joseph Lister discovered, just after the Civil War ended, that spraying carbolic acid during surgery and covering a wound with a bandage soaked in carbolic acid would significantly reduce wound infections. This information, published in 1867, was the beginning of modern antiseptic practice. However, during the American Civil War, some surgeons already used carbolic acid for antiseptic and disinfecting purposes.

Besides carbolic acid, antiseptics included potassium iodide, potassium permanganate, liquid iodine, bromine, turpentine, powdered charcoal, nitric acid, nitrate of silver, sulphuric acid, hydrochloric acid, corrosive sublimate (bichloride of mercury), creosote, and alcohol. Bromine and several other antiseptics were used quite effectively to treat erysipelas and hospital gangrene.

The U.S. Sanitary Commission issued a pamphlet on disinfectants, naming sulfate of lime, quicklime, chloride, and bromine among other useful disinfectants. Union medical purveyors issued such disinfectants as carbolic acid, sulphate of iron, nitrate of lead, chlorinated lime, permanganate of potash, and charcoal. In hospitals especially, conscientious medical officers tried to ensure that walls were whitewashed properly, which was supposed to be disinfecting. Some doctors washed their hands in chlorinated soda when possible, a technique developed in the 1840s to prevent the spread of a dangerous childbirth fever. At least one surgeon painted scratches and scrapes on his own hands with bromine to avoid infections. Carbolic acid and chlorinated lime were frequently used to disinfect latrines.

Doctors and hospitals that used antiseptics and disinfectants effectively had lower infection and higher recovery rates.

See also: Erysipelas; Gangrene, Hospital; Gunshot Wounds, Treatment of; Infections, of Wounds; Latrines; Medical Purveyors; Miasms; Sanitation; United States Sanitary Commission.

Bibliography

Adams, George Worthington. *Doctors in Blue: The Medical History of the Union Army in the Civil War.* New York: Schuman, 1952; reprint, Dayton, OH: Morningside, 1985.

Bollet, Alfred Jay. *Civil War Medicine: Challenges and Triumphs.* Tucson, AZ: Galen, 2002.

ARMY MEDICAL MUSEUM

On May 21, 1862, the new Union surgeon general, William A. Hammond, issued Circular No. 2 establishing the Army Medical Museum. He projected two purposes for the museum: to prepare *The Medical and Surgical History of the War of the Rebellion* and to collect specimens of diseased and wounded anatomy that would be valuable for the study of military medicine and surgery.

In Circular No. 5 of June 9, 1862, Hammond recalled two doctors, Joseph J. Woodward and John H. Brinton, from other duties and assigned them to prepare the medical and surgical portions of the history, respectively. On August 1, Brinton became the first curator of the museum, with orders to arrange the specimens that had accumulated thus far and to collect more. The first specimens were three dried, varnished bones.

Just after the Battle of Antietam in September 1862, Hammond ordered Brinton to the battlefield. He was to help wherever he could, sometimes performing surgery or supervising the transportation of the wounded. But Brinton's main purpose was to collect specimens of gunshot wounds, and their case histories, for the museum. He was also to encourage and instruct surgeons in how to collect material themselves. Initially, Brinton dug up trenches full of amputated limbs, but later on he gained the cooperation of the field surgeons.

A specimen was to be partly cleaned, given an identification tag, and stored in a keg of whiskey or other alcoholic substance. When the keg was full of specimens, it would be shipped to the surgeon general's office. Of course, not all wounds were in amputated limbs and many of the patients otherwise wounded survived. On several occasions Brinton took along an artist who sketched and painted pictures of these other types of wounds, many of which ultimately illustrated the published history. In addition to Antietam, Brinton visited the battlefields of Fredericksburg, Chancellorsville, and Gettysburg, among others. Brinton's staff included professional specimen preparators, illustrators, clerks, and, after the summer of 1864, a photographer.

The museum grew rapidly. On January 1, 1863, Brinton issued its first catalog detailing 1,349 items, mostly gunshot wound specimens, but also 133 "projectiles" that had been removed from wounds. By 1865 the collection had grown to 7,630 specimens, including models of tents, ambulances, and other medical equipment. Soon after the war the collection contained the amputated leg of General Daniel E. Sickles; the bullet that killed President Abraham Lincoln and the probe used to locate it (Woodward was one of the doctors who performed Lincoln's autopsy); the section of spinal cord with cervical vertebrae of Lincoln's assassin John Wilkes Booth, showing where he was fatally shot; and sections of the spine, neck, and right arm of Henry Wirz, the commander of the camp for Union prisoners of war at Andersonville, Georgia, who was hanged for alleged abuse of prisoners in November 1865. After Brinton was removed as curator in September 1864, surgeon George A. Otis replaced him, remaining curator until he had a stroke in May 1877.

Initially the museum was located on shelves in Brinton's office and then in some other rooms that it soon outgrew. In the fall of 1863 the museum moved to the so-called Corcoran schoolhouse building. In 1866 it moved again, to Ford's Theatre, which had been confiscated by the government after Lincoln's assassination. Here it remained for twenty years. The museum has changed its name and location several times since then. Now serving all branches of the armed forces, it continues its mission of collecting and dispensing medical information, to civilians as well as the military. Known since 1989 as the National Museum of Health and Medicine, it is located on the Walter Reed Army Medical Center campus in Washington, DC.

See also: Alcohol, Abuse of; Alcohol, Medicinal Uses of; Ambulances; Amputation; Andersonville Prison; Antietam, Battle of; Brinton, John Hill; Gettysburg, Battle of; Gunshot Wounds; Hammond, William Alexander; Hospitals, Field; Lincoln, Abraham; *The Medical and Surgical History of the War of the Rebellion;* Minié Balls; Sickles, Daniel Edgar; Woodward, Joseph Janvier.

Bibliography

Brinton, John H. *Personal Memoirs of John H. Brinton, Civil War Surgeon, 1861–1865.* New York: Neale, 1914; reprint, Carbondale: Southern Illinois University Press, 1996.

Graf, LeRoy P., Ralph W. Haskins, and Paul H. Bergeron, eds. *The Papers of Andrew Johnson*. Vol. 15. Knoxville: University of Tennessee Press, 1967–2000.

Henry, Robert S. *The Armed Forces Institute of Pathology: Its First Century, 1862–1962*. Washington, DC: Government Printing Office, 1964.

ARTIFICIAL LIMBS

Surgeons performed more than 50,000 amputations during the Civil War and nearly 75 percent of the patients survived. While some men lost fingers or toes, thousands of others had some substantial part of a leg or an arm removed. Many of these patients were candidates for an artificial limb, which federal and state governments, as well as voluntary organizations, sought to supply during and after the war.

While there were a number of designs for artificial limbs before the Civil War, the needs of soldiers stimulated eighty-eight new patents for artificial legs between 1861 and 1873, as well as patents for arms, crutches, and wheelchairs (known at the time as invalid chairs). While artificial arms could be functional to some extent, they were not able to provide fine movements, and they were often considered to be merely cosmetic.

Artificial legs, however, enabled many amputees to return to a nearly normal lifestyle. Artificial legs were made in a variety of styles, from the utilitarian peg leg to those realistically shaped like the missing limb. Artificial legs and arms were made of wood, wood and leather, or wire cloth. They might be covered with parchment, painted appropriate flesh tones. Later, some were covered with india rubber to make them feel more natural to the touch. Most artificial legs had joints at the knee and ankle. These could involve cords, levers, springs, or balls and sockets made of metal or gutta-percha (a hard substance derived from a particular kind of tree sap and used as we would use plastic). Artificial legs also had a system of straps and buckles to fasten onto the stump. Whatever materials they were made of, artificial legs needed to be strong enough to support the wearer and survive hard use, yet light enough for easy mobility.

Among the notable manufacturers of artificial limbs was B. Franklin Palmer of Philadelphia, himself an amputee, who had been making such limbs since well before the Civil War. Many other people got into the business to meet the soldiers' needs. Private James E. Hanger, a Confederate cavalryman who lost his leg in June 1861, became a designer and manufacturer as a result of his own need, founding a company that was still supplying orthopedic items in the late twentieth century. An April 1864 article in the *Confederate States Medical and Surgical Journal* described how locksmiths, gunsmiths, instrument makers, or good mechanics could manufacture artificial legs based on copies of plans published in the U.S. Patent Office Reports, found in Confederate libraries.

Several generals managed to remain on active duty with artificial legs, including Confederates John Bell Hood and Richard S. Ewell and Union general Daniel E. Sickles. Union cavalryman Ulric Dahlgren, one of the leaders of the Kilpatrick-

Dahlgren raid on Richmond in February 1864, had lost his leg at the Battle of Gettysburg and made the raid with an artificial one. After Dahlgren died in the raid, his high-quality leg was given to and worn by a Confederate amputee.

Not all the veterans could or would wear artificial limbs, however. In some cases, the stump was too short to buckle anything onto. In other cases, the stump was too sore because of scar tissue, unhealed areas, skin irritation, or a bone protruding or just below the skin. Some veterans found that their artificial limb never fit right and wore it only on formal occasions. Some amputees learned that crutches provided better mobility than an artificial leg. Finally, some found an empty sleeve or pant leg more useful politically, as did three veterans with amputated arms who were eventually elected governor of Wisconsin, Louisiana, and Arkansas.

The U.S. Congress passed an act on July 16, 1862, that allowed amputee soldiers fifty dollars to buy an artificial arm or seventy-five dollars for a leg. In 1868 this allowance was offered to commissioned officers as well. Soldiers could have free transportation to fittings for their artificial limbs and new limbs every five years, as a result of acts passed in 1866 and 1870, respectively.

In January 1864 Confederates in Richmond, Virginia, organized an Association for the Relief of Maimed Soldiers to provide artificial limbs for military amputees. Within a few days they had raised $50,000 and were soliciting further donations. Committee members believed that they could have enough legs manufactured in the Confederacy to meet the need. For obvious reasons, the Federal government did not provide aid for Confederate amputees after the war. In February 1866 North Carolina became the first former Confederate state to help its veterans by providing free legs or an allowance of seventy dollars to amputees who did not want one. In 1867 the legislature also included arms or a commutation of fifty dollars. Governor Jonathan Worth contracted with Jewett's Patent Leg Company of Washington, DC, to set up a factory in Raleigh, North Carolina. South Carolina, Mississippi, Virginia, and Arkansas also established state-supported artificial limbs programs in 1866 and 1867.

See also: Amputation; *Confederate States Medical and Surgical Journal;* Ewell, Richard Stoddert; Gunshot Wounds, Treatment of; Hood, John Bell; Sickles, Daniel Edgar.

Bibliography

"Artificial Limbs—How to Make Them." *Confederate States Medical and Surgical Journal* 1 (April 1864): 59.

"Association to Purchase Artificial Limbs for Maimed Soldiers." *Confederate States Medical and Surgical Journal* 1 (March 1864): 44.

Figg, Laurann, and Jane Farrell-Beck. "Amputation in the Civil War: Physical and Social Dimensions." *Journal of the History of Medicine and Allied Sciences* 48 (October 1993): 454–475.

Wegner, Ansley Herring. *Phantom Pain: North Carolina's Artificial Limbs Program for Confederate Veterans.* Raleigh: Office of Archives and History, North Carolina Department of Cultural Resources, 2004.

ASSOCIATION OF ARMY AND NAVY SURGEONS OF THE CONFEDERATE STATES

The Association of Army and Navy Surgeons of the Confederate States was a wartime organization designed to promote the collection, discussion, and dissemination of information about topics that would be useful to medical officers in both the hospitals and the field.

The association was founded in late August 1863 under the auspices of Surgeon General Samuel P. Moore, who became its president. It was supposed to meet every other Saturday at the medical school in Richmond at 7:00 or 8:00 p.m. (depending on the time of year). In addition to the president, the officers consisted of two vice presidents, two recording secretaries, two corresponding secretaries, and a treasurer. Any surgeon or assistant surgeon in the Confederate army or navy could join by paying ten dollars and signing the group's constitution. Dr. Conrad, a naval surgeon, served as second vice president. Otherwise, participants seem to have been army doctors.

Although only members stationed in Richmond and its environs could attend the meetings, the association welcomed corresponding members who sent their views on the topics under discussion as well as descriptions of cases they had treated. These materials from correspondents were to be read at the meetings and combined into reports. The plan was to propose a topic of interest for members to consider and discuss at the next meeting in two weeks. While this arrangement worked to some extent, information received later from correspondents, as well as from members who wished to consider additional aspects of a subject, might cause a topic to reappear at several later meetings. For example, tetanus was discussed from the end of January to at least the end of March 1864.

Minutes survive for at least twenty-one meetings of the association. Topics discussed included the criteria used to determine whether a gunshot wound was made by the entrance or exit of a bullet, secondary hemorrhages of gunshot wounds, the use of chloroform, the possibility of there being two types of gangrene, cold-water dressings for wounds, and gunshot wounds of the chest, featuring the case of a soldier whose wound forced a gold pocket watch into his lungs. (The patient coughed up many small parts of the watch and survived.)

Beginning in January 1864, Surgeon General Moore oversaw the publication of the *Confederate States Medical and Surgical Journal.* This monthly, which lasted through February 1865, printed accounts of some of the association's meetings, as well as other material sent by corresponding doctors.

See also: Confederate States Medical and Surgical Journal; Education, Medical; Gangrene, Hospital; Gunshot Wounds; Gunshot Wounds, Treatment of; Moore, Samuel Preston; Richmond, Virginia; Tetanus.

Bibliography
Confederate States Medical and Surgical Journal, January 1864–February 1865; reprint, Metuchen, NJ: Scarecrow, 1976; reprint, San Francisco: Norman, 1992.

ASSOCIATION OF MEDICAL OFFICERS OF THE ARMY AND NAVY OF THE CONFEDERACY

The Association of Medical Officers of the Army and Navy of the Confederacy (1874–1875, 1898–ca. 1917) was a postwar organization of Confederate surgeons of all ranks, as well as hospital stewards, chaplains, soldiers who became doctors after the war, and doctors who were the sons of Confederate veterans. Founded in Atlanta, Georgia, in 1874, the association collapsed due to lack of effective leadership after its meeting in Richmond, Virginia, in 1875. Refounded in 1898, again in Atlanta, the group always met at the same time and place at the United Confederate Veterans annual reunion. The purpose of the association was to collect as much material as possible about the Confederate medical experience. The doctors attempted to use themselves as primary sources to replace information that had been lost when the Confederate medical records burned at the fall of Richmond in April 1865.

In the early 1900s the organization numbered more than 400 members. Meeting attendance peaked at about 150 in 1902 and 1903 but soon declined; only several dozen members were ever very active. During the meetings doctors presented accounts of their medical experiences that were then published by Deering J. Roberts in the *Southern Practitioner,* a Nashville-based medical journal. The organization faded away about 1917 because of the old age and death of most of its members.

See also: Southern Practitioner; Stout, Samuel Hollingsworth.

Bibliography
Schroeder-Lein, Glenna R. "'While the Participants Are Yet Alive': The Association of Medical Officers of the Army and Navy of the Confederacy." In *Inside the Confederate Nation: Essays in Honor of Emory M. Thomas,* ed. Lesley J. Gordon and John C. Inscoe, pp. 335–348. Baton Rouge: Louisiana State University Press, 2005.
Southern Practitioner 22–39 (1900–1917).

AUTENRIETH MEDICINE WAGON

The Autenrieth medicine wagon was one of several designs, produced by the Union medical department, for a wagon to resupply medicine and materials to surgeons and hospitals in the field. None of the sources identify Autenrieth, the designer, more fully.

Early in the Civil War, medical supplies, beyond what the surgeons and hospitals had on hand for immediate use, were packed in large, heavy boxes in army wagons that traveled with the supply train and were seldom available when needed during a battle. The first attempt to solve this problem involved specially designed "panniers" or wooden boxes with spaces for certain amounts of the most necessary medicines and supplies. They were supposed to be carried by pack mules or horses, but were too awkward and heavy, so they were usually placed in an ambulance.

The prototype medicine wagon, designed by surgeon Jonathan Letterman, was constructed in March 1862. In April the reviewing committee gave it wholehearted approval and urged that it be field-tested. A wagon designed on this plan solved all the previous supply problems and was so practical that the doctors were surprised that such a wagon had not been used before.

The goal of the medicine wagon was to provide three months' worth of medicine and surgical supplies for a regiment and, later, for a brigade. The interior of the wagon had built-in trays, drawers, and shelves, with specific items assigned to each space to provide the proper amount of material and to prevent shifting and breakage in transit. The wagon also included pots and pans, some bedding, a lantern, a hatchet, and an amputating table. When supplies were exhausted, the army medical purveyor refilled what was lacking.

The army medical department considered several different designs for medicine wagons. They rejected the Dunton design of November 1862, which looked like a Conestoga wagon with doors opening in the side of the wagon box. The examining doctors believed that it was improperly constructed and would not hold enough supplies. The Perot wagon and the Autenrieth design were more boxy-looking and more conveniently arranged, but the Perot was more expensive to construct and fill, so the Autenrieth seems to have become the standard. Both types of wagons seem to have been in use, however. In mid-1862 some of the early Autenrieths proved top-heavy and were easily upset. They were also provided to the army without brakes, but these problems were soon remedied.

When fully stocked medicine wagons were available, Union surgeons were better able to treat their wounded in the field.

See also: Ambulances; Hospitals, Field; Letterman, Jonathan; Medical Purveyors.

Bibliography

Barnes, Joseph K., ed. *The Medical and Surgical History of the War of the Rebellion (1861–1865)*. Vols. 2, 12. Washington, DC: Government Printing Office, 1870–1888; reprint, Wilmington, NC: Broadfoot, 1990.

B

BANDAGES

Caring for wounds during the Civil War usually involved the use of dressings and bandages of some sort. At the first aid station an attendant would apply a bandage to stop the bleeding. This could be a rolled bandage of clean cotton or linen from a well-stocked medicine chest or wagon. Or, during a desperate battle with crowds of patients exhausting the supplies, the bandage could be a strip of the doctor's shirt.

Once the wound had been cleaned and any necessary operation performed, the wound was often covered with cerate (a beeswax ointment) and then a dressing made of lint (fibers scraped from old linen cloth) or raw cotton (sometimes baked until charred). Most doctors used a cold-water dressing, keeping the pad moist with cold water through frequent applications or a continual drip. Some used warm dressings, but these usually produced infection ("laudable pus"). On occasion some doctors used dry dressings with successful healing and fewer infections.

Dressings were held on the wounds with bandages. Many women, North and South, gave up sheets, bedspreads, skirts, and other material to be torn into strips and rolled for bandages, which were used in addition to manufactured bandages. While these bandages were clean after a fashion, they were never sterile. In many hospitals, bandages were washed and reused, often because of shortages, sometimes spreading infections. In other hospitals, doctors refused to reuse bandages because they suspected that reused bandages hindered healing. Although not elastic, bandages could also be used in the manner of modern elastic bandages to affix splints to broken limbs.

Civil War doctors also used "adhesive plaster." This sticky bandage was made by spreading a mixture of resin, olive oil, lard, and lead monoxide on thin muslin. The dried bandage was then rolled for storage and transportation. It could be cut in strips of any length and width for a variety of uses, such as holding the edges of a wound together, holding dressings and bandages in place, and helping to stabilize fractures. However, adhesive plaster bandages could not simply be stuck on; they had to be heated to make them stay. Many doctors kept a can of hot water handy and put the back of the adhesive strip around it until it was sticky enough for use. The bandages could also be heated over the flame of a spirit lamp. If all else failed, rubbing the bandage between the thumb and forefinger might warm the bandage enough for use. Because of the problems of heating the adhesive plaster bandages and because they sometimes irritated the patient's skin, not all doctors used them.

Plaster bandages, such as are used to make casts, were uncommon and were not a regular part of the hospital supplies.

See also: Amputation; Antiseptics and Disinfectants; Gunshot Wounds, Treatment of; Splints.

Bibliography

Barnes, Joseph K., ed. *The Medical and Surgical History of the War of the Rebellion (1861–65)*. Washington, DC: Government Printing Office, 1870–1888; reprint, Wilmington, NC: Broadfoot, 1990.

Cunningham, H.H. *Doctors in Gray: The Confederate Medical Service*. Baton Rouge: Louisiana State University Press, 1958; reprint, Gloucester, MA: Peter Smith, 1970.

Rokicki, Ryan. "Artifact Under Exam: Adhesive Plaster: The Sticky Bandage." *Surgeon's Call* 8 (Spring 2003): 15.

BARNES, JOSEPH K. (1817–1883)

Joseph K. Barnes, Union surgeon general during the latter part of the Civil War, was born in Philadelphia, Pennsylvania, on July 21, 1817. His father, also named Joseph Barnes, was a judge in the district court in Philadelphia. Young Barnes studied at Round Hill School in Northampton, Massachusetts, and attended Harvard until forced by poor health to drop out. He studied medicine with naval surgeon Thomas Harris and graduated from the University of Pennsylvania's medical school in 1838. After a year as a hospital resident and another as a visiting physician, Barnes passed the army medical board examination and was commissioned assistant surgeon on June 15, 1840. At some point he married Mary Fauntleroy of Winchester, Virginia.

After a brief assignment at West Point, Barnes served eight different posts in Florida (1840–1842) during the Seminole War. Stationed in Louisiana from 1842 to 1846, Barnes then served during the Mexican War in both Zachary Taylor's army in northern Mexico and with Winfield Scott in the siege of Vera Cruz and the Mexico City campaign. After the end of the war, Barnes was stationed at various times in Texas, Kansas, California, the Pacific Northwest, Maryland, and Pennsylvania. On August 29, 1856, he was promoted to surgeon with the rank of major.

Barnes was at Fort Vancouver, Washington Territory, when the Civil War began. Ordered east, he served with troops in Missouri before being assigned to duty in Washington, DC, in May 1862. Here he became a friend of and personal physician to Secretary of War Edwin M. Stanton. On February 9, 1863, Barnes became a medical inspector with the rank of lieutenant colonel and was promoted to medical inspector general with the rank of colonel on August 10, 1863.

Stanton and Surgeon General William A. Hammond had never gotten along. Stanton sent Hammond on an inspecting tour to the armies and hospitals away from Washington, replacing him on September 3, 1863, with Barnes as acting surgeon general. It took almost a year longer for Stanton to maneuver Hammond out of office, but on August 18, 1864, Hammond was dismissed on trumped-up charges related to contracts for medical supplies. Barnes officially became surgeon general on August 22, 1864, with the rank of brigadier general.

Interestingly, with Barnes as surgeon general, Stanton was much more concerned and cooperative about the medical needs of the army. The war department issued orders to give medical officers authority over military officers in hospitals as well as control of hospital transports. Barnes was evidently more diplomatic than Hammond. He also continued the work begun by Hammond of collecting specimens for the Army Medical Museum and information for *The Medical and Surgical History of the War of the Rebellion*. Because Barnes remained surgeon general for seventeen years after the war, he was able to continue these programs. Four of the six volumes of the *Medical History* were published while he was still surgeon general. He also encouraged the development of the Army Medical Library.

Barnes was present at the bedside of the dying Abraham Lincoln and attended the president's autopsy. Barnes helped to treat Secretary of State William H. Seward when he was wounded in an assassination attempt at the same time Lincoln was shot. In 1881 Barnes cared for President James A. Garfield as he declined for three months before finally dying from the effects of the assassin Charles Guiteau's bullet.

In 1882 Congress passed a law requiring army officers to retire when they reached the age of sixty-four. Barnes was forced to retire on June 30, 1882, because he was nearly a year older. Already in poor health, he died of chronic nephritis (kidney inflammation) on April 5, 1883, in Washington, DC.

See also: Army Medical Museum; Hammond, William Alexander; Hospital Ships; Inspectors, Medical; Lincoln, Abraham; *The Medical and Surgical History of the War of the Rebellion*; Surgeon General.

Bibliography
Phelan, James M. "Joseph K. Barnes." *Army Medical Bulletin* 52 (April 1940): 47–51.

BARTON, CLARA (1821–1912)

Probably the best known of all the women involved in the Civil War, Clara Barton was born December 25, 1821, in North Oxford, Massachusetts. Clarissa Harlowe Barton, who always used the name Clara, was the fifth child of Captain Stephen Barton and Sarah Stone Barton. Because Clara was eleven years younger than her nearest sibling, she essentially grew up with six adult teachers. Never taken seriously by her family, she became self-conscious and shy, always feeling herself to be a burden. A bright child who started school at age three, Clara impressed her teachers with her intelligence and academic success, but she was not comfortable socializing with her fellow students and always felt out of place.

Clara's father was a farmer and miller who had been in the army fighting Indians in the Northwest Territory. She loved hearing his stories and the adventures of her Revolutionary War ancestors. She participated in many activities with her boy cousins, beating them at many sports and games. Throughout her life Barton was happiest in what were considered men's pursuits and was frequently discouraged, restricted, or frustrated because of her gender when she tried to participate, both as a young girl and as an adult.

Her family emphasized the importance of hard work. Barton was still young when she realized that being useful earned her appreciation. She began to see her self-worth as based on her ability to be of service to others, a perspective that lasted for the rest of her life and triggered serious depressions when she had no area of service.

During her teen years Clara cared for her injured brother, her sister's children, and numerous ailing neighbors. At about age eighteen she began teaching school. She was very successful and much loved by her students in several different locations in Massachusetts and New Jersey. However, Barton was extremely discouraged when, after she had established and developed the public school in Bordentown, New Jersey, the school board brought in a man to be the principal and made her his lower-paid assistant. Barton evidently had several suitors during her life, but little is known about them, sometimes not even their names, because she said and wrote little about them. In any case, she never married any of them.

Beginning in July 1854, Barton worked as a clerk in the Patent Office in Washington, DC, one of the few women in government positions. Although she was an excellent copyist and more productive than most of her male colleagues, she met with salary reductions and job loss due to political and gender issues. She worked there regularly or intermittently from 1854 to 1857 and from 1860 to 1865. This position supported her during her Civil War relief activities.

Clara Barton's work during the Civil War was made possible in part because she gained some influential backers, such as Massachusetts senator Henry Wilson, the chairman of the senate military affairs committee. When she did not have backers, Barton generally found her way obstructed, both because she was a woman and because she was independent of the U.S. Sanitary Commission as well as the female nurses headed by Dorothea Dix.

Barton's first wartime activity was caring for wounded Massachusetts troops who had been attacked by a mob in Baltimore on April 19, 1861, on their way to Washington. The government was completely unprepared to care for the soldiers, whether wounded or well, most of whom had had their luggage stolen by the mob. Barton solicited and purchased food, clothing, and other necessities for them.

Barton had friends and former students among the Massachusetts, New York, and New Jersey troops arriving in the capital, and she visited them frequently. Friends began to send supplies to her because they believed she would be able to get them to the troops. Soon she began to solicit supplies so they would be available when a battle took place. She took delicacies to hospitalized soldiers and met boats and trains arriving with sick and wounded soldiers needing care.

In early 1862 Barton spent some weeks caring for her ailing father, who encouraged her to serve her country. After his death on March 21, she went back to Washington, where she finally got passes that enabled her to take her supplies to the field. Her first battle scene was at Culpepper, Virginia (also known as Cedar Mountain and Cedar Run), where she arrived on August 13, four days after the battle. She provided shirts, salves, bandages, beverages, food, and other items that the doctors desperately needed. She and two assistants worked without a break for two days and nights, cooking, making bandages, cleaning, and doing whatever nursing they could to meet the need.

She next took relief supplies to the wounded at Fairfax Station, Virginia, essentially a makeshift hospital from which soldiers wounded at the Second Battle of Bull Run (Manassas) on August 29–30 were being shipped to Washington. The doctors had no supplies besides what Barton brought. She left with the last train of wounded, just before Confederates attacked and burned the station. Then, on September 14, Barton arrived with supplies just after the battle ended at South Mountain, Maryland.

The Battle of Antietam (Maryland), fought on September 17, 1862, was the bloodiest single day of the Civil War. Barton arrived at the Poffenberger farm on the field, which had become a hospital for an estimated 1,500 of the most seriously wounded men, with four wagons loaded with desperately needed supplies. Again, Barton did what she could, bandaging wounds, giving drinks of water, making pots of gruel, and holding limbs during amputations. She even removed a bullet from a soldier's face. After Antietam, Barton became ill with typhoid fever and was unable to work for a month.

Barton arrived at Falmouth, across the Rappahannock River from Fredericksburg, Virginia, on December 7, 1862. She cared for patients at the Lacy House even before the battle of December 13, during which she was under fire while working in a hospital in the town. She then returned to the Lacy House and nursed patients until the end of December, when they all had either died or been shipped to Washington.

Barton spent the winter gathering further supplies. However, by the time of the spring campaign, many of the army medical department reforms that she and others had urged had been adopted. Both the department and the Sanitary Commission opposed independent relief workers such as Barton, limiting her activities. In April 1863 she went to Hilton Head, South Carolina, where her brother, David, had been appointed an assistant quartermaster. There she had an active social life, apparently including a love affair with the quartermaster, Colonel John J. Elwell. However, she was frustrated by her inability to serve the soldiers in any significant way. Barton did care for some of the wounded on Morris Island after the Battle of Fort Wagner, fought on July 18, 1863, but disagreements with the commanding officer limited even that opportunity.

During the spring campaign of 1864 Barton worked in Fredericksburg, to which many of the wounded from various battles were moved. In June she began to work in a field hospital that was part of the medical services for General Benjamin F. Butler's Army of the James. In the tent hospital, which moved when the army moved, Barton served as hospital cook and performed other duties for forty to one hundred patients. She remained with the hospital until January 1865.

In the late spring and early summer of 1865, Barton was in Annapolis, Maryland, where she established an office to which people could write who were seeking information about a missing soldier. She published lists of these names in the hope that someone who knew what had happened to the soldier would contact her and she could pass the information on to his family. In July and August 1865 she went to Andersonville prison camp in Georgia with Dorence Atwater, a former Andersonville prisoner, and a work crew. Atwater had kept a list of the names of all the soldiers who had died at the prison and where they were buried. The group went to properly mark the graves. After this trip, Barton continued her missing persons office as well as she could with her limited finances until she finally got some government aid in 1866.

Although Barton worked hard during the war and performed important services, she was by no means the only woman worker on the battlefields, in the hospitals, or bringing supplies. However, she became better known than the rest partly through her own efforts to publicize her work, both at the time and after the war. From 1866 through 1868 she lectured around the country, captivating her audiences and, at times, exaggerating the importance of her activities. The common soldiers, whom she had nursed, loved her, and after the war, in gratitude, many of them named a daughter after her.

Barton is best known for founding the American Red Cross in 1877. Promoting the Red Cross became her full-time occupation for many years. After several years of declining health and a long bout with pneumonia, Barton died at her home in Glen Echo, Maryland, on April 12, 1912.

See also: Andersonville Prison; Antietam, Battle of; Bull Run (Manassas), Second Battle of; Cooks; Dix, Dorothea Lynde; Fredericksburg, Battle of; Hospitals, Field; Nurses; Quartermasters; Tents, Hospital; Typhoid Fever; United States Sanitary Commission; Washington, DC; Women, as Hospital Workers.

Bibliography

Oates, Stephen B. *A Woman of Valor: Clara Barton and the Civil War.* New York: Free Press, 1994.

Pryor, Elizabeth Brown. *Clara Barton, Professional Angel.* Philadelphia: University of Pennsylvania Press, 1987.

Schultz, Jane E. "Between Scylla and Charybdis: Clara Barton's Wartime Odyssey." *Minerva: Quarterly Report on Women and the Military* 14 (Fall/Winter 1996): 45–68.

BEAN, JAMES BAXTER (1834–1870)

James Baxter Bean, a Civil War dentist, was born in Washington County in East Tennessee, the son of gunsmith Robert Bean and his wife, Mary Hunter Bean. Little is known about Bean's childhood and youth except that his father died when James was two years old. Bean attended and may have graduated from Washington College in Limestone, Tennessee. By the late 1850s he was living in Micanopy, Florida, where he practiced medicine (nothing is known about his training) and collected bird eggs and other specimens for the Smithsonian Institution. In March 1860 Bean graduated from the Baltimore College of Dental Surgery after attending its five-month course. On October 30, 1860, Bean married Hester Bovell in Jonesborough, Tennessee. The couple eventually had a son and a daughter, both of whom died in childhood.

Bean apparently suffered from chronic rheumatism and, therefore, was unable to do military service during the Civil War. He moved to Atlanta, Georgia, where he had a private dental practice and worked for Brown and Hape, the only company manufacturing dental products in the Confederacy. In late 1863 Bean met Samuel H. Stout, medical director of hospitals for the Army of Tennessee, and volunteered to spend one day per week providing dental care for soldiers.

Bean worked as a civilian, apparently paid from the hospital fund, at the Medical College Hospital in Atlanta. After the evacuation of that city in the summer of 1864, he worked at the Blind School Hospital in Macon, Georgia. In each place Bean treated soldiers who had suffered broken jaws because of gunshot wounds. Previously, treatment involved a sort of papier-mâché splint that often resulted in facial deformities. Bean's important treatment innovation was the "interdental splint." This consisted of a vulcanized rubber mouthpiece with indentations for the teeth and an opening in the front to admit liquids. It was held in place by a cap of straps on top of the head, attached to a padded piece under the chin, which kept the mouth closed. The splint had numerous advantages over previous treatments: (1) it was neat; (2) it allowed patients to consume liquids easily; (3) it was difficult to dislodge; (4) it kept the teeth and jaw properly aligned; and (5) it prevented facial deformities.

Stout was so pleased with the results of Bean's treatment that he ordered all jaw fracture cases in the Army of Tennessee to be sent to the hospital where Bean was working. When Surgeon General Samuel P. Moore heard about the interdental splint, he ordered Bean to Richmond to demonstrate it and instruct Richmond dentists how to use it. After the fall of Richmond, Moore ordered Bean to go to Charlotte, North Carolina, where Moore was attempting to reestablish his hospital center; however, the collapse of the transportation system prevented Bean from going.

Bean successfully treated more than 140 cases, including General James Patton Anderson, who suffered a jaw wound in the Battle of Jonesboro, Georgia, in 1864. However, Bean never wrote up case reports after the war and little would have been known about his treatment if Edward N. Covey, a Confederate medical inspector, had not published an article about the splint in the *Richmond Medical Journal* in 1866.

After the war Bean practiced dentistry briefly in Atlanta and then moved his practice to Baltimore. He (and ten others) froze to death in a blizzard while climbing Mont Blanc in the French Alps in September 1870. He was buried in the Protestant Cemetery in Chamonix, France.

See also: Dentistry; Gunshot Wounds, Treatment of; Hospital Fund; Hospitals, General; Moore, Samuel Preston; Stout, Samuel Hollingsworth.

Bibliography
Baxter, Colin F. "Dr. James Baxter Bean, Civil War Dentist: An East Tennessean's Victorian Tragedy." *Journal of East Tennessee History* 67 (1995): 34–57.

BEERS, FANNIE A. (1840?–FL. 1888)

Fannie A. Beers, a Confederate hospital matron, was born in the North, probably in Connecticut, where she grew up. In the 1850s she married Augustus P. Beers, who had studied at Yale. The couple moved to New Orleans, where, despite her upbringing, she became an ardent Southern partisan. At the outbreak of the war Beers was in Connecticut, in poor health, awaiting the birth of a baby. The new-born infant died, and Beers was soon in grave danger from the townspeople, who were upset by her Southern sympathies. She and her young son, Georgie, fled to Richmond, Virginia, where she was reunited with her husband, who was serving in Dreux's Battalion.

Beers wanted to nurse Confederate soldiers. Although her husband approved, the doctors thought her too young and delicate. She finally gained some experience at the Soldier's Rest, a small private hospital run by several ladies in a schoolhouse. She then served as the matron of the Second Alabama Hospital in Richmond until she became ill and went to Alabama to recuperate with her husband's relatives.

Shortly after the Battle of Shiloh in 1862, Beers answered an advertisement and became matron of the Buckner Hospital, which she helped Dr. William T. McAllister to organize in Gainesville, Alabama. Over the course of the war, Beers moved with this Army of Tennessee hospital to Ringgold, Newnan, and Fort Valley, all in Georgia. As matron she was responsible for supervising hospital cleanliness and bedding, as well as the cooking for the sick. However, she also took personal care of the sick and wounded herself. In Newnan the hospital had 1,000 beds. During a Federal raid on that town, every able-bodied Confederate male fled the hospital and Beers was in charge for a day, aided in nursing only by some patients who were barely convalescent themselves.

After the Battle of Jonesboro in the summer of 1864, the Buckner Hospital moved to Fort Valley but received few patients. Because Beers was compulsive about being of service, she asked to be sent to a hospital nearer the front. After a few weeks in Macon, Georgia, she went to a primitive tent hospital in Lauderdale Springs, Mississippi, which suffered from severe supply shortages. Here she spent the winter of 1864–1865 nursing patients through a smallpox epidemic.

Her nursing career ended when her health failed in February 1865 and she returned to her husband's relatives in Alabama. Reunited with her husband and son, Beers and her family eventually returned to New Orleans, where she wrote articles and stories and served as assistant editor for the *Southern Bivouac*. Beers promoted remembrance of the "Lost Cause" by attending veterans' meetings. Her most important contribution was the publication of *Memories: A Record of Personal Experience and Adventure During Four Years of War* (1888), an account of her hospital experiences with the Army of Tennessee. Unfortunately, her wartime diary had been stolen during a raid, so she was not able to be as detailed about dates and people as she might otherwise have been. Her book contains little information about her personal life. The date of her death is not known.

See also: Diet, of Hospital Patients; Hospital Relocations; Matrons; Nurses; Richmond, Virginia; Shiloh, Battle of; Tents, Hospital; Women, as Hospital Workers.

Bibliography

Beers, Fannie A. *Memories: A Record of Personal Experience and Adventure During Four Years of War.* Philadelphia: J.B. Lippincott, 1888; reprint, Alexandria, VA: Time-Life, 1985.

BELLOWS, HENRY WHITNEY (1814–1882)

Henry Whitney Bellows, Unitarian minister and president of the U.S. Sanitary Commission, was born in Boston, the son of John and Betsy Eames Bellows, on June 11, 1814. He graduated from Harvard in 1832. After teaching school in Cooperstown, New York, and tutoring on a Louisiana plantation, Bellows attended Harvard Divinity School, from which he graduated in 1837. Ordained a Unitarian minister, Bellows served a church in Mobile, Alabama, for about a year before accepting the pastorate of All Souls Unitarian Church in New York City in 1839.

In August 1839 Bellows married Eliza Nevins Townsend of New York; they eventually had five children. In the mid-1840s Bellows became the editor of the *Christian Inquirer*. He was also instrumental in founding such New York groups as the Century Club, the Union League, and the Harvard Club of New York. As a pastor, he was a good preacher but not a theological scholar. He was more interested in practical ways to meet the needs of his parishioners. He was also involved with various humanitarian causes in the antebellum period.

Upon the outbreak of the Civil War, Bellows became very concerned about the care of Union soldiers. With Dr. Elisha Harris, the physician in charge of the quarantine hospital on Staten Island, Bellows led a meeting of New York City women on April 25, 1861, which called a second meeting four days later, organizing the Woman's Central Association of Relief. Within a few weeks Bellows, Harris, and two other New York physicians went to Washington, DC, to investigate the conditions of the volunteer troops gathering there. Discovering that the soldiers lacked many supplies and that the medical department had made no preparations to take care of the sick and wounded, the committee proposed to establish a sanitary commission to assist the medical department.

The army's medical hierarchy did not believe that it needed assistance from civilians. It was only after several weeks of visiting officials that the committee persuaded Secretary of War Simon Cameron to draw up and President Abraham Lincoln to sign an order establishing the U.S. Sanitary Commission in June 1861.

Bellows became the Sanitary Commission's president and a member of its executive committee, headquartered in New York City. He attended nearly daily meetings in New York, as well as frequent meetings in Washington. He often lobbied government officials, including Lincoln and General George B. McClellan, for reforms desired by the Sanitary Commission, such as a competent surgeon general and an ambulance corps. In addition, Bellows traveled much during the war, on occasion to inspect troop conditions but later mostly to promote and encourage the Sanitary Commission and its various branches. In 1864, for example, he traveled to California, after the death of the commission's greatest supporter there, to preach in his stead, organize branch commissions, establish fund-raising methods, and resolve conflicts between commission supporters in California and Oregon.

Bellows did not manage the day-to-day functioning of the Sanitary Commission, which was the responsibility of Frederick Law Olmsted, the executive secretary, and his successors. Instead, Bellows preached and published sermons, gave speeches, and wrote private and public letters to inspire support for the commission's work. He also tried to smooth over and mediate quarrels that arose with the government, within the commission, and with other organizations. Bellows was a good, clear speaker, regarded as wise and public-spirited by his supporters. His critics, however, saw him as egotistical. Some local relief organizations, objecting to the nationalizing, centralizing commission, remained independent, as did the Western Sanitary Commission (despite its name). In addition, some evangelical Christians refused to support an organization headed by Bellows, who, as a Unitarian, did not believe Jesus was the Son of God. They formed their own relief organization, the U.S. Christian Commission.

After the war Bellows continued his pastorate, in addition to editing the *Christian Examiner* (1866–1877) and helping to found and lead the National Conference of Unitarian Churches. He also became very active in promoting civil service reform. Bellows's wife died in August 1869. In June 1874 he married Anna Huidekoper Peabody of Boston, by whom he had two children. After nearly forty-four years as pastor of the All Souls Unitarian Church, Bellows died in New York City on January 30, 1882.

See also: Ambulance Corps; Nightingale, Florence; Olmsted, Frederick Law; Strong, George Templeton; United States Christian Commission; United States Sanitary Commission; Western Sanitary Commission.

Bibliography

Maxwell, William Quentin. *Lincoln's Fifth Wheel: The Political History of the United States Sanitary Commission.* New York: Longmans, Green, 1956.

BICKERDYKE, MARY ANN BALL ("MOTHER") (1817–1901)

Mary Ann Ball Bickerdyke was a Union nurse and U.S. Sanitary Commission agent with the western armies. The daughter of Hiram and Annie Rodgers Ball, Mary Ann Ball was born in Knox County, Ohio, on July 19, 1817. Because her mother died when Mary Ann was seventeen months old, she was mostly raised by her maternal grandparents and, after their deaths, by an uncle and his family. She grew up on farms, gaining many practical skills but little formal education.

For a few years she lived near Cincinnati and may have studied at the Physio-Botanic Medical School, which would explain why she later practiced botanic medicine. On April 27, 1847, she married Robert Bickerdyke, a Cincinnati sign and ornamental painter as well as a bass viol player. He was a widower with two sons and a daughter, whom Mary Ann helped to raise. Robert and Mary Ann also had two sons and a daughter, who died at the age of two. In 1856 the family moved to Galesburg, Illinois, where Robert died suddenly in 1859. Mary Ann then supported the family as a "botanic physician."

Because of her recognized organizational abilities, Bickerdyke was selected by her church, the Brick Congregational Church of Galesburg, to take a shipment of supplies to Galesburg troops suffering in Cairo, Illinois, shortly after the Civil War began. She arrived on June 9, 1861, and proceeded to clean up the filthy hospitals, bathe the patients, and prepare more digestible food for them. She also taught the soldiers and company cooks how to fix food properly so that poor cooking would not make them sick.

Devoted to the well being of ordinary soldiers, Bickerdyke did anything she could to improve their health, personally pitching in to clean, cook, wash, and haul supplies. The soldiers, in turn, loved her and already by the summer of 1861 were calling her "Mother." Refusing to be bossed around, she had many conflicts with doctors and other officials because she was blunt, truthful, and forceful in defense of the needs of the sick and wounded and her right to meet those needs. Yet the clear benefits of her work gained her the support of such generals and army commanders as John A. Logan, Stephen A. Hurlbut, Ulysses S. Grant, and William T. Sherman. Sherman famously responded to one complainer that he could not oppose Bickerdyke because she outranked him, since she believed that God had called her to her work. The generals provided her with passes for herself, her assistants, and her supplies. In addition to several detailed soldiers, Bickerdyke employed a number of "contrabands" (escaped slaves) at numerous tasks.

In February 1862, after working in Cairo for some months, Bickerdyke cared for wounded soldiers from the Battle of Fort Donelson on the Sanitary Commission ship *City of Memphis.* Accompanying Grant's army, she also nursed the wounded from the Battle of Shiloh (April 6–7, 1862). In many cases she appropriated Sanitary Commission supplies for her wounded. In the spring of 1862, the commission made her one of its official agents. On several occasions during the war, she took a couple of weeks to visit her sons, left behind in boarding situations, and her supporters in Galesburg. She also made speeches to raise funds and supplies for the Sanitary Commission in Chicago and elsewhere.

After Shiloh, Bickerdyke cleaned up and managed a hospital that was established in Farmington and then moved to Corinth, Mississippi, caring for the sick of the Corinth campaign. In Memphis, Tennessee, Bickerdyke ministered to sick and wounded hospital patients from Grant's lengthy Vicksburg campaign in late 1862 and 1863. During the summer of 1863, Sherman appointed Bickerdyke to work with the Fifteenth Corps. She traveled south with it on a difficult march, arriving just before the Battle of Chattanooga (November 23–25, 1863), during which she worked in a makeshift hospital. Her famous ability to stretch supplies was put to good use during a period of serious shortages after the battle.

Bickerdyke went along on Sherman's Atlanta campaign in the spring and summer of 1864, but not on the March to the Sea in the fall of that year. In Wilmington, North Carolina, she nursed Union prisoners of war who were in terrible physical condition after their release from the prison camp at Andersonville, Georgia. Throughout the summer of 1865 she worked getting hospitalized soldiers in Louisville, Kentucky, and then Huntsville, Alabama, ready to go home. She remained a Sanitary Commission agent until the last Illinois soldier was mustered out on March 21, 1866.

After the war Bickerdyke worked for a year as a cook and housekeeper at Chicago's Home for the Friendless. Then she helped displaced veterans to settle and learn how to farm in the Salina, Kansas, area, where she kept a hotel/boarding house for several years. From 1870 to 1874 Bickerdyke instructed individuals and families in matters of cooking, sanitation, and health, working toward cleaning up the slums of New York City. She traveled and spoke around the Midwest and East, raising 200 carloads of supplies for the Kansas families whose livelihoods had been wiped out by the grasshopper plague of 1874. She served as an agent and advocate for veterans' pensions and worked at the mint in San Francisco.

Bickerdyke won wide recognition for her achievements. On May 24, 1865, she rode with General Logan on the second day of the Grand Review in Washington, DC. In her old age, living with her son, Jimmy, in Bunker Hill, Kansas, she collected a special government pension of $25 per month. Grateful veterans in the Grand Army of the Republic, Kansas branch, staged a huge celebration in honor of her eightieth birthday on July 19, 1897. Mary Ann Bickerdyke died on November 8, 1901, in Kansas, from the effects of a stroke, and was buried in Galesburg, Illinois, with her husband.

See also: Alternative Medicines; Andersonville Prison; Blacks, as Hospital Workers; Cooks; Diet, of Hospital Patients; Diet, of Troops; Hospital Support Staff; Hospitals, General; Laundresses; Livermore, Mary Ashton Rice; Nurses; Sanitation; Shiloh, Battle of; United States Sanitary Commission; Women, as Hospital Workers.

Bibliography
Baker, Nina Brown. *Cyclone in Calico: The Story of Mary Ann Bickerdyke*. Boston: Little, Brown, 1952.
Livermore, Mary A. *My Story of the War*. Hartford, CT, 1887; reprint, New York: Da Capo, 1995.

BLACKS, AS HOSPITAL WORKERS

Blacks, whether slave, free, or "contraband" (escaped slaves), proved crucial to medical efforts during the Civil War in both Union and Confederate hospitals.

In the South, slave laborers built or remodeled buildings for hospital use. They also provided other types of manual labor such as caring for livestock, raising food for the patients, and hauling supplies. Slaves could be hired from their owners or forcibly impressed into service to prevent their owners from taking them out of the area. Free blacks were also hired, and even impressed for hospital work, as early as May 1862 in Tennessee.

Blacks constituted a growing percentage of the hospital staff as the war progressed, replacing detailed and convalescent soldiers who returned to the field and providing worker stability that was missing with the frequent turnover of soldiers. Both male and female blacks did much of the hospital cooking. Most laundresses were black women, who sometimes also did cleaning and nursing. More black men than women were nurses, however.

An analysis of records for the Confederate Army of Tennessee hospitals in northern Georgia in 1863 shows that blacks were about 46 percent of all hospital workers. This percentage increased during the first half of 1864 until in some hospitals blacks made up more than 70 percent of the workforce. Hundreds of blacks also worked at the Chimborazo and Winder hospitals in Richmond, Virginia. Undoubtedly blacks composed an equivalent proportion of the workers in other Confederate hospitals for which records no longer survive.

Other Southern blacks contributed to the medical and war effort by working in the medical purveyor's office or at one of the medical laboratories. Slaves often accompanied their mistresses on hospital visits to bring supplies, while still others went to the battlefield with masters as part of relief association efforts.

Blacks, free and contraband, were employed in similar capacities in Union hospitals. However, more of them worked in hospitals located in the slave states than in hospitals where there was a lower black population. Compiled Service Records (CSRs) for women who served with the Union army show that 2,096, or 10 percent of the women whose services were recorded, were black. They constituted 36 percent of female cooks, 14 percent of female laundresses, and 6 percent of female nurses (although many laundresses provided nursing care without receiving the title or the pay). Twelve black physicians also served with the U.S. Colored Troops (USCT): Anderson R. Abbott, Alexander T. Augusta, Benjamin A. Boseman, Cortlandt Creed, John De Grasse, William B. Ellis, Joseph D. Harris, David O. McCord, William Powell, Charles Burleigh Purvis, John Rapier, and Alpheus Tucker. Augusta, De Grasse, and McCord had commissions while the others served as contract (acting assistant) surgeons.

See also: Chimborazo Hospital; Convalescents; Cooks; Hospital Support Staff; Laboratories, Medical; Laundresses; Medical Purveyors; Nurses; Richmond, Virginia; Women, as Hospital Workers.

Bibliography

Glatthaar, Joseph T. "The Costliness of Discrimination: Medical Care for Black Troops in the Civil War." In *Inside the Confederate Nation: Essays in Honor of Emory M. Thomas*, ed. Lesley J. Gordon and John C. Inscoe, pp. 251–271. Baton Rouge: Louisiana State University Press, 2005.

Green, Carol C. *Chimborazo: The Confederacy's Largest Hospital.* Knoxville: University of Tennessee Press, 2004.

Mohr, Clarence L. "The Atlanta Campaign and the African American Experience in Civil War Georgia." In *Inside the Confederate Nation: Essays in Honor of Emory M. Thomas*, ed. Lesley J. Gordon and John C. Inscoe, pp. 272–294. Baton Rouge: Louisiana State University Press, 2005.

Schultz, Jane E. *Women at the Front: Hospital Workers in Civil War America.* Chapel Hill: University of North Carolina Press, 2004.

Slawson, Robert G. *Prologue to Change: African Americans in Medicine in the Civil War Era.* Frederick, MD: NMCWM, 2006.

BLACKS, HEALTH OF

Blacks, slave and free, suffered many illnesses during the antebellum and Civil War eras. Due to environmental and living conditions, discrimination, and occasional genetic factors, blacks contracted certain diseases more or less frequently than whites.

Many Southern doctors believed that whites and blacks were medically different. Blacks were supposed to be immune, or at least less susceptible, to certain diseases, making them naturally able to do hard work in hot climates. Doctors sometimes studied the physical traits of blacks, such as color, facial features, odor, and brain size. The goal of most of these studies was political, to prove that blacks were inferior and, consequently, to justify slavery. Some Southern doctors also tried experimental surgeries and other treatments on blacks before attempting them on whites.

When slaves became ill, masters were generally concerned because of their financial investment. A master also could have an emotional attachment to a slave or worry that the disease might spread from the slave to the white family. Many owners would try home treatment of the slave at first, calling a doctor only if the patient continued to get worse. While a "regular" physician might be called, some masters consulted homeopaths or Thomsonian doctors, black herb doctors, or even, on occasion, conjurers. While some masters were reluctant to spend money to treat slaves, many other slaveholders provided the best medical attendance possible.

Free blacks, who generally earned low incomes, were often unable to afford medical attendance. Sometimes they received treatment from local physicians as charity cases or at dispensaries associated with medical schools in large cities.

Most blacks, whether slave or free, worked and lived in crowded, unsanitary conditions that contributed to the spread of disease (as did similar conditions for lower-class whites). Both blacks and whites tended to have two different seasons of sickness. During the cold months, people were confined and crowded indoors most of the time or exposed to inclement weather outdoors. These conditions led to many respiratory illnesses, from colds to pneumonia. During the warm season, people suffered from many intestinal illnesses, caused by polluted water, spoiled food, and contaminated soil. Some of these diseases were spread by flies and other insects. Mosquitoes also spread malaria and yellow fever in the South.

Although blacks and whites suffered from the same health problems generally, there were actually a few differences between the two races that were confirmed by researchers during the twentieth century. The most important of these was sickle cell anemia, a genetic red blood cell disease inherited by some blacks. Persons with the sickle cell trait were themselves healthy but had a chromosome that could pass on the disease to their children if both parents had the trait. A person with sickle cell disease could be quite ill with severe joint pain and other problems such as susceptibility to lung diseases. Half of all children with sickle cell disease died before the age of twenty, probably contributing to the high mortality among slave children. Sickle cell trait or disease generally made the person immune to malaria, however.

The major causes of death for slaves in the 1850s were infectious diseases. Tuberculosis was the leading cause of death, followed by other respiratory ailments, such as pneumonia, and by gastrointestinal problems, such as typhoid fever and other diseases that caused diarrhea and extreme dehydration.

Blacks who joined the Union army suffered severely from illnesses during the Civil War, as did white soldiers, North and South. However, black soldiers tended to have some additional problems. Because of racial discrimination, many black regiments were stationed in unhealthy areas. Some regiments also had difficulty getting doctors who were competent and willing to care for them. In some cases, black regiments had to make do with poorly trained hospital stewards as their only source of medical care. Few white women were willing to nurse black soldiers; one exception was Esther Hill Hawks, who helped to care for sick and wounded black soldiers in the South Carolina Sea Islands, where her husband was a doctor.

In general, however, the black soldiers fared better when treated in their regiment than when sent to a general hospital.

One historian who has studied the mortality of black troops has determined that the death rate of black soldiers from disease was two and a half times the death rate for white soldiers with the same illnesses.

See also: Alternative Medicines; Diarrhea and Dysentery; Hawks, Esther Hill; Hospitals, Field; Hospitals, General; Malaria; Mortality, of Soldiers; Mosquitoes; Nurses; Pneumonia; Stewards, Hospital; Surgeons; Tuberculosis; Typhoid Fever.

Bibliography

Glatthaar, Joseph T. "The Costliness of Discrimination: Medical Care for Black Troops in the Civil War." In *Inside the Confederate Nation: Essays in Honor of Emory M. Thomas*, ed. Lesley J. Gordon and John C. Inscoe, pp. 251–271. Baton Rouge: Louisiana State University Press, 2005.

Savitt, Todd L. *Medicine and Slavery: The Diseases and Health Care of Blacks in Antebellum Virginia*. Urbana: University of Illinois Press, 1978.

Schwartz, Gerald, ed. *A Woman Doctor's Civil War: Esther Hill Hawks' Diary*. Columbia: University of South Carolina Press, 1984, 1989.

BLOCKADE

On April 19, 1861, just days after the Confederates fired on the Union garrison at Fort Sumter in the harbor at Charleston, South Carolina, beginning the Civil War, President Abraham Lincoln declared a blockade of all Southern ports. This early war measure was designed to shorten the war by preventing the South from importing manufactured goods, especially military supplies, and from exporting its major crop, cotton. Because the South had very little industry, a blockade had great potential for damaging the Southern cause.

At first the idea of the blockade seemed laughable because only twelve of the Union navy's forty-two ships were available for blockade duty. The Confederacy had 3,500 miles of coastline, including ten major ports and 180 bays and other shallow areas that could be visited by small ships. There were land and river borders as well. However, even as early as May 1861 the threat of the blockade was beginning to cause shortages and rising prices in the South.

By June 1861 three dozen Union ships were involved in the blockade and more were added almost daily by purchase and charter. Ultimately, about 500 ships of various types participated in the blockade, with about 150 on duty at any one time. Initially, the blockaders caught only one of every dozen blockade-runners, but by 1864, runners had a one-in-three chance of being caught, and by 1865 a one-in-two chance. Wilmington, North Carolina, was the last major Southern port open. It closed when Fort Fisher fell to Union forces in January 1865.

During the war, blockade-runners made about 8,000 successful trips. Blockaders captured or destroyed about 1,500 ships. During the four years before the war, 20,000 ships had visited what became Confederate ports. Historians have calculated that the blockade, by sea and land, ultimately reduced Southern trade to less than one-third of the normal amount, at a time when even more imports were needed to provide for the war effort and to replace materials destroyed by military action. This trade reduction caused great shortages and contributed to the terrible inflation experienced by the Confederacy.

Medical supplies were among the items declared contraband of war and affected by the blockade. These included medical instruments and many medicines that could not be domestically produced easily, especially quinine, morphine, and chloroform. Confederates searched with limited success for indigenous plants that could be used to manufacture substitutes for scarce medicines. Blockade-runners usually included medicines in their cargoes because they were small and light and would sell for a high price. Other people also attempted to smuggle quinine and other medicines through the lines into the Confederacy. A number of women attached packages to their hoopskirts or other parts of their clothing or anatomy. One ingenious smuggler hid medicine in the carcass of a dead mule being hauled outside the lines for burial. However, smuggling, domestic manufacture, and supplies captured from the enemy could not fully meet the shortages that resulted from the blockade.

See also: Anesthesia; Laboratories, Medical; Morphine; Quinine; *Resources of the Southern Fields and Forests*; Substitutes, for Supplies.

Bibliography

Basler, Roy P., ed. *The Collected Works of Abraham Lincoln*. Vol. 4. New Brunswick, NJ: Rutgers University Press, 1953.

Flannery, Michael A. *Civil War Pharmacy: A History of Drugs, Drug Supply and Provision, and Therapeutics for the Union and Confederacy*. New York: Pharmaceutical Products Press, 2004.

Massey, Mary Elizabeth. *Ersatz in the Confederacy: Shortages and Substitutes on the Southern Homefront*. Columbia: University of South Carolina Press, 1952, 1993.

McPherson, James M. *Battle Cry of Freedom: The Civil War Era*. New York: Oxford University Press, 1988; reprint, New York: Ballantine, 1989.

Wise, Stephen R. *Lifeline of the Confederacy: Blockade Running During the Civil War*. Columbia: University of South Carolina Press, 1988.

"BLUE MASS" *See* Calomel.

BRINTON, JOHN HILL (1832–1907)

Union surgeon and medical museum curator John Hill Brinton was born in Philadelphia on May 21, 1832. He was a cousin of General George Brinton McClellan. John Brinton received a classical education before he entered the University of

Pennsylvania in 1848. Graduating with a bachelor's degree in 1850, he received a master's degree (largely an honorary degree in those days) in 1852. In the same year, he graduated from the Jefferson Medical College in Philadelphia. Unlike most young doctors of the period, Brinton was able to spend a year of postgraduate clinical training in Paris and Vienna. Upon his return, he was hired by his alma mater as a demonstrator and then lecturer in operative surgery. Eventually he was appointed professor of the principles and practice of surgery. Brinton held this succession of positions from 1853 until 1861, when he enlisted in the army medical service.

After passing his examination, Brinton was commissioned a brigade surgeon in August 1861 and sent west. He organized a military hospital in Mound City, Illinois, and several times served as medical director for General Ulysses S. Grant, both in Cairo, Illinois, and during the campaign against Forts Henry and Donelson in early 1862. Besides performing surgery, Brinton assisted and trained subordinate doctors who had had little surgical experience. He also supervised the transportation and general treatment of the patients. Brinton briefly served on the staffs of General John A. McClernand and General Henry W. Halleck. He was always in supervisory positions throughout his military career, never serving at the basic levels of regimental or hospital surgeon.

In May 1862 Brinton was ordered to Washington, DC, where on June 9 Surgeon General William A. Hammond made him responsible for gathering information to prepare the surgical part of the projected *The Medical and Surgical History of the War of the Rebellion*. On August 1 Hammond appointed Brinton the first curator of the Army Medical Museum.

Brinton's tasks during his time in Washington were quite varied. He generally spent mornings doing office work and in the afternoons visited the museum and then some hospital in the Washington area. He also helped devise new forms for reporting the numbers of sick and wounded soldiers. He served on a number of medical examining boards, whose purpose was to determine the qualifications of prospective army doctors.

Brinton was also responsible for gathering medical specimens for the museum. In this connection, he was ordered to the field soon after such major battles as Antietam, Fredericksburg, Chancellorsville, Gettysburg, and some of the battles in the spring campaign of 1864. At first Brinton had to get his specimens by digging up trenches full of amputated arms and legs in order to select the most illustrative examples of wounds. However, he was soon able to interest other surgeons in furnishing the specimens for him. Brinton's presence on the field served a practical purpose as well, as he assisted wherever he could, performing surgery or arranging transportation. At other times Hammond sent Brinton to inspect hospitals with gangrene problems or to gather information on casualties.

Unfortunately for Brinton, Secretary of War Edwin M. Stanton was vindictive toward those he disliked, including Surgeon General Hammond and General McClellan. In September 1864, after Hammond was court-martialed and dismissed from the service, Brinton was abruptly recalled from battlefield work in Winchester, Virginia, relieved of his posts in Washington, and sent to St. Louis, Missouri, where he became field medical director for General William S. Rosecrans. This sudden change was apparently the result of Brinton's close working relationship with Hammond and his kinship with McClellan. Brinton eventually served as superintendent and director of general hospitals at Nashville, Tennessee, at the time of the battles around Nashville in November and December 1864.

On February 16, 1865, Brinton resigned his commission because the war was nearly over and he needed to care for his widowed mother and unmarried sisters. After his resignation was accepted in March, Brinton returned to Philadelphia, where he resumed his post at the Jefferson Medical College. Beginning in 1882, he was professor of both bacteriology and clinical surgery there.

Soon after the war, Brinton married Sarah Wade, a woman about four years his junior, who had been born in India. By 1880 they had at least five children. In order to communicate something about himself and his war experiences to his children and their descendants, he wrote his *Personal Memoirs*, based on his correspondence during the war and completed in June 1891. His family had the book published in 1914, seven years after Brinton died of a stroke on March 18, 1907.

See also: Alcohol, Abuse of; Amputation; Antietam, Battle of; Army Medical Museum; Education, Medical; Examining Boards, Medical; Gangrene, Hospital; Gettysburg, Battle of; Gunshot Wounds; Hammond, William Alexander; Hospitals, Field; Hospitals, General; *The Medical and Surgical History of the War of the Rebellion*; Medical Directors, Field; Medical Directors, of Hospitals; Surgeons, Brigade.

Bibliography

Brinton, John H. *Personal Memoirs of John H. Brinton, Civil War Surgeon, 1861–1865.* New York: Neale, 1914; reprint, Carbondale: Southern Illinois University Press, 1996.
United States Census, 1880, Pennsylvania, Philadelphia, Philadelphia, 448C.

BRONCHITIS *See* Catarrh.

BULL RUN (MANASSAS), FIRST BATTLE OF (1861)

The First Battle of Bull Run (so named by the Union forces after a nearby creek) or Manassas (named by the Confederates for a nearby town) was the first large battle of the Civil War. It took place on July 21, 1861, between inexperienced armies in the Virginia countryside, nearer to Washington, DC, than to Richmond, Virginia.

Many of the Union troops under General Irvin McDowell were coming to the end of their three-month enlistments and there was considerable pressure from the public and the federal government for a decisive battle. McDowell's army was supposed to attack Confederates under General P.G.T. Beauregard at Manassas, an important railroad junction. Unknown to McDowell, the day before the battle Beauregard was reinforced by troops under General Joseph E. Johnston, who had come by railroad from the Shenandoah Valley. Although at first the Union attack on July 21 successfully pushed back the Confederates, they rallied on Henry House Hill under the command of Thomas J. Jackson, who earned his nickname "Stonewall" there. About 3:30 p.m. one more Confederate brigade arrived and attacked the Union troops, who began a retreat that turned into a disorganized rout.

As a result of the battle, the Confederates reported 387 killed, 1,582 wounded, and 13 missing (probably killed or captured). Union troops lost 418–460 killed, 1,011–1,124 wounded, and 1,216–1,460 missing. The casualty figures depend on who was doing the counting; the variations result from the absence of properly prepared reports. Although these figures are low compared to those from many of the major battles later in the war, at the time they were shocking.

Neither side was medically prepared for the battle. William S. King, medical director of McDowell's army, anticipated only a skirmish and failed to exercise more leadership than to fill out paperwork. He expected each regiment's medical officers to care for its own wounded. Unfortunately, many of the regiments were poorly supplied. The First Connecticut Infantry, for example, had between 600 and 700 men but only one ambulance, two hospital tents, and no hospital supplies, no litters, and no attendants except for the regimental band.

Many of the regimental medical officers did the best they could with what they had, improvising field hospitals in available buildings or treating individual wounded soldiers where they lay. Some doctors treated only their own men and turned away wounded soldiers from other regiments. Some doctors found their stations overwhelmed with wounded, while others had no one to treat. King eventually established one official Union field hospital, at Sudley Church, which quickly filled and overflowed into nearby outbuildings and an orchard. There was a shortage of both food and medical supplies for the wounded. The situation was chaotic and unsupervised.

Removing the wounded from the field presented further difficulties. The fortunate wounded were those able to walk back to Washington themselves. There were only a few ambulances, mainly driven by civilians. In the midst of battle most of these drivers, determined to save their own hides, fled back to Washington, not taking any patients with them. Eventually improvised wagon trains removed some of the wounded soldiers. Others were transported on the bare floors of railroad cars. Some wounded soldiers remained on the field as much as a week after the battle before being removed. Once the Union wounded arrived in Washington, they continued to face disorganized conditions and supply shortages in hospitals hastily established in public buildings.

The Confederates retained possession of the battlefield, including some Union wounded who could not be moved and the doctors who remained to care for them. Over the next two weeks the Confederates slowly moved the wounded soldiers to Richmond, where they overwhelmed the available hospitals. Mayor Joseph Mayo called a mass meeting of citizens and organized committees to bring the wounded from the battlefield, gather food and supplies, and set up new hospitals in churches, hotels, and private homes. Most of these were closed after the emergency had passed and the Confederate military reorganized the hospitals in Richmond. One of the exceptions was the Robertson Hospital, headed by Sally Tompkins, which remained open for the rest of the war.

The first battle at Bull Run (Manassas) showed that the war would last longer than many people had supposed. It demonstrated the need for medical resources and official organization on both sides. It also stimulated the work of the U.S. Sanitary Commission in the North, as well as other civilian aid societies on both sides that prepared and procured medical supplies. Nevertheless, the Union medical establishment under Surgeon General Clement A. Finley initially remained resistant to many of the changes needed to improve patient care, although William King was immediately replaced as army medical director by Charles S. Tripler.

See also: Ambulance Corps; Ambulances; Finley, Clement Alexander; Hospitals, Field; Hospitals, General; Medical Department, Organization of; Medical Directors, Field; Prisoners of War; Richmond, Virginia; Tompkins, Sally Louisa; Tripler, Charles Stuart; United States Sanitary Commission; Washington, DC.

Bibliography

Calcutt, Rebecca Barbour. *Richmond's Wartime Hospitals.* Gretna, LA: Pelican, 2005.

Davis, William C. *Battle at Bull Run: A History of the First Major Campaign of the Civil War.* Baton Rouge: Louisiana State University Press, 1977.

Duncan, Louis C. *The Medical Department of the United States Army in the Civil War.* Washington, DC: Author, 1914; reprint, Gaithersburg, MD: Butternut, 1985.

Rutkow, Ira M. *Bleeding Blue and Gray: Civil War Surgery and the Evolution of American Medicine.* New York: Random, 2005.

BULL RUN (MANASSAS), SECOND BATTLE OF (1862)

The Second Battle of Bull Run (Manassas) was fought on August 29–30, 1862, on nearly the same ground as the first battle, which had occurred about thirteen months previously. Like the first battle, the second was a Confederate victory.

In an effort to aid General George B. McClellan and the Army of the Potomac in the Peninsula Campaign against Richmond, Abraham Lincoln and the Union war department organized the new Army of Virginia by combining the armies of John C. Frémont, Nathaniel Banks, and Irvin McDowell, all of which had been operating unsuccessfully in the Shenandoah Valley. In addition to protecting that valley, the purpose of the new army was to protect Washington, DC, from the Confederates and to both pressure and distract General Robert E. Lee so that he would send some of his troops away from the Richmond area, giving McClellan a better chance. Lincoln selected General John Pope as the new commander. Pope managed to offend nearly everyone with an address to the troops comparing them unfavorably to the western soldiers he had previously led. Lincoln's plan was for Pope's 50,000 troops to move from the north and McClellan's 90,000 soldiers to come from the east to trap Lee. However, Pope and McClellan hated each other and McClellan, having retreated from Richmond, was not moving back toward it. In addition, the Army of the Potomac had many sick soldiers and was approaching the sickliest season of the year. Therefore, Lincoln decided that McClellan should withdraw from the peninsula by water and join Pope.

Meanwhile, Lee determined to attack Pope before Pope could be reinforced. Taking a great risk because Pope's forces already outnumbered the Confederates, Lee split his army and sent half of his forces with General Thomas J. "Stonewall" Jackson around Pope's right to cut his supply line (August 25–26). Marching more than fifty miles, Jackson's troops destroyed Pope's supply depot at Manassas. Pope, realizing that Lee's army was split, wanted to crush Jackson's troops before General James Longstreet and the rest of Lee's army arrived.

On the evening of August 28 elements of Jackson's and Pope's armies tangled at the Battle of Groveton, where Confederate general Richard S. Ewell was so badly wounded in the left knee that he had to have his leg amputated. The main battle at Bull Run began on August 29 when Pope ordered his troops to make a number of uncoordinated attacks on Jackson's men, who were defensively situated in an unfinished railroad cut. Union troops under General Fitz-John Porter were on the field for hours before Pope ordered Porter to attack Jackson's flank. By this time, Longstreet's forces had arrived and occupied the ground on Jackson's flank. Thus Porter could not and did not attack Jackson's troops, an alleged disobedience of orders that got Porter court-martialed and dismissed from the service a few months later.

During the night Jackson pulled back a few troops to strengthen his lines. Pope, who still did not know that Longstreet had arrived, decided that Jackson was retreating. About noon on August 30, when Pope sent troops to head off the supposed Confederate retreat, the men ran directly into Jackson's soldiers, leading to further hard fighting at the railroad cut. Lee ordered Longstreet's entire corps to attack Pope's left, where the Union forces were weakest. This move allowed the Confederates to push the Union troops back to Henry House Hill, where they made a stand. Overnight the Union troops withdrew from the field, leaving many casualties behind.

During the two-day battle, more than 75,000 Union troops fought, suffering 1,724 killed, 8,372 wounded, and 5,958 missing, for a total of 16,054 casualties, more than 21 percent of the force. The more than 48,000 Confederates lost 1,481 killed, 7,627 wounded, and 89 missing, totaling 9,197 casualties, or 19 percent of the force. Medical care for these injured soldiers was a tremendous problem during and after the battle.

Although army medical director Jonathan Letterman recently had ordered the establishment of a trained and supplied ambulance corps for the Army of the Potomac, that corps was still getting organized. Furthermore, McClellan had not sent many of his troops to join Pope, and those who went were rushed off without their ambulances or supplies. Letterman was not at Second Bull Run. Pope's medical director, Thomas McParlin, was in charge.

Instead of setting up field hospitals, McParlin decided to establish one large hospital, using regimental hospitals as dressing stations. Unfortunately, the hospital was so far behind the lines that it was four to seven miles away from various parts of the battlefield, making a long ride for wounded soldiers in such ambulances as were available. The hospital had a severe shortage of supplies, in some cases because supply trains were captured by the Confederates. The hospital also was seriously understaffed because most of the surgeons stayed with their regiments. On August 31, Secretary of War Edwin M. Stanton issued a call for civilian doctors and nurses, some of whom were able to provide useful service.

Transportation of the wounded was the biggest nightmare of the battle. The best-equipped Union corps had forty-five ambulances instead of the 170 it was supposed to have. However, most of those forty-five were unavailable since they had broken down and been abandoned before getting to the field. In a move reminiscent of First Bull Run, the medical department in Washington impressed wagons, cabs, and other wheeled vehicles to send to the field. Many of the civilian drivers fled the field, refused to make more than one trip, or raided the medicinal whiskey and became drunk. Unless a wounded soldier could walk, he was likely to lie on the field, unattended in the blistering heat and pouring rain, for some time. Three days after the battle there were still 3,000 Union wounded on the field, and the last soldiers were not retrieved for six or seven days. Undoubtedly many died because of this lack of attention.

The fact that the field remained in Confederate possession created some problems, although Lee was generous about allowing removal of the Union wounded. He refused to allow the Union forces to bring in supply wagons, however. Confederate doctors treated wounded Union soldiers, but were unable to feed them. The hospitals in Richmond were already overflowing with Confederate wounded, and supplies were limited. Once again, Richmond citizens did all they could to help the patients.

McParlin had neglected to ship the Union wounded back to Washington as soon as they were stabilized, creating a bottleneck at the field hospital. Once shipment began, the dangerously wounded, who should not have been sent, were included. When the wounded reached Washington, they overcrowded the hospitals already established there, so patients were housed in the U.S. Capitol and the patent office building.

As a result of Second Bull Run, it was obvious to most concerned people in the North that the Union army badly needed an organized hospital corps. On September 7, 1862, Surgeon General William A. Hammond wrote to Secretary of War Stanton urging the establishment of an ambulance corps. Stanton, who had a personal vendetta against Hammond, and General-in-Chief Henry W. Halleck, who generally disliked innovation, both disapproved of the idea. No amount of pressure from the U.S. Sanitary Commission or others would budge Stanton or Halleck on this issue. However, Letterman was already setting up an ambulance corps in the Army of the Potomac, which worked well at the Battle of Antietam in September 1862. The idea spread to Ulysses S. Grant's army in the west and to the other armies. By the time an official ambulance corps was established on March 11, 1864, virtually all the Union armies already had them. Second Bull Run was the last battle where shortage of transportation caused such serious damage to Union wounded.

See also: Alcohol, Medicinal Uses of; Ambulance Corps; Ambulances; Antietam, Battle of; Bull Run (Manassas), First Battle of; Ewell, Richard Stoddert; Hammond, William Alexander; Hospitals, Field; Jackson, Thomas Jonathan ("Stonewall"): Letterman, Jonathan; Medical Directors, Field; Peninsula Campaign; Surgeon General.

Bibliography

Adams, George Worthington. *Doctors in Blue: The Medical History of the Union Army in the Civil War.* New York: Schuman, 1952; reprint, Dayton, OH: Morningside, 1985.

Duncan, Louis C. *The Medical Department of the United States Army in the Civil War.* Washington, DC: Author, 1914; reprint, Gaithersburg, MD: Butternut, 1985.

Hennessy, John J. *Return to Bull Run: The Campaign and Battle of Second Manassas.* New York: Simon and Schuster, 1993.

C

CALOMEL

Calomel was a mercury-based medicine favored by both Union and Confederate doctors during the Civil War. It came in two main forms. "Blue pills" contained a mixture of mercury with licorice, rose water, powdered rose, honey, and sugar. The other, "blue mass," was a lump of mercurous chloride from which dispensing doctors pinched off a piece. In neither case were the doses standardized or measured.

Nineteenth-century doctors feared constipation and calomel was one of their main methods to keep the bowels "open." However, physicians also dispensed calomel as a remedy for diarrhea and dysentery. Many doctors seemed unaware that their treatments with calomel and tartar emetic, a related compound, could cause problems worse than the original disease. Often dispensed in large or frequent "heroic" doses, the mercury medicines led to excessive salivation (as much as a pint to a quart per day). In addition, many patients suffered "mercurial gangrene," or the death of cheek and mouth tissue, leading to permanent facial deformities. Mercury also loosened the patient's teeth. A number of people died from mercury poisoning.

In Circular No. 6 of May 4, 1863, Union surgeon general William A. Hammond removed both calomel and tartar emetic from the medical supply table because the problems they caused far outweighed any benefits produced. This pronouncement caused a tremendous upheaval in the Union medical service because most doctors, who dispensed calomel moderately, regarded it as absolutely essential. These doctors supposed that anyone who opposed the use of calomel was a member of a fringe medical sect rather than a standard medical professional. The upheaval over calomel became a part of Secretary of War Edwin M. Stanton's excuse for removing Hammond, whom he did not like, from the post of surgeon general.

The dangers of dosing with mercury were not acknowledged by the medical profession until after the Civil War.

See also: Barnes, Joseph K.; Diarrhea and Dysentery; Hammond, William Alexander; Tartar Emetic.

Bibliography

Adams, George Worthington. *Doctors in Blue: The Medical History of the Union Army in the Civil War.* New York: Schuman, 1952; reprint, Dayton, OH: Morningside, 1985.

Bollet, Alfred Jay. *Civil War Medicine: Challenges and Triumphs.* Tucson, AZ: Galen, 2002.

Flannery, Michael A. *Civil War Pharmacy: A History of Drugs, Drug Supply and Provision, and Therapeutics for the Union and Confederacy.* New York: Pharmaceutical Products Press, 2004.

CAMP FEVER *See* Fevers.

CAMP ITCH

"Camp itch" was a painful skin disease, involving itching, lesions, and inflammation, suffered by soldiers both North and South during the Civil War. Doctors debated the cause of the itch. Certainly some cases were really scabies, a very contagious skin disease caused by mites and quickly spread by shared blankets as well as in crowded conditions. Some doctors, however, stated that camp itch was not scabies as no "animaliculae" were present. Whether scabies or not, the itch resulted from the poor hygiene of troops who bathed infrequently, suffered numerous scratches and bites, and were generally very dirty. Then, when afflicted, the men scratched, making the problem worse. The itch became so severe in some cases that 31,947 Union troops and quite a number of Confederates had to be hospitalized for treatment of the infections that followed.

The standard remedies were evidently sulphur and arsenic taken internally, plus external alkaline baths. Some doctors also prescribed a wash of sulphur and lime. Because many ingredients were difficult to get in the South, Confederate doctors sought to develop treatments using indigenous plants, some of which were tested on patients at Chimborazo Hospital in Richmond, Virginia. Several doctors reported their treatments in the *Confederate States Medical and Surgical Journal.*

Surgeon John H. Claiborne, in charge of the hospitals in Petersburg, Virginia, reported success in mild cases of camp itch by having the patient change clothes frequently and bathe in a decoction (prepared by boiling) of poke root once or twice daily, followed by washing with soap and water. This regimen generally produced a cure in a week to ten days. Patients with more serious cases found the poke baths too irritating. For them, Claiborne recommended washing with a decoction of broom-straw root or slippery elm, three or four times per day, until the soldier was able to take the poke root baths. Claiborne also recommended a diet of vegetables and grains, as well as a light laxative for the patient. If mercury and arsenic were available, he would give the usual doses in addition to his other treatments.

In the January 1865 issue of the *Confederate States Medical and Surgical Jour-*

nal, Assistant Surgeon S.R. Chambers published the recipe for an ointment that he claimed had *"never failed"* to cure the itch. It consisted of the boiled inner bark of the elder tree, combined with lard, a little sweet gum, Basilicon ointment, olive oil, and sulphur flour. The patient was to wash with soap and water, dry well, and apply the ointment to the affected parts twice daily. Chambers suggested that the patient wear the same underwear for a week because it would become saturated with ointment, reducing the need to reapply the medicine.

While not a fatal disease itself, camp itch clearly made the afflicted soldiers' lives miserable. Any treatment that involved improved cleanliness and a soothing ointment or wash seemed to help.

See also: Blockade; Calomel; Chimborazo Hospital; *Confederate States Medical and Surgical Journal*; Diet, of Hospital Patients; *Resources of the Southern Fields and Forests*; Sanitation; Substitutes, for Supplies.

Bibliography

Bollet, Alfred Jay. *Civil War Medicine: Challenges and Triumphs*. Tucson, AZ: Galen, 2002.

Chambers, S.R. "On the Treatment of Camp Itch." *Confederate States Medical and Surgical Journal* 2 (January 1865): 10.

Claiborne, John H. "On the Use of Phytolacca Decandra in Camp Itch." *Confederate States Medical and Surgical Journal* 1 (March 1864): 39.

CATARRH

Catarrh (the h is silent) was a nineteenth-century term for such respiratory infections as colds and bronchitis, but not the more serious pneumonia. Colds were often listed as "epidemic catarrh."

In addition to contracting measles and other childhood diseases, new recruits in both the Northern and Southern armies soon caught colds, which they often spread to the veterans. At least one doctor commented that recent recruits could be distinguished at night by the amount of coughing coming from their tents.

Many colds worsened into bronchitis, which was also a common aftereffect of a bout with measles. The continuous presence of smoke from campfires undoubtedly worsened many cold and bronchitis cases, as did exposure to bad weather, damp clothes, and lack of proper clothing in cold weather. The number of cases of catarrh and bronchitis usually peaked during the winter and decreased during the summer. Few of these cases were fatal unless they turned into pneumonia.

At the end of June 1862, the Union medical department changed its reporting forms, dropping the term *catarrh* altogether and replacing it with *acute bronchitis*.

See also: Measles; Mortality, of Soldiers; Pneumonia.

Bibliography

Barnes, Joseph K., ed. *The Medical and Surgical History of the War of the Rebellion (1861–1865)*. Vol. 6. Washington, DC: Government Printing Office, 1870–1888; reprint, Wilmington, NC: Broadfoot, 1990.

Bollet, Alfred Jay. *Civil War Medicine: Challenges and Triumphs*. Tucson, AZ: Galen, 2002.

Steiner, Paul E. *Disease in the Civil War: Natural Biological Warfare in 1861–1865*. Springfield, IL: C.C. Thomas, 1968.

CHAMBERLAIN, JOSHUA LAWRENCE (1828–1914)

Joshua Lawrence Chamberlain, Union brigadier general, was born in Brewer, Maine, on September 8, 1828, the oldest of the five children of Joshua and Sarah Dupee Chamberlain. After intense study, Chamberlain entered Bowdoin College in Brunswick, Maine, in February 1848, where he proved himself a scholar, eventually learning nine languages besides English. Due to a severe illness when he was twenty-one, Chamberlain did not graduate until the summer of 1852. In August 1855 he received his master's degree and also graduated from the theological seminary. Although he did not really want to be a college professor, he joined the faculty at Bowdoin. After a lengthy courtship, Chamberlain married Frances Caroline ("Fannie") Adams (1825–1905) on December 7, 1855. The couple eventually had five children, of whom only two survived.

In August 1862, despite Fannie's protests, Joshua volunteered for the Union army and became lieutenant colonel of the Twentieth Maine infantry regiment. Although he had no previous experience, Chamberlain loved military life, studied tactics diligently, and became an excellent leader. The Twentieth Maine's first battle was Antietam in September 1862, although the troops were not in action. At Fredericksburg on December 13, 1862, Chamberlain was slightly wounded when a bullet grazed his neck and right ear. On May 20, 1863, when Adelbert Ames, the colonel of the Twentieth Maine, was promoted to brigadier general, Chamberlain succeeded him in regimental command. Chamberlain suffered sunstroke in June 1863 and was still rather weak when he became a hero during the battle of Gettysburg. As immortalized in Michael Shaara's novel *The Killer Angels* (1974) and in *Gettysburg* (1993), the movie made from it, Chamberlain led the Twentieth Maine in the defense of Little Round Top on the far Union left on July 2, 1863. This action culminated in a bayonet charge when the Union forces ran out of ammunition, leading to the defeat and capture of many opposing Confederate troops. Chamberlain suffered only a cut to his right foot and a bruise to his left thigh from a spent bullet.

In late July and August Chamberlain had sick leaves due to nervous prostration (probably the equivalent of what is called post–traumatic stress disorder today) and then a bout with malaria, from which he suffered the rest of his life. On August 26 he was given command of his brigade, although attempts to promote him to brigadier general failed. In November 1863, a severe attack of malaria, perhaps complicated by typhoid fever, forced him to be hospitalized in Georgetown, DC. While recuperating, he served on court-martial duty until the opening of the spring campaign in May 1864.

On June 18, 1864, Chamberlain was severely wounded leading an attack on Rives's Salient at Petersburg in Virginia. A minié ball hit him in the right thigh near the hip and went all the way through his body at an angle to the left hip, cutting arteries, damaging his urethra and bladder, and fracturing his left pelvic bones. On June 20, General Ulysses S. Grant gave Chamberlain a "deathbed" promotion to brigadier general. However, much to everyone's surprise, Chamberlain survived. Two surgeons in the field hospital did the best repairs they could. On June 19 a relay of soldiers carried Chamberlain sixteen miles by stretcher to City Point, where he was taken by the hospital ship *Connecticut* to the naval academy hospital in Annapolis. Here, due to a catheter problem, he developed a urethral fistula (abnormal opening) through which urine leaked and which caused him problems for the rest of his life. After five months of convalescence in hospitals and in Maine, he impatiently returned to the army in November 1864 before he could either walk very far or ride a horse. In January 1865 he had some corrective surgery (the first of at least four operations), returning to the army in February.

Chamberlain was a leading figure in the battles in Virginia during the last days of the war. He was wounded in an attack on Quaker Road on March 29, 1865, when a bullet, going through his horse's neck and his own arm, struck him in the chest below the heart. Here it was deflected by a leather case full of dispatches and a brass-backed mirror. The bullet followed around two ribs and came out his back. Although in pain and bleeding, Chamberlain led his troops heroically. He was also heavily involved at the Battle of Five Forks several days later. Grant chose Chamberlain to receive the formal Confederate surrender at Appomattox Court House on April 12, 1865.

After the war, Chamberlain's original discharge was revoked so he could have further surgery, and he was discharged with the rank of brevet major general in January 1866. Elected governor of Maine in September 1866, Chamberlain served four single-year terms. He then served as president of Bowdoin from 1871 to 1883. From the 1880s on, he suffered severely from his wounds, battling chronic pain and frequent debilitating infections. Nevertheless, at the age of seventy, in 1898, he volunteered for service in the Spanish-American War, an offer that was not accepted.

Awarded the Congressional Medal of Honor in 1893 for his actions at Gettysburg, Chamberlain frequently spoke and eventually wrote about the war. His book *The Passing of the Armies* was published after his death. After years of suffering, Chamberlain died from the effects of his wounds on February 24, 1914.

See also: Antietam, Battle of; Fredericksburg, Battle of; Gettysburg, Battle of; Gunshot Wounds; Hospital Ships; Infections, of Wounds; Minié Balls; Post–Traumatic Stress Disorder.

Bibliography

Harmon, William J. "The Lion of the Union: The Pelvic Wound of Joshua Lawrence Chamberlain." *Journal of Civil War Medicine* 6 (April–June 2002): 30–33.

Smith, Jennifer Lund. "The Reconstruction of 'Home': The Civil War and the Marriage of Lawrence and Fannie Chamberlain." In *Intimate Strategies of the Civil War: Military Commanders and Their Wives*, ed. Carol K. Bleser and Lesley J. Gordon, pp. 157–177. New York: Oxford University Press, 2001.

Trulock, Alice Rains. *In the Hands of Providence: Joshua L. Chamberlain and the American Civil War*. Chapel Hill: University of North Carolina Press, 1992.

Welsh, Jack D. *Medical Histories of Union Generals*. Kent, OH: Kent State University Press, 1996.

CHAPLAINS

During the Civil War chaplains served in both the Union and Confederate armies to promote the spiritual and physical welfare of the troops, as they had served during the colonial and Revolutionary wars, the War of 1812, and the Mexican War. When the Civil War began, there were thirty chaplains at various army posts. Although the U.S. Congress considered abolishing the position in order to cut costs and to maintain the separation of church and state, such ideas were soon overruled.

Both the Union and Confederate congresses quickly passed laws establishing the position of chaplain, one per regiment. Both sides regarded chaplains as somewhat equivalent to captains, but there were many unsettled and sometimes awkward issues because their rank was not clear. Both sides readjusted the pay of chaplains (usually downward) as well as what rations, quarters, and forage for horses they were entitled to. About 2,300 men served the Union as regimental chaplains. President Abraham Lincoln eventually appointed chaplains to large, permanent hospitals as well.

At first the Union's only requirement for chaplains was that they be regularly ordained Christian ministers. In 1862 this wording was changed to include the ministers of any "religious denomination" in order to allow Jewish rabbis to serve. (The vast majority of chaplains were Christians, however). Laws passed at this time also required more documentation of a prospective chaplain's ministerial qualifications. Nevertheless, there were no educational requirements for either Union or Confederate chaplains, so there was tremendous variation in preparation, depending on the criteria set by each denomination.

Generally, the officers of a regiment selected the chaplain, usually a minister from the regiment's home area and, if possible, belonging to the denomination of the majority of the regiment's members. Some chaplains were poorly suited to the work or soon lost their health and left the service, but many others ministered effectively for substantial periods of time.

The one required duty for a chaplain was to hold a weekly public worship service. Many chaplains held more than one or augmented them with prayer meetings and Bible studies. Many of the services were nondenominational because chaplains had to minister to troops from a variety of denominations. A number of soldiers and ministers commented on the frequent and productive interdenominational cooperation during the war. Chaplains also provided individual counseling and administered the sacraments of baptism and Holy Communion. Most chaplains also took on other duties as the needs of the men dictated.

Chaplains accompanied troops on the march and into battle, where some chaplains dug rifle pits and even took up arms to fire on the enemy. At least sixty-six Union chaplains died in the line of duty during the war. On the battlefield most chaplains attended the wounded, helping them to the field hospital, administering basic first aid or a drink of water or medicinal whiskey, helping the surgeons, and comforting the dying. Both regimental and hospital chaplains visited soldiers in the hospitals, writing letters for the incapacitated and offering spiritual comfort. Chaplains attended the dying, recording their last words and Christian testimonies to relay to loved ones at home, and performed burial services. In addition, many chaplains kept patient records for future reference.

Other tasks performed by chaplains included forwarding the soldiers' pay to their families, distributing mail, maintaining and developing the regimental or hospital library, teaching illiterate soldiers to read, and promoting temperance and morality generally. The chaplains provided significant physical, moral, and spiritual aid to numerous soldiers during the Civil War. Because of their work with the wounded and dying, their letters and reminiscences can be helpful for the study of Civil War medicine.

See also: Alcohol, Medicinal Uses of; Death, Attitudes Toward; Quintard, Charles Todd.

Bibliography

Armstrong, Warren B. *For Courageous Fighting and Confident Dying: Union Chaplains in the Civil War.* Lawrence: University Press of Kansas, 1998.

Quintard, Charles Todd. *Doctor Quintard, Chaplain C.S.A. and Second Bishop of Tennessee: The Memoir and Civil War Diary of Charles Todd Quintard.* Sewanee, TN: University Press of Sewanee, 1905; reprint, ed. Sam Davis Elliott. Baton Rouge: Louisiana State University Press, 2003.

Schroeder, Glenna R. "The Civil War Diary of Chaplain Stephen C. Bowers." *Indiana Magazine of History* 79 (June 1983): 167–185.

CHICKAMAUGA, BATTLE OF (1863)

The Battle of Chickamauga, fought in Georgia on September 19–20, 1863, was the largest battle in the western theater and one of the bloodiest battles of the Civil War. The Union Army of the Cumberland, led by General William S. Rosecrans, faced the Confederate Army of Tennessee, commanded by General Braxton Bragg and reinforced by troops from Virginia under General James Longstreet.

After losing Tullahoma, Tennessee, to Rosecrans in the summer of 1863, Bragg retreated to Chattanooga, Tennessee. Rosecrans slowly pursued. Finally deciding not to defend Chattanooga, Bragg evacuated the town on September 6. After some days of maneuvering, the two armies fought each other with inconclusive results on September 19. After both armies switched troops around during the night, a misunderstanding about troop location on the morning of September 20 caused Rosecrans to order a movement that left a large gap in his line. Coincidentally, at that moment Longstreet's Confederates struck that very spot, pushing the Union troops back. Rosecrans and several other generals, believing that all was lost, fled to Chattanooga. However, General George H. Thomas rallied some Union soldiers and managed to delay the Confederates until dusk, when he retreated. The Confederates were unable to take full advantage of their victory, but did besiege the Union troops in Chattanooga for a few weeks.

An estimated 58,222 Union and 66,326 Confederate soldiers participated in the battle. Of these, approximately 1,657 Federals and 2,312 Confederates were killed, with 9,756 Union and 14,674 Confederates wounded. Including missing soldiers, the casualties totaled 16,170 for the Union and 18,454 for the Confederacy, about 28 percent of the soldiers involved for each army.

Both armies had a number of field hospitals to care for their wounded. The Union army set up a hospital for each division of each army corps. Although several were located north of the battle area, most of the hospitals were set up on September 19 at Crawfish Spring, which was slightly southwest of Lee and Gordon's Mills. All the hospitals needed water, which made the spring an important attraction. Although several division medical directors attempted to move their hospitals closer to the fighting, military actions forced them to return to the spring. The hospitals at Crawfish Spring were evacuated on the afternoon of September 20 when all available ambulances, as well as baggage and supply wagons, were pressed into service to haul the wounded that could be moved to Chattanooga. About 2,500 of the very seriously wounded were left behind with fifty-two Union surgeons, all of whom were captured by the Confederates.

The Confederates evidently had divisional field hospitals as well, but little is known about them, probably because the reports were destroyed with other papers in the surgeon general's office when Richmond burned in April 1865. It is known that there was one hospital near Snodgrass Hill. Most of the rest were probably along Chickamauga Creek because the Confederate hospitals needed water, just as the Union hospitals did. Confederate general John B. Hood suffered a serious wound and had his right leg amputated by Dr. Tobias G. Richardson in one of these field hospitals.

The Confederates held the field at the end of the battle, but had considerable difficulty removing the wounded from the field. Using supply wagons padded with the soft part of pine branches, they carted the wounded to the nearest railroad depot. A shortage of trains left thousands of wounded soldiers lying on the ground at Tunnel Hill and the "Wood Shed near Burnt Bridge" for several days with minimal care because of a lack of medical officers, attendants, and supplies. Several doctors, as well as the Army of Tennessee's medical director of hospitals, Samuel H. Stout, bitterly complained about a number of quartermasters who refused to take any responsibility for providing transportation for the wounded. In addition, a complete breakdown of communication between Stout and the army's field medical director, E.A. Flewellen, hindered coordination of care for the patients.

On September 18, the day before the battle, Union surgeon Israel Moses arrived in Chattanooga to prepare hospitals to receive the prospective wounded. He found some hospital buildings recently abandoned by the Confederates when they evacuated Chattanooga. These buildings were able to hold a few hundred, but not as many patients as Moses anticipated. As the wounded arrived, Moses established hospitals wherever he could, ultimately treating at least 4,000 patients in nine improvised hospitals, sending as many as possible on to hospitals in Bridgeport and Stevenson, Alabama. Only 800, who were too dangerously ill for further movement, remained in Chattanooga by September 23. At that point no patients could be transferred because the Confederates besieged the Union forces in Chattanooga.

Many Confederate general hospitals had been established in new locations shortly before Chickamauga. Beginning in July, Medical Director Stout had evacuated patients from Chattanooga south into Georgia, but in late August and early September he had to move all the hospitals located in small towns north of Resaca, Georgia, to Marietta, Georgia, and towns south of Atlanta. As a result of Chickamauga, the Confederate hospitals in Atlanta, which had 1,800 beds, received 10,000 patients. Stout's whole department had 7,500 beds. To relieve the overcrowding, Stout sent some patients out of his department to hospitals in Montgomery, Alabama, and Macon, Columbus, and Augusta, Georgia. Other patients were placed in private homes or, if nearly well, sent to convalescent camps. Some, who needed time rather than medical care to heal, received furloughs.

Although many of the problems resulted from factors beyond the control of the medical directors, both sides received much criticism for failures of medical care after Chickamauga. Both General Rosecrans and General Bragg, however, commended the work of their medical departments.

See also: Ambulances; Convalescents; Flewellen, Edward Archelaus; Hood, John Bell; Hospital Relocations; Hospitals, Field; Hospitals, General; Medical Directors, Field; Medical Directors, of Hospitals; Prisoners of War; Quartermasters; Stout, Samuel Hollingsworth.

Bibliography

Barnes, Joseph K., ed. *The Medical and Surgical History of the War of the Rebellion (1861–65)*. Washington, DC: Government Printing Office, 1870–1888; reprint, Wilmington, NC: Broadfoot, 1990.
Cawood, Hobart G. *The Medical Service at Chickamauga*. Fort Oglethorpe, GA: Chickamauga and Chattanooga National Military Park, 1964.

Cozzens, Peter. *This Terrible Sound: The Battle of Chickamauga.* Urbana: University of Illinois Press, 1992.

Duncan, Louis C. *The Medical Department of the United States Army in the Civil War.* Washington, DC: Author, 1914; reprint, Gaithersburg, MD: Butternut, 1985.

Schroeder-Lein, Glenna R. *Confederate Hospitals on the Move: Samuel H. Stout and the Army of Tennessee.* Columbia: University of South Carolina Press, 1994.

CHIMBORAZO HOSPITAL

Chimborazo Hospital was the largest hospital, North or South, during the Civil War. It was located just outside Richmond, Virginia, on Chimborazo Hill, which had been named for a peak in Equador. Sunny in winter but with the best breezes in the area during the summer, Chimborazo was an ideal place to establish a hospital.

Surgeon General Samuel P. Moore appointed Dr. James B. McCaw head and commander of Chimborazo Hospital. McCaw did the planning for the hospital, which was established in October 1861 and running within a couple of weeks. Chimborazo was designed as a pavilion hospital with separate one-story buildings, about 80 feet by 28 feet, for each ward.

The wards were arranged in rows angled to receive the best breezes, with wide streets between the buildings for the best ventilation. Each ward held forty to sixty patients, depending upon how crowded the hospital was. Eventually Chimborazo had 150 wards split into five divisions, each headed by a surgeon in charge and functioning to some degree as a separate hospital, although ultimately still directed by McCaw. The divisions and wards tended to be organized as much as possible by state. While some people complained about the state-orientated nature of this system, which might become discriminatory, it had some advantages for keeping track of patients, properly directing visiting family members, and distributing supplies received from a particular state.

The Chimborazo site had only two prewar buildings, which the hospital leased for offices. Many more buildings were constructed in addition to the wards and other offices to support patient care. Besides a central storehouse, Chimborazo had latrines, bath houses, kitchens, a bakery producing up to 10,000 loaves of bread per day, a soap manufactory, five ice houses, stables, staff housing for some workers, a chapel, a carpenter shop, a blacksmith shop, pharmacies, a guardhouse for imprisoning the unruly, and five morgues. Just outside the hospital grounds proper were a brewery, a dairy, and a sawmill. The hospital used tents during periods of overcrowding and also to house contagious patients, such as those with wound infections.

Several miles away, the hospital had a large garden and ran a farm with goats and cows. Seven wells and three springs furnished water for the hospital. Chimborazo also had a canal boat to bring supplies such as vegetables and poultry from as far away as Lynchburg and Lexington, Virginia. By the end of the war, however, Chimborazo was suffering the severe supply shortages experienced by all Richmond residents.

Dr. McCaw and the five hospital division heads were apparently the only full surgeons on the Chimborazo staff. The rest were assistant surgeons or acting assistant (contract) surgeons—forty to fifty of them. Each of these doctors was in charge of one to three wards, depending on the number of patients in the hospital and the number of doctors available. Two wards, totaling about eighty patients, was the average load. The hospital staff also included stewards, ward masters, matrons, nurses, druggists, clerks, chaplains, baggage masters, forage masters, wagon masters, cooks, bakers, carpenters, shoemakers, inspectors, and ambulance drivers. Convalescents and permanently disabled soldiers filled some of these positions.

According to surviving hospital records, now in the National Archives in Washington, DC, the Chimborazo staff treated a total of 77,889 patients. The great majority of the patients were sick, while the wounded constituted about 14 percent before 1863 and 20 percent after. Most of the wounded had already been treated in the field hospitals before arriving at Chimborazo. During some of the battles around Richmond, however, a number of patients came directly from the field. The majority of wounds, as many as 65 percent, were to the arms or legs. Chest, head, and abdominal wounds were seen less frequently because soldiers whose vital organs were damaged were more likely to die on the battlefield, in transit, or in the field hospitals before they ever got to general hospitals such as Chimborazo behind the lines.

Of the patients, about 2,700 died at the hospital, 19,500 returned to duty, 14,500 were transferred to other hospitals, 5,500 received furloughs, 700 were discharged, 1,000 deserted, and the fate of the rest could not be determined. The mortality rate at Chimborazo has been figured in various ways. In the January 1864 *Confederate States Medical and Surgical Journal*, Dr. McCaw reported that from November 1, 1861, to November 1, 1863, a total of 47,196 patients had been admitted, of whom 3,031 died, a mortality rate of 6.62 percent. Twenty-first-century historians have estimated the mortality rate as between 9 and 11 percent.

In a number of ways Chimborazo served as a teaching hospital. Students from the Medical College of Virginia, the only medical school open in the Confederacy throughout the war, did rounds with McCaw. Many students also gained experience by serving as stewards in the hospital. As the Confederates tried to develop effective medications from various indigenous plants, Chimborazo doctors tested some of them on the hospital's patients.

In general, Chimborazo was well organized and provided care that was as good as or better than that found in other Civil War hospitals.

After the war, Chimborazo became a school for freed slaves and by 1866 was also being used as a refugee camp. From 1870 to 1874 a brewery operated there with little success. In 1874 the premises became a city park. From 1909 to 1954 the U.S. Weather Bureau operated a station on the site. Finally, in 1959, the National Park Service established the Richmond National Battlefield Park, including a part of Chimborazo. The rest became housing developments.

See also: Confederate States Medical and Surgical Journal; Education, Medical; Hospital Buildings; Hospitals, General; Hospitals, Pavilion; Infections, of Wounds;

McCaw, James Brown; Mortality, of Soldiers; Pember, Phoebe Yates Levy; *Resources of the Southern Fields and Forests*; Richmond, Virginia; Stewards, Hospital; Substitutes, for Supplies; Surgeons, Acting Assistant (Contract); Surgeons, Assistant; Tents, Hospital; Ventilation.

Bibliography

Green, Carol E. *Chimborazo: The Confederacy's Largest Hospital*. Knoxville: University of Tennessee Press, 2004.

Johns, Frank S., and Johns, Ann Page. "Chimborazo Hospital and J.B. McCaw, Surgeon in Chief." *Virginia Magazine of History and Biography* 62, no. 2 (1954): 190–200.

Pember, Phoebe Yates. *A Southern Woman's Story: Life in Confederate Richmond*. 1879; reprint, ed. Bell Irvin Wiley. Jackson, TN: McCowat-Mercer, 1959; reprint, Covington, GA: Mockingbird, 1974.

CHISOLM, JOHN JULIAN (1830–1903)

J. Julian Chisolm, Confederate surgeon, author, and medical purveyor, was born on April 16, 1830, in Charleston, South Carolina, the second son of Robert Trail and Harriet Emily Schutt Chisolm. Little is known about his life until he graduated from the Medical College of the State of South Carolina in March 1850. He spent the rest of that year and most of 1851 studying in Paris and London, especially focusing on diseases of the eye.

Chisolm opened his private practice in Charleston in 1852 and was soon a skilled surgeon. During the same year, he married his cousin Mary Edings Chisolm, with whom he eventually had two children. Chisolm was part of a group of doctors who began a medical preparatory school that offered free evening lectures and a summer medical school in 1853. In 1857, he helped to open a free hospital for slaves. Although he was elected to the chair of surgery at his alma mater in 1858, Chisolm first traveled to Europe, visiting military hospitals in Italy during the wars for Italian unification, before assuming his teaching post in 1860.

When the Civil War began, Chisolm was the first doctor to be granted a Confederate medical commission. He spent the war in several different capacities. Because most Confederate medical officers had had little experience with wounds or surgery and because the Union blockade of Southern ports cut off instructional materials from Europe, Chisolm saw a need for a surgical manual. Based on his own experiences and the most recent publications in German, French, and English, Chisolm prepared *A Manual of Military Surgery for the Use of Surgeons in the Confederate Army, with an Appendix of the Rules and Regulations of the Medical Department of the Confederate Army*. This all-purpose volume was published in July 1861 in Richmond and revised in 1862 and 1864. In addition to the sections on military surgery, Chisolm included chapters on appropriate food, clothes, and sanitation for the troops, how to preserve their health, the field and camp duties of surgeons, the regulations of the Confederate medical department, and samples of the forms to be used for making reports.

For a time Chisolm was chief surgeon at a hospital in Richmond, but he soon returned to South Carolina, where he became a medical purveyor. Chisolm also ran a government pharmaceutical laboratory that manufactured "blue mass" (a mercurial preparation), mercurial ointment, sweet spirit of nitre, and sulphuric ether. The largest Confederate Treasury Department warrant known to have been issued to a medical purveyor for the purchase of supplies was granted to Chisolm on April 13, 1864, for $850,254.57.

At the conclusion of the war, Chisolm returned to his private practice and professorship in Charleston. However, he spent 1866 in Paris studying diseases of the eye and ear. Because of various frustrations caused by Reconstruction, Chisolm moved to Baltimore, where he practiced his specialty and held a professorship in diseases of the eye and ear at the University of Maryland School of Medicine until 1896. During his career there he helped found two hospitals, published a number of medical articles, and was active in several medical associations.

After his first wife died in 1888, Chisolm married Elizabeth Steel, a much younger woman, in January 1894. They had one child. Unfortunately, the same year he remarried, Chisolm had a stroke from which he never fully recovered. However, he tried to practice medicine until 1898, when the family moved to Petersburg, Virginia. Chisolm died there on November 2, 1903.

See also: Blockade; Calomel; Laboratories, Medical; Medical Purveyors; Sanitation.

Bibliography

Chisolm, John Julian. *A Manual of Military Surgery.* Richmond, VA: West and Johnston, 1861; reprint, San Francisco: Norman, 1989.

Cunningham, H.H. *Doctors in Gray: The Confederate Medical Service.* Baton Rouge: Louisiana State University Press, 1958; reprint, Gloucester, MA: Peter Smith, 1970.

CHLOROFORM *See* Anesthesia.

CHRISTIAN COMMISSION *See* United States Christian Commission.

COMMISSARY DEPARTMENT *See* Subsistence Department.

CONFEDERATE STATES MEDICAL AND SURGICAL JOURNAL

The *Confederate States Medical and Surgical Journal*, the organ of the Association of Army and Navy Surgeons of the Confederate States, was published in Richmond,

Virginia, and edited by surgeon James B. McCaw. The only medical journal published in the Confederacy, it ran from January 1864 to February 1865. The March 1865 issue was destroyed when Richmond burned on April 2, 1865. All Confederate medical officers were urged to subscribe at a cost of ten dollars the first year and twenty dollars the second.

The purpose of the journal was to increase the knowledge and skills of Confederate military physicians. Each issue contained a variety of materials, including reports of the association meetings, case histories of various kinds of treatments for particular wounds and diseases, statistics on certain wounds or diseases, and reports on new treatments. Some reports included relevant line drawings. Most of the material came from the Richmond area, but there were some articles from military physicians in North Carolina as well as from the Army of Tennessee. Each issue also included reprints from European journals, particularly British, but also French translations. There were more foreign reprints in the later issues of the journal than in the earlier issues. Most of the articles pertained to military medicine, but other topics, such as obstetrics, were also included.

See also: Association of Army and Navy Surgeons of the Confederate States; Education, Medical; Gunshot Wounds, Treatment of; McCaw, James Brown.

Bibliography
Confederate States Medical and Surgical Journal, January 1864–February 1865; reprint, Metuchen, NJ: Scarecrow, 1976; reprint, San Francisco: Norman, 1992.

CONSUMPTION *See* Tuberculosis.

CONTRACT SURGEONS *See* Surgeons, Acting Assistant (Contract).

CONVALESCENTS

During the Civil War, a convalescent soldier was one who was no longer suffering the acute phases of his illness or his wound. He needed little attention from nurses or doctors. However, while he was recovering, he needed time to rest and a nutritious diet. He needed to regain his strength because he was not yet able to do full duty, march for any distance, or withstand exposure to bad weather.

There were no set criteria to determine when a patient would be considered convalescent. Much depended on the location of the hospital and the need for beds. During a slow period, a convalescent might remain in the hospital. Before a battle, however, as many beds as possible would be emptied to provide space for the expected wounded. In this case, some soldiers who were barely convalescent would be sent away.

The destination of a convalescent soldier depended on his location, the period of the war, and the expected length of his recovery. Soldiers with a recovery period of at least thirty days could be sent home on furlough if they were able to travel. Some soldiers, however, could not be furloughed because their homes were behind enemy lines. Later in the war, some Southern generals opposed furloughs out of fear that the soldiers would never return to the army, where manpower was badly needed.

The solution, in many cases, was a separate convalescent ward or camp. These tent wards on the hospital grounds or camps elsewhere were supposed to provide lots of fresh air and often some light duty for the convalescents. Some were well managed and most patients recovered rapidly. Some Union camps housed a mixture of convalescents and healthy soldiers who were waiting to be sent to their regiments.

A number of convalescent camps or hospitals faced serious problems with discipline. Soldiers with little to do snuck away to drink and visit brothels in nearby towns. At a Confederate convalescent hospital on Lookout Mountain near Chattanooga, Tennessee, the convalescents refused to use the latrines, leaving their excrement outside the "sinks." Similar problems occurred at the vast Union camp at Alexandria, Virginia, a collection point for convalescents throughout the East. Begun after Second Bull Run (Manassas) in August 1862, the camp was not well situated. Nevertheless, the convalescents did nothing to promote sanitation. Excrement mixed with mud spread over acres and infected the water supply. "Camp Misery" inmates experienced a shortage of clothing, blankets, and food as well, and suffered severely during the freezing winter, despite help from both the Sanitary and the Christian commissions. Many soldiers sickened and died rather than convalesced. After some men froze to death, the camp was moved and gradually improved, but was still known as "Camp Relapse." It did not become a well-managed convalescent camp until late 1863.

Many convalescents were assigned to some sort of light duty rather than sent to camps. In hospitals, convalescents worked as clerks, cooks, and guards. They also served as nurses, a carryover from antebellum hospitals where convalescents were expected to care for those sicker than themselves. Unfortunately, most convalescents were inexperienced or unwilling nurses who provided poor patient care. About the time the convalescents finally became competent nurses, they would be well enough to return to their regiment. Louisa May Alcott reported in *Hospital Sketches* that some convalescent nurses were not strong enough for the hard work of nursing and had a relapse themselves, sometimes with fatal results.

Convalescents also provided extra personnel for local defense, joining militia during threatened raids. They turned out from hospitals to meet threats to Richmond, Virginia, and Washington, DC, as well as many smaller locations. In June 1864 at Lynchburg, Virginia, authorities considered a convalescent to be anyone who could walk. These patients were sent out to join the militia at the Battle of Lynchburg. In some small Georgia towns, where the militia was tiny or nonexistent, convalescents in the Confederate hospitals, fearing capture, fled to the woods with the able-bodied doctors and male nurses at the threat of a Yankee raid. In Chattanooga, Tennessee, convalescent soldiers helped to pack up the hospitals to move when the Confederates evacuated the city.

The goal of all convalescent treatment was to send a healthy soldier back to his regiment. Both Northern and Southern armies eventually set up examining boards to determine when a soldier was ready to return to duty. Boards composed of medical personnel tended to be sympathetic to the needs of the soldiers, while those made up primarily or entirely of military officers focused solely on the army's manpower needs. As a result, some soldiers were sent back to their regiments before they were sufficiently recovered and soon ended up in some other hospital.

See also: Alcott, Louisa May; Bull Run (Manassas), Second Battle of; Cooks; Hospital Support Staff; Hospitals, Antebellum; Latrines; Mosquitoes; Nurses; Sanitation; Tents, Hospital; United States Christian Commission; United States Sanitary Commission; Ventilation; Wittenmyer, Annie Turner.

Bibliography

Adams, George Worthington. *Doctors in Blue: The Medical History of the Union Army in the Civil War.* New York: Schumann, 1952; reprint, Dayton, OH: Morningside, 1985.
Alcott, Louisa May. *Hospital Sketches.* 1863; reprint, Boston: Applewood, 1986.
Schroeder-Lein, Glenna R. *Confederate Hospitals on the Move: Samuel H. Stout and the Army of Tennessee.* Columbia: University of South Carolina Press, 1994.

COOKS

Civil War military and hospital cooks, both North and South, frequently had no prior culinary experience. Soldiers cooked for themselves, their messmates, or their company and often prepared indigestible messes, contributing to poor troop health. The soldiers in a few Union regiments received some basic cooking instructions from professional chefs, with consequent improvement in their health. Others learned through experience or gave responsibility to the best cook among their messmates, but troop diet was generally deficient throughout the war.

A hospital cook could be nearly anyone: black or white; slave, contraband, or free; male or female; detailed soldier, convalescent, or civilian. However, the authorities on both sides, especially later in the war, avoided having able-bodied soldiers serving in hospitals in any capacity. At least in established general hospitals, doctors realized that good nutrition, as they understood it, played a key part in patient recovery. While they sought to employ competent cooks, many cooks learned on the job.

The hospital cook was most likely to be a man, assisted by a number of convalescents and/or blacks, depending upon the size and location of the hospital. This department cooked for those who could eat a regular diet. Women, especially hospital matrons in the South, were more likely to be in charge of providing special diets for the very sick and severely wounded who needed broth, chicken, or various delicacies to tempt their appetites. By the middle of the war, cooks on both sides had access to special diet recipes prepared by chef Alexis Soyer during the Crimean War.

In 1864 Union relief worker Annie Wittenmyer developed special, well-equipped diet kitchens for more than 100 of the larger Union hospitals. These kitchens featured two experienced women supervising the male cooks. This improved nutrition was credited with saving the lives of many Union soldier patients.

See also: Blacks, as Hospital Workers; Convalescents; Cumming, Kate; Diet, of Hospital Patients; Diet, of Troops; Matrons; Pember, Phoebe Yates Levy; Wittenmyer, Annie Turner; Women, as Hospital Workers.

Bibliography

Cumming, Kate. *Kate: The Journal of a Confederate Nurse, 1862–1865.* 1866; reprint, ed. Richard Barksdale Harwell. Baton Rouge: Louisiana State University Press, 1959, 1987; Savannah, GA: Beehive, 1975.

Davis, William C. *A Taste for War: The Culinary History of the Blue and Gray.* Mechanicsburg, PA: Stackpole, 2003.

Wittenmyer, Annie. *Under the Guns: A Woman's Reminiscences of the Civil War.* Boston: E.B. Stillings, 1895.

CRIMEAN WAR *See* Nightingale, Florence.

CUMMING, KATE (CA. 1827–1909)

Kate Cumming, who became a matron and nurse in the Confederate Army of Tennessee hospitals, was born in Edinburgh, Scotland. Although 1835 has been accepted as her birth year, her obituary in 1909 stated that she was eighty years old, and the 1850 census listed her as twenty-three. Therefore, she probably was born between 1827 and 1829. Kate (Catharine) was the fourth of at least ten children born to David Cumming and his wife Janet. The family moved to Montreal, Canada, and then, before 1850, to Mobile, Alabama, where Kate absorbed many Southern attitudes.

After the Civil War broke out, Cumming, like many other women North and South, gathered supplies for the hospitals. After hearing about a sermon by the Reverend Benjamin M. Miller urging women to go to the hospitals to nurse the sick and wounded, she determined to do so, despite much opposition from her family. She left on April 7, 1862, with Miller and a group of women, for Okolona and then Corinth, Mississippi, where she nursed soldiers wounded at the Battle of Shiloh, Tennessee (April 6–7).

Although Cumming had no nursing experience, she soon learned, and she continued nursing, mainly as a supervising matron, for the rest of the war. She worked in hospitals in Chattanooga, Tennessee, from September 1862 until the town was evacuated in August 1863; in Newnan, Georgia, until August 1864; in Americus, Georgia, until November 1864; and in Griffin, Georgia, until May 1865. She briefly visited and worked in other places, as well, and she spent a month or two in Mobile each winter.

Cumming kept a detailed diary of her experiences caring for soldiers, a version of which she published in 1866 as *A Journal of Hospital Life in the Confederate Army of Tennessee from the Battle of Shiloh to the End of the War: With Sketches of Life and Character, and Brief Notices of Current Events During That Period.* Although not especially popular in the 1860s, the book was reprinted three times during the twentieth century under the shorter title *Kate: The Journal of a Confederate Nurse.*

Cumming's book is a very important source for studying the general hospitals of the Confederate Army of Tennessee because it presents so many specific details about the duties of a hospital matron, the care of the patients, the facilities used for hospitals in a number of locations, and the relationships of the staff members. Her account includes the names of staff and patients, as well as rumors and reports about the progress of the war. In 1895 Cumming published a shorter, revised version called *Gleanings from Southland*, in which the information presented earlier is watered down.

Cumming never married but lived with her family in Mobile and then with her father in Birmingham, Alabama. She taught school and was active in the United Confederate Veterans, the United Daughters of the Confederacy, and the Episcopal church. She died in Birmingham on June 5, 1909, and was buried in Mobile.

See also: Hospital Relocations; Hospitals, General; Matrons; Nurses; Shiloh, Battle of; Women, as Hospital Workers.

Bibliography

Cumming, Kate. *Kate: The Journal of a Confederate Nurse, 1862–1865.* 1866; reprint, ed. Richard Barksdale Harwell. Baton Rouge: Louisiana State University Press, 1959, 1987; reprint, Savannah, GA: Beehive, 1975.

Schroeder-Lein, Glenna R. *Confederate Hospitals on the Move: Samuel H. Stout and the Army of Tennessee.* Columbia: University of South Carolina Press, 1994.

United States Census, 1850, Alabama, Mobile, Mobile, 653.

CUPPING AND BLISTERING

Cupping and blistering had long histories as "depletive" treatments for certain illnesses before the Civil War and continued to be used by both sides during the conflict.

A patient suffering from an infectious illness characterized by a high fever, a rapid pulse, and delirium was considered to have an inflammation caused by congestion of the blood vessels and excited tissues. In the terminology of the time this was called a "sthenic" disease. The category included such illnesses as typhoid fever and pneumonia.

Doctors believed that the way to reduce the inflammation was by depleting the fluids. This could be done through bloodletting by cutting a vein or an artery or, less drastically, by using leeches to suck a smaller amount of blood. Bleeding was practiced infrequently by the time of the Civil War. Only four instances were recorded in *The Medical and Surgical History of the War of the Rebellion*.

Depletion could also be achieved by the use of "counter-irritants." These substances and procedures were supposed to provide a sort of distraction for the body by drawing blood to the surface of the skin and thus relieving the inflammation. Cupping consisted of heating a glass or metal cup and placing it on the skin—for example, on the chest or back of a pneumonia patient. As the glass or metal cooled, it pulled the patient's skin into the cup, creating a painful irritation. Blistering could be achieved by mustard plasters, poultices, or specific substances applied to the part to be irritated.

Although counter-irritants did not cure any illnesses, they continued to be used into the twentieth century.

See also: Fevers; Pneumonia; Stewards, Hospital; Typhoid Fever.

Bibliography

Bollet, Alfred Jay. *Civil War Medicine: Challenges and Triumphs*. Tucson, AZ: Galen, 2002.

Welsh, Jack D. *Medical Histories of Confederate Generals*. Kent, OH: Kent State University Press, 1995.

D

DAVIS, JEFFERSON (1808–1889)

Jefferson Davis, the president of the Confederacy, was born on June 3, 1808, or possibly 1807, in Christian County, Kentucky. The tenth and last child of Samuel Emory Davis and Jane Cook Davis, he allegedly was given the middle name Finis (meaning last), but he never used it. The family briefly moved to Louisiana and then settled in Mississippi. In 1816, eight-year-old Jefferson was sent to a Catholic school in Kentucky for several years. After further education in Mississippi, Davis attended Transylvania University in Kentucky and then went to West Point. He graduated in 1828 and, because of his relatively low ranking (twenty-third of thirty-three), became a second lieutenant in the infantry.

Davis was not particularly happy in the military as he was stationed at several small forts in the upper Midwest. In 1831, while supervising the construction of a sawmill on the Yellow River in Michigan Territory, he suffered what was evidently the first really serious illness of his life, a bout with pneumonia. He apparently had pneumonia again in December 1833. Family members and historians have suggested that these illnesses at least predisposed Davis to other serious episodes of bronchitis and pneumonia for the rest of his life.

In 1835 Davis resigned from the army, intending to become a planter at Brierfield, land purchased for him in Mississippi by his oldest brother, Joseph Emory Davis (1784–1870), who functioned as a father figure for Jefferson for many years. On June 17, 1835, Jefferson Davis married Sarah Knox Taylor (1814–1835), daughter of his commanding officer Zachary Taylor. No sooner had the newlyweds reached Mississippi than both of them became very ill, probably with malaria. Sarah died on September 15, 1835. Jefferson needed several months to recover from his illness and had relapses, often annually, for the rest of his life.

Although Davis continued as a planter, he also began to become interested in politics about 1840. He first campaigned for state representative as a Democrat in 1843; although he lost, he did very well on short notice. On February 26, 1845, Davis married Varina Banks Howell (1826–1906), eighteen years his junior, with whom he eventually had six children (the four sons all predeceased him). During the same year Davis was elected one of Mississippi's representatives in Congress. While campaigning, he suffered from inflammation in both eyes. In Congress he had similar eye problems, as well as fevers and earaches. Doubtless some of his ailments were due to overwork and exhaustion as Davis threw himself into all the details of his position, staying up until the early hours of the morning to attend to his correspondence with constituents. He was evidently unable to distinguish between the important and the trivial, a problem that also plagued him as Confederate president.

Soon after the Mexican War began in May 1846, Davis volunteered to lead Mississippi troops and was elected colonel of the First Mississippi Volunteers. He played important roles in the battles of Monterrey and Buena Vista, serving under his former father-in-law Zachary Taylor. However, at Buena Vista on February 23, 1847, Davis was painfully wounded in the right foot near the ankle. Apparently the bullet pushed fragments of spur and sock into his foot. Davis spent the next two years on crutches as pieces of shattered bone worked up to the surface, causing great pain. He continued to have discomfort in his foot as late as 1887.

After a year in the service, Davis, now a war hero, was mustered out. Mississippi's governor promptly appointed him to the U.S. Senate to complete the term of recently deceased senator Jesse Speight. In the Senate, Davis opposed the Compromise of 1850 and, after the death of John C. Calhoun, became the leading spokesman for state's rights and other Southern perspectives. In 1851 he resigned his Senate seat to run for governor of Mississippi, a race that he lost. During the campaign he was ill from malaria, exhaustion, and a terrible eye inflammation. Doctors have surmised that, based on Davis's description of his symptoms, he suffered from herpetic keratitis (a type of herpes simplex infection) with ulceration of the left cornea. Such eye problems cannot be cured, but they can periodically improve or get worse. A combination of heat, sunlight, malaria or other fever, and emotional stress tended to trigger Davis's painful ophthalmic attacks. Eventually a film formed over his left eye, and during the Civil War he became blind in that eye, able only to distinguish light and dark.

When Franklin Pierce became president of the United States in 1853, he selected his friend Jefferson Davis to serve as his secretary of war. Davis was much more involved in the workings of the War Department than were many of his predecessors. Ironically, he made a number of modernizing improvements to the military establishment, including the introduction of new technology, which was used against the South during the Civil War. At the conclusion of Pierce's term in March 1857, the Mississippi state legislature promptly reelected Davis to the U.S. Senate. He served until January 21, 1861, when he got up from his sickbed to give his resignation speech because Mississippi had seceded from the Union.

In February 1861 Davis was chosen provisional president of the Confederacy and soon thereafter elected to a six-year term. He evidently would have preferred to be the Confederate commanding general or secretary of war. While Davis may have been the best person available for the presidential post, his personality caused difficulties. He had frequent conflicts with people in key positions whom he did not like, but was fiercely loyal to his friends, such as General Braxton Bragg and Commissary General Lucius B. Northrop, even when their incompetence for office was evident. Davis was often indecisive, but once he made a decision, he was inflexible. When he had come to a conclusion, Davis felt that he was right and expected everyone else to agree with him. He was unable and unwilling to admit that he ever made a mistake. He was also caught up in the minutiae of the War Department and failed to delegate responsibilities that others should have borne.

Davis also suffered from chronic poor health. In addition to bouts of malaria, bronchitis, and eye inflammation, he experienced painful facial neuralgia and digestive discomforts generally called dyspepsia. All these ailments were exacerbated by stress and exhaustion. Many people who saw Davis during the war mentioned that he was thin and pale, with a drawn face and a fragile, though dignified, appearance. Of course Davis's ill health contributed to his touchiness in dealing with people. It may also have made him less perceptive about national and military matters than he might otherwise have been. On many occasions only Davis's iron will and determination kept him going.

Despite his liabilities, Davis did a creditable job of overseeing the administrative arm of the Confederate government, enabling it to perform as well as it did for as long as it did. Because Davis was president, people had a tendency to blame him for whatever went wrong, whether he had any direct connection with a problem or not.

Although Davis wanted to continue fighting, using guerrilla tactics, when the Confederacy collapsed, his generals rejected the idea. Davis was captured near Irwinville, Georgia, on May 10, 1865. For the next two years he was imprisoned at Fortress Monroe, Virginia. While initially held in close confinement, guarded around the clock, he eventually received more comfortable and private quarters. Although he lost some weight and suffered bouts of his usual ailments while imprisoned, his health did not seriously deteriorate. Varina Davis, however, frequently cited her husband's bad health when urging President Andrew Johnson to release him from confinement. As a result, Johnson sent various observers to check on Davis's health and he had regular visits from a physician.

The federal government intended to try Davis for complicity in the assassination of Abraham Lincoln. After the excitement over the assassination died down, however, it became evident that the charges against Davis were either trumped up or the result of perjured testimony. Also, whether he would have a civil or a military commission trial became a matter of great controversy. Eventually Davis was released on a writ of habeas corpus, and in December 1868 Chief Justice Salmon P. Chase of the U.S. Supreme Court dismissed the indictment entirely.

After his release, Davis and his family lived in genteel poverty. Although he served as the figurehead president of an insurance company for a few years (it failed during the Panic of 1873), he rarely found remunerative employment. However, in 1877 a benefactress, Sarah Dorsey, set him up in a cottage on her property, Beauvoir, near Biloxi, Mississippi, where he wrote his two-volume *Rise and Fall of the Confederate Government* (1881).

After his imprisonment, Davis generally had fewer and less serious episodes of his usual malaria, neuralgia, and eye problems, but he had difficulties related to old age or accidents. In early November 1889, Davis developed an upper respiratory infection. It turned into acute bronchitis and may have been complicated by an attack of malaria. Finally it became pneumonia, from which Davis died in New Orleans on December 6, 1889.

See also: Catarrh; Eye Ailments; Malaria; Pneumonia; Subsistence Department.

Bibliography

Cooper, William J., Jr. *Jefferson Davis, American.* New York: Knopf, 2000.

Davis, William C. *Jefferson Davis: The Man and His Hour.* New York: HarperCollins, 1991.

Riley, Harris D., Jr. "Jefferson Davis and His Health, Part I: June, 1808–December, 1860." *Mississippi History* 49 (August 1987): 179–202.

_____. "Jefferson Davis and His Health, Part II: January, 1861–December, 1889." *Mississippi History* 49 (November 1987): 261–287.

DEATH, ATTITUDES TOWARD

During the Civil War, people's attitudes toward death were similar in the North and the South. These attitudes were not monolithic, however; there was some variety. Attitudes also varied between those at home and those on the battlefield, as well as between classes, at least in the ways death could be mourned. Many attitudes toward death were influenced to some degree by Christianity.

In the nineteenth century many Americans were Christians. No matter what denomination they belonged to, they shared certain basic beliefs. They believed that Jesus Christ was the Son of God who had come to earth. After a few years of teaching and ministering to people and leading a perfect life, Jesus died on the cross for the sins of everyone, and three days later he rose from the dead. Although Jesus returned to heaven, he invited people to believe in him, repent of their sins, receive forgiveness, and anticipate eternal life in heaven with him once they died.

Belief in these teachings caused many differences in attitudes between Christians and non-Christians. Soldiers of both viewpoints might believe that it was their duty to go to war to fight for their country and possibly to die for it. However, soldiers who were Christians believed in God's power and "providence," as they called it. This meant that God was in control of everything. Therefore, if a soldier died in battle or of disease, or if a family member died at home, God had a reason for this death that was beyond human understanding. Christians understood death as a temporary separation from loved ones, and they could look forward to a reunion some day in heaven, if all were Christians.

These beliefs provided Christians with a sense of peace and joy at the prospect of battle that the non-Christians did not share. Confederate general Thomas J. "Stonewall" Jackson so strongly believed in the providence of God that he felt as safe on the battlefield as in bed. In fact, many soldiers on both sides were converted during the war (that is, came to believe in Jesus) because of the example of

Christian fellow soldiers, as well as the preaching and care provided by regimental chaplains. Both Northern and Southern armies saw large revivals, involving numerous prayer meetings, frequent church services, and many conversions.

It was especially important for relatives at home to know that their soldier was properly prepared to die or had died a "good death." The concept of a "good death" in this period meant that the dying person was surrounded by family members during the last hours. The dying person would be able to affirm faith in Christ and give precious last farewells, admonitions, and encouragement to loved ones. Because families whose soldier relative died suddenly in battle or in a hospital with no family member present felt robbed of this experience, they often sought out those who could report on their loved one's final hours. Fellow soldiers, as well as nurses in hospitals, frequently wrote letters to the family members of the deceased, reporting the attitude, conversion experiences, and last words of the soldier that indicated his faith and demonstrated that he had died well.

While many soldiers took a profound comfort from their faith and prepared themselves in case they should die, the battlefield experience itself left little time for meditation. The clash and movement of battle gave soldiers little opportunity to deal with the deaths of loved ones or comrades. While most soldiers tried to give their fellows a decent burial in a marked grave, this was often impossible, especially for the side that lost a battle and possession of the field. Soldiers could become callous at the sight of so much death and had limited time to mourn even those they were closest to. When the body of a soldier who had died in battle could be found and identified, or when a soldier died in a hospital, an embalmer might prepare the body for shipment home for a funeral and proper burial.

On the home front, especially in the middle and upper classes, social rituals associated with mourning determined the clothing that the bereaved wore and restricted their social activities. These mourning customs, which especially affected women, were based on those practiced in England and developed particularly during the nineteenth century. The adult female relatives of the deceased wore black dresses made of certain dull materials and carried black accessories. They wore no jewelry or else special mourning jewelry made of jet (polished coal), the hair of the deceased, or a small picture of the deceased. There were four degrees of mourning from the deepest first mourning to half mourning, when a woman could wear gray or purple. The amount of time spent in each degree of mourning depended upon the relationship of the mourner to the deceased. Deep mourning also restricted the activities a woman could participate in. For example, she would not go to the theater for six months. The lengthiest mourning was that of a wife for her husband, the various degrees of which lasted for two and a half years.

Mourning clothes could be quite fashionable. Large cities had special stores featuring mourning garb and accessories. Women of the lower classes who could not afford the expense of mourning clothes or the restriction of their activities would make token gestures toward mourning with whatever black materials they had available. Men in mourning had few restrictions and were most likely to indicate their sorrow with a black band around their hat or around their upper arm. After Abraham Lincoln's assassination, the citizens of Illinois wore crepe bands on their left arms and their hats for six weeks. Men and women who could afford it wrote their letters on stationery with a black border.

Not all relatives of the deceased found that conventional Christian principles met their needs. Spiritualism, or communicating with the spiritual world through the use of a human medium in séances and similar gatherings, had been gaining followers since the late 1840s. The practice grew tremendously during the Civil War as survivors sought to communicate with their deceased relatives. Mary Lincoln, for example, attended séances, several of them in the White House, in an effort to contact the Lincolns' son Willie after he died in February 1862. Séances continued to be popular even after Christian ministers denounced them and many mediums proved to be charlatans.

See also: Chaplains; Embalming; Jackson, Thomas Jonathan ("Stonewall"); Nurses; United States Christian Commission.

Bibliography

Faust, Drew Gilpin. "The Civil War Soldier and the Art of Dying." *Journal of Southern History* 67 (February 2001): 3–38.

Masson, Ann, and Bryce Reveley. "When Life's Brief Sun Was Set: Portraits of Southern Women in Mourning, 1830–1860." *Southern Quarterly* 27 (Fall 1988): 33–56.

McPherson, James M. *For Cause and Comrades: Why Men Fought in the Civil War.* New York: Oxford University Press, 1997.

Weisberg, Barbara. *Talking to the Dead: Kate and Maggie Fox and the Rise of Spiritualism.* San Francisco: HarperSanFrancisco, 2004.

Woodworth, Steven E. *While God Is Marching On: The Religious World of Civil War Soldiers.* Lawrence: University Press of Kansas, 2001.

DEATH RATES *See* Mortality, of Soldiers.

DEBILITAS

Debilitas (Latin) or *debility* were diagnostic terms used by Civil War surgeons, especially Confederates, to describe general, severe, disabling weakness in a patient. Some doctors also used the term *cachexia* for such weakness. Both Union and Confederate forms for listing the number of patients with each type of diagnosis included debility in the category "all other diseases."

Debility was a vague diagnosis for weakness not otherwise classified. There were two general types of debility. First, it was seen as the result of and associated with some other severe illness, such as "Debility from Acute Dysentery" or "Chronic Diarrhea with Debility." Patients who were unable to eat, or unable to retain what they ate because of vomiting or diarrhea, would naturally have resulting weakness. Many soldiers received furloughs because of associated disease and debility, and some died.

The second type of debility was a weakness apparently not associated with any disease. The soldier had a poor appetite and little energy, was lethargic and depressed, and complained of various aches and pains. Some soldiers with these symptoms were described as having "lack of morale" or a "poor attitude"; some were accused of malingering. Most of these soldiers were in the field, trying to do their duty, while feeling quite unwell. In many cases, this condition may have been the early stage of scurvy, before the symptoms appeared that conclusively identified the disease. Substantial parts of an army often developed scurvy at the same time, leading to diminished effectiveness on the battlefield. Scurvy-induced debility could be improved by including fruits and vegetables in the soldiers' diet, foods that are now known to contain vitamin C.

See also: Diarrhea and Dysentery; Diet, of Troops; Scurvy.

Bibliography

Bollet, Alfred Jay. *Civil War Medicine: Challenges and Triumphs.* Tucson, AZ: Galen, 2002.
Cunningham, H.H. *Doctors in Gray: The Confederate Medical Service.* Baton Rouge: Louisiana State University Press, 1958; reprint, Gloucester, MA: Peter Smith, 1970.

DELEON, DAVID CAMDEN (CA. 1818–1872)

David Camden DeLeon, the first Confederate surgeon general, was born in Camden, South Carolina, and apparently went by his middle name. His brother Edwin was U.S. consul general in Egypt at the outbreak of the Civil War, but resigned to join the South and served as a Confederate diplomat in Europe. His other brother, Thomas Cooper DeLeon, wrote two gossipy books about Richmond, Virginia, and its people during the Civil War: *Belles, Beaux and Brains of the 60's* (1909) and *Four Years in Rebel Capitals* (1890).

Virtually nothing is known about Camden DeLeon's youth, education, and early career. He was commissioned as an assistant surgeon in the U.S. Army on August 21, 1838, and promoted to surgeon, with the rank of major, on August 29, 1856. At the time of the 1860 census, DeLeon lived in Washington, DC. He resigned his army post on February 19, 1861, in order to support the Southern cause.

DeLeon went to New Orleans to procure medical supplies for the garrison at Pensacola in April 1861. In the Confederate capital, Montgomery, Alabama, he was appointed the country's first surgeon general, possibly on May 6, 1861 (sources conflict). DeLeon shared a rented house with Confederate adjutant general Samuel Cooper, quartermaster general Abraham C. Myers, his brother Thomas DeLeon, and several other men. Their porch became a rendezvous for various members of Confederate society. Camden DeLeon served with Myers on a board to choose a design for the Confederate uniform.

DeLeon was evidently considered only an acting surgeon general. References to him generally suggest that he was incompetent. Mary Chesnut, the Confederate diarist, who knew the DeLeon family in South Carolina, recorded that there was considerable competition for the post and that DeLeon had an alcohol problem. He resigned on July 12, 1861. Charles H. Smith served for a week or two and was succeeded by Samuel P. Moore, who remained surgeon general for the rest of the war. DeLeon continued serve the Confederacy, however, inspecting a hospital site on Roanoke Island in January 1862 and briefly serving as medical director for the Army of Northern Virginia in June 1862.

DeLeon apparently did not marry. By 1870 he was practicing medicine in Santa Fe, New Mexico. DeLeon died on September 3, 1872.

See also: Moore, Samuel Preston; Surgeon General.

Bibliography

DeLeon, Thomas Cooper. *Four Years in Rebel Capitals.* Mobile, AL: Gossip Printing, 1890; reprint, Alexandria, VA: Time-Life, 1983.

Heitman, Francis B. *Historical Register and Dictionary of the United States Army, From Its Organization, September 29, 1789, to March 2, 1903.* Washington, DC: Government Printing Office, 1903.

United States Census, 1860, District of Columbia, Washington, 1st Ward, 209.

United States Census, 1870, New Mexico, Santa Fe, Santa Fe, 3rd Precinct, 349.

Woodward, C. Vann, ed. *Mary Chesnut's Civil War.* New Haven, CT: Yale University Press, 1981.

DENTISTRY

By the time of the Civil War, dentistry was an established profession in the United States. Its practitioners cleaned tartar from teeth, filled cavities, pulled teeth that were beyond repair, and made dentures. The first dental school in America, the Baltimore College of Dentistry, opened in 1840 with five students. By 1860 there were three schools that together had graduated about 400 dentists. However, like physicians, many more trained by apprenticeship than by formal schooling; about 5,500 men listed themselves as dentists in city directories and censuses. Approximately 1,000 of those men lived in the Confederate states, although none of the dental schools was in the South.

During the 1850s several officials, including the then-Secretary of War Jefferson Davis, had attempted to set up an army dental corps with six dentists, but nothing had come of the plan. As a consequence, the U.S. Army medical department did not have dentists at the beginning of the Civil War, nor did it establish such a group during the war. Regimental surgeons performed basic dental care, such as pulling teeth and lancing boils on the gum. For more serious problems soldiers visited civilian dentists and paid their own expenses. For example, when General William T. Sherman's troops reached Savannah, Georgia, in December 1864, many of the men rushed to the civilian dentists in that city with dental problems.

U.S. Army recruits could be rejected because of bad teeth. It was especially important that soldiers have their four front teeth in order to hold and tear the paper cartridge while loading their guns. Soldiers rejected for lacking these front teeth were noted on the paperwork as "4F," an abbreviation eventually expanded to mean any kind of physical disability preventing military service.

Confederate soldiers, like their Union counterparts, frequently had poor dental hygiene. However, the Confederate medical department was sympathetic to their needs. Surgeon General Samuel P. Moore arranged to have dentists commissioned as captains or majors, and when dentists were drafted, beginning in 1863, they were assigned to treating soldiers' dental needs. The large military hospitals had an assigned dentist who examined and treated the patients. These dentists were busy men, performing an average of twenty-five fillings, twenty extractions, and uncountable amounts of tartar cleaning daily. A soldier who needed dentures had to visit a civilian dentist at his own expense, a costly proposition given Confederate monetary inflation during the war.

Small fillings were usually made with gold foil and large ones with cheaper tin foil. In some cases dentists used an amalgam of silver, tin, and mercury for hard-to-fill places. One Confederate grave held a corpse whose tooth had been filled with lead and shotgun pellets. Although gold had formerly been used as a base for dentures, by the time of the Civil War many dentists were using "vulcanite," a type of vulcanized hard rubber.

James Baxter Bean, a civilian dentist who treated many Confederate soldiers in Atlanta, Georgia, developed an "interdental splint" for immobilizing fractures of the lower jaw. His success rate prompted Surgeon General Moore to have him introduce the method in the Richmond, Virginia, hospitals as well. Evidently a Northern dentist, Dr. Thomas B. Gunning, developed a similar apparatus independently at about the same time and used it to treat Secretary of State William H. Seward after he fractured his jaw in a carriage accident on April 5, 1865.

See also: Bean, James Baxter; Education, Medical; Moore, Samuel Preston.

Bibliography

Baxter, Colin F. "Dr. James Baxter Bean, Civil War Dentist: An East Tennessean's Victorian Tragedy." *Journal of East Tennessee History* 67 (1995): 34–57.
Bollet, Alfred Jay. *Civil War Medicine: Challenges and Triumphs.* Tucson, AZ: Galen, 2002.
Cunningham, H.H. *Doctors in Gray: The Confederate Medical Service.* Baton Rouge: Louisiana State University Press, 1958; reprint, Gloucester, MA: Peter Smith, 1970.

DIARRHEA AND DYSENTERY

Diarrhea and dysentery were endemic in all armies, both North and South, during the Civil War. Although the statistics come from Union records, the Confederates suffered similarly. "Acute" diarrhea, loose and frequent bowel movements over the course of several days, was most common. "Chronic" diarrhea lasted for weeks, months, or even years, severely weakening the patient. The term *dysentery* was not clearly defined during the Civil War. It is usually interpreted to mean blood in the bowel movement or a more severe case. Because it is not evident what differences doctors intended by their choice of terms, diarrhea and dysentery will be treated together here.

Union medical records show as many as 641 cases of acute diarrhea and dysentery per 1,000 troops per year, for a total of 1,528,098 cases. Even this figure is an underrepresentation because many soldiers with diarrhea did not bother to report to sick call, and, if they did go to get some medicine, they were not counted unless they were sick enough to be hospitalized. Soldiers frequently referred to episodes of diarrhea in their letters and diaries, often using such slang terms as "Virginia quickstep" or "Tennessee trots." Everyone from generals to privates was likely to suffer at least several bouts per year.

There were a variety of causes of acute diarrhea. Poor sanitation was certainly a major factor, especially in recently assembled armies. Improperly dug, covered, or located latrines, and soldiers who chose to relieve themselves wherever convenient, rather than in the latrines, could pollute the water supply as well as contaminate the area generally. Contact with the excrement of the ill could further spread disease. Increased discipline and location to a new campsite sometimes improved the health of the troops.

Food also proved a major source of acute diarrhea. Contaminated, spoiled, or improperly cooked rations affected the soldiers' digestion, sometimes with food poisoning. In addition, quantities of unripe fruit, available to marauding soldiers at some times of the year, usually resulted in cases of acute diarrhea.

Although the incidence of acute diarrhea tended to be somewhat higher at the beginning of the war and during the summers, it was relatively consistent throughout the war. Death rates from acute diarrhea and dysentery were relatively low (about 20 per 1,000 cases). However, the prevalence of diarrhea had an effect on battles because it could reduce the numbers of men available to fight. Soldiers who fought when they were sick might not fight as well as when they were healthy. In addition, wounded soldiers who were already weakened by diarrhea could have more difficulty recovering.

The most common and effective treatment for diarrhea was opiates, either in alcohol solution, such as laudanum, or in pills. Belladonna was used to treat intestinal cramps. Other treatments, which were either useless or further cleaned out the system rather than stopping the problem, included calomel, turpentine, castor oil, and quinine.

While acute diarrhea usually cleared up in a few days, chronic diarrhea lingered on, leading to weight loss, weakness, and emaciation. Chronic diarrhea was the leading cause of death from disease, with 288 deaths per 1,000 cases, and the third-highest cause of medical discharges, after gunshot wounds and consumption (tuberculosis). Many soldiers who contracted chronic diarrhea suffered from it for the rest of their lives, years after the war ended. Diarrhea was often a symptom of other diseases, such as typhoid fever. While some chronic diarrhea may have been caused by intestinal tuberculosis or various microbes, much of it was associated with malnutrition, vitamin deficiencies, and such nutrition-related diseases as scurvy and pellagra. Chronic diarrhea increased in armies on the march or with reduced rations. It was also the leading cause of death in prisons. When doctors detected a "scorbutic taint" in the diseases of their armies, they hastened to get the commissary to issue onions, potatoes, or other fresh vegetables if at all possible. Soldiers found blackberries an especially good aid to recovery. The fact that fresh vegetables and fruits were the only remedies that worked for many cases of chronic diarrhea indicates that this disease was frequently nutrition-related, because most ordinary diarrhea is worsened when the patient eats vegetables and fruits.

Recent research suggests that chronic diarrhea can also result from intestinal damage suffered during one or more bouts of acute diarrhea. Such problems, labeled "irritable bowel syndrome" in the twenty-first century, are still difficult to diagnose and treat.

See also: Alcohol, Medicinal Uses of; Andersonville Prison; Calomel; Diet, of Troops; Elmira Prison; Latrines; Laudanum; Malnutrition; Medication, Administration of; Morphine; Mortality, of Soldiers; Opiate Use and Addiction; Quinine; Sanitation; Scurvy; Surgeon's Call; Tuberculosis; Typhoid Fever.

Bibliography

Bollet, Alfred Jay. *Civil War Medicine: Challenges and Triumphs.* Tucson, AZ: Galen, 2002.

Kohl, Rhonda M. "'This Godforsaken Town': Death and Disease at Helena, Arkansas, 1862–63." *Civil War History* 50 (March 2004): 109–144.

Welsh, Jack D., and Thomas P. Lowry. "Chronic Diarrhea During and After the Civil War: Post-Gastroenteritis Chronic Diarrhea." *Journal of Civil War Medicine* 6 (October–December 2002): 118–120.

DIET, OF HOSPITAL PATIENTS

Hospital patients suffering from serious illnesses, wounds, and malnutrition resulting from lengthy periods of poor nutrition in the field often could not eat the hardtack, salt pork, and similar staples of the typical diet of Civil War troops on both sides. The sickest needed special diets featuring broths, toast, and rice. Chicken, eggs, milk, custards, pickles, onions, lemonade, and vegetables and fruits of all sorts were among the items used to tempt the feeble soldier with a poor appetite to take some nourishment.

In both the North and the South, the recipes for special diets were based on the ideas of Alexis Soyer (1809–1859), a notable French chef working in England at the time of the Crimean War. Hearing about the poor condition of the soldiers, he volunteered to go to the Crimea in 1855–1856, where he worked with Florence

Nightingale to improve the soldiers' diet. He published a book about his experiences, *Soyer's Culinary Campaign* (1857), as well as his own cookbook.

Joseph Janvier Woodward, of the Union army, included forty-seven of Soyer's recipes in his *Hospital Steward's Manual* (1862), while *Regulations for the Medical Department of the Confederate States Army* (1863) contained fifteen of the same recipes. These recipes included beef tea with several variations (such as mutton tea); chicken broth; arrowroot, rice, or barley water; variations on lemonade (some with citric acid or limes rather than lemons); a fig and apple drink; egg soup; tapioca pudding; and a number of other liquid concoctions.

Depending upon the patient's condition, his doctor would prescribe a certain type of diet with precisely determined amounts of particular items. In 1863 the Confederates had a very complex list of ten different diets, including Tea Diet, Milk Diet, Chicken Diet, and Half Diet (a smaller portion of the regular diet). This system proved impractical, however, and most hospitals simply used low (or light), half, and full diets or a diet for the sick and one for convalescents.

In the South, a number of the matrons supervised or did the special diet cooking, while a steward supervised the meals for the convalescents. In the North, relief worker Annie Wittenmyer observed that special diets were often poorly prepared. She devised a plan for special diet kitchens with female superintendents directing the cooking. Beginning in early 1864 Wittenmyer established these kitchens in the large hospitals with the aid of supplies furnished by the U.S. Christian Commission. The kitchens worked so well that they were used in about a hundred hospitals by the end of the war. Wittenmyer also prepared a cookbook, published in 1864, for the diet kitchens. Despite recipes and diet plans, in some cases matrons or cooks took what was available and tried to make it taste like the patient's mother's cooking in order to tempt his appetite.

Hospitals had a number of sources of food to feed their patients. Basics such as beef and rice could be obtained from the commissary. If possible, eggs, chickens, milk, fruits, and vegetables would be purchased from farmers in the surrounding area using money from the hospital fund or, in some places in the South, bartering with pottery or cotton thread. At Chimborazo Hospital in Richmond, Virginia, and a number of the Army of Tennessee hospitals in Georgia, the servants and convalescents planted vegetable gardens and kept cows for milk. Supplies also came from relief agencies, usually organized by groups of local women in both the North and the South. In the North both the U.S. Sanitary Commission and the U.S. Christian Commission collected and distributed vast amounts of supplies to the field and general hospitals.

Hospital diets could only be as good as the supplies received. Even patients in Union hospitals could be poorly fed when supplies failed to arrive. Hospitals not on a main supply route could have difficulties procuring food. In both North and South, hospital staff complained about quartermasters who failed to give hospital supplies any priority. Hospitals located in areas that had been foraged bare had difficulty finding food to purchase. In Richmond, despite a far-reaching foraging system, patients had fewer food options than they did in corresponding hospitals in Georgia. One matron defused a rebellion among her patients by reminding them that she had stewed the rats they had caught when the cook refused to do so. Stewed rat was not ordinarily on hospital menus, however.

In general, surgeons and hospital workers recognized that hospital patients had different dietary needs from healthy troops in the field and did their best to provide special diets with the food available.

See also: Chimborazo Hospital; Convalescents; Cooks; Diet, of Troops; Hospital Fund; Malnutrition; Matrons; Nightingale, Florence; Quartermasters; Stewards, Hospital; Subsistence Department; United States Christian Commission; United States Sanitary Commission; Wittenmyer, Annie Turner; Women's Hospital Auxiliaries and Relief Societies; Woodward, Joseph Janvier.

Bibliography

Cumming, Kate. *Kate: The Journal of a Confederate Nurse, 1862–1865.* 1866; reprint, ed. Richard Barksdale Harwell. Baton Rouge: Louisiana State University Press, 1959, 1987; Savannah, GA: Beehive, 1975.

Gill, Gillian. *Nightingales: The Extraordinary Upbringing and Curious Life of Miss Florence Nightingale.* New York: Ballantine, 2004.

Pember, Phoebe Yates. *A Southern Woman's Story: Life in Confederate Richmond.* 1879; reprint, ed. Bell Irvin Wiley. Jackson, TN: McCowat-Mercer, 1959; reprint, Covington, GA: Mockingbird, 1974.

Regulations for the Medical Department of the Confederate States Army. Richmond, VA: Richie and Dunnavant, 1863.

Schroeder-Lein, Glenna R. *Confederate Hospitals on the Move: Samuel H. Stout and the Army of Tennessee.* Columbia: University of South Carolina Press, 1994.

Wittenmyer, Annie. *Under the Guns: A Woman's Reminiscences of the Civil War.* Boston: E.B. Stillings, 1895.

Woodward, Joseph Janvier. *The Hospital Steward's Manual: For the Instruction of Hospital Stewards, Ward-Masters, and Attendants, in Their Several Duties.* Philadelphia: J.B. Lippincott, 1862; reprint, San Francisco: Norman, 1991.

DIET, OF TROOPS

Although both Union and Confederate armies developed tables indicating the appropriate rations to distribute to their troops, the ability to fulfill these guidelines varied widely depending on the location of the troops, the season of the year, and the period of the war. The shortages, poor quality, and lack of nutritional variety of the rations led to many digestive diseases and other ailments related to nutrient imbalance. While some soldiers suffered only briefly from these illnesses, many others found their health permanently impaired.

A single ration (for each man, each day) in the Union army was supposed to consist of 12 ounces pork or bacon or 1 pound 4 ounces salt or fresh beef, and 1 pound 6 ounces soft bread or flour or 1 pound hard bread (hardtack) or 1 pound

4 ounces corn meal. In addition, for each hundred rations certain items were distributed in bulk to be equally divided among the troops: 1 peck beans or peas, 10 pounds rice or hominy, 10 pounds green coffee or 8 pounds roasted and ground coffee or 1 pound 8 ounces tea, 15 pounds sugar, 2 quarts salt, 4 quarts vinegar, 4 ounces pepper, ½ bushel potatoes, and 1 quart molasses. Substitutes included small amounts of vegetables, dried fruits, pickles, pickled cabbage (to prevent scurvy), desiccated (dried) potatoes, or desiccated vegetables. Southern rations were similar but did not include hardtack or desiccated vegetables. Both sides often had to make substitutions, depending upon what was available. Southerners rarely received full rations, especially as the war progressed. Considerably reduced rations were dispensed on the march, consisting of 1 pound hard bread, ¾ pound salt pork or ½ pound fresh meat, sugar, coffee, and salt. Commissioned officers did not receive rations. Instead, they received money to purchase food from the commissary.

Fresh beef rations could include meat from any part of the cow. Salt beef rations were universally despised because the meat was preserved with saltpeter. Often called "salt horse," the beef smelled vile, was frequently spoiled, and needed to be soaked overnight before cooking, preferably in a running stream, to make it edible. Salt pork was the most common meat ration. It was usually prepared boiled, fried, or broiled, but also used in soups or, in cases of desperation, eaten raw by the troops. It frequently arrived spoiled.

The desiccated (or, as the soldiers joked, "desecrated") vegetables distributed as part of the Union rations were unpopular with the troops. Close examination indicated that the vegetables consisted of cabbage leaves, turnip greens, carrots, turnips, parsnips, and a little onion, shredded, layered, and dried. A soldier would receive a block of these dried vegetables and break off a small piece, soaking it in water to reconstitute it before cooking, or adding it to soup.

Late in the war massive bakeries in Washington, DC, Alexandria, Fortress Monroe, and City Point, Virginia, supplied the Union Army of the Potomac with several hundred thousand loaves of bread per day. But hardtack was essential for Union armies on the march and often in camp as well. Confederates ate hardtack when it was captured from the enemy, but otherwise usually had cornbread.

Unfortunately, rations of any sort issued to Union and Confederate troops might well be of poor quality. Unscrupulous manufacturers supplied poor or possibly adulterated products. Contractors or commissaries could damage the items during shipment or storage by careless handling, exposure to the weather, or failure to protect the food from vermin infestation.

Soldiers could supplement their army rations by two methods: foraging and purchases from sutlers. Foraging meant gathering food from the vicinity. Soldiers might pick wild greens, berries, and nuts or take the plant or animal produce of nearby farms, with or without the farmers' permission. At times army commanders authorized their men to forage. In other instances, soldiers foraged on their own initiative, sometimes showing no scruples about what they took.

Sutlers supplied fresh and canned food as well as other items to troops who could afford to purchase them. These civilians had permits and pitched their tents or wagons near camp. Sutlers' wares were quite expensive because of the cost of purchasing and transporting them, as well as the risk of loss should the army move suddenly. Most sutlers did not deliberately cheat their customers, though some unscrupulous sutlers were raided by soldiers frustrated at being overcharged or receiving defective products. Local women might also sell the soldiers baked goods or culinary treats on a smaller scale.

Most troops who joined the army were incompetent as cooks. Cooking was considered women's work, and soldiers, except for a few professional chefs, simply had no experience with it. In camp, company cooks, who were excused from other responsibilities, often prepared the rations for the group. A good company cook was a treasure. The inexperienced could produce some awful concoctions, especially when they had been cooked in the same pots used to boil laundry. Later in the war it became common to organize cooking by three- or four-man messes. Soldiers had limited cooking utensils—usually a tin cup and plate or half an old canteen that served as a frying pan. On the march each man was responsible for his own food. Usually soldiers were ordered to take three days' worth of cooked rations. Hungry men who ate theirs all at once then had nothing else to eat but what they might forage or beg until the commissary distributed more rations.

In several Union regiments troop health rapidly improved when chefs gave the soldiers some cooking instruction. One of these teachers, James M. Sanderson, a New York hotel operator and member of the U.S. Sanitary Commission, published a cookbook, *Camp Fires and Camp Cooking; or, Culinary Hints for the Soldier*, in January 1862. It is not known how widely soldier cookbooks were distributed, but most soldiers probably did not benefit from them. None were produced in the South. In the Confederacy some soldiers brought slaves to cook for them and some men, North and South, hired free black cooks.

The main beverages drunk by the soldiers were coffee and water. Whiskey was rarely issued, usually only for medicinal purposes. Of course some soldiers managed to procure whiskey for themselves through theft or illicit purchase. Soldiers on both sides considered coffee an absolute staple. Southerners often suffered from coffee shortages and had to drink substitutes made from other plant products, such as rye, acorns, and other nuts and seeds. Soldiers collected water from whatever sources were available—streams, wells, or even contaminated puddles, depending on how desperate was the situation.

Contaminated water, spoiled food, and indigestibly prepared food all contributed to the ubiquitous diarrhea from which most soldiers frequently, if not continuously, suffered. Many soldiers were hospitalized for diarrhea-related debility. In addition, a consistent diet of hardtack and salt pork led to cases of scurvy. Diarrhea and scurvy also made other diseases worse. Many soldiers suffered permanent health problems and even died as a result of food- and water-related disease.

See also: Alcohol, Abuse of; Alcohol, Medicinal Uses of; Cooks; Diarrhea and Dysentery; Diet, of Hospital Patients; Hardtack; Malnutrition; Scurvy; Subsistence Department; Substitutes, for Supplies; United States Sanitary Commission.

Bibliography

Billings, John D. *Hardtack and Coffee: The Unwritten Story of Army Life.* Boston: George M. Smith, 1887; reprint, Lincoln: University of Nebraska Press, 1993.

Davis, William C. *A Taste for War: The Culinary History of the Blue and Gray.* Mechanicsburg, PA: Stackpole, 2003.

DISINFECTANTS *See* Antiseptics and Disinfectants.

DIX, DOROTHEA LYNDE (1802–1887)

Dorothea Lynde Dix, who served as superintendent of women nurses for the Union Army during the Civil War, was born April 4, 1802, in Hampden, Maine, the daughter of Joseph and Mary Bigelow Dix. An only child until she was ten, Dix had difficult relationships with various family members. In fact, throughout her life Dix was touchy and had problems with many relationships, at least in part because she was very intense and morally self-righteous, emotionally isolated, and a loner who never married.

Dix rejected her father's ardent Methodism and became a devout Unitarian. Sober and self-disciplined, she taught in several schools where she imparted her ideas of discipline, moral values, and perseverance. She was extremely strict and so uncompromising that she often had difficulties with her students. Dix wrote several books, including *Conversations on Common Things* (1824), which conveyed miscellaneous information through the medium of a mother-daughter dialogue. Because of a physical collapse in 1836, Dix spent some time in Europe.

Dix found the major direction of her life after a visit to the jail in Middlesex County, Massachusetts, in March 1841. Concerned about the treatment of prisoners, she was even more concerned about the care of the insane poor, who were often jailed as well. Of several possible treatment options for the insane, she advocated moral treatment, the goal of which was to develop self-control through therapy in the carefully controlled, orderly environment of the insane asylum, under the personal direction of the asylum superintendent.

As a result of a tour of Massachusetts facilities housing the insane, Dix began her advocacy work in January 1843 with a recommendation to the Massachusetts state legislature for an asylum for the incurably insane. She was soon touring other states, advocating proper care or state asylums, depending on what provisions for the insane were available already in that state. Eventually regarded as an expert, she was invited to some states to further their campaigns for care for the insane. Some state facilities were developed or improved because of her work, although her efforts were sometimes defeated because of political maneuvering. Nevertheless, by the time of the Civil War, she was one of the best-known and most highly respected women in America.

Dix saw the Civil War as a crisis between self-control and passion and believed that nonpartisan benevolence was the cure for both secessionism and abolitionism, two attitudes that she regarded as types of insanity. As soon as the Southerners fired on Fort Sumter, Dix caught a train to Washington, DC, where she went to the White House and, on April 19, 1861, volunteered herself and a group of women (yet unselected) to nurse sick and wounded soldiers without pay. Accepting her offer, Secretary of War Simon Cameron appointed her superintendent of women nurses on June 10. Initially she was to assign women to hospitals in the Washington area. Dix also saw herself as a hospital inspector, promoting improvements to hospitals established around Washington, much as she had done with insane asylums. In many respects, she saw herself, and was so regarded by many people, as an American Florence Nightingale, following in the footsteps of the woman who had done so much to improve British hospital care during the Crimean War.

As superintendent of women nurses, Dix determined to be very selective about the women chosen as nurses. She preferred to employ a small number of women who would spread a positive influence, because she saw their moral and spiritual qualifications as more important than any experience or training as a nurse. The women were to be between the ages of thirty-five and fifty, plain-featured, plainly and soberly dressed in brown or black, without hoop skirts, jewelry, curls, or ornaments of any sort. Although Dix wanted, reasonably, to avoid employing young women who had come to husband-hunt rather than to nurse, she rejected a number of capable young women because of their age. It is not known exactly how many women Dix appointed, but some estimates suggest 3,200. Nevertheless, other avenues to appointment soon opened and many women rejected by Dix provided good service under other auspices.

Although Dix did have some supporters, many people were unhappy with her because she was so confrontational and had conflicts with nearly everyone. She had fierce battles with many army doctors and failed to cooperate with the Woman's Central Association of Relief and the U.S. Sanitary Commission. She saw nuns as competitors against her nurses. Even her own nurses found Dix patronizing and distant. Dix did not get along with Surgeon General William A. Hammond either. He did his best to diminish what little authority Dix had. An October 1863 order, issued by Acting Surgeon General Joseph K. Barnes, permitted women to apply for a nursing appointment through the secretary of war rather than through Dix, placing them under the command of surgeons instead of under Dix. Although she was tired, lost weight, and had little enthusiasm for her post, Dix continued as superintendent, with diminished authority, until the end of the war.

After the Civil War Dix continued her involvement with insane asylums, but to a lesser degree, especially after 1868. She lived in special quarters at several of her favorite mental hospitals, finally settling permanently in the one at Trenton,

New Jersey, in October 1881. After years of increasing feebleness, Dix died there on July 18, 1887.

See also: Barnes, Joseph K.; Hammond, William Alexander; Nightingale, Florence; Nuns; Nurses; United States Sanitary Commission; Woman's Central Association of Relief.

Bibliography

Brown, Thomas J. *Dorothea Dix: New England Reformer.* Cambridge, MA: Harvard University Press, 1998.

Schultz, Jane E. *Women at the Front: Hospital Workers in Civil War America.* Chapel Hill: University of North Carolina Press, 2004.

DYSENTERY *See* Diarrhea and Dysentery.

E

EDUCATION, MEDICAL

All the commissioned medical officers in both the Union and the Confederate service had similar basic medical training. With few exceptions they were required to have a degree from a "regular" medical school (not from one of the homeopathic or other medical sects). From the 1830s to the 1850s, when most of the doctors who participated in the Civil War were trained, the standard curriculum consisted of seven subjects, each usually taught by a different professor unless the school was very small. Over the five-month term (usually mid-October to mid-March), the student attended classes in theory and practice of physic (medicine), chemistry, surgery, anatomy, materia medica (pharmacy), institutes of medicine (physiology), and obstetrics and diseases of women and children. Each class was taught in lecture format with demonstrations performed by the professor. Students did not have any hands-on clinical or laboratory experience as part of the required classes, although a professor might offer an optional extra class before or after the regular term that included hospital visitation, for example.

The student's primary personal experience with patients came through an apprenticeship to a practicing physician, often in the student's hometown. This might begin before a student took medical classes and usually continued after the term of classes was over. There was no set length of time for these apprenticeships, but they usually lasted several years. Especially in rural areas, doctors trained solely by apprenticeship, but they were not eligible for commissions during the Civil War. However, a number of them served as contract physicians in emergencies or worked as hospital stewards.

After the period of apprenticeship, the fledgling doctor returned to the medical school for another five-month term, during which he took exactly the same seven courses as he had taken the first time. There was no distinction made between medical students taking their first or their second term. However, those in their second term wrote a thesis on some medical subject, normally based on lecture notes and textbook readings rather than on original research. They also had to pass a final examination. They then received their degree and were able to practice wherever they could find the patients. Some doctors, however, went on to further training in association with hospitals or to study in Europe.

The most prestigious medical schools were located in Philadelphia and New York City. Many Southerners, as well as Northerners, trained in these schools. By the 1850s a number of medical schools had been opened in the South, in Richmond, Virginia; Augusta, Georgia; Charleston, South Carolina; Nashville, Tennessee; and New Orleans, Louisiana. Some Southern nationalists urged that Southerners should be educated at home because of alleged physical and medical differences between blacks and whites as well as distinctive Southern diseases. In December 1859, in response to John Brown's raid on Harpers Ferry, Virginia, 250 students withdrew from the medical colleges in Philadelphia and returned to the South to complete their education.

Many doctors who served as medical officers during the Civil War soon realized that their basic education and their civilian practice had not adequately prepared them for the challenges of military medicine. Early in the war Union physicians stationed in southern Illinois organized the Army Medical and Surgical Society of Cairo, which met weekly for discussions at the medical purveyor's office. Union surgeon general William A. Hammond was not pleased with the skill level of many who passed the examinations for surgeon and assistant surgeon and wanted to set up a special postgraduate medical school, to meet in the basement of the Army Medical Museum. He proposed to have distinguished surgeons lecture on various aspects of military medicine and proper hygiene. However, Secretary of War Edwin M. Stanton refused to grant permission for the project.

By the second year of the Civil War, the Medical College of Virginia in Richmond was the only medical school still open in the Confederacy. Because of an increased need to provide military physicians, special arrangements were made for stewards and ward masters in Richmond hospitals who already had some medical background: in addition to their work, they could attend classes at the medical college during the term. Some students who had not yet attended two terms and graduated were permitted to take the examination for assistant surgeon and commissioned when they passed. Leniency to nondegreed doctors was not permitted outside Richmond, however.

Confederate medical officers in Richmond in August 1863 organized the Association of Army and Navy Surgeons of the Confederate States with Surgeon General Samuel P. Moore as president. The group met twice a month and was open to any Confederate medical officer who signed the constitution of the association and paid ten dollars annually. The organization's object was to further the knowledge of military medicine through collection and dissemination of data and the discussion of relevant topics, such as treatment of certain wounds, treatment of diseases, and the use of anesthesia. From January 1864 through February 1865 the group published the *Confederate States Medical and Surgical Journal* monthly. The journal contained reports of the group meetings as well as data and articles on various topics. Medical officers outside Richmond were encouraged to subscribe and contribute articles. This was the only medical journal published in the Confederacy.

See also: Alternative Medicines; Anesthesia; Army Medical Museum; Association of Army and Navy Surgeons of the Confederate States; *Confederate States Medical and Surgical Journal*; Examining Boards, Medical; Gunshot Wounds, Treatment of; Hammond, William Alexander; Hospitals, Antebellum; Materia Medica; Medical Purveyors; Moore, Samuel Preston; Richmond, Virginia; Stewards, Hospital; Surgeons; Surgeons, Acting Assistant (Contract); Surgeons, Assistant; Ward Masters.

Bibliography

Brinton, John H. *Personal Memoirs of John H. Brinton, Civil War Surgeon, 1861–1865.* New York: Neale, 1914; reprint, Carbondale: Southern Illinois University Press, 1996.

Confederate States Medical and Surgical Journal. January 1864–February 1865; reprint, Metuchen, NJ: Scarecrow, 1976; reprint, San Francisco: Norman, 1992.

Kaufman, Martin. "American Medical Education." In *The Education of American Physicians: Historical Essays*, ed. Ronald L. Numbers, 7–28. Berkeley: University of California Press, 1980.

Schroeder-Lein, Glenna R. *Confederate Hospitals on the Move: Samuel H. Stout and the Army of Tennessee.* Columbia: University of South Carolina Press, 1994.

ELMIRA PRISON

The camp for Confederate prisoners of war at Elmira, New York, officially known as Barracks No. 3 or Camp Chemung, is considered to have been the worst of the Union prison camps, with the poorest conditions and highest death rate.

Located in Chemung County, in western New York just north of the Pennsylvania border, Elmira had a prewar population of about 8,800. The town had a number of small manufacturing enterprises and was a transportation center with a canal and a railroad. Early in the war, the fairgrounds at Elmira became a state and then a federal military camp where ultimately 20,796 Union soldiers gathered for organization and processing into the army. By the spring of 1864 fewer soldiers were being routed through Elmira. At the same time, because prisoners of war were not being exchanged, the prisoner of war camps were full. In mid-May Assistant Adjutant General E.D. Townsend, in Washington, DC, proposed that some vacant barracks at Elmira could be used for prisoners.

Commissary General of Prisoners Colonel William Hoffman notified Lieutenant Colonel Seth Eastman, post commander at Elmira, to prepare the camp for 8,000 to 10,000 prisoners of war, even though Eastman repeatedly told Hoffman that the area allotted could hold 4,000 or at most 5,000. Hoffman paid no attention, and at its peak on September 1, 1864, the camp contained 9,480 prisoners.

The prison consisted of thirty-two acres enclosed with a twelve-foot-high fence. A platform four feet from the top along the outside of the fence connected the forty sentry boxes for the 300-man guard detail. There was no "deadline" to keep the prisoners away from the fence as at Andersonville. Thirty barracks housed 3,000 to 4,000 men while the rest occupied tents, some even into the winter.

The first prisoners, from the camp at Point Lookout, Maryland, arrived on July

6, 1864. More than 4,000 men occupied Barracks No. 3 by the end of July. The prisoners were organized into companies of 84 (later 112), commanded by a Union officer. All the prisoners' clothing except underwear, socks, and shoes was supposed to be gray. Consequently there was a serious shortage of clothing. The diet was essentially bread with a little meat in the morning, and bread and a thin soup in the afternoon. At first the prisoners were able to supplement this diet by purchasing fruits and vegetables from the camp sutler. However, Hoffman's Circular No. 4 of August 10 prevented the prisoners from buying food from sutlers or receiving boxes of food from outside the camp unless the prisoner were officially sick. This policy resulted in many serious cases of scurvy and malnutrition among the prisoners, worsening any other disease they contracted. Prison officials and local newspaper reporters claimed that the prisoners were well fed, however.

At first the prison had no hospital. Even after one was constructed, there were never enough beds for the patients. The prison had no chief surgeon until after the camp had been open for a month. One of the major sources of disease at Elmira was Foster's Pond, a large, stagnant pool filled with filth, which polluted the drinking water and caused many intestinal diseases. Although inspectors reported the potential dangers of the pond almost immediately, it was not until October 23 that Hoffman finally permitted prisoners to begin work on a drainage ditch and wooden pipeline to flush the pond.

The two post commanders, Seth Eastman and his successor, Colonel Benjamin Franklin Tracy, were both military sticklers who obeyed orders exactly and did not exercise discretion when it was possible to improve conditions for the prisoners. Some historians of the Elmira camp suggest that Hoffman and other officers may have tried to retaliate against the Confederates for mistreating Union prisoners of war. It was not clear during the war that most of the Confederacy was suffering from a food shortage, a mitigating circumstance affecting prisoner rations there. Local shortages could not be an excuse for Barracks No. 3, however, as the Elmira area had a bountiful harvest in 1864.

During the severe cold of the winter of 1864–1865, the prisoners at Elmira were poorly clothed, housed, and fed. Many sickened and died. Prisoner of war exchanges finally began in February 1865 and the last 256 Confederates left Elmira on July 11. During the year the camp was open, 2,950 prisoners of the total 12,122 inmates died, a 24.3 percent death rate. This compares to an overall 11.7 percent rate among prisoners of war in Northern camps and 15.3 percent in Southern camps. Elmira had the highest death rate of any prisoner of war camp in the North.

See also: Andersonville Prison; Diarrhea and Dysentery; Malnutrition; Mortality, of Soldiers; Prisoners of War; Sanitation; Scurvy.

Bibliography

Gray, Michael P. "Elmira, a City on a Prison-Camp Contract." *Civil War History* 45 (December 1999): 322–338.

Horigan, Michael. *Elmira: Death Camp of the North*. Mechanicsburg, PA: Stackpole, 2002.

Robertson, James I. "The Scourge of Elmira." *Civil War History* 8, no. 2 (1962): 80–97; reprint, *Civil War Prisons*, ed. William B. Hesseltine. Kent, OH: Kent State University Press, 1972.

EMBALMING

Embalming of the dead became much more common during the Civil War than it had been previously because of the tremendous number of war casualties. Before the war, few people were embalmed except for the wealthy, particularly politicians. Generally, funerals were conducted soon after death and, if necessary, the body could be packed in ice for short-term preservation. The purpose of embalming during the war was to preserve the body sufficiently for it to travel, in good condition, the often-considerable distance from the battlefield or the hospital to the soldier's home.

During the Civil War, with few exceptions, only Northerners were able to have the bodies of their fallen kin embalmed, and even then, most Northern soldiers were not embalmed. Many battle casualties were not identified and were buried on the field or in other unmarked graves. Even when a comrade identified the soldier and marked the grave, the body became too decomposed for embalming. Many Northerners were unable to travel to retrieve the bodies of their relatives or chose not to do so, even if the whereabouts of the remains were known.

The persons most likely to be embalmed were officers and soldiers who died in the hospital, especially with family or friends present. When Colonel Elmer Ellsworth of the Eleventh New York Infantry was shot and killed on May 24, 1861, after lowering a Confederate flag from the roof of a hotel in Alexandria, Virginia, he became not only the first Northern martyr of the war, but one of the first embalmed. The fact that Ellsworth's body could be kept presentable for viewing at funerals in several cities received a lot of newspaper attention, making many Northerners aware of the possibilities of embalming.

All of the embalmers were civilians. Although at least one of them, Dr. Daniel Prunk, had served as an acting assistant (contract) surgeon in Nashville, Tennessee, none of the embalmers operated under military auspices. They were required to have military permission, however, which was not always granted. At one point, General Benjamin F. Butler banned embalmers from his area of command because he was afraid that their presence would discourage the soldiers and be bad for morale. By April 1865, all embalmers were required to have a license.

Many of the embalmers were physicians or at least had some medical training. Many learned the trade by working for another embalmer. Prunk established branch offices in several Tennessee cities, run by men whom he had trained.

The business proved quite lucrative during the war. Embalmers commonly charged fifty dollars to prepare the body of an officer and ship it home, while the family of a private would pay twenty-five dollars. By the end of the war, charges had risen to eighty and thirty dollars, respectively.

Thomas Holmes, the "father of American embalming," who had embalmed Elmer Ellsworth, also made quite a bit of money selling his embalming fluid, but many embalmers made their own. There were several recipes. One of the most common preservatives was zinc chloride, which was prepared by dissolving strips of zinc sheets in hydrochloric acid. Other preparations were made with arsenic, sugar of lead, and other acids and alkalies. The proportions could be adjusted with more or less preservative depending on whether the body would be making a long or short trip. Some embalmers added potassium nitrate to the solution to give the corpse a pinker complexion. Certain combinations of ingredients turned the body hard and marble-like.

The embalmer might or might not drain the blood from the corpse first. In either case, the embalming process involved injecting the embalming fluid into a slit cut in an artery, usually the femoral artery in the thigh, using the equivalent of a large hypodermic syringe, sometimes attached to a type of pump. Once the body was embalmed, it was placed in a metallic coffin or a wooden one lined with zinc. It usually was shipped by train if possible.

The most famous person embalmed during the Civil War was President Abraham Lincoln after his assassination by John Wilkes Booth in April 1865. After two surgeons performed an autopsy, Dr. Charles D. Brown, undertaker in the firm of Brown and Alexander in Washington, DC, who had also embalmed Lincoln's son Willie when he died in February 1862, prepared the body. With the help of his assistant, Brown drained Lincoln's blood through the jugular vein and pumped embalming fluid through the femoral artery, using a chemical that hardened the body. Lincoln's corpse was put through more stress than most, traveling more than 1,600 miles and being exhibited at twelve funerals before his burial in a temporary receiving vault in Oak Ridge Cemetery in Springfield, Illinois, on May 4. Dr. Brown traveled on the funeral train and had to do a good deal of touch-up work at various stops after Lincoln's face began to deteriorate.

Following the Civil War, embalming continued to become more common, in part because it put to rest the fears of survivors that their loved one might be buried alive.

See also: Death, Attitudes Toward; Lincoln, Abraham; Surgeons, Acting Assistant (Contract).

Bibliography

Berman, Gary E. "Civil War Embalming: A Short History." *Journal of Civil War Medicine* 1 (July–August 1997): 3–4.

Bollet, Alfred Jay. *Civil War Medicine: Challenges and Triumphs.* Tucson, AZ: Galen, 2002.

Johnson, Edward C., and Gail R. Johnson, eds. "A Civil War Embalming Surgeon: The Story of Dr. Daniel H. Prunk." *The Director* [National Funeral Directors Association], January 1970; reprint, *Museum News* [Illinois Funeral Service Foundation], June 1970: 2–4.

Kunhardt, Dorothy Meserve, and Philip B. Kunhardt Jr. *Twenty Days.* New York: Castle, 1965.

ERYSIPELAS

Erysipelas is a severe streptococcal skin infection that often proved fatal to those who contracted it during the Civil War. It could affect soldiers suffering from major wounds as well as nurses, doctors, and hospital visitors who had a slight scratch that became infected. Because erysipelas was so contagious, these patients were moved to a separate building or hospital tent. There they were furnished with their own towels, and no dressings or bandages were reused.

Erysipelas began in a break in the patient's skin, causing redness, tenderness, and inflammation at the point of infection. Erysipelas could remain confined to the infected area, but was likely to spread under the skin, quickly destroying tissues. If the infection spread to the lymph nodes and then the bloodstream, Civil War physicians called it blood poisoning or pyemia. Pyemia patients developed further internal infections on heart valves and lungs. The fatality rate was greater than 90 percent.

Erysipelas was successfully treated in some cases with applications of bromine solution. The infection still exists in the twenty-first century, but is not as serious because it can be treated effectively with antibiotics.

See also: Antiseptics and Disinfectants; Gangrene, Hospital; Infections, of Wounds; Mortality, of Soldiers; Tents, Hospital.

Bibliography

Bollet, Alfred Jay. *Civil War Medicine: Challenges and Triumphs.* Tucson, AZ: Galen, 2002.

ETHER *See* Anesthesia.

EWELL, RICHARD STODDERT (1817–1872)

Confederate lieutenant general Richard Stoddert Ewell was born on February 8, 1817, in Georgetown, DC, the third son and sixth child of the ten children of Thomas Ewell, a doctor, and Elizabeth Stoddert Ewell. The Ewells had land but little cash. Thomas Ewell died, after bouts of alcoholism and poor health, when Richard was only nine. Mostly educated at home in Virginia by his oldest sister, Ewell then attended West Point, beginning in 1836 when he was nineteen. He graduated thirteen of forty-two in the class of 1840 and chose appointment to the dragoons (cavalry).

Stationed in Cherokee Territory, Ewell escorted some traders from Fort Leavenworth to Santa Fe in 1843. En route he contracted malaria, from which he continued to suffer effects for the rest of his life. During the Mexican War he served with the troops guarding commanding general Winfield Scott. While in Mexico, Ewell was bitten by a scorpion and had several bouts of malaria. Between the end of the Mexican War and the beginning of the Civil War, he was stationed in various parts of the territory that became New Mexico and Arizona.

Home in Virginia on sick leave when the Civil War broke out, Ewell resigned from the U.S. Army on April 24, 1861. Although he opposed secession, he believed that he had to go with his state. Appointed a lieutenant colonel, Ewell was the first Confederate field officer wounded when, on June 1, 1861, he received a slight shoulder wound during a skirmish at Fairfax Court House, Virginia.

On June 17, 1861, Ewell became a brigadier general, commanding a brigade with three regiments. Although he saw little action for some months, he was appointed a major general and placed in command of a division in January 1862.

Ewell was distinctive-looking with a mostly bald head, prominent eyes, and a beaked nose. His nervously active movements and piping voice reminded many people of a bird. In addition, he had some odd dietary beliefs, was easily angered, and was very profane in speech. In the spring of 1862 he was assigned to the army commanded by Thomas J. "Stonewall" Jackson. At first Ewell was very critical of Jackson, but became one of Jackson's biggest supporters when they worked together during the Shenandoah Valley Campaign in Virginia.

Ewell was bruised by a ricocheting bullet at the Battle of Gaines's Mill on June 27, 1862, during the Peninsula Campaign in Virginia. Then, on August 28 at Groveton, just before the Battle of Second Bull Run (Manassas), Ewell was kneeling to observe the action when a minié ball hit him in the center of his left kneecap, splitting it in two and then traveling down the bone marrow for six inches, splintering the bone of his lower leg. As a result, Dr. Hunter H. McGuire and another surgeon amputated Ewell's left leg above the knee on August 29.

Ewell nearly died after the operation, and as he began to recover, he had to flee Union cavalry, carried for many miles on a litter to Charlottesville. Here Ewell's femur poked through the stump of his leg so that he had to have another inch of bone removed. By mid-November Ewell was convalescing in private quarters in Richmond. He was able to navigate on crutches but suffered a severe setback on December 25 when he slipped on ice and fell, knocking a piece of bone off his stump and reopening his wound. Ewell spent the next several months bedridden.

Ewell's fiancée helped to care for him during his convalescence. Lizinka Campbell Brown was a cousin of Ewell's whom he had courted while in his teens. When he went to West Point, she married someone else. Now a wealthy widow, Lizinka became engaged to Ewell on December 1, 1861. They were married on May 26, 1863, at St. Paul's Episcopal Church in Richmond. Many of Ewell's staff members did not care for Lizinka because she was very bossy. During his convalescence Ewell experienced a religious conversion and stopped swearing.

After the death of Stonewall Jackson on May 10, 1863, Robert E. Lee reorganized the Army of Northern Virginia and gave Jackson's former corps to Ewell. Although Ewell's health was still fragile, he took command on June 1. He was bruised in the chest by a spent ball on June 14, 1863, at the Battle of Second Winchester (Virginia). He won this battle, creating unrealistic expectations that he was a "second Jackson."

On the first day of the Battle of Gettysburg (July 1), Ewell and his troops were very active and effective. Nevertheless, he has often been criticized for not attacking the Union troops on Cemetery Hill in the afternoon, thus "losing" the battle for the Confederates. Given Lee's conflicting orders to Ewell, the numerous Union troops already on the hill, and the failure of several of Ewell's subordinate generals to arrive on time, Ewell's decision seems understandable. However, Lee began to lose confidence in Ewell thereafter. At Gettysburg Ewell fell off his horse when it was wounded, and he was hit by a bullet in his wooden leg.

In mid-November 1863 a poorly fitting wooden leg caused Ewell's stump to become ulcerated. Lee relieved Ewell of command and sent him to the rear to recover, replacing him with Jubal A. Early. Lee refused to reinstate Ewell until after the end of the Mine Run Campaign (Virginia). Then, in January 1864, Ewell had to give up command again after his horse slipped on ice and rolled over on him. Throughout the rest of the war Ewell's health was both a genuine concern for those who knew him and an excuse for relieving him from command. At times he looked frailer than he actually was.

Ewell was capable enough to effectively manage a part of the Battle of the Wilderness on May 5–6, 1864. However, in late May he suffered from diarrhea and Lee once again removed him from command, this time permanently, replacing him with Early. Ewell's feelings were hurt when he was assigned to the more sedentary command of the defense of Richmond, but he did so as effectively as he could with the third-rate troops available to him. Because he protested against burning the tobacco warehouses when Richmond was evacuated on April 2, 1865, he later objected to being blamed for the destruction of Richmond.

Ewell and his troops were defeated and captured at Sayler's Creek, Virginia, on April 6, 1865. Unlike those who surrendered at Appomattox on April 9, Ewell was treated as a prisoner of war and incarcerated at Fort Warren in Boston harbor until July 19. After his release, he visited Philadelphia to get a new artificial leg and then settled with his wife on her 3,000-acre farm, Spring Hill, in Maury County, Tennessee. He managed both it and a cotton plantation in Mississippi for a time. Ewell suffered much from neuralgia (nerve pain) and dyspepsia (indigestion). He also tended to wear himself out with overwork. He died of pneumonia on January 25, 1872, three days after his wife died of a respiratory illness.

Ewell frequently has been faulted for his supposedly poor performance as a leader during the latter half of the Civil War. These opinions are often based on criticisms by contemporaries who had much to gain from Ewell's demotion. The critics usually suggest that Ewell lost his nerve and decisiveness along with his leg. Much contemporary evidence suggests that Ewell, in fact, remained an effective leader.

See also: Amputation; Artificial Limbs; Diarrhea and Dysentery; Gettysburg, Battle of; Gunshot Wounds, Treatment of; Jackson, Thomas Jonathan ("Stonewall"); McGuire, Hunter Holmes; Malaria; Minié Balls; Pneumonia; Prisoners of War.

Bibliography

Pfantz, Donald C. *Richard S. Ewell: A Soldier's Life.* Chapel Hill: University of North Carolina Press, 1998.

Welsh, Jack D. *Medical Histories of Confederate Generals.* Kent, OH: Kent State University Press, 1995.

EXAMINING BOARDS, MEDICAL

Medical examining boards, usually consisting of three qualified physicians serving on a short-term basis, were appointed in both the North and South to examine the professional qualifications of doctors who sought military medical appointments. Such examinations were first administered in the U.S. Army in 1832 when a board of examiners traveled to the various army posts testing the doctors who were already in the service. These examinations continued to be required for those wishing to be surgeons and assistant surgeons in the regular army.

With the outbreak of the Civil War, both the Union and the Confederacy raised large numbers of volunteer troops. Each regiment, permitted to select its own surgeon and assistant surgeon, usually chose popular local doctors. While many of these were very competent, if inexperienced with the details of military routine, others clearly should have stayed in civilian practice where the stresses, expectations, and patient load were lower. By 1862, the medical service on both sides (the Southern service was modeled upon that of the North) was administering exams to the volunteer surgeons in order to weed out incompetents. Both armies also used examinations to determine promotions from assistant surgeon to surgeon.

The Union exams were at first very difficult. After writing a brief medical autobiography, the candidate had to take a written examination with questions on anatomy, surgery, and the practice of medicine. This was followed by an oral exam on the same subjects, as well as general pathology, chemistry, physiology, hygiene, toxicology, and pharmacy. Some candidates even endured examinations on history, geography, zoology, literature, natural philosophy, and languages, most of which had little to do with their competence as physicians. Some candidates had to undergo a clinical examination with patients in a hospital and perform surgery on a cadaver. Many candidates failed the exam and some complained bitterly about their lack of time to study because of their medical responsibilities. During the summer of 1862, Secretary of War Edwin M. Stanton, insisting that the army needed more doctors, required the examining board to relax its standards somewhat. Some exceptions were also made for doctors with lots of practical medical skills but limited knowledge of languages, geography, and other general subjects.

The Confederate exams, while challenging, do not seem to have been as difficult as those administered by the Union boards, but all Confederate medical officers were required to be graduates of medical colleges. Thomas Hart Benton Williams, assistant surgeon of the Ninth Mississippi Regiment, took (and passed) a typical written exam for promotion to surgeon. Forty-eight questions on four pages asked the meaning of various terms, the proper dosages of various medications, the antidotes to certain poisons, the route of blood circulating from particular organs to the heart, the circumstances rendering amputation necessary, procedures for the treatment of gunshot wounds, and the nature, diagnosis, and treatment of particular diseases. Like their Union counterparts, Confederates took oral as well as written exams.

Both Union and Confederate armies also had another type of medical examining board, also made up of three officers. The purpose of this type of board was to examine soldiers who had been hospitalized for some time with illness or wounds. The board was to determine whether a soldier was sufficiently convalescent to return to duty, whether he needed a furlough for further convalescence at home, or whether he would never recover enough to return to the service and should be discharged.

See also: Alternative Medicines; Education, Medical; Gunshot Wounds, Treatment of; Surgeons; Surgeons, Assistant.

Bibliography

Adams, George Worthington. *Doctors in Blue: The Medical History of the Union Army in the Civil War.* New York: Schuman, 1952; reprint, Dayton, OH: Morningside, 1985.

Blustein, Bonnie Ellen. *Preserve Your Love for Science: Life of William A. Hammond, American Neurologist.* Cambridge, UK: Cambridge University Press, 1991.

Brinton, John H. *Personal Memoirs of John H. Brinton, Civil War Surgeon, 1861–1865.* New York: Neale, 1914; reprint, Carbondale: Southern Illinois University Press, 1996.

Schroeder-Lein, Glenna R. *Confederate Hospitals on the Move: Samuel H. Stout and the Army of Tennessee.* Columbia: University of South Carolina Press, 1994.

EXCISION *See* Resection.

EYE AILMENTS

During the Civil War many Union and Confederate soldiers suffered from eye problems. These problems tended to fall into three categories: disease, injury, and nutritional deficiency. Though Civil War physicians treated eye problems according to current knowledge, one important innovation on both sides was to establish special wards or hospitals devoted to eye disease and staffed by a skilled doctor. The Union forces had eye infirmaries in St. Louis, Missouri, and Washington, DC, while in 1864 the Confederate Army of Tennessee had the Ophthalmic Hospital in Athens, Georgia.

Eye diseases were often labeled ophthalmia, meaning a severe inflammation of the eye or eyes. Then, as now, these problems could be caused by germs or irritants. A number of soldiers developed ophthalmia as a consequence of having measles, a "childhood disease" that spread rapidly through new regiments when they joined the army. Eye injuries resulted from accidents or gunshot wounds.

Night blindness, the inability to see at night while having normal vision during the day, is a result of vitamin A deficiency. Not surprisingly, the problem became worse as the war progressed because more soldiers had had poor nutrition for a longer period of time. At the time some doctors observed an increase in night blindness when scurvy increased. This is logical because both are related to vitamin deficiency, although not the same vitamins. Other doctors considered complaints of night blindness to be a form of malingering. It seemed particularly to be an excuse to get a furlough because night blindness tended to disappear at home where the soldiers ate a more balanced diet. Few soldiers were hospitalized for night blindness because they could function perfectly well to fight during the day. There were significant problems with night blindness among William T. Sherman's Union troops during the Atlanta Campaign and also in Robert E. Lee's Confederate Army of Northern Virginia.

See also: Diet, of Troops; Malingerers; Malnutrition; Measles; Scurvy.

Bibliography
Bollet, Alfred Jay. *Civil War Medicine: Challenges and Triumphs.* Tucson, AZ: Galen, 2002.

F

FEVERS

Fevers of numerous types were common to soldiers both North and South during the Civil War. Doctors tended to consider a fever to be itself a disease rather than a symptom. As physicians diagnosed and categorized these fevers, they often used terms unfamiliar in the twenty-first century. All the fevers involved an elevated temperature in the patient, but beyond that their characteristics varied.

Eruptive fevers included those diseases that caused skin eruptions or spots. Among the illnesses in this category were measles, smallpox, and scarlet fever. They were understood to be contagious.

Intermittent fevers were associated with malaria. The name described the periodic nature of the attacks of the disease. Sometimes doctors added the descriptors *quotidian*, *tertian*, or *quartan* to indicate that the symptoms returned daily, every other day, or every third day, respectively.

Continued fevers were those in which the patient's temperature did not return to normal at all, but remained elevated. For the Confederates this term included typhoid fever, typhus fever, and other less defined illnesses. Union doctors stopped using this diagnostic term in July 1862.

Remittent fever was one of the most common. Doctors recorded 286,490 cases among white Union troops and a proportional number among black soldiers. In remittent fever, the patient's temperature varied several degrees daily but did not return to normal. This diagnostic classification could be applied to a variety of diseases and would be equivalent to the contemporary "fever of unknown origin." Remittent fever patients had a low death rate.

The general term *camp fever* was applied to a number of diseases such as yellow fever, typhoid fever, malaria, typhomalarial fever, and continued fever.

See also: Malaria; Measles; Mortality, of Soldiers; Smallpox; Typhoid Fever; Typhomalarial Fever.

Bibliography

Barnes, Joseph K., ed. *The Medical and Surgical History of the War of the Rebellion (1861–1865).* Washington, DC: Government Printing Office, 1870–1888; reprint, Wilmington, NC: Broadfoot, 1990.

Bollet, Alfred Jay. *Civil War Medicine: Challenges and Triumphs.* Tucson, AZ: Galen, 2002.

Cunningham, H.H. *Doctors in Gray: The Confederate Medical Service.* Baton Rouge: Louisiana State University Press, 1958; reprint, Gloucester, MA: Peter Smith, 1970.

Welsh, Jack D. *Medical Histories of Confederate Generals.* Kent, OH: Kent State University Press, 1995.

Woodward, Joseph Janvier. *Outlines of the Chief Camp Diseases of the United States Armies, As Observed During the Present War.* Philadelphia: Lippincott, 1863; reprint, San Francisco: Norman, 1992.

FINLEY, CLEMENT ALEXANDER (1797–1879)

Clement Alexander Finley, who served as surgeon general for the Union forces for slightly less than a year, was born at Newville, Pennsylvania, on May 11, 1797. He grew up in Chillicothe, Ohio, and attended Dickinson College in Carlisle, Pennsylvania, graduating in 1815. He graduated from the University of Pennsylvania's medical school in 1818, and on August 10 of that year he was commissioned a surgeon's mate in the First Infantry. In 1832 he married Elizabeth Moore of Philadelphia.

During his forty-three years in the army, Finley was stationed at various times in Louisiana, Arkansas, Florida, Missouri, Kansas, Illinois, Wisconsin, Virginia, New York, Pennsylvania, and Kentucky. During the Mexican War he was briefly medical director of the armies of first Zachary Taylor and then Winfield Scott; but in each case illness soon intervened and Finley was sent back to the North. He also served on medical examining boards.

When Surgeon General Thomas Lawson died unexpectedly on May 15, 1861, President Abraham Lincoln chose Finley, then sixty-four years old and the senior medical officer, to replace Lawson. Opinion of Finley's performance as surgeon general has tended to be negative, focusing on his age and his inability to overcome his old army lethargy in order to provide the sort of energetic, change-oriented leadership needed for the vastly expanded Civil War medical service. Finley was parsimonious about providing supplies and failed to prepare the medical corps for battle casualties. The medical chaos at First Bull Run (Manassas) was blamed on him.

In the fall of 1861 the medical director of the South Carolina expedition led by General Thomas W. Sherman ordered a hospital constructed for the troops in South Carolina. Finley countermanded the order because he claimed that the mild climate of South Carolina made a hospital unnecessary. As a result, editor Horace Greeley published a blistering attack on Finley in the *New York Tribune*. Finley also managed to run afoul of both the U.S. Sanitary Commission, whose aid he resisted, and Secretary of War Edwin M. Stanton, who essentially forced Finley to retire on April 14, 1862. Finley was replaced by William A. Hammond.

After leaving the medical service, Finley lived in West Philadelphia, where he died on September 8, 1879.

See also: Bull Run (Manassas), First Battle of; Hammond, William Alexander; Lawson, Thomas; Medical Department, Organization of; Surgeon General; United States Sanitary Commission.

Bibliography

Bollet, Alfred Jay. *Civil War Medicine: Challenges and Triumphs.* Tucson, AZ: Galen, 2002.
Phalen, James. "Clement Alexander Finley." *Army Medical Bulletin* 52 (April 1940): 38–41.

FLEWELLEN, EDWARD ARCHELAUS (1819–1910)

Edward Archelaus Flewellen, medical director for the Confederate Army of Tennessee, was born in Warren County, Georgia, on September 17, 1819. He attended Randolph-Macon College in Virginia, and graduated from Jefferson Medical College in Philadelphia, Pennsylvania, on March 18, 1851. Practicing medicine in Thomaston, Georgia, Flewellen also served in the state legislature.

When the Civil War began, Flewellen enlisted and in May 1861 was commissioned as surgeon of the Fifth Georgia Infantry Regiment. He was in charge of a hospital in Pensacola, Florida, for a time. After serving with his regiment in several locations and suffering a serious illness at Cumberland Gap on the Tennessee-Kentucky-Virginia border, Flewellen had charge of hospitals at LaGrange, Tennessee. In June 1862 he became assistant medical director of the Army of Tennessee. He succeeded A.J. Foard as medical director in January 1863, when Foard joined the staff of General Joseph E. Johnston in the Department of the West.

As medical director, Flewellen was in charge of field medical services for the army, which was then commanded by General Braxton Bragg. Flewellen supervised and coordinated with Samuel H. Stout, the medical director of hospitals for the army, as both sought to assign doctors and other medical personnel to the locations where they could be most useful to the sick and wounded. During the several weeks surrounding the Battle of Chickamauga in Georgia, in September 1863, communication between Stout and Flewellen broke down because of military movements and the inability to get messages through, leading to confusion and disruption of medical services for wounded soldiers.

In November 1863 Flewellen resigned as medical director due to ill health and unwillingness to serve under General Johnston, who was named to army command. Foard replaced Flewellen in February 1864. During the final months of the war, Flewellen assisted Foard and also served as a hospital inspector. In this capacity, he examined the prison hospital at Andersonville, Georgia, but his report has been lost.

After the war, Flewellen, a life-long bachelor, returned to Georgia, where he served as superintendent of public works, as a member of the state constitutional convention in 1877, and as a state senator (1896–1897). He was in charge of several railroads at various times. After Flewellen's death on December 9, 1910, his Civil

War medical papers were given to the federal government and were eventually placed in the National Archives in Washington, DC.

See also: Andersonville Prison; Chickamauga, Battle of; Foard, Andrew Jackson; Hospitals, Field; Hospitals, General; Inspectors, Medical; Medical Directors, Field; Medical Directors, of Hospitals; Stout, Samuel Hollingsworth.

Bibliography

"E.A. Flewellen, M.D." *Southern Practitioner* 24 (April 1902): 207, 209.
Obituary, "Dr. E.A. Flewellen." *Confederate Veteran* 20 (January 1912): 33.
Schroeder-Lein, Glenna R. *Confederate Hospitals on the Move: Samuel H. Stout and the Army of Tennessee.* Columbia: University of South Carolina Press, 1994.
Tombstone, Edward A. Flewellen, Glenwood Cemetery, Thomaston, Georgia.

FOARD, ANDREW JACKSON (CA. 1829–1868)

Andrew Jackson Foard, field medical director for the Confederate Army of Tennessee, was born in Milledgeville, Georgia. Almost nothing is known about his early years except that he graduated from Jefferson Medical College in Philadelphia by 1852. He studied medicine privately with Dr. White in Milledgeville and Dr. Francis O. Smith in Philadelphia.

Foard's first known medical job was serving as an acting assistant (contract) surgeon, replacing an absent assistant surgeon, at Fort Capron, Florida, from late 1852 into 1853. On May 11, 1853, having been approved by the examining board, Foard was commissioned an assistant surgeon in the U.S. Army. He probably continued to serve in Florida at first, but from August 25, 1855, to the summer of 1860 he worked at various posts in Texas. After Georgia, his home state, had seceded, Foard resigned on April 1, 1861, and offered his services to the Confederacy, where he was immediately appointed a surgeon.

Assigned to duty in Pensacola, Florida, Foard organized the hospitals and field medical services for General Braxton Bragg's forces there. Bragg, impressed by Foard's unusual organizing ability, made Foard his medical director. Foard did further important medical organization in the spring of 1862 during the confusion of combining several armies into what eventually became the Army of Tennessee, with Bragg commanding. Bragg and Foard soon realized that it was too difficult for one person to adequately supervise both the army's field hospitals and its general hospitals. In an order of August 22, 1862, Bragg appointed Samuel H. Stout, an excellent hospital administrator in Chattanooga, Tennessee, the medical director for all the army's general hospitals in Tennessee and northern Georgia. Foard remained field medical director.

In this position Foard inspected hospital and medical arrangements and directed medical officers in their preparations and activities. With Stout, Foard coordinated the appointment of doctors to the field or hospital service. Based on army movements, Foard directed Stout when to move hospitals out of a particular area and where to move them in order to prevent their capture, while still keeping them within a reasonable distance of the army.

In December 1862 Foard became medical director for the Department of the West, commanded by General Joseph E. Johnston. This department, which never worked very well, included Bragg's army as well as that of John C. Pemberton in the Vicksburg area. Foard's duties in this department mainly involved inspections.

Edward A. Flewellen, assistant medical director of the Army of Tennessee, succeeded Foard as medical director. When Flewellen stepped down because of ill health, Foard was named medical director again in November 1863, although he apparently did not resume his responsibilities until February 1864. He served until the end of the war under Johnston and General John B. Hood during the Atlanta campaign and Hood's Tennessee campaign. Foard was in Augusta, Georgia, when the war ended.

After the war, Foard began a private medical practice in Columbus, Georgia, which evidently was not successful. In the summer of 1867 he became professor of anatomy at the medical school of Washington University in Baltimore. He taught only one term before becoming very ill with double pneumonia, which apparently aggravated latent tuberculosis. Foard died in Charleston, South Carolina, on March 8, 1868.

See also: Examining Boards, Medical; Flewellen, Edward Archelaus; Hood, John Bell; Hospital Relocations; Hospitals, Field; Hospitals, General; Medical Directors, Field; Medical Directors, of Hospitals; Stout, Samuel Hollingsworth; Surgeons; Surgeons, Acting Assistant (Contract); Surgeons, Assistant; Tuberculosis.

Bibliography
Foard, Andrew Jackson, file. Personal Papers of Medical Officers and Physicians. Adjutant General's Office. RG 94, National Archives, Washington, DC.
"The Late Dr. A.J. Foard." *Nashville* (Tennessee) *Republican Banner*, May 16, 1868.
Schroeder-Lein, Glenna R. *Confederate Hospitals on the Move: Samuel H. Stout and the Army of Tennessee*. Columbia: University of South Carolina Press, 1994.

FORMENTO, FELIX (1837–1907)

Felix Formento, Confederate surgeon and author, was the son of Felix Formento Sr., a physician and native of Italy, and his wife, Palmyra Lauve Formento. The younger Felix was born in New Orleans on March 16, 1837. He attended Jefferson College in New Orleans. When the family moved to Italy in 1851, young Felix, following in his father's footsteps, studied at the Royal University of Turin, where he earned his medical degree in 1857. After studying with his father and attending a semester of medical lectures in Paris, he practiced medicine briefly in Paris and Nice, France. When France and Sardinia declared war on Austria in 1859, young

Felix, at his father's request, joined the Franco-Sardinian army as a surgeon, participating in the Italian campaign of that year, including the battles of Magenta and Solferino. In 1860 both Felix Formentos returned to New Orleans, where the younger became a visiting surgeon at the Charity Hospital.

By the time the Civil War began, Formento thus had the advantages of a European medical education, military medical experience, and hospital experience. With the support of the Louisiana Soldier's Relief Association, Formento went to Richmond, Virginia, and by October 1861 had opened the Louisiana Hospital, a 300-bed facility with an additional, smaller hospital for officers. Its main purpose was to treat Louisiana soldiers. Located about a mile from Richmond, the hospital consisted of a number of small wards located both in buildings and hospital tents. Formento, a strong advocate of good ventilation, cleanliness, and the use of all known hygienic methods, claimed that the hospital site had plenty of fresh air and good water. He also was aware of the dangers of contagious diseases such as measles, smallpox, and the wound infections gangrene and erysipelas. At the first sign of any contagious disease in a patient, Formento ordered the man removed to a contagious disease ward or an isolated hospital tent.

Formento strongly believed that patients healed more rapidly in tents than in crowded hospital wards, citing a number of instances of dying patients restored to health after they had been moved to a tent. He also advocated the use of female nurses, who were more attuned to patient comfort than were untrained convalescents or soldiers assigned to the hospitals to serve as nurses. He believed that the Louisiana Hospital had one of the lowest mortality rates of any of the hospitals in Richmond.

In late 1863 Formento published *Notes and Observations on Army Surgery*, based on his experiences with over 5,000 patients during two years as surgeon in charge at the Louisiana Hospital. In the book he discussed many aspects of patient care, including treatments he had found successful for smallpox, wound infections, and various other diseases. He compared conditions that determined whether a limb wounded by a gunshot should be amputated, resected, or saved. Formento also discussed other gunshot wounds and gave case studies of several successful and unsuccessful treatments. It is not known how widely this book circulated during the war, but it has been cited in postwar studies of Confederate medicine.

Formento remained in charge of the Louisiana Hospital until September 1864, when he resigned due to his own poor health and that of his wife, Celestine Voorhies, whom he had married in 1861. Returning to New Orleans, he established a successful private medical practice. He studied epidemiology and infectious diseases, served on the state board of health for two terms (1880–1884, 1890–1894), and was an active member of a number of professional organizations. Formento and his wife were the parents of one son. After his wife's death in 1875, Formento married Louise Chiapella in 1878. He died in New Orleans of heart disease on June 4, 1907.

See also: Amputation; Convalescents; Erysipelas; Gangrene, Hospital; Gunshot Wounds, Treatment of; Hospital Buildings; Hospitals, General; Hospitals, "Pest" (Smallpox); Measles; Mortality, of Soldiers; Nurses; Resection; Richmond, Virginia; Sanitation; Tents, Hospital; Ventilation; Women, as Hospital Workers.

Bibliography

Cunningham, H.H. *Doctors in Gray: The Confederate Medical Service.* Baton Rouge: Louisiana State University Press, 1958; reprint, Gloucester, MA: Peter Smith, 1970.

Formento, Felix, Jr. *Notes and Observations on Army Surgery.* New Orleans: L.E. Marchand, 1863; reprint, San Francisco: Norman, 1990.

FREDERICKSBURG, BATTLE OF (1862)

The Battle of Fredericksburg in December 1862 was the first in which the medical department of the Army of the Potomac was prepared before the battle to care for the needs of the Union wounded.

On November 7, 1862, General Ambrose E. Burnside replaced General George B. McClellan as commander of the Army of the Potomac. Because McClellan had done virtually nothing militarily after the Battle of Antietam in September, Burnside, who lacked confidence in his own capacity for overall command, was under pressure from all sides for a speedy, effective campaign. The army's march to Fredericksburg was relatively rapid, but the pontoon train, needed to bridge the Rappahannock River, did not arrive for several weeks. This delay ruined any element of surprise by the Union forces and enabled General Robert E. Lee to entrench the Army of Northern Virginia in excellent defensive positions on the hills behind Fredericksburg.

Although the situation had changed, Burnside did not change his plans. The Union engineers managed to complete the five pontoon bridges on December 11, after considerable difficulty and loss of life, despite a major Union artillery bombardment of the town.

The main battle took place on December 13 in two unconnected parts. Some of the Union forces crossed the river and fought south of the town. The rest attacked firmly entrenched Southern forces on Marye's Heights behind Fredericksburg. The attacks were particularly lethal for the Union soldiers, who had to cross a large open area before they got to the foot of the hill where the Confederates had an effective defense in a sunken road behind a stone wall. Burnside ordered repeated attacks that achieved nothing but casualties. Although Burnside wished to renew the attack on December 14, his subordinate commanders persuaded him not to do so. Union troops withdrew from Fredericksburg on the night of December 15.

The Union army suffered 1,284 dead, 9,600 wounded, and 1,769 captured or missing, for a total of 12,653. Confederate casualties totaled 5,309, of whom 595 were killed, 4,061 were wounded, and 653 were captured or missing. Because the battlefield was unusually open and more people saw much more of the battle than was normally the case, estimates of Union losses tended to be even higher, most often around 20,000.

The Confederates initially took their wounded from straw pallets in the woods to field hospitals in abandoned houses and barns. On December 14 they began to move the casualties by railroad to hospitals in Richmond and Charlottesville. When more than 800 wounded soldiers arrived in Richmond on December 15, the mayor called for assistance from the citizens. Women brought coffee, tea, soup, and milk to the train station. Due to a shortage of ambulances, other wheeled vehicles were also pressed into service to take the wounded to the hospitals.

The Army of the Potomac's medical department had taken advantage of the lengthy delay before the battle to make preparations based on the organizational changes recently implemented by the department's director, Jonathan Letterman. Union doctors had stockpiles of medical supplies and blankets and had set up ten division hospitals in the Falmouth area. Once the army crossed the Rappahannock, the doctors set up seven field hospitals in buildings in Fredericksburg.

Because of the exposed nature of the terrain, many of the Union wounded could not be removed from the battlefield until after nightfall on December 13. In some areas, ambulances could get close enough to remove the wounded efficiently. In other areas, litter-bearers carried the wounded, while some were taken to the rear on boards or other makeshift stretchers by their comrades. Most of the wounded had been removed from the battlefield to Fredericksburg by the morning of the fourteenth. The night was very chilly but not below freezing, so accounts of great numbers of wounded soldiers freezing to death after the battle are inaccurate.

All the wounded were moved back across the river to the division hospitals on December 15. Letterman wanted to leave them there to recover, but Burnside had other campaigning in mind and insisted that all the wounded be removed to hospitals in Washington, DC. This evacuation process began on December 16 and was completed on December 27, when the most severely wounded arrived in Washington. All the wounded had to travel in open railroad cars, often without enough straw or blankets, about eleven miles to Aquia Creek landing. Here the U.S. Sanitary Commission maintained a feeding station to provide the patients with nourishment before they were put on the boats for transport to Washington, a distance of about sixty miles. The entire trip generally took sixteen to eighteen hours. About 6,000 patients made the journey.

Although some people complained about conditions after Fredericksburg, the complainers generally had no idea how much care for the wounded had improved since previous battles.

See also: Ambulance Corps; Ambulances; Antietam, Battle of; Barton, Clara; Hospitals, Field; Hospitals, General; Letterman, Jonathan; Richmond, Virginia; United States Sanitary Commission; Washington, DC.

Bibliography

Duncan, Louis C. *The Medical Department of the United States Army in the Civil War.* Washington, DC: Author, 1914; reprint, Gaithersburg, MD: Butternut, 1985.

Rable, George C. *Fredericksburg! Fredericksburg!* Chapel Hill: University of North Carolina Press, 2002.

GANGRENE, HOSPITAL

Hospital gangrene was a severe streptococcal wound infection that proved fatal to many soldiers, both North and South, during the Civil War. Because it was much more serious than other types of gangrene and developed only in large hospitals in major cities where many kinds of infections were treated, researchers suggest that it may have resulted from a combination of several types of bacteria.

Hospital gangrene was extremely contagious and fast moving. A soldier with a healthy wound could contract the disease and be dead in several days. The edges of the infected wound turned a grayish color and the surrounding tissue was destroyed rapidly, as much as an inch per hour in some severe cases. The gangrene caused blood clotting in the small arteries leading to the tissue, causing the tissue to die and drop off, leaving gaping wounds.

The first step in caring for a hospital gangrene patient was to move him to a tent or separate building to prevent the further spread of gangrene. Here he and fellow sufferers were provided with their own sponges, towels, and sheets, which were frequently washed. Dressings and bandages were often reused elsewhere but not in the gangrene ward.

The patient was then anesthetized so his wound could be cleaned with such caustic agents as nitric acid, iodine, or carbolic acid, a painful process if the patient was conscious. In 1864 many doctors began to use a bromine solution to clean the wound and to inject into the affected tissue area, with considerable success. They also used it with good results to prevent the spread of the disease among those who worked with the gangrene patients.

In cases where gangrene affected a limb, doctors might amputate to prevent the spread of the disease. Where gangrene infected a previous amputation, doctors might amputate again further up the stump. Despite all medical efforts, about 46 percent of hospital gangrene patients died. Many of the survivors had permanent deformity in the affected area.

Hospital gangrene was rare during the first year of the war, became common during the second and third years, and then decreased, either because of the use of bromine or because the bacteria disappeared. Hospital gangrene cases were unusual after the Civil War except in other war situations. Necrotizing fasciitis is a similar wound infection that occurs in the twenty-first century and is fatal to about 20 percent of patients.

See also: Amputation; Anesthesia; Antiseptics and Disinfectants; Erysipelas; Infections, of Wounds; Mortality, of Soldiers; Tents, Hospital.

Bibliography

Bollet, Alfred Jay. *Civil War Medicine: Challenges and Triumphs.* Tucson, AZ: Galen, 2002.

GETTYSBURG, BATTLE OF (1863)

The three-day battle waged in and around Gettysburg, Pennsylvania, on July 1–3, 1863, was the largest battle ever fought in the United States, producing more than 50,000 casualties (killed, wounded, and missing).

In June 1863 Confederate general Robert E. Lee led the Army of Northern Virginia toward Pennsylvania. He believed that such a movement would draw Union troops away from threatening Richmond, Virginia, and from Vicksburg, Mississippi, as well. In addition, he expected to get supplies for the army in Pennsylvania and hoped to provoke European support for the South. However, the Northerners became very angry as the Southerners invaded Pennsylvania, taking livestock, food, wagons, and whatever else was available.

Neither Lee nor General George G. Meade, the new commander of the Union's Army of the Potomac, planned to fight at Gettysburg, a crossroads town in Adams County where ten roads met. The town had two colleges, numerous businesses, and a population of about 2,400. Confederate infantry came to Gettysburg allegedly looking for shoes. Instead they found Union cavalry. Fighting began on the northwest side of town on the morning of July 1. Both armies rushed additional troops to the area. The Union cavalry fought back numerous Confederate charges until reinforced by infantry from the Army of the Potomac's First Corps, whose commander, General John F. Reynolds, was killed by a Confederate sharpshooter just after he arrived on the battlefield. Various buildings in Gettysburg, including the courthouse, churches, warehouses, and private homes, were commandeered immediately as impromptu hospitals. Some of the wounded remained in these buildings even after the Confederates captured the town and pushed the Union defenders to Cemetery Hill and Cemetery Ridge on the north and east sides of town.

On the morning of July 2, the Union line resembled a large hook, occupying Culp's Hill on the northeast side of town, curving around to the north on Cemetery Hill, and then running more or less straight south on Cemetery Ridge to the hills Little Round Top and Round Top. It was an excellent defensive position and Confederate general James Longstreet urged Lee to flank (go around) the position rather than attack, advice that Lee rejected. Lee planned attacks on the flanks (ends) of the Union line with Longstreet attacking in the Round Top area and a secondary attack by troops under General Richard S. Ewell on Culp's Hill and Cemetery Hill. Because Longstreet's troops had to take an indirect road, the attack did not begin until late afternoon. Union general Daniel E. Sickles had moved his soldiers out of line, leaving some areas undefended. The battle raged in areas that became famous as the Peach Orchard, the Wheat Field, Devil's Den, and Little Round Top (an action commemorated in Michael Shaara's novel *The Killer Angels* and the movie *Gettysburg*). Sickles was wounded and had to have his right leg amputated. Despite an artillery barrage and hard fighting, the Confederates made little progress at Cemetery Hill and Culp's Hill.

On July 3 early morning fighting at Culp's Hill and a cavalry battle three miles from town were overshadowed by a two-hour artillery duel followed by Pickett's Charge, an attack by 15,000 Confederates on the center of the Union line at about three in the afternoon. The Confederates were decimated, no more than half of the Southerners being able to return to their own lines. Neither side attacked on July 4, and that night Lee began to withdraw. Meade, who had been commander of the Army of the Potomac only since June 28, did not pursue the Confederates with vigor, and they escaped across the Potomac a few days later.

Wounded and dead soldiers overwhelmed the town of Gettysburg and its environs. At least 160 locations served as hospitals, including the courthouse, college and seminary buildings, businesses and warehouses, hotels, churches, schools, forty-five homes in town, barns, farmhouses, and outbuildings. Yet many wounded soldiers remained lying in the open air in the rain. The Union forces were initially handicapped because, despite the protests of his medical director Jonathan Letterman, Meade had ordered the medical supply wagon trains to park near Westminster, Pennsylvania, about twenty-five miles from the fighting, so that ammunition transport would not be obstructed. As a consequence, all but the Twelfth Corps (which somehow did not receive or obey the command) had only their ambulances and medicine wagons, no hospital tents, food, clothing, utensils, or other supplies needed for the wounded. No tents arrived until July 5.

Many Gettysburg civilians did what they could to nurse and feed the patients, but their own supplies were low because of Confederate raiding a few days before the battle. A dozen Daughters of Charity of St. Vincent de Paul came from Emmitsburg, Maryland, on July 5 to nurse the wounded physically and spiritually. More nuns soon arrived from Baltimore and other places. Civilian doctors and a number of women came to help from outside the area. Members of the U.S. Sanitary Commission and the U.S. Christian Commission arrived with wagon trains of supplies (the railroad had been cut) before the military wagons arrived. In fact, the Sanitary Commission was providing supplies already on July 1.

Most of the wounded left within Union lines were gathered up and taken to field hospitals within hours of the end of the battle. The members of the ambulance corps worked diligently to move all they could during the battle, at great risk to their own lives. Five members of the corps died and seventeen were wounded during the fighting.

The care of the wounded was complicated by the Confederate withdrawal. The Southerners took as many of their wounded as they could in a train of 1,200 unpadded wagons that stretched for miles, traveling as rapidly as possible through mud and rain in order to avoid capture. Many patients suffered severely from lack of food and water for thirty-six hours as well as from the pain caused by the lurching wagons. In addition, they had no medical care at all since only guards and drivers accompanied them. The 6,802 more severely wounded Confederates remained behind with some medical officers in field hospitals to the west of Gettysburg. The Union military and relief agencies provided supplies for their care as well as for the 14,193 Union wounded. Doctors on both sides worked themselves to exhaustion treating the wounded and performing amputations for four or five days.

With the reopening of the railroad on July 6, the supply situation improved dramatically. Trains also took those patients able to be moved to Baltimore for transfer to other hospitals. As the crisis passed, the medical department established a consolidated hospital on the George Wolf farm about one and a half miles east of Gettysburg. Camp Letterman, as it was called, had at least 400 hospital tents arranged in neat rows, each tent housing eight to ten patients. The camp was located by the railroad for ease of transferring supplies and patients. The hospital opened on July 22, but transporting the wounded to the hospital took about two weeks. By October 18, only 326 patients remained at Camp Letterman, and the camp closed entirely on November 20, 1863.

Although the exact numbers can never be known, approximately 3,155 Union and 4,500 Confederate soldiers died during the Battle of Gettysburg. An additional 14,530 Union and 18,750 Confederates were wounded, roughly 75 percent of whom survived their wounds. More than 5,000 on each side were missing (captured, killed, or otherwise unaccounted for). Thus, casualties for the three days of battle (there are no accurate figures for each day) totaled more than 51,000, over 25 percent of the Union army and more than one-third of the Confederate.

See also: Ambulance Corps; Amputation; Autenrieth Medicine Wagon; Chamberlain, Joshua Lawrence; Ewell, Richard Stoddert; Hospitals, Field; Letterman, Jonathan; Nuns; Nurses; Sickles, Daniel Edgar; Tents, Hospital; United States Christian Commission; United States Sanitary Commission; Women, as Hospital Workers.

Bibliography

Coco, Gregory A. *A Vast Sea of Misery: A History and Guide to the Union and Confederate Field Hospitals at Gettysburg, July 1–November 20, 1863.* Gettysburg, PA: Thomas, 1988.

Duncan, Louis C. *The Medical Department of the United States Army in the Civil War.* Washington, DC: Author, 1914; reprint, Gaithersburg, MD: Butternut, 1985.

Maust, Roland R. *Grappling with Death: The Union Second Corps Hospital at Gettysburg.* Dayton, OH: Morningside, 2001.

Sheldon, George. *When the Smoke Cleared at Gettysburg: The Tragic Aftermath of the Bloodiest Battle of the Civil War.* Nashville, TN: Cumberland, 2003.

GUILD, LAFAYETTE (1825–1870)

Lafayette Guild, medical director for the Confederate Army of Northern Virginia, was a native of Tuscaloosa, Alabama. The son of James and Mary Williams Guild, he was born on November 23, 1825. Little is known about most of his life. He trained in medicine at the Jefferson Medical College in Philadelphia, graduating in 1848. On March 2, 1849, he was appointed an assistant surgeon in the U.S. Army. He married Martha "Pattie" Aylette Fitts (1831–1902) in 1851.

Guild remained in the army medical service until the Civil War, serving at various posts in the South and Southwest. From 1857 to 1861 he was assigned to the Second Dragoons and was with them in northern California in a campaign against the Indians. Evidently at that time Guild and his wife adopted two young Indian boys.

When the Civil War broke out, Guild returned from California and offered his services to the Confederacy. He was commissioned a surgeon and became medical director for the Army of Northern Virginia on June 27, 1862, serving on the staff of General Robert E. Lee. A number of his reports to Surgeon General Samuel P. Moore and other orders and correspondence survive. They show Guild's concern about provisions for the soldiers, both the healthy, whom he wanted to keep well, and the sick and wounded. As medical director, he had the authority to issue orders specifying, for example, the number of shirts, pairs of drawers, and blankets to be packed in each divisional medical wagon, to provide comfort and warmth for the wounded. Other problems that were out of his control—such as a chronic shortage of ambulances, the poor quality of surgical instruments manufactured in the Confederacy, and the poor quality and quantity of army rations that were completely deficient in vegetables—he could only report and hope for improvement. Guild remained medical director until Lee surrendered at Appomattox Court House, Virginia, in April 1865.

After the war Guild moved to Mobile, Alabama, where he had a private medical practice and, from 1866 to 1869, was quarantine inspector for the port, attempting to keep out yellow fever. In 1869 he moved to San Francisco, where he was visiting surgeon at the San Francisco City and County Hospital until his death on July 4, 1870. He was buried in Tuscaloosa.

See also: Ambulances; Diet, of Troops; Malnutrition; Medical Directors, Field; Moore, Samuel Preston.

Bibliography

Cunningham, H.H. *Doctors in Gray: The Confederate Medical Service.* Baton Rouge: Louisiana State University Press, 1958; reprint, Gloucester, MA: Peter Smith, 1970.

Guild, Pattie. "Journey to and from Appomattox." *Confederate Veteran* 6 (1898): 11–12.

Who Was Who in America: Historical Volume, 1607–1896. Chicago: Marquis, 1963.

GUNSHOT WOUNDS

By far the largest number of wounds during the Civil War resulted from gunshots. Minié balls caused the most injuries, often very severe ones with torn tissue and shattered bones. Round musket balls caused wounds at the beginning of the war, and pistol shots wounded troops throughout the conflict. Artillery ammunition—whether grape and canister (projectiles containing a number of smaller balls) or solid shot—was more likely to cause immediate death, by removing a head or limb or mangling the torso, rather than a treatable wound. Sabers and bayonets, which could be used only when soldiers fought in close proximity, produced a tiny percentage of wounds.

The physicians who assembled *The Medical and Surgical History of the War of the Rebellion* worked hard to gather the most accurate statistics they could, but even they could only make an educated estimate of the number of Union soldiers who suffered from gunshot wounds. Union hospitals, for example, treated about 175,000 gunshot wounds of the extremities, but this figure does not include those with minor wounds who were not hospitalized or those who died of their wounds before reaching a hospital. Medical historian Alfred Jay Bollet suggests that about four or five soldiers were wounded for every one killed in battle.

Men could be wounded in whatever part of their anatomy happened to be exposed at the wrong moment. Trenches tended to protect the legs and lower torso, while the hands and head were exposed when firing. Participating in a charge left all parts of the body vulnerable. Estimates suggest that 31 percent of all battlefield injuries (both killed and wounded) were to the upper extremities (arms and hands); 30 percent to the lower extremities (legs and feet); 15 percent to the head, face, and neck; and 23 percent to the torso or trunk. However, of those killed in battle, roughly 51 percent had trunk wounds and 42 percent were hit in the head or neck. Only about 8 percent of those killed in battle died of wounds to the extremities. In those situations, the limb was either blown off or hit in a major artery, as was the case with General Albert Sidney Johnston at the Battle of Shiloh. Roughly 70 percent of the hospitalized wounded had arm and leg injuries.

In their records, many Confederate doctors still used Latin terms for medical conditions. Thus a gunshot wound would be recorded as *vulnus sclopeticum* or *v.s.*

See also: Amputation; Gunshot Wounds, Treatment of; Johnston, Albert Sidney; *The Medical and Surgical History of the War of the Rebellion*; Minié Balls; Mortality, of Soldiers.

Bibliography

Barnes, Joseph K., ed. *The Medical and Surgical History of the War of the Rebellion (1861–65)*. Washington, DC: Government Printing Office, 1870–1888; reprint, Wilmington, NC: Broadfoot, 1990.

Bollet, Alfred Jay. *Civil War Medicine: Challenges and Triumphs*. Tucson, AZ: Galen, 2002.

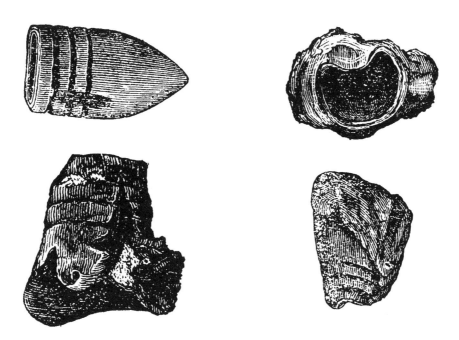

Minié balls, like the nearly intact one at the top left, were made of soft lead that distorted on impact, shattering bones and tearing tissue. The other three drawings show damaged minié balls removed from dead and wounded soldiers. (*Surgical History*, Vol. 2, Part 1, p. 589)

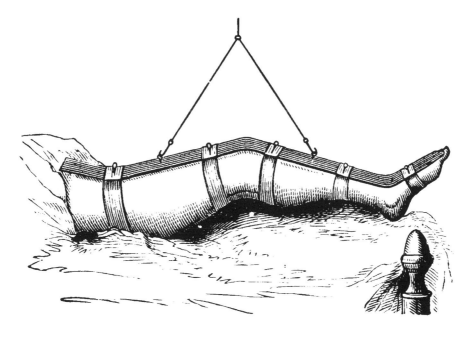

Smith's anterior splint suspended a broken leg with the splint on top of the leg, attached by bands as shown. The process was completed by wrapping the entire leg with a rolled bandage (not shown). (*Surgical History*, Vol. 2, Part 3, p. 346)

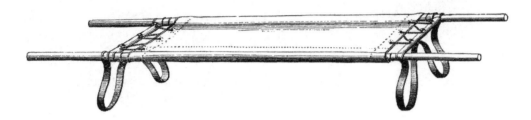

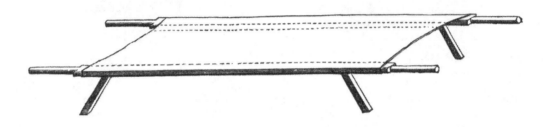

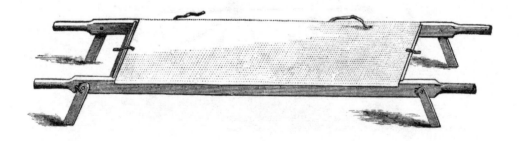

Examples (top to bottom) of the Satterlee and Halstead litters, used by the Union army, as well as a Confederate stretcher. (*Surgical History,* Vol. 2, Part 3, pp. 923–25)

This drawing of an Autenrieth medicine wagon shows the various shelves, trays, and drawers in this specially designed vehicle for transporting medicine. (*Surgical History,* Vol. 2, Part 3, p. 918)

A Finley ambulance, one of the two-wheeled type, was so uncomfortable for wounded soldiers that they called such vehicles "avalanches." (*Surgical History*, Vol. 2, Part 3, p. 946)

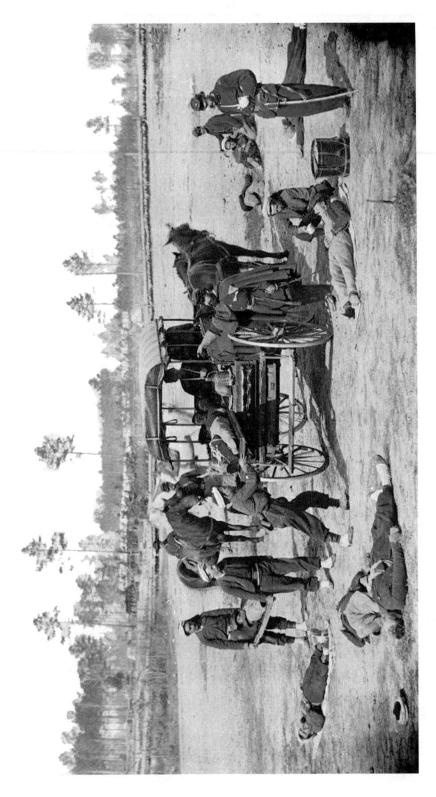

Zouave troops were so named because of their distinctive French-style uniforms. The ambulance corps of an unidentified Zouave regiment posed for a photographer during a drill, bringing "wounded" to, and loading them into, a four-wheeled ambulance. (Library of Congress-DIG-cwpb-03950)

Many wounded soldiers were shipped to hospitals behind the lines on the floors of boxcars or in other impro-vised railcar arrangements. However, in some areas medical officers developed special hospital or ambulance railroad cars to transport the sick and wounded. This drawing shows the interior of one design. (*Surgical History*, Vol. 2, Part 3, p. 958)

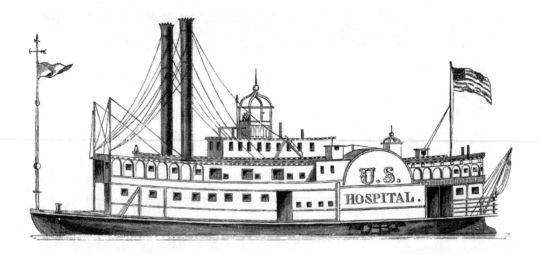

The *D.A. January* was one of a number of boats remodeled as hospital transports. These drawings show how each of the four decks was arranged for patient care. The ship made a total of 81 trips, carrying 23,738 sick and wounded soldiers on the western rivers between April 11, 1862, and September 4, 1865. (*Surgical History,* Vol. 2, Part 3, pp. 977–79)

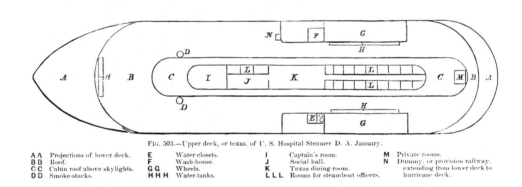

FIG. 503.—Upper deck, or texas, of U. S. Hospital Steamer D. A. January.

A A	Projections of lower deck.	E	Water-closets.	I	Captain's room.	M	Private rooms.
B B	Roof.	F	Wash-house.	J	Social hall.	N	Dummy, or provision railway,
C C	Cabin roof above skylights.	G G	Wheels.	K	Texas dining-room.		extending from lower deck to
D D	Smoke-stacks.	H H H	Water-tanks.	L L L	Rooms for steamboat officers.		hurricane deck.

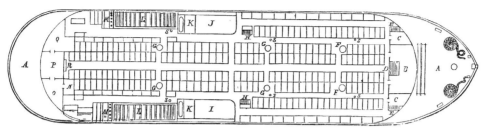

FIG. 504.—Cabin deck of U. S. Hospital Steamer D. A. January.

A A	Projections of lower deck.	**F F**	Steamboat chimneys.	**K K**	Bath-rooms, hot and cold.	**P** Surgery.
B	Office.	**G G**	Stoves.	**L L**	Steamboat's wheels.	**Q** Linen-room.
C C	Private rooms.	**H H**	Middle ward stairs.	**M M**	Water-closets.	**R** Space occupied by the mirror.
D	Front stairs.	**I**	Nurses' dining-room.	**N**	Private room.	**S S** Cold-water pipes.
E E	Texas stairs.	**J**	Kitchen.	**O**	Drug-store.	

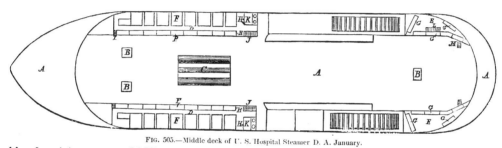

FIG. 505.—Middle deck of U. S. Hospital Steamer D. A. January.

A A	Lower deck.	**D D E E**	Middle deck.	**I** Side or middle deck.	**K K**	Water-closets.
B B B	Hatchways.	**F F**	Space for sick.	**J** { Stairs to lower deck.	**L**	Nurses' stairs from cabin deck.
C .	Boilers.	**G G**	Nurses' quarters.	**J** { Stairs to upper deck.	**M M**	Nurses' stairs to lower deck.
		H H	Cold water.			

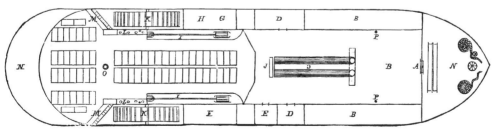

FIG. 506.—Lower Boiler Deck of the U. S. Hospital Steamer D. A. January.

A	Foot of stairs.	**E**	Pastry room.	**I**	Engines.	**M M** Water-closets.
B B	Space for wood and coal.	**F**	Kitchen.	**J**	Donkey engine.	**N N** Main deck.
C	Boilers.	**G**	Carpenter's shop.	**K K**	Wheels.	**O** Stoves.
D	Stores.	**H**	Blacksmith's shop.	**L**	Washstands	**P P** Cold water.

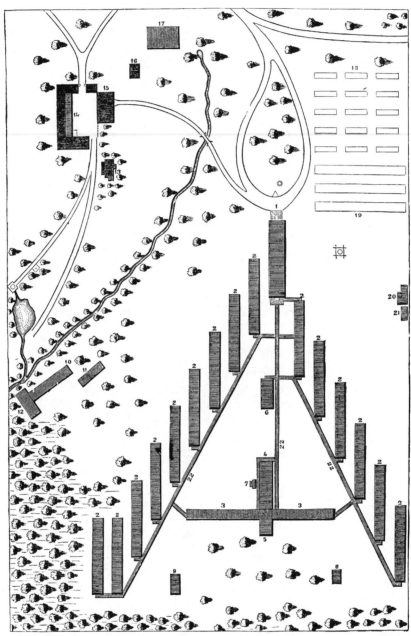

HAREWOOD HOSPITAL, WASHINGTON, D. C.

Scale $\frac{1}{21600}$: 1, Administration building ; 2, 2, 2, Wards ; 3, Dining-room ; 4, 5, Kitchen ; 6, Knapsack-room ; 7, Ice-house ; 8, Dead-house ; 9, Guard-house; 10, Laundry ; 11, Laundresses' quarters; 12, Engine-room; 13, Quarters for female nurses; 14, Brick building used as bakery and commissary store-house ; 15, Brick stable; the loft used as store-house ; 16, Store-house ; 17, Barn ; 18, Hospital tents ; 19, Old barracks ; 20, Sutler; 21, Coal ; 22, Covered pathway. Sinks in movable boxes placed on the flanks of the triangle.

Map of the layout of the Harewood Hospital in Washington, DC. A pavilion hospital, Harewood was located on the farm of W.W. Corcoran on the 7th Street Road near the Soldier's Home. (*Medical History*, Vol. 1, Part 3, p. 941)

April 1864 exterior view of the Harewood Hospital near Washington, DC, showing a row of pavilion wards. The cap tol dome can be seen in the distance on the right. (Library of Congress-DIG-cwpb-04248)

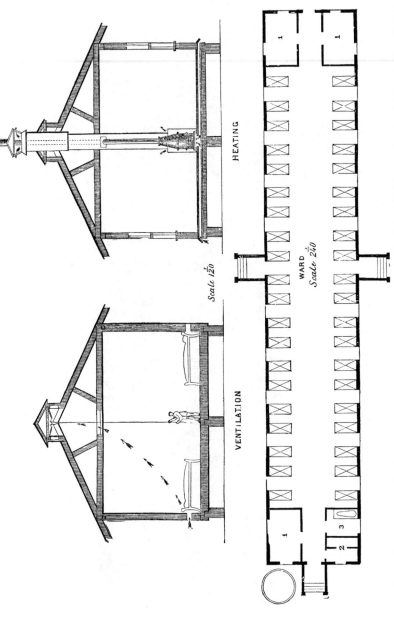

VENTILATION   HEATING

Scale $\frac{1}{120}$

WARD
Scale $\frac{1}{240}$

SEDGWICK HOSPITAL, GREENVILLE, LA.—Plans of ward, ventilation and heating: 1, 1, 1, Nurses' rooms; 2, Water-closets; and 3, Bath-rooms, at the free end of the ward. The double-lined circle indicates the position of the rain-water tank.

Plans for a pavilion ward at the Sedgwick Hospital (Union) in Greenville, Louisiana, are representative of pavilion designs in most places. The lower illustration shows the layout for a forty-bed ward. The two upper drawings depict methods for ventilating and heating the wards. (*Medical History*, Vol. 1, Part 3, p. 948)

GUNSHOT WOUNDS, TREATMENT OF

Although the vast majority of wounds during the Civil War were caused by bullets (mostly minié balls), wounds resulting from artillery, sabers, and bayonets, as well as accidental injuries, were treated in the same ways.

When a wounded soldier walked or was carried to a first aid station or field hospital, the doctor would examine him to determine the nature of his wound. A soldier with anything beyond a minor flesh wound would probably be sent from the first aid station to the field hospital for further treatment. If there was no exit wound, the doctor at the hospital would probe for the bullet, first with his little finger and then with a nelaton (ceramic-tipped) probe, if the bullet was more than finger deep. If possible, the bullet would be removed. Sometimes, however, due to the bullet's location, removal was not possible. Occasionally a bullet worked itself out of the body after many months or years, or the soldier retained the bullet for the rest of his life.

Whether the bullet was still in or already out of the body, the wound needed to be cleaned. After removing scraps of clothing, dirt, grass, bone fragments, and any other foreign matter, the doctor would clean the wound with bromine or some other antiseptic, if it were available. A wound might be sewed closed with silk or horsehair that had been boiled to make it flexible. Cerate, an ointment made with beeswax, was often applied to the wound, which might be left open or packed with lint and bandaged. Many doctors espoused using cold water on dressings to keep the wound from forming a painful crust or scab (which is now known to be a part of healing). The majority of wounds became infected, but often not seriously.

In some hospitals where cleanliness was a problem, flies laid eggs in the patient's wounds, and the eggs hatched into maggots. Nasty as they were, the maggots ate unhealthy tissue and the wounds actually healed faster than in other hospitals where maggots were removed from the wounds.

Many wounds were not straightforward but involved seriously mangled tissue and nerves, as well as shattered bones. When these were wounds of the extremities—arms, legs, hands, and feet—amputation was sometimes the best way to preserve the soldier's life. Especially later in the war, surgeons performed some excisions and resections. These operations removed the injured section of bone, leaving a shortened, but sometimes at least partially functional limb. The affected limb would be immobilized with a splint after the operation until the wound healed.

The most complicated wounds were those of the head, chest, and abdomen. Before the Civil War physicians rarely tried to operate in any of these areas because the death rate from infection was so high. However, during the war several skilled doctors tried innovative experiments to save lives. Confederate surgeon Hunter Holmes McGuire used the tine of a fork to raise a depressed skull fracture. Assistant Surgeon Benjamin Howard (U.S.) developed a way to "hermetically seal" chest wounds that would otherwise result in a collapsed lung. After closing the wound, he covered it with dry lint and a few drops of collodion, a chemical that dries as a seal. This procedure solved the immediate problem of shortness of breath, but Howard had trouble finding out what eventually happened to the patients after they were transferred to other hospitals. Evidently, when the patients got an infection, only those whose wounds unsealed survived.

For all wounded patients, doctors prescribed opiates for the pain. Most patients took the medicine orally but some had morphine dusted directly into the wound. Doctors also ordered the most nourishing diet the patient could eat and the resources of the hospital would allow in order to help the soldier regain his strength.

See also: Amputation; Antiseptics and Disinfectants; Bandages; Diet, of Hospital Patients; Gunshot Wounds; Hospitals, Field; Infections, of Wounds; Maggots; McGuire, Hunter Holmes; Medication, Administration of; Minié Balls; Morphine; Mortality, of Soldiers; Opiate Use and Addiction; Resection; Splints.

Bibliography

Bollet, Alfred Jay. *Civil War Medicine: Challenges and Triumphs.* Tucson, AZ: Galen, 2002.

Kuz, Julian E., and Bradley P. Bengtson. *Orthopaedic Injuries of the Civil War: An Atlas of Orthopaedic Injuries and Treatments During the Civil War.* Kennesaw, GA: Kennesaw Mountain, 1996.

Wegner, Ansley Herring. *Phantom Pain: North Carolina's Artificial Limbs Program for Confederate Veterans.* Raleigh: Office of Archives and History, North Carolina Department of Cultural Resources, 2004.

HAMMOND, WILLIAM ALEXANDER (1828–1900)

William Alexander Hammond, reform-minded surgeon general for the Union army during part of the Civil War, was born in Annapolis, Maryland, on August 28, 1828. He was the second son of Dr. John Wesley Hammond (a physician who did not practice much) and his wife, Sarah Pinckney Hammond. William grew up in Harrisburg, Pennsylvania, and was educated, with an excellent background in classics, by private tutors. In 1844 he began privately studying medicine in New York City with William Holme Van Buren. He then attended the Medical Department of the University of the City of New York (1847–1848), from which he graduated in March 1848, despite the fact that graduates were supposed to be at least twenty-one years old.

Hammond became a resident medical student at the Pennsylvania Hospital in Philadelphia and applied for a post as assistant surgeon in the U.S. Army. He received his commission on July 3, 1849, and the following day he married Helen Nisbet, the daughter of a Philadelphia attorney. The couple eventually had five children, two of whom died in infancy. On July 8, the Hammonds left on the three-month journey to William's first post, Santa Fe, New Mexico Territory. Hammond spent eleven years as an army assistant surgeon, mostly in the New Mexico and Kansas territories. In addition to caring for the medical needs of the soldiers at his posts, he participated in some natural history surveys and did research on scurvy, urine, and other topics in physiological chemistry. After suffering several bouts of illness, Hammond, who desired to spend more time doing research, resigned from the army in 1860 and took a job as professor of anatomy and physiology at the University of Maryland Medical School.

However, the Civil War broke out in April 1861. On April 19 Hammond helped to treat soldiers of the Sixth Massachusetts Infantry who were wounded by a mob as they came through Baltimore. He then resigned his professorship and reenlisted as an assistant surgeon, although, despite his previous service, he lost his former rank. He was ordered to organize military hospitals in Pennsylvania and Maryland and then sent to inspect other hospitals. The surgeon general, Colonel Clement A. Finley, was in his sixties and had little understanding about how to organize and manage the huge enterprise that the medical bureau had suddenly become.

The U.S. Sanitary Commission urged numerous medical reforms, including the appointment of a new surgeon general. The commission favored Hammond for surgeon general because he had eleven years of military medical experience; he was known in the civilian medical world because of his research and teaching; he was the American expert on hospital design; he was self-confident and enthusiastic, with an impressive physical presence and military bearing; and he was an energetic thirty-three years old, unlike his predecessors. President Abraham Lincoln appointed him despite the opposition of Secretary of War Edwin M. Stanton, and Stanton became Hammond's greatest enemy.

Appointed to his post on April 25, 1862, Hammond promptly set out to increase the efficiency of the medical department. He employed several men who managed the day-to-day business of the surgeon general's office, such as paying bills and answering questions about wounded soldiers. He developed more stringent requirements for physicians joining the volunteer service and established examination boards to determine the qualifications of candidates. To improve hospital care, he began a hospital inspection system and carefully supervised hospital construction. Hammond improved the methods of recording medical statistics, began an ambulance corps to remove the wounded from the field, appointed a board to standardize the medication table, improved ways to get supplies, established laboratories to manufacture medicines, started the Army Medical Museum, and began to collect information for what eventually became *The Medical and Surgical History of the War of the Rebellion*. Because there was no book available on the subject of hygiene, Hammond wrote one himself, *Treatise on Hygiene with Special Reference to the Military Service* (1863).

Members of the Sanitary Commission and other reformers lauded Hammond's efforts, but he also gained many enemies. Army doctors who resisted change, such as removing calomel from the supply table, or who ranked higher than Hammond and resented being passed over when he was chosen, disliked him. Some found him demanding and pompous. His strong personality clashed with Stanton's from the beginning. In July 1863 Stanton appointed a special committee to investigate the medical department. Strongly biased against Hammond, the committee was headed by one of his enemies, former Kansas governor Andrew H. Reeder. In August Stanton ordered Hammond to undertake an inspection tour of western hospital posts, replacing him with Stanton's own personal physician and friend, Joseph K. Barnes, as acting surgeon general. Stanton refused to order Hammond back to Washington. Hammond unwisely requested a court-martial to justify himself. The trial, which began January 19, 1864, and lasted until August, was rigged against Hammond and involved essentially trumped-up charges pertaining to the purchase of blankets, as well as that catch-all accusation, "conduct unbecoming" an officer. Hammond was found guilty and dismissed from the service on August 18. His conviction was finally overturned in August 1879.

Hurt, disillusioned, and financially strapped, Hammond moved to New York City, where friends helped him to recover financially. His medical reputation had not suffered, and he soon became the leading neurologist (a new specialty) in America. He wrote medical books and articles as well as a number of novels. In 1887 he retired from his practice and moved to Washington, DC, where he established a hospital for patients with nervous system diseases. Hammond died of a heart attack in Washington on January 5, 1900, and was buried in Arlington Cemetery.

See also: Ambulance Corps; Army Medical Museum; Barnes, Joseph K.; Calomel; Examining Boards, Medical; Finley, Clement Alexander; Hospital Buildings; Inspectors, Medical; *The Medical and Surgical History of the War of the Rebellion;* Medical Department, Organization of; Surgeon General; United States Sanitary Commission.

Bibliography

Blustein, Bonnie Ellen. *Preserve Your Love for Science: Life of William A. Hammond, American Neurologist.* Cambridge: Cambridge University Press, 1991.

Freemon, Frank R. "Lincoln Finds a Surgeon General: William A. Hammond and the Transformation of the Union Army Medical Bureau." *Civil War History* 33 (March 1987): 5–21.

HARDTACK

Hardtack, also known as hard bread, army crackers, crackers, or biscuits, was a staple of the Union army diet. Made of flour and water, the crackers measured about three inches square (or slightly longer and narrower) and one-half inch thick. They were shipped to the troops in wooden crates (cracker boxes) containing fifty pounds of hardtack and usually issued in quantities of nine or ten crackers for a day's bread ration. The Confederates did not manufacture hardtack, but they certainly ate it when captured from the Yankees, either in supply trains or from the haversacks of deceased soldiers.

Soldiers complained that hardtack suffered from three unwholesome conditions. Some hardtack was too hard to bite, probably because it was stale, and had to be broken by force. Even when soaked, it became rubbery rather than soft. Other hardtack was moldy or wet when distributed. Observers blamed manufacturers who boxed the bread too soon after baking or commissary agents and quartermasters who stored the hardtack improperly, unprotected from the weather. Wet, moldy hardtack could be exchanged for better quality crackers at the next ration distribution. A third problem often found in hardtack was insect infestation, usually weevils, less commonly maggots. Soldiers nicknamed hardtack "worm castles" and joked that the insects supplemented the daily meat ration. Weevils, which were about one-eighth inch long and had no taste, might be driven out by heating the hardtack or drowned by crumbling it in coffee. Many soldiers preferred to eat their "worm castles" at night when they could not see the creatures. Soldiers blamed inspectors who failed to do their jobs as well as cheating supply contractors for the poor quality of the rations.

Troops came up with a number of creative, if not necessarily nutritious, methods to prepare hardtack. Certainly the most common ways to consume it were to eat it plain (often a necessity on the battlefield or on the march) or to crumble it in coffee. A dish called skillygalee consisted of hardtack soaked in cold water and then fried brown in pork fat. Hardtack might be toasted on a split stick and spread with butter purchased from a sutler (a licensed civilian vendor). If a soldier were wealthy enough to buy condensed milk at seventy-five cents per can, he could have milk-toast. Hardtack accidentally dropped in the fire and charred was considered a good remedy for diarrhea. Crumbled hardtack also served as an ingredient in soups and stews.

While hardtack kept the troops from starving, diets relying on hardtack could contribute to digestive and nutritional problems among the soldiers. A type of hardtack, called ship biscuit, is still used by the U.S. Navy and the Peace Corps.

See also: Cooks; Diarrhea and Dysentery; Diet, of Troops; Maggots; Malnutrition; Quartermasters; Subsistence Department.

Bibliography

Billings, John D. *Hardtack and Coffee: The Unwritten Story of Army Life.* Boston: George M. Smith, 1887; reprint, Lincoln: University of Nebraska Press, 1993.

Robertson, James I., Jr. *Soldiers Blue and Gray.* Columbia: University of South Carolina Press, 1988.

Wiley, Bell Irvin. *The Life of Johnny Reb: The Common Soldier of the Confederacy.* Garden City, NY: Doubleday, 1943, 1971.

HAWKS, ESTHER HILL (1833–1906)

One of a small number of women who practiced medicine at the time of the Civil War, Esther Hill Hawks belonged to an even tinier number of female physicians who treated soldiers during the conflict. Esther Jane Hill was born on August 4, 1833, in Hooksett, New Hampshire, the fifth of Parmenas and Jane Kimball Hill's eight children. She attended public schools, high school, and an academy, after which she taught school in several New Hampshire towns.

Esther met Dr. John Milton Hawks (ca. 1826–1910), about seven years her senior, in 1850. After an intermittent courtship, much of which Milton spent in the South, the couple were married in New Hampshire on October 5, 1854. On a lengthy wedding trip to Florida, Esther began to read her husband's medical books. After the couple returned to Manchester, New Hampshire, Esther continued to study his books as well as clerk in his drugstore and visit his patients. In the fall of 1855 she entered the New England Female Medical College. After attending two sessions, she graduated in 1857 and returned to Manchester to establish a practice.

Milton Hawks was a zealous abolitionist and reformer. Esther Hawks shared his interest to some degree. However, the couple had a number of personality differences that at times caused considerable tension between them.

When the Civil War began, Esther went to Washington, DC, to volunteer but was rejected as a nurse by Dorothea Dix. Nevertheless, Esther remained in Washington volunteering under other auspices until October, when she returned to Manchester. Milton then left for Washington in an unsuccessful search for a job while Esther continued her medical practice and supervised the bottling of a patent medicine elixir that Milton had invented and sold. She also gathered supplies for sick and wounded soldiers. In April 1862 Milton went to the South Carolina Sea Islands as a plantation superintendent for the National Freedman's Relief Association. There he cared for, supervised, and taught the blacks who had come under Union control when their masters fled the islands, leaving their slaves behind.

After General Rufus Saxton became the commander of the so-called "Port Royal experiment" (the plantations of freedmen on the Sea Islands) in June 1862, Milton was appointed physician at the hospital for blacks in Beaufort, South Carolina. He became a U.S. Army acting assistant (contract) surgeon in the fall of 1862 and was the physician to the First South Carolina Infantry, the first regiment of blacks to be mustered into the U.S. Army.

In October 1862 Esther went to the Sea Islands as a teacher for the Freedman's Aid Society. Besides teaching blacks, both soldiers and civilians, she also practiced medicine, assisting her husband in surgery and treating wounded black soldiers, as well as needy civilian blacks. She helped care for the men of the Fifty-fourth Massachusetts Infantry who were wounded in the attack on Fort Wagner near Charleston, South Carolina, as well as the wounded from the Battle of Olustee (or Ocean Pond), Florida. Near the end of the war she helped to found an orphanage for black children in Charleston, South Carolina. She recorded her experiences in a diary. Three volumes of it (October 1862–November 1866) were discovered in a trash bin in 1975 and published as *A Woman Doctor's Civil War* in 1984.

After the war Esther and Milton went to Florida, where he set up a land and lumber company to be run by freedmen, a business that failed. Esther taught blacks and also practiced medicine. While her husband continued land speculation, charitable activities, and Republican politics in Florida, Esther returned to New England, where she set up a medical practice in Lynn, Massachusetts, mostly treating gynecological cases. She was also involved in various charitable and educational causes and was a woman's suffrage activist. Esther spent many winters in Florida, and Milton lived with her in Massachusetts at times.

After an illness of about three months, Esther Hill Hawks died on May 6, 1906, in Lynn, Massachusetts.

See also: Dix, Dorothea Lynde; Education, Medical; Surgeons, Acting Assistant (Contract); Women, as Doctors.

Bibliography

Schwartz, Gerald, ed. *A Woman Doctor's Civil War: Esther Hill Hawks' Diary*. Columbia: University of South Carolina Press, 1984, 1989.

HEART DISEASE

During the Civil War, as in other eras, some people suffered from congenital or early onset heart defects, including heart murmurs, valve malfunctions, enlargement, and other problems, that caused a recruit to be rejected and a soldier to be discharged, if detected.

In the days before electrocardiograms and other modern imaging tests, Civil War doctors relied on the methods of percussion and auscultation. These involved tapping the area of the chest and listening to the resulting sound, such as dullness or shifting fluid, with the ear or with a stethoscope. Although some writers on Civil War medicine have claimed that Civil War surgeons rarely used the stethoscope, recent research demonstrates that some physicians were quite skilled in its use.

During the Civil War soldiers suffered from two main types of heart problems: rheumatic fever and "soldier's heart." Rheumatic fever, frequently called acute rheumatism during the period, was especially prevalent during the winter. Now known to be a streptococcal infection, rheumatic fever begins with a sore throat and progresses to extremely painful swollen joints. More seriously, rheumatic fever can involve inflammation of the sac around the heart and the heart valves, leading to abnormal heart function or even heart failure and death. The illness usually lasted one to two months. Patients were treated with opiates, quinine, baths, and compresses to reduce the pain and inflammation. Many soldiers who survived had to be discharged because of resulting heart problems.

"Soldier's heart" or "irritable heart" was first studied and described during the Civil War by Dr. Jacob Da Costa, a physician who worked with a ward of cardiac patients at Turner's Lane Hospital in Philadelphia. The symptoms of irritable heart included palpitations, rapid heartbeat, and lightheadedness. Evidently the syndrome was related to severe mental or emotional stress. The patients recovered best when given an extended opportunity to rest.

The most notable person who apparently had heart disease during the Civil War was Confederate general Robert E. Lee. However, historians have engaged in considerable controversy about what type of heart disease he had. Some have suggested that he had coronary artery disease, others that he had pericarditis (inflammation of the sac around the heart) since that was what his physicians diagnosed. Yet others suggest angina pectoris, arteriosclerosis (thickening of the artery walls), or rheumatic fever with resulting heart disease. Whatever Lee had seems to have begun with an illness in March and April 1863, from which he never fully recovered and which cannot now be conclusively diagnosed.

See also: Mortality, of Soldiers; Rheumatism; Turner's Lane Hospital.

Bibliography

Bollet, Alfred Jay. *Civil War Medicine: Challenges and Triumphs.* Tucson, AZ: Galen, 2002.

Thomas, Emory M. *Robert E. Lee: A Biography.* New York: Norton, 1995.

Welsh, Jack D. *Medical Histories of Confederate Generals.* Kent, OH: Kent State University Press, 1995.

HERMETIC SEALING OF WOUNDS *See* Gunshot Wounds, Treatment of.

HISTORIOGRAPHY, MEDICAL

A huge number of books have been written and published about the American Civil War, especially its military history and prominent figures. A very small fraction of those books relate specifically to Civil War medicine. This article is not a complete bibliography but examines representative works, arranged chronologically from the Civil War itself to the twenty-first century. Some lengthy titles have been shortened.

During the Civil War both the Union and the Confederate medical departments sponsored and encouraged the publication of material that would help doctors and other medical workers become more knowledgeable about the best care and most successful treatments available for their soldier patients. Union volumes included *The Hospital Steward's Manual: For the Instruction of Hospital Stewards, Ward-Masters, and Attendants, in Their Several Duties* (1862) and *Outlines of the Chief Camp Diseases of the United States Armies, As Observed During the Present War* (1863), both by Joseph Janvier Woodward; and Charles R. Greenleaf's *A Manual for the Medical Officers of the United States Army* (1864). S. Weir Mitchell, George R. Morehouse, and William W. Keen discussed their discoveries in *Gunshot Wounds and Other Injuries of Nerves* (1864), while the U.S. Sanitary Commission issued a number of reports on various topics. Something quite different, for the general reader, was Louisa May Alcott's *Hospital Sketches* (1863), an account of her own experiences as a Union nurse, thinly fictionalized as those of Nurse Tribulation Periwinkle.

In the South, John Julian Chisolm published *A Manual of Military Surgery* (1861) early in the war. Francis Peyre Porcher's *Resources of the Southern Fields and Forests, Medical, Economical and Agricultural* (1863) proposed indigenous substitutes for medications that were scarce in the South due to the Union blockade. The *Confederate States Medical and Surgical Journal,* published in Richmond, Virginia, monthly from January 1864 through February 1865, attempted to get helpful medical information to military physicians throughout the Confederacy.

The immediate postwar period featured the publication of important wartime memoirs by medical personnel, especially women. Kate Cumming's *A Journal of Hospital Life in the Confederate Army of Tennessee from the Battle of Shiloh to the End of the War* (1866) is more commonly known by its title as a reprint, *Kate: The Journal of a Confederate Nurse* (1959). Both Cumming and Mrs. S.E.D. [Susan] Smith, who published *The Soldier's Friend: Being a Thrilling Narrative of Grandma Smith's Four Years Experience . . .* (1867) the following year, worked as matrons in the general hospitals of the Confederate Army of Tennessee. Union memoirs included Mrs. A.H. [Jane] Hoge's *The Boys in Blue: or, Heroes of the "Rank and File"* (1867), about her experiences with soldiers as a U.S. Sanitary Commission representative, and Jane Stuart Woolsey's *Hospital Days* (1868), which detailed her experiences as a nurse and supervisor at several places in the East. L.P. Brockett and Mary C. Vaughan memorialized a number of Union women in *Women's Work in the Civil War: A Record of Heroism, Patriotism, and Patience* (1867). Some surgeons also reminisced—for example, medical director Jonathan Letterman in *Medical Recollections of the Army of the Potomac* (1866).

The 1870s and 1880s were notable for the publication of the multivolume, tremendously detailed *The Medical and Surgical History of the War of the Rebellion* (1870–1888), nominally under the editorship of Surgeon General Joseph K. Barnes. These volumes, which collected surgeons' reports, patient case studies of all types of diseases and injuries, illustrations, and statistics, remain an important source for mostly Union medical information. Further nurse or matron accounts were published, including those by Confederates Phoebe Pember, *A Southern Woman's Story: Life in Confederate Richmond* (1879), and Fannie Beers, *Memories: A Recollection of Personal Experiences During Four Years of War* (1888). Union Sanitary Commission worker Mary A. Livermore published *My Story of the War* (1887). Poet Walt Whitman published *Memoranda During the War* (1875), which related his work as a visitor in Washington, DC, hospitals.

Between 1890 and 1920 the Civil War soldiers and medical workers aged and many of them died. The veterans' organizations—the Grand Army of the Republic (Union) and the United Confederate Veterans—peaked and began to decline. Former Confederate surgeons founded the Association of Medical Officers of the Army and Navy of the Confederacy and, to preserve their medical recollections, published a number of reminiscences in the monthly journal *Southern Practitioner* (1900–1917). These articles sometimes included reflections on what the surgeons could or could not do during the war because of what they did or did not know, specifically the fact that they did not know about germs. During this time also the periodical *Confederate Veteran* published articles and obituaries, including those of medical officers and female matrons.

Some medical officers published their own reminiscences, as did Ferdinand Eugene Daniel, *Recollections of a Rebel Surgeon* (1899). Other memoirs, written but not published during the writer's lifetime, were edited and published by heirs or friends, as was the case with both Charles Todd Quintard's *Doctor Quintard, Chaplain C.S.A. and Second Bishop of Tennessee* (1905) and John H. Brinton's *Personal Memoirs of John H. Brinton, Civil War Surgeon* [USA] (1914).

Mary Gardner Holland published a collection of short reminiscences by Union women who had served, *Our Army Nurses: Stories from Women in the Civil War* (1895). As part of the centenary celebration of Abraham Lincoln's birth in 1909, friends finally persuaded Charles A. Leale to discuss his experiences caring for the dying president; Leale's speech was privately published as *Lincoln's Last Hours: Address Delivered Before the Commandery of the State of New York Military Order of the Loyal Legion of the United States*. Evidently Louis C. Duncan was one of the first to write an extended history of Civil War medicine; he privately printed *The Medical Department of the United States Army in the Civil War* in 1914.

Although not a lot of work was published on Civil War medicine between 1920 and 1950, one significant article must be mentioned. George Worthington Adams's article "Confederate Medicine," *Journal of Southern History* 7 (May 1940): 151–166, opened with the statement that "the Civil War was fought in the very last years of the medical middle ages." Since that time, this opinion has seriously influenced the attitudes of much Civil War writing, in both scholarly and popular books and articles as well as in documentary and other presentations.

Three path-breaking and still very important books on Civil War medicine were published in the 1950s. George W. Adams's *Doctors in Blue: The Medical History of the Union Army in the Civil War* (1952) is still a standard in the field, as is H.H. Cunningham's study of the other side, *Doctors in Gray: The Confederate Medical Service* (1958). The third work is William Quentin Maxwell's *Lincoln's Fifth Wheel: The Political History of the United States Sanitary Commission* (1956). In addition, the quarterly journal *Civil War History*, which began publication in 1954, has printed several scholarly articles and numerous book reviews on medical topics.

The 1961–1965 Civil War centennial brought a flood of publications, a few of which pertained to Civil War medicine. These included *Medicines for the Union Army: The United States Army Laboratories During the Civil War* (1962) by George Winston Smith; *Physician-Generals in the Civil War* (1966) and *Disease in the Civil War: Natural Biological Warfare in 1861–1865* (1968), both by Paul E. Steiner; and *Field Medical Services at the Battles of Manassas (Bull Run)* (1968) by H.H. Cunningham. *Civil War Times Illustrated* (later *Civil War Times*), which started publishing popularly oriented Civil War articles in 1961, has included a number related to medicine. In the 1970s James O. Breeden published a good study of a Confederate medical researcher, *Joseph Jones, M.D.: Scientist of the Old South* (1975).

Since the 1980s, articles and books related to Civil War medicine have been published in greater numbers. These studies have been facilitated by reprints of Civil War–era works. From 1989 to 1992 Norman Publishing in San Francisco issued several dozen titles of Civil War medical manuals with introductions by Ira M. Rutkow. The Broadfoot company in Wilmington, North Carolina, reprinted *The Medical and Surgical History,* with a helpful index, in 1990. Other primary sources, such as letters and diaries of medical personnel, have also been discovered, edited, and published. These include Jean V. Berlin, ed., *A Confederate Nurse: The Diary of Ada W. Bacot, 1860–1863* (1994); Peter Josyph, ed., *The Wounded River: The Civil War Letters of John Vance Lauderdale, M.D.* [USA] (1993); James M. Greiner, Janet L. Coryell, and James R. Smither, eds., *A Surgeon's Civil War: The Letters and Diary of Daniel M. Holt, M.D.* [USA] (1994); John Herbert Roper, ed., *Repairing the*

"March of Mars": The Civil War Diaries of John Samuel Apperson, Hospital Steward in the Stonewall Brigade, 1861–1865 (2001); Gerald Schwartz, ed., *A Woman Doctor's Civil War: Esther Hill Hawks' Diary* [USA] (1984); and Donald B. Koonce, ed., *Doctor to the Front: The Recollections of Confederate Surgeon Thomas Fanning Wood, 1861–1865* (2000).

A few recent publications have provided some type of synthesis. The most thorough and useful for research is Alfred Jay Bollet's *Civil War Medicine: Challenges and Triumphs* (2002). Frank R. Freemon's *Gangrene and Glory: Medical Care during the Civil War* (1998) is shorter with more illustrations. Despite its title, Ira M. Rutkow's *Bleeding Blue and Gray: Civil War Surgery and the Evolution of American Medicine* (2005) examines the Union army in the East.

Not surprisingly, authors have written biographies of medical personnel. There have been two studies of Clara Barton. Elizabeth Brown Pryor's *Clara Barton, Professional Angel* (1987) studied Barton's entire life, while Stephen B. Oates's *A Woman of Valor: Clara Barton and the Civil War* (1994) focused on the war years. There are also two recent studies of the controversial Union doctor Mary Edwards Walker: *A Woman of Honor: Dr. Mary E. Walker and the Civil War* (2001) by Mercedes Graf and, for general audiences, Dale E. Walker's *Mary Edwards Walker: Above and Beyond* (2005). Walt Whitman has been the subject of several books, including *The Better Angel: Walt Whitman in the Civil War* (2000) by Roy Morris Jr. Bonnie Ellen Blustein studied a Union surgeon general in *Preserve Your Love of Science: Life of William A. Hammond, American Neurologist* (1991).

Historians have also studied a variety of special topics. Glenna R. Schroeder-Lein looked at the entire general hospital system for the Confederate Army of Tennessee in *Confederate Hospitals on the Move: Samuel H. Stout and the Army of Tennessee* (1994), while in *Two Confederate Hospitals and Their Patients, Atlanta to Opelika* (2005), Jack D. Welsh examined two of those hospitals in greater detail. Rebecca Barbour Calcutt discussed *Richmond's Wartime Hospitals* (2005) and Carol C. Green studied one of those facilities in *Chimborazo: The Confederacy's Largest Hospital* (2004). At least two books evaluated the hospitals after the Battle of Gettysburg: Gregory A. Coco, *A Vast Sea of Misery: A History and Guide to the Union and Confederate Field Hospitals at Gettysburg, July 1–November 20, 1863* (1988) and Roland R. Maust, *Grappling with Death: The Union Second Corps Hospital at Gettysburg* (2001).

In addition to biographies and diaries, a number of studies deal with the various medical roles of women during the war. Jeanie Attie analyzed the activities of women with the U.S. Sanitary Commission in *Patriotic Toil: Northern Women and the American Civil War* (1998); Jane E. Schultz discussed issues of race, class, and gender in *Women at the Front: Hospital Workers in Civil War America* (2004); and Sister Mary Denis Maher focused on the role of nuns in *To Bind Up the Wounds: Catholic Sister Nurses in the U.S. Civil War* (1989).

Thomas P. Lowry dealt with venereal disease and other sexual issues in *The Story the Soldiers Wouldn't Tell: Sex in the Civil War* (1994), while Lowry and Jack

D. Welsh presented the cases of Union doctors accused of negligence and other detrimental conduct in *Tarnished Scalpels: The Court-Martials of Fifty Union Surgeons* (2000). Welsh also studied the medical rather than the military backgrounds of the Union and Confederate generals in *Medical Histories of Confederate Generals* (1995) and *Medical Histories of Union Generals* (1996).

Julian E. Kuz and Bradley P. Bengtson provided illustrated examples in *Orthopaedic Injuries of the Civil War: An Atlas of Orthopaedic Injuries and Treatments During the Civil War* (1996). William C. Davis analyzed the diet of Civil War soldiers in *A Taste for War: The Culinary History of the Blue and Gray* (2003). In *Civil War Pharmacy: A History of Drugs, Drug Supply and Provision, and Therapeutics for the Union and Confederacy* (2004), Michael A. Flannery tackled the subject of medicines.

A number of historians have examined specific prisoner of war camps or the system generally, all of which studies have a medical component: *Elmira: Death Camp of the North* (2002) by Michael Horigan; *While in the Hands of the Enemy: Military Prisons of the Civil War* (2005) by Charles W. Sanders Jr.; *Rebels at Rock Island: The Story of a Civil War Prison* (2000) by Benton McAdams; *Life and Death in Civil War Prisons: A Story of Hardship, Horror and Extraordinary Courage* (2004) by J. Michael Martinez; and *Andersonville: The Last Depot* (1994) by William Marvel.

More information about books and articles pertaining to Civil War medicine can be found in the bibliography in this book as well as in Frank R. Freemon's *Microbes and Minié Balls: An Annotated Bibliography of Civil War Medicine* (1993), a rather idiosyncratic but useful guide to works published before the early 1990s.

See also: Alcott, Louisa May; Andersonville Prison; Association of Medical Officers of the Army and Navy of the Confederacy; Barton, Clara; Beers, Fannie A.; Chimborazo Hospital; Chisolm, John Julian; *Confederate States Medical and Surgical Journal;* Cumming, Kate; Diet, of Troops; Elmira Prison; Hammond, William Alexander; Hawks, Esther Hill; Hospitals, General; Jones, Joseph; Laboratories, Medical; Leale, Charles Augustus; Letterman, Jonathan; *The Medical and Surgical History of the War of the Rebellion;* Nuns; Nurses; Pember, Phoebe Yates Levy; Prisoners of War; *Resources of the Southern Fields and Forests; Southern Practitioner;* United States Sanitary Commission; Venereal Disease; Walker, Mary Edwards; Whitman, Walt; Women, as Hospital Workers; Woodward, Joseph Janvier.

HOGE, JANE CURRIE BLAIKIE (1811–1890)

Jane C. Hoge, one of the associate managers of the Northwestern Sanitary Commission in Chicago during the Civil War, was born in Philadelphia on July 31, 1811, the daughter of merchant George Dundas Blaikie and Mary Monroe Blaikie. She was a good student, particularly in music, and graduated from the Young Ladies

College in Philadelphia. On June 2, 1831, she married Abraham Holmes Hoge of Pittsburgh, a union that lasted until his death fifty-nine years later. The couple had thirteen children, of whom eight survived to adulthood.

While living in Pittsburgh, Jane Hoge joined the Presbyterian church and was an active member. She was also secretary of the orphan asylum. In September 1848 the Hoge family moved to Chicago. Here, in 1857, she became one of the founders and important supporters of the Home for the Friendless. She met Mary Livermore when both were on the board of directors for the home.

At the beginning of the Civil War two of Hoge's sons joined the Union army. Hoge soon found herself at Camp Douglas in Chicago, caring for sick soldiers in the regiment of her son, future brigadier general George Blaikie Hoge. Jane Hoge and Mary Livermore became involved with the Northwestern Sanitary Commission (the Chicago branch of the U.S. Sanitary Commission) when it was organized in the fall of 1861. At first the two women gathered supplies for the troops. However, in March 1862 the Chicago commission sent Hoge and Livermore to Mound City and Cairo, Illinois, to visit hospitals supplied by the commission, to be sure that the materials were being used properly. The women also visited hospitals in St. Louis to see what could be learned there. The resulting report helped lead to reform in other hospitals.

In November 1862 Hoge and Livermore attended a women's council in Washington, DC, to discuss the Sanitary Commission's work. When they returned to Chicago, they were appointed associate managers of the Northwestern Sanitary Commission, work that occupied them full time. Hoge and Livermore stimulated many women in the Northwest (today's Midwest) to gather supplies and participate in other commission activities. The two women encouraged involvement through extensive correspondence, distributing numerous circulars, and visiting aid association meetings all over the Northwest to discuss the soldiers' needs and how women could efficiently meet them. Two years of effort by Hoge and Livermore are said to have raised over 50,000 aid packages and $400,000.

In January 1863 Hoge attempted to visit Ulysses S. Grant's army across the river from Vicksburg, Mississippi, but she and her supplies were waylaid. She ended up nursing soldiers with measles and pneumonia during a campaign in Arkansas. The troops had no medical supplies besides those Hoge brought. A few weeks later she did visit Grant's troops at Young's Point. Discovering signs of scurvy, Hoge returned to Chicago, where she solicited many bushels of potatoes and onions to alleviate the problem. In June 1863 Hoge went to the Vicksburg area once more to nurse her son, who had been wounded.

Hoge and Livermore first proposed the idea of a "sanitary fair" to raise money so the Sanitary Commission could continue to provide supplies for sick and wounded soldiers. Although most of the men in the Northwestern Sanitary Commission scoffed at the idea and expected the fair to be a failure, the women of Chicago rallied and organized, collected exhibits, gathered donations for sale, recruited entertainment and food supplies, and publicized the event. The two-week

Chicago fair, held October 27–November 7, 1863, netted $100,000, four times the $25,000 that the organizers originally hoped to raise. Hoge and Livermore spread information about the sanitary fair to other Northern women who gathered at another women's council in Washington in January 1864. Hoge and Livermore also spearheaded a second fair in Chicago in 1865, but the war was already over before the fair took place.

After the war, Hoge continued to work with the Home for the Friendless. She published a book detailing her war experiences, *The Boys in Blue,* in 1867. From 1872 to 1885 she headed the Woman's Presbyterian Board of Foreign Missions of the Northwest. Jane Hoge died in Chicago on August 26, 1890, as a result of a broken hip and old age.

See also: Livermore, Mary Ashton Rice; Measles; Pneumonia; Sanitary Fairs; Scurvy; United States Sanitary Commission; Women's Hospital Auxiliaries and Relief Societies.

Bibliography

Attie, Jeanie. *Patriotic Toil: Northern Women and the America Civil War.* Ithaca, NY: Cornell University Press, 1998.

Brockett, L.P., and Mary C. Vaughan. *Women's Work in the Civil War: A Record of Heroism, Patriotism, and Patience.* Philadelphia: Zeigler, McCurdy, 1867.

Forsyth, Henry H., et al. *In Memorium* [Jane C. Hoge]. Chicago: Illinois Printing and Binding Co. [ca. 1890].

Hoge, Mrs. A.H. *The Boys in Blue; or Heroes of the "Rank and File."* New York: E.B. Treat, 1867; Chicago: C.W. Lilley, 1867.

Livermore, Mary A. *My Story of the War.* Hartford, CT, 1887; reprint, New York: Da Capo, 1995.

Temple, Wayne C. "Jane Currie Blaikie Hoge." In *Notable American Women, 1607–1950: A Biographical Dictionary,* ed. Edward T. James, et al. Cambridge, MA: Belknap Press of Harvard University Press, 1971.

HOOD, JOHN BELL (1831–1879)

John Bell Hood, the son of John W. and Theodosia French Hood, was born June 29, 1831, in Owingsville, Kentucky. He graduated from West Point, forty-fourth out of the fifty-two members of the class of 1853. Assigned to the infantry, Hood, a second lieutenant, was stationed first in northern California. In 1855 he transferred to the newly organized Second Cavalry, posted in Texas, and was promoted to first lieutenant in 1858.

Although his home state of Kentucky did not secede from the Union, Hood resigned from the U.S. Army in April 1861 and joined the Confederate army from his adopted state of Texas. Initially sent to train cavalry in Richmond, he became colonel of the Fourth Texas Infantry on October 1, 1861. In March 1862 he was promoted to brigadier general, commanding what came to be known as Hood's

Texas Brigade. In the Battle of Gaines's Mill on June 27, 1862, Hood led a charge that was crucial to the Confederate victory and the prolongation of the war. On August 30, the second afternoon of Second Manassas (Bull Run), he led another important attack. Finally, at Antietam, on September 17, Hood and his brigade performed vital service in holding the Confederate left. In each of these battles Hood's troops suffered massive losses. Hood became a major general on October 10, 1862, and received command of a division in General James Longstreet's corps in November.

During Longstreet's charge on the second day of the battle at Gettysburg, July 2, 1863, a shell exploded above Hood and pieces of shrapnel struck him in the left hand, forearm, elbow, and biceps. He had to leave the field and go to a hospital, where the doctor was able to save his arm. Hood evidently suffered major nerve damage, however, and permanent paralysis of his left hand.

After several months of convalescence, Hood joined his division in September on its way to Georgia. On September 20, at the Battle of Chickamauga, while he was riding to rally his old Texas brigade, he was struck in the right leg by an "exploding" bullet. The wound shattered the bone, necessitating an amputation at the upper third of the thigh. This was a very risky location for amputation, with about a 50 percent survival rate. Hood's amputation, performed by Dr. Tobias G. Richardson, assistant field medical director of the Army of Tennessee, healed quickly. However, Hood had pain in the stump, which was so short that it was difficult to attach an artificial leg to it. His former brigade raised more than $3,000 to purchase a cork or wood leg for him. By January 1864, he was able to ride horseback, although he had to be lifted onto his horse, and was determined to return to the army. In February 1864 Hood was appointed a lieutenant general and ordered to the Army of Tennessee to command a corps under Joseph E. Johnston.

Hood was able to ride twelve to twenty miles a day, wearing a boot and spur on his artificial leg as well as his real one. Nevertheless, his injuries limited his physical mobility. After he succeeded Johnston as commander of the Army of Tennessee on July 17, 1864, these limitations may have caused him to give his subordinate generals a lot of discretion in carrying out his orders because he could not be there. (He also was influenced by Robert E. Lee's similar command style, however.)

Hood was unable to keep Atlanta from falling to the Union forces of General William T. Sherman at the beginning of September. Later in the fall of 1864, in an attempt to draw Sherman out of Georgia, Hood marched the Army of Tennessee into Alabama and Tennessee, where his forces were decimated in the battles of Franklin and Nashville in November and December. Jefferson Davis removed Hood from army command in January 1865.

Hood's decisions have often been criticized, at the time and by later historians. In many ways, given his limited options, Hood's choices were reasonable, but his subordinate commanders were too inexperienced to carry out his plans without much more specific direction. His failures of logistical planning led to uncertainty about enemy movements because of poor reconnaissance, breakdowns in transportation, and lack of food and other supplies. Some historians have suggested that his use of laudanum or other opiates for pain may have impaired Hood's judgment. While this may be true, most of his actions seem to be part of a consistent pattern, suggesting that he was not competent to command anything larger than a brigade.

After the war Hood settled in New Orleans, where he initially became a cotton factor and commission merchant. He switched to a career in insurance, which provided a comfortable living for his family until economic problems began in 1878. During the Civil War Hood had courted and been engaged to the flirtatious socialite Sally "Buck" Preston, but the relationship foundered because her parents objected. On April 13, 1868, Hood married Anna Marie Hennen. In eleven years of marriage they had eleven children—eight girls and three boys—including three sets of twins. Hood died in a yellow fever epidemic on August 30, 1879, within a week of his wife and oldest daughter. He had spent a great deal of his last few years trying to justify his Civil War career. His memoir, *Advance and Retreat,* was published posthumously (1880).

See also: Amputation; Artificial Limbs; Bull Run (Manassas), Second Battle of; Chickamauga, Battle of; Gettysburg, Battle of; Gunshot Wounds, Treatment of; Laudanum; Opiate Use and Addiction.

Bibliography

McMurray, Richard M. *John Bell Hood and the War for Southern Independence.* Lexington: University Press of Kentucky, 1982.

Welsh, Jack D. *Medical Histories of Confederate Generals.* Kent, OH: Kent State University Press, 1995.

HOPKINS, JULIET ANN OPIE (1818–1890)

Juliet Opie Hopkins was instrumental in organizing, supplying, and managing hospitals in Richmond for sick and wounded Alabama soldiers. She was born in Jefferson County, Virginia, on May 7, 1818. Her father, Hierome Lindsay Opie, was a U.S. senator and wealthy plantation owner with 2,000 slaves by the mid-1830s. He had his daughter educated at home by English tutors and also sent her to Miss Ritchie's school in Richmond. When Juliet was sixteen, her mother, Margaret Muse Opie, died. Juliet left school to help manage her father's estate. In 1837 she married Alexander George Gordon, a lieutenant in the U.S. Navy. He died in 1849. She married Arthur Francis Hopkins in 1854 in New York City and moved with him to Mobile, Alabama. Hopkins, a leading Alabama Whig, who served briefly as chief justice of the Alabama supreme court and as U.S. senator from Alabama, was twenty-four years older than Juliet. She adopted her niece, also named Juliet Opie, as her daughter.

When the Civil War began, both Juliet and her husband quickly became involved in recruiting supplies for the Alabama soldiers who were sick and wounded in Virginia. Although Alabama governor John Gill Shorter appointed Judge Hopkins as agent for the Alabama hospitals in November 1861, the judge was nearly seventy and somewhat of an invalid. He apparently contributed mostly in the way of finances, influence, and support of his wife, who did the active work. The Hopkinses evidently sold property in Alabama, New York, and Virginia, and reportedly contributed between $200,000 and $500,000 (sources vary) for the care of sick and wounded Alabama Confederates. Neither accepted any payment for their efforts except for expenses.

Juliet Hopkins, authorized by the Alabama state legislature, established a supply depot in Richmond to store and distribute the food and clothing sent by Alabama ladies' associations and other patriotic citizens. In December 1861 she rented two large tobacco factories, establishing Alabama Hospitals No. 1 and No. 2 with capacities of 200 and 170, respectively. In April 1862 she set up Alabama Hospital No. 3, holding 170 patients, in another tobacco factory. She recruited and hired the nurses and other attendants and oversaw their training.

As hospital administrator, Hopkins carried on an enormous correspondence, requesting supplies, notifying senders when materials arrived, answering questions from patients' relatives, and sending personal effects and locks of hair to the families of those who had died. She personally purchased supplies for the hospitals and visited the wards daily.

Hopkins was extremely energetic, determined, and decisive. Although she was firm when necessary, reprimanding staff members who neglected their duty, she was very kind to the patients and would do everything possible to meet their needs. Hopkins even went to the battlefield on occasion. On May 31, 1862, at the Battle of Seven Pines, she was hit twice in the left hip while helping to remove the wounded from the field. Because a bone fragment had to be removed from her leg, she always walked with a limp thereafter, although she otherwise recovered.

In 1862 the Confederate medical department began changing to a new philosophy, closing small hospitals and consolidating the patients in much larger facilities holding several thousand patients on the edge of town. These large hospitals included Chimborazo, Winder, Howard's Grove, and Jackson. As a result of this policy, the Alabama patients were moved to Jackson and other hospitals, and Alabama Hospital No. 1 closed in June 1863, No. 2 in September, and No. 3 in December.

At this point Arthur and Juliet Hopkins moved back to Alabama, where much less is known about Juliet's activities, except that she briefly managed a hospital in Montgomery and one at Camp Watts in Notasulga. Many Alabamians expressed their gratitude to her in various ways. The state even put her picture on the fifty-cent and one-hundred-dollar Alabama Confederate currency.

Arthur Hopkins died in 1866, soon after the end of the war. Juliet then moved to New York City. Little is known about her postwar activities except that she often visited her adopted daughter, Juliet, and her husband, Romeyn B. Ayres, in

Washington, DC. Juliet Opie Hopkins died there on March 9, 1890, and was buried with military honors at Arlington Cemetery.

See also: Beers, Fannie A.; Chimborazo Hospital; Richmond, Virginia; Women, as Hospital Workers; Women's Hospital Auxiliaries and Relief Societies.

Bibliography
Beers, Fannie A. *Memories: A Recollection of Personal Experiences During Four Years of War.* Philadelphia: J.B. Lippincott, 1888; reprint, Alexandria, VA: Time-Life, 1985.

Calcutt, Rebecca Barbour. *Richmond's Wartime Hospitals.* Gretna, LA: Pelican, 2005.

Griffith, Lucille. "Mrs. Juliet Opie Hopkins and Alabama Military Hospitals." *Alabama Review* 6, no. 2 (1953): 99–120.

HOSPITAL BUILDINGS

Before the Civil War, hospitals were generally few in number and confined to large cities. When the war started producing thousands of sick and wounded soldiers in a short period of time, hospitals for their care had to be established on short notice and often under very makeshift conditions. As a result, nearly any type of building was used as a hospital.

In the field, doctors used whatever buildings were most convenient, particularly houses and barns, but also other outbuildings that were large enough to hold patients or serve as operating rooms.

Hospitals behind the lines were located in nearby towns, as well as in major cities far from the fighting, such as Philadelphia, New York City, or, for a time, Atlanta, Georgia. If hospital expansion was necessary but not an emergency, medical officers tried to select and rent buildings that would cause the least inconvenience to townspeople while still meeting medical needs. However, when towns received a sudden large influx of patients, doctors felt justified in impressing whatever structures they needed.

Hospitals were established in warehouses, factories, hotels, stores, and resorts, such as Cherokee Springs, Georgia. Both elementary schools and colleges served as hospitals. Many of the schools had already closed because their students went off to war. Churches of various denominations became hospitals, although doctors tried to leave at least one church in a town open for worship. Many courthouses and other public buildings were also converted into hospitals. In Washington, DC, for example, the Patent Office housed patients in the storerooms among the models of inventions.

While many buildings were used without alteration, those that were not well suited for hospital purposes were altered if possible. These adjustments included removing inappropriate furniture, placing boards across pew backs to make beds, and removing walls to expand room size. Some hospitals were augmented by using tents, constructing sheds, or building sturdier additional wards.

Although the main function of a hospital building was to provide space for patient care, some other rooms and buildings were required to support that care. Hospitals needed kitchens, often more than one, depending on the size of the hospital. They needed a laundry, latrines and bathing facilities for the patients, and storerooms for food, linens, medicines, and other supplies. Convalescents also needed a dining room. Many hospitals even had a library of sorts, as well as staff offices. In addition, hospitals had to have a dead house or morgue where deceased patients could be taken before burial.

In some more permanent hospital locations, doctors had the luxury of supervising the construction of new facilities. Many, North and South, were built on a pavilion model, with separate, single-story, ward-size buildings arranged in rows or a semicircle and designed for good ventilation. These hospitals had additional buildings for kitchens and other supportive services. Later in the war, as the Confederates fell back, they were rarely able to construct new hospitals. In a number of cases, such as in Chattanooga, Tennessee, the Union medical department took over and used the former Confederate hospitals.

See also: Chimborazo Hospital; Hospital Relocations; Hospitals, Antebellum; Hospitals, Field; Hospitals, Pavilion; Latrines; Tents, Hospital; Turner's Lane Hospital; Ventilation.

Bibliography

Schroeder-Lein, Glenna R. *Confederate Hospitals on the Move: Samuel H. Stout and the Army of Tennessee.* Columbia: University of South Carolina Press, 1994.

HOSPITAL FUND

The hospital fund was a method designed to pay for the food and supplies used for patients in military hospitals during the Civil War. A procedure devised by the prewar U.S. Army, the hospital fund concept was retained by both Union and Confederate forces.

The concept was based on the assumption that hospitalized soldiers would not be able to eat any or all of their normal rations. This was partly true because the sick and wounded would find hardtack and salt pork indigestible, although other parts of the ration, such as rice, could be useful. The surgeon in charge was to calculate the total number of uneaten rations monthly, based on the number of patients in the hospital, and multiply it by the standardized monetary value of a ration (usually thirty cents). The total figure was the hospital fund, from which the surgeon was to buy chickens, eggs, milk, vegetables, and other "delicacies" needed for the patients' diet.

While the concept may have made sense in theory, it was difficult to carry out satisfactorily. Surgeons in both the Union and Confederate armies, joining the military from civilian life, had great difficulty figuring out how to calculate the fund. This led to several kinds of problems. Some surgeons wasted their share of the fund because they failed to claim it and so their patients suffered from shortages. Other surgeons failed to understand how to apply the funds properly and became subject to disciplinary actions, such as courts-martial, for misappropriation of funds. Even if the funds were properly used and adequate, the surgeon might be unable to buy the proper supplies locally because the area had already been overforaged by one or both armies.

Union surgeon general William A. Hammond concluded that the amount of the hospital fund was not sufficient to meet the patients' needs, but did not attempt to change the calculation.

See also: Diet, of Hospital Patients; Diet, of Troops; Hammond, William Alexander; Hardtack; Negligence, by Medical Staff; Subsistence Department.

Bibliography

Lowry, Thomas P., and Jack D. Welsh. *Tarnished Scalpels: The Court-Martials of Fifty Union Surgeons.* Mechanicsburg, PA: Stackpole, 2000.

Schroeder-Lein, Glenna R. *Confederate Hospitals on the Move: Samuel H. Stout and the Army of Tennessee.* Columbia: University of South Carolina Press, 1994.

HOSPITAL PAPERWORK

Keeping records on sick and wounded soldier patients was an important duty for medical officers in the Union and Confederate armies. Accurate records could help to trace the spread and abatement of epidemic disease, determine mortality rates, track the effectiveness of treatments, determine the proportion of the army incapacitated for duty, and track the whereabouts of individual patients for their commanders and their families. The ultimate goal of Union record collection, as planned by Surgeon General William A. Hammond, was postwar publication of the information in what eventually became the six-volume *The Medical and Surgical History of the War of the Rebellion* (1870–1888).

Collecting these records meant that medical officers were responsible for a great deal of paperwork. The British army, during the Crimean War in the 1850s, had been the first to keep really detailed military medical records. The Union army based its information-gathering system on the British methods, as did the Confederates, whose leading medical officers had been in the Union army. However, Union doctors switched to listing diseases by their English names, while the Confederates retained the Latin terminology.

On both sides, the regimental surgeon kept records of those excused from duty or sent to the hospital because of illness. However, he did not list those who received medicine at sick call but returned to duty. In all reports, diseases were often vaguely labeled (for example, intermittent fever) because the lack of modern diagnostic equipment made it difficult to pinpoint the illness.

Paperwork flourished at the hospitals on both sides. By 1864 the manual for the Union medical officers listed more than two-dozen types of reports, while the Confederate Army of Tennessee general hospitals had twenty-seven different standardized forms. On both sides the surgeon in charge of a hospital had to report each morning how many patients he had and how many empty beds. These daily reports were summarized in the weekly report and all were sent to the medical director of the army or of hospitals. These statistical reports were crucial during campaigning season in determining where to send the wounded in order to avoid overcrowding, if possible.

Monthly reports were the most numerous for the Union medical service (Confederate reports were similar). The surgeon general was to receive a report on the sick and wounded, a statement of the hospital fund, a report on sick and wounded prisoners of war, and a report of the commissioned officers treated. The adjutant general needed a list of people at the post. The medical director was supposed to receive a muster roll of the contract nurses. The commissary general of prisoners required monthly lists of paroled and deceased prisoners of war. The provost marshal general had to have a report of deserters. The quartermaster general required a list of all quartermaster department property at the hospital, requisitions for fuel and for forage for government animals, and accounts of postage and telegraph expenses. Finally, reports on the hospitalized men had to be sent to their company commanders. In addition to these reports were several that had to be done quarterly or annually.

Summary reports were not the only kind of paperwork required. In the Confederacy, each patient was supposed to have his descriptive roll or identifying papers that described his medical problems and went with him whenever he transferred to another hospital. With the overwhelming influx of wounded after a battle, these rolls were often done improperly or not at all, causing annoyance at hospitals that received the patients. Tags also had to be filled out to identify knapsacks and other property that was stored for patients during their hospitalization. Confederate surgeons also had to keep a hospital register, casebook, prescription book, diet book, and copies of all correspondence. Records on both sides had to be duplicated by hand copying.

It is no wonder that surgeons newly in charge of hospitals could easily feel overwhelmed. Many medical directors and other officials, such as Confederate surgeon general Samuel P. Moore, were sticklers for accuracy, completeness, and promptness of reports. A number of Northern hospitals put a surgeon or assistant surgeon in charge of record keeping. Most Southern hospitals had at least a clerk to help the surgeon in charge. Still, records were often poorly kept and incomplete, although their quality tended to improve after the first year of the war as formerly civilian doctors became more attuned to military protocol.

Samuel H. Stout, medical director of hospitals for the Confederate Army of Tennessee, found a unique way to improve the efficiency and cost-effectiveness of record keeping. Because the cost of forms was taken out of the hospital fund,

Stout believed that it would be cheaper for the hospital department to own a printing press than to pay local printers. In 1864 Stout spent $16,000 for the printing equipment of the former Winchester, Tennessee, *Bulletin,* employed a disabled private and two assistants, and had at least $25,000 worth of forms printed in the first three months the press operated.

The majority of Union records survived the war and were analyzed in *The Medical and Surgical History of the War of the Rebellion.* However, the bulk of Confederate records were destroyed in the fires that accompanied the evacuation of Richmond on April 2, 1865. Nevertheless, some collections of material survived, such as the 1,500 pounds of Army of Tennessee hospital records preserved by Samuel H. Stout. These collections provide some basis for comparison with Union records.

See also: Hammond, William Alexander; Hospital Fund; Hospitals, General; *The Medical and Surgical History of the War of the Rebellion;* Medical Directors, of Hospitals; Moore, Samuel Preston; Mortality, of Soldiers; Stout, Samuel Hollingsworth; Surgeon in Charge; Surgeons.

Bibliography

Adams, George Worthington. *Doctors in Blue: The Medical History of the Union Army in the Civil War.* New York: Schuman, 1952; reprint, Dayton, OH: Morningside, 1985.

Bollet, Alfred Jay. *Civil War Medicine: Challenges and Triumphs.* Tucson, AZ: Galen, 2002.

Greenleaf, Charles R. *A Manual for the Medical Officers of the United States Army.* Philadelphia: J.B. Lippincott, 1864; reprint, San Francisco: Norman, 1992.

Schroeder-Lein, Glenna R. *Confederate Hospitals on the Move: Samuel H. Stout and the Army of Tennessee.* Columbia: University of South Carolina Press, 1994.

HOSPITAL RELOCATIONS

During the Civil War, field hospitals migrated with the troops of both sides to treat the sick and wounded as quickly as possible. General hospitals for longer-term care were established in towns and cities behind the lines where they remained until no longer needed. The major exception to this rule was the system of general hospitals of the Confederate Army of Tennessee, because most of these hospitals moved more than once to escape incursions by Federal troops, especially those of General William T. Sherman in Georgia in 1864.

The first Army of Tennessee general hospital post to be evacuated was Nashville, Tennessee, in February 1862, after the fall of Fort Henry and Fort Donelson to the Union forces. The Confederate departure was panicked and haphazard, with a number of government officials, including the quartermaster, fleeing the town and their responsibilities. As a result, many supplies were simply abandoned. The patients were shipped to hospitals elsewhere and the doctors were sent individually to new posts, to fit into existing hospitals or organize new ones.

Samuel H. Stout experienced the mess created by the evacuation of Nashville, and when he became medical director of (general) hospitals for the Army of Tennessee, he developed a more efficient plan. He, too, would ship patients to some previously organized hospital away from the enemy. But he would otherwise preserve the hospital intact, with doctors, nurses, and other attendants taking as much hospital furniture and as many supplies as possible and setting up the hospital again in a more secure location. Stout and his subordinates were continually looking for suitable hospital sites, so they were prepared when the hospitals had to move.

The first test of Stout's mobilization plan came with the evacuation of Chattanooga, Tennessee, in August 1863, shortly before the Battle of Chickamauga, when most of the hospitals from that town were sent to Marietta, Georgia, just north of Atlanta. Soon after, all the hospitals in Georgia north of Resaca had to be moved south and west of Atlanta.

Much more difficult was the almost continuous hospital mobilization that began with Sherman's movements in May 1864. All hospitals in his path or exposed to raids by his troops had to move, often on short notice, and frequently more than once. During the summer of 1864 the list of Army of Tennessee hospital locations changed weekly. Many hospitals moved out of Georgia into Alabama and even Mississippi and were forced to use makeshift facilities. Some hospitals suffered shortages of supplies and serious overcrowding. Quartermasters often treated hospitals, their needs, and their property with little respect and no priority, forcing them to abandon bulky furniture, such as bunks, and then refusing to replace the materials when the hospitals reached their destination.

As the war continued, Confederate transportation resources—railroads, wagons, and ships—all deteriorated. By late 1864, hospitals that attempted to follow the Army of Tennessee north on General John Bell Hood's fateful march into Tennessee found themselves stranded for days or weeks awaiting transportation, a problem that continued until the end of the war.

Despite the many difficulties caused by mobilization, most of the Army of Tennessee hospitals were able to avoid capture and remain operating until the end of the war because they moved intact.

See also: Chickamauga, Battle of; Hood, John Bell; Hospital Buildings; Hospitals, Field; Hospitals, General; Quartermasters; Stout, Samuel Hollingsworth.

Bibliography
Schroeder-Lein, Glenna R. *Confederate Hospitals on the Move: Samuel H. Stout and the Army of Tennessee*. Columbia: University of South Carolina Press, 1994.

HOSPITAL SHIPS

Both Union and Confederate forces used hospital ships during the Civil War. However, little is known about those of the Confederacy because of the destruction of records in Richmond at the close of the war. Hospital ships might be boats of various sizes impressed to meet a particular emergency, or they might be vessels remodeled for long-term patient care. They could be floating hospitals, in use because of a lack of shore facilities. Most commonly, hospital ships served as floating ambulances, transporting the sick and wounded from field hospitals to general hospitals far behind the lines in the Northern states.

The first known hospital ship during the Civil War was prepared by the Confederates in Charleston, South Carolina. A barge, with its cabin holding eight to ten beds served by a doctor, was attached to a floating battery during the attack on Fort Sumter in April 1861. The Confederates also had several hospital ships on the western rivers during the early part of the war. The *Star of the West*, captured by the Confederates in April 1861, became the *St. Philip*, a hospital ship that cared for 130 patients on the lower Mississippi River from September 18, 1861, to April 20, 1862. The Confederates also had two hospital ships at Fort Henry, Tennessee, when the fort fell in February 1862. The *Patton* surrendered with sixty patients while the *Samuel Orr* was destroyed to keep it from being captured. Evidently the Confederates rarely used ships to transport the wounded.

The Union forces used both floating hospitals and transports primarily on two fronts, the western rivers and the Virginia campaign area. The use of such ships really began in the west as a result of the campaign against Fort Henry and Fort Donelson in February 1862. Because of the forts' river location, hospital ships were natural and convenient. While some vessels were pressed into service by the army, usually without adequate supplies, others were leased and equipped by the U.S. Sanitary Commission and the Western Sanitary Commission. Chartering these ships temporarily cost $200 to $600 each per day. The *City of Memphis*, the first ship used as a hospital transport, served from February 7 to July 17, 1862. It took the wounded from the two forts to Paducah, Kentucky. Ultimately the *City of Memphis* made fourteen trips, carrying a total of 7,221 patients.

Hospital transport ships traveled between various ports, depending on the location of the battle and available hospital beds. The *D.A. January*, a side-wheel steamer that the U.S. Army purchased on April 1, 1862, saw immediate use following the Battle of Shiloh on April 6–7, 1862. Along with other boats, it traveled from Pittsburg Landing, Tennessee, to Keokuk, Iowa; Cincinnati, Ohio; St. Louis, Missouri; Paducah, Kentucky; Louisville, Kentucky; Columbus, Kentucky; Memphis, Tennessee; Helena, Arkansas; and Cairo and Mound City, Illinois. During return trips the crew cleaned the ship and prepared for the next patients. In its first three months the *D.A. January* carried 3,000 patients and sailed more than 8,000 miles. In September 1862 it was completely remodeled as a hospital ship and it remained in service until August 1865, carrying a total of 23,738 patients. The medical department was so proud of the *D.A. January* that it had a model made for the 1876 Centennial Exposition in Philadelphia, a model that is still on display at the National Museum of Health and Medicine in Washington, DC.

The first Union ship actually to be outfitted for hospital service was the *Red*

Rover, which began service on the Mississippi on June 10, 1862, and continued in use until November 17, 1865. A ship specifically prepared for hospital use could have walls removed to make larger wards, ice storage, steam heating, distilled water, operating rooms, laundries, bathrooms, storage space, tiers of bunks, space for additional cots, kitchens, elevators to move the patients between decks, and staff quarters. Most hospital ships had several women as part of their nursing staff and also employed free or contraband (escaped slave) blacks. As many as sixty people cared for the patients and ran the ship. Because the patients were generally on board only two or three days, the doctors were unable to pursue extensive treatments or follow up on patients.

In the West, the majority of hospital transports were added after the battles at Forts Henry and Donelson (February 1862), Shiloh (April 1862), and during the lengthy Vicksburg campaign (ending in July 1863). Although some hospital ships continued in use until the end of the war, fewer of them were needed as the wartime action moved away from the Mississippi Valley.

In the East, hospital transport ships were needed for General George B. McClellan's army as soon as the Peninsula Campaign began in the spring of 1862. The evacuation system was very poor. Dr. Charles S. Tripler, the army medical director, was not an adequate administrator for the needs of the sick and wounded of such a large army. He also did not have the cooperation of the quartermaster department.

In April 1862 Frederick Law Olmsted, executive secretary and general administrator for the U.S. Sanitary Commission, organized and took charge of the Hospital Transport Service. As in the West, the U.S. Sanitary Commission chartered and supplied a number of boats to use as hospital transports, but had a good deal of trouble with conflicting orders from various army officers.

After the Battle of Seven Pines, Virginia, (May 31–June 1, 1862), trainloads of wounded were sent to White House Landing without any medical care or nourishment. There the men were loaded onto the overcrowded U.S. Sanitary Commission boats, where doctors and nurses scrambled frantically to care for them en route to Washington, DC; Annapolis, Maryland; Boston; or New York City. Boats provided by the army or other organizations had even more problems with filth and lack of staff, as well as little or no food, water, or medical supplies. A number of eastern society women volunteered and served well, nursing and cleaning on the hospital transports. These women also wrote letters, some of which were published, describing the terrible conditions. These reports affected the image of the army medical department, even after conditions improved.

On June 27, 1862, the Union army and the hospital transports evacuated White House Landing and moved to Harrison's Landing. Here conditions improved because Jonathan Letterman became army medical director. With better army organization, the U.S. Sanitary Commission ships, which had transported between 8,000 and 10,000 casualties, were consolidated under army control. Union sick and wounded continued to be evacuated by water from Virginia throughout the rest of the war from such locations as Aquia Landing and City Point.

See also: Army Medical Museum; Blacks, as Hospital Workers; Letterman, Jonathan; Medical Directors, Field; Nurses; Olmsted, Frederick Law; Peninsula Campaign; Quartermasters; Shiloh, Battle of; Tripler, Charles Stuart; United States Sanitary Commission; USS *Red Rover;* Western Sanitary Commission; Women, as Hospital Workers; Woolsey Sisters.

Bibliography

Bacon, Georgeanna Woolsey, and Eliza Woolsey Howland. *My Heart Toward Home: Letters of a Family During the Civil War.* 1898; reprint, Roseville, MN: Edinborough, 2001.

Bollet, Alfred Jay. *Civil War Medicine: Challenges and Triumphs.* Tucson, AZ: Galen, 2002.

Josyph, Peter, ed. *The Wounded River: The Civil War Letters of John Vance Lauderdale, M.D.* East Lansing: Michigan State University Press, 1993.

Roca, Steven Louis. "Presence and Precedents: The USS *Red Rover* During the American Civil War, 1861–1865." *Civil War History* 44 (June 1998): 91–110.

Rybczynski, Witold. *A Clearing in the Distance: Frederick Law Olmsted and America in the 19th Century.* New York: Scribner, 1999.

Waddell, Ronald. "Ships of War—Ships of Hope: The Women and Their Hospital Ships in the Mississippi Valley Campaigns of the Civil War." *Journal of Women's Civil War History* 2 (2002): 86–119.

HOSPITAL SUPPORT STAFF

Any hospital, North or South, required a sizable staff to support the work of the surgeons in caring for sick and wounded soldiers. While the support staff was largely male, most hospitals eventually had female workers in some posts. The male staff could include detailed and convalescent soldiers as well as civilians. In the South, a large percentage of the laboring staff was black slaves, hired or impressed from their masters. Some free blacks also worked in the hospitals. While most of the hospital staff was paid, some women and civilian men offered their services without compensation. The number of any particular type of workers was supposed to be proportional to the number of patients in the hospital or expected to arrive there. For example, there was supposed to be a nurse for every ten patients.

White men could, and did, fill virtually any position at the hospital. As stewards they managed the procurement of supplies and preparation of food, as well as serving as the hospital pharmacist. Ward masters oversaw all aspects of the care and provisions for the men in their ward. Nurses provided all types of patient care and cleaned the wards. Clerks managed the masses of paperwork related to supply procurement, patient records, and numerous reports. Other workers constructed or remodeled hospital buildings, set up tents when needed, dug wells and privies, and provided other manual labor. Cooks prepared food for the patients. Male workers occasionally did laundry; in the Confederate Army of Tennessee hospital at Cherokee Springs, Georgia, for example, a soldier and his wife did the laundry.

Black men did much of the manual labor of construction, cleaning, nursing, and also cooking. This was a given in the South, but Union hospitals also used the services of blacks when available. Black women chiefly worked as laundresses or nurses. Sometimes those officially hired as laundresses ended up working as nurses as well, especially when the hospitals overflowed with wounded after a battle.

In both the North and the South the idea of white women working in a hospital was controversial. Many people believed that white women were too delicate to deal with gruesome wounds and miserable illnesses and too modest to care for the bodies of men unrelated to them. Most women in both sections, but especially in the South, gave in to these pressures and served their cause by providing supplies or other aid. However, some white women did work as nurses, cooks, and laundresses. Women of the upper classes were most likely to become hospital matrons (in the South) or supervisors who had management responsibilities. They oversaw the cooking for invalid patients with special diets, the laundry, and the general cleanliness of the hospital.

The purpose of all the members of the hospital staff was to make the patients as comfortable as possible by keeping the hospital orderly and clean, administering medicines, serving food, and dressing wounds as directed. Their success at achieving these goals depended on the experience, attitude, and number of the staff, as well as their location and access to supplies.

See also: Blacks, as Hospital Workers; Convalescents; Cooks; Diet, of Hospital Patients; Hospital Paperwork; Laundresses; Matrons; Nurses; Stewards, Hospital; Ward Masters; Women, as Hospital Workers.

Bibliography

Bollet, Alfred Jay. *Civil War Medicine: Challenges and Triumphs.* Tucson, AZ: Galen, 2002.

Green, Carol C. *Chimborazo: The Confederacy's Largest Hospital.* Knoxville: University of Tennessee Press, 2004.

Schroeder-Lein, Glenna R. *Confederate Hospitals on the Move: Samuel H. Stout and the Army of Tennessee.* Columbia: University of South Carolina Press, 1994.

HOSPITAL TRAINS *See* Ambulance Trains.

HOSPITALS, ANTEBELLUM

During the period before the Civil War, most Americans never went to a hospital for any reason; if they became ill or injured, they were cared for at home. Because no large, specialized medical equipment was used in treatment, home care provided by family members and/or hired nurses, under the supervision of a physician who made house calls, was very practical. What hospitals there were, were located mainly in large Northern cities. They were designed to care for the sick but worthy (noncriminal) poor and travelers who became ill during their journey.

Hospitals were designed to give the illusion of home care for those who had no home or were far away from it.

Such hospitals as existed were generally small and were managed by civilian administrators. The doctors who visited the patients were often associated with a nearby medical school. They were paid little or nothing for their services, but could use the patients as subjects when training their medical students. A hospital post also increased a doctor's reputation and attracted private, paying patients to his practice.

Nursing was not a profession, as it is in the twenty-first century, and was usually done by family members or persons who had learned nursing skills by caring for family members. Because hospitals were essentially charity institutions, convalescents were expected to nurse those who were sicker than they, as well as to clean the premises.

Because of the nature and reputation of antebellum hospitals, few Civil War soldiers had had, or wanted to have, a hospital experience. However, the widespread use of hospitals became necessary during the war because of the masses of sick and wounded soldiers who needed close attention from doctors and could not be sent home for treatment.

After the war, until about the twentieth century, hospitals again became charity institutions for the indigent and transient.

See also: Convalescents; Gunshot Wounds, Treatment of; Hospitals, Attitudes Toward; Nurses.

Bibliography
Rosenberg, Charles E. *The Care of Strangers: The Rise of America's Hospital System*. New York: Basic Books, 1987.

HOSPITALS, ATTITUDES TOWARD

Many people, North and South, expressed an opinion about Civil War hospitals. These opinions varied depending on the time and place during the war, as well as the person's actual experience with wartime hospitals.

There were few hospitals before the war. Those that did exist were designed to care for the impoverished or for travelers who could not be treated at home. As a result, few Civil War soldiers had ever been in a hospital, and nearly all, officers as well as enlisted men, initially regarded the idea with horror. Women, too, were horrified at the idea that their sons, husbands, or other male relatives might be sent to a hospital, and tried to persuade the regimental officers not to allow that to happen.

The mid–nineteenth-century ideal of care for the sick was nursing them at home under the supervision of a physician who made periodic house calls. As a result, hospital care was inevitably compared to home care. In the early months of the war, medical care in military camps, improvised field hospitals, and impromptu general hospitals often compared very poorly, due to shortages of supplies, doctors, attendants of all sorts, and properly equipped buildings. Reports of these problems by patients, comrades, friends, and newspapers influenced the opinions of those at home. Even after conditions were much improved, bad first impressions remained. Many people never got over the idea that a hospital provided second-class care. They thought that the patients should be sent home for proper nursing.

While most civilians faced the prospect of a loved one in the hospital at some point, many also saw hospitals come to them. In the border states and the South, civilians living near battlefields willingly or unwillingly saw their homes, barns, and outbuildings turned into temporary hospitals. People in towns and cities found large buildings of many sorts impressed for hospital purposes. Some towns offered homes, businesses, and other buildings willingly, out of compassion for the needs of the sick and wounded soldiers, but many people, especially in the South, objected to the loss of these buildings for their original civilian purposes. It was inconvenient for travelers to be unable to stay at a hotel, for local governments to be ousted from their meeting and office space in the courthouse, and for religious congregations to give up their churches. In the Confederate Army of Tennessee, military medical officials tried to keep at least one church in a town open for services.

Some civilians also feared that their loss of occupancy would be permanent. They suspected that hospital use would cause so much damage that buildings could never be restored to their original purpose, at least not without great expense. A number of Southerners opposed having hospitals in their towns because they feared the spread of disease from the soldiers to the civilians. Some doctors displayed poor attitudes or behavior in their relations with the civilians, reinforcing the citizens' disapproval of the hospital. In other instances, doctors established such good relationships that the townspeople were sorry to see them go.

Having hospitals in a town could provide numerous business opportunities. In the North, politicians lobbied to have general hospitals quartered in their districts, while town officials eagerly anticipated profits. In the South, however, many towns with hospitals found them a drain on the economy, sucking up the produce of the region while issuing government promissory notes that were unlikely to be paid or offering Confederate currency that continued to lose value. As a result, many farmers refused to sell their produce to the hospitals unless they received something tangible, such as cloth, thread, or pottery, in payment.

Most women, North and South, at some point aided the hospitals at least by donating supplies. Some women became very active in local relief organizations or, in the North, gathered supplies for distribution by the U.S. Sanitary Commission. Other women went to work in hospitals as nurses, matrons, laundresses, or cooks. Louisa May Alcott's book *Hospital Sketches* (1863), a slightly fictionalized account of her own brief nursing experiences at the Union Hotel Hospital in Georgetown, DC, contributed to interest in hospitals in the North.

Many soldiers who had been reluctant to go to the hospital expressed their opinions about the experience once they were there. The level of complaint tended to vary depending on the seriousness of a soldier's medical condition. Those who were not very sick complained the most about the building, the quality of care, the lack of cleanliness, the food, the smell, and alleged favoritism to enemy prisoners of war who were patients. On the other hand, some men preferred the hospital to the field and feigned illnesses in order to stay there. Some former patients commended the doctors, matrons, nurses, or general care at a particular hospital, sometimes comparing several hospitals where they had been patients.

See also: Alcott, Louisa May; Cooks; Hospital Buildings; Hospitals, Antebellum; Hospitals, Field; Hospitals, General; Laundresses; Malingerers; Matrons; Nurses; Prisoners of War; Sanitation; Surgeons; United States Sanitary Commission; Woman's Central Association of Relief; Women, as Hospital Workers; Women's Hospital Auxiliaries and Relief Societies.

Bibliography

Alcott, Louisa May. *Hospital Sketches.* 1863; reprint, Boston: Applewood, 1986.

Schroeder-Lein, Glenna R. *Confederate Hospitals on the Move: Samuel H. Stout and the Army of Tennessee.* Columbia: University of South Carolina Press, 1994.

Smith, Mrs. S.E.D. *The Soldier's Friend: Being a Thrilling Narrative of Grandma Smith's Four Years Experience and Observation, as Matron, in the Hospitals of the South . . .* Memphis, TN: Bulletin Publishing, 1867.

HOSPITALS, CONVALESCENT *See* Convalescents.

HOSPITALS, DEPOT *See* Hospitals, Receiving and Distributing.

HOSPITALS, DIVISION *See* Hospitals, Field.

HOSPITALS, FIELD

The goal of a field hospital in both the Union and Confederate armies during the Civil War was to provide medical care for sick and wounded soldiers while they were still in the field. The location and permanence of a field hospital depended on whether the soldiers were in camp or on the battlefield.

Initially, field hospitals were established by regiments and staffed by the regimental surgeon with one or two assistant surgeons (depending on the size of the regiment), a steward, soldiers detailed as nurses, and cooks and laundresses as necessary. In camp the hospital could be established in tents, a nearby house, or another appropriate building. Although always temporary, such camp hospitals might be used for a number of months, until the regiment moved. Field hospitals in camps primarily treated soldiers who were too sick to remain in their quarters, such as those with typhoid fever, or who needed to be isolated, such as patients with measles or smallpox.

During a battle, field hospitals were established as close to the site of the battle as possible while still being outside the range of enemy artillery. Because the lines often shifted position as one side or the other gained the advantage, field hospitals frequently came under fire and had to relocate if they could. Hospital tents were often kept away from the battle, in the baggage train, and were not available during the fight itself. Doctors set up their field hospitals in houses, barns, outbuildings, and under shade trees when no structures were available.

On the field itself, the assistant surgeons remained just behind the lines, providing first aid or triage for the newly wounded. These assistant surgeons bandaged wounds, stopped bleeding, splinted broken bones, and gave opiates or whiskey to dull the pain so that the patient could be moved to the field hospital.

Once the patient arrived in the field hospital, surgeons examined his wounds more closely. Given the often overwhelming numbers of wounded, the medical officers had to make quick decisions about who was most likely to survive and how best to treat him. If the bullet was still present, doctors would remove it if possible. They would also clean the wound, removing grass, dirt, clothing scraps, bone fragments, and other debris. They would then bandage and, if necessary, splint the wound. If the bones and tissue of a wounded arm or leg were severely mangled, the doctors in the field hospital would perform an amputation.

After stabilizing the patient, the doctors prepared him for travel if he was well enough to be moved by ambulance, train, or boat to a general hospital for long-term care. Those with slight wounds and a short expected recovery time, as well as those likely to die if moved, remained in the field hospital. Once the wounded had been cared for and as many sent to the general hospitals as possible, the field hospitals might be consolidated in the best remaining facilities. The situation of field hospitals also depended on whether the army remained on or retained control of the battlefield, as well as the availability of supplies.

Regimental field hospitals presented a number of problems, however. They were small, poorly supplied, and often lacked skilled surgeons or enough nurses and other attendants. In addition, depending on which troops were most actively fighting, some regimental hospitals could be swamped with wounded, while others saw no patients because they were not supposed to treat the members of other regiments. After the terrible medical care fiasco of the Peninsula Campaign and the Second Battle of Bull Run (Manassas) in 1862, Union surgeon general William A. Hammond and Jonathan Letterman, the new medical director of the Army of the Potomac, reorganized the army's medical department. Not only did they develop an ambulance corps, they reorganized field hospitals by division.

A division, or sometimes corps, hospital was to have a surgeon in charge, as well as two assistant surgeons with administrative responsibilities. One was in charge of providing food, water, shelter, and fuel for the hospital while the other was in charge of keeping records of the wounded and deceased. In addition, the hospital was to have three medical officers to perform operations and three to assist them, all chosen by skill rather than by rank. Other doctors to attend less serious wounds, nurses, stewards, and cooks were assigned as necessary. Confederate field hospitals were also arranged by brigade or division after the early part of the war and performed similar care for the wounded.

Good care in a field hospital could mean the difference between life and death for a sick or wounded Civil War soldier.

See also: Ambulance Corps; Amputation; Bull Run (Manassas), Second Battle of; Cooks; Gunshot Wounds, Treatment of; Hammond, William Alexander; Hospital Buildings; Hospital Paperwork; Hospitals, General; Letterman, Jonathan; Measles; Medical Directors, Field; Nurses; Peninsula Campaign; Smallpox; Stewards, Hospital; Surgeons; Surgeons, Assistant; Tents, Hospital; Typhoid Fever.

Bibliography

Cawood, Hobart G. *The Medical Service at Chickamauga.* Fort Oglethorpe, GA: Chickamauga and Chattanooga National Military Park, 1964.

Cunningham, H.H. *Doctors in Gray: The Confederate Medical Service.* Baton Rouge: Louisiana State University Press, 1958; reprint, Gloucester, MA: Peter Smith, 1970.

Duncan, Louis C. *The Medical Department of the United States Army in the Civil War.* Washington, DC: Author, 1914; reprint, Gaithersburg, MD: Butternut, 1985.

Greenleaf, Charles R. *A Manual for the Medical Officers of the United States Army.* Philadelphia: J.B. Lippincott, 1864; reprint, San Francisco: Norman, 1992.

HOSPITALS, GENERAL

General hospitals were established by both the Union and the Confederate medical services. Initially, a sick or wounded soldier would be treated by his regimental surgeon and/or in a field hospital. If his condition was likely to be of short duration or too grave for him to be moved, he would remain in the field hospital; otherwise he would be sent to a general hospital for further treatment and convalescence.

These general hospitals, so called because they usually were not restricted to the members of a particular regiment or corps, were established in cities or towns behind the lines. Washington, DC, and Philadelphia, for the Union, and Richmond, Virginia, for the Confederacy, became major hospital centers, but Nashville, Tennessee; Atlanta, Georgia; Lynchburg, Virginia; Frederick, Maryland; and numerous other towns also housed general hospitals holding hundreds of patients.

Each hospital had a surgeon in charge, as well as a number of surgeons, assistant surgeons, and nurses proportional to the capacity of the hospital. During crises caused by the influx of wounded men after a battle, wards could be severely overcrowded and the number of attendants painfully inadequate. Stewards, cooks, laundresses, and other staff members helped to meet the needs of the patients.

Most general hospitals treated all types of cases although they might set aside separate wards for contagious diseases or a particular type of wound. A few entire hospitals were established to treat particular problems, such as the venereal disease hospital in Nashville, the nerve wound and disease hospital (Turner's Lane) in Philadelphia, and smallpox hospitals in various places.

General hospitals were initially established in existing buildings such as hotels, churches, schools, courthouses, and other available structures, but later in the war pavilion wards and other similar buildings were constructed specifically for the hospitals. These general hospitals, once established, did not usually move except in the Confederate Army of Tennessee, where the movements of Union troops continually pushed the Confederates back, forcing frequent relocation of their general hospitals.

A patient could expect to stay in a general hospital until he either recovered enough to be sent to his regiment or a convalescent camp, was declared unable to return to duty and sent home on furlough or permanently discharged, or died.

See also: Chimborazo Hospital; Convalescents; Cooks; Hospital Buildings; Hospital Relocations; Hospital Support Staff; Hospitals, Field; Hospitals, Pavilion; Hospitals, "Pest" (Smallpox); Laundresses; Nurses; Stewards, Hospital; Stout, Samuel Hollingsworth; Surgeon in Charge; Turner's Lane Hospital; Venereal Disease; Ventilation.

Bibliography

Adams, George Worthington. *Doctors in Blue: The Medical History of the Union Army in the Civil War.* New York: Schuman, 1952; reprint, Dayton, OH: Morningside, 1985.

Cunningham, H.H. *Doctors in Gray: The Confederate Medical Service.* Baton Rouge: Louisiana State University Press, 1958; reprint, Gloucester, MA: Peter Smith, 1970.

Schroeder-Lein, Glenna R. *Confederate Hospitals on the Move: Samuel H. Stout and the Army of Tennessee.* Columbia: University of South Carolina Press, 1994.

HOSPITALS, MOBILIZATION OF *See* Hospital Relocations.

HOSPITALS, OFFICERS'

The military forces of the United States have always been hierarchical. In addition to being paid more, officers are separated from enlisted men in various ways, including living quarters. Separation of officers and men also characterized their medical treatment during the Civil War in both the Union and the Confederacy.

If an officer was sick, he would be treated in his quarters as long as possible (as was also true for enlisted men). If the officer was chronically ill or facing a slow recovery, he could be sent home on a furlough (enlisted men were treated similarly here as well). If the officer was too sick to travel, he might be placed in a private hospital. However, many government hospitals began to establish separate floors or wings for officers. There was an officers' floor at the Armory Square Hospital in Washington, DC, for example.

A separate officers' hospital opened in Philadelphia in the winter of 1862–1863, about the same time that one opened in Memphis, Tennessee, now under Union control. Because officers were paid more and received a food allowance, they were expected to procure their own food, even when hospitalized, unlike enlisted soldiers. Initially, some officers' hospitals were also restricted in everything else they provided. In Memphis the hospital furnished only medicine and doctors—no beds, nurses, food, or any other assistance. These conditions improved when the Western Sanitary Commission took control of the hospital.

After December 1862 there were at least two Confederate officers' hospitals in Richmond, Virginia—General Hospitals No. 4 and No. 10. Each had a capacity of more than 300 patients. Chimborazo Hospital functioned as an overflow facility and at several times served some officers. These men tended to be sent to private quarters as soon as they were able to leave the hospital.

In March 1864 the Union war department issued a general order that established officers' hospitals in each military department. There were ten of them by December 1864, varying widely in size from twenty beds in Beaufort, South Carolina, to 409 beds in Annapolis, Maryland, for a total of slightly over 1,000 beds. Each officer was to pay one dollar for each day he was hospitalized, plus an extra thirty cents per day if he had a servant. This fee was collected at the end of each month and the end of the officer's hospitalization. Each officer's hospital was to have a treasurer to handle the rather complicated procedures involved in collecting the charges. These fees irritated some officers. Despite the daily fee, new buildings were not to be erected for officers' hospitals without special permission.

As in any Civil War hospital, the quality of officers' care varied depending on the surgeon in charge of the hospital and his attitude toward patient care. Although officers were treated separately from enlisted men, they were not necessarily treated better. Sick and wounded generals, such as Thomas J. "Stonewall" Jackson, Richard S. Ewell, and Daniel E. Sickles, were cared for in private homes or hotels.

See also: Chimborazo Hospital; Ewell, Richard Stoddert; Jackson, Thomas Jonathan ("Stonewall"); Sickles, Daniel Edgar; Western Sanitary Commission.

Bibliography

Adams, George Worthington. *Doctors in Blue: The Medical History of the Union Army in the Civil War.* New York: Schuman, 1952; reprint, Dayton, OH: Morningside, 1985.

Green, Carol E. *Chimborazo: The Confederacy's Largest Hospital.* Knoxville: University of Tennessee Press, 2004.

Greenleaf, Charles R. *A Manual for the Medical Officers of the United States Army.* Philadelphia: J.B. Lippincott, 1864; reprint, San Francisco: Norman, 1992.

HOSPITALS, PAVILION

Hospitals designed in the pavilion style were constructed in both the North and the South during the Civil War. Based on principles developed in Europe in the 1850s during the Crimean War, these hospitals were advocated by Florence Nightingale. The pavilion plan required a large amount of space and new construction; it could not be applied to buildings converted from other uses.

Although there were some variations from hospital to hospital, the plan was based on the idea of an individual single-story building for each ward. These pavilions could be from 80 to 150 feet long and 22 to 30 feet wide. They held from thirty-two to sixty patients each, depending on arrangement and proximity to battlefield casualties. Some, such as Chimborazo Hospital in Richmond, had wider wards with four rows of beds separated by aisles, while the Confederate Army of Tennessee hospitals in Chattanooga, Tennessee, and Georgia had narrower wards with only two rows of beds. A hospital might have as many as 150 of these ward buildings.

The chief advantage of the pavilion hospital was good ventilation, a primary concern of hospital designers and doctors during the Civil War. Because physicians believed that miasms and odors in the air from vegetable matter and bodily secretions caused or worsened disease, they thought that good ventilation, providing "pure" air, would reduce the spread of disease and help patients to get well sooner. In fact, the small wards gathered fewer people to spread germs to each other and the fresh air did alleviate the bad odors of illness, although it also made some of the wards rather hard to heat in winter.

The pavilion wards were quickly constructed wooden frame buildings with plank floors and numerous windows. These windows had shutters, sometimes sliding ones, that could be opened or closed. Most wards had openings under the ridge of the roof to draw the contaminated air out. The design advocated by Medical Director Samuel H. Stout of the Army of Tennessee also included openings one foot high and two feet wide just above the floor and just below the ceiling at each bed. Stout claimed that with their sliding shutters open, the wards aired out in just a few minutes without subjecting the patients to drafts.

The pavilion wards were arranged in several designs. Those in the Confederacy tended to be in rows. Union hospitals, such as the Hammond General Hospital at Point Lookout, Maryland, and the Mower General Hospital in Chestnut Hill, Pennsylvania, tended to have a circular arrangement. The wards radiated out like spokes from a central area containing the various service buildings and were connected by roofed corridors that were open on the sides. Whatever the arrangement, the wards were separated from each other by spaces or, in row hospitals, "streets," that were at least twelve feet wide to permit maximum air circulation.

Each hospital had a number of buildings devoted to supporting patient care—administrative offices, quarters for staff, kitchens, laundries, bathhouses, storerooms (for food, linens, soldiers' knapsacks, and other supplies), ice houses, bakeries,

156

breweries, guardhouses, morgues, carpenter shops, chapels, libraries, and other buildings as needed by particular hospitals. Some of the hospitals also had gardens on the premises or nearby, farmed in part by convalescent soldiers, who raised vegetables and fruits and pastured livestock to provide food for the patients.

Some of the hospitals continued to be used after the Civil War. Pavilion-style construction remained common for military hospitals into the mid-twentieth century.

See also: Chimborazo Hospital; Convalescents; Hospital Buildings; Hospitals, General; Miasms; Stout, Samuel Hollingsworth; Ventilation.

Bibliography

Adams, George Worthington. *Doctors in Blue: The Medical History of the Union Army in the Civil War.* New York: Schuman, 1952; reprint, Dayton, OH: Morningside, 1985.

Bollet, Alfred Jay. *Civil War Medicine: Challenges and Triumphs.* Tucson, AZ: Galen, 2002.

Green, Carol C. *Chimborazo: The Confederacy's Largest Hospital.* Knoxville: University of Tennessee Press, 2004.

Schroeder-Lein, Glenna R. *Confederate Hospitals on the Move: Samuel H. Stout and the Army of Tennessee.* Columbia: University of South Carolina Press, 1994.

Stout, Samuel H. "On the Best Models and Most Easily Constructed Military Hospital Wards for Temporary Use in War." *Transactions of the International Medical Congress* 9th session, vol. 2 (1887): 88–91.

HOSPITALS, "PEST" (SMALLPOX)

Because smallpox was such a deadly and contagious disease, doctors in both the Union and Confederate armies quickly determined that smallpox patients should be isolated from the rest of the sick and wounded. Depending on the size of the hospital or post and the number of cases involved, the smallpox victims might be isolated in one or more tents or in separate buildings.

In large towns, the post surgeons established separate smallpox hospitals, often called "pest" hospitals. Sometimes these were known as "eruptive" hospitals because they also received patients with other contagious diseases that produced spots or lesions, such as measles or erysipelas. Well-informed doctors isolated patients with different diseases in separate wards or tents. Smallpox patients usually had a staff detailed solely to their care.

While some smallpox hospitals occupied buildings, others used tents. Many doctors believed that the increased ventilation of tents improved patients' health and reduced mortality. In addition, should the hospital need to evacuate, as was often the case in the Confederate Army of Tennessee, the tents, bedding, and hospital clothing of the smallpox ward could be burned to prevent accidental use by noninfected patients.

Union forces had a 750-bed smallpox hospital in Memphis by 1864. One of the largest Confederate smallpox hospitals was Howard's Grove in Richmond, Virginia, built in what had been a popular picnic area. Smallpox cases discovered in other

Richmond hospitals were immediately transported to Howard's Grove, which also accepted civilian smallpox patients. Howard's Grove eventually had a capacity of over 1,800, although not all parts of the hospital were used for contagious diseases. After Richmond fell, Union forces continued to use Howard's Grove as a smallpox hospital.

See also: Erysipelas; Hospital Relocations; Measles; Richmond, Virginia; Tents, Hospital; Ventilation.

Bibliography

Adams, George Worthington. *Doctors in Blue: The Medical History of the Union Army in the Civil War.* New York: Schuman, 1952; reprint, Dayton, OH: Morningside, 1985.

Waitt, Robert W., Jr. *Confederate Military Hospitals in Richmond.* Richmond, VA: Richmond Civil War Centennial Committee, 1964.

HOSPITALS, PRE–CIVIL WAR *See* Hospitals, Antebellum.

HOSPITALS, RECEIVING AND DISTRIBUTING

Receiving and distributing hospitals, also called depot hospitals or clearing hospitals in the North, were located in large cities that were hospital centers or at transfer points where patients changed modes of transportation. The purpose of these hospitals was to serve as triage centers, in modern terminology. The doctors assigned patients to other hospitals in the city or forwarded them to another town. The hospitals also provided short-term medical care until the patients could be taken to their destination.

In Chattanooga, Tennessee, in 1862–1863 the Confederate Army of Tennessee used a hotel across the street from the railroad depot as a receiving and distributing hospital, while in Atlanta, Georgia, the army used a large shed. At City Point, Virginia, on the James River, the sick and wounded from the Union Army of the Potomac's Petersburg Campaign in 1864–1865 arrived by rail and waited in a depot hospital, consisting of wooden pavilions and hospital tents, for hospital boats to take them north to Washington, DC, or other hospital centers.

The distinguishing factor of receiving and distributing hospitals was the short stay and constant turnover of the patients. Ideally, patients remained for just a few hours, resting and receiving food, water, medication, and limited medical attention, such as having their dressings changed. In Atlanta, the surgeon in charge of the receiving and distributing hospital used the fact that the patients spent only a few hours in the bed while wearing their dirty clothes as an excuse to change and wash the bed linen only twice a month. In some cases, such as the City Point depot hospital, which had more than 8,000 beds, a patient might remain several days.

After a battle, hundreds of patients could arrive at a receiving and distributing hospital in a single day. More than 65,000 soldiers passed through three Union depot hospitals in Virginia in the summer of 1864 alone.

Similar to receiving and distributing hospitals, wayside hospitals were mostly rest and feeding stations that did not provide much medical care, nor did they assign patients to hospitals.

See also: Hospital Ships; Hospitals, Pavilion; Hospitals, Wayside; Tents, Hospital.

Bibliography
Bollet, Alfred Jay. *Civil War Medicine: Challenges and Triumphs.* Tucson, AZ: Galen, 2002.

Schroeder-Lein, Glenna R. *Confederate Hospitals on the Move: Samuel H. Stout and the Army of Tennessee.* Columbia: University of South Carolina Press, 1994.

HOSPITALS, REGIMENTAL *See* Hospitals, Field.

HOSPITALS, WAYSIDE

Wayside hospitals developed in both the South and the North to provide food and a brief rest for soldiers in transit to or from the field. They were located at depots along railroad lines or where soldiers transferred from trains to boats. Often there were no other hospitals in the area.

Although they were similar to receiving and distributing hospitals, wayside hospitals were less involved in acute care and did not assign patients to other hospitals. They especially helped convalescents on the way to or from furloughs at home, as well as those who had medical discharges.

Wayside hospitals were often initially developed and at least partially staffed by local women's relief organizations to meet the needs of soldiers passing through. In a law passed on May 1, 1863, the Confederate Congress specifically directed the surgeon general to establish such "way hospitals." There were seventeen in Virginia and North Carolina, as well as others in Georgia, South Carolina, Alabama, and Mississippi. In the North, members of the U.S. Sanitary Commission or the U.S. Christian Commission set up feeding stations that functioned as wayside hospitals.

See also: Convalescents; Hospitals, Receiving and Distributing; United States Christian Commission; United States Sanitary Commission; Women's Hospital Auxiliaries and Relief Societies.

Bibliography
Cunningham, H.H. *Doctors in Gray: The Confederate Medical Service.* Baton Rouge: Louisiana State University Press, 1958; reprint, Gloucester, MA: Peter Smith, 1970.

INFECTIONS, OF WOUNDS

Because of the general lack of cleanliness during the Civil War and the medical profession's ignorance of the role of bacteria, most wounds, from minor cuts and scrapes to major gunshot wounds, became infected to some degree. Doctors, both North and South, were generally surprised when a wound healed "by first intention," meaning without infection.

In order to prevent infection, doctors knew that it was important to clean the wound by removing bullets, grass, dirt, bits of clothing, chips of bone, and dead tissue; but it was difficult to remove everything, so infection usually followed. Because minié balls often created messy wounds, immediate amputation was often regarded as the best way to save the patient from death by infection, even at the cost of his limb.

Doctors who observed that a wound had "laudable pus" did not mean that pus was necessary, but that "good" pus represented a minor infection from which the patient was likely to recover. Minor infections were the most common types of infection. Malodorous pus tended to indicate the presence of pyemia, or "blood poisoning," a dreaded infection, now known to be streptococcal, that killed more than 90 percent of those who contracted it.

More common than pyemia but equally feared were two other serious streptococcal infections, erysipelas and hospital gangrene. Erysipelas, a severe skin infection, was extremely contagious and could be contracted in even the smallest scratch or mosquito bite. It caused redness, swelling, and damage to tissues beneath the skin. If it infected the lymph nodes, it spread through the bloodstream as pyemia.

Hospital gangrene was very uncommon early in the war and also uncommon in field or temporary hospitals. Since it appeared and spread quickly in larger urban hospitals, it may have been a virulent combination of several types of bacteria. A person with hospital gangrene developed a gray edge to his wound that sloughed off and spread rapidly.

Patients with hospital gangrene and erysipelas were moved to a separate building or tent to prevent the spread of infection to other patients. The most effective treatment was to clean the wound with nitric acid, iodine, carbolic acid, or bromine, a procedure so painful that the patient was anesthetized first. In the later years of the war bromine seems to have been used with better results than the other solutions. Nevertheless, serious wound infections proved fatal to many soldiers who otherwise would have recovered.

See also: Amputation; Anesthesia; Antiseptics and Disinfectants; Erysipelas; Gangrene, Hospital; Minié Balls; Mortality, of Soldiers; Tents, Hospital.

Bibliography
Bollet, Alfred Jay. *Civil War Medicine: Challenges and Triumphs.* Tucson, AZ: Galen, 2002.

INSANITY

At the time of the Civil War the definition of insanity was not very precise but included three categories: (1) mania—agitation without evident physical cause, such as a fever; (2) melancholia—extreme depression or lethargy; and (3) dementia—problems with the thinking processes. Not a large number of soldiers suffered from insanity during the Civil War, but those who did had to be cared for.

Volunteers who were known to be insane before they joined the service were promptly rejected by examining doctors. However, some soldiers developed mental problems as a result of diseases such as high fevers or the late stages of syphilis. A number had head injuries caused by saber wounds, gunshot wounds, or accidents that left them with mental impairments such as insanity, "partial insanity," or "temporary insanity." Some men probably also suffered from what is today called post–traumatic stress disorder. Doctors tended to be suspicious of soldiers who had symptoms of insanity without any obvious physical cause, as malingerers sometimes tried to feign insanity.

In the North, 819 white soldiers were listed as discharged from the service because of insanity, 432 of them in 1863. After 1863, soldiers with mental problems were supposed to be sent to the Government Hospital for the Insane in Washington, DC, rather than be discharged by the local military officers. Despite this policy, a number of the insane were committed to local asylums or the care of their families. President Abraham Lincoln ordered one man pardoned and discharged rather than shot for desertion because the soldier was insane.

Evidently not enough Confederate soldiers suffered from insanity to cause a significant problem until June 1864, when one medical director suggested establishing a hospital for the insane in North Carolina. Nothing came of this recommendation. In Virginia, at least, soldiers exhibiting signs of insanity were to be brought before a justice of the peace and committed to the nearest civilian insane asylum. Not until March 27, 1865, was the Louisiana Hospital in Richmond, Virginia, selected for a mental hospital, and by then the war was ending.

See also: Gunshot Wounds; Malingerers; Post–Traumatic Stress Disorder; Venereal Disease.

Bibliography

Barnes, Joseph K., ed. *The Medical and Surgical History of the War of the Rebellion (1861–65)*. Washington, DC: Government Printing Office, 1870–1888; reprint, Wilmington, NC: Broadfoot, 1990.

Cunningham, H.H. *Doctors in Gray: The Confederate Medical Service*. Baton Rouge: Louisiana State University Press, 1959; reprint, Gloucester, MA: Peter Smith, 1970.

Dean, Eric T., Jr. *Shook Over Hell: Post-Traumatic Stress, Vietnam, and the Civil War*. Cambridge, MA: Harvard University Press, 1997.

INSPECTORS, MEDICAL

Both the North and the South used official and unofficial medical inspectors to improve the conditions of army life and, especially, patient care for hospitalized soldiers. The healthier the soldiers were, the more of them would be available to fight, an important consideration during the Civil War.

In 1861, in the North, the newly organized U.S. Sanitary Commission immediately acted upon its concern about poor sanitation and lack of supplies for the troops by sending out qualified civilian inspectors. These were usually doctors who were too elderly to enlist or whose medical practices were too busy for them to join the army, but who worked as inspectors on a temporary basis, usually for a month.

The inspectors arrived unexpectedly at any hour of the day or night and usually received good cooperation from the medical officers on duty. The commission devised a questionnaire with 175 to 200 questions about all aspects of camp or hospital life to be examined in detail by the inspectors. At first the commission operated without cooperation from Surgeon General Clement A. Finley. However, after William A. Hammond became surgeon general in April 1862, he invited the commission inspectors to continue their work. The peak period for Sanitary Commission inspectors seems to have been from September 1862 to May 1863.

In December 1862, Congress passed legislation establishing the office of medical inspector general for the army with sixteen subordinate inspectors. These inspectors were to receive the rank and pay of a lieutenant colonel of cavalry. Although some people complained that the army inspectors focused more on military minutiae than on sanitary issues, the inspectors generally did what the Sanitary Commission had done. As the new department geared up, the commission inspectors gradually phased out. Indeed, after 1864, the new surgeon general, Joseph K. Barnes, who was not fond of the Sanitary Commission, refused to allow commission men to inspect. However, by this time conditions had improved markedly, and with the army inspectors in place, there was little need for commission inspectors.

The Confederates did not have a Sanitary Commission, but they did have a small number of regional medical inspectors, six in the field and seven in the hospitals, as of 1864. However, a great many Confederate inspections seem to have been performed by people who were not officially titled inspectors. As early as the summer of 1861, an experienced military officer inspected the hospital of the

Third Tennessee Regiment and explained what needed to be done to bring it up to military standards. General Braxton Bragg, accompanied by several doctors, personally performed a very thorough inspection of hospitals in Chattanooga, Tennessee, in July 1862.

At the most local level, the officer of the day in a general hospital was supposed to perform a thorough inspection of the hospital premises. Surgeons in charge of hospitals usually held a weekly inspection. A temporary commission of several doctors might be formed to inspect and report on a particular problem and recommend a solution. Surgeons from one location might be sent to inspect possible sites where new hospitals could be established. In addition, departmental medical directors and their assistants, as well as post surgeons, performed inspections.

The purpose of inspections on both sides included preventive measures to resolve sanitation and other issues before they caused illness. In addition to making extensive reports to supervisors and the surgeon general, the inspectors were supposed to make recommendations on the spot to solve problems quickly.

Inspectors were to examine conditions not only in hospitals, but in camps and on troop and hospital transports as well. Buildings were inspected for good repair, cleanliness, ventilation, drainage, light, heat, and overcrowding. Were latrines or water closets functioning, clean, and odor-free? Did the soldiers use them? What type of water supply served the camp or hospital? Was it subject to contamination by sewage, cooking waste, or drainage problems? Were there enough bathing facilities and did the soldiers use them regularly? Was the diet of the troops or patients adequate? Was the food plentiful, in good condition, properly stored, and well cooked? Were there appropriate delicacies for the very ill? Were the diet tables for patients properly followed? Were the kitchens clean, properly arranged, and equipped with enough cooking utensils and plates, bowls, and cups for serving?

Did there seem to be any epidemic disease in the area and was there any evident cause? Were there any local sources of malaria, such as marshes? Did the sick and wounded have enough doctors, nurses, and other attendants? Did these helpers know how to perform their jobs and did they care for the patients well? Were sufficient medicines available, stored and dispensed according to regulations? Were there clean and adequate bedding and hospital clothing? Were the hospital wards quiet and orderly? Was the transportation for the sick and wounded—ambulances, wagons, trains, and ships—appropriate, adequate, as comfortable as possible, and clean?

Inspections, whether by official or unofficial inspectors, contributed tremendously to improvements in camp and hospital cleanliness and troop health. By the end of the war, most doctors, hospitals, and army camps operated in significantly more sanitary ways than they had at the beginning of the conflict.

See also: Ambulances; Ambulance Trains; Barnes, Joseph K.; Diet, of Hospital Patients; Diet, of Troops; Finley, Clement Alexander; Hammond, William Alexander; Hospital Buildings; Hospital Ships; Hospitals, Field; Hospitals, General; Latrines;

Malaria; Officer of the Day; Sanitation; Surgeon General; Surgeons, Post; United States Sanitary Commission; Ventilation.

Bibliography

Bollet, Alfred Jay. *Civil War Medicine: Challenges and Triumphs.* Tucson, AZ: Galen, 2002.

Greenleaf, Charles R. *A Manual for the Medical Officers of the United States Army.* Philadelphia: J.B. Lippincott, 1864; reprint, San Francisco: Norman, 1992.

Schroeder-Lein, Glenna R. *Confederate Hospitals on the Move: Samuel H. Stout and the Army of Tennessee.* Columbia: University of South Carolina Press, 1994.

INTERMITTENT FEVERS *See* Malaria.

INVALID CORPS

Both the North and the South developed an "invalid corps," a group of soldiers who, as a result of disease or injuries, were no longer able to endure service in the field but could perform guard duty, clerical tasks, or other light activities. Later in the war the North called this group the Veteran Reserve Corps.

The Invalid Corps in the North was organized in April 1863. It consisted of 161 companies divided into two battalions. The First Battalion was made up of men who were able to do guard duty at various sites, including hospitals. The Second Battalion included men who were able to serve as nurses, cooks, clerks, and other attendants, particularly in general hospitals behind the lines. Most of the men were transferred to the corps from general hospitals or convalescent camps, although some came from the field. Some soldiers were assigned to the corps immediately after enlistment, such as those who were extremely nearsighted. By October 1863 Acting Surgeon General Joseph K. Barnes thought that the Invalid Corps showed real promise for providing permanent nursing and other staff for the hospitals.

There were some problems with the Invalid Corps, however. Rumors spread that it was a place for cowards, malingerers who were faking disabilities, disagreeable enlisted men, and incompetent officers. Some soldiers preferred to be furloughed home or discharged if they could not return to their regiment. Members of the corps resented the teasing and harassment from healthy soldiers and hospital patients implying that corps members were cowards, fakers, or physical wrecks. Making the harassment even worse was a distinctive corps uniform and badge with *IC* for Invalid Corps. As it happened, the quartermaster department used the abbreviation *IC* to mark broken equipment and animals as "inspected and condemned" for disposal.

In March 1864 the Invalid Corps was reorganized as the Veteran Reserve Corps (VRC). Although the corps contained the same structure of two battalions with the same responsibilities, it had somewhat different membership. Soldiers who had completed their three-year enlistment and did not wish to reenlist for combat could enlist in the VRC instead. The provost marshal general was the commander of the corps and appointed the officers, squelching rumors of officer incompetence.

One important duty of Second Battalion corps members was to handle the paperwork of the hospitals. The senior VRC officer was in charge of the paperwork. VRC clerks checked in new patients, prepared muster rolls for payment and discharge of soldiers, kept track of soldiers' clothing and equipment, managed their descriptive rolls, prepared inventories of the belongings of soldiers who died, and saw that the deceased were properly buried. According to the regulations, all hospital clerks, ward masters, nurses, cooks, and similar attendants were supposed to be members of the VRC. Physically fit soldiers were not permitted to be detailed to hospital duty. At least some reports suggest that the VRC members made good clerks but less successful nurses.

Members of the First Battalion of the corps performed service as hospital guards, especially to prevent convalescent patients from sneaking out of the hospital and getting into trouble in bars and brothels. In addition, members of the VRC helped to defend Washington, DC, against Confederate general Jubal Early's raid in the summer of 1864. About 60,000 men served in the IC and the VRC during the Civil War.

The Confederacy's Invalid Corps was organized almost a year later than the Union corps. In December 1863, President Jefferson Davis proposed the establishment of an invalid corps to do many light-duty tasks, thus allowing healthy soldiers on detached service to return to the field. The Confederate Congress passed "An Act to Provide an Invalid Corps," which went into effect on February 17, 1864.

The Confederate corps was somewhat different than its Union counterpart. A smaller number of men, roughly 6,200, were members of the Invalid Corps. Those able to do light duty served as guards and clerks, as did the Northerners; but about one-third of the Confederate members were listed as totally disabled. They remained in the corps on retired or discharged status, essentially getting a sort of disability pay. Each member of the corps was supposed to have a physical examination every six months to see if his status had changed. Anyone who was restored to health was to return to his command.

See also: Barnes, Joseph K.; Cooks; Convalescents; Davis, Jefferson; Hospital Paperwork; Hospital Support Staff; Hospitals, General; Malingerers; Nurses; Ward Masters.

Bibliography

Adams, George Worthington. *Doctors in Blue: The Medical History of the Union Army in the Civil War.* New York: Schuman, 1952; reprint, Dayton, OH: Morningside, 1985.

Cunningham, H.H. *Doctors in Gray: The Confederate Medical Service.* Baton Rouge: Louisiana State University Press, 1958; reprint, Gloucester, MA: Peter Smith, 1970.

Greenleaf, Charles R. *A Manual for the Medical Officers of the United States Army.* Philadelphia: J.B. Lippincott, 1864; reprint, San Francisco: Norman, 1992.

J

JACKSON, THOMAS JONATHAN ("STONEWALL") (1824–1863)

Thomas Jonathan Jackson, nicknamed "Stonewall," who became one of the most successful and famous of Southern generals, was born on January 21, 1824, in Clarksburg, now West Virginia. His father, Jonathan Jackson, an impecunious lawyer, and his older sister, Elizabeth, died of typhoid fever when Thomas was two. His mother, Julia Beckwith Neale Jackson (Woodson) died when Thomas was seven, leaving him and his younger sister Laura to be raised by Jackson uncles.

Thomas's early education was quite weak, leaving him barely able to pass the entrance exams when he was admitted to West Point. He studied diligently and raised his ranking until he graduated seventeenth of fifty-nine in the class of 1846. Jackson earned assignment to the artillery, the branch of service he wanted. He went to Mexico immediately and served under General Winfield Scott in the siege of Vera Cruz and the Mexico City campaign. Jackson's actions with his battery at Contreras and Chapultepec resulted in two brevets. While stationed in Mexico, he began a serious study of the Bible and Christianity, having already been converted when in his teens.

In his youth Jackson had suffered from dyspepsia (indigestion), which became worse while he was stationed at Fort Hamilton, New York. He devised strict dietary rules for himself to cope with what was probably reflux esophagitis. He also developed an eye inflammation and began to take water cures as a useful remedy for his ailments. Historians have noted that Jackson seemed to be extremely health-conscious and even a hypochondriac while in fairly inactive positions, stationed in New York or teaching at the Virginia Military Institute (VMI). However, his health improved dramatically at West Point, in Mexico, and during the Civil War.

After a bad experience with his superior in Florida, Jackson resigned from the U.S. Army and accepted a job at VMI in Lexington, teaching natural and experimental philosophy (basically physics) and artillery tactics. He was not a good teacher because he was totally inflexible, humorless, and unable to give helpful explanations. He joined the Presbyterian church in 1851, eventually becoming a deacon and teaching a Sunday school class for slaves. On August 4, 1853, he married Elinor Junkin, who bled to death after the birth of a stillborn son on October

22, 1854. Jackson married his second wife, Mary Anna Morrison, on July 16, 1857. Their first daughter died in 1858 at the age of three weeks. Both Mary Anna and their second daughter, Julia, born November 23, 1862, outlived Jackson.

On December 2, 1859, Jackson led a detachment of VMI cadets at the hanging of abolitionist and Harpers Ferry raider John Brown in Charlestown, [West] Virginia. Although Jackson was a Unionist during the secession crisis, he supported his state and joined the Confederacy when Virginia seceded. He left Lexington with the VMI cadets on April 21, 1861. Commissioned a colonel, Jackson was ordered to Harpers Ferry, where he shaped raw recruits into a disciplined brigade. He became a brigadier general in June 1861.

At the First Battle of Bull Run (Manassas) on July 21, 1861, Jackson and his brigade earned the nickname "Stonewall" for their firm stand on Henry House Hill. During this battle, Jackson was wounded in his left middle finger. A bullet broke the bone and carried away a small piece of it. Jackson did not go to a field hospital until after the battle. The first doctor he saw wanted to amputate the finger, so Jackson left the hospital and found Dr. Hunter Holmes McGuire. McGuire put a splint on the finger and wrapped it in lint, telling Jackson to keep the dressing wet with cold water. Although Jackson obeyed scrupulously, pouring cups of what turned out to be contaminated cold water on the wound contributed to infection. Jackson suffered pain for some time, but his finger healed without deformity.

Jackson had few other major medical problems during the war. After his successful campaign in the Shenandoah Valley in 1862, he suffered extreme exhaustion that dulled his ability to command effectively during the Seven Days battles. On September 6, 1862, a horse reared and fell on him, stunning him and causing enough pain that he had to ride in an ambulance for a few days. In January 1863 Jackson suffered a severe earache, forcing him to move from a tent into a plantation office building for protection from the elements.

None of these difficulties hampered his leadership at the battles of Second Bull Run, Antietam, Fredericksburg, and Chancellorsville. On May 2, 1863, at Chancellorsville, Jackson took a large part of Robert E. Lee's Army of Northern Virginia on a long flanking march around portions of the Union army in order to strike and successfully rout the unsuspecting corps of Union general Oliver O. Howard. Later that evening, Jackson and eighteen others went on a reconnaissance. As they were returning to Confederate lines, Southern troops mistakenly opened fire on the party, killing four and wounding Jackson and three others.

Jackson, in pain, had to be helped to the rear as the group came under Union artillery bombardment. Part of the time he was carried on a litter, which was dropped when one of the litter-bearers was shot and wounded, and then a second time when a litter-bearer tripped over a root or vine. Finally, he was taken to a field hospital by ambulance. By this time Jackson was in shock. It was 2:00 a.m. before doses of whiskey and water revived him enough that he could receive chloroform and have his wounds examined by Dr. McGuire and three other experienced surgeons.

Jackson had been hit by three bullets. The least serious shot went through the palm of his right hand, breaking two fingers. The doctors removed the ball, splinted the hand, and applied a lint and cold-water dressing. The other two shots were so serious that they rendered the amputation of Jackson's left arm necessary. One bullet had gone through his forearm from the outside, about an inch below the elbow, to the inside, about an inch above the wrist. The other had gone through the arm about three inches below the shoulder, breaking the bone and cutting an artery. Dr. McGuire amputated the arm two inches below the shoulder.

Initially, Jackson's wound and amputation healed well. Since 82 percent of soldiers with an amputation of Jackson's type recovered, Jackson was expected to recover as well. He was moved further away from the lines to the office outbuilding on the Chandler plantation at Guiney Station. Here, on May 7, the doctors discovered that he had developed pneumonia, probably because of lung injuries when the litter-bearers dropped him. No medical treatments of the period could cure him, and Jackson died at 3:15 p.m. on May 10, 1863. Because of Jackson's prominence, his wounding and death made him one of the most famous casualties of the Civil War.

See also: Alcohol, Medicinal Uses of; Ambulances; Amputation; Anesthesia; Antietam, Battle of; Bull Run (Manassas), First Battle of; Bull Run (Manassas), Second Battle of; Fredericksburg, Battle of; Gunshot Wounds, Treatment of; Hospitals, Field; Infections, of Wounds; McGuire, Hunter Holmes; Pneumonia; Splints.

Bibliography

Robertson, James I., Jr. *Stonewall Jackson: The Man, the Soldier, the Legend.* New York: Macmillan, 1997.

Welsh, Jack D. *Medical Histories of Confederate Generals.* Kent, OH: Kent State University Press, 1995.

JOHNSTON, ALBERT SIDNEY (1803–1862)

Confederate general Albert Sidney Johnston, the highest-ranking officer on either side to be killed during the Civil War, was born in Washington, Kentucky, on February 2, 1803, the son of John and Abigail Harris Johnston. Because his physician father wanted his son to follow in his career footsteps, Johnston went to Transylvania University in 1818. Here, in 1821, he met Jefferson Davis, with whom he developed a friendship that continued when both attended West Point. Johnston graduated from the military academy eighth in the class of 1826.

Assigned to the Sixth Infantry as a second lieutenant, Johnston served in several posts and participated in the Black Hawk War in 1832. In 1829 he had married Henrietta Preston of Louisville, Kentucky. By 1834 they had three small children and Henrietta was suffering from tuberculosis. Because of his wife's illness, Johnston resigned from the army. In 1835 Henrietta and a daughter died, and Johnston was having no luck with farming. As a result, in 1836 he joined the army of the Republic of Texas, serving in several high-ranking capacities and, briefly, as secretary of war.

In 1843 he married Eliza Griffin, the cousin of his first wife. The family moved to Galveston, Texas, where Johnston had his usual lack of success as a planter. During the Mexican War, Johnston was a temporary staff officer for Zachary Taylor, distinguishing himself at the Battle of Monterrey. After the war, Taylor, then president, got Johnston appointed paymaster for the forts in western Texas. Then, in 1854, Jefferson Davis, now secretary of war, gave Johnston command of the Second Cavalry regiment. Johnston also commanded, with considerable tact, an 1859 expedition against rebellious Mormons.

Johnston had just been assigned to a command on the Pacific Coast when the Civil War began. When his adopted state of Texas seceded, Johnston resigned his commission, traveled cross country, and arrived in Richmond, Virginia, in September 1861, where he reported for duty to his friend Davis, now the Confederate president.

Davis had a high regard for Johnston and by various statements contributed to inflated expectations of what Johnston, now a full general, could achieve as commander of the Confederacy's western department. Johnston immediately encountered a number of problems beyond his control. First, the department was huge, including parts of Mississippi, Alabama, Louisiana, Tennessee, Arkansas, Kentucky, Missouri, Kansas, and Indian Territory. Second, although he never had enough men and equipment, he was unable to persuade Davis that there was an urgent need for both. Third, Johnston had a great deal of trouble with his subordinates. General Leonidas Polk, who had been Johnston's roommate at West Point, was guilty of gross insubordination by ignoring Johnston's numerous orders about fortifying strategic places. All three senior commanders at Fort Donelson were incompetent, finally surrendering the fort. P.G.T. Beauregard planned the march to and battle at Shiloh poorly, making matters overly complicated for inexperienced troops. Johnston put more faith in these men than was warranted, without checking up on them.

At the Battle of Shiloh on April 6, 1862, Johnston was riding with his medical director, Dr. David W. Yandell, and Tennessee governor Isham G. Harris. Johnston ordered Yandell to stay behind to care for some Federal wounded. Johnston was soon hit by a spent ball on his right thigh, a shell fragment just above and back of his right hip, and a minié ball, which cut the sole of his left boot. He was also shot in the right leg, below the knee. The bullet went about halfway into the leg and tore an artery, right where it divided into two other arteries. Because no one located where this serious wound was, Johnston lost consciousness and bled to death within half an hour. Ironically, he had a tourniquet in his pocket, which Yandell had given to him earlier.

Ever since, much lost cause speculation has centered on whether the South would have won at Shiloh, and perhaps even won the war, if Albert Sidney Johnston, a high-ranking general, had not died at an early stage of the war.

See also: Davis, Jefferson; Gunshot Wounds; Medical Directors, Field; Minié Balls; Shiloh, Battle of (1862).

Bibliography

Castel, Albert. "Dead on Arrival: The Life and Sudden Death of General Albert Sidney Johnston." *Civil War Times* (March 1997): 30–37.

Engle, Stephen D. "'Thank God, He Has Rescued His Character': Albert Sidney Johnston, Southern Hamlet of the Confederacy." In *Leaders of the Lost Cause: New Perspectives on the Confederate High Command,* ed. Gary W. Gallagher and Joseph T. Glatthaar, 133–163. Mechanicsburg, PA: Stackpole, 2004.

Welsh, Jack D. *Medical Histories of Confederate Generals.* Kent, OH: Kent State University Press, 1995.

Woodworth, Steven E. "When Merit Was Not Enough: Albert Sidney Johnston and Confederate Defeat in the West, 1862." In *Civil War Generals in Defeat,* ed. Steven E. Woodworth, 9–27. Lawrence: University Press of Kansas, 1999.

JOHNSTON, JOSEPH EGGLESTON (1807–1891)

Confederate general Joseph Eggleston Johnston was born at Cherry Grove near Farmville, Virginia, on February 3, 1807, the son of Peter and Mary Wood Johnston. Peter had been a Revolutionary War soldier, which influenced Joseph's attitudes and career, mainly because of expectations that Joseph put upon himself. When Joseph was about four, the family moved to Abingdon, Virginia, where his father was a judge.

Joseph attended West Point and graduated in 1829, thirteenth in the same class in which Robert E. Lee graduated second. This rivalry established at West Point eventually would be damaging to the Confederate war effort because Johnston was always exceedingly ambitious and fiercely protective of his own rank. After graduation, Johnston served in the Black Hawk War in Illinois, as well as in Virginia, South Carolina, Alabama, and Florida. A first lieutenant, Johnston resigned his commission in May 1837 because someone had been promoted over him.

Johnston became a civilian topographical engineer and joined a military expedition against the Seminole Indians in Florida. On January 15, 1838, Johnston took command when the expedition's officers were wounded. He also received a serious head injury from a bullet. During the summer of 1838 Johnston rejoined the U.S. Army as a first lieutenant in the topographical engineers unit, serving in Texas, New York, Washington, DC, and Florida and with various coast, waterway, and boundary surveys.

On July 10, 1845, Johnston married Lydia McLane of Baltimore. He was soon assigned to General Winfield Scott's forces during the Mexican War. Johnston was wounded twice in the battle at Cerro Gordo and once in the action at Chapultepec, earning several brevet ranks. After the war Johnston again worked with the topographical engineers until he became lieutenant colonel of the First Cavalry in 1855. Beginning June 30, 1860, he held the post of quartermaster general for the U.S. Army with the rank of brigadier general. Although he opposed secession, he resigned his commission on

April 22, 1861, because he felt obligated to go with his state when Virginia seceded.

Johnston soon accepted appointment in the Confederate army, rather than the Virginia state forces, because he believed he would get a higher rank. Confederate president Jefferson Davis assigned Johnston to command at Harpers Ferry, Virginia (now West Virginia). Immediately deciding that he could not defend it, Johnston planned to and withdrew his forces, a pattern that he followed wherever he was assigned throughout the war. While it was true that Harpers Ferry probably could not be defended because of its location, Johnston could have held it longer while removing more machinery and supplies, rather than destroying equipment that the Confederacy could not replace.

Possibly Johnston's best military action was rushing his troops by train in time for the First Battle of Manassas (or Bull Run, as the Union forces called it) in July 1861. Johnston evidently made the successful Confederate troop dispositions at the battle and was very unhappy that the public gave the credit to his colleague, General P.G.T. Beauregard, who had been in command of the troops in the area before Johnston came.

During the winter of 1861–1862, Johnston's relationships with President Davis, Davis's adviser Robert E. Lee, and other Confederate leaders continually worsened. Johnston always complained that he was not given enough troops and supplies, and he squabbled over issues of rank and authority. He also failed to inform Davis about his plans.

During the spring 1862 Peninsula Campaign, when Union general George B. McClellan brought his forces by ship to Fortress Monroe and then slowly marched them up the peninsula between the James and York rivers toward Richmond, Johnston commanded the Confederate forces. However, he could never see any location as worth fighting for. He was always afraid that his troops would be outflanked by Union ships on the York River. He lost the navy yard at Norfolk, Virginia, and much other material. To the alarm of most Confederates, Johnston retreated until the army was just a few miles from Richmond.

Johnston did attack Union forces at Seven Pines on May 31, 1862, but the battle did not go well because he did not give his orders clearly to all who needed them, resulting in much confusion. At about 7:00 p.m. Johnston was wounded by a musket ball that entered his right shoulder, breaking the shoulder blade, and a shell fragment that hit him in the chest and broke two ribs. Not surprisingly, he fell from his horse unconscious. As Dr. Edwin S. Gaillard was dressing Johnston's wounds, the doctor was himself wounded in the arm and had to have it amputated.

Unfortunately, Johnston's treatment included bleeding, blistering, and purging, which depleted his system as intended, leaving him still weak a month after he was wounded. Johnston expected that he would recover quickly and return to the command of the Army of Northern Virginia. Neither expectation came to pass. The day after Johnston was wounded, Jefferson Davis gave the army command to Johnston's competitor Robert E. Lee, who, of course, retained it until he surrendered at Appomattox Court House on April 9, 1865.

When Johnston finally returned to duty in November 1862, he still suffered pain. Davis assigned Johnston to command the Department of the West, a rather vague creation that covered most of the Confederacy west of the Appalachian Mountains and included supervision of armies under Braxton Bragg in Tennessee and John C. Pemberton in Mississippi. Johnston had little authority and did very little except argue on paper with the authorities in Richmond. During the crises of the spring and summer of 1863, Johnston did nothing to assist Pemberton at Vicksburg except to tell him to retreat and save his army, advice Pemberton did not take.

Although Johnston had been consistently obnoxious to Davis, Davis had a shortage of high-ranking generals, and in December 1863 he assigned Johnston to replace Bragg as commander of the Army of Tennessee. Johnston immediately began demanding more supplies, although he did not understand enough about administrative record keeping to monitor what he did have. He also failed to understand how the patient statistics in hospital morning reports related to the number of men available for duty. Never a fan of hospitals, Johnston blamed furloughs of the sick and wounded for the army's shrinking manpower. As the spring campaign of 1864 began, Johnston's slow retreat through Georgia caused massive problems for the medical department of the Army of Tennessee because the general hospitals behind the lines had to move again and again.

On July 17, 1864, Davis replaced Johnston, now on the outskirts of Atlanta, with the more aggressive John Bell Hood. This change did not save Atlanta and, during Hood's Tennessee campaign in the fall of 1864, cost much of the remaining strength and manpower of the Army of Tennessee. Davis put Johnston in command of the regiment on February 25, 1865, and Johnston surrendered to William T. Sherman on April 26, 1865.

After the war Johnston did civil engineering for several railroad companies and made a good deal of money working for an insurance company. He continued his written war against Jefferson Davis and other ex-Confederates with a book, *Narrative of Military Operations* (1874), and a number of vituperative articles in which Johnston always justified his own actions and viewpoint.

Johnston died on March 21, 1891, in Washington, DC, reportedly as a result of catching a cold while participating in William T. Sherman's funeral procession. However, his death certificate said he died of heart failure caused by fatty degeneration of the heart.

See also: Bull Run (Manassas), First Battle of; Cupping and Blistering; Davis, Jefferson; Gunshot Wounds, Treatment of; Hood, John Bell; Hospital Relocations; Hospitals, General; Peninsula Campaign.

Bibliography

Downs, Alan. "'The Responsibility Is Great': Joseph E. Johnston and the War in Virginia." In *Civil War Generals in Defeat,* ed. Steven E. Woodworth, 29–70. Lawrence: University Press of Kansas, 1999.

Krick, Robert K. "'Snarl and Sneer and Quarrel': General Joseph E. Johnston and an Obses- sion with Rank." In *Leaders of the Lost Cause: New Perspectives on the Confederate High Command,* ed. Gary W. Gallagher and Joseph T. Glatthaar, 165–203. Mechanicsburg, PA: Stackpole, 2004.

Schroeder-Lein, Glenna R. *Confederate Hospitals on the Move: Samuel H. Stout and the Army of Tennessee.* Columbia: University of South Carolina Press, 1994.

Welsh, Jack D. *Medical Histories of Confederate Generals.* Kent, OH: Kent State University Press, 1995.

JONES, JOSEPH (1833–1896)

Joseph Jones, a Confederate medical researcher, was born in Walthourville, Lib- erty County, Georgia, on September 6, 1833. The son of Charles Colcock Jones, a Presbyterian minister and plantation owner, and Mary Jones Jones, Joseph attended South Carolina College before graduating from Princeton in 1853. An avid scientific researcher, even as a youth, Jones graduated from the University of Pennsylvania medical school in 1856. Before the Civil War he briefly taught chemistry or natural science at Savannah Medical College, the University of Georgia (Athens), and the Medical College of Georgia (Augusta).

An ardent secessionist and Southern partisan, Jones served the Confederacy first as surgeon of the Liberty Independent Troop (October 1861–March 1862) and then as a contract physician at the general hospital in Augusta, Georgia. Always more interested in research than in practicing medicine, Jones began to study the diseases suffered by the Southern army. During the course of the war he focused on malaria, tetanus, pneumonia, typhoid fever, and hospital gangrene.

In November 1862 Jones passed the examination for Confederate surgeon, but was assigned to continue his research and report his findings to Surgeon General Samuel P. Moore rather than to serve with a regiment or in a hospital. From his home base of Augusta, he traveled to do research in South Carolina; Richmond, Charlottesville, and Lynchburg, Virginia; certain coastal areas of the South; the Army of Tennessee hospitals in and around Atlanta; and the camp for Union prisoners of war at Andersonville, Georgia. At each place Jones copied hospital records, made statistical studies of the diseases found there, and observed the progress of the diseases by studying the patients. At Andersonville he tried to discover the cause of the high mortality among the prisoners. His detailed report on the conditions at the prison led to his being called as a witness at the trial of post commander Henry Wirz in October 1865.

Jones also tried to gain information from other physicians by sending out exten- sive questionnaires, but most of the recipients were too busy treating casualties to respond. In fact, a number of physicians had a rather low opinion of Jones because they did not appreciate his poking around doing research when they desperately needed help to treat patients. Jones prepared at least four lengthy reports for the surgeon general during the war.

On October 26, 1859, Jones married Caroline Smelt Davis, by whom he had four children. After her death he married Susan Rayner Polk (June 21, 1870), and they eventually had three children. Jones spent most of his long postwar career as professor of chemistry and clinical medicine (1868–1894) at the University of Louisiana (Tulane). He died in New Orleans on February 17, 1896.

See also: Andersonville Prison; Gangrene, Hospital; Malaria; Moore, Samuel Preston; Pneumonia; Prisoners of War; Surgeons, Acting Assistant (Contract); Tetanus; Typhoid Fever.

Bibliography

Breeden, James O. *Joseph Jones, M.D.: Scientist of the Old South.* Lexington: University Press of Kentucky, 1975.

Myers, Robert Manson, ed. *Children of Pride: A True Story of Georgia and the Civil War.* New Haven, CT: Yale University Press, 1972.

L

LABORATORIES, MEDICAL

During the Civil War both the Union and the Confederate medical departments had supply tables that listed the types of medicines that could be stocked and prescribed for patients. Medical purveyors purchased and distributed these drugs. However, both sides experienced shortages and high prices, among other problems, which caused their respective surgeons general to establish medical laboratories to manufacture, test, and package medicines.

The U.S. Naval Laboratory had been functioning successfully since 1852. It was Surgeon General William A. Hammond's idea, by the fall of 1862, to create such a laboratory for the army. Hammond intended the laboratory to test the purity of liquors, drugs, and raw materials before the army purchased them from suppliers. The laboratory then was to produce or redistribute unadulterated medicines of standardized dosage in uniform packaging, saving the government the money being paid as profits to the drug companies, controlling the prices of medicines, and making sure that there was an adequate supply of medicine at all times.

Although a more or less authorized laboratory opened in St. Louis, Missouri, in 1863, it was closed by July because it manufactured inferior products. Two laboratories were finally established, in Astoria, New York, near New York City, and in Philadelphia. Instead of going through Secretary of War Edwin M. Stanton, whom Hammond expected to refuse permission to establish the laboratories, Hammond associated the facilities with the medical purveying depots, enabling the laboratories to use medical department funds. The Philadelphia lab began the rebottling of liquor and production of medicines in late April 1863. It produced well over 100 kinds of tinctures, extracts, powders, and pills. While some medicines were prepared from the raw ingredients, others, bought in bulk, were tested for quality and then repackaged for distribution. The Philadelphia lab also had a sewing department that produced bedding, curtains, towels, and hospital clothing. The lab employed several hundred workers, at least half of them women and girls.

The laboratory at Astoria was smaller and more controversial than that at Philadelphia. Drug manufacturers objected to government competition. However, in New York there was conflict between the purveyor and the laboratory director as well. The Astoria lab did not produce much until September 1863 and was not fully functional until February 1864. As at Philadelphia, about half of the workers were women, who rolled pills and tested and bottled the alcohol. At various times Astoria produced or packaged 105 medicines and medicinal liquors. On February 13, 1865, an accidental fire in the wood frame laboratory buildings ended production at Astoria, although the workers continued to bottle and package drugs and liquor manufactured elsewhere.

Although the medical laboratories probably saved the U.S. government some money, it is unclear how much, because the medical directors did not factor in other expenses paid by the government, such as rent and transportation costs covered by the quartermaster's department. The laboratories may have affected drug prices somewhat, especially with the threat to manufacture more products. However, other factors also affected the prices, such as need, availability, gold prices, and tariffs on imports. Although the laboratory products had uniform packaging, the medicines as a whole did not because the medical department still purchased much of the needed medicine from commercial manufacturers.

Neither Hammond nor his successor as surgeon general, Joseph K. Barnes, expected the government labs to continue after the war. Many of the surplus medicines and hospital supplies were sold at auction. The Astoria laboratory was completely closed by November 1865, and the Philadelphia lab by March or April 1868.

Less is known about the Confederate laboratories than about their Union counterparts because of the destruction of many records when Richmond, Virginia, burned in April 1865. There were, however, more Confederate medical laboratories. The first evidently opened in Richmond by late January 1862. The others, probably begun between mid-1862 and mid-1863, were located in Columbia, South Carolina; Arkadelphia, Arkansas; Atlanta and Macon, Georgia; Charlotte and Lincolnton, North Carolina; Mobile and Montgomery, Alabama; and possibly Little Rock, Arkansas; Jackson, Mississippi; Knoxville, Tennessee; and a few other places. Due to the threat of Union troops, the Arkadelphia lab moved to Tyler, Texas, and the one in Atlanta moved to Augusta, Georgia. There was evidently also a naval medical lab in Richmond, but virtually nothing is known about it.

The Confederates had serious drug shortages because the Union blockade of Southern ports prevented importation of needed medicines. Blockade-runners and the capture of Union supplies provided some medicines, but not a consistent or predictable amount. As a result, the medical laboratories were supposed to manufacture necessary drugs, such as the anesthetics ether and chloroform. The labs also experimented with indigenous plants in order to produce remedies that could replace such vital medicines as quinine, which were difficult to import.

The laboratories were usually, but not always, associated with a purveying depot and headed by a medical purveyor, such as John Julian Chisolm at the Columbia lab. In addition, the labs employed surgeons, hospital stewards, civilian pharmacists and chemists, disabled soldiers, and free blacks. Some labs had their own gardens where the staff grew opium poppies, sorghum, and flax, among other plants. However, virtually all the labs encouraged civilians to gather or, sometimes, to grow certain potentially medicinal plants. Although the labs planned to grind and process plants and minerals into extracts, tinctures, and other preparations, the Confederates generally had less and poorer equipment than the Union labs. Some of the medicine manufactured was of poor quality. Like the Union labs, the Confederates also distilled some medicinal liquors. None of the Confederate laboratories operated beyond the end of the war.

See also: Alcohol, Medicinal Uses of; Anesthesia; Barnes, Joseph K.; Blockade; Chisolm, John Julian; Hammond, William Alexander; Materia Medica; Medical Purveyors; Medication, Administration of; Quinine; *Resources of the Southern Fields and Forests*; Substitutes, for Supplies; Supply Table.

Bibliography

Flannery, Michael A. *Civil War Pharmacy: A History of Drugs, Drug Supply and Provision, and Therapeutics for the Union and Confederacy.* New York: Pharmaceutical Products Press, 2004.

Hasegawa, Guy R., and F. Terry Hambrecht. "The Confederate Medical Laboratories." *Southern Medical Journal* 96 (December 2003): 1221–1230.

Smith, George Winston. *Medicines for the Union Army: The United States Army Laboratories During the Civil War.* Madison, WI: American Institute for the History of Pharmacy, 1962; reprint, New York: Pharmaceutical Products Press, 2001.

LATRINES

Latrines were commonly called "sinks" by soldiers North and South during the Civil War. Improper preparation of latrines, and the failure of some soldiers to use them, caused great discomfort and much disease in virtually all the armies at times.

The common sink was a trench 10 to 12 feet long, 1 to 2 feet wide, and 6 to 8 feet deep. A crotched stick was placed at each end to hold a pole that functioned as a seat. Improvements on the conventional sink included boards with holes placed over the trench and, in the Union Army of the Cumberland, board platforms with kegs or cracker boxes for seats. Each day six inches of dirt was supposed to be shoveled into the sink to cover the waste. Ideally, carbolic acid or chlorinated lime would also be added to deodorize and sanitize the area. Some regiments surrounded the sink with brush to provide minimal privacy. When the sink was filled to within one and a half to two feet of the edge, it was supposed to be filled in and a new sink dug. Each regiment was supposed to have a sink on the left and right ends of the camp as well as a third sink for the officers.

Sinks were the source of a variety of problems. Early in the war many regiments failed to construct sinks at all. Soldiers from rural areas were used to using convenient bushes and continued the practice in camp. This habit led to filthy, offensive, and malodorous sites that quickly caused diseases such as typhoid fever, diarrhea, and dysentery. Even regiments that dug sinks could have similar problems if the officers did not enforce discipline and insist that the men use the sinks. One probably effective punishment, applied in some Union camps, was to force the offender to wear a barrel with his head protruding over the top and excrement piled under his nose.

Some sinks were poorly maintained. Soldiers in charge failed to cover the deposits with dirt every day. Men who were lazy or too ill to control themselves missed the sink, producing nasty areas around the edges of the latrine. The offensive smell caused some soldiers to avoid the sinks while others sought the bushes because of modesty. These actions only contributed to the problem.

Even a sink that was well maintained might be poorly located, in a place where the sewage seeped, drained, or overflowed into the camp water supply. Wells and streams were easily polluted with germs that caused intestinal diseases. Some latrines were located close to camp kitchens or cooking areas, where flies spread disease from the excrement to the food. In October 1861, the surgeon of the Third Tennessee Regiment (Confederate) complained that the men of the Eighteenth Tennessee were digging a sink right next to his regimental hospital. He protested that the latrine would contribute to the spread of disease and undo all the progress he had made toward cleanliness in his regiment.

Permanently located hospitals also had to provide latrines for their patients. Confederate Army of Tennessee surgeons searching for locations to establish hospitals behind the lines considered whether the site had a rapidly moving river or stream where an outhouse could be built over the water so the waste would be carried away.

A number of hospitals had indoor water closets of some sort. They might have a rudimentary flush mechanism activated by pulling the chain to a cistern. The water carried the waste directly into a sewer, but there was nothing to keep noxious odors and gases from coming back up into the water closet. A hospital in Central Park in New York City had water closets on all the floors, but the building was so tall that the pressure was insufficient to get water for flushing to the upper floors.

Some hospitals had toilets that had to be flushed by using a bucket of water. Since that water usually had to be hauled from a distance, the facilities were not flushed as often as they should have been. Another variety, especially popular in Philadelphia hospitals, was a long, slightly slanted zinc trough. The trough had a cover with a number of seat holes. At the upper end was a faucet that could be turned on to flush the waste down a sewer hole at the other end. Ideally the water was always on to keep the trough clean, but, practically, this used too much water, so waste and odor accumulated between periodic flushes.

An indoor latrine did little good if the soldiers did not know how to use it. The patients at the Gordon Hospital in Nashville, Tennessee, in November 1861 used the water closets like a trash can, throwing in paper, sticks, cloth, and other rubbish. Not surprisingly, the drainpipes plugged up and filthy sewage overflowed the hospital to such an extent that the patients had to be moved out and the hospital closed and thoroughly cleaned.

The efforts of the U.S. Sanitary Commission in the Union army, as well as medical inspectors, surgeons, and army officers on both sides, led to considerable improvement in sanitation as the war progressed. It was evident that well-disciplined regiments, with properly prepared and used latrines, had much less sickness than unsanitary regiments.

See also: Antiseptics and Disinfectants; Diarrhea and Dysentery; Hospitals, General; Inspectors, Medical; Sanitation; Stout, Samuel Hollingsworth; Typhoid Fever; United States Sanitary Commission.

Bibliography

Adams, George Worthington. *Doctors in Blue: The Medical History of the Union Army in the Civil War.* New York: Schuman, 1952; reprint, Dayton, OH: Morningside, 1985.

Calhoun, J. Theodore. "Rough Notes of an Army Surgeon's Experience During the Great Rebellion." *Medical and Surgical Reporter* Whole Series no. 316, New Series vol. 9, no. 6 (November 8, 1862): 149–150; reprint, *Journal of Civil War Medicine* 9 (January–March 2005): 17–18.

Schroeder-Lein, Glenna R. *Confederate Hospitals on the Move: Samuel Hollingsworth Stout and the Army of Tennessee.* Columbia: University of South Carolina Press, 1994.

Woodward, Joseph Janvier. *The Hospital Steward's Manual: For the Instruction of Hospital Stewards, Ward-Masters, and Attendants, in Their Several Duties.* Philadelphia: J.B. Lippincott, 1862; reprint, San Francisco: Norman, 1991.

LAUDANUM

Laudanum was an opiate widely used as a painkiller in the nineteenth century. Both civilians and the military used it during the Civil War. Probably the most easily available of the opiates, laudanum was a liquid with about 10 percent opium in an alcohol solution. It did not require a prescription and could be procured from physicians, druggists, and patent medicine salespeople. It was administered to both adults and children.

Besides being used as a painkiller, laudanum was also a sedative and an effective treatment for diarrhea. Because physicians and patients during the nineteenth century had little idea that opiates could be habit-forming, their widespread use in treating common medical problems led to many instances of opiate addiction.

See also: Alcohol, Medicinal Uses of; Diarrhea and Dysentery; Morphine; Opiate Use and Addiction.

Bibliography

Bollet, Alfred Jay. *Civil War Medicine: Challenges and Triumphs.* Tucson, AZ: Galen, 2002.

LAUNDRESSES

Both Union and Confederate hospitals were authorized to employ laundresses at the rate of one for every twenty patients. The laundresses were selected and hired by the surgeon in charge of the hospital. Union laundresses were to be paid six dollars per month plus a daily ration, while the Confederates offered eight dollars per month and a ration. These relatively low wages for washing very messy and often infectious clothing and bedding frequently made it difficult to hire laundresses at all. Eventually the Union medical department used the term *matron* to refer to those who did the laundry in hospitals while calling those who did washing for the soldiers in the field laundresses.

Soldiers' wives received priority in hiring, but other white women also worked as laundresses, as did black women, both slave and free. Some soldiers also worked as "laundresses." At the Confederate hospital for chronic cases in Cherokee Springs, Georgia, in 1863, a soldier and his wife did the washing.

In Union hospitals the surgeon in charge had the option to decide whether laundry should be done on the hospital premises or at the home of the laundress. For those who worked on the hospital grounds, laundry facilities might consist of sheds, tents, or trees as protection from the weather. However, one Confederate post surgeon in Kingston, Georgia, refused to provide any shelter because his mother and grandmother had done their washing in the open air and, therefore, he insisted, no one else needed any protection.

Surgeons had varying philosophies on hospital cleanliness and, as a result, some hospitals made better use of laundresses than others. Some washed the clothes of incoming patients as a matter of course while others simply packed the dirty clothes in the soldier's knapsack for him to put back on when he left the hospital. One of the worst examples of laundry failure was in the receiving and distributing hospital that was located in a shed in Atlanta, Georgia. Because the patients were only in the bed for an hour or two before being sent to some other hospital, the surgeon thought it sufficient to wash the sheets and pillowcases once each month, having changed them only once or twice during the period.

A number of laundresses, both North and South, ended up doing nursing during periods of crisis. Those attached to regiments cared for soldiers who were sick in the field. Hospital laundresses augmented the regular nursing staff when hospitals overflowed with wounded after a battle. Some laundresses received acknowledgment for their nursing, but many did not.

See also: Blacks, as Hospital Workers; Cumming, Kate; Hospitals, Receiving and Distributing; Matrons; Sanitation; Surgeons, Post; Women, as Hospital Workers.

Bibliography

Cumming, Kate. *Kate: The Journal of a Confederate Nurse, 1862–1865.* 1866; reprint, ed. Richard Barksdale Harwell. Baton Rouge: Louisiana State University Press, 1959, 1987; Savannah, GA: Beehive, 1975.

Regulations for the Army of the Confederate States, 1862. Richmond, VA: J.W. Randolph, 1862; reprint, San Francisco: Norman, 1992.

Schroeder-Lein, Glenna R. *Confederate Hospitals on the Move: Samuel H. Stout and the Army of Tennessee.* Columbia: University of South Carolina Press, 1994.

Schultz, Jane E. *Women at the Front: Hospital Workers in Civil War America.* Chapel Hill: University of North Carolina Press, 2004.

Woodward, Joseph Janvier. *The Hospital Steward's Manual for the Instruction of Hospital Stewards, Ward-Masters, and Attendants, in Their Several Duties.* Philadelphia: J.B. Lippincott, 1862; reprint, San Francisco: Norman, 1991.

LAWSON, THOMAS (1789–1861)

Thomas Lawson, Union surgeon general at the beginning of the Civil War, was born into a prominent family in southeastern Virginia on August 29, 1789. Nothing is known about his medical education, but he was probably trained by apprenticeship to a physician.

At the age of nineteen he began his military medical career, serving as a surgeon's mate in the navy from March 1, 1809, to January 12, 1811. He then became a garrison surgeon's mate in the army. From May 21, 1813, to the end of the War of 1812, Lawson was surgeon of the Sixth Infantry. He became surgeon of the Seventh Infantry on May 17, 1815. From 1821 he ranked as the senior surgeon in the army medical corps. He seems to have been rather a complainer and curmudgeon. In 1832, after the War Department ordered examinations for army medical officers, Lawson headed the board that traveled to army posts to test the doctors already in the service. On occasion Lawson performed other nonmedical military duties as well, such as those of adjutant or quartermaster. From February 5 to May 15, 1836, Lawson was the lieutenant colonel of a Louisiana volunteer regiment during the Seminole War.

After the death of the previous surgeon general, Joseph Lovell, Lawson was appointed to the post on November 30, 1836. Lawson seemed to prefer field service to his Washington office, however. He was with troops during the Seminole War until May 1838. During the Mexican War, Lawson accompanied General Winfield Scott's expedition to Vera Cruz and Mexico City. Lawson served only as an adviser, however, since Scott had other medical directors.

During his twenty-four years as surgeon general, Lawson worked hard to achieve such improvements for the medical corps as military rank, an increase in numbers, enlisted hospital stewards, and extra pay for soldiers detailed for medical duty. He also oversaw the preparation and publication by his subordinates of three volumes of *Army Medical Statistics* and two volumes of the *Meteorological Register.* Lawson had a volatile temper and could be unkind when he felt threatened, but he was compassionate to the properly subordinate.

As a veteran of the War of 1812, Lawson was too physically infirm to handle the increased responsibilities of his post at the outbreak of the Civil War. In the spring of 1861 he went to Norfolk, Virginia, for medical treatment, and he died there of a stroke on May 15.

See also: Examining Boards, Medical; Finley, Clement Alexander; Stewards, Hospital; Surgeon General.

Bibliography

Gillett, Mary C. "Thomas Lawson, Second Surgeon General of the U.S. Army: A Character Sketch." *Prologue* 14 (Spring 1982): 15–24.

Phalen, James M. "Thomas Lawson." *Army Medical Bulletin* 52 (April 1940): 33–37.

LEALE, CHARLES AUGUSTUS (1842–1932)

Charles Augustus Leale was the first physician to reach and treat Abraham Lincoln after the president was shot at Ford's Theatre on April 14, 1865. Leale was born in New York City on March 26, 1842, the son of Captain William Pickett Leale and his wife, Anna Maria Burr Leale.

Young Leale attended Bellevue Hospital Medical College in New York City. In addition to the regular courses, he had private instruction from Dr. Austin Flint Sr. in diseases of the heart and lungs and from Dr. Frank H. Hamilton in gunshot wounds and surgery. From February 17, 1864, to February 17, 1865, Leale served as a medical cadet, probably at the Armory Square Hospital in Washington, DC. Starting as a wound dresser, he probably advanced to full responsibility for a ward by the end of his cadet year.

On March 1, 1865, Leale received his medical degree from Bellevue. He had evidently been a contract or acting assistant surgeon and was now appointed an assistant surgeon of volunteers effective April 8, 1865. At this time he was in charge of a ward for wounded officers at the Armory Square Hospital.

On April 11 Leale was part of the crowd at the White House that heard Abraham Lincoln give what turned out to be his last speech. Because he wanted to see Lincoln again, Leale went to Ford's Theatre on April 14, after he had finished his evening duties at the hospital. Leale arrived about 8:15, after the play had started but before the Lincoln party arrived. He was too late to get a seat in the orchestra section, but found a seat in the dress circle less than forty feet from Lincoln's box.

After Lincoln was shot, someone in the box called for a doctor. Leale vaulted the intervening rows of chairs and was admitted to the box, where he found Lincoln being held in the rocking chair by his wife Mary. The president was nearly dead, in a coma with no pulse and long pauses between breaths. With the help of two men, Leale got Lincoln flat on the floor and began to examine him, looking for a stab wound because he had seen assassin John Wilkes Booth waving a knife. The pupil of one eye was very large and the other very small, indicative of brain damage. Leale gently probed with his fingers through Lincoln's hair until he found the bullet wound. He removed a blood clot and probed the wound with his little finger, looking for the bullet, but was unable to locate it. With the removal of the blood clot, Lincoln's breathing and pulse improved somewhat, as they did every time a clot was removed during the rest of the night.

In consultation with two other doctors, Charles Sabin Taft and Albert F.A. King, who had joined him in the box, Leale determined to move Lincoln out of the theater to a house across the street. Leale already realized, and had stated, that the president's wound was mortal, and he believed that Lincoln would die on the way if taken back to the White House.

The three doctors and several soldiers managed to carry Lincoln across the street to the Peterson house, where a resident told them to bring the dying president into the back bedroom. Because Lincoln was too tall for the bed and the foot-board could not be removed, Leale had the president laid diagonally, propping his head on pillows, and kept him warm with hot water bottles, warm blankets, and a mustard plaster. Leale then sent for Robert K. Stone, the Lincolns' family physician; Surgeon General Joseph K. Barnes; D. Willard Bliss, the surgeon in charge of Armory Square Hospital; Lincoln's pastor, the Reverend Phineas Gurley; Lincoln's son Robert; and the members of the cabinet.

Although Leale had only recently received his medical degree, he had had a lot of experience with gunshot wounds. His treatments were approved and continued by the senior surgeons who took over the case. Leale stayed with the president, holding Lincoln's right hand, until he died at 7:22 on the morning of April 15. Leale believed that prolonging Lincoln's life for nine hours gave government leaders time to act, ensuring a smooth transition of government.

Although Leale was invited to Lincoln's autopsy, he did not attend because he needed to care for his wounded patients. However, he did attend Lincoln's funeral on April 19 at the White House, where he sat at the head of the casket. In the procession to the Capitol, he was assigned to the carriage just ahead of the catafalque. In the ceremonies at the Capitol, he was also at the head of the casket. Later Leale was honored with a grandstand seat at the Grand Review of the troops in Washington on May 24.

Leale was brevetted captain on January 4, 1866, and honorably mustered out of the service on January 20. He went to Europe where he studied Asiatic cholera. Later in 1866 he returned to New York City and opened a private medical practice. He also held positions at the Northwestern Dispensary (1866–1871), the Central Dispensary, and several other hospitals, at least as a consultant. He was involved in several medical societies and served as their president.

On September 3, 1867, Leale married Rebecca Medwin Copcutt. The couple's six children all lived to adulthood. Leale retired from medical practice in 1928 and died on June 13, 1932, at the age of 90.

Within a day or two of the assassination, Leale wrote an account of the event that he used as the basis for a letter to Benjamin F. Butler and the congressional committee he headed that was investigating the assassination in the summer of

1867. Refusing to take advantage of his potential celebrity, however, Leale never spoke about his experiences until fellow members of the New York commandery of the Military Order of the Loyal Legion persuaded him to share his information in February 1909 in honor of the centennial of Lincoln's birth. The bloodstained shirt cuffs that Leale was wearing on the night of the assassination are in the National Museum of Health and Medicine in Washington, DC.

See also: Barnes, Joseph K.; Gunshot Wounds, Treatment of; Lincoln, Abraham; Medical Cadets; Surgeons, Acting Assistant (Contract); Surgeons, Assistant.

Bibliography

Leale, Charles A. *Lincoln's Last Hours: Address Delivered Before the Commandery of the State of New York Military Order of the Loyal Legion of the United States.* New York: privately printed, 1909.

Read, Harry. "A Hand to Hold While Dying: Dr. Charles A. Leale at Lincoln's Side." *Lincoln Herald* 79 (Spring 1977): 21–26.

LETTERMAN, JONATHAN (1824–1872)

Jonathan Letterman, medical director for the Union Army of the Potomac, was born on December 11, 1824, in Cannonsburg, Pennsylvania, the son of Jonathan Letterman, a physician, and his wife, Anna Ritchie Letterman. Young Jonathan was educated by private tutors and then at Jefferson College in Cannonsburg, from which he graduated in 1845. He received his medical training at Jefferson Medical College in Philadelphia. After graduating in 1849, he passed the examination for appointment as a U.S. Army physician. Letterman received his commission on June 29, 1849, at the same time as William A. Hammond, and the two became good friends.

In the period before the Civil War, Letterman was stationed in Florida, Minnesota, and New Mexico. Hammond was also serving in New Mexico Territory, where both he and Letterman collected specimens for the young Smithsonian Institution. After tours of duty as a medical purveyor at Fortress Monroe, Virginia, and in New York, Letterman was serving in California when the Civil War began.

Letterman was ordered east, where his first assignment was as medical director for the area that soon became West Virginia. It was then under the command of General George B. McClellan, and Hammond was the department medical inspector.

In July 1861 McClellan became commander of the Army of the Potomac, which had just been defeated by the Confederates at the Battle of First Bull Run (Manassas). In April 1862 Hammond became surgeon general for the Union medical department. McClellan's abortive Peninsula Campaign in the late spring and early summer of 1862 left roughly 20,000 men, about one-quarter of the army, sick or wounded at Harrison's Landing, Virginia, in a chaotic situation that McClellan's medical director, Charles S. Tripler, was unable to manage. Letterman officially replaced Tripler as medical director on June 23, 1862, but was not on duty until July 4. He soon realized that McClellan's army was suffering from an epidemic of scurvy. Letterman requisitioned large amounts of potatoes, onions, cabbage, tomatoes, squash, beets, and fresh bread to improve the soldiers' diet, and the scurvy cleared up immediately.

Letterman had excellent organizational skills and experience as a medical purveyor, qualifications that he quickly put to good use during the summer of 1862, to reorganize medical care for the Army of the Potomac. He first addressed the problem of removing the wounded from the battlefield quickly by establishing an ambulance corps. This plan specified a certain number of trained stretcher-bearers and ambulances for each regiment. These vehicles were not to be used for nonmedical purposes. Letterman also reorganized the field hospital system. Letterman's reforms got their first real test at the Battle of Antietam in Maryland on September 17, 1862. The wounded were removed by the stretcher-bearers and taken to the field dressing stations for immediate first aid. Those who needed further treatment were then taken to the large field hospitals set up in tents. While the reorganization worked well, Letterman discovered that the supply system itself was deficient because the surgeons and other attendants quickly ran low on crucial items.

In October 1862 Letterman announced a new system that allotted a particular quantity of medical supplies to each brigade for a month or for each battle. The medical directors were to see that the supplies were always replenished in a timely manner and always available.

Letterman had field and divisional hospitals set up and supplied before the Battle of Fredericksburg in December 1862. However, he was unable to set up in advance at Gettysburg because the location of the three-day battle (July 1–3, 1863) was not planned. Supplies did not arrive until after the fighting had begun. Letterman used churches, homes, barns, and other buildings for hospitals initially, but set up large tent hospitals to care for the wounded after the battle.

Because Letterman was a friend of William A. Hammond, the controversies surrounding the surgeon general evidently affected Letterman as well. Letterman asked to be relieved as medical director in January 1864. The new surgeon general, Joseph K. Barnes, replaced Letterman with Dr. Thomas McParlin and gave Letterman some rather paltry assignments. Letterman finally resigned from the army entirely on December 22, 1864.

In October 1863 Letterman had married Mary Lee. After his resignation from the military, the couple moved to California, where Letterman practiced medicine and wrote *Medical Recollections of the Army of the Potomac* (1866). He also served two terms as coroner for San Francisco. Mary Letterman died suddenly in 1867. Letterman himself died, apparently as a result of a chronic intestinal problem, on March 15, 1872. The military hospital in San Francisco was named for him.

See also: Ambulance Corps; Ambulances; Antietam, Battle of; Barnes, Joseph K.; Bull Run (Manassas), First Battle of; Fredericksburg, Battle of; Gettysburg, Battle of; Hammond, William Alexander; Hospitals, Field; Medical Directors, Field; Medical Purveyors; Peninsula Campaign; Stretchers; Tents, Hospital; Tripler, Charles Stuart.

Bibliography

Bollet, Alfred Jay. *Civil War Medicine: Challenges and Triumphs*. Tucson, AZ: Galen, 2002.

Dammann, Gordon E. "Jonathan A. Letterman, Surgeon for the Soldiers." *Caduceus* 10 (Spring 1994): 23–34.

LICE

Lice, small insects that thrive in dirty places, were ubiquitous in the clothes and on the bodies of Civil War soldiers, North and South. Although soldiers with high standards of personal cleanliness might delay getting lice, sooner or later everyone from the lowliest private to the highest general suffered their presence.

The initial discovery of lice on one's person embarrassed many soldiers, who sought to rid themselves of the pests in private. However, most soldiers soon realized that lice were a universal problem, and "skirmishing" for "graybacks" became a communal social event as soldiers sat around in a group examining their clothing, removing the vermin, and squishing them. At times, bored soldiers held "vermin fairs" and louse-jumping contests to see whose insect hopped the farthest.

Skirmishing for lice provided temporary and partial relief, as did the rare opportunity to acquire a new uniform and burn one's old clothes. The only lasting way to get lice out of apparel was to boil the clothes in water, preferably with a little salt. Most soldiers had or took few opportunities to boil their clothes or bathe frequently, so lice remained a constant problem.

Civil War soldiers saw lice as a nuisance, not as spreaders of disease. Lice transmit typhus, but surprisingly few cases of typhus were reported during the war. However, the lice caused unpleasant itching, and the resultant scratching of dirty skin led to numerous skin infections.

See also: Camp Itch; Sanitation.

Bibliography

Billings, John D. *Hardtack and Coffee: The Unwritten Story of Army Life*. Boston: George M. Smith, 1887; reprint, Lincoln: University of Nebraska Press, 1993.

Bollet, Alfred Jay. *Civil War Medicine: Challenges and Triumphs*. Tucson, AZ: Galen, 2002.

LINCOLN, ABRAHAM (1809–1865)

Lawyer, legislator, and president of the United States during the Civil War, Abraham Lincoln was born to Thomas and Nancy Hanks Lincoln near Hodgenville,

Kentucky, on February 12, 1809. In 1816 the Lincoln family moved to Perry (later Spencer) County, Indiana. On October 5, 1818, Nancy Lincoln died from the "milk sickness," caused by drinking the milk of cattle that had eaten poisonous white snakeroot. Thomas soon married a widow, Sarah Bush Johnston, who proved a compassionate stepmother for Abraham.

In 1830 the Lincoln family moved to Illinois, and in 1831 Abraham himself settled in New Salem, where he was a storekeeper, surveyor, postmaster, and state legislator. He read law, was admitted to the bar, and moved to Springfield in 1837, where he practiced in succession with John T. Stuart, Stephen T. Logan, and William H. Herndon. On November 4, 1842, Lincoln married Mary Todd, with whom he had four sons: Robert Todd (1843–1926); Edward "Eddie" Baker (1846–1850), who died of tuberculosis; William "Willie" Wallace (1850–1862), who died of typhoid fever in the White House while Lincoln was president; and Thomas "Tad" (1853–1871).

Lincoln served a single term in Congress (1847–1849) as a Whig. After the Whig Party disappeared, Lincoln joined the new Republican Party in 1856 and made many political speeches opposing the spread of slavery into the territories. In 1860 Lincoln became the first president elected by the Republicans; he was reelected in 1864. During his term in office the Southern states seceded from the Union and fought a civil war with the North, which Lincoln led to victory. The war was almost over when Southern sympathizer John Wilkes Booth shot Lincoln in the head at Ford's Theatre on the evening of April 14, 1865. Lincoln died at 7:22 in the morning on April 15.

Lincoln's life has been and continues to be the subject of intense examination in all respects. Thousands of books and articles provide the minute details of his life and career. Lincoln's medical experiences have provoked considerable speculation. For example, researchers have suggested that Lincoln may have had Marfan syndrome, an inherited genetic disease of the connective tissue that can cause serious, and eventually fatal, problems, such as a sudden rupture of the aorta. Many people who have the syndrome are tall and thin, with long limbs and large hands and feet. While Lincoln clearly fit that physical description, other evidence that he had Marfan syndrome is slim, mainly that several distant relatives in the twentieth century had the disease. The idea was first proposed in 1964. Although it was refuted in 1981, the issue of Marfan syndrome continues to resurface. Researchers have wanted to do DNA testing on the known samples of Lincoln's blood and tissue. However, based on the advice of a committee of scholars and scientists that met in 1991 and 1992, the National Museum of Health and Medicine, which houses the specimens, has refused to permit the testing until a technique is developed that will not destroy the sample during the analysis and until more is known about the genetic variations of Marfan syndrome.

Researchers have also proposed that Lincoln could have had ataxia, another genetic disease that causes problems with muscle control. Here too the main evidence is that other distant Lincoln relatives (there are no longer any direct descendants) had the disorder in the twentieth century. In addition, people have conjectured that Lincoln was a homosexual. Most evidence to support this view comes from a misunderstanding of common nineteenth-century social practices.

Although these speculations about Lincoln's physical condition can be neither proven nor completely dismissed, some facts about Lincoln's health at various points during his life are known. About 1818, soon after the Lincolns moved to Indiana, Abraham was kicked in the forehead by a horse. He may have sustained some facial bone fractures that made the right side of his face asymmetrical and could have contributed to later headaches. One researcher has proposed, though with little evidence, that the injury caused Lincoln to have petit mal (mild) epileptic seizures for the rest of his life.

Lincoln is also known to have had a melancholy temperament, which especially manifested itself in several severe depressions while he was a young man. His first major depression occurred in the late summer of 1835, shortly after the death of Ann Rutledge. Some historians and storytellers claim that Lincoln loved Ann Rutledge, was actually engaged to her, went into a near-suicidal depression, and never got over her death. Others believe that Lincoln and Rutledge were merely friends and that her death saddened Lincoln at the time, but did not have a lasting effect. In the twenty-first century, one student of the problem has suggested that Lincoln's breakdown could have been set off by overwork while studying law during a period of continuous gloomy weather.

Lincoln's other notorious bout with depression occurred after the "fatal" first of January 1841. Historians have generally attributed Lincoln's distress to a broken engagement with Mary Todd, but there is no conclusive evidence that the couple broke up on that date. Another possible cause was Lincoln's despair over damage to his career resulting from an economic decline that caused the failure of the internal improvements Lincoln had supported so ardently in the state legislature, a failure that produced a major state debt. Additional causes may have been mixed feelings about Mary Todd, a crush on a young woman named Matilda Edwards, and the plans of his closest friend, Joshua Speed, to move back to Kentucky.

In any case, Lincoln spent a week in bed and was treated by Dr. Anson G. Henry, a practitioner of "heroic" regular medicine. Henry may well have used bleeding, purging, and mercurial medicines on Lincoln. The treatment did not help, but made Lincoln look worse. Lincoln was still recovering from his depression during the summer of 1841. He evidently suffered bouts of depression for the rest of his life, but he learned how to deal with them and they were never again so severe.

During the Civil War Lincoln contracted varioloid, a mild form of smallpox. He first showed symptoms on November 19, 1863, on the train on the way back from the cemetery dedication at Gettysburg. Lincoln was sick for at least three weeks, during which he saw only a few visitors, such as cabinet members with important business.

In addition to his own personal medical concerns during the Civil War, Lincoln, as president, was necessarily concerned about decisions about the medical care of others. He instituted a blockade of Southern ports, declaring medical supplies to be contraband of war. He was slow to agree to the establishment of the U.S Sanitary Commission and to appoint William A. Hammond as surgeon general. He also failed to interfere with Secretary of War Edwin M. Stanton's efforts to remove Hammond. Nor did Lincoln take any steps to ensure better conditions for prisoners of war. Although he has been criticized for these decisions, it is important to realize that as president Lincoln was in charge of the entire Union war effort. Medical care was only a part of his concern. Lincoln was not a micromanager, and he allowed knowledgeable leaders to carry out their responsibilities unless or until they proved themselves unable to do so.

As president, Lincoln was under enormous strain throughout the war. He often did not eat properly, so he lost weight. At times he suffered from headaches and exhaustion. Pictures taken over the course of the war show that he aged dramatically. However, Lincoln was still in excellent physical shape at the end of the war, able to chop wood and hold an ax out horizontally with one arm. Even the doctors who cared for Lincoln after he was shot were surprised by his good physical condition, which they thought enabled him to survive as long as he did.

On April 14, 1865, John Wilkes Booth shot Lincoln at close range with a derringer. The bullet entered Lincoln's head in the back, about one and a half inches to the left of the center, traveled more than seven inches across the brain carrying bone fragments with it, and stopped behind one of his eyes. (Some doctors who attended the autopsy said the right eye while others said the left). In an attempt to locate the bullet, Charles A. Leale, the first doctor on the scene, probed the wound with his little finger. Later Surgeon General Joseph K. Barnes used a nelaton probe with a ceramic tip that would discolor on contact with the bullet, but no one found the bullet until the autopsy, performed on Lincoln's head on April 15. Lincoln's brain injuries were very severe. It is unlikely that even twenty-first-century medicine could have kept Lincoln alive, much less restored him to functional ability.

See also: Army Medical Museum; Barnes, Joseph K.; Blockade; Gunshot Wounds, Treatment of; Hammond, William Alexander; Leale, Charles Augustus; Smallpox; Typhoid Fever; United States Sanitary Commission; Varioloid; Woodward, Joseph Janvier.

Bibliography

Donald, David Herbert. *Lincoln.* New York: Simon and Schuster, 1995.

Henry, Robert S. *The Armed Forces Institute of Pathology: Its First Century, 1862–1962.* Washington, DC: Government Printing Office, 1964.

Kauffman, Michael W. *American Brutus: John Wilkes Booth and the Lincoln Conspiracies.* New York: Random, 2004.

Lattimer, John K. *Kennedy and Lincoln: Medical and Ballistic Comparisons of Their Assassinations.* New York: Harcourt Brace Jovanovich, 1980.

Leale, Charles A. *Lincoln's Last Hours: Address Delivered Before the Commandery of the State of New York Military Order of the Loyal Legion of the United States.* New York: privately printed, 1909.

Miers, Earl Schenck. *Lincoln Day by Day*. Washington, DC: Lincoln Sesquicentennial Commission, 1960.

Reilly, Philip R. *Abraham Lincoln's DNA and Other Adventures in Genetics*. Cold Spring Harbor, NY: Cold Spring Harbor Laboratory Press, 2000.

Shenk, Joshua Wolf. *Lincoln's Melancholy: How Depression Challenged a President and Fueled His Greatness*. Boston: Houghton Mifflin, 2005.

Shutes, Milton H. *Lincoln and the Doctors: A Medical Narrative of the Life of Abraham Lincoln*. New York: Pioneer, 1933.

"Study Traces Gene Defect in Abe's Family." Springfield (IL) *State Journal-Register*, November 2, 1994.

LIVERMORE, MARY ASHTON RICE (1820–1905)

Mary Ashton Rice Livermore, a U.S. Sanitary Commission activist during the Civil War, was born in Boston on December 19, 1820. Her parents, Timothy and Zebiah Ashton Rice, were strict Calvinists. Mary graduated from the Charlestown (Massachusetts) Female Seminary at the age of seventeen and then taught Latin, French, and Italian there. In 1839 she began tutoring children on a Virginia plantation, a three-year experience that caused her to become an abolitionist. She then returned to New England where she became headmistress of a school in Duxbury, Massachusetts.

In 1845 Mary married Daniel Parker Livermore, a Universalist minister whose spiritual message of love and hope she found more appealing than her own religious background. The Livermores had three daughters; the oldest child died when she was four. By 1858 the family had moved to Chicago where Daniel edited a Universalist paper, the *New Covenant*. Mary, who wrote poems, essays, and stories for various publications, served as his assistant editor. In this capacity she was the only female journalist to attend the Republican convention in Chicago in 1860, when Abraham Lincoln was nominated for the presidency.

Mary Livermore advocated temperance and served on the board of directors of the Home for the Friendless in Chicago. Once the Civil War began, she became active in the Northwestern Sanitary Commission (the Chicago branch of the U.S. Sanitary Commission), which was founded in October 1861. She initially rolled bandages and gathered supplies for the troops. In March 1862, soon after the fall of Fort Donelson, Livermore and her colleague Jane C. Hoge made a hospital inspection trip to St. Louis, Missouri, and Mound City and Cairo, Illinois, studying how to organize hospitals efficiently and ensuring that supplies sent by the Sanitary Commission were being used properly. During the tour Livermore and Hoge also nursed and comforted sick and wounded soldiers.

In November 1862 Livermore and Hoge attended the meeting of the Women's Council of the Sanitary Commission in Washington, DC. On December 8, after their return to Illinois, they became associate managers of the Chicago branch. As paid professionals, they made many hospital inspection tours, conducted a voluminous correspondence with individuals and groups about supplies, met with aid society members to further their efforts, and sought to help family members seeking news of their soldier relatives. They also tried to find places for women looking for nursing jobs. Livermore did a great deal of traveling to organize aid societies and raise funds, although she did not speak at the meetings herself until March 1864. She was a good administrator who was often able to cut through tangles of red tape. Throughout all these activities, Livermore continued to write two or three articles per week for the *New Covenant,* promoting relief work.

Livermore and Hoge proposed what became the first sanitary fair, held in Chicago from October 27 to November 7, 1863. The men of the Sanitary Commission had scoffed at the idea of such an event to raise money for the needs of sick and wounded soldiers. However, the women of the commission persisted and put on a highly successful fair that raised about $100,000 and served as a prototype for a succession of fairs around the country.

As a result of her Civil War experiences, during which she was often discriminated against or disparaged because she was a woman, Livermore became an advocate of women's rights, including better education, equal-paying jobs, and legal and political rights. She wrote many articles and edited several women's suffrage newspapers, including the *Agitator* in Chicago (1869) and the *Woman's Journal* in Boston (1870–1871). Livermore published an account of her Civil War experiences, as well as the accomplishments of other women during the war, called *My Story of the War* (1887). Both this book and her autobiography, *The Story of My Life* (1897), sold very well. Livermore died in Melrose, Massachusetts, on May 23, 1905.

See also: Bandages; Hoge, Jane Currie Blaikie; Sanitary Fairs; United States Sanitary Commission; Women's Hospital Auxiliaries and Relief Societies.

Bibliography

Brockett, L.P., and Mary C. Vaughan. *Women's Work in the Civil War: A Record of Heroism, Patriotism, and Patience.* Philadelphia: Zeigler, McCurdy, 1867.

Livermore, Mary A. *My Story of the War.* Hartford, CT: 1887; reprint, New York: Da Capo, 1995.

Venet, Wendy Hamand. "The Emergence of a Suffragist: Mary Livermore, Civil War Activism, and the Moral Power of Women." *Civil War History* 48 (June 2002): 143–164.

M

MAGGOTS

Infestations of maggots were fairly common in the wounds of Civil War soldiers, both North and South, especially where there were many flies and sanitation standards were low. Flies deposited their eggs in open wounds or those covered with moist dressings. The maggots quickly hatched. While they caused the soldiers no pain, their wiggling was annoying, and, of course, they looked revolting.

In reality, maggots provided a useful service because they ate dead and diseased tissue, cleaning out the wound without disturbing the healthy tissue and thus promoting quick healing. As a result, wounded soldiers in unsanitary facilities, who got maggots, often healed better than patients without maggots in cleaner hospitals. Confederate surgeon and medical researcher Joseph Jones noted the beneficial effects of maggots, and some Confederate surgeons encouraged their use.

See also: Gunshot Wounds, Treatment of; Infections, of Wounds; Jones, Joseph; Sanitation.

Bibliography
Adams, George Worthington. *Doctors in Blue: The Medical History of the Union Army in the Civil War.* New York: Schuman, 1952; reprint, Dayton, OH: Morningside, 1985.
Bollet, Alfred Jay. *Civil War Medicine: Challenges and Triumphs.* Tucson, AZ: Galen, 2002.

MALARIA

Malaria was a disease prevalent in the South and parts of the Midwest during the Civil War, especially in the summer and early fall. It was known as chills and fever, fever and ague, and intermittent fever because of its distinctive symptoms.

A person contracted the disease from the bite of an infected anopheles mosquito, with an incubation time of seven to fourteen days after the bite. The first symptom was a strong chill with violent shivering. This was succeeded by a fever that could reach as high as 106 degrees, producing tremendous amounts of perspiration that would soak the bedclothes. An attack usually lasted ten to fifteen hours. A person with malaria could have attacks every day, every other day, or every third day. The doctors called the fever "quotidian," "tertian," and "quartan" respectively, based on the frequency of episodes. Between attacks the patient would feel pretty well. Unfortunately, those who had suffered from malaria did not develop immunity to it. The parasite that caused the illness lingered in the bloodstream for months or years, and malaria would recur when the patient's immune system was disturbed by fatigue, stress, malnutrition, or some other illness.

Malaria was second only to diarrhea and dysentery as a cause of illness during the Civil War. The Union army recorded nearly 1 million cases, with about 1,800 cases per year for every 1,000 white soldiers and 1,200 cases per 1,000 per year for black troops. Extant statistics show that Confederate troops probably had more cases of malaria than Union soldiers, but more Union troops died of the disease.

Although malaria had a rather low fatality rate, it had a major effect on the Civil War. Many patients suffering from malaria did not go to the hospital but remained in their quarters when suffering an attack. At certain seasons of the year and in particular locations, the fighting ability of armies on both sides was weakened because of the illness.

Malaria could be treated effectively with quinine and other derivatives of cinchona bark. Given in the proper quantity, quinine could derail the recurring attacks of malaria. By the time of the Civil War, some doctors realized that quinine could also be given to prevent malaria. However, the doses given were often too small or too inconsistent to be very effective.

Because malaria had such a serious effect on the armies, surgeons and military officers did their best to keep the troops from getting it. However, the illness was difficult to prevent because no one realized that mosquitoes spread the disease. Theories about the causes of malaria blamed sleeping in wet blankets, bad drinking water, and rapid climate changes. Other theories had to do with "bad air" (*malaria* in Italian). Though some doctors thought that bad air was caused by crowded camps or some sort of poisonous airborne fungi, most theorists settled on "miasms," or malodorous vapors, from swamps, decomposing vegetation, and standing water.

The doctors realized that setting up camps in dry, elevated places, away from swamps and standing water, reduced the incidence of malaria dramatically. For the wrong reason, these officers did the right thing, keeping the troops away from the mosquitoes' breeding grounds.

See also: Diarrhea and Dysentery; Miasms; Mosquitoes; Quinine.

Bibliography
Bollet, Alfred Jay. *Civil War Medicine: Challenges and Triumphs*. Tucson, AZ: Galen, 2002.

Spielman, Andrew, and Michael D'Antonio. *Mosquito: The Story of Man's Deadliest Foe*. New York: Hyperion, 2001.

Woodward, Joseph Janvier. *Outlines of the Chief Camp Diseases of the United States Armies, as Observed During the Present War*. Philadelphia: Lippincott, 1863; reprint, San Francisco: Norman, 1992.

MALINGERERS

Also known as a "hospital rat," a malingerer was a soldier who feigned illness in order to go to or stay in a field or general hospital and thus avoid active military service. Some soldiers were quite creative in their development of pains, "fits," laryngitis, rheumatism, deafness, and other ailments whose symptoms could be easily imitated. Although malingerers were relatively uncommon during the Civil War, the memoirs of a number of doctors and matrons described how the medical staff outsmarted and exposed a false patient (or, occasionally, were unable to do so). Sometimes doctors used anesthesia for the purpose, leading to a miraculous "recovery" when the patient awoke.

Some nutrition-related diseases produced weakness, night blindness, and other problems. In their early stages, these diseases could not be diagnosed and sufferers with the symptoms were suspected of malingering.

See also: Anesthesia; Hospitals, Field; Hospitals, General; Rheumatism; Surgeon's Call.

Bibliography

Bollet, Alfred Jay. *Civil War Medicine: Challenges and Triumphs.* Tucson, AZ: Galen, 2002.

Beers, Fannie A. *Memories: A Recollection of Personal Experiences During Four Years of War.* Philadelphia: J.B. Lippincott, 1888; reprint, Alexandria, VA: Time-Life, 1985.

Lyon, A.A. "Malingerers." *Southern Practitioner* 26 (September 1904): 558–564.

Schroeder-Lein, Glenna R. *Confederate Hospitals on the Move: Samuel H. Stout and the Army of Tennessee.* Columbia: University of South Carolina Press, 1994.

MALNUTRITION

Because the diet of troops in both the Union and the Confederacy was often very restricted in variety and quantity, many soldiers in the ranks and most of those held in prisoner of war camps suffered from malnutrition to some degree.

A shortage of food was often a problem for troops on the march or going into battle. When soldiers were told to take three days' cooked rations on a march, many did not comply fully. Most commonly, a hungry soldier ate all his food on the first day because there simply was not enough of it, leaving him to beg from his fellows, scavenge what he could, or go hungry. Many men fell behind on the march or wearied during battle due to lack of food. Even if a soldier ate his rations sparingly, there was no guarantee that the food supply would be replenished on schedule. The regiment's commissary wagons were often far in the rear and unable to resupply the troops in a timely manner. Even if they could, the troops might not have time to cook the food.

The rations issued to soldiers, especially on the march, focused on hardtack or some other type of bread, pork or beef, and coffee (or its substitute). Although other foodstuffs were supposed to be issued as well, they usually were not. Such a restricted diet deprived the soldiers of necessary vitamins. Unless the troops were in an area with plentiful fruits and vegetables that they could either buy or confiscate to supplement their rations, troops tended to develop a "scorbutic taint," as the doctors called it. In other words, they had scurvy, a disease caused by lack of vitamin C. Symptoms included general weariness and weakness, gum problems and loose teeth, and skin and joint hemorrhages. In the early stages of the disease, when scurvy could not be positively diagnosed, sufferers were sometimes suspected of malingering.

The lack of vegetables and fruits also caused several other medical conditions, including night blindness (caused by a lack of vitamin A) and chronic diarrhea (frequently associated with scurvy). The lack of vitamin A tended to affect certain cells in the bronchial tubes that protect against infection, probably contributing to the incidence of bronchitis and pneumonia among the troops. In prison camps such as Andersonville, where the diet was largely cornmeal, prisoners probably suffered from pellagra, a serious illness caused by lack of the B vitamin nicotinic acid. (This diagnosis has been suggested by later research and was not determined at the time.) Symptoms of many of these illnesses hindered a soldier's effectiveness long before the condition became severe enough for him to seek medical aid. These nutritional deficiencies tended to make other illnesses and wounds worse as well.

Doctors at the time of the Civil War knew how to prevent malnutrition, but were often unable to do so. Even when they recommended issues of vegetables and fruits, commanders did not necessarily attempt to provide them. Given the limitations of transportation during the period, commanding officers and quartermasters were more likely to fill the available space with ammunition rather than fresh vegetables. Onions and potatoes were often used as antiscorbutics (against scurvy) because they survived shipping better than many other vegetables. Soldiers also recognized the health benefits of blackberries and would pick and eat them whenever they could find them. The availability of fresh vegetables and fruits could quickly and drastically improve the health of an army.

See also: Andersonville Prison; Debilitas; Diarrhea and Dysentery; Diet, of Troops; Elmira Prison; Eye Ailments; Hardtack; Malingerers; Prisoners of War; Quartermasters; Scurvy; Subsistence Department.

Bibliography
Bollet, Alfred Jay. *Civil War Medicine: Challenges and Triumphs.* Tucson, AZ: Galen, 2002.

MATERIA MEDICA

One of the seven branches of medicine that made up the usual curriculum in nineteenth-century medical schools, *materia medica* was the period name for pharmacy. The term involved the knowledge of medicinal plants, as well as the uses of all available medicines for treatment. Every Civil War physician, North and South, had training in materia medica.

See also: Alcohol, Medicinal Uses of; Calomel; Education, Medical; Laudanum; Morphine; Opiate Use and Addiction; Porcher, Francis Peyre; Quinine; *Resources of the Southern Fields and Forests*; Substitutes, for Supplies.

Bibliography

Cowen, David L. "Materia Medica and Pharmacology." In *The Education of American Physicians: Historical Essays*, ed. Ronald L. Numbers, 95–121. Berkeley: University of California Press, 1980.

Flannery, Michael A. *Civil War Pharmacy: A History of Drugs, Drug Supply and Provision, and Therapeutics for the Union and Confederacy.* New York: Pharmaceutical Products Press, 2004.

Smith, George Winston. *Medicines for the Union Army: The United States Army Laboratories During the Civil War.* Madison, WI: American Institute for the History of Pharmacy, 1962; reprint, New York: Pharmaceutical Products Press, 2001.

MATRONS

In both the North and the South, women with the title "matron" worked in general hospitals behind the lines. However, the two sides varied in their concept of a matron's duties.

The position of matron was established in the Confederacy by legislation passed on November 25, 1862. Each hospital was to have two chief matrons to supervise the entire "domestic economy" of the hospital. There were also supposed to be two assistant matrons in charge of the laundry and patients' clothing, and two ward matrons for each ward of 100 patients, who made sure that each patient received suitable bedding, food, and medicine.

In practice, the number of matrons depended upon the size of the hospital and the willingness of the doctor in charge to appoint them. Their duties also varied, involving many kinds of hands-on hospital work in addition to their supervisory roles. Matrons often cooked for patients with special diet needs, making toddies, eggnog, or recipes that some soldier's mother used to make, in order to appeal to delicate appetites. Matrons sometimes fed the concoctions to the patients as well. In many hospitals matrons controlled the key to the medicinal liquor supply, dispensing whiskey only by proper prescription. Matrons sometimes did the same tasks as nurses, such as washing the hands, faces, and wounds of patients. In addition, matrons comforted patients, offered spiritual counsel, sat with the dying, and wrote to patients' families to inform them about the soldier's location or, if necessary, his demise.

Matrons worked long hours, in some cases from 4:00 a.m. until midnight. Many matrons became ill from exhaustion, as well as disease, and had to leave the hospital to recuperate. Among the most famous of the Confederate matrons were Phoebe Pember, at Chimborazo Hospital No. 2 in Richmond, and Ella Newsom, Fannie Beers, and Kate Cumming, who worked at various locations with the Army of Tennessee. Pember, Beers, and Cumming later wrote books about their experiences.

Officially, as of 1863, one Union matron was to be appointed for every twenty beds to perform the duty in hospitals that laundresses performed in the field. However, the term *matron* was also used in other contexts to apply to women working as nurses, cooks, chambermaids, or ward supervisors, a position similar to what Confederates meant by the term. Jane Woolsey, for example, seems to have served as a matron in the supervisory sense.

The position of matron evidently was more important and prestigious for the Confederates. Although some people objected to matrons, as they did to the presence of women in hospitals in any capacity, patients generally seem to have benefited from matrons' care.

See also: Alcohol, Medicinal Uses of; Beers, Fannie A.; Chimborazo Hospital; Cooks; Cumming, Kate; Diet, of Hospital Patients; Hospital Support Staff; Hospitals, General; Laundresses; Newsom (Trader), Ella King; Nurses; Pember, Phoebe Yates Levy; Women, as Hospital Workers; Woolsey Sisters.

Bibliography

Beers, Fannie A. *Memories: A Recollection of Personal Experiences During Four Years of War.* Philadelphia: J.B. Lippincott, 1888; reprint, Alexandria, VA: Time-Life, 1985.

Cumming, Kate. *Kate: The Journal of a Confederate Nurse, 1862–1865.* 1866; reprint, ed. Richard Barksdale Harwell. Baton Rouge: Louisiana State University Press, 1959, 1987; reprint, Savannah, GA: Beehive, 1975.

Greenleaf, Charles R. *A Manual for the Medical Officers of the United States Army.* Philadelphia: J.B. Lippincott, 1864; reprint, San Francisco: Norman, 1992.

Pember, Phoebe Yates. *A Southern Woman's Story: Life in Confederate Richmond.* 1879; reprint, ed. Bell Irvin Wiley. Jackson, TN: McCowat-Mercer, 1959; reprint, Covington, GA: Mockingbird, 1974.

Schroeder-Lein, Glenna R. *Confederate Hospitals on the Move: Samuel H. Stout and the Army of Tennessee.* Columbia: University of South Carolina Press, 1994.

Schultz, Jane E. *Women at the Front: Hospital Workers in Civil War America.* Chapel Hill: University of North Carolina Press, 2004.

MCCAW, JAMES BROWN (1823–1906)

James Brown McCaw, surgeon in charge of the Chimborazo Hospital in Richmond, Virginia, during the Civil War, was a native of Richmond. Born on July 12, 1823, he was the son of William Reid McCaw and Ann Ludwell Brown McCaw. James McCaw studied at the Richmond Academy and then earned his medical degree from the University of the City of New York in 1844, becoming a fourth-generation physician.

Returning to Richmond, McCaw established a private practice specializing in the diseases of women and children. In 1845 he married Delia Patteson. The couple had nine children, three of whom became physicians. McCaw edited several medical journals and, in 1858, became professor of chemistry and pharmacy at the Medical College of Virginia.

Although McCaw remained a civilian throughout the Civil War, he was appointed a Confederate surgeon on October 9, 1861, and given the responsibility of planning, organizing, and commanding Chimborazo Hospital using military principles. He had overall administrative control of the five divisions of the hospital, the largest in the Confederacy. McCaw took daily walks through the hospital to encourage the staff and to make sure he understood what was going on. He hired many of the workers himself and influenced the choice of doctors to be assigned there. He also mediated between quarreling staff members, applying wisdom and humor in sticky situations. He cared about the patients and staff and usually was able to get needed tasks accomplished. During the war he not only managed the hospital, but also continued his private practice, taught at the Medical College of Virginia, and edited the *Confederate States Medical and Surgical Journal*.

After the war McCaw continued teaching at the Medical College of Virginia, where, in 1869, he became professor of the practice of medicine. He served as dean of the faculty for twelve years, but retired in 1883 because he was tired of dealing with faculty disputes. He practiced medicine in Richmond until 1901 and was involved in a number of medical associations and community activities. He died in Richmond on August 13, 1906.

See also: Chimborazo Hospital; *Confederate States Medical and Surgical Journal*; Education, Medical; Richmond, Virginia.

Bibliography

Green, Carol E. *Chimborazo: The Confederacy's Largest Hospital*. Knoxville: University of Tennessee Press, 2004.

Johns, Frank S., and Anne Page Johns. "Chimborazo Hospital and J.B. McCaw, Surgeon in Chief." *Virginia Magazine of History and Biography* 62, no. 2 (1954): 190–200.

MCGUIRE, HUNTER HOLMES (1835–1900)

Hunter Holmes McGuire, noted Confederate surgeon, was born in Winchester, Virginia, on October 11, 1865, the son of Hugh Holmes McGuire and Eliza Moss McGuire. Hugh McGuire, a surgeon, ophthalmologist, and professor of surgery at Winchester Medical College, undoubtedly influenced his son's choice of vocation.

Educated first at Winchester Academy, Hunter McGuire graduated from Winchester Medical College in 1855. He taught there as professor of anatomy and practiced medicine with his father for two years before furthering his medical education in Philadelphia with classes at the medical college of the University of

Pennsylvania and Jefferson Medical College in the fall of 1858. McGuire taught a medical tutoring class in Philadelphia with Dr. Francis E. Luckett. In December 1859 McGuire and Luckett helped lead several hundred Southern students who seceded from the Philadelphia medical schools because of the sympathy some citizens of Philadelphia showed for abolitionist John Brown. Many of the students completed their degrees at the Medical College of Virginia or other Southern schools. McGuire taught a tutoring class at the New Orleans School of Medicine until the Civil War broke out.

As soon as Virginia seceded from the Union, McGuire returned to his native state and joined the Second Virginia Infantry as a private. However, he soon went to Richmond to apply for a medical post. In May 1861 he became medical director of the Army of the Shenandoah at Harpers Ferry, then commanded by Thomas J. Jackson (soon to be known as "Stonewall"). McGuire remained Jackson's medical director through several command changes.

McGuire's responsibilities included arranging for the removal of Confederate wounded from the battlefield, often a very complex logistical problem. He helped Jackson set up the parole and exchange of some captured Union surgeons in May 1862. McGuire also treated wounded officers. Although he is best known for amputating Stonewall Jackson's wounded left arm in May 1863, McGuire also amputated General Richard S. Ewell's left leg above the knee. Yet McGuire did not perform amputations unless he believed that they were really necessary. In fact, when Jackson was wounded in the middle finger of his left hand during the Battle of First Manassas (Bull Run), McGuire prevented another doctor from amputating and saved the finger by using cold-water dressings and a splint. After Jackson's death from pneumonia, on May 10, 1863, McGuire continued as medical director of the Second Corps of the Army of Northern Virginia under Richard S. Ewell and Jubal Early.

During the war McGuire met Mary Stuart of Staunton, Virginia, when both were attendants in a wedding. The pair was married in Staunton on December 19, 1866. Between 1867 and 1885 they had nine children, including two sets of twins.

McGuire served as professor of surgery at the Medical College of Virginia in Richmond until 1881, as well as conducting a successful private practice. In 1893 he became president of the rival University College of Medicine. He also established a hospital, St. Luke's Home for the Sick (1883). McGuire was active in various medical organizations, wrote articles, and gave talks on medical, surgical, and historical subjects. He was best known for his account of the death of Stonewall Jackson. During the 1890s he headed a Confederate veterans organization committee that analyzed history textbooks to make sure that the Southern viewpoint was presented fully and correctly.

On March 19, 1900, McGuire had a stroke. Although he regained his ability to walk, he could neither speak nor swallow. He died on September 19, 1900. His medical heritage lived on, as at least two of his sons, a grandson, and two great-grandsons also became doctors.

See also: Amputation; Bull Run (Manassas), First Battle of; Ewell, Richard Stoddert; Jackson, Thomas Jonathan (Stonewall); Pneumonia; Prisoners of War.

Bibliography

"Death of Dr. Hunter McGuire." *Southern Practitioner* 22 (October 1900): 466–468.
Shaw, Maurice F. *Stonewall Jackson's Surgeon, Hunter Holmes McGuire: A Biography.* Lynchburg, VA: H.E. Howard, 1993.

MEASLES

Until the advent of immunization for the disease in the late twentieth century, measles, along with mumps and chicken pox, was a common childhood illness. Characterized by a fever, cough, and rash, measles could make the immune system vulnerable to serious aftereffects, which doctors at the time of the Civil War called sequelae.

A highly contagious disease, measles quickly spread through newly recruited regiments, both Union and Confederate, especially those in which the soldiers came from rural areas and had not previously been exposed to the disease, as had many urban recruits. Measles epidemics could affect from one-third to the majority of a regiment. For example, 800 of the 1,200 men in the Twelfth North Carolina Infantry contracted the disease. Union statistics showed a total of 76,318 cases resulting in 5,177 deaths. However, Dr. Joseph Janvier Woodward (USA) wrote during the war that measles was underrepresented statistically because most cases occurred early in a regiment's history, either while soldiers were still in state-controlled training camps or soon after they were mustered into the army, when regimental surgeons were still learning how to properly prepare their paperwork.

A measles epidemic usually lasted one to two months, infecting all the susceptible soldiers and effectively rendering the regiment useless for military purposes during that time. Most measles cases occurred from the fall of 1861 to the spring of 1862. However, throughout the war new recruits continued to get measles. There were 2,207 cases in the Confederate general hospitals in Virginia from October 1, 1862, to January 31, 1864. In the later part of the war, the Confederates tried to leave new regiments in camp until their disease phase was finished.

Because measles was known to be a disease that ran a certain course and could not be shortened, doctors merely tried to alleviate the worst symptoms of each phase and provide the patient with appropriate nourishment. Far more serious than measles itself were its sequelae, other diseases that affected the measles-weakened system after the original disease had run its course. Acute bronchitis and pneumonia seem to have been the most common aftereffects, but doctors also reported eye problems, dysentery or diarrhea, typhoid fever, and tuberculosis. Many more patients died from these sequelae than from the original disease. Others were permanently disabled by the aftereffects. Doctor Woodward urged that measles convalescents should not be exposed to cold and damp conditions or sent back to their regiments until two to three weeks after the rash had disappeared or until they completely stopped coughing, in order to avoid contracting these additional diseases.

See also: Convalescents; Diarrhea and Dysentery; Diet, of Hospital Patients; Eye Ailments; Hospitals, General; Mortality, of Soldiers; Pneumonia; Tuberculosis; Typhoid Fever; Woodward, Joseph Janvier.

Bibliography

Cunningham, H.H. *Doctors in Gray: The Confederate Medical Service.* Baton Rouge: Louisiana State University Press, 1958; reprint, Gloucester, MA: Peter Smith, 1970.

Woodward, Joseph Janvier. *Outlines of the Chief Camp Diseases of the United States Armies, As Observed During the Present War.* Philadelphia: Lippincott, 1863; reprint, San Francisco: Norman, 1992.

THE MEDICAL AND SURGICAL HISTORY OF THE WAR OF THE REBELLION

The Medical and Surgical History of the War of the Rebellion is a monumental work published from 1870 to 1888. Its six large volumes (reprinted more conveniently in twelve) covered the medical and surgical aspects of the Civil War as comprehensively as possible, primarily using Union sources.

Union surgeon general William A. Hammond announced the plan for such a history in a circular of June 9, 1862. Hammond delegated assistant surgeons Joseph J. Woodward and John H. Brinton to prepare the medical and surgical parts of the study respectively. Hammond also assigned Brinton to collect and organize medical specimens from the battlefields and hospitals for the Army Medical Museum, which would become a source of examples for the book. In addition, Hammond revised the forms used to report the sick and wounded in order to collect more useful statistical information.

Brinton was removed from his post and succeeded by Assistant Surgeon George A. Otis about the same time that Hammond was ousted as surgeon general. The new surgeon general, Joseph K. Barnes, continued the history and museum projects and was eventually listed as the editor of the volumes. Secretary of War Edwin M. Stanton, who was interested in the history, helped influence Congress to grant an appropriation, on June 8, 1868, for publishing 5,000 copies.

The content of the six volumes (three medical, three surgical) is based on reports of all sorts collected during the war, as well as on specimens from the museum, which also serve as illustrations, both photographs and line drawings. The authors were able to discover the outcome of a number of cases by using the U.S. pension records for soldiers wounded during or disabled by the war. They used as much Confederate material as they could find, but the end result is heavily Union-based.

The first medical volume consists of numerous statistical tables summarizing the data from monthly reports about illnesses and deaths. The statistics are organized by white and colored troops, then by region, by military department within that region, and, finally, by hospital. The second part of the volume, called the appendix, contains appropriate excerpts from the reports of medical directors and other medical officers, beginning with the first Bull Run (Manassas) campaign and continuing through the end of the war, arranged chronologically by region. This volume, compiled by Woodward, was published in 1870.

The huge second medical volume, published in 1879 and also edited by Woodward, is a study of diarrhea and dysentery, consisting of statistics, reports, detailed case studies of individual patients, and discussions of specific symptoms and treatments. Because of Woodward's own poor health, Surgeon Charles Smart succeeded Woodward as head preparer of the medical volumes in 1883 and published the last one in 1888. This volume contains data on camp fevers and every other disease suffered by the troops.

The surgical volumes, also three of them, discuss all the types of gunshot wounds, with case studies and illustrations. They are arranged according to the part of the body wounded. The first volume, compiled by George A. Otis and published in 1870, deals with wounds and injuries to the head, face, neck, spine, and chest. Otis's second volume (1876) presents data on wounds of the abdomen, pelvis, genitourinary area, and arms. The final volume (1883), completed by D.L. Huntington after Otis's death, covers leg wounds, as well as wound infections.

The enormous amount of work undertaken by these authors, their clerks, and the men who collected the data has provided an invaluable source of information on most aspects of Civil War medicine.

See also: Army Medical Museum; Barnes, Joseph K.; Brinton, John Hill; Diarrhea and Dysentery; Fevers; Gunshot Wounds; Gunshot Wounds, Treatment of; Hammond, William Alexander; Infections, of Wounds; Woodward, Joseph Janvier.

Bibliography

Barnes, Joseph K., ed. *The Medical and Surgical History of the War of the Rebellion (1861–65).* Washington, DC: Government Printing Office, 1870–1888; reprint, Wilmington, NC: Broadfoot, 1990.

Henry, Robert S. *The Armed Forces Institute of Pathology: Its First Century, 1862–1962.* Washington, DC: Government Printing Office, 1964.

MEDICAL CADETS

The corps of medical cadets was a group of Union men between the ages of eighteen and twenty-three who had some medical training and worked as assistants to surgeons, usually in hospitals. The corps, which was approved by Congress on August 3, 1861, contained up to fifty (later seventy) cadets at a time. These cadets already had two years of private study with a physician and one term of medical college courses (two terms were required for graduation). Applicants who passed the examination enlisted for a year at a noncommissioned officer's rank. They were paid thirty dollars per month, plus living quarters, fuel for cooking and heating, and transportation. In 1862 they were also granted a daily food ration. The cadets received only practical experience, not formal medical training such as was available to some of the Confederate hospital stewards in Richmond, Virginia.

The first cadets were selected in November 1861 and the corps was officially abolished in July 1866. Between those two dates 273 men served as medical cadets, at least twenty-six of them for more than a single term. While some served in field hospitals and on hospital transport ships, most cadets worked in army general hospitals, about half of them in the area of Washington, DC, Maryland, Pennsylvania, and Virginia. These cadets were usually paired with a medical officer to care for patients in specific wards. Cadets' duties included dressing wounds, assisting with postmortem examinations, and helping with administrative chores such as issuing clothes to patients. Some cadets assisted at, and may even have performed, surgeries. (Certainly cadets practiced on deceased soldiers, amputating limbs). During periods when the hospitals were flooded with patients and understaffed, some medical cadets had complete responsibility for one or more wards and functioned as assistant surgeons. Benefiting from this very practical medical training, 111 of the medical cadets went on to become commissioned or contract military medical officers. Among them were Assistant Surgeon Charles A. Leale, the first physician to reach Abraham Lincoln after John Wilkes Booth shot him at Ford's Theatre, and Surgeon Edward Curtis, who assisted at Lincoln's postmortem examination.

There were also "acting medical cadets," civilians with just one year of study with a physician, who contracted to work for the medical department for at least three months. Though they were paid only living quarters and rations, an unknown number of men chose to serve in order to gain practical experience.

See also: Education, Medical; Hospital Ships; Hospitals, Field; Hospitals, General; Leale, Charles Augustus; Lincoln, Abraham; Stewards, Hospital; Surgeons; Surgeons, Acting Assistant (Contract); Surgeons, Assistant.

Bibliography

Hasegawa, Guy R. "The Civil War's Medical Cadets: Medical Students Serving the Union." *Journal of the American College of Surgeons* 193 (July 2001): 81–89.

MEDICAL DEPARTMENT, ORGANIZATION OF

The Northern and Southern armies began the Civil War with a similar structure for their medical departments because Southern organizers based their new department on the Union model with which they were familiar. As a result, both sides began with a medical department that was much too small to meet the needs of the sick and wounded of their rapidly growing armies, and both sides eventually made some changes to their organization.

In both cases, the department was headed by a surgeon general who was in charge of all aspects of military medical care, both in the field and in the general hospitals. The surgeon general needed a talent for organization, a quality that the first two Union surgeons general, Thomas Lawson and Clement A. Finley, did not possess. The surgeon general ranked as a colonel. On April 16, 1862, the U.S. Congress passed an act promoting the surgeon general to brigadier general. The Confederate Congress discussed, but did not pass, such a promotion.

At the outbreak of the war, the Union surgeon general had a small administrative staff of several surgeons, assistant surgeons, and clerks. The April 1862 legislation that reorganized the medical department established the office of sanitary inspector general, as well as a number of subordinate inspectors. The act also made all posts dependent on merit rather than military seniority, opening the way for the appointment of the innovative William A. Hammond as surgeon general.

In the Confederacy, a law of February 26, 1861, created the medical department. Subsequent acts enlarged the department until President Jefferson Davis was able, by August 1861, to appoint as many medical officers as needed.

On both sides, the medical officers who cared for the patients in the field and the hospitals were divided into three ranks: surgeons, assistant surgeons, and acting assistant (or contract) surgeons. The surgeons had the best education and the most experience, usually at least five years in medical practice. They provided the most complex treatments and also handled administrative tasks. Assistant surgeons, with less experience, were, like the surgeons, commissioned officers; they provided initial or continuing patient care. Acting assistant surgeons were temporarily employed by contract during a crisis, generally because they were too old or weak for military service, they did not wish to leave an established practice, or they were not yet qualified for a commission. Each regiment was supposed to have a surgeon and one or two assistant surgeons. Armies also eventually had brigade, division, corps, and army medical directors, as appropriate, each supervising the medical officers of his army unit. The top official reported to the surgeon general.

General hospitals usually had surgeons in supervisory positions and assistant or acting assistant surgeons each responsible for one or two wards, reporting to the surgeon in charge of the hospital. In turn, that doctor reported to the surgeon in charge of the post or, in the North, to the local army commander. In the South, an order of March 12, 1863, established the position of medical director of hospitals, a medical officer in charge of all the general hospitals in a particular region. Although these medical directors of hospitals cooperated with field medical directors of armies, both types of medical directors reported to the surgeon general.

In addition, both the Northern and Southern medical departments included medical inspectors, laboratories for manufacturing medicines, and medical purveyors for distributing those medicines. However, construction of facilities and transportation of patients and supplies almost always were under the control of the quartermaster department. This arrangement sometimes caused tremendous hardships because the medical department could not manage its own equipment to meet the patients' needs.

In the North, the performance of the department improved tremendously under the prodding of the U.S. Sanitary Commission and the administrative skill of Surgeon General William A. Hammond. In the South, Surgeon General Samuel P. Moore managed one of the best-organized departments of the Confederacy. Although it suffered from the shortages common to the breakdown of the rebel effort, the medical department was still functioning well when the war ended.

See also: Finley, Clement Alexander; Hammond, William Alexander; Hospitals, General; Inspectors, Medical; Laboratories, Medical; Lawson, Thomas; Medical Directors, Field; Medical Directors, of Hospitals; Medical Purveyors; Moore, Samuel Preston; Quartermasters; Surgeon General; Surgeon in Charge; Surgeons; Surgeons, Acting Assistant (Contract); Surgeons, Assistant; Surgeons, Brigade; Surgeons, Post; United States Sanitary Commission.

Bibliography

Adams, George Worthington. *Doctors in Blue: The Medical History of the Union Army in the Civil War.* New York: Schuman, 1952; reprint, Dayton, OH: Morningside, 1985.

Cunningham, H.H. *Doctors in Gray: The Confederate Medical Service.* Baton Rouge: Louisiana State University Press, 1958; reprint, Gloucester, MA: Peter Smith, 1970.

Schroeder-Lein, Glenna R. *Confederate Hospitals on the Move: Samuel H. Stout and the Army of Tennessee.* Columbia: University of South Carolina Press, 1994.

MEDICAL DIRECTORS, FIELD

Each army, North and South, had a medical director during the Civil War. Later on, when the armies were reorganized, each army corps and division also had a medical director. It was the medical director's responsibility to organize the medical system to ensure that the troops remained in the best health possible.

The medical director was supposed to make sure that the army had enough medicines and supplies and the means to replenish supplies that were used up. He arranged for ambulances and stretchers to remove the wounded from the field, hospital beds for the sick and wounded, and adequate doctors, nurses, and other attendants. The medical director inspected camps and hospital sanitation. He also assigned, supervised, and trained subordinate medical officers.

Supervising an entire army's medical system required administrative skills that some of the early Union medical directors did not possess. Those who had served in the pre–Civil War army, rising to the top of the department through seniority, tended to apply army regulations rigidly and failed to understand the need to be prepared for thousands of sick or wounded soldiers They did not know how to organize their subordinates, nor did they have medical inspectors to help. Union soldiers wounded at First Bull Run (Manassas) in July 1861 and during the Peninsula Campaign in the spring of 1862 suffered severely as a result.

At first, there were no regulations that detailed the powers and authority of the medical director. As a result, a medical director needed a cooperative army commander to give him the authority and support for organizational reform. General George B. McClellan of the Union Army of the Potomac worked with his medical directors Charles S. Tripler and then Jonathan Letterman. Tripler made some progress but was overwhelmed by the size of the army and the accompanying chaos, particularly during the Peninsula Campaign. Although he suggested organizing an ambulance corps, it was his successor, Jonathan Letterman, who actually did so, ensuring its efficiency by placing it under the control of the medical rather than the quartermaster's department. Letterman also reorganized the medical supply system for the army. The advent of William A. Hammond as surgeon general in the spring of 1862 contributed tremendously to the ability of Letterman and other medical directors to organize field medical systems.

Even though they had to establish every part of the medical system from the beginning, the Confederates had the advantage of the organizational stickler Samuel P. Moore serving as surgeon general from the summer of 1861 on. The Confederate army medical directors had responsibilities similar to those of their Union counterparts. However, they also had to supervise the general hospitals behind the lines in their department, a task Union medical directors did not have. In order to promote better medical administration of both the armies and the hospitals, on March 12, 1863, the Adjutant and Inspector General's Office in Richmond ordered the appointment of eight medical directors of hospitals to relieve the field medical directors of that responsibility. In the Army of Tennessee, for example, field medical directors Andrew J. Foard and Edward A. Flewellen cooperated with hospital medical director Samuel H. Stout to get the patients to the hospitals and to let Stout know when military movements would force those hospitals to evacuate and relocate.

Improved organization enabled field medical directors on both sides to carry out their responsibilities better during the second half of the war, although the Confederates were hampered by increasing supply problems.

See also: Ambulance Corps; Blockade; Bull Run (Manassas), First Battle of; Flewellen, Edward Archelaus; Foard, Andrew Jackson; Hammond, William Alexander; Hospital Relocations; Hospitals, Field; Hospitals, General; Letterman, Jonathan; Medical Department, Organization of; Medical Directors, of Hospitals; Moore, Samuel Preston; Peninsula Campaign; Quartermasters; Sanitation; Stout, Samuel Hollingsworth; Surgeon General; Tripler, Charles Stuart.

Bibliography

Adams, George Worthington. *Doctors in Blue: The Medical History of the Union Army in the Civil War*. New York: Schuman, 1952; reprint, Dayton, OH: Morningside, 1985.

Brinton, John H. *Personal Memoirs of John H. Brinton, Civil War Surgeon, 1861–1865.* New York: Neale, 1914; reprint, Carbondale: Southern Illinois University Press, 1996.

Cunningham, H.H. *Doctors in Gray: The Confederate Medical Service.* Baton Rouge: Louisiana State University Press, 1958; reprint, Gloucester, MA: Peter Smith, 1970.

Schroeder-Lein, Glenna R. *Confederate Hospitals on the Move: Samuel H. Stout and the Army of Tennessee.* Columbia: University of South Carolina Press, 1994.

MEDICAL DIRECTORS, OF HOSPITALS

Medical directors of hospitals were surgeons who had administrative responsibility for a large number of general hospitals in a particular region of the Confederacy. The Union medical service did not have this position.

Problems with the chain of command, including surgeons in charge of hospitals receiving conflicting orders from the surgeon general, field medical directors, and army commanders, led to the development of this position. General Braxton Bragg first promulgated the idea on August 22, 1862, in Special Orders No. 160, by placing surgeon Samuel H. Stout in charge of all the Army of Tennessee general hospitals currently located or thereafter to be established between Chattanooga, Tennessee, and Atlanta, Georgia.

On March 12, 1863, Surgeon General Samuel P. Moore and the Confederate War Department extended the plan to all the Confederate armies. The surgeon general would give orders to the medical directors of hospitals, who would pass them on to the post surgeons in towns with two or more hospitals or directly to surgeons in charge of hospitals in smaller posts. In return, reports to the surgeon general would be sent by way of the medical director of hospitals. By the fall of 1864 there were eight medical directors and districts, which varied in size. The three largest were North Carolina with twenty-one hospitals, Virginia with thirty-nine, and Georgia/Alabama (Stout's district) with more than sixty.

Besides serving as a conduit for messages, the medical director had a number of important duties. He was responsible for assigning doctors, stewards, and matrons to the various hospitals, supervising all the medical officers, and managing personnel problems that were beyond the scope of his subordinates. (In Stout's case, this meant responsibility for several hundred doctors and several thousand other staff members.) The medical director was responsible for getting often scarce resources to the hospitals that needed them, negotiating with quartermasters and other agents when necessary. The medical director also selected, supervised, and sometimes designed new hospital sites, a responsibility especially undertaken by Stout because of the mobile nature of many of his hospitals during the campaigns in Georgia. The medical director would have several assistants, depending on the size of his department, and would visit his hospitals personally whenever possible.

In short, medical directors of hospitals provided overall supervision and troubleshooting for a number of hospitals, often in widely spaced locations.

See also: Hospital Buildings; Hospital Relocations; Hospitals, General; Matrons; Moore, Samuel Preston; Quartermasters; Stewards, Hospital; Stout, Samuel Hollingsworth; Surgeon General; Surgeon in Charge; Surgeons, Post.

Bibliography

Cunningham, H.H. *Doctors in Gray: The Confederate Medical Service.* Baton Rouge: Louisiana State University Press, 1958; reprint, Gloucester, MA: Peter Smith, 1970.

Schroeder-Lein, Glenna R. *Confederate Hospitals on the Move: Samuel H. Stout and the Army of Tennessee.* Columbia: University of South Carolina Press, 1994.

MEDICAL IMPORTANCE OF THE CIVIL WAR

Many historians have viewed the medical aspects of the Civil War as unimportant, or at least brutally primitive because the war took place before scientists discovered the nature of germs. Few historians have noted medical developments—significant medical discoveries or changes in medical practice—in their analyses of the results of the Civil War.

Yet surgeons, both North and South, did learn a number of medical lessons from the Civil War. Men on both sides kept statistics, wrote up cases, and reported treatments that did or did not work. In the South, some of this information was published during the war in the *Confederate States Medical and Surgical Journal* (January 1864–February 1865) and disseminated as widely as possible to army medical officers. In the North, the material was gathered, analyzed, and published after the war in the six massive volumes of *The Medical and Surgical History of the War of the Rebellion* (1870–1888). Collected specimens also became the nucleus of the Army Medical Museum (now the National Museum of Health and Medicine), an institution initiated by Surgeon General William A. Hammond. Surgeons general on both sides made important wartime changes in medical procedures.

Because of the vast numbers of patients available, Civil War doctors sometimes tested treatments to determine if they actually were effective. Physicians discovered that doses of quinine could prevent malaria. Southern medical officers tested some of the botanical remedies proposed in Francis P. Porcher's *Resources of the Southern Fields and Forests*, determining that few of them were of any value. Other doctors found that bleeding was not a useful treatment. Union surgeon general William A. Hammond restricted the use of calomel, surely an important step, although it caused a furor among physicians who believed that calomel was still an important remedy.

Although few specific inventions occurred during the Civil War, John Julian Chisolm developed an inhaler to administer chloroform, while James Baxter Bean invented an interdental splint for the treatment of jaw fractures. Several splints for legs and arms were improved during the war.

Doctors on both sides took steps toward specialized medicine by setting aside separate wards or even hospitals for people with specific types of diseases, conditions, or wounds, such as jaw fractures, eye ailments, neurological problems, heart disease, venereal diseases, and hernias. Because of wartime experiences, specialties in orthopedics and neurology began soon after the war.

Before the war few American doctors ever had to do more surgery than stitching up occasional cuts. During the war many doctors gained extensive surgical experience. They discovered that ligatures (stitches) were generally better for stopping bleeding than tourniquets. Several surgeons performed plastic surgery, doing facial reconstruction for severely wounded soldiers. Some surgeons successfully used a trephine (circular bone saw) to remove bone and relieve pressure in depressed skull fractures, proving Crimean War experiences to be wrong. Doctors on both sides tried innovative measures to save lives and frequently succeeded.

Over the course of the war, the medical departments and individual doctors learned how to deal with massive numbers of casualties, both sick and wounded. The development of an ambulance corps in the North and mobilized hospitals, especially in the Confederate Army of Tennessee, provided examples that were followed as late as World War II.

The experiences of enormous numbers of patients in hospitals, especially those hospitals that were well run, began to change the attitudes of the general populace toward the possibilities of hospital care. Innovations such as the pavilion hospital provided examples for postwar hospital design. Women's good service in hospitals stimulated the founding of nursing schools after the war, some of them run by women who had been Civil War nurses. The emphasis by many doctors and nurses on the importance and benefits of cleanliness, good sanitation, and good ventilation influenced the development of postwar public health movements.

In general, as a result of the Civil War, large numbers of doctors around the country had better training and experience than ever before to meet the needs of their patients. Even doctors in small towns were able to operate on their own patients rather than sending them to the city.

See also: Ambulance Corps; Army Medical Museum; Bean, James Baxter; Calomel; Chisolm, John Julian; *Confederate States Medical and Surgical Journal*; Eye Ailments; Gunshot Wounds, Treatment of; Hammond, William Alexander; Heart Disease; Hospital Relocations; Hospitals, Attitudes Toward; Hospitals, Pavilion; Malaria; *The Medical and Surgical History of the War of the Rebellion*; Nurses; Porcher, Francis Peyre; Quinine; *Resources of the Southern Fields and Forests*; Sanitation; Splints; Turner's Lane Hospital; Venereal Disease; Ventilation; Women, as Hospital Workers.

Bibliography

Cunningham, H.H. *Doctors in Gray: The Confederate Medical Service.* Baton Rouge: Louisiana State University Press, 1958; reprint, Gloucester, MA: Peter Smith, 1970.

Flannery, Michael A. *Civil War Pharmacy: A History of Drugs, Drug Supply and Provision, and Therapeutics for the Union and Confederacy.* New York: Pharmaceutical Products Press, 2004.

Gaillard, Edwin S. *The Medical and Surgical Lessons of the Late War*. Louisville, KY: Louisville Journal Job Print, 1868.

Green, Carol C. *Chimborazo: The Confederacy's Largest Hospital*. Knoxville: University of Tennessee Press, 2004.

Kuz, Julian E., and Bradley P. Bengtson. *Orthopaedic Injuries of the Civil War: An Atlas of Orthopaedic Injuries and Treatments During the Civil War*. Kennesaw, GA: Kennesaw Mountain Press, 1996.

Rutkow, Ira M. *Bleeding Blue and Gray: Civil War Surgery and the Evolution of American Medicine*. New York: Random, 2005.

MEDICAL INSPECTORS *See* Inspectors, Medical.

MEDICAL OFFICERS *See* Surgeons.

MEDICAL PURVEYORS

Medical purveyors, in both the North and the South, were physicians employed as the equivalent of quartermasters for medical supplies. It was their responsibility to acquire, store, and distribute medicines for both hospitals and armies in the field.

There were essentially two types of medical purveyors—those in charge of depots and those in the field. Depot purveyors purchased materials and oversaw the manufacture of medicines and supplies. The Union army had two major depots, in New York City and Philadelphia, with thirty other subdepots around the country. The Confederates established nine districts, each with a depot and purveyor. However, due to military necessity, a number of the Confederate depots had to be relocated, in some cases several times. Depots held vast amounts of supplies to be distributed, according to specific quantities listed on the standard supply table, to all the hospitals and armies in the area. Purveyors had to keep accurate records of the quantities of material acquired, on hand, dispensed, lost, damaged, or destroyed, making several kinds of monthly, semimonthly, and quarterly reports to their surgeon general.

Purveyors acquired medicines from a number of sources, including purchases from civilians, manufacture in government laboratories, and importation from Europe (through the Union blockade in the case of the South). In the Confederacy, purveyors encouraged civilians to gather and turn in certain indigenous plants from which medicines could be prepared. In addition to medicines, which included alcohol, purveyors supplied surgical instruments, hospital bedding and furniture, medical books, bandages, and all the utensils needed for the care of the sick and wounded. Some items, such as bowls, pitchers, spoons, chamber pots, and lanterns, could evidently be procured from either the purveyor or the quartermaster.

Transportation was the responsibility of the quartermaster department, however, except in cases of emergency.

At least in the Union army, a few purveyors were assisted by medical store-keepers, skilled pharmacists who were directly responsible for storing, guarding, and issuing the medicines and supplies. These storekeepers also served as acting medical purveyors when the purveyor was absent from his post.

Field purveyors were to have enough supplies on hand to meet the probable medical needs of their army. It was a challenge to keep enough materials available to care for an emergency influx of patients while avoiding large stockpiles that could be captured or would have to be relocated or destroyed in case of sudden military movements.

Although most purveyors tried hard to avoid shortages that would prove harmful to the patients, they often encountered problems beyond their control. At times, especially in the Confederacy, purveyors were unable to get supplies because of shortages or transportation failures. Even when supplies of drugs were available, Confederate purveyors sometimes lacked jars, bottles, and corks. Purveyors urged medical officers to return all empty medicinal containers for reuse. Sometimes medical personnel misunderstood orders for supplies; sometimes supplies were damaged, adulterated, lost, or stolen in transit. Medicinal whiskey was particularly subject to theft during shipping. Medical purveyors found it impossible to solve many of these difficulties.

See also: Alcohol, Medicinal Uses of; Blockade; Laboratories, Medical; Quartermasters; Substitutes, for Supplies; Supply Table.

Bibliography

Flannery, Michael A. *Civil War Pharmacy: A History of Drugs, Drug Supply and Provision, and Therapeutics for the Union and Confederacy.* New York: Pharmaceutical Products Press, 2004.

Greenleaf, Charles R. *A Manual for the Medical Officers of the United States Army.* Philadelphia: J.B. Lippincott, 1864; reprint, San Francisco: Norman, 1992.

Smith, George Winston. *Medicines for the Union Army: The United States Army Laboratories During the Civil War.* Madison, WI: American Institute for the History of Pharmacy, 1962; reprint, New York: Pharmaceutical Products Press, 2001.

MEDICAL SECTS *See* Alternative Medicines.

MEDICATION, ADMINISTRATION OF

During the Civil War era, as now, medications came in a variety of formats for internal or external administration. Few drugs were commercially produced, although a number of laboratories were established both North and South during the war. Physicians or local druggists compounded most medicines themselves. During the war a number of these druggists became hospital stewards with responsibility for preparing the medications for their patients. Most medications were derived from plant products, although some were metal based, such as the mercury compound calomel.

There were three general methods for administering medications internally: powder, pill, and liquid. The plant or metal product was usually ground into a powder no matter how it would be dispensed. Some medicines were retained in powder form, measured into appropriate doses, and wrapped in paper, to be mixed with water or other liquid before being swallowed. Powders were easy to carry and administer. However, the powder format was sensitive to light, moisture, and humidity, which could dissolve it prematurely. In addition, powders generally tasted awful.

Pills were the most popular way to take medicine. A nineteenth-century pill, however, was not a standard-sized, compressed tablet, such as an aspirin. Instead, the druggist took the proper amount of medicinal powder and mixed it with something to hold it together, such as honey, molasses, or gum arabic. The mixture was then rolled into a small ball or pill.

Liquid formats included tinctures (a medicine usually of plant origin, dissolved in a water or alcohol base) and fluid extracts (plant juices of the appropriate consistency and strength for the proper dosage). Elixirs, mixtures whose evil taste was masked by a sweetened alcohol base, were available for a few medicines, but became much more common after the Civil War.

External medications were primarily used to soothe and heal, though some external medications were used to deliberately irritate the skin in order to draw out poisons or create a counterirritant to cure some other condition. Healing preparations included dressings, poultices, and ointments. Morphine, although most commonly taken orally, could be applied as a powder to a wound, usually with a doctor's bare fingertip. In some cases morphine was injected by syringe, but because doctors did not have sharp needles, they had to make a small cut in order to insert the point of the syringe. Although morphine applied externally relieved pain, the application process could spread infection.

See also: Alcohol, Medicinal Uses of; Calomel; Cupping and Blistering; Materia Medica; Medical Purveyors; Morphine; Opiate Use and Addiction; Porcher, Francis Peyre; Stewards, Hospital.

Bibliography

Bollet, Alfred Jay. *Civil War Medicine: Challenges and Triumphs.* Tucson, AZ: Galen, 2002.
Flannery, Michael A. *Civil War Pharmacy: A History of Drugs, Drug Supply and Provision, and Therapeutics for the Union and Confederacy.* New York: Pharmaceutical Products Press, 2004.

MIASMS

Miasm (or *miasma*) was a term used during the Civil War to indicate airborne sources of infection. Miasms were supposedly poisonous vapors given off by decomposing plant matter, such as in swamps. The Italian term for bad air, *malaria*, was applied to certain fevers that seemed to come from the emanations of swamps. Odors caused by sewage, bodily waste, unwashed bodies, and human and animal corpses caused army camps and many other locations to smell vile. These foul odors were also believed to cause disease.

The premise of miasms was wrong because odors do not cause disease. However, attempts to prevent the effects of bad air proved beneficial by reducing the spread of germs and the presence of insects that transmitted disease. For example, pitching camps away from swamps and mosquitoes decreased the number of cases of malaria. Quarantining ships coming into New Orleans and cleaning up the dock area helped prevent the mosquito-borne yellow fever epidemics that so often occurred before the Civil War. Improved camp cleanliness reduced the contamination that was the actual cause of diseases such as typhoid fever.

See also: Diarrhea and Dysentery; Fevers; Latrines; Malaria; Mosquitoes; Sanitation; Typhoid Fever.

Bibliography
Bollet, Alfred Jay. *Civil War Medicine: Challenges and Triumphs.* Tucson, AZ: Galen, 2002.

MINIÉ BALLS

Minié balls were a type of bullet used in Springfield and Enfield rifles by soldiers of both the North and the South during the Civil War.

In this period nearly all muskets and rifles were single shot and muzzle loading. This meant that the bullet and gunpowder were inserted and rammed down from the same end that the bullet would be fired out of. Until the 1850s, and even at the beginning of the Civil War, most of these guns had a smooth bore (the inside of the barrel) and fired round balls. A rifle differed from a smoothbore because it had spiral grooves cut inside the barrel. These grooves caused the bullet to spin, enabling it to travel further and more accurately. Although these principles were known, rifles were too slow for most military uses because they were difficult to load and required frequent cleaning.

Two men made rifles practical by inventing a new type of ammunition. In the 1840s, Captain Claude-Étienne Minié, of the French army, developed the bullet that bore his name. Rather than being round, it was bullet-shaped, with a base of iron or wood that expanded to fit into the rifling (grooves) when the gun was fired. Although these bullets were easier to load, they were expensive to produce and often functioned improperly.

James H. Burton, who worked at the U.S. armory in Harpers Ferry, Virginia, made the improvements that produced the minié ball used during the Civil War. The main change was in the base, which was hollow with ridges on the outside. When the powder exploded to fire the gun, it caused a gas that enlarged the hollow base of the minié ball, permitting it to expand to fit the rifling.

Minié balls were made of soft lead and were fairly large (.58 caliber). They tended to produce wounds more devastating than those made by the previously used musket balls. Musket balls generally entered and exited the body more cleanly. Minié balls usually flattened or deformed in other ways upon contact, tearing tissue, shattering bone, and leaving a larger exit than entrance wound if they went all the way through. Even spent balls, which had hit something else first, could do a great deal of damage. Because the bullet would bring clothing scraps and other dirt and debris into the wound, minor or sometimes serious wound infections almost always resulted. Physicians were unable to do delicate reconstructive procedures on shattered bones, although sometimes they did an excision or resection, removing portions of damaged bone. Often, even if a wounded arm or leg healed, the patient would have little use of it. In many cases doctors performed amputations of extremities to avoid more serious problems. Minié balls created the largest percentage of wounds of known origin treated by Northern doctors and reported in *The Medical and Surgical History of the War of the Rebellion.*

Rifles loaded with minié balls had a tremendous impact on the Civil War. Smoothbores had a maximum range of 250 yards, but were unlikely to hit anything further than 80 yards away. Rifles had a maximum range of about 1,000 yards and were effective to about 400 yards. This meant that a soldier with a rifle could hit an attacker five times further away than one armed with a smoothbore. This change favored defenders, made frontal assaults more deadly, and reduced the effect of cavalry charges against infantry. However, many commanders on both sides, who had been trained with smoothbores, took a long time to change their tactics, resulting in the killing and wounding of many additional soldiers.

See also: Amputation; Artificial Limbs; Gunshot Wounds; Gunshot Wounds, Treatment of; Infections, of Wounds; *The Medical and Surgical History of the War of the Rebellion;* Mortality, of Soldiers; Resection.

Bibliography

Bollet, Alfred Jay. *Civil War Medicine: Challenges and Triumphs.* Tucson, AZ: Galen, 2002.

McPherson, James M. *Ordeal by Fire: The Civil War and Reconstruction.* New York: Knopf, 1982.

MITCHELL, SILAS WEIR (1829–1914)

Silas Weir Mitchell (usually known as S. Weir Mitchell), a Union contract surgeon and neurologist, was the son of a physician, John Kearsley Mitchell, and his wife, Sarah Matilda Henry Mitchell. Born in Philadelphia, on February 15, 1829, young Mitchell attended University Grammar School before entering the University of Pennsylvania in 1844 when he was fifteen. Mitchell dropped out during his senior year, due to either his own illness or his father's (sources differ on this point). Since a college degree was not required to study medicine, Mitchell attended Jefferson Medical College (where his father taught), graduating in 1850. Mitchell then studied with several notable physicians in France, returning to Philadelphia in 1851 and joining his father's private practice. As his father's health declined, Mitchell took more and more responsibility for the practice, and for his family's financial well being, until his father died in 1858.

In that same year, Mitchell married Mary Middleton Elwyn. They had two sons before she died of diphtheria in 1862. In 1874 he married Mary Cadwalader. They had a daughter who died young.

In addition to his medical practice and his family concerns, Mitchell was always busily engaged in research and writing. Between 1852 and 1863 he studied various aspects of blood, poisons, medicinal plants, and physiology, publishing nearly thirty papers on these topics.

When the Civil War broke out, Mitchell became an acting assistant (contract) surgeon for the Union army, serving at both the Filbert Street and the Christian Street hospitals in Philadelphia. Here he first became interested in patients suffering from nerve diseases and injuries. These patients were difficult to treat, and most doctors were only too happy to send them to Mitchell in exchange for one of his patients with a different disease. After his friend William A. Hammond became surgeon general, Mitchell proposed setting up a separate hospital for nerve patients, an idea that Hammond approved. Renting an estate in the Philadelphia suburbs, Mitchell established Turner's Lane Hospital in August 1863. It accommodated 275 or 400 patients (accounts differ).

At Turner's Lane, Mitchell and his colleagues George Read Morehouse and William Williams Keen (who had been a regimental assistant surgeon earlier in the war) studied all sorts of nerve injuries, such as contracted limbs, burning sensations in the hands and feet, phantom pain in amputated limbs, and other crippling problems. They did all the observation and note-taking themselves and devised helpful treatments in many instances. The three men published several papers as well as the important study *Gunshot Wounds and Other Injuries of Nerves* (1864). Mitchell worked entirely in the Philadelphia hospitals except for service on the field after the third day at Gettysburg.

After the war Mitchell became a prominent neurologist, a new specialty. He worked at the Philadelphia Orthopaedic Hospital and Infirmary for Nervous Diseases for more than forty years. In the 1870s he developed a rest cure regimen for the treatment of nervous disorders, especially the "hysteria" experienced by women. This cure included rest, nutritious food, massage, electrotherapy, and physical therapy. At the time it was regarded as a humane treatment, sympathetic to the needs of women. More recently it has been severely criticized for assuming that women were, and should be, weak and dependent, under the absolute authority of the doctor.

Mitchell used his Civil War experiences as the basis for further research and for writings both medical and fictional. He wrote more than 170 medical papers during his career, as well as several neurology books. After the war he also wrote short stories, poetry, and fifteen novels, many of which included realistic Civil War descriptions, based on Mitchell's own experiences. The novel *In War Time*, for example, contains an account of the Filbert Street Hospital.

Mitchell died on January 4, 1914.

See also: Amputation; Gettysburg, Battle of; Gunshot Wounds, Treatment of; Hammond, William Alexander; Hospital Buildings; Hospitals, Pavilion; Surgeons, Acting Assistant (Contract); Turner's Lane Hospital.

Bibliography

Freemon, Frank R. "The First Neurological Research Center: Turner's Lane Hospital During the American Civil War." *Journal of the History of the Neurosciences* (April 1993): 135–142.

Middleton, William S. "Turner's Lane Hospital." *Bulletin of the History of Medicine* 40 (January/February 1966): 14–42.

Mitchell, S. Weir. "Some Personal Recollections of the Civil War." *Transactions of the College of Physicians of Philadelphia*, 3rd series, 27 (1905); reprint, *Journal of Civil War Medicine* 1 (May–June 1997): 5–7.

Mitchell, Silas Weir, George Read Morehouse, and William Williams Keen. *Gunshot Wounds and Other Injuries of Nerves*. Philadelphia: J.B. Lippincott, 1864; reprint, San Francisco: Norman, 1989.

MOORE, SAMUEL PRESTON (1813–1889)

Samuel Preston Moore, Confederate surgeon general, was born in Charleston, South Carolina, on September 16, 1813, the sixth of the nine children of Stephen West Moore and Eleanor Screven Gilbert Moore. Educated in Charleston, he graduated from the Medical College of South Carolina in 1834. On March 14, 1835, Moore was commissioned an assistant surgeon in the U.S. Army. Before the Mexican War, he served at forts in Kansas, Iowa, Texas, and several places in Florida. In Pensacola, Florida, he met Mary Augusta Brown, daughter of a regimental commander. The couple was married in June 1845 and eventually had three children, two of whom lived to adulthood.

During the Mexican War, Moore served sick and wounded troops in hospitals along the Rio Grande—on Brazos Island, Texas, and in Camargo, Mexico—rather than with either invading army. Promoted to surgeon on April 30, 1849, Moore served at Jefferson Barracks, Missouri; Fort Laramie, in the future Wyoming Territory; San Antonio and Brownsville, Texas; and Fort Columbus on Governor's Island, New York. Moore was the surgeon at West Point military academy (1855–1860) and then medical purveyor at New Orleans until he resigned from the army on February 25, 1861.

Moore evidently had no desire to be involved in the Civil War on either side, so he moved to Little Rock, Arkansas, to practice medicine and manage family property. However, when David C. DeLeon proved unsuitable for the post of Confederate surgeon general, Moore accepted the office, believing it was his duty. He was appointed acting surgeon general on July 30, 1861, with formal appointment as surgeon general in late November.

Moore drew on his twenty-six years of experience as a Union medical officer as he began to organize the Confederate medical department out of nothing. He used the same structure and operations as the U.S. Army medical department, but he had to recruit appropriate physicians to fill positions in both regiments and hospitals. Only twenty-four of the approximately 3,000 medical officers who ultimately served the Confederacy had previous army experience. In order to get properly qualified doctors and to weed out unqualified physicians who had become surgeons of volunteer regiments in the early days of the war, Moore instituted a medical examining board. He encouraged the preparation of new doctors through a program for hospital stewards at the Medical College of Virginia in Richmond. He also promoted continuing education for practicing military physicians through the Association of Army and Navy Surgeons of the Confederate States, which met in Richmond, and its monthly publication, the *Confederate States Medical and Surgical Journal*.

Moore also needed to provide medical supplies for all the regiments and hospitals in the Confederacy, a task made more difficult by the Union blockade of Southern ports, which identified medical supplies as contraband. Moore sponsored the study of Southern plants and their uses prepared by Francis Peyre Porcher, *Resources of the Southern Fields and Forests*. He established laboratories at seven locations in the Confederacy to manufacture needed medicines, to the extent possible with local resources. Moore also set up four distilleries to manufacture 600 gallons per day of alcoholic beverages for medicinal purposes.

Moore also supervised all the Confederate medical officers, working closely with the medical directors of armies and hospitals, who then supervised the regimental and ward physicians, respectively. Moore was a stickler for accurate, thorough, and timely completion of paperwork. He was also a strict disciplinarian, although fair in his judgments. Because of Moore's brusque nature, many doctors were glad to avoid direct contact with him. To the extent to which it depended on Moore rather than quartermasters or other military and civilian officials, the medical department was one of the most efficient government agencies in the Confederacy.

When Richmond was evacuated on April 2, 1865, Moore left with the other Confederate officials. Most of his departmental records and his own personal papers were consumed in the fires that followed. Moore soon returned to Richmond and took the amnesty oath on June 22, 1865. However, he never practiced medicine again. He served on the Richmond school board and the board of the Virginia Agricultural Society, and he joined a Confederate veterans group. He was elected president of the Association of Medical Officers of the Army and Navy of the Confederacy during the short-lived attempt to establish it in the 1870s. Moore died in Richmond on May 31, 1899, and was buried there in Hollywood Cemetery.

See also: Association of Army and Navy Surgeons of the Confederate States; Association of Medical Officers of the Army and Navy of the Confederacy; Blockade; *Confederate States Medical and Surgical Journal*; DeLeon, David Camden; Education, Medical; Examining Boards, Medical; Medical Directors, Field; Medical Directors, of Hospitals; Medical Purveyors; Porcher, Francis Peyre; *Resources of the Southern Fields and Forests*; Substitutes, for Supplies; Surgeon General.

Bibliography

Cunningham, H.H. *Doctors in Gray: The Confederate Medical Service.* Baton Rouge: Louisiana State University Press, 1958; reprint, Gloucester, MA: Peter Smith, 1970.

Farr, Warner Dahlgren. "Samuel Preston Moore: Confederate Surgeon General." *Civil War History* 41 (March 1995): 41–56.

Lewis, Samuel E. "Samuel Preston Moore, M.D., Surgeon General of the Confederate States." *Southern Practitioner* 23 (August 1901): 381–386.

MORPHINE

Morphine was one of the most important painkillers used by both sides during the Civil War. Morphine is a derivative of opium, discovered by a German pharmacist in 1803 or 1804. It could be administered in three ways: as a pill taken orally, as a powder dusted directly on the wound or placed in it with a fingertip, or as a fluid injected from a syringe into a small cut. All three methods were effective, although the oral administration required a larger dose.

Doctors on the battlefield and in hospitals who needed to provide pain relief for the wounded generally used morphine. At Turner's Lane Hospital for neurological diseases and injuries in Philadelphia, surgeons prescribed morphine to treat severe nerve pain.

Although Confederate surgeon general Samuel P. Moore urged Southern citizens to plant poppies, few of their products were actually made into opium. Nearly all the morphine used in the South came through the Union blockade, although occasionally some was captured from the Union forces.

See also: Blockade; Gunshot Wounds, Treatment of; Materia Medica; Medication, Administration of; Moore, Samuel Preston; Opiate Use and Addiction.

Bibliography

Bollet, Alfred Jay. *Civil War Medicine: Challenges and Triumphs.* Tucson, AZ: Galen, 2002.

MORTALITY, OF SOLDIERS

No one knows exactly how many soldiers died during the Civil War. The most generally accepted estimate is 620,000—roughly one-third killed in action or dying of battle wounds (as well as other injuries) and the other two-thirds dying of disease. The total breaks down to about 110,000 Union deaths from gunshot wounds and 250,000 from disease, for a total of 360,000, plus 95,000 Confederate battle-related deaths and 165,000 deaths from disease, totaling 260,000.

Approximately 2.1 million soldiers (including 150,000 blacks) served in the Union armies during the war, while 800,000 fought for the Confederacy. At the beginning of the war, there were about three and a half times as many white men of military age in the North as in the South. Just over half of the eligible men in the North served, while close to four-fifths of Confederate men fought. The basic statistical analysis of the Civil War, still generally used, is Thomas L. Livermore's *Numbers and Losses in the Civil War in America, 1861–1865* (1901). Historians who come up with other figures generally start with Livermore as the authority to dispute. Most medical analyses rely heavily on the statistics in *The Medical and Surgical History of the War of the Rebellion*, but may interpret those statistics differently.

While historians have been able to make some good estimates, the exact numbers of soldiers who served, or their mortality, cannot be known because of inaccurate statistics. Some records were improperly kept. For example, the same soldier might be counted as a separate person each time he transferred to another hospital. When the battlefield or hospital was very busy, some soldiers might not be recorded at all. Some wounded men died in out-of-the-way places and their bodies were never found. Diseases were often incorrectly diagnosed, attributing deaths to the wrong cause. Some soldiers died at home on furlough or after discharge from wounds or disease directly attributable to their military service, yet their numbers were not included in the statistics. Many records, especially Confederate papers, were destroyed; others were lost. In some cases, no one kept records at all. As a result, the actual soldier mortality may be somewhat higher or lower than the generally accepted statistics.

A soldier was most likely to be killed in action or die on the field if he was wounded in the head, neck, chest, or abdomen. A wound in an arm or a leg was unlikely to kill the soldier at once unless he was hit in an artery or had a limb blown off. Because minié balls, the bullets most commonly used during the Civil War, often shattered bone and severely mangled tissue, the best treatment for a limb wound was sometimes amputation. Nearly 30,000 amputations were performed upon Union soldiers, with about a 25 percent fatality rate. In general, the mortality rate for leg amputations was higher than for arm amputations; the mortality rate for amputations close to the trunk of the body was higher than for amputations elsewhere; and the mortality rate for amputations at a joint was higher than for amputations elsewhere on a limb.

In the Union army, 1,739,135 soldiers with diarrhea and dysentery were hospitalized, with 44,558 men dying, mostly chronic sufferers. The second most fatal disease was typhoid fever, with 34,833 deaths out of 148,631 cases. Of the 77,335 pneumonia patients, 19,971 died, as did 10,063 out of 1,315,955 malaria sufferers. Tuberculosis caused 6,946 fatalities out of 29,510 patients, while 7,058 of the 18,952 ill with smallpox or varioloid died. Smaller numbers of patients died from a wide variety of other diseases as well. Available Confederate statistics show similar proportions of deaths from disease.

One researcher calculates mortality from disease among Union soldiers as 53.4 per 1,000 soldiers (5.3 percent). Although this figure sounds high to people in the twenty-first century, the statistic compares favorably with figures from other mid–nineteenth-century wars. During the Mexican War (1846–1848), American deaths averaged 110 per 1,000 soldiers (11 percent), while during the Crimean War (1853–1856), British soldiers died from disease at the rate of 232 per 1,000 (23.2 percent).

Prisoners of war on both sides suffered greatly from lack of food, clothing, adequate shelter, clean water, and proper sanitation. Conditions varied widely among the camps, but many prisoners developed sanitation-related diseases and malnutrition. The death rate was very high. Roughly 23,000 of the 127,000 Union soldiers in Confederate prisons, or about 18 percent, died. Approximately 10 percent, or 26,000 out of 220,000 Confederate prisoners, died in Northern prisons. It has been estimated that prisoner of war deaths accounted for about 10 percent of all Civil War soldier deaths.

See also: Amputation; Andersonville Prison; Diarrhea and Dysentery; Elmira Prison; Gunshot Wounds, Treatment of; Malaria; Malnutrition; *The Medical and Surgical History of the War of the Rebellion*; Minié Balls; Pneumonia; Prisoners of War; Sanitation; Scurvy; Smallpox; Tuberculosis; Typhoid Fever; Varioloid.

Bibliography
Barnes, Joseph K., ed. *The Medical and Surgical History of the War of the Rebellion (1861–65)*. Washington, DC: Government Printing Office, 1870–1888; reprint, Wilmington, NC: Broadfoot, 1990.

Bollet, Alfred Jay. *Civil War Medicine: Challenges and Triumphs*. Tucson, AZ: Galen, 2002.

Faust, Drew Gilpin. "'Numbers on Top of Numbers': Counting the Civil War Dead." *Journal of Military History* 70 (2006): 995–1009.

Kuz, Julian E., and Bradley P. Bengtson. *Orthopaedic Injuries of the Civil War: An Atlas of Orthopaedic Injuries and Treatments During the Civil War*. Kennesaw, GA: Kennesaw Mountain Press, 1996.

Steiner, Paul E. *Disease in the Civil War: Natural Biological Warfare in 1861–1865*. Springfield, IL: C.C. Thomas, 1968.

MORTALITY, OF SURGEONS

During the Civil War the Union army employed more than 12,000 physicians altogether, while the Confederates commissioned 3,236 doctors and temporarily hired an unknown number by contract. These men were exposed to harsh living conditions, to the diseases suffered by their patients, and to military action.

Not surprisingly, a number of medical officers, as well as nurses, matrons, and other members of the hospital staff, sickened and died. Some also suffered wounds. In the Union army nineteen doctors died in battle with an additional ten mortally wounded. Seventy-three others were wounded, but survived. Thirteen doctors were killed by rioters or assassins, while nine died because of accidents in the line of duty. An additional four died in prison, and 281 died of unspecified disease, for a total of at least 336 deaths.

One historian of Civil War medicine has compiled a list of 178 Confederate doctors known to have died during the Civil War. Of the 117 whose cause of death is known, twenty-eight were killed in action, fourteen were mortally wounded, three were murdered, and seven died as a result of accident (including two drownings and two train wrecks). One physician committed suicide. The remaining sixty-four medical officers died of disease, including typhoid fever (seven), pneumonia (five), yellow fever (four), diarrhea and dysentery (four), liver problems (three), heart disease (two), and a number of other diagnoses. Twenty-five died of unspecified diseases.

See also: Diarrhea and Dysentery; Heart Disease; Hospital Support Staff; Nurses; Pneumonia; Surgeons; Tuberculosis; Typhoid Fever.

Bibliography

Barnes, Joseph K., ed. *The Medical and Surgical History of the War of the Rebellion (1861–65).* Washington, DC: Government Printing Office, 1870–1888; reprint, Wilmington, NC: Broadfoot, 1990.

Hambrecht, F.T. Biographical data on Confederate physicians who died during the American Civil War. Unpublished research in progress, May 20, 2006.

Mitchell, S. Weir. "Some Personal Recollections of the Civil War." *Transactions of the College of Physicians of Philadelphia,* 3rd series, 27 (1905); reprint, *Journal of Civil War Medicine* 1 (May–June 1997): 5–7.

MOSQUITOES

Mosquitoes are flying insect pests known worldwide. Various types of mosquitoes are found in different locations. Female mosquitoes are the ones that bite because they need blood products for the gestation of their eggs. Many types of mosquitoes prefer the blood of birds and animals rather than humans, transferring their bites to humans only when their preferred mammal or bird is unavailable. Mosquitoes spread a number of diseases, but only certain types of mosquitoes are carriers for any particular disease, and many individual mosquitoes are not infected. At the time of the Civil War, mosquitoes were seen merely as a nuisance; their disease-carrying potential was unknown.

Female mosquitoes lay rafts of eggs (as many as 240) in standing water. Within two weeks those eggs that survive various natural predators have gone through larval and pupal stages to emerge as adult mosquitoes. Mosquitoes can bite more than once. When they do bite, they suck in blood and deposit various microbes in the animal or person on whom they are feeding. If these microbes originated in an infected person or animal that the mosquito bit previously, disease spreads.

The two most serious diseases spread by mosquitoes at the time of the Civil War were malaria, spread by *Anopheles* mosquitoes, and yellow fever, carried by *Aedes aegypti* mosquitoes.

People justly feared yellow fever, a terrible disease with no effective treatment or cure, characterized by severe muscle pains, internal bleeding, and black vomit. Epidemics ravaged many coastal cities in the antebellum period, especially New Orleans, and a fatality rate of nearly 50 percent of those who contracted the disease was not uncommon. Those who survived yellow fever developed permanent immunity. No one during the period understood how the disease spread, but they did realize that it was not directly contagious from person to person and that it often came to port on a ship from some area of the Caribbean that already had an epidemic.

Although fear of yellow fever was common during the Civil War, there were comparatively few instances of the disease. Only 1,355 Union soldiers suffered yellow fever during the entire war. Of these, 436 died. There was no yellow fever in New Orleans at all, which surprised its regular residents, who had hoped that yellow fever would drive out the hated Yankee occupiers. The good health of the city was directly attributable to the Union commander, General Benjamin F. Butler, who enforced a strict forty-day quarantine of incoming ships and supervised a city cleanup, removing many of the mosquitoes' breeding areas.

Small epidemics of yellow fever occurred in Union-held Southern cities, including Galveston, Texas; Pensacola and Key West, Florida; New Bern, North Carolina; and Hilton Head, South Carolina, as well as among the Confederates at Charleston, South Carolina, and Wilmington, North Carolina. News of the Wilmington epidemic in the summer and fall of 1862 delayed a Union attack on that city. In general, the Union blockade of Southern ports not only kept many goods out of the South during the war, it also reduced the incidence of yellow fever.

Some ships in both the Union and Confederate navies, as well as some Confederate blockade runners, altered their strategies or supply bases because of yellow fever outbreaks in the Caribbean islands. Some ships had an isolated case of yellow fever among the crew—generally a person who had contracted the disease from a mosquito on shore—but the fever did not spread to the rest of the crew because there were no mosquitoes on the ship.

Both the Union and the Confederate populace were fortunate that there were no major yellow fever outbreaks during the war, for such an epidemic could have been devastating.

The other major mosquito-borne illness, malaria, had a much greater impact on the war (and is treated in detail in a separate article). Malaria was common and chronic throughout the South and Midwest. Unlike yellow fever, it did not have a high mortality rate, but it also did not confer immunity. Those who contracted malaria, with its alternating extremes of chills and fever, were liable to a recurrence any time that the balance of the body's immune system was upset by stress, exhaustion, malnutrition, or some additional illness. As a consequence, many soldiers had periodic and sometimes prolonged absences from duty because of malaria. Quinine proved an effective treatment for malaria and was also used successfully as a prophylactic to ward off the disease.

Although no one knew the role of mosquitoes in the spread of malaria, some perceptive commanders and doctors took steps that avoided them. Doctors choosing hospital sites for the Confederate Army of Tennessee looked for places that were somewhat elevated and had good drainage after a rainstorm. Careful commanders on both sides tried to avoid having their men camp near a swamp. Although these officers were not explicitly trying to avoid mosquitoes, choosing dry locations was known to lower the incidence of malaria.

See also: Blockade; Davis, Jefferson; Fevers; Hospital Relocations; Malaria; Miasms; Mortality, of Soldiers; Quinine; Sanitation; Typhomalarial Fever.

Bibliography
Bollet, Alfred Jay. *Civil War Medicine: Challenges and Triumphs.* Tucson, AZ: Galen, 2002.

Schroeder-Lein, Glenna R. *Confederate Hospitals on the Move: Samuel H. Stout and the Army of Tennessee.* Columbia: University of South Carolina Press, 1994.

Spielman, Andrew, and Michael D'Antonio. *Mosquito: The Story of Man's Deadliest Foe.* New York: Hyperion, 2001.

MUDD, SAMUEL ALEXANDER (1833–1883)

Samuel Alexander Mudd was the doctor who set John Wilkes Booth's broken leg on the morning after Booth shot Abraham Lincoln. Born on December 21, 1833, at the family's plantation near Bryantown, Charles County, Maryland, Samuel was the third of the ten children of Henry Lowe Mudd and Sarah Ann Reeves Mudd. He attended Frederick College in Frederick, Maryland, and graduated from Georgetown College in Georgetown, District of Columbia, in 1854. Mudd received his medical degree from the University of Maryland Medical School in Baltimore in 1856 and then apprenticed with his cousin George Mudd in the Bryantown area. On November 26, 1857, Mudd married Sarah Frances Dyer, a neighbor whom he had courted for years. They eventually had nine children and lived on a farm near Bryantown where Mudd raised tobacco and practiced medicine.

Although it remained in the Union, Maryland was a divided state during the Civil War. Confederate couriers came through the Bryantown area and Federal troops often harassed the residents. Mudd joined no military force, but continued as a farmer and physician despite declining profits. Mudd's neighbors evidently regarded him as a Unionist. There are no records suggesting that he was suspected of or participated in Confederate activity, except that he once briefly hid his brother-in-law and two friends.

Mudd met Booth in December 1864 when the actor came to Charles County allegedly looking for property and a horse to buy. Later, Mudd ran into him at least once in Washington, DC. Some students of the Lincoln assassination have attempted to show Mudd as a member of the Confederate underground and an active conspirator with Booth. Others have viewed Mudd as a doctor doing his duty, but unfortunately in the wrong place at the wrong time. The evidence is not conclusive for either alternative.

Booth shot President Lincoln on April 14, 1865, during a performance of the play *Our American Cousin* at Ford's Theatre in Washington. Most contemporary and secondary accounts indicate that Booth broke his leg jumping from the president's box to the stage. Recent research suggests that Booth may have broken his leg not when he landed, but when his horse fell on him after he left Washington. In any case, Booth and his fellow conspirator David Herold arrived at Mudd's home about four o'clock on the morning of April 15, asking for help. Mudd treated Booth for a broken left fibula (the smaller bone in the lower leg) that did not pierce the skin, a clean break about two inches above the ankle. Mudd made a splint from part of a bandbox (a thin wood or cardboard clothes box) and had his gardener make crutches for the patient. Booth disguised his voice, kept his face turned or otherwise hidden, and used an assumed name while at Mudd's home. Neither Mudd nor his wife recognized the actor.

Arrested more than a week later on ill-defined charges of conspiracy in the president's assassination, Mudd was imprisoned in Washington, DC, and tried with seven other alleged conspirators by a military commission (May 9–June 30, 1865). Because of laws and customs in place at the time, Mudd and the other accused suspects did not testify in their own defense. Mudd was convicted and sentenced to life imprisonment at hard labor at Fort Jefferson in the Dry Tortugas, islands near Key West, Florida.

In 1867 a yellow fever epidemic sickened many of the prisoners and soldiers at the fort, claiming the life of the regimental surgeon. Mudd took over the medical duties, probably saving the lives of some patients. In gratitude, members of the garrison sent several petitions to President Andrew Johnson urging that Mudd be pardoned. These were no more successful than the appeals Mudd's wife and his attorney, Thomas Ewing Jr., had been sending since 1865. Nevertheless, various people continued to urge Mudd's release because he was doing his duty as a doctor when he treated Booth's leg.

Johnson pardoned Mudd on February 8, 1869. It took a month for the pardon to reach Fort Jefferson and Mudd did not arrive home until March 20. He continued to farm and practice medicine until his death on January 10, 1883, probably from pleurisy contracted while making house calls in bad weather.

Long after Mudd's death, family members, led by his grandson Dr. Richard D. Mudd, sought for about seventy-five years to have the federal government declare Mudd innocent. These legal efforts ended in failure in 2002.

See also: Lincoln, Abraham; Splints.

Bibliography

Carter, Samuel, III. *The Riddle of Dr. Mudd.* New York: Putnam, 1974.

Graf, LeRoy P., Ralph W. Haskins, and Paul H. Bergeron, eds. *The Papers of Andrew Johnson,* vols. 8–15. Knoxville: University of Tennessee Press, 1967–2000.

Kauffman, Michael W. *American Brutus: John Wilkes Booth and the Lincoln Conspiracies.* New York: Random House, 2004.

MUSICIANS, AS MEDICAL ASSISTANTS

Musicians were an essential part of both the Union and the Confederate armies. Each company generally had two field musicians. Fifers or buglers and drummers accompanied the infantry, while buglers were necessary for the cavalry and artillery. These musicians sounded calls from reveille to taps, signaling the daily activities of camp such as breakfast, sick call, cleanup, and guard duty. Musicians also played during drills, inspections, and funerals. During battle, bugle calls communicated orders for charge, retreat, and other maneuvers, orders that could not have been heard over the noise otherwise.

Brigades, and sometimes regiments, also had bands that played marches, popular and patriotic songs, and other music. They participated in parades, receptions, and numerous concerts for troops, visiting notables, and civilians. Sometimes they played for their hospitalized comrades. These bands had an important role in keeping up soldiers' morale.

Military musicians had to learn several dozen bugle calls, many pieces of music for performance, and even new instruments requiring different skills. John A. Widney of the 112th Illinois Infantry, a bass drummer, also learned to play a bass horn. These responsibilities required considerable individual and group practice time. While the musicians ordinarily did not fight during battles, they participated in a variety of other military activities. They stood guard, did camp cleanup, dug fortifications, and went on foraging expeditions.

During battles, musicians were supposed to serve as stretcher-bearers to remove the wounded from the field, as well as assist the surgeons in the field hospitals. They were supposed to be drilled in these responsibilities by the regimental surgeon. Some musicians did receive basic first aid training. Assigning musicians to be medical assistants, however, brought mixed results. In some cases the men were untrained, inexperienced, and unwilling to serve. If they could, they fled the field, and surgeons complained that the musicians had to be watched and forced to do their duty. Some musicians were more of a hindrance than a help when they did show up to assist. Such problems provoked some Union medical directors to urge the establishment of a trained ambulance corps.

Band members at Resaca, Georgia, however, were reported to be more efficient at moving the wounded from the field than the ambulance corps was. At Gettysburg, band members of the 150th New York Infantry, the 114th Pennsylvania Zouaves, and the Twentieth Maine Infantry were particularly helpful to the Union surgeons. Other bands assisted at Chickamauga and the Wilderness.

In addition to moving the wounded, musicians aided by carrying water, cleaning surgical instruments, nursing the wounded, holding limbs during amputations, and burying amputated limbs. One Confederate claimed that several band members of the "Stonewall Brigade" could amputate an arm or a leg as well as any of the surgeons, a claim which may have been an exaggeration.

See also: Ambulance Corps; Amputation; Chickamauga, Battle of; Gettysburg, Battle of; Hospitals, Field.

Bibliography

Abel, E. Lawrence. "Rattle, Toot, Tweet." *Civil War Times Illustrated* 40 (October 2001): 52–59.

Davis, James A. "More Work Than Play: Insights from the Letters of J. Herbert George, Civil War Musician." *Journal of American Culture* 26 (December 2003): 464–473.

Olson, Kenneth E. *Music and Musket: Bands and Bandsmen of the American Civil War.* Westport, CT: Greenwood, 1991.

Widney, John A. Unpublished diaries, 1862–1865. SC 1653. Manuscripts Department, Abraham Lincoln Presidential Library, Springfield, IL.

NEGLIGENCE, BY MEDICAL STAFF

Although most military physicians and other medical personnel during the Civil War performed their duties competently by the standards of the day, many were nevertheless charged with some sort of negligence. These charges tended to fall into three categories: administrative issues, medical incompetence, and inappropriate or criminal behavior.

Few doctors, North or South, knew anything about military administrative matters when they began their service. Either because of failure to understand the regulations (which were often poorly explained, if at all) or from frustration with petty record keeping, doctors violated protocol. As a result, they were censured for not properly filling out forms, for improperly using the hospital fund, and for eating food intended for patients. Military officers, often sticklers for rank, accused doctors of lack of respect for superior officers, failure to go through the proper chain of command, and eating with enlisted men. These charges often resulted from disputes between doctors and local commanders over the control of patients in the hospital. If these accusations led to a court-martial, the doctor would frequently be charged with "conduct unbecoming an officer and a gentleman" or "conduct to the prejudice of good order," categories that could cover just about any violation.

Doctors were often blamed for conditions caused by lack of supplies, such as shortages of food, shelter, and transportation for the wounded. Actually, these problems were likely to be the result of lack of support by commissaries, and especially quartermasters, whose failures to give any priority to medical supplies and transportation were a source of almost universal complaint by Northern and Southern medical personnel.

Other charges against doctors related to incompetence in medical treatment. Initially, before examinations and experience weeded out inept volunteers, some doctors had little idea what they were doing. Other charges, with foundation in a few early cases, accused doctors of performing unnecessary amputations for practice. One doctor was charged with mutilating a corpse because he performed an autopsy (a rarity at the time). Some charges of inexperience, inefficiency, unclean hospitals, cruelty to patients, and refusal to treat patients at all or in a timely manner undoubtedly were accurate. But other charges targeted doctors who were exhausted

227

and overworked, had a poor bedside manner, provoked the enmity of colleagues, or failed to live up to the unrealistic expectations of the complainant.

Inappropriate or criminal behavior included the theft of hospital supplies, such as patient food, for the medical attendant's personal use or for sale to persons outside the hospital. Hospital regulations were unclear as to exactly how the attendants were to procure their own food, but some people clearly had criminal intent when they sold hospital food to a nearby boardinghouse for their own profit. Illegal sale of items often involved selling any sort of whiskey to patients or selling medicinal whiskey to nonpatients. Doctors and attendants were frequently charged with imbibing hospital whiskey and getting drunk on duty. Certainly these accusations were sometimes valid, but the number of such instances seems to have been exaggerated. Other criminal charges included cowardice, consorting with prostitutes, and absence without leave.

These complaints and charges could be made in a variety of ways—gossip, direct verbal accusations, letters to military superiors and other influential persons, and formal court-martial proceedings. Records of numerous Union courts-martial survive in the National Archives in Washington, DC. Other accounts of complaints and difficulties can be found in letter collections, diaries, and memoirs written by those involved with the medical departments on both sides. Although most surviving information relates to doctors, charges of medical incompetence, criminal activity, and administrative sins could also be leveled against nurses, matrons, stewards, and ward masters.

Charges were dealt with in a variety of ways. In some cases, superior officers doubtless considered the source of the complaint and ignored it. An alleged offender might be warned or helped to correct the problem through increased training or changed behavior. An offender could also be forced to resign under threat of a court-martial.

A formal trial, or court-martial, was the last resort. Some alleged offenders were brought before such a tribunal against their will, while others asked for a court-martial in order to clear their name. The results of these trials were inconsistent. Although some offenses initially sounded terrible, detailed examination showed that the charges were seriously exaggerated or trumped up because of personal conflict and spite. Some defendants received a fair trial and punishment that fit the case. Others received serious punishment (such as dismissal from the army) for relatively insignificant offenses. Such injustice tended to occur especially when the offenses involved alleged disrespect to army discipline and hierarchy. Certainly the most famous case of this sort was the court-martial and dismissal of Union surgeon general William A. Hammond. Other accused medical personnel were found guilty but merely reprimanded. Still others were declared not guilty when evidence to the contrary seems pretty clear. Because courts-martial usually were conducted by local officers who knew the defendant, the results could be biased by personal attitudes. An estimated 3 percent of Union surgeons were court-martialed (no figure exists for the Confederates).

See also: Alcohol, Abuse of; Alcohol, Medicinal Uses of; Examining Boards, Medical; Hammond, William Alexander; Hospital Fund; Hospital Paperwork; Matrons; Nurses; Quartermasters; Stewards, Hospital; Subsistence Department; Ward Masters.

Bibliography

Lowry, Thomas P., and Jack D. Welsh. *Tarnished Scalpels: The Court-Martials of Fifty Union Surgeons.* Mechanicsburg, PA: Stackpole, 2000.

Schroeder-Lein, Glenna R. *Confederate Hospitals on the Move: Samuel H. Stout and the Army of Tennessee.* Columbia: University of South Carolina Press, 1994.

NEWSOM (TRADER), ELLA KING (CA. 1833–1919)

Ella King Newsom, a Confederate nurse, was born in Brandon, Mississippi. Her father, T.S.N. King, a Baptist minister, soon moved his family to Arkansas, where Ella grew up. There she met and married Dr. Frank Newsom of Tennessee. He died less than two years later, leaving her quite wealthy. She rented a house in Winchester, Tennessee, where her younger sisters and several other young women lived with her while they attended Mary Sharp College.

When the Civil War began, Newsom sent the young ladies home, gathered five servants and a railroad car full of supplies purchased with her own funds, and went to Memphis to care for wounded soldiers. There she worked at the city hospital, the Southern Mothers' Home hospital, and the Overton Hospital. However, when it became evident that the women of Memphis were providing adequately for the patients there, Newsom took her servants and supplies to Bowling Green, Kentucky. Here she often worked from 4:00 a.m. to midnight to organize the hospitals and care for the patients.

Moving to Nashville about the time of the fall of Forts Henry and Donelson, Newsom helped to evacuate patients from Nashville to Winchester before Nashville fell to Union forces. She later cared for wounded soldiers from the Battle of Shiloh in several hospitals in Corinth, Mississippi. Then she became matron of the Foard Hospital, located in the Crutchfield House hotel in Chattanooga, Tennessee. Because of her tremendous services to the cause, another Chattanooga hospital was named in her honor. The Newsom Hospital retained its name even when it was evacuated to other locations. Newsom continued her nursing work in Marietta and Atlanta, Georgia, as well as other locations in the area, until the end of the war.

Considered a beautiful, gentle, and devoutly Christian woman, Newsom exhausted her fortune during the war. She remarried in 1867. Her new husband, Colonel W.H. Trader of North Carolina, was a Confederate veteran. They had several children, but only their daughter Mary lived to adulthood. Colonel Trader died in 1885. Soon after, Ella and her daughter both took clerical jobs in the pension office in Washington, DC. By 1913, Newsom, nearly eighty, was blind in one eye and deaf. The United Confederate Veterans and the United Daughters of the Confederacy raised funds for her support. Newsom died at her daughter's home in Washington on January 18, 1919, after a lengthy illness.

See also: Hospital Relocations; Matrons; Nurses; Shiloh, Battle of; Women, as Hospital Workers.

Bibliography
"The Florence Nightingale of the South." *Confederate Veteran* 27 (February 1919): 46.

Lewis, Samuel W. "The Florence Nightingale of the South." *Southern Practitioner* 30 (September 1908): 420–424.

Manlove, Anna Gaut. "Mrs. Ella King Newsom Trader." *Confederate Veteran* 21 (July 1913): 343–344.

NIGHTINGALE, FLORENCE (1820–1910)

Florence Nightingale was a British reformer whose ideas on sanitation and nursing, especially during the Crimean War, influenced Americans during the Civil War. The younger daughter of William Edward Nightingale, a wealthy industrialist, and Frances (Fanny) Smith Nightingale, she was born in Florence, Italy, on May 12, 1820. Throughout her life she had a relationship of love and conflict with her parents and her sister Parthenope (1819–1890) because Florence did not wish to adhere to Victorian upper-middle-class expectations for women.

The Nightingales had a Unitarian and Anglican background and believed in education for girls. Florence was a precocious, brilliant, and opinionated child with a talent for languages and mathematics. Beginning when she was seven, Florence spent two and a half years under a governess, Sarah Christie, who was very severe with Florence in order to break her spirit and make her a nice, proper girl. This period evidently led to lifelong attitude difficulties, preoccupation with guilt, and anger at her family. William Nightingale then taught his daughters himself. Florence flourished, studying Latin, Greek, Italian, mathematics, geography, and history, as well as reading widely in her father's extensive library. She also enjoyed investigating nature and caring for her younger cousins, animals, and sick people. In her teens, Florence was already extremely efficient and well organized. About 1837, when she was sixteen, Florence believed that she had received a call from God but was not sure what it was a call to do.

By 1845 Nightingale, then twenty-five, had read a great deal about public health and wanted to be a nurse (not a doctor, given the "heroic" methods of bleeding and purging that doctors often used). However, nursing had a low reputation and was not a respected profession. There were no schools where she could find training. Her goals led to repeated conflict with her family as she avoided social obligations when possible and rejected two suitable marriage proposals. Finally, in 1853, Nightingale became superintendent of the Institution for Ill Gentlewomen in London, a private home for sick governesses, which she managed with great efficiency and wise frugality until she left for the Crimea in the fall of 1854.

The Crimean War (1854–1856) pitted Russia against Turkey and its allies, Britain and France. It began with Russian incursions into Turkish land that need not have led to war since the Russians retreated each time when confronted. Popular sentiment, which portrayed Turkey (actually a corrupt, autocratic regime) as a victim of the Russian bully, finally goaded a reluctant British government into the war.

The British army was singularly unprepared for war because it was led by aged officers, without experience, who had purchased their rank. Supply functions were decentralized among several ministries and consequently extremely disorganized. Many of the doctors and medical assistants cared little about their patients unless they had an interesting wound. Sanitation was ignored, leading to numerous cases of dysentery, cholera, and other deadly diseases wherever the British army camped in the Constantinople area, including Varna, Scutari, and Balaclava. The British tended to choose poor campsites, particularly the badly situated and difficult-to-supply Balaclava during the siege of Sevastopol. Although the Turks gave the British a large hospital building and a huge barracks to use as hospitals at Scutari, the facilities were overcrowded, undersupplied, understaffed, and filthy, with many soldiers dying daily. The British newspapers publicized the situation and the public was shocked.

Florence Nightingale was already planning to go to the Crimea in October 1854 before she was officially invited to do so by her friend Sidney Herbert, the war minister. She had difficulty finding suitable women to take along to serve as nurses. One-quarter of her party was Roman Catholic nuns, which appalled many of the Protestant women and caused factions in the group. When they got to Scutari, Nightingale found conditions at the Barracks Hospital abysmal. There were hardly any mops and buckets, let alone adequate cooking and eating utensils. Clothes and linens, such as they were, were seldom, if ever, washed. The doctors refused to allow the women to work in the hospital until suddenly hundreds of wounded arrived, at which point the doctors accepted all the help they could get.

Much of what Nightingale accomplished in Scutari was administrative, organizing the purchase of items such as basic cleaning supplies, linens, and food for special diets. Under her guidance the wards and corridors were cleaned, suitable food was cooked and served, the men were bathed, they had clean sheets and clothes, and the wounded had their bandages changed regularly. Yet, in this patriarchal society, Nightingale met much opposition from men in any leadership position (including many of the doctors), as well as from women workers, who refused to accept her authority. She also did nursing, often caring for the dying and visiting the wards at night, earning the title "the Lady with the Lamp." She went to work in Balaclava three times and in May 1855 became very ill with a fever, requiring several months of recovery. The Crimean War ended with a peace treaty in the spring of 1856. Nightingale remained until the Scutari hospitals were closed in late July.

After the war Nightingale returned to England and worked with a group of men to influence Parliament to reform the army medical corps so that such a tragic loss of life would never occur again. She prepared an 830-page report, *Notes Affecting the Health, Efficiency, and Hospital Administration of the British Army* (1858). She never testified personally before commissions, but her report provided much of the information for those who did. Nightingale also wrote *Notes on Nursing: What It Is and What It Is Not*, published for the general public in England in December 1859 and in the United States the following year. In it she stressed the importance of providing a clean, warm, well-lighted, well-ventilated environment, clean bedding and clothes, and appropriate, nutritious food, so that the patient could heal. During the American Civil War, members of the U.S. Sanitary Commission and others interested in the health of the troops read Nightingale's writings and accounts by others of her work. Many doctors tried to implement her ideas on ventilation, particularly.

In 1857 Nightingale was seriously ill, probably with a nervous breakdown and perhaps a relapse of the illness she had in the Crimea. Some historians have suggested that she had chronic severe brucellosis, a bacterial disease caused by drinking milk from infected goats or sheep. (It is now treatable with antibiotics.) Nightingale suffered terribly for years and became a reclusive invalid, working hard for her public health causes, but doing most of her business by writing, only occasionally seeing people individually by appointment.

Nightingale lived to the age of ninety but was evidently rather senile during her last few years. She died on August 13, 1910.

See also: Nuns; Nurses; Sanitation; United States Sanitary Commission; Ventilation.

Bibliography

Gill, Gillian. *Nightingales: The Extraordinary Upbringing and Curious Life of Miss Florence Nightingale*. New York: Ballantine, 2004.

Nightingale, Florence. *Notes on Nursing: What It Is and What It Is Not*. New York: D. Appleton, 1860; reprint, Mineola, NY: Dover, 1969.

NOSTALGIA *See* Post–Traumatic Stress Disorder.

NUNS

During the Civil War approximately 617 Roman Catholic nuns (sisters) served as nurses for sick and wounded soldiers on both sides. They came from twenty-one convent communities of twelve different orders. Most people, unaware of or confused by the distinctions, called all of them Sisters of Charity or Sisters of Mercy.

Because most of the nuns belonged to orders that had conducted small hospitals before the war, they were the only trained, experienced nurses in the nation when the war began. Their services were also desirable because the sisters obeyed orders, cooperated with the doctors, did not complain about or avoid hard, unpleasant work, and were completely reliable. The sisters were also impartial politically. About a hundred of them worked in Confederate hospitals. Members of the Daughters of Charity of St. Vincent de Paul from Emmitsburg, Maryland, served in hospitals in both Washington, DC, and Richmond, Virginia.

Some of the nuns began to nurse soldiers when their convents or hospitals were taken over by the military after a battle. Sometimes government officials at the national, state, or local level requested the nuns' assistance. In other cases the sisters volunteered their services. Some of them served only briefly while others cared for soldiers during much of the war. The nuns of several teaching orders also became nurses. However, only a fraction of all the nuns in the United States at the time cared for soldiers during the Civil War. About ten of them are known to have died as a result of diseases contracted while nursing.

The nuns nursed the sick because of their commitment to serving Jesus and performing charitable works. Having taken vows of poverty, chastity, and obedience, they worked anywhere they were needed—in large and small, urban and battlefield hospitals and on hospital transport ships. The sisters performed all kinds of work: administering hospitals, supervising wards or departments, distributing supplies sent by aid societies, dispensing medicine, dressing wounds, helping with surgery, cooking, cleaning, doing laundry, mediating quarrels between staff members or patients, taking care of the occasional female soldier, comforting the dying, providing religious counsel and baptism, and preparing the dead for burial. Sisters often took care of prisoners of war, patients who had serious contagious illnesses, those whom no one else wanted to care for, and those whom the doctors had given up on. Many soldiers who survived credited the sisters, rather than the doctors, for their survival.

It is not clear, in many cases, whether the sisters were paid because they often do not appear in official hospital records. Sometimes they clearly received the same pay as other female nurses. In other instances they received transportation, lodging, and food, usually of the most basic type. At least in settled hospitals, the sisters usually insisted on having a room for a chapel and, if at all possible, a priest so they could have regular services.

Reactions to the sisters varied. At first some soldiers were suspicious of the nuns or frightened by their unusual clothing. At least one of the orders wore hats (cornettes) that looked like large white wings. Some Protestant patients and coworkers were prejudiced against the nuns because they were Catholic. There were some serious conflicts with other women workers over issues of authority, particularly with Dorothea Dix and her nurses. However, many doctors supported the nuns as soon as they saw their work, and some women coworkers were anxious to learn their skills. Many prejudices were overcome by the sisters' patient, tender care. Although the nuns did not force their faith on their patients, a number of soldiers did become Catholics.

See also: Cooks; Dix, Dorothea Lynde; Hospital Ships; Hospitals, General; Nurses; Prisoners of War; Women, as Hospital Workers.

Bibliography

Fitzpatrick, Michael F. "The Mercy Brigade: Roman Catholic Nuns in the Civil War." *Civil War Times Illustrated* 36 (October 1997): 34–40.

Maher, Sister Mary Denis. *To Bind Up the Wounds: Catholic Sister Nurses in the U.S. Civil War.* Westport, CT: Greenwood, 1989.

NURSES

During the Civil War a variety of mostly untrained people served as nurses for the sick and wounded of both sides in the field and in hospitals. In this period there were no professional nursing schools and people learned by the experience of nursing.

The majority of nurses were male, since many people considered it inappropriate for women to tend the bodily needs of men to whom they were not related. Male nurses were often soldiers detailed from the ranks to meet a particular need—after a battle, for example. These soldiers were subject to recall to their regiments on very short notice, usually about the time they had learned something about nursing and become useful.

Another group of male nurses were convalescent soldiers. In the period before the Civil War, recuperating hospital patients were expected to care for those sicker than they were, a tradition continued during the war. Unfortunately, these convalescents were inexperienced and, in many cases, too weak for the tasks assigned, sometimes having serious, even fatal, relapses. Those convalescents who became skilled at nursing were usually returned to their regiments when they had recovered, once again leaving the hospitals with inexperienced staff.

Free blacks and slaves, both men and women, also worked as nurses. Slaves could be hired from their owners or impressed. Slave women who already had experience nursing their masters' families were particularly useful. A number of black women, both slave and free, were listed in the records as laundresses or cooks, but actually worked as nurses as well.

The only trained nurses at the time of the Civil War were members of the Roman Catholic nursing orders, such as the Sisters of Charity. Although many doctors did not want women in their hospitals, they were more likely to accept nuns because these women were used to taking orders. Despite their initial resistance, many doctors came to appreciate female nurses because their wards tended to be cleaner and their patients often recovered better under the care of these surrogate mothers and sisters. Nurses could be of any social standing, but many of the women who served on both sides came from the middle and upper classes. In the South, many women became nurses by default when they opened their homes to patients after a nearby battle.

The Woman's Central Association of Relief was organized in New York City in April 1861 to prepare women nurses for service. For a short time it ran programs at Bellevue Hospital and New York Hospital, where some women trained to be head nurses by attending lectures and visiting the wards for a month. However, most women who nursed had only the prior experience of caring for their own families and the on-the-job training provided at the hospitals.

The Union developed an official women's nursing corps directed by Dorothea Dix, who served as superintendent beginning in June 1861. She had stringent requirements for the women whom she employed. They had to be at least thirty years old, plain of feature, and simply and modestly dressed in black or brown. The women employed under Dix's auspices worked mainly in the hospitals around Washington, DC. Many women who nursed, however, did so independently of Dix. In both the Union and the Confederacy (which had no official department to recruit women), mothers, wives, and sisters who had gone to a hospital to care for a relative remained working there after their patient had recovered or died. Others responded to the need for nurses after a battle or desired to aid the war effort. Women nurses generally had no set period of service. Some worked only after a single battle; others served for the duration of the war or until felled by disease.

Nursing was hard work, involving long hours, especially after battles or when the hospital was otherwise full. Soldiers who worked as nurses might receive as much as $7.50 per month extra pay, a strong motivation for privates whose base pay was $13 per month. Female Union nurses usually earned about $12 per month if white, $10 per month if black, plus a daily ration. When pay rates were raised to $18, parsimonious government officials quickly returned them to $12. Even then, many nurses went for months without pay or never received the complete amount due them. By 1864 white and free black Southern women working at Chimborazo Hospital in Richmond were earning $40 per month, but this meant little because of the rampant inflation in the Confederacy. Many nurses on both sides served as volunteers, entirely without pay.

Most nurses of either gender on both sides served in hospitals, although some assisted with the transportation of wounded soldiers on trains or hospital ships. Few women besides those who lived in close proximity worked in field hospitals. Nursing duties involved all aspects of caring for the needs of the sick and wounded. While female nurses bathed the patients' hands and faces, male nurses were more likely to bathe the rest of the body and move patients. Male nurses were also more likely to assist at surgeries and help dress wounds, although some female nurses also performed these tasks. Nurses of both genders fed patients, attended patients throughout the night, and sat with the sick and dying. Many nurses were devout Christians who ministered to the spiritual needs of the patients through prayer, Bible reading, and sharing their faith. Nurses often wrote letters for patients and, if they died, wrote the details of their demise to their families. Women might work as ward supervisors or matrons, cook special diets, or supervise the laundry. Much depended on the situation: individual nurses did whatever was necessary for the well being of the patients.

A number of nurses suffered serious illnesses as a result of their work. Some contracted diseases from their patients while others collapsed from exhaustion. Although some were able to return to nursing, others found their health permanently damaged. A number died because of their service.

Many female nurses wrote diaries, letters, or memoirs about their experiences, which have been published, but accounts by male nurses are rare.

See also: Alcott, Louisa May; Barton, Clara; Beers, Fannie A.; Bickerdyke, Mary Ann Ball ("Mother"); Blacks, as Hospital Workers; Convalescents; Cooks; Cumming, Kate; Dix, Dorothea Lynde; Hospital Support Staff; Laundresses; Matrons; Newsom (Trader), Ella King; Nuns; Pember, Phoebe Yates Levy; Women, as Hospital Workers; Woman's Central Association of Relief; Woolsey Sisters.

Bibliography

Alcott, Louisa May. *Hospital Sketches.* 1863; reprint, Boston: Applewood, 1986.

Beers, Fannie A. *Memories: A Recollection of Personal Experiences During Four Years of War.* Philadelphia: J.B. Lippincott, 1888; reprint, Alexandria, VA: Time-Life, 1985.

Berlin, Jean V., ed. *A Confederate Nurse: The Diary of Ada W. Bacot, 1860–1863.* Columbia: University of South Carolina Press, 1994.

Holland, Mary Gardner. *Our Army Nurses: Stories from Women in the Civil War.* 1895, 1897; reprint, Roseville, MN: Edinborough, 1998.

Schultz, Jane E. *Women at the Front: Hospital Workers in Civil War America.* Chapel Hill: University of North Carolina Press, 2004.

Winters, William. *The Musick of the Mocking Birds, the Roar of the Cannon: The Civil War Diary and Letters of William Winters,* ed. Steven E. Woodworth. Lincoln: University of Nebraska Press, 1998.

Woolsey, Jane Stuart. *Hospital Days: Reminiscence of a Civil War Nurse.* 1868; reprint, Roseville, MN: Edinborough, 1996, 2001.

NUTRITION *See* Diet.

OFFICER OF THE DAY

The officer of the day was the surgeon on call at a general hospital. In the Confederate Army of Tennessee hospitals, the surgeons and assistant surgeons rotated the responsibility. Beginning at 7:00 a.m., the medical officer was on duty for twenty-four hours. He was to be fully uniformed, complete with sash and sword, and ready for any emergency, especially those during the night when the other doctors were not on duty. His other responsibility was to make an inspection of the entire hospital and to write a report on his findings before going off duty the next morning. Most of these reports were prosaic accounts. However, when there were few patients in the hospital, a bored officer might occasionally become creative. One officer wrote pages of pompous verbosity to say that the bread was burned. On another occasion he lapsed into poetry about the predicament of a pig that had allegedly fallen into the sink (latrine) behind Ward 3. This literary foray earned a mild reproof from the medical director of hospitals, who thought that the officer should regard his duties more seriously.

See also: Hospital Paperwork; Hospitals, General; Latrines; Surgeons; Surgeons, Assistant.

Bibliography
Schroeder-Lein, Glenna R. *Confederate Hospitals on the Move: Samuel H. Stout and the Army of Tennessee.* Columbia: University of South Carolina Press, 1994.

OLMSTED, FREDERICK LAW (1822–1903)

Frederick Law Olmsted, who became a noted landscape architect, was executive secretary of the U.S. Sanitary Commission during the Civil War. He was born in Hartford, Connecticut, on April 26, 1822, the older son of John Olmsted, a dry goods merchant, and Charlotte Hull Olmsted. When Frederick was three, his mother died of an overdose of laudanum. His father married again just over a year later, and this second marriage produced six children. Frederick was a bright, curious child with a short attention span. He attended several schools away from home until he was fifteen.

Olmsted tried a variety of occupations before he finally settled on a career. He apprenticed to a surveyor, clerked for a dry goods importer, shipped as a crew member on a boat to China, became a scientific farmer and landscaper, and visited Europe, where he wrote an agricultural travelogue that was published in America. Two trips in the American South during the early 1850s resulted in three books and a series of columns for the *New York Daily Times*. Olmsted briefly served as managing editor for *Putnam's Monthly Magazine*. In 1857 he became designer and superintendent of construction for Central Park in New York City, a project with which he had a stormy association for a number of years.

On June 13, 1859, Olmsted married Mary Olmsted, the widow of his younger brother John; he raised her three children as his own. The couple also had four children themselves, of whom two survived. Olmsted broke his leg during the late summer of 1860. The accident left him with a permanent limp and prevented him from joining the military when the Civil War broke out. However, on June 20, 1861, he was offered the position of executive secretary for the newly established U.S. Sanitary Commission. He accepted the post and took a leave of absence from Central Park.

The Sanitary Commission was headed by a board of managers (including Henry W. Bellows, president, and George T. Strong, treasurer), most of whom lived in New York City. Olmsted, as executive secretary, managed the organization's relief operations from Washington, DC. He set up the administrative system, which he headed, and appointed three regional undersecretaries. He also hired sanitary inspectors to visit Union military camps and hospitals in order to note problems, to try to prevent such problems by giving instruction, and to provide supplies where they were lacking. Olmsted directed the inspectors to gather comprehensive statistics, which were used in writing numerous commission reports.

Olmsted was discouraged by his first visits to the Union troops around Washington, DC, in 1861 because their camps were filthy and undisciplined. The military medical department, headed by Clement A. Finley, was very obstructionist; Finley and his subordinates claimed to have enough supplies and resented civilian meddling. When the First Battle of Bull Run (Manassas) in July 1861 proved a medical nightmare, Olmsted wrote a report on the conditions that was so critical of the army that the Sanitary Commission managers would not publish it as written.

Convinced that it was the army medical department's responsibility to care for the soldiers' medical needs, Olmsted and other commissioners agitated, through meetings with politicians and written reports, for reform and reorganization of the medical department. On April 16, 1862, Congress passed a medical department reform bill, and on April 25, without the blessing of Secretary of War Edwin M. Stanton, the commission's candidate, William A. Hammond, was appointed surgeon general.

Meanwhile, Olmsted oversaw the collection of supplies from civilians and channeled them to the areas of the army where they were most needed. During the Peninsula Campaign from April through June 1862, Olmsted organized, personally

OLMSTED, FREDERICK LAW (1822–1903)

accompanied, and directed a small fleet of ships equipped as hospital transports to evacuate sick and wounded soldiers to Washington, Annapolis, Boston, and New York City. Exhausted by the grueling work, Olmsted contracted jaundice and had to convalesce for several months. However, in September 1862 he directed supplies to be sent to the Army of the Potomac by wagon train, the first supplies to arrive on the field after the Battle of Antietam.

Olmsted deplored sectionalism and factionalism in relief work, just as he did in the country as a whole. Believing that all relief efforts should be funneled through the Sanitary Commission, he vigorously fought against such competing organizations as the Western Sanitary Commission and the U.S. Christian Commission.

Olmsted was an impatient, hard-driving planner and organizer. Although he got along well enough with the individual members of the commission's managing board, Olmsted tended to have conflicts with them as a group. When the board decreased his responsibilities, Olmsted was unhappy and began to get more involved with other projects outside the commission. On September 1, 1863, Olmsted resigned as executive secretary of the Sanitary Commission.

Olmsted achieved his greatest personal success after the Civil War. Although his first endeavor, managing an estate in northern California, failed because of financial collapse, Olmsted gained several opportunities for creative landscape planning, such as Mountain View Cemetery in Oakland, California.

Olmsted finally focused on landscape architecture starting in the late 1860s. Over the following years he worked with several colleagues, eventually including his stepson and son, on many landscape architecture projects. Some of Olmsted's design proposals were never built or only partly completed, while others contributed to his fame. His best-known projects included the grounds for the World's Columbian Exposition in Chicago in 1893 and the Biltmore Estate in Asheville, North Carolina.

By 1895 Olmsted was beginning to have severe memory lapses and suffering other signs of dementia. When his family could no longer care for him, he spent the last few years of his life in Waverly, Massachusetts, in an asylum for which he had designed the grounds. Olmsted died on August 28, 1903.

See also: Ambulances; Antietam, Battle of; Bellows, Henry Whitney; Bull Run (Manassas), First Battle of; Finley, Clement Alexander; Hammond, William Alexander; Hospital Ships; Laudanum; Peninsula Campaign; Sanitation; Strong, George Templeton; United States Christian Commission; United States Sanitary Commission; Western Sanitary Commission; Woman's Central Association of Relief.

Bibliography

Censer, Jane Turner, ed. *The Papers of Frederick Law Olmsted.* Vol. 4, *Defending the Union, 1861–1863.* Baltimore: Johns Hopkins University Press, 1986.

Maxwell, William Quentin. *Lincoln's Fifth Wheel: The Political History of the United States Sanitary Commission.* New York: Longmans, Green, 1956.

Rybczynski, Witold. *A Clearing in the Distance: Frederick Law Olmsted and America in the 19th Century.* New York: Scribner, 1999.

OPIATE USE AND ADDICTION

A number of types of opiates were available to treat civilians and soldiers on both sides during the Civil War. Opiates were the most effective painkillers of the period and were also used as sedatives and for the treatment of diarrhea.

Opium is made from poppies and is also processed to produce derivatives, most importantly morphine. Morphine, the strongest of the painkillers, could be administered in pill form, as a powder dusted on the wound, or as a liquid injected by syringe into a small cut. Opium itself could be given in a powdered or pill form or as a tincture (liquid made with alcohol) such as laudanum and paregoric.

Because opiates worked, physicians prescribed them for many conditions. For soldiers suffering from diarrhea and dysentery, opiates relieved cramps and had a constipating effect. Opiates were also used as cough suppressants for patients with pneumonia, pleurisy, asthma, bronchitis, influenza, and tuberculosis (or "consumption," as it was then called). Opiates provided pain relief for patients with wounds and injuries, as well as many other ailments such as stomachaches, headaches, gallstones, hemorrhoids, tetanus, typhoid fever, malaria, syphilis, and neuralgia. Those suffering from restlessness, delirium tremens, insanity, and depression received opiates for their sedative effects.

Union physicians dispensed nearly 10 million opium pills, nearly 3 million ounces of other opiates, and nearly 30,000 ounces of morphine during the war. No figures are available for the Confederates, but their physicians, who had similar medical training, used opiates for the same purposes in whatever quantity was available. Southerners obtained opiates primarily by importing them through the Union blockade or capturing them from the Union forces.

Historians have suggested that several Civil War generals who had serious health problems may have made poor military choices because they were under the influence of painkilling opiates. There has been particular speculation about Confederate general John Bell Hood at the Battle of Franklin, Tennessee, in December 1864, because Hood certainly suffered chronic pain from his wounded left arm and his amputated right leg. The truth of these speculations cannot be determined, however.

Mid–nineteenth-century physicians were not aware of the addictive nature of opiates. A soldier who received an occasional pill or dose of laudanum would not have a problem, but those with a chronic condition who took opiates over an extended period could become addicted. The chances of addiction depended on the type of opiate, the quantity taken, the frequency with which it was taken, the length of time for which it was taken, the method by which it was administered, and the general physiology of the patient.

The amount of opiates administered and the numerous chronic illnesses and wounds that resulted from the war suggest that eventually a number of soldiers became addicted after the conflict. However, there are no records to this effect. Historians dispute whether veterans suffered from what some called the "old soldier's disease"—that is, opium addiction—and whether veterans contributed significantly to an increase in opium addiction in the late nineteenth century. At least some historians have concluded that Civil War veterans may have represented a small part of the increase, but were always a minority of opium addicts. Most of the addicts were women who took opiates for "female complaints" such as migraines and menstrual cramps.

See also: Alcohol, Abuse of; Blockade; Diarrhea and Dysentery; Gunshot Wounds, Treatment of; Hood, John Bell; Laudanum; Medication, Administration of; Morphine; Pneumonia; Tetanus; Tuberculosis; Typhoid Fever.

Bibliography
Bollet, Alfred Jay. *Civil War Medicine: Challenges and Triumphs.* Tucson, AZ: Galen, 2002.

Courtwright, David T. "Opiate Addiction as a Consequence of the Civil War." *Civil War History* 24 (June 1978): 101–111.

McMurray, Richard M. *John Bell Hood and the War for Southern Independence.* Lexington: University Press of Kentucky, 1982.

Stout, James, Jr. "Under the Influence: Did Civil War Soldiers Depend on Drugs and Alcohol?" *Civil War Times Illustrated* 27 (May 1988): 30–35.

P

P.A.C.S.

P.A.C.S. stands for Provisional Army of the Confederate States. Medical officers who were part of the Confederate army, in contrast to the medical officers serving state troops, sometimes used it as part of their title when signing documents—for example, Name, Surgeon, P.A.C.S.

See also: Hospital Paperwork; Medical Department, Organization of; Surgeons.

Bibliography

Barnes, Joseph K., ed. *The Medical and Surgical History of the War of the Rebellion (1861–65).* Washington, DC: Government Printing Office, 1870–1888; reprint, Wilmington, NC: Broadfoot, 1990.

PAIN MANAGEMENT *See* Opiate Use and Addiction.

PEMBER, PHOEBE YATES LEVY (1823–1913)

Phoebe Pember, a hospital matron in Richmond, Virginia, was born in Charleston, South Carolina, on August 18, 1823. She was the fourth of the six daughters of Jacob Clavius Levy and Fanny Yates Levy, a wealthy Jewish couple. The family moved to Savannah, Georgia, in the 1850s. Although nothing is known about Phoebe's education, it is clear from her writing style that she was well educated. Sometime before the Civil War she married Thomas Pember of Boston. Unfortunately, he contracted tuberculosis and died in Aiken, South Carolina, on July 9, 1861, at the age of thirty-six.

Pember moved back to Savannah and lived with her parents, "refugeeing" with them to Marietta, Georgia, because of Yankee activity in the Savannah area. Pember, a strong-willed woman, had conflicts with her family, especially her father. Through her acquaintance with Mrs. George W. Randolph, the wife of the Confederate secretary of war, Pember was offered a position as matron at her choice of several hospitals. She picked Chimborazo Hospital in Richmond. Although in her recollections she repeatedly indicates that she worked in the hospital for four years, official records show that she assumed her responsibilities on December 18, 1862. Pember stayed until the hospital closed after the war ended in April 1865.

Chimborazao was such a large hospital that it was partitioned into five divisions. Pember was the matron for the second division. Initially she had to find living quarters—eventually she had quarters both at the hospital and with a family in town—and learn her duties, which included making requisitions for supplies. Much of her knowledge came through trial and error rather than any explicit instruction. Though she occasionally took part in Richmond's social life, her main concern was to care for the patients in her hospital. She was particularly in charge of preparing special diets for the very ill, using her ingenuity when supplies were short or patients desired unusual food. Pember frequently walked through her wards, checking on the needs of the patients and mothering many of them. At times she helped treat their wounds as well.

Sometime between 1865 and 1879 Pember wrote her recollections of her experiences during the war, publishing them in 1879. She recounted both amusing and sad incidents and tended to be critical of some of the surgeons and other attendants. The book described her ongoing struggle for control of the whiskey rations, which were supposed to be guarded by the matron and dispensed on physicians' orders, for medicinal purposes only. She combated the wily schemes of assistant surgeons, attendants, and "hospital rats" (malingerers) who wanted the liquor for their own consumption, rather than for the medical needs of the patients.

After the war, Pember traveled in America and abroad. She died in Pittsburgh, Pennsylvania, on March 4, 1913, and was buried with her husband in Laurel Grove Cemetery in Savannah, Georgia.

See also: Alcohol, Addiction to; Alcohol, Medicinal Uses of; Chimborazo Hospital; Malingerers; Matrons; Richmond, Virginia; Women, as Hospital Workers.

Bibliography
Pember, Phoebe Yates. *A Southern Woman's Story: Life in Confederate Richmond.* 1879; reprint, ed. Bell Irvin Wiley. Jackson, TN: McCowat-Mercer, 1959; reprint, Covington, GA: Mockingbird, 1974.

PENINSULA CAMPAIGN (1862)

The Peninsula Campaign (also called the Peninsular Campaign) was a series of maneuvers and battles in the spring and summer of 1862 on the peninsula between the York and the James rivers in Virginia. It began in mid-March when General George B. McClellan sent the Union Army of the Potomac by boat to Fortress Monroe, at the tip of the peninsula, with the goal of marching about sixty-five miles up the peninsula to capture Richmond.

The Army of the Potomac began its march on April 4. On April 5, at Yorktown, Confederate general John B. Magruder maneuvered his soldiers to make it look like he had far more troops than the 4,000 that he actually had. McClellan, fooled, settled down for a month-long siege, which ended only when the Confederates evacuated the trenches during the night of May 3. The Battle of Williamsburg, on May 4–5, resulted in 2,249 Union and 1,703 Confederate casualties (killed, wounded, and missing) before the Confederates withdrew from the field.

General Joseph E. Johnston, Confederate commander, preferred not to fight if he could maneuver. As a result, the Confederates evacuated the Norfolk navy yard, destroyed the ironclad *Merrimack* (CSS *Virginia*), and kept retreating up the peninsula until, to the Confederate nation's alarm, McClellan's forces were in sight of Richmond. At the major Battle of Seven Pines (or Fair Oaks) on May 31–June 1, Johnston's orders were not very clear and his troops did not end up where they needed to be. When Johnston reached the field on May 31, he was severely wounded in the right shoulder and ribs.

Robert E. Lee succeeded Johnston as Confederate commander on June 1 and soon turned the military situation around, literally. During most of June McClellan did very little with his troops, giving Lee time to reorganize and prepare. Confederate cavalry under Jeb Stuart even rode all the way around the Union army on June 12–15. The Seven Days battles, June 25–July 1, were the bloodiest of the Peninsula Campaign and included major fights at Mechanicsville (June 26), Gaines's Mill (June 27), Glendale or Frayser's Farm (June 30), and Malvern Hill (July 1). The ultimate result of these battles was to push the Union forces away from Richmond, back toward a new base that McClellan established at Harrison's Landing on the James River. McClellan's superiors were unable to send him the 35,000 to 50,000 men he claimed to need before he could take further action. General-in-chief Henry W. Halleck, concerned about the potential for further disease in the army during the late summer, ordered McClellan to withdraw from the peninsula, beginning in late August.

As near as it is possible to calculate from surviving figures, the Union forces suffered 23,141 battle casualties (killed, wounded, and missing), while the Confederate casualties totaled 28,551 during the Peninsula Campaign. These amounted to less than 11 percent of the Army of the Potomac and about 20 percent of the Army of Northern Virginia. However, both sides, particularly the Union, also had other serious medical problems to deal with during the campaign.

The Army of the Potomac had suffered a great deal from diseases of various kinds, both contagious and sanitation-related, during the nine months before the Peninsula Campaign began. Some soldiers were weakened by previous illness while others developed diseases on the peninsula to which they had been exposed before they arrived. As much as 20 percent of the army was sick at any one time. From April to August, 124,027 cases of illness were treated in Union field hospitals, including 48,912 cases of diarrhea or dysentery, 7,715 cases of intermittent fever (malaria), and 2,805 cases of typhoid. These numbers indicated only those who were treated in the hospital, not those who remained in their quarters and reported to sick call. While only 1,940 deaths were registered (279 from typhoid), many of the sick were shipped to general hospitals in the North, where information on whether they recovered, died, or were discharged could no longer be related to statistics from the peninsula. McClellan himself was ill with dysentery for several weeks in May and June.

Many of the Union army's problems stemmed from poor supplies of food, water, shelter, and medical care. The troops were so poorly fed that many were suffering from malnutrition and scurvy by July 1862. Polluted drinking water was a problem. A number of soldiers aboard ships en route to the peninsula, not provided with water, drank from the filthy Potomac and were sick with diarrhea and dysentery before they ever got to the peninsula. The weather was hot and there was a great deal of rain during the campaign, making camp conditions uncomfortable and muddy and contributing to swampy breeding grounds for mosquitoes. Rivers, such as the Chickahominy, flooded at times. Sanitation was often miserable.

Many of the medical problems for both the sick and the wounded of the Army of the Potomac would have been less severe had the army had adequate medical supplies and doctors. Unfortunately, Charles S. Tripler, medical director for the Army of the Potomac, was not up to the challenge of supervising the medical care of such a large number of men.

Tripler set up major hospitals at Fortress Monroe, Yorktown, and White House Landing on the York River. However, these were by no means adequate for the number of sick and, after the Battle of Williamsburg on May 5–6, wounded patients. Ships had to be found to carry patients to hospitals in Washington and Georgetown, DC; Alexandria, Virginia; Baltimore and Annapolis, Maryland; Philadelphia; Boston; and New York City. Many of those ships, commandeered by the quartermaster's department, had been hauling supplies to the troops, including livestock. As a result, the boats were completely unsuitable for transporting sick and wounded patients because they were filthy and had no bedding, food, medical staff, or medical supplies. The U.S. Sanitary Commission came to the rescue in April 1862, outfitting several boats. A number of upper-class women from New York City served as nurses on these vessels, which transported about 8,000 patients.

The Army of the Potomac lacked doctors as well. Medical officers suffered from many of the same diseases as the soldiers. Some became exhausted because of overwork. Tripler finally refused to give doctors leaves of absence because so many did not return to the field. He hired 100 contract surgeons, many of whom resigned because of the poor conditions. Tripler continually complained about the medical officers because they were not regular army men. However, the difficulties they faced were more often due to lack of supplies than to incompetence. Medical supplies were usually inadequate because stocks were not refilled when the materials were used or because supplies were abandoned or destroyed during retreats. In June, for example, a receiving hospital with 3,000 patients at Savage Station was abandoned, leaving the men to become prisoners. McClellan also abandoned his main supply depot at White House Landing at the end of June, moving across the peninsula to Harrison's Landing on the James River. Despite all these problems, Tripler reported that the army on the peninsula was the healthiest of any in the U.S. service!

On July 4, Tripler was replaced as medical director by Jonathan Letterman. Letterman discovered that the army was suffering from a scurvy epidemic, which turned out to be the worst of the war. The new medical director hastened to order antiscorbutics, such as potatoes, onions, cabbages, tomatoes, squash, and beets, for the soldiers. The addition of vegetables and fruits to their diet quickly improved soldier health in general. Letterman also made a number of recommendations about camp hygiene that McClellan ordered put into practice, but the results for the army were inconsistent. Letterman began to reorganize the hospital system and establish an ambulance corps as well.

The Confederate troops surely suffered from the heat, rain, mosquitoes, and generally unpleasant conditions of the peninsula, as did their Union opponents. However, the Confederates had several advantages because they were so close to Richmond. Although the capital was crowded with refugees, government employees, and soldiers, straining the amount of supplies available, the residents did the best they could to care for the enormous numbers of Confederate sick and wounded, as well as the Union prisoner of war patients. During this period Richmond had more hospitals than at any other time. New hospitals were continually being established in any available public building or private home because the wounded, including 5,000 from Seven Pines and 16,000 from the Seven Days battles, overflowed the hospitals already in use. By September 1862 Richmond had fifty hospitals, a number that gradually decreased as the hospitals were consolidated into larger establishments such as the Winder, Jackson, and Chimborazo hospitals on the edge of town.

The Peninsula Campaign was generally a medical nightmare for both sides because of the tremendous number of sick and wounded who suffered due to the inadequate facilities and supplies.

See also: Ambulance Corps; Chimborazo Hospital; Diarrhea and Dysentery; Diet, of Troops; Hospital Buildings; Hospital Ships; Hospitals, Field; Johnston, Joseph Eggleston; Letterman, Jonathan; Malaria; Medical Directors, Field; Mosquitoes; Nurses; Olmsted, Frederick Law; Richmond, Virginia; Scurvy; Surgeon's Call; Tripler, Charles Stuart; Typhoid Fever; United States Sanitary Commission; Women, as Hospital Workers.

Bibliography

Bollet, Alfred Jay. *Civil War Medicine: Challenges and Triumphs.* Tucson, AZ: Galen, 2002.

Calcutt, Rebecca Barbour. *Richmond's Wartime Hospitals.* Gretna, LA: Pelican, 2005.

Furgurson, Ernest B. *Ashes of Glory: Richmond at War.* New York: Knopf, 1996.

Miller, William J., comp. "The Grand Campaign: A Journal of Operations in the Peninsula Campaign, March 17–August 26, 1862." In *The Peninsula Campaign of 1862: Yorktown to the Seven Days*, vol. 1, ed. William J. Miller, 177–205. Campbell, CA: Savas Woodbury, 1993.

Steiner, Paul E. *Disease in the Civil War: Natural Biological Warfare in 1861–1865*. Springfield, IL: C.C. Thomas, 1968.

Thomas, Emory M. *The Confederate State of Richmond: A Biography of the Capital*. Austin: University of Texas Press, 1971.

PHTHISIS *See* Tuberculosis.

PNEUMONIA

Pneumonia is a serious disease of the lungs that afflicted soldiers on both sides during the Civil War. Often known at the time as inflammation of the lungs, it involves one or both lungs filling with fluid, causing chest pain, cough, and inability to breathe properly. Pneumonia can be a complication of some other disease, such as a cold, bronchitis, measles, or typhoid fever, or the result of a bacterial infection. In many cases pneumonia occurs because a weak or sick person is unable to take deep breaths when lying in bed in a single position. Some Civil War soldiers were diagnosed with "typhoid pneumonia." This could mean that they had both diseases or that they had a serious lung infection as well as abdominal swelling

The greatest number of pneumonia cases occurred in the early years of the war, since the new recruits suffered diseases of all sorts while they adjusted to the conditions of service. Pneumonia was also more prevalent during the winter rather than the summer, and among the armies stationed further north rather than those near the Gulf of Mexico. Confederate prisoners of war in Northern camps suffered more from pneumonia than did Federal soldiers in Southern prison camps. Although there were fewer cases in the later years of the war, the mortality rate was higher; about 31 percent of the pneumonia patients died, possibly because they were weaker from poor nutrition over a longer period of time. Overall, about one-quarter of white Union soldiers who got pneumonia died from it.

Confederate surgeon Joseph Jones, studying available field and hospital disease statistics for January 1862 to July 1863, found that about 18 percent of the Confederate army suffered from pneumonia, with the disease accounting for 3.15 percent of all general hospital admissions. Jones found that more pneumonia patients got well when treated in the field hospitals than in the general hospitals. However, the general hospitals tended to receive the more serious cases. The most famous Confederate to die of pneumonia during the war was General Thomas J. "Stonewall" Jackson, who developed pneumonia possibly from a bruise to his lung when he was dropped while being carried from the field after he was wounded at Chancellorsville, Virginia, in May 1863.

Earlier in the century, bleeding the patient had been a standard treatment for pneumonia, but in the 1830s the French physician Pierre Louis had determined that it was not effective and bleeding was not used much by the time of the Civil War. Blistering and cupping were still used on the chest as counterirritants. Small doses of tartar emetic were given as well as mercurials and opium to reduce fever, inflammation, and cough. The U.S. Sanitary Commission opposed bleeding and blistering because they annoyed the patient without producing useful results. The commission encouraged the use of supportive treatments such as tonics, alcoholic stimulants, and nutritious diets.

The roughly 25 percent mortality rate was typical of, and even slightly lower than, the civilian mortality rate for pneumonia until at least the 1930s. Sulfa drugs and penicillin improved the survival rate for pneumonia cases drastically, although pneumonia remains a significant cause of death among the elderly. However, in the twenty-first century, persons at risk can receive a pneumonia vaccination.

See also: Calomel; Catarrh; Cupping and Blistering; Diet, of Hospital Patients; Diet, of Troops; Hospitals, Field; Hospitals, General; Jackson, Thomas Jonathan ("Stonewall"); Jones, Joseph; Malnutrition; Measles; Mortality, of Soldiers; Opiate Use and Addiction; Prisoners of War; Tartar Emetic; United States Sanitary Commission.

Bibliography

Bollet, Alfred Jay. *Civil War Medicine: Challenges and Triumphs.* Tucson, AZ: Galen, 2002.

Cunningham, H.H. *Doctors in Gray: The Confederate Medical Service.* Baton Rouge: Louisiana State University Press, 1958; reprint, Gloucester, MA: Peter Smith, 1970.

Edwards, C.J. "Pneumonia in the Confederate Army." *Southern Practitioner* 33 (September 1911): 478–480.

Flannery, Michael A. *Civil War Pharmacy: A History of Drugs, Drug Supply and Provision, and Therapeutics for the Union and Confederacy.* New York: Pharmaceutical Products Press, 2004.

Welsh, Jack D. *Medical Histories of Confederate Generals.* Kent, OH: Kent State University Press, 1995.

PORCHER, FRANCIS PEYRE (1825–1895)

Francis Peyre Porcher, Confederate physician and botanist, was born on December 14, 1825, in St. John's, Berkeley County, South Carolina. He was the son of William Porcher, a physician, and Isabella Sarah Peyre Porcher. Young Porcher attended the Mount Zion Academy in Winnsboro, South Carolina, followed by South Carolina College, from which he graduated with a Bachelor of Arts degree in 1844. He studied at the Medical College of the State of South Carolina, graduating as valedictorian of his class in 1847. Although all medical school graduates had to write a thesis on some medical subject, few performed original research for their paper. However, Porcher's "A Medico-Botanical Catalogue of the Plants and Ferns of St. John's, Berkeley County, South Carolina" made a contribution to knowledge and was published that year in Charleston. The topic showed the direction of his future career.

From the fall of 1847 through the winter of 1849, Porcher studied medicine in Paris with the famous doctor Pierre Louis. He also studied in Florence, Italy. Upon his return to South Carolina in 1849, Porcher began practicing medicine in Charleston. In 1852 he helped to establish a medical preparatory school in that city. After another study trip to Europe, he taught clinical medicine, materia medica (pharmacy), and therapeutics at the medical college from which he had graduated. In 1855 he married Virginia Leigh of Richmond, Virginia, by whom he had two daughters and a son.

In the midst of teaching and establishing a family, Porcher continued his medicinal plant research and also studied diseased human tissues through a microscope. He gave and published several papers on these subjects. Porcher worked with J. Julian Chisolm to establish a hospital for slaves in Charleston, and he also edited a medical journal.

When the Civil War began, Porcher joined the Confederates as a surgeon, caring for the troops of the Holcombe Legion until March 1862. He then served at the naval hospital in Norfolk, Virginia, and finally at the South Carolina Hospital in Petersburg, Virginia. Porcher's main contribution to the Confederate war effort, however, was his book *Resources of the Southern Fields and Forests, Medical, Economical and Agricultural; Being Also a Medical Botany of the Confederate States; with Practical Information of the Useful Properties of Trees, Plants, and Shrubs*, published in Charleston in 1863. Surgeon General Samuel P. Moore had asked Porcher to write this book in order to help Southerners find and use indigenous resources to replace medicines that were no longer being imported into the South because of the Union blockade of Southern ports. Unfortunately, Porcher was unable to find a substitute for such crucial imports as quinine.

After the war Porcher resumed his teaching at the South Carolina medical college, served on the staff of City Hospital in Charleston (1866–1887), became an authority on yellow fever, and continued to write and publish on medical topics. Porcher's first wife died in 1866. In 1877 he married Margaret Ward and the couple had four children. In the fall of 1895 Porcher suffered a stroke and died on November 19.

See also: Blockade; Chisolm, John Julian; Materia Medica; Moore, Samuel Preston; Quinine; *Resources of the Southern Fields and Forests*; Substitutes, for Supplies.

Bibliography

Bollet, Alfred Jay. *Civil War Medicine: Challenges and Triumphs*. Tucson, AZ: Galen, 2002.

Porcher, Francis Peyre. *Resources of the Southern Fields and Forests, Medical, Economical and Agricultural; Being Also a Medical Botany of the Confederate States; with Practical Information of the Useful Properties of Trees, Plants, and Shrubs*. Charleston, SC: Evans and Cogswell, 1863; reprint, San Francisco: Norman, 1991.

POST SURGEON *See* Surgeons, Post.

POST–TRAUMATIC STRESS DISORDER

Post–traumatic stress disorder (PTSD) is a term devised after the Vietnam War to describe a variety of psychological and associated physical symptoms caused by exposure to combat or some other major stress. It is roughly equivalent to the conditions described as "nostalgia" or "homesickness" during the Civil War, "shell shock" during World War I, and "combat fatigue" during World War II.

The symptoms, which affected both Union and Confederate soldiers of all ranks, as well as medical personnel, might begin during or soon after a battle or perhaps not until months or even years after the war was over. Symptoms varied from the mild to the debilitating. They could be managed and overcome by many soldiers, but in some cases led to violence and insanity.

Symptoms of PTSD, which varied in number and severity from one individual to another, included any combination of flashbacks, unpleasant recollections triggered by sights or sounds, nightmares, extreme and unrealistic anxiety, hallucinations, depression, startle reactions, withdrawal from society, mental disorientation, violent threats and acts, insomnia, fear of going outside, delusions, crying spells, restlessness, shaking, an extreme sense of guilt, hyperactivity, heart palpitations, memory problems, insanity, and attempted or successful suicide. These symptoms could also develop after gunshot wounds or severe bouts of disease and were, at times, related to exhaustion from intense marching on a limited diet. While mild depression, nightmares, recollections, and startle reactions would be normal responses to difficult combat experiences, some soldiers had much more traumatic responses. Some ran or hid because of their anxieties when ordered into battle. Others began to behave strangely during or after a battle and ended up being sent to a local insane asylum or, if they were Union soldiers, to the government hospital for the insane in Washington, DC.

However, PTSD was difficult to diagnose, and in many cases doctors did not recognize the symptoms, thinking instead that the patient was a malingerer or shirker. Late–twentieth-century historians believed that some soldiers might have deserted from the army because of the effects of PTSD.

After the war most veterans suffering from psychological problems were cared for at home. But when they became dangerous to themselves and others, they were confined in jails and state or local insane asylums. Some received veterans' pensions, especially if they also suffered from a physical condition.

See also: Gunshot Wounds; Insanity; Malingerers.

Bibliography

Dean, Eric T., Jr. *Shook Over Hell: Post–Traumatic Stress, Vietnam, and the Civil War*. Cambridge, MA: Harvard University Press, 1997.

PRISONERS OF WAR

During the course of the Civil War, soldiers of both the North and the South captured thousands of their opponents. While some were released on parole or exchanged, many others spent months or even years in prisoner of war facilities, usually in conditions ranging from difficult to wretched.

A major reason for the suffering of prisoners of war during the Civil War was that neither side was prepared to deal with prisoners, especially in large numbers. Disorganization contributed to poor conditions. The Union forces tended to house their prisoners in old forts or at military training camps (such as Camp Morton at Indianapolis, Indiana, or the camp at Elmira, New York), eventually remodeling them to some extent to house more men. Later the Union constructed a few new facilities such as the barracks at Rock Island, Illinois. The Confederates initially used a variety of jails and warehouses to hold prisoners. Libby Prison in Richmond, Virginia, is an example. Later, when the Richmond prisons were overwhelmed, the Confederates constructed stockades with high fences but virtually no shelter, as at the notorious Andersonville prison camp in Georgia and several other locations in Georgia and South Carolina. Altogether there were at least 150 prisons operating at some time in the North and South.

Initially many captured soldiers were paroled. This meant that they signed a paper promising not to fight again until they were properly exchanged. They would be released to return to their own lines, where they might be sent home temporarily or housed in a special camp. Sometimes men ignored their paroles and returned to the fight, a move that could be dangerous if they were recaptured.

The exchange process could be complicated. Generally, a prisoner was exchanged for an opponent of equal rank, such as a private for a private. However, an officer might also be exchanged for a certain number of privates and lower officers. Although paroles and exchanges occurred earlier, a cartel, or agreement, of July 22, 1862, made the process official. However, problems and violations arose on both sides. In July 1863 U.S. secretary of war Edwin M. Stanton insisted on several specific changes, such as man-for-man (of equal rank) exchanges only. The Confederates rejected the proposal, so most exchanges stopped by the fall of 1863. This immediately led to overcrowding of prisons on both sides and the construction of new ones. Most of these new facilities were hastily and poorly constructed. Sanitation was terrible in most of the camps. In addition, clothing and food supplies were cut, deliberately in many cases, leading to tremendous suffering and a high mortality rate in the winter of 1863–1864. Inspectors on both sides reported the problems, but few improvements were made. No priority was ever given to supplies for prisoners of war on either side.

When the Confederates finally agreed to the exchange cartel alterations in August 1864, Union commander Ulysses S. Grant refused to reinstate the exchanges. The public reason was that the South would not exchange black soldiers. Grant, however, also privately refused the exchanges because each soldier returned to fight in the Southern army prolonged the war. Although Grant realized that his refusal would mean more suffering and death for Union prisoners of war, he believed that refusing to exchange troops would shorten the war, resulting in fewer deaths overall. As a consequence, the prison conditions became even worse than previously.

Exact numbers of prisoners of war cannot be known, and figures vary widely. However, the best recent estimate suggests that about 194,743 Union soldiers spent time in Confederate prisons while about 214,865 Southerners were imprisoned in the North. Of these 409,608 prisoners, roughly 30,218 Federals and 25,976 Confederates died. About one-seventh of the total number of Civil War soldiers became prisoners and about one-seventh of those prisoners died. Important causes of death included digestive diseases, malnutrition, scurvy, and pneumonia. Several prisons also had many smallpox cases. The highest death rate in the North occurred in the prison at Elmira, in the South at Andersonville.

Medical care for prisoners of war varied widely. Wounded prisoners were often treated initially by the doctors and in the hospitals of their opponents. Most medical officers tried to provide the same care as they gave to their own soldiers. Sometimes townspeople or fellow patients complained about equal care for the enemy, and some nurses refused to provide it. Others went out of their way to give equal care to all. Sometimes local women who sympathized with, or allegedly sympathized with, the enemy brought delicacies to the hospitalized captives, stimulating complaints from the loyal. Some prisoners of war were paroled or exchanged because of their medical conditions. Others recovered enough to be sent to a prisoner of war camp.

As in any hospital, doctors assigned to the prisoner of war camps on both sides varied in quality and in compassion for the patients. Some doctors objected to or tried to get out of assignment to a prison. Those who did serve in prisons generally worked under adverse conditions, with a shortage of hospital buildings, tents, clothing, medical supplies, bedding, beds, cooking utensils, food, and medicine. Repeated requisitions might only be partially filled. Too few doctors had to treat too many patients, who were nursed reluctantly and inexpertly by fellow prisoners. Doctors' reports on abysmal living and sanitary conditions were often ignored rather than resolved. Yet most doctors did the best they could with the resources they had.

Some doctors became prisoners of war themselves. At the beginning of the war there were no guidelines about what to do with captured physicians, and some medical officers refused to stay behind with patients too severely wounded to move for fear that the doctors might be captured. Some doctors were released, while others spent up to a year in prison.

In May 1862, after the Shenandoah Valley campaign in Virginia, Confederate general Thomas J. "Stonewall" Jackson and his medical director Hunter H. McGuire negotiated the parole and exchange of a number of Union surgeons. After

June, following negotiations between generals George B. McClellan and Robert E. Lee, surgeons on both sides were usually regarded as noncombatants, able to stay with and treat their soldiers without fear of imprisonment. This arrangement failed for about five months during 1863, resulting in the capture of some surgeons at Gettysburg (July 1863) and Chickamauga (September 1863) who were not released for several months. Dr. Mary Walker, who served as a Union contract surgeon, was captured on April 10, 1864, and, suspected of being a spy (which she may have been), imprisoned in Castle Thunder, Richmond, Virginia, for four months.

The topic of prisoners of war during the Civil War tends to be a sensitive issue. Many works attempt to fix blame, presenting the topic in a very judgmental way. Former prisoners themselves were hardly neutral commentators. Those who wrote memoirs many years after the fact (as opposed to those whose diaries have been published) tended to exaggerate, making poor conditions sound even worse. Conditions in Northern camps actually did become worse because of miserly Union officials, especially commissary general of prisoners William C. Hoffman. In addition, Northerners thought that imprisoned rebels should suffer as punishment for taking up arms against the Union or in retaliation for alleged Southern mistreatment of Union prisoners. In the South serious supply shortages and transportation breakdowns affected prisoners of war as well as the Confederate army and civilians generally.

See also: Andersonville Prison; Chickamauga, Battle of; Diarrhea and Dysentery; Elmira Prison; Gettysburg, Battle of; Jackson, Thomas Jonathan ("Stonewall"); McGuire, Hunter Holmes; Malnutrition; Nurses; Sanitation; Scurvy; Smallpox; Walker, Mary Edwards.

Bibliography

Horigan, Michael. *Elmira: Death Camp of the North.* Mechanicsburg, PA: Stackpole, 2002.

Leonard, Elizabeth D. *Yankee Women: Gender Battles in the Civil War.* New York: Norton, 1994.

Marvel, William. *Andersonville: The Last Depot.* Chapel Hill: University of North Carolina Press, 1994.

McAdams, Benton. *Rebels at Rock Island: The Story of a Civil War Prison.* DeKalb: Northern Illinois University Press, 2000.

Robertson, James I. "The Scourge of Elmira." *Civil War History* 8, no. 2 (1962): 80–97; reprint, William B. Hesseltine, ed. *Civil War Prisons.* Kent, OH: Kent State University Press, 1972.

Sanders, Charles W., Jr. *While in the Hands of the Enemy: Military Prisons of the Civil War.* Baton Rouge: Louisiana State University Press, 2005.

PROSTHESES *See* Artificial Limbs.

QUARTERMASTERS

The quartermaster department, in both the North and South, had vast and varied responsibilities for supplying the physical and military needs of their respective armies during the Civil War. Because quartermasters had such huge responsibilities, often complicated by a shortage of supplies and transportation, they were the focus of much complaint throughout the war.

The structure and responsibilities of the departments were the same in both sections because the Confederates based their system on the Union military regulations. At the top of each department was the quartermaster general. Montgomery C. Meigs held the office in the North while Abraham C. Myers was the first Confederate quartermaster general, succeeded by Alexander R. Lawton in August 1863. All three men had graduated from West Point and served in the prewar U.S. Army, although Lawton had resigned after a year or less.

Beneath them were a number of assistant quartermasters, stationed at supply depots, in hospitals, and with the armies in the field. The chief quartermasters at supply depots made most of the contracts for purchasing and manufacturing supplies. Each army had a chief quartermaster who was in charge of ordering, storing, and delivering supplies for his whole army. Within that army each progressively smaller group—corps, division, brigade, and regiment—had its own quartermaster to arrange transportation and distribution of supplies.

Although this was the plan, there were never enough quartermasters, only 919 in the Union army during the entire war. Quartermasters were supposed to have a business background and to be bonded, with papers signed by wealthy, reputable persons. Serving as a quartermaster could be a thankless task, with often overwhelming amounts of work unrewarded by commensurate rank and pay. Quartermasters were assisted by civilian clerks, manufacturers, and workers to load and unload materials. Often slaves, "contrabands" (escaped slaves), or free blacks provided muscle, while some women worked at manufacturing and clerical tasks.

Quartermasters were responsible for providing almost everything the army needed except food for the soldiers (furnished by the subsistence or commissary department), medicines and some related supplies (provided by the medical purveyor), ammunition (the responsibility of the ordnance department), and the soldier's wages (handled by paymasters). Quartermasters had to provide living quarters, offices, and hospitals for the armies. This meant tents, straw, bedding, blankets, cooking gear, wood for fuel and construction, cots, bunks, and rented or constructed rooms. Records at all levels required stationery, envelopes, ledgers, pens, ink, pencils, glue, "red tape" (cloth tape to tie up bundles of papers), sealing wax, and blank forms. Cavalry and artillery horses and mules, along with their food, shoes, veterinary medicines, and the vehicles they pulled, came from the quartermaster. Clothing for soldiers and hospital patients was provided by the quartermaster as well.

All supplies, whether furnished by the quartermaster or not, had to be stored and transported by the quartermaster department. Storing enormous amounts of supplies meant that quartermasters had to rent, impress, or build numerous buildings and sheds to protect the supplies. Sometimes the supplies were simply stacked outside, liable to spoil or be ruined by inclement weather.

Transporting all the supplies required working railroads with enough locomotives and cars, as well as track in good repair. River- and ocean-going vessels and horse-drawn wagons were also essential. A shortage in any of these areas could deprive troops of critical supplies at a crucial time, leading to possible failure of a campaign and certainly misery for the soldiers.

Although quartermasters were not in charge of the soldier payroll, they had responsibility for paying many expenses, such as the wages of day laborers, postage and express charges for official mail and packages, the costs of holding courts-martial, the costs of pursuing deserters, the burial expenses of officers and men who died in the service, the expenses of spies and guides, the charges for veterinarians and any medicine they prescribed for horses, as well as every other army expense not paid by some other department. It is no wonder that the quartermaster department spent more money than all the other sections of the War Department combined.

In order to supply the armies, the quartermasters had to procure the supplies from somewhere. Supplies could be purchased if they were available and the quartermaster had money to buy them or, sometimes in the South, useful products to barter. Southern quartermasters, and sometimes Northerners as well, could impress materials if their owners would not sell at a reasonable price. Both Northern and Southern quartermasters made arrangements with existing factories or established new ones to provide the enormous amounts of material necessary to keep the huge armies functioning.

The quartermaster department required a large number of forms at all levels so it could monitor what supplies were on hand and prevent dishonesty and loss. Sending quartermasters were supposed to provide detailed lists of what each shipment contained. Receiving quartermasters were to inspect the shipment and receipt for the items. All the Northern paperwork eventually had to be examined in Washington before most bills could be paid. In both regiments and hospitals, officers had to fill out lengthy forms monthly, detailing the specific amount of all supplies received and on hand and accounting for the use or loss of all supplies listed in the previous report.

Because the quartermaster department was so large and had such varied responsibilities, it is no surprise that it faced many problems at all levels. Some people did not know how to fill out forms properly. Payment could be delayed for months while forms were in transit. Quartermasters were often shifted from place to place to fill urgent vacancies, and paperwork might take months to catch up with them for signatures before the expenses could finally be paid. Despite all the regulations, shipments could be short because officers other than those for whom the shipment was intended removed materials, with or without giving a proper receipt.

Quartermasters were frequently blamed for poor-quality materials and food as well as shortages of supplies, even though many problems were due to forces beyond the quartermaster's control, such as bad weather, flooded rivers, and enemy depredations. Many problems resulted from lack of transportation. Although the North had extensive resources for constructing wagons, railroads, and ships, nevertheless, in many places such transport was in short supply. The situation was even more critical in the South, where worn-out transportation could not be replaced. Even when transportation was available, the lack of coordination between quartermasters in charge of different districts caused delays. Furthermore, quartermasters and those in need of supplies often disagreed about what should have priority for transportation. In general, troops and ammunition took priority over food and especially over anything to do with the medical department.

Doctors, both Union and Confederate, often complained about quartermasters, frequently with some cause. After the Battle of Chickamauga in September 1863, the medical director for the Confederate Army of Tennessee's general hospitals complained about several obstructionist quartermasters who refused to provide transportation for the wounded, to requisition blacks to care for the wounded, or to supply a coffin for a dead soldier. In other instances, quartermasters ordered wagons to the front that were supposed to carry wounded to the hospitals, used lumber prepared for hospital construction to build storage sheds, and ordered hospitals being relocated to leave behind bulky property such as bunks without providing any replacement beds at the new location. Doctors on both sides also complained about the quartermasters' failure to give any priority to the transportation of the sick and wounded from the field to the hospital. Doctors also objected when freight cars or ships that had just been used to haul livestock were assigned to carry patients without being cleaned.

Although certainly some quartermasters were irresponsible, incompetent, obstructionist, or corrupt, the majority performed their duty as faithfully as they were able under the circumstances.

See also: Ambulance Trains; Chickamauga, Battle of; Hospital Buildings; Medical Purveyors; Subsistence Department.

Bibliography

Regulations for the Army of the Confederate States, 1862. Richmond, VA: J.W. Randolph, 1862; reprint, San Francisco: Norman, 1992.

Schroeder-Lein, Glenna R. *Confederate Hospitals on the Move: Samuel H. Stout and the Army of Tennessee.* Columbia: University of South Carolina Press, 1994.

Taylor, Lenette S. *"The Supply for Tomorrow Must Not Fail": The Civil War of Captain Simon Perkins Jr., a Union Quartermaster.* Kent, OH: Kent State University Press, 2004.

Weigley, Russell F. *Quartermaster General of the Union Army: A Biography of M.C. Meigs.* New York: Columbia University Press, 1959.

Wilson, Harold S. *Confederate Industry: Manufacturers and Quartermasters in the Civil War.* Jackson: University Press of Mississippi, 2002.

QUININE

Quinine is an effective medicine used for treating malaria. It is made from the ground bark of the cinchona tree, which grows in South America. Thus, in the nineteenth century it was often called "Peruvian bark." Spanish Jesuit missionaries first observed the indigenous peoples of South America using cinchona bark to treat malaria in the sixteenth century. In the 1820s, French chemists developed quinine from the bark. The derivative proved to be more effective than the crude bark and was soon widely used in malarious areas of the United States. Quinine was dispensed either as a powder dissolved in a liquid or as a pill. A dose would be given to a malaria patient upon diagnosis and then usually at the beginning of each successive chill. Overdoses of quinine could result in ringing in the ears and other symptoms.

Shortly before the Civil War, it was discovered that small doses of quinine could be given on a regular basis to prevent malaria. Both Union and Confederate doctors prescribed these doses in malarious regions, but the bad taste of the drug made troops reluctant to take it unless it was dispensed in whiskey. Southerners were less able to use quinine as a preventive because of the shortage of quinine in the Confederacy.

Because the drug could not be produced in the United States, all quinine had to be imported. Since the Union blockade of the Confederacy included medicines, the inability to import quinine became a major problem for the South, where malaria affected most regions. Confederate surgeons were more concerned about a potential shortage of quinine than any other medicine. As early as September 1861, Confederate surgeon general Samuel P. Moore urged doctors to use it conservatively. Because quinine worked so well for malaria, doctors also prescribed it for other conditions: to reduce fever, to relieve pain, to stop diarrhea, and to treat bone inflammations resulting from wounds (osteomyelitis). Quinine was not effective for any of these problems, but doctors continued to prescribe it, in effect wasting medicine that, in the South at least, was in short supply and was needed to combat malaria.

Southerners attempted to alleviate the quinine shortage in a number of ways. Blockade-runners often included the product in their cargoes because a package of quinine was small, light, and could be sold for a high price. Women with permission to cross enemy lines sometimes smuggled in quinine and other medicines by hiding them in their hoop skirts or elsewhere on their person. Some quinine was also captured from the Federals on the battlefield. But all of these sources were not enough, and Surgeon General Moore ordered doctors to use substitutes whenever possible. Indigenous plant materials used, alone or in combination, as quinine substitutes included the root and bark of the chinquapin, willow bark, knotgrass, Georgia bark, boneset tea, tulip tree bark, dogwood, cottonseed tea, the inner bark of the holly, and external applications of turpentine. Late in the war, doctors in Richmond hospitals were urged to try out quinine substitutes on their malaria patients. Unfortunately for the Confederates, none of the substitutes was particularly effective. This was also a major problem for the citizens at home who had to rely on substitutes because they were usually unable to get quinine. The government monopolized for the army whatever quinine entered the country, and any that might be sold to the public was prohibitively expensive.

See also: Blockade; Intermittent Fevers; Malaria; Moore, Samuel Preston; Mosquitoes; Porcher, Francis Peyre; Substitutes, for Supplies.

Bibliography
Adams, George Worthington. *Doctors in Blue: The Medical History of the Union Army in the Civil War.* New York: Schuman, 1952; reprint, Dayton, OH: Morningside, 1985.
Bollet, Alfred Jay. *Civil War Medicine: Challenges and Triumphs.* Tucson, AZ: Galen, 2002.
Cunningham, H.H. *Doctors in Gray: The Confederate Medical Service.* Baton Rouge: Louisiana State University Press, 1958; reprint, Gloucester, MA: Peter Smith, 1970.
Massey, Mary Elizabeth. *Ersatz in the Confederacy: Shortages and Substitutes on the Southern Homefront.* Columbia: University of South Carolina Press, 1952, 1993.
Porcher, Francis Peyre. *Resources of the Southern Fields and Forests, Medical, Economical and Agricultural: Being Also a Medical Botany of the Confederate States; with Practical Information of the Useful Properties of Trees, Plants, and Shrubs.* Charleston, SC: Evans and Cogswell, 1863; reprint, San Francisco: Norman, 1991.

QUINTARD, CHARLES TODD (1824–1898)

Charles Todd Quintard served the Confederate Army of Tennessee as both a chaplain and an assistant surgeon. Born in Stamford, Connecticut, on December 22, 1824, Quintard studied at Trinity School in New York City and received a Master of Arts degree from Columbia College. In 1847 he graduated as a medical doctor from the University of the City of New York and practiced for a year at Bellevue Hospital in that city. He then practiced medicine in Athens, Georgia. While there, he married Eliza Catherine Hand (1826–1905). The couple eventually had five children, of whom three survived to adulthood. In 1851 Quintard accepted the chair of physiology and pathological anatomy at the Medical College of Memphis, Tennessee.

Dissatisfied with his medical career, Quintard became a candidate for holy orders in the Episcopal Church in January 1854. After studying theology with James H. Otey, Bishop of Tennessee, Quintard was ordained a deacon in January 1855 and a priest in 1856. After a brief stint as rector of Calvary Church in Memphis, he became rector at the Church of the Advent in Nashville, Tennessee, later in 1856. Quintard was considered a powerful preacher who exerted a good influence on young men. In 1859 these young men elected him chaplain of the Rock City Guard, a militia group. Although Quintard had been a Unionist, he accepted the chaplainry of the Confederate First Tennessee Volunteer Infantry Regiment, when elected, because he believed that he could be of more spiritual service to the soldiers than he could be to his congregation as a whole.

As chaplain, Quintard preached to soldiers and to civilian congregations in whatever town or city he happened to be. For a time he served as chaplain-at-large in Atlanta, founding and serving as rector of St. Luke's Church until it was damaged in General William T. Sherman's bombardment of the city in 1864. Quintard offered Holy Communion frequently, baptized and confirmed numerous people, and officiated at a number of officers' weddings. Spiritual conversations with Quintard evidently influenced the lives of several generals, including Braxton Bragg, inspiring them to join the Episcopal Church. Quintard held frequent services at the hospitals. He performed burial services for countless soldiers and also several generals, including Leonidas Polk, Episcopal bishop of Louisiana, killed near Atlanta in June 1864, and John Adams and Patrick Cleburne, killed at the Battle of Franklin, Tennessee, on November 30, 1864.

Although Civil War chaplains spent much of their time with sick and wounded soldiers, Quintard did so to an unusual degree because he could care for the soldiers physically as well as spiritually, often functioning as an assistant surgeon while never officially holding the position. Quintard recruited supplies from civilians for hospitalized soldiers at various times. More than once he was left behind to care for sick soldiers or sent with ambulance trains of wounded. He dressed the wounds of Union soldiers as well as Confederates. At the Battle of Perryville, Kentucky, in October 1862, he worked as an assistant surgeon for much of the day and all night without food or rest until he collapsed from exhaustion. Because he had torn up his shirt to use for bandages, he also caught a cold. At Murfreesboro, Tennessee, from December 1862 to January 1863, Quintard essentially functioned as regimental surgeon because that officer was absent. In October 1863, after the Battle of Chickamauga, he served as an assistant surgeon in the hospitals in Marietta, Georgia. Because of his spiritual and medical services to the Army of Tennessee, Quintard Hospital was named for him.

On September 6, 1865, soon after the war ended, Quintard was made second bishop of the diocese of Tennessee, replacing Bishop Otey who had died during the war. Quintard faced major challenges because many churches had been damaged or destroyed and many parishioners displaced or killed. A number of former soldiers, to whom he had ministered, became supportive members of the Episcopal Church. Quintard was particularly influential in establishing the University of the South at Sewanee, Tennessee, and overseeing its development. He lived at Sewanee in the summer and in Memphis during the winter. He worked on his memoir relating his Civil War experiences about 1896, but did not finish it before his death on February 15, 1898, in Darien, Georgia, where he had gone to rest. Arthur Howard Noll edited the memoir, added an introduction and two concluding chapters, and published the work in 1905.

See also: Ambulances; Chaplains; Chickamauga, Battle of; Hospitals, General; Surgeons, Assistant.

Bibliography

Quintard, Charles Todd. *Doctor Quintard, Chaplain C.S.A. and Second Bishop of Tennessee: The Memoir and Civil War Diary of Charles Todd Quintard.* Sewanee, TN: University Press of Sewanee, 1905; reprint, ed. Sam Davis Elliott. Baton Rouge: Louisiana State University Press, 2003.

R

RECORD KEEPING *See* Hospital Paperwork.

RED ROVER *See* USS *Red Rover.*

REMITTENT FEVER *See* Fevers.

RESECTION

Resection and excision, methods of surgically treating a gunshot wound of the extremities without resorting to amputation, were practiced by surgeons in both the North and the South during the Civil War.

Because minié balls often shattered the bone as well as destroying tissue, amputation of the arm or leg was sometimes the best way to treat a serious wound and preserve the life of the patient. However, if the nerves and arteries were uninjured, particularly in an arm, the surgeons might try excision. This meant that they would remove the two or three inches of fragmented bone, but otherwise leave the limb intact. If the doctors removed a shattered joint, at least in the Confederacy, this would be called a resection. However, the terms are often used interchangeably in the literature. After either a resection or an excision, the recovered soldier would have minimal to near normal use of his limb, although it would be shorter than its fellow. Arm excisions and resections tended to be more successful because a weak, resected leg might actually be more troublesome than an artificial leg.

Records show 174,206 gunshot wounds of the extremities treated by Union surgeons (there were probably more). Of these, 20 percent were treated with surgery. Of these operations, 29,143 were amputations, while 4,656 were excisions or resections. These operations had a higher fatality rate (27.5 percent) than amputations (25.8 percent), and a significantly higher rate for arm excisions and resections (23.8 percent) than for arm amputations (12.6 percent). Both amputation and reconstructive treatments of legs had at least a 40 percent fatality rate. Only fragmentary Confederate statistics are available.

Union doctors obviously performed far fewer resections and excisions than they did amputations, and, according to one medical historian, they performed fewer resections and excisions as the war went on. Confederate surgeons, however, who seemed to regard resection and excision as conservative measures, recalled more attempts to save limbs later in the war.

See also: Amputation; Artificial Limbs; Gunshot Wounds; Gunshot Wounds, Treatment of; *The Medical and Surgical History of the War of the Rebellion*; Minié Balls; Mortality, of Soldiers.

Bibliography

Bollet, Alfred Jay. *Civil War Medicine: Challenges and Triumphs.* Tucson, AZ: Galen, 2002.

Cunningham, H.H. *Doctors in Gray: The Confederate Medical Service.* Baton Rouge: Louisiana State University Press, 1958; reprint, Gloucester, MA: Peter Smith, 1970.

Formento, Felix, Jr. *Notes and Observations on Army Surgery.* New Orleans: L.E. Marchand, 1863; reprint, San Francisco: Norman, 1990.

Taylor, William. "Conservatism in Army Surgery—Some Field Reminiscences." *Southern Practitioner* 27 (November 1905): 625–628.

RESERVE SURGICAL CORPS

The reserve surgical corps was a Confederate innovation to supply extra, well-qualified surgeons to care for the wounded during battles. Both Northerners and Southerners had sent extra doctors to the battlefield previously. After Fredericksburg, for example, the Union forces hired a group of "reserve surgeons," civilians who were paid as contract surgeons. But this Confederate reserve corps was the first attempt to organize the effort, using doctors already in the army, before the emergency arose.

The plan was developed by Samuel H. Stout, medical director of hospitals for the Confederate Army of Tennessee. On February 23, 1864, his second in command, Samuel M. Bemiss, issued Circular No. 6, which set up the corps. Each surgeon in charge of hospitals at any general hospital post under Stout's control was to select his best surgeon or surgeons at a ratio of one for each 500 beds. These doctors would be continually on call, ready to leave for the front on a moment's notice when a battle began, but meanwhile continuing with their usual hospital duties. When called, the surgeons were to bring surgical and medical supplies, stimulants such as whiskey and coffee, and cooked rations for the wounded patients.

Dudley D. Saunders, post surgeon at Marietta, Georgia, commanded the reserve corps, which, in February 1864, consisted of fourteen surgeons, eight assistant surgeons, and some male members of local soldier's relief committees in Atlanta and Griffin, Georgia. Andrew J. Foard, field medical director for the Army of Tennessee, was responsible for calling the corps into action.

The corps received an immediate test. On February 25, Foard ordered the corps to Dalton, Georgia, because of various enemy movements. When the Federal troops withdrew after a few skirmishes, Foard dismissed the corps on February 27. He was very pleased that everyone had arrived within twenty-four hours, some from as far as 300 miles away, with plenty of supplies to minister to several thousand wounded, had there been an actual battle. As a result of this successful effort, Surgeon General Samuel P. Moore, on March 15, 1864, ordered each of the other Confederate armies to set up a similar corps. Doctors from Chimborazo Hospital in Richmond, Virginia, participated in a reserve corps in the area.

Once the spring campaign of 1864 got under way, with Sherman's troops gradually pushing the Confederates south through Georgia toward Atlanta, some problems became evident with the reserve surgical corps. When a battle seemed likely, Foard would call out the corps. However, once they reported, they might wait for some days, doing nothing, before the battle began. Meanwhile, the hospitals from which they had come were understaffed while dealing with an influx of sick and wounded sent from hospitals nearer the front, which were trying to empty beds in order to have room for the new patients that were expected after the battle. On June 4, 1864, Foard promised Stout that he would not call out the corps until a battle actually began. Nevertheless, some post surgeons resisted sending away their best surgeons when they needed them most, causing them to rely on local contract surgeons with less skill.

Despite these problems, the reserve surgical corps successfully fulfilled its purpose until the end of the war.

See also: Foard, Andrew Jackson; Hospitals, General; Moore, Samuel Preston; Stout, Samuel Hollingsworth; Surgeons; Surgeons, Acting Assistant (Contract); Surgeons, Post.

Bibliography

Bollet, Alfred Jay. *Civil War Medicine: Challenges and Triumphs.* Tucson, AZ: Galen, 2002.
Schroeder-Lein, Glenna R. *Confederate Hospitals on the Move: Samuel H. Stout and the Army of Tennessee.* Columbia: University of South Carolina Press, 1994.

RESOURCES OF THE SOUTHERN FIELDS AND FORESTS

In 1863, at the request of Confederate surgeon general Samuel P. Moore, Francis Peyre Porcher, South Carolina physician and Confederate surgeon, published a monumental work on Southern botany titled *Resources of the Southern Fields and Forests, Medical, Economical and Agricultural; Being Also a Medical Botany of the Confederate States; with Practical Information of the Useful Properties of Trees, Plants, and Shrubs.* The purpose of this 594-page book by a botanical authority was to enable Confederate physicians, as well as other Southerners, to make full use of indigenous remedies and resources to replace Northern and foreign products that were difficult to procure because of the Union blockade.

The entries, organized by families of plants, listed the Latin botanical name, followed by the common English name or names of the species. Porcher then indicated where the plant commonly grew. (Many were native to South Carolina, Porcher's area of expertise.) The entry then explained the parts of the plant (such as leaves or bark) that were useful in what form (decoction or poultice, for example) for what purpose. While many of the plants had medicinal value, others were good for dyes, basket weaving, or durable fence posts. For each entry, Porcher listed his sources, such as people who had used and recommended the plant or books and journals reporting a particular treatment. At times Porcher requested doctors to further test remedies and report the results to him.

Southern newspapers published excerpts from the book. Because of this widespread circulation of the information, a number of citizens collected appropriate plants that they took to army medical purveyors. Some students of the war have suggested that the use of indigenous materials, stimulated by the book, prolonged the Confederate war effort. A revised version of Porcher's book was printed in 1869.

See also: Blockade; Medical Purveyors; Porcher, Francis Peyre; Substitutes, for Supplies.

Bibliography

Porcher, Francis Peyre. *Resources of the Southern Fields and Forests, Medical, Economical and Agricultural; Being Also a Medical Botany of the Confederate States; with Practical Information of the Useful Properties of Trees, Plants, and Shrubs.* Charleston, SC: Evans and Cogswell, 1863; reprint, San Francisco: Norman, 1991.

RHEUMATISM

During the Civil War, *rheumatism* was the term used in both the North and the South for several kinds of diseases that caused inflammation and serious pain of the joints. Although these diseases, classified as "acute" and "chronic" rheumatism, had a low fatality rate, they incapacitated many soldiers temporarily or permanently.

Medical historians now believe that acute rheumatism was usually rheumatic fever, which resulted from a streptococcal infection (such as strep throat). It caused swelling, tenderness, and excruciating pain in the joints, which made it hard for the patient to move. Most common in winter, the disease usually lasted one to two months. In many cases the disease went beyond the joints and caused pericarditis, the inflammation of the sac around the heart, as well as damage to the heart valves, possibly leading to heart failure. These problems could cause death from "rheumatism."

Rheumatic fever was common in civilian life. The resulting heart defects caused the rejection of about 2 percent of Civil War recruits if they were given a careful preenlistment physical. Many other soldiers were later discharged from the service because of their disability. One historian suggests that General Robert E. Lee may have had rheumatic fever with resulting heart damage. Although very rare in the twenty-first century because of antibiotics, rheumatic fever was common up through World War II.

Chronic rheumatism was a vague classification that evidently included a number of diseases such as extended cases of rheumatic fever, arthritis, and rheumatoid arthritis. One historian suggests that it was often reactive arthritis, a lengthy and frequently deformative inflammation of joints or the spine developing after a patient has suffered from such diseases as gonorrhea or dysentery. Since both venereal and intestinal diseases were common, this diagnosis could account for many of the chronic cases.

Acute and chronic rheumatism caused about 280,000 cases of disease in the Union army, the most of any disease grouping in the noncontagious category. Of these cases, only 710 men died; another 12,000 were discharged because of rheumatic disability. Confederate records, although not complete for the entire war, indicate 59,772 cases of rheumatism in the armies east of the Mississippi River during 1861–1862, with 1,842 discharges resulting. During the war, Chimborazo Hospital in Richmond, Virginia, treated almost 2,000 patients with rheumatism, of whom eighty died.

Treatments for rheumatism were limited and often ineffective. Some Confederate patients with chronic rheumatism were not treated at all. The best that doctors could do was to prescribe opiates for pain. They also administered quinine, potassium iodide, baths, and compresses to reduce inflammation. Late in the war, Samuel H. Stout, medical director of the hospitals behind the lines for the Confederate Army of Tennessee, ordered rheumatism patients sent to a hospital in Eufaula, Alabama, where they could be treated with a galvanic battery.

Because it involved aches and pains that could be felt by the patient but not seen by an observer, rheumatism became one of the favorite diseases feigned by malingerers.

See also: Diarrhea and Dysentery; Heart Disease; Malingerers; Mortality, of Soldiers; Opiate Use and Addiction; Quinine; Stout, Samuel Hollingsworth; Venereal Disease.

Bibliography
Bollet, Alfred Jay. *Civil War Medicine: Challenges and Triumphs.* Tucson, AZ: Galen, 2002.

Cunningham, H.H. *Doctors in Gray: The Confederate Medical Service.* Baton Rouge: Louisiana State University Press, 1958; reprint, Gloucester, MA: Peter Smith, 1970.

Steiner, Paul E. *Disease in the Civil War: Natural Biological Warfare in 1861–1865.* Springfield, IL: C.C. Thomas, 1968.

RICHMOND, VIRGINIA

Richmond, the capital of the state of Virginia, also became the capital of the Confederacy in May 1861. The Confederate legislature had found accommodations rather lacking in Montgomery, Alabama, the new nation's first capital. Richmond was among the largest cities in the South. Moving the capital there would ensure that Virginia joined the Confederacy. It would also make Richmond the symbolic goal of Union military efforts throughout the war.

Richmond was the most industrialized city in the South. The Tredegar Iron Works there was the key producer of large metal products. During the Confederate era, Tredegar manufactured more than 1,600 cannons, armor for ironclad gunboats, machinery for making weapons, and hundreds of thousands of artillery shells. Richmond also had seven flour mills, a woolen mill, a paper mill, fifty tobacco factories, and numerous smaller businesses, including fifty iron and metal works of various sorts. In addition, it was a regional transportation center on the James River, with the James River and Kanawha Canal and five railroads (although none of the tracks joined together and all products had to be unloaded and transferred).

Richmond had a population of about 38,000 when the war broke out, more than one-third of them slaves or free blacks. The city was a major center for the slave trade. The white population was very much divided by class, with a proud elite group. Richmond had thirty churches, three synagogues, and more educational institutions than was usual in a Southern city. It soon became the governmental, manufacturing, hospital, prison, and railroad center of the Confederacy. The government eventually employed more than 70,000 civilians in Richmond, overwhelming and overcrowding the facilities available and requiring creativity, change of building use, and more construction. The tremendous number of people, both military and civilian, also led to increased instances of theft, violence, and prostitution.

During the war, 25 percent of the battles and 60 percent of the casualties occurred within seventy-five miles of Richmond, so it naturally became a hospital center. The earliest battle to affect the city was the First Battle of Manassas (or Bull Run, as the Union called it), fought on July 21, 1861. The casualties came in three waves: those with minor wounds, some of whom walked to the city themselves; the dead; and finally, the seriously wounded. The day after the battle, Richmond mayor Joseph Mayo called a mass meeting in Capitol Square to establish committees to bring the wounded from the field, select buildings to serve as hospitals, and find food and supplies for the patients. Richmond citizens, especially the women, rallied to meet the needs of the sick and wounded soldiers.

Richmond only had five hospitals when the war began. Makeshift hospitals quickly opened in churches, hotels, tobacco factories, private homes, and the city's new almshouse. Citizens of other states living in Richmond opened some hospitals specifically for soldiers from Alabama, Georgia, and South Carolina. Although many of these temporary facilities closed after the First Manassas emergency ended, some remained in use for at least part of the war or reopened during the next crisis. Chimborazo Hospital, which ultimately treated more than 76,000 patients, the largest total in the Confederacy, was constructed on the edge of town and opened in October 1861.

In the spring of 1862, Union general George B. McClellan began what is known as the Peninsula Campaign. His troops were transported by boat to Fortress Monroe and then, in early April, began moving up the peninsula between the York and James rivers toward Richmond. After delay by a siege at Yorktown, the Federal and Confederate forces fought several significant battles near Richmond, particularly Seven Pines (May 31–June 1) and the Seven Days battles (June 25–July 1). The thousands of soldiers wounded in these battles inundated Richmond once again, requiring the establishment of numerous new hospitals in tobacco warehouses and private homes. Howard's Grove, a large pavilion-style hospital on a former picnic ground, opened in June. By July Richmond had about fifty hospitals, which, by September 1862, had treated nearly 100,000 patients, of whom 7,600 (nearly 8 percent) died. More patients came to Richmond directly from the field in 1862 than during any other year. Local women again furnished what food and supplies they could.

In addition to the wounded, Federal prisoners of war contributed to the crowding in Richmond, as did refugees from areas affected by battles. Supplies of all sorts were already becoming scarce and prices were rising by the summer of 1862. These problems only got worse. By January 1863 prices in the city were ten times higher than they had been in 1860. When Richmond had a smallpox epidemic (November 1862–February 1863), the city council paid for vaccinations for 734 people who could not afford to pay for their own. On March 13, 1863, an explosion at the Confederate ordnance laboratory killed thirty-five workers, mostly women and girls. Then, on April 2, a number of women waged a bread riot, leading the city council to set up two free food depots to provide for those who were actually needy.

In 1863 Surgeon General Samuel P. Moore and the Confederate medical department issued orders closing many of the small hospitals in Richmond. They favored extending larger establishments on the outskirts of the city, such as Chimborazo, Howard's Grove, Winder, and Jackson, with a capacity of more than 1,000 patients each. Some small hospitals remained, however, including the Robertson Hospital, managed by Captain Sally Tompkins. By the end of the war about 100 different hospitals had been open at some point in the city. The average total hospital capacity in Richmond was between 10,000 and 15,000, but during times of medical emergency, the hospitals held as many as 20,000.

The winter of 1863–1864 brought more hardships and shortages to Richmond. In January 1864 the Confederate Congress increased the salaries of government workers whose wages were not keeping up with inflation. Conditions of scarcity and inflation worsened through the last year of the war because it was difficult to get food to Richmond. Everyone who lived in the capital, including hospital patients, suffered much hardship. Some hospital wards had to be closed because there was no fuel to heat them.

When evacuating Confederate troops burned supplies in Richmond on April 2, 1865, the out-of-control fire destroyed at least fifty-four blocks in the heart of the city containing more than 900 homes and businesses. Confederate medical records burned as well. When the Union troops took over, about 5,000 patients remained in nine hospitals.

See also: Bull Run (Manassas), First Battle of; Chimborazo Hospital; Hospital Buildings; Hospitals, General; Hospitals, Pavilion; Moore, Samuel Preston; Peninsula Campaign; Prisoners of War; Smallpox; Tompkins, Sally Louisa; Vaccination, Smallpox; Women's Hospital Auxiliaries and Relief Societies.

Bibliography

Calcutt, Rebecca Barbour. *Richmond's Wartime Hospitals.* Gretna, LA: Pelican, 2005.

Furgurson, Ernest B. *Ashes of Glory: Richmond at War.* New York: Knopf, 1996.

Green, Carol C. *Chimborazo: The Confederacy's Largest Hospital.* Knoxville: University of Tennessee Press, 2004.

Thomas, Emory M. *The Confederate State of Richmond: A Biography of the Capital.* Austin: University of Texas Press, 1971.

Waitt, Robert W., Jr. *Confederate Military Hospitals in Richmond.* Richmond, VA: Richmond Civil War Centennial Committee, 1964.

S

SANITARY COMMISSION *See* United States Sanitary Commission.

SANITARY FAIRS

Sanitary fairs were a method of fund-raising used in the North, mainly for the benefit of the U.S. Sanitary Commission but also for the Western Sanitary Commission, the U.S. Christian Commission, and local soldier's aid organizations. The fairs not only raised money, they also restored morale, educated the public about the work of the relief agencies, and recruited volunteers for the work.

The first such fair was held in Chicago from October 27 to November 7, 1863. It was followed by a host of others, both in major cities and small towns: Boston (December 14–21, 1863); Cincinnati, Ohio (December 21, 1863–January 9, 1864); Brooklyn, New York (February 22–March 11, 1864); St. Louis, Missouri (the Mississippi Valley Sanitary Fair, May 17–June 18, 1864); Dubuque, Iowa; Kalamazoo, Michigan; and Chelsea, Massachusetts, among at least thirty altogether.

The most profitable fair, held in New York City (April 4–23, 1864), raised $1,183,506.23, closely followed by the Great Central Sanitary Fair in Philadelphia (June 7–28, 1864), which earned $1,035,398.96. Most totals were more modest. Taylorsville, California, and Bridgeport, Connecticut, did their part by raising $3,744.12 and $200, respectively.

The fairs raised money in a variety of ways. All charged admission. Philadelphia's fair cost fifty cents for basic admission (double on the day President Abraham Lincoln attended) with additional separate charges to visit the horticultural building and the art gallery. Many people donated items for sale, ranging from food, agricultural, and household products to President Lincoln's autograph, which he provided for several fairs. He sent his original draft of the Emancipation Proclamation to the Chicago fair, where it sold to T.B. Bryan for $3,000. This earned Lincoln the prize—a gold watch—for donating the item that raised the most money. The fairs featured numerous exhibits from the historical to miscellaneous curiosities (there were ninety departments at Philadelphia), as well as parades, concerts, dances, and other entertainment. Some fairs held raffles, which became the subject of protests by antigambling forces. Several fairs raised considerable sums when people voted for their favorite general at one dollar per vote. (The results varied based on the location of the fair and the stage of the war). Lincoln attended and spoke briefly at the fairs in Washington, DC (March 18, 1864), Baltimore, Maryland (April 18, 1864), and Philadelphia (June 16, 1864).

Together the fairs raised about $4,392,980.92 of which the central office of the U.S. Sanitary Commission received $2,736,868.84. Interestingly, the leaders of the U.S. Sanitary Commission thought that the sanitary fairs distracted the people involved from the true work of the commission. However, the commissioners tolerated the fairs because they did raise so much money.

See also: Lincoln, Abraham; Livermore, Mary Ashton Rice; United States Christian Commission; United States Sanitary Commission; Western Sanitary Commission.

Bibliography

Basler, Roy P., ed. *The Collected Works of Abraham Lincoln*, vol. 7. New Brunswick, NJ: Rutgers University Press, 1953.

Bender, Robert Patrick. "'This Noble and Philanthropic Enterprise': The Mississippi Valley Sanitary Fair of 1864 and the Practice of Civil War Philanthropy." *Missouri Historical Review* 95 (January 2001): 117–139.

Thompson, William T. "Sanitary Fairs of the Civil War." *Civil War History* 4 (March 1958): 51–67.

SANITATION

Sanitation during the Civil War was very inconsistent. There were few uniform standards about what constituted sanitation in either the North or the South, and what military regulations there were often were not enforced. Many soldiers had less than a rudimentary idea of sanitation. Coming from a rural background where they relieved themselves outside wherever nature called, these men continued their habits in camp rather than using the latrines. In addition to repulsive sights and smells, these sanitation problems contributed to the spread of a variety of contamination-related diseases, such as diarrhea and typhoid fever. When these soldiers entered a hospital with an indoor water closet, they did not know how to use it, plugging it up with sticks, paper, and other debris, rather than reserving it for bodily waste.

The conditions of life in camp and on the march contributed to poor habits of cleanliness in other respects. Many soldiers rarely bathed, washed their clothes, or were in any way clean, often through no fault of their own. Some commanding officers were better about enforcing discipline than others. But even those who insisted that their men keep a tidy camp and use the latrines might defeat their own sanitation attempts by ordering the latrines dug too close to the regimental hospital or in a location that polluted the water supply and spread disease.

Among medical personnel, concepts of sanitation also varied widely from the truly abysmal to the fairly effective. Because germs had not yet been discovered, doctors had inaccurate ideas about what caused the spread of disease. Some, physicians however, suspected that some sort of invisible "animaliculae" were involved, because patients recovered better and contracted fewer infections when doctors washed their hands. Frequency of hand washing was strictly a personal decision for medical personnel.

Standards of hospital cleanliness varied greatly. In the same town one hospital might routinely wash incoming patients' clothes and another might not. In gross breaches of sanitation, some nurses refused to take bedpans to the latrine, instead emptying them wherever they chose. Nurses and doctors used the same sponge and water to clean all the wounds in a ward, thereby spreading infection. Attendants did not wash the dishes before serving food on them to a second group of patients. Stories are common, as well, about the bloody appearance of amputating surgeons who merely wiped their knives on their dirty aprons between operations.

However, some medical officers had high standards for at least the appearance of cleanliness, setting regular times for cleaning wards, whitewashing hospital walls, using what they considered to be disinfectants, and emphasizing ventilation, or airing out the wards as much as possible.

Women tended to have better concepts of sanitation than men. Hospitals with matrons and female nurses (whether nuns or not) tended to have cleaner wards and patients who recovered more quickly. In the North, the U.S. Sanitary Commission urged regulations and other measures to protect the health of the men, in and out of the hospitals, with some success.

See also: Antiseptics and Disinfectants; Diarrhea and Dysentery; Infections, of Wounds; Latrines; Matrons; Negligence, by Medical Staff; Nuns; Nurses; Typhoid Fever; United States Sanitary Commission; Ventilation; Women, as Hospital Workers.

Bibliography

Bollet, Alfred Jay. *Civil War Medicine: Challenges and Triumphs.* Tucson, AZ: Galen, 2002.
Schroeder-Lein, Glenna R. *Confederate Hospitals on the Move: Samuel H. Stout and the Army of Tennessee.* Columbia: University of South Carolina Press, 1994.

SCURVY

Scurvy, a disease caused by a deficiency of vitamin C, affected many soldiers, North and South, during the Civil War. Scurvy's earliest symptoms included sluggishness, depression, and muscular weakness (possibly what many doctors diagnosed as "debility" or *debilitas*). The patient then developed a sallow complexion, gum problems, and loose teeth. Although doctors at the time of the Civil War might have suspected a "scorbutic taint" to a soldier's disease, they could not conclusively diagnose scurvy until the next stage, when skin hemorrhages began to appear.

Because scurvy patients also had internal bleeding of the joints, they often suffered pains that were sometimes attributed to rheumatism. Many scurvy patients also had chronic diarrhea. If such a patient did not receive food with vitamin C, he suffered further weakness, bleeding, damage to internal organs, and, finally, death.

Scurvy had long been recognized among sailors and had also been identified in land armies by at least the time of the Crusades. The British surgeon James Lind published a work in 1753 identifying citrus fruits as important antiscorbutics (effective against and preventive of scurvy). Lind's work resulted in regular issues of lime or lemon juice to British sailors and their improved health.

In addition to citrus fruits, onions, raw potatoes, and fresh green vegetables also contain vitamin C. Such grains as wheat, barley, oats, and rye, which formed the armies' bread staple, do not. Many of the antiscorbutics were difficult to transport before they spoiled, with the result that the frontier army before and after the Civil War suffered from scurvy as much as or more than the Civil War armies did.

Frederick Law Olmsted, executive secretary of the U.S. Sanitary Commission, recognized as early as July 1861 that Union troops were at great risk for developing scurvy because of the diet issued to the soldiers—meat and bread, but no fresh vegetables. Olmsted's concerns were soon realized. The earliest and largest scurvy epidemic took place in George B. McClellan's army in the spring and summer of 1862 during the Peninsula Campaign. When Jonathan Letterman replaced Charles S. Tripler as medical director of that army on June 19, he ordered potatoes, onions, cabbage, tomatoes, squash, and beets sent to the troops, and the scurvy cleared up immediately.

Major outbreaks of scurvy occurred among Union troops during the sieges of Vicksburg and Petersburg and the Atlanta Campaign. Crew members on some of the ships in the Union blockading squadron also suffered scurvy outbreaks and had to return to port for vegetables. The Confederate forces also had severe problems with scurvy—in Robert E. Lee's Army of Northern Virginia, for example. However, extensive Confederate statistics are lacking. Prisoners of war on both sides suffered severely from scurvy.

One attempt made by the Union army to solve the scurvy problem was to issue "desiccated vegetables" to the troops. These dried, pressed blocks of vegetables supposedly included carrots, onions, beets, turnips, and string beans. They required several hours of soaking and cooking to prepare properly, time which the soldiers frequently did not have. The soldiers hated what they called "desecrated" vegetables. Since no one at the time knew about vitamins, they did not know what it was that provided the benefit in their food. No one realized that vitamin C is sensitive to heat and that, therefore, these overcooked vegetables contained little or no antiscorbutic benefit.

Even doctors who ordered antiscorbutics often encountered opposition to their orders or found them ignored by commanding officers and quartermasters who did not comprehend that fresh vegetables would keep an army in better health and fighting condition. These officers used what transportation was available for ammunition rather than food. Confederate surgeon Samuel H. Stout, when in charge of the Gordon Hospital in Nashville, Tennessee, early in the war, prescribed raw onions for the men in his hospital. The smell angered the members of the ladies' association in charge of the hospital, until Stout explained the importance of the onions as an antiscorbutic.

Other women did understand the importance of fresh vegetables and fruits and sent them to the soldiers through local aid associations in the South or the U.S. Sanitary Commission in the North. Foraging for food, including fresh vegetables, wild greens, and fruits, also tended to improve an army's health.

Although only 771 Union deaths were officially attributed to scurvy and only 46,000 cases merited a diagnosis of scurvy, many more soldiers on both sides suffered from the disease at some time or other. Scurvy certainly contributed to many more illnesses and deaths than were officially recognized.

See also: Debilitas; Diarrhea and Dysentery; Diet, of Hospital Patients; Diet, of Troops; Letterman, Jonathan; Malnutrition; Mortality, of Soldiers; Olmsted, Frederick Law; Quartermasters; Rheumatism; Stout, Samuel Hollingsworth; Subsistence Department; Tripler, Charles Stuart; United States Christian Commission; United States Sanitary Commission; Western Sanitary Commission; Women's Hospital Auxiliaries and Relief Societies.

Bibliography

Bollet, Alfred Jay. *Civil War Medicine: Challenges and Triumphs.* Tucson, AZ: Galen, 2002.

Schroeder-Lein, Glenna R. *Confederate Hospitals on the Move: Samuel H. Stout and the Army of Tennessee.* Columbia: University of South Carolina Press, 1994.

SEXUALLY TRANSMITTED DISEASES *See* Venereal Disease.

SHILOH, BATTLE OF (1862)

The Battle of Shiloh (also known as Pittsburg Landing), which took place on April 6 and 7, 1862, produced more than 23,000 casualties, the largest number in any battle in American history to that point. The battle is known by the name of a small church (Shiloh), established about 1846 when Methodists in the area split over issues related to slavery. Pittsburg Landing, Tennessee, was the local port on the Tennessee River, and Savannah, Tennessee, was the nearest town.

In mid-March 1862 about 50,000 Union troops under General Ulysses S. Grant had moved into the area on their way to attack Corinth, Mississippi, an important railroad junction. Grant's troops (the Army of the Tennessee) were waiting for the arrival of the Army of the Ohio under General Don Carlos Buell. While camped, many of the soldiers contracted terrible diarrhea from drinking the Tennessee River water, so they were already physically weakened before the battle.

Meanwhile, Confederate general Albert Sidney Johnston decided not to sit and wait in Corinth but to attack Grant's forces before Buell's troops arrived. Despite delays and confusion, the Confederates managed to surprise their enemies, who were unaware of the number of Confederates close by until just before the Southerners attacked around dawn on April 6. Over the course of the day, Johnston's troops managed to push the Union soldiers back several miles to the area of their defenses around Pittsburg Landing, which Union artillery helped to hold. Johnston himself was hit in the leg by a bullet and bled to death around 2:30 p.m. He was succeeded in command by General P.G.T. Beauregard. As night fell, Beauregard halted the attacks.

Beginning in the late afternoon of April 6, Buell's forces began to arrive, providing Grant with fresh soldiers when the battle resumed on April 7. After much hard fighting, the Union troops retook the area they had lost on the first day. The Confederates retreated to Corinth, leaving many dead and wounded behind. Ever since the battle, soldiers and historians have debated such questions as where the hottest fighting was, whether the South would have won if General Johnston had not died, and whether Beauregard kept the South from winning by stopping the attacks on April 6.

On the first day, the Confederates overran nearly all the Union camps and plundered them. While these movements replenished Confederate stocks of medical supplies, they deprived the Union forces of most of the medicines, surgical instruments, stretchers, blankets, and wagons needed to treat and transport their own wounded. Also, there were not enough Union medical officers, a situation made even worse when a number of them were captured at their field stations.

The only structure usable for a hospital was a fifteen- by thirty-foot log building. Few tents were available to augment it. Since most of the stretchers and wagons had been captured, the Northerners had no way to transport the wounded to the hospital. The friends of the wounded could not take them because they were still busy fighting. Those who made it to the hospital on the first day generally walked there by themselves. The most seriously wounded remained on the field, where they were soaked by heavy rainfall on both the nights of April 6 and 7.

Those who got to the hospital enjoyed only marginally better conditions because the hospital provided so little shelter. With little hay to lie on, most patients ended up on the wet, muddy ground. The medical staff killed a couple of bulls and made some soup, but had no other cooking and serving utensils. On Sunday, April 6, many of the retreating troops came right through the hospital. The next morning, Confederate artillery fire landed among the wounded, but there was no place else to move them. As the Federals pushed the Confederates back on Monday, many of the wounded from the previous day, including a number of Confederates, began to come into the lines and the hospital.

Assistant surgeon B.J.D. Irwin was able to seize tents and cooking utensils from one of the few camps that had not been looted. He set up a tent hospital for 300, considered the first completely equipped tent field hospital ever established.

General Grant ordered all available tents and surgeons to the main hospital. In addition, troop transports began to carry the wounded seven miles down the river to Savannah, Tennessee, which was soon overcrowded as well.

Beginning on Tuesday, April 8, the day after the battle, major efforts began to ship the wounded away from the battlefield. The effort involved government ships and some chartered by the U.S. Sanitary Commission and the Western Sanitary Commission, which also sent supplies. Other local aid societies created some problems by trying to restrict their assistance to wounded soldiers from their own state or region. The transports took patients to hospitals in Mound City, Illinois; Louisville, Kentucky; Cincinnati, Ohio; Evansville and New Albany, Indiana; and St. Louis, Missouri. Surgeons performed amputations and other operations on board as the boats sailed. By the end of the week after the battle, all the wounded had been removed from the field.

Although the Confederates had to leave more than 1,000 of their wounded behind, they took those whom they could transport along on the retreat to Corinth, where they turned every building that they could into a hospital. The Tishomingo Hotel, for example, had patients on every kind of bed or cot, plus on the floor and in the yard.

Out of more than 62,000 Union soldiers engaged in the Battle of Shiloh, Grant and Buell lost 1,754 killed, 8,408 wounded, and 2,885 missing, for a total of 13,047. The Confederate figures were 1,723 killed, 8,012 wounded, and 959 missing, totaling 10,694 out of 40,000 troops. The casualties of Shiloh, greater than any yet seen in the war, shocked both North and South. Later in the spring, General Henry W. Halleck led the combined Union forces against Corinth. The Confederates evacuated the city on May 29 without a fight, leaving an opening for further Union movements in the Mississippi River Valley.

See also: Diarrhea and Dysentery; Hospital Buildings; Hospital Ships; Hospitals, Field; Johnston, Albert Sidney; Stretchers; United States Sanitary Commission; Western Sanitary Commission.

Bibliography

Barnes, Joseph K., ed. *The Medical and Surgical History of the War of the Rebellion (1861–65)*. Washington, DC: Government Printing Office, 1870–1888; reprint, Wilmington, NC: Broadfoot, 1990.

Daniel, Larry J. *Shiloh: The Battle That Changed the Civil War*. New York: Simon and Schuster, 1997.

Fahey, John H. "The Fighting Doctor: Bernard John Dowling Irwin in the Civil War." *North and South* 9 (March 2006): 36–50.

Smith, Timothy B. *The Untold Story of Shiloh: The Battle and the Battlefield*. Knoxville: University of Tennessee Press, 2006.

SICK CALL *See* Surgeon's Call.

SICKLES, DANIEL EDGAR (1819–1914)

Congressman, diplomat, and Union general during the Civil War, Daniel Edgar Sickles tended to provoke strong opinions both during and after his lifetime. His biographers used larger-than-life descriptors, such as "incredible" or "scoundrel," to reflect his often controversial actions.

The only child of George Garret and Susan Marsh Sickles, Daniel was a native of New York City. Although born in 1819, Sickles in his later years said he was born in 1825 and people believed him because he looked much younger than his age. Bright and willful as a youth, he quit school and became a typesetter. He was tutored for several years in the home of his mentor, the Italian scholar Lorenzo Da Ponte, but gave up continuing his higher education at New York University when Da Ponte died. Sickles read law with Benjamin F. Butler and was admitted to the New York bar in 1843. He also became a leading Democratic politician, heavily involved with the political machine Tammany Hall, and was elected to the New York state legislature in 1847.

Sickles was an elegant dresser, a frequent theatergoer, a connoisseur of food, a crony of politicians and influential men, and an inveterate womanizer. Once he introduced a prostitute, under an assumed name, to Queen Victoria. Because he spent money extravagantly and always needed more, Sickles was frequently accused of questionable financial dealings, but was never convicted.

On September 27, 1852, Sickles, then almost thirty-three, married Teresa Bagioli (1836–1867), a charming sixteen-year-old whom Sickles had known since she was very young. Laura (1853–1891) was their only child. Busy with his post as corporation lawyer for New York City, his political machinations, his numerous sexual escapades, his position as secretary of legation for American minister James Buchanan in London (1853–1855), and a term in the state senate (1856–1857), Sickles usually neglected his wife and daughter.

He did take them to Washington, DC, for the first part of his tenure in the U.S. House of Representatives (1857–1861). Here Teresa had an affair with District Attorney Philip Barton Key, a widower whose father, Francis Scott Key, was the author of "The Star Spangled Banner." Defending his "honor," Sickles shot and killed Key in February 1859. His eight-man legal defense team, which included future Secretary of War Edwin M. Stanton, managed to get Sickles acquitted using, for the first time, the temporary insanity defense. Sickles then scandalized people further by taking back his repentant wife, although he paid her no more attention than he had previously.

Soon after the Civil War broke out in 1861, Sickles recruited a brigade and became a brigadier general, although his rank was not confirmed by the Senate until May 1862. He was promoted to major general in November of that year. Sickles led troops in the Peninsula Campaign, at Antietam (Sharpsburg), Fredericksburg, and Chancellorsville. Closely associated with his commanding officer General Joseph Hooker, Sickles was displeased when General George Gordon Meade replaced

Hooker as commander of the Army of the Potomac. His distrust of Meade led to virtual disobedience of orders on July 2, 1863, the second day at Gettysburg, when Sickles, believing his troops could make a stronger stand in the Peach Orchard, moved them out of alignment. This costly movement devastated his troops and led to much future controversy.

Near the end of the day Sickles, then on horseback, was struck in the right leg by a cannon ball and severely injured. Unlike his Confederate counterpart Albert Sidney Johnston, Sickles knew what to do: he ordered one of his subordinates to make a tourniquet out of a saddle strap. In order to give his men confidence, Sickles smoked a cigar while being carried from the field on a stretcher. Taken behind the lines to the Third Corps hospital near the Taneytown Road, Sickles received chloroform and then had his right leg amputated about one-third of the way up the thigh by Dr. Thomas Sim, medical director of the Third Corps. The leg was placed in a small casket and Sickles donated it to the recently founded Army Medical Museum, where, in his later years, he sometimes went to visit his severed limb. (The bones can still be seen in the National Museum of Health and Medicine, successor to the Army Medical Museum, in Washington, DC.)

In the two days following his surgery, Sickles was carried by relays of stretcher-bearers to the nearest train station and taken to Washington, where Dr. Sim personally oversaw his care and President Abraham Lincoln came to visit him. By July 23, Sickles was learning to use crutches. In mid-October 1863, after trips to New York City and to several spas for a period of convalescence, Sickles briefly returned to the field seeking reassignment to his command, but it was clear that he was in no physical condition for such a post and he never had a field command again. He was fitted for a wood and leather artificial leg in December 1863 and although he used it, he came to prefer maneuvering on crutches.

In May 1864 Lincoln sent Sickles on a confidential trip to visit Tennessee military governor Andrew Johnson and to observe several other Union-held areas in the South. Sickles was on a government mission to Colombia, South America, when Lincoln was assassinated. After Sickles's return to the United States, President Andrew Johnson appointed him military governor of South Carolina, where he served from July 1865 to March 1867, and then commander of the Second Military District (North Carolina and South Carolina). His actions in that post, with which the president did not agree, led Johnson to remove him from command in August 1867. Sickles retired from the army with the rank of major general in April 1869.

In May 1869 President Ulysses S. Grant appointed Sickles minister to Spain, where he served until 1873. On November 28, 1871, Sickles, by now a widower, married Caroline de Creagh, by whom he had a daughter Eda (born in 1875) and a son George Stanton (born in 1876). He treated his second family no better than he had his first, and the couple lived apart for the remainder of Sickles's life.

In his later years Sickles served another term in the U.S. House of Representatives (1893–1895) and was very active in efforts to place commemorative monuments at Gettysburg. Sickles died on May 3, 1914, from the effects of a stroke.

See also: Amputation; Anesthesia; Army Medical Museum; Artificial Limbs; Gettysburg, Battle of; Gunshot Wounds, Treatment of; Insanity; Johnston, Albert Sidney.

Bibliography
Keneally, Thomas. *American Scoundrel: The Life of the Notorious Civil War General Dan Sickles.* New York: Nan A. Talese/Doubleday, 2002.
Schroeder-Lein, Glenna R., and Richard Zuczek. *Andrew Johnson: A Biographical Companion.* Santa Barbara, CA: ABC-Clio, 2001.
Swanberg, W.A. *Sickles the Incredible.* New York: Charles Scribners' Sons, 1956.
Welsh, Jack D. *Medical Histories of Union Generals.* Kent, OH: Kent State University Press, 1996.

SINKS *See* Latrines.

SISTERS OF CHARITY *See* Nuns.

SLAVES, HEALTH OF *See* Blacks, Health of.

SMALLPOX

Smallpox was a highly contagious, often fatal disease. Its symptoms included severe headache, high fever, general aches and pains, and possible delirium. However, the characteristic symptom was the "pox," small, red, pus-filled blisters, also called pustules, which could appear on any part of the body. As the patient recovered, the pustules dried and formed a scab, which eventually dropped off, leaving a pitted scar. Some doctors called mild cases of the disease varioloid. Early in the war some of the mild cases may actually have been chicken pox because there was no separate reporting category on the forms for that childhood disease.

Although smallpox could be prevented by vaccination, many people had not been vaccinated at the time of the Civil War, either because they had no opportunity or because they resisted the idea and procedure. Surgeons general on both sides soon gave orders that all soldiers should be vaccinated, but this did not always happen. Some camps were casual or careless about making sure that all the men were vaccinated. Doctors also did not realize that some soldiers, vaccinated years previously, needed re-vaccination. Sufficient vaccine was not always available and some of it was not effective, so that the vaccination did not "take." Especially later in the war, some vaccine was contaminated, leading to "spurious vaccination," including the development of huge sores, sometimes necessitating amputation and even causing death.

Generally, a large portion of the white Union troops was vaccinated, leading to a rate of about five cases of smallpox per 1,000 troops per year. However, black troops had evidently not been vaccinated as slaves, and many seem not to have been vaccinated when they entered the army either. As a result, they averaged about thirty-six cases of smallpox per 1,000 troops per year.

Despite vaccinations, there were several smallpox epidemics, especially in the Confederacy. The first broke out just after the Antietam campaign in the fall of 1862. Although the exact source of the contagion is unknown, several medical officers theorized that troops had been exposed while they were in Maryland, that prisoners returning from Fort Delaware brought the disease, or that it broke out in the prisons and hospitals of Richmond. Indicating the seriousness of the problem, Richmond's smallpox hospital admitted 250 patients during the week of December 12–19, 1862, alone. Of these, 110 died, a fairly average mortality rate for smallpox (29 of the patients had some other illness as well). The Army of Northern Virginia and the citizens of Richmond suffered a second epidemic during the fall of 1863 and the following winter. In both years, authorities tried to derail the epidemic by isolating the sick, quarantining soldiers who had been exposed, and vaccinating soldiers and civilians.

Although Union troops did not experience smallpox epidemics to the same degree, except among the black soldiers, Washington, DC, suffered an epidemic in the fall of 1863 that peaked from December 1863 to January 1864. Many people were seriously alarmed and sought to avoid contagion by staying away from such public places as theaters and streetcars. President Abraham Lincoln contracted varioloid in November 1863 during this epidemic. Republican senator Lemuel J. Bowden of Virginia died in Washington on January 2, 1864, from smallpox.

There was no effective treatment for smallpox. When doctors diagnosed the disease, they isolated the patients in separate tents, wards, or hospitals (often called "pest" hospitals). Many physicians, believing that good ventilation helped smallpox patients recover, always assigned them to tents. Some doctors had a good success rate when they prescribed no medication for their patients. Others used a salve on the pustules and washed the eyes with a vinegar/water solution to prevent eye disease. Some doctors prescribed medicines to keep the bowels open and opiates to calm restlessness. Some also promoted a nourishing diet.

Whatever the treatment, smallpox was a very serious disease, with a fatality rate of from 20 to 40 percent.

See also: Amputation; Blacks, Health of; Hospitals, "Pest" (Smallpox); Lincoln, Abraham; Mortality, of Soldiers; Prisoners of War; Richmond, Virginia; Tents, Hospital; Vaccination, Smallpox; Varioloid; Ventilation; Washington, DC.

Bibliography

Bollet, Alfred Jay. *Civil War Medicine: Challenges and Triumphs.* Tucson, AZ: Galen, 2002.

Cunningham, H.H. *Doctors in Gray: The Confederate Medical Service.* Baton Rouge: Louisiana State University Press, 1958; reprint, Gloucester, MA: Peter Smith, 1970.

SMALLPOX VACCINATIONS *See* Vaccination, Smallpox.

SOUTHERN PRACTITIONER

The *Southern Practitioner* was a monthly medical journal published in Nashville, Tennessee, from 1878 to 1918. Its publisher, Deering J. Roberts (1840–1925), was a surgeon in the Twentieth Tennessee Infantry, serving the wounded at Vicksburg, Chickamauga, and Atlanta, among other battles in the western theater. He was captured at Franklin, Tennessee, and spent several weeks as a prisoner of war. Roberts returned to Nashville and practiced medicine there for more than fifty years.

Roberts's journal contained a variety of typical articles on diseases, treatments, and medical association meetings. However, in 1900, Roberts offered to add sixteen pages to each issue in order to print "Records, Recollections, and Reminiscences" of the Civil War service of members of the Association of Medical Officers of the Army and Navy of the Confederacy. As a result of the addition, many issues (1900–1917) contained papers given at the association's annual meetings, minutes of the annual meetings, a series (1900–1903) by Samuel H. Stout detailing his experiences in the Army of Tennessee hospitals, and obituaries of the association members and other Confederate medical veterans. These articles preserved information about the Confederate medical service that would otherwise have been lost.

See also: Association of Medical Officers of the Army and Navy of the Confederacy; Stout, Samuel Hollingsworth.

Bibliography

Obituary, "Deering J. Roberts." *Confederate Veteran* 33 (June 1925): 228.

Schroeder-Lein, Glenna R. "'While the Participants Are Yet Alive': The Association of Medical Officers of the Army and Navy of the Confederacy." In *Inside the Confederate Nation: Essays in Honor of Emory M. Thomas*, ed. Lesley J. Gordon and John C. Inscoe, 335–348. Baton Rouge: Louisiana State University Press, 2005.

Southern Practitioner 22–39 (1900–1917).

SPLINTS

The purpose of a splint, during the Civil War as in the twenty-first century, was to keep an injured limb immobilized so that it could heal. A splint might be made of any material that would serve that purpose. During the Civil War, doctors employed fence rails, thin wood from bandboxes used to store clothes, heavy wire, plaster, or whatever was available at the time.

Splints were used to set fractures caused by accidents or gunshots, to immobilize limbs from which bone fragments or sections had been removed by excision or resection, and to immobilize stumps so they could heal after an amputation. In most of these cases, the splint had to be open so that the wound could drain, if necessary, and the doctor could tend to it.

One of the most important kinds of splints, commented on in both the North and the South, was "Smith's anterior splint." This splint for the leg was developed before the Civil War by Dr. Nathan Ryno Smith, who held the chair of surgery at the University of Maryland for many years. Initially Smith made the splint of inch-thick wood, but later he made it of sturdy wire wrapped in muslin. When the leg was stretched out, but slightly bent at the ankle, knee, and hip, the splint was attached to the top or front (anterior) of the leg. Smith fastened slings around the leg and the splint at four places and then wrapped the entire leg and splint with a cotton or linen bandage (much as a twenty-first century doctor would use an elastic bandage). The splinted leg was then suspended above the bed with cords attached to hooks on the splint. Suspending a leg in this manner from the roof of an ambulance caused less pain for a wounded soldier who had to travel.

Several other types of splints were developed during the war, including one that made a sort of wooden cradle for the leg. Union surgeon Gurdon Buck devised another kind that provided traction with a weight and pulley. Although doctors designed the most elaborate splints for legs, similar types of splints were developed for arm fractures, including one that suspended the arm on a pad with wires or straps. Plaster casts were occasionally used, but they took too long to apply, they could easily become too tight, and they did not permit treatment of a wound on the limb.

See also: Ambulances; Amputation; Bandages; Gunshot Wounds, Treatment of; Resection.

Bibliography

Barnes, Joseph K., ed. *The Medical and Surgical History of the War of the Rebellion (1861–65).* Washington, DC: Government Printing Office, 1870–1888; reprint, Wilmington, NC: Broadfoot, 1990.

Cunningham, H.H. *Doctors in Gray: The Confederate Medical Service.* Baton Rouge: Louisiana State University Press, 1958; reprint, Gloucester, MA: Peter Smith, 1970.

Hamilton, Frank Hastings. *A Practical Treatise on Fractures and Dislocations.* Philadelphia: Blanchard and Lea, 1860; reprint, San Francisco: Norman, 1991.

STEWARDS, HOSPITAL

The hospital steward, both North and South, was essentially his hospital's chief administrator as well as its pharmacist. He supervised all aspects of the hospital and was usually the person in charge when the surgeon was absent. Stewards served in both field and general hospitals.

In order to become a steward, a man needed to be between eighteen and thirty-five years old, healthy, honest, temperate, of good character, and generally intelligent. To fulfill his responsibilities, he had to have a good knowledge of English, to spell well, to write legibly, to have a basic knowledge of pharmacy and of cooking, to know how to change dressings and bandages, and to have experience with such minor surgery as pulling teeth.

Stewards could be appointed from the enlisted ranks or be civilians who volunteered for that role. Stewards ranked with ordnance sergeants as noncommissioned officers, outranking all other hospital employees except doctors and commissioned officers. In the Union army a steward initially received $22 per month, but after April 1862 he earned $30 per month, as well as one ration per day, a room, and allowances for firewood and clothing. In some cases acting hospital stewards filled a temporary vacancy or worked for a probationary period before receiving a regular appointment.

Among those who became hospital stewards were doctor's assistants, pharmacists, doctors who had trained entirely by apprenticeship, medical students who had not finished their degree, doctors who were waiting to be examined for a commission, and doctors who had failed those exams. In the Confederacy some stewards in Richmond, Virginia, were able to take courses at the Medical College of Virginia, followed by the examination for assistant surgeon.

The steward's considerable responsibilities were outlined in *The Hospital Steward's Manual*, prepared by Joseph J. Woodward, a Union assistant surgeon, under the auspices of Surgeon General William A. Hammond and published in Philadelphia in 1862. As a supervisor, the steward enforced the hospital rules and regulations. He was in charge of all hospital personnel except the doctors and responsible for daily roll calls of patients and employees. He recorded the admission and discharge or death of patients. Twice daily he was supposed to inspect the entire hospital, making sure that it was clean and tidy, checking the ventilation, heating, lighting, latrines, laundries, and storerooms. The steward supervised the preparation and serving of food, using the regulation diet tables when possible. He also was responsible for ordering all food and other supplies and keeping records of what was on hand. He prepared and dispensed medicines for all the patients. He also performed minor operations such as cupping, pulling teeth, and injections.

A steward's tasks generally kept him busy, but many of his responsibilities meant supervising the work of others, such as nurses, cooks, and clerks, rather than doing all the work himself. A single steward was enough for a hospital of up to 150 patients. A larger hospital would have two stewards, with one in charge of administration and the other handling the rest of the duties. In a 500-bed hospital, three stewards would divide the tasks, one doing the administration, the second serving as pharmacist, and the third supervising the cooking. The administrative steward was always the chief steward.

It is not known how many men served as stewards during the war because their number varied from time to time. However, at one point there were more than 700 stewards in the Union service.

Although many stewards met the qualifications, some did not. A number learned their duties on the job and came to perform them well. Others were difficult to work with or neglected their responsibilities. In the spring of 1864 a Confederate steward in the Blind School Hospital in Macon, Georgia, was so busy studying to take the assistant surgeon's exam that he failed to take an accurate inventory for several weeks and thus did not know or report that the acting ward master had apparently stolen some supplies.

The importance of hospital stewards in the South, just as in the North, is shown by the Confederate surgeon general's circular of July 8, 1864. In a period of severe manpower shortage, stewards were the only able-bodied white men aged seventeen to forty-five employed in hospitals who were exempt from field duty.

See also: Cooks; Cupping and Blistering; Diet, of Hospital Patients; Hospital Paperwork; Hospital Support Staff; Hospitals, Field; Hospitals, General; Latrines; Moore, Samuel Preston; Negligence, by Medical Staff; Nurses; Surgeon General; Ventilation; Ward Masters.

Bibliography

Flannery, Michael A. *Civil War Pharmacy: A History of Drugs, Drug Supply and Provision, and Therapeutics for the Union and Confederacy.* New York: Pharmaceutical Products Press, 2004.

———. "The Life of a Hospital Steward: The Civil War Journal of Spencer Bonsall." *Pharmacy in History* 42, no. 3–4 (2000): 87–98.

Roper, John Herbert, ed. *Repairing the "March of Mars": The Civil War Diaries of John Samuel Apperson, Hospital Steward in the Stonewall Brigade, 1861–1865.* Macon, GA: Mercer University Press, 2001.

Woodward, Joseph Janvier. *The Hospital Steward's Manual: For the Instruction of Hospital Stewards, Ward-Masters, and Attendants, in Their Several Duties.* Philadelphia: J.B. Lippincott, 1862; reprint, San Francisco: Norman, 1991.

STOUT, SAMUEL HOLLINGSWORTH (1822–1903)

Samuel Hollingsworth Stout, doctor and medical director of hospitals for the Confederate Army of Tennessee, was born in Nashville, Tennessee, on March 3, 1822, the fourth son and fifth child (of seven) of carriage maker Samuel Van Dyke Stout and his wife, Catherine Tannehill Stout. Young Stout received his education at Moses Stevens's classical and mathematical seminary and the University of Nashville (BA 1839, MA 1842). He taught school at several locations and also studied medicine in Nashville with his older brother Josiah and Josiah's partner R.C.K. Martin. Stout attended two terms at the University of Pennsylvania Medical School in Philadelphia and graduated in 1848. Although he passed the examination for assistant surgeon in the U.S. Navy, he declined the commission. Instead, on April 6, 1848, Stout married Martha Moore Abernathy, with whom he eventually had seven children. Stout practiced medicine in Nashville with Josiah for several years before moving his family to Giles County, Tennessee, where he continued to practice medicine and became a farmer, owning twenty slaves in 1860.

On May 17, 1861, Stout was commissioned surgeon of the Third Tennessee Regiment, composed mainly of his Giles County neighbors. In this position he learned the basics of military medicine and administration. In mid-November 1861, he was assigned to head the Gordon Hospital, a general hospital in Nashville. Here he took control from the local women's hospital society and improved hygiene, discipline, and record keeping, with much effort. After the fall of Forts Henry and Donelson in February 1862, Stout was permitted to evacuate from Nashville and in March was ordered to take charge of the several small hospitals in Chattanooga, Tennessee. The town soon became a major hospital center and Stout's responsibilities expanded to include supervision of all the hospitals serving the soldiers of the Army of Tennessee behind the lines in northern Georgia.

From mid-1863 on, as medical director of hospitals for the Army of Tennessee, Stout had a number of responsibilities. He assigned doctors, stewards, and matrons to hospitals, handling such personnel matters as mediation of quarrels and discipline for various infractions. In conjunction with field medical directors Andrew J. Foard and Edward A. Flewellen, he decided which doctors should be sent to field service and when they should be transferred to other hospitals to meet the army's needs. Stout selected hospital sites, especially crucial during the campaigns of 1864 when his hospitals had to move frequently, and designed structures when existing buildings were inadequate. He oversaw general obedience to orders from Richmond and made sure that his subordinates completed their voluminous paperwork properly. He also prodded quartermasters, commissaries, and medical purveyors who were often slow to get needed supplies to the hospitals. That Stout competently performed these duties for more than fifty hospitals demonstrates that he had administrative skills unusual in the Confederacy. When difficulties arose, they were generally the result of transportation and supply failure rather than inadequate administration.

Stout preserved 1,500 pounds of hospital records with which, in the postwar period, he proposed to write several large volumes about the Confederate medical service. However, due to his need for remunerative employment to support his family, he never wrote more than several dozen articles, including a series for the medical journal *Southern Practitioner* (1900–1903).

After the war, Stout lost his farm in Tennessee and settled in Atlanta, Georgia, where he briefly taught in the Atlanta Medical College, practiced medicine, helped to establish the Atlanta public schools, and sold textbooks. In 1882 he moved his family to Cisco, Texas, where he again practiced medicine and was superintendent of the public schools. In 1893 the family moved to Dallas, where, in 1898, he celebrated his fiftieth anniversary in medical practice. He died in Clarendon, Texas, on September 18, 1903, after an illness of a few weeks.

Stout's two daughters, Margaret and Katherine, eventually sold his Civil War papers to several repositories and private collectors. By the late twentieth century, most of these papers were housed at the University of Texas at Austin; Emory

University in Atlanta; the Southern Historical Collection at the University of North Carolina, Chapel Hill, and Duke University, Durham, North Carolina (both microfilm collections); the Tennessee State Library and Archives in Nashville; and the Museum of the Confederacy in Richmond, Virginia. These papers present a rich source of material about hospitals in the Confederate western theater.

See also: Association of Medical Officers of the Army and Navy of the Confederacy; Chickamauga, Battle of; Flewellen, Edward Archelaus; Foard, Andrew Jackson; Hospital Buildings; Hospital Paperwork; Hospitals, General; Medical Directors, of Hospitals; Medical Purveyors; Quartermasters; *Southern Practitioner*; Subsistence Department.

Bibliography
Schroeder-Lein, Glenna R. *Confederate Hospitals on the Move: Samuel H. Stout and the Army of Tennessee.* Columbia: University of South Carolina Press, 1994.

STRETCHERS

During the Civil War, armies on both sides needed stretchers to remove their wounded from the battlefields. Typically each ambulance was supposed to contain two stretchers. The Union medical department purchased 52,489 stretchers during the course of the war. These were of various types as new styles were developed during the conflict. The Satterlee and Halstead models were the most commonly used.

The Satterlee litter was the official type in use at the beginning of the war. It was 27 inches wide and 5 feet 10 inches long. The center part was made of canvas with wide hems on both sides where the carrying poles were inserted. The frame of the stretcher was made of ash wood. There were also bars with wrought iron bands, as well as legs so the litter could be turned into a cot if necessary. The Satterlee model was very bulky and, at 24½ pounds, fairly heavy.

The Halstead model was a little lighter—23¾ pounds. It was slightly narrower (23½ inches) and longer (5 feet 11 inches) and its canvas was fastened to the outside of the wooden frame with tacks. This version also had folding legs attached, as well as a horsehair pillow covered with canvas. While both the Satterlee and the Halstead stretchers actually carried the patient on a canvas sling, at least one other type had wooden laths for the wounded man to lie on.

Although less is known about Confederate stretchers, at least one type used duck cloth or sacking (similar to canvas). The edges were tacked to grooves in the frame and the grooves were covered with a wooden lath so that the canvas could not rip off under the weight of the patients during repeated use.

The stretchers described were those used by official stretcher-bearers, band members, or the ambulance corps. However, comrades of the wounded and volunteers used whatever was available to remove injured soldiers from the field. These improvisations included coats with poles or muskets run through the sleeves; gates, window shutters, or doors removed from their normal locations; ladders; poles strung with wire; blankets tied to poles; and the two-person, four-arm clasp to make a seat now known as a "fireman's carry."

See also: Ambulance Corps; Ambulances; Musicians, as Medical Assistants.

Bibliography

Bollet, Alfred Jay. *Civil War Medicine: Challenges and Triumphs.* Tucson, AZ: Galen, 2002.

Haller, John S., Jr. *Farmcarts to Fords: A History of the Military Ambulance, 1790–1925.* Carbondale: Southern Illinois University Press, 1992.

Moone, Debby. "Artifact Under Exam–Wooden Stretcher Bed." *Surgeon's Call* 3 (March 1998): 2, 10.

STRONG, GEORGE TEMPLETON (1820–1875)

George Templeton Strong, treasurer of the U.S. Sanitary Commission, was born in New York City on January 26, 1820. An extremely precocious student who read widely and voraciously, Strong entered Columbia College at age fourteen. In 1838 Strong became a clerk in his father's law office and was admitted to the bar in 1841, remaining a member of his father's firm. On May 15, 1848, Strong married Ellen Ruggles, daughter of one of the founders of the Erie Railroad. The Strongs had a happy marriage that produced a daughter, stillborn, and then three sons who survived.

Strong, a member of the New York City elite, was very active in a number of public causes. He was a trustee of Columbia College and one of the organizers of its School of Mines, a vestryman of Trinity (Episcopal) Church, a founder of the Philharmonic Society, a member of the Century Club, and, during the Civil War, a founder of the Union League Club of New York. However, he is best known for his work as treasurer of the Sanitary Commission, a post he assumed at its second meeting, in June 1861, and performed without pay to the end of the war.

Strong began keeping a diary in 1835, when he was fifteen. The volume for the Civil War years is fascinating, informative, and highly opinionated. His Sanitary Commission duties involved nearly daily meetings with other commission officials in New York City. He presided over the raising and expenditure of nearly $5 million for the health and comfort of Union soldiers. He also made numerous trips to Washington, DC, and occasionally to other cities, for meetings of the commission. On these occasions he met President Abraham Lincoln, Secretary of War Edwin M. Stanton, and other government notables, both on business and social occasions. He also traveled to army camps and battlefields to observe conditions. In 1862 his wife spent several weeks as a nurse aboard hospital transport ships.

Following the war, Strong continued his law practice and voluntary activities. After years of failing health, he died on July 21, 1875.

See also: Bellows, Henry Whitney; Diet, of Hospital Patients; Diet, of Troops; Hammond, William Alexander; Hospital Ships; Lincoln, Abraham; Medical Department, Organization of; Olmsted, Frederick Law; Sanitary Fairs; Sanitation; Surgeon General; United States Christian Commission; United States Sanitary Commission; Western Sanitary Commission.

Bibliography

Strong, George Templeton. *Diary of the Civil War, 1860–1865,* ed. Allan Nevins. New York: McMillan, 1962.

SUBSISTENCE DEPARTMENT

The army subsistence department, also called the commissary department, contracted for, received, stored, and distributed the food products consumed by the armies during the Civil War. The Confederate department was based on the Union regular army model.

An act of April 14, 1818, established the U.S. army's department, to be headed by a commissary-general of subsistence with the rank of colonel. George Gibson, the original commissary-general, was still holding the post when the Civil War began. In poor health, Gibson died in September 1861 and was replaced by another career commissary officer, Joseph Pannel Taylor (1796–1864), the brother of President Zachary Taylor. On February 9, 1863, a congressional act promoted the commissary-general to the rank of brigadier general and provided for several assistant commissaries-general. When Joseph Taylor died on June 29, 1864, he was succeeded by Amos Beebe Eaton (1806–1877), who had been serving as assistant commissary-general.

The Confederate commissary-general for most of the war was Lucius Bellinger Northrop (1811–1894), a West Point graduate who was wounded in 1839 during the Seminole War. While on sick leave from the army for many years, he studied and practiced medicine in Charleston, South Carolina. Appointed commissary-general by his good friend Jefferson Davis, Northrop made Confederate supply difficulties even worse by his cantankerous personality. On February 15, 1865, Northrop was removed from his post and replaced the next day by Isaac Munroe St. John (1827–1880), head of the Nitre and Mining Bureau.

The subsistence department had to procure the food for the armies. When properly done, this meant advertising for bids to provide the foodstuffs wanted. Northern agents most often purchased supplies in large cities, such as New York, Boston, Philadelphia, Cincinnati, Louisville, Baltimore, and St. Louis. They thus drew on products from many parts of the country and, ideally, got supplies to the armies quickly, requiring minimum transportation and causing few bottlenecks. From these major cities, the food was shipped to supply depots nearer to the armies and ultimately to the armies themselves for distribution to the soldiers.

Not surprisingly, at the beginning of the war the needs of a suddenly greatly enlarged army led to a certain amount of chaos. It was difficult for the department officials in Washington, DC, to find out the details of the subsistence situation in the armies outside the Washington area. Much confusion also arose because many of the new commissaries had recently enlisted from civilian life and did not understand the masses of paperwork, sometimes requiring five copies. As a result, inappropriate contracts were made and canceled, armies got supplies from the wrong depot or failed to get them at all, and there were many inaccuracies in the forms filled out. Regimental officers also had to learn how to fill out requisitions correctly so they received the proper amount of food for their troops. In the first fiscal year of the war (July 1, 1861–June 30, 1862), the Union army subsistence department spent $48,701,122.98.

Even after the commissaries were better organized and more experienced, military movements could cause a shortage of food for the troops. In addition, although the commissary usually provided fresh beef or salt pork, as well as flour or hardtack, it issued fruits or vegetables less often, leading at times to scurvy and other nutrition-related diseases.

The subsistence department had to rely on the quartermaster's department to ship massive amounts of food. For example, during 1863 the quartermaster department shipped an average of 7,000 packages of subsistence per day from the port of New York. Shortages of transportation could lead to shortages of food. Although the commissary-general claimed in his annual reports that the troops had been supplied with an "abundance of good, wholesome food," soldiers often received food that was spoiled, infested by bugs, or soaked by rain as a result of poor storage. Nevertheless, Union troops generally had more and better food than the Confederates.

The Southern armies faced great obstacles in supplying food to their troops. While Northern farmers were able to continue to produce food, Southern farming was disrupted. The Union blockade of Confederate ports drastically restricted coastal shipping of foodstuffs. In addition, many supplies were destroyed by evacuating or invading armies, both in supply depots and while growing in the field. Confederates had to resort to a tax-in-kind, foraging, and confiscation to supply even a partial ration for their troops at times. The Confederates also had serious transportation problems, since wagons and railroads that wore out or were destroyed could not be replaced. In the latter part of the war, Confederate troops rarely, if ever, received a full ration.

See also: Blockade; Diet, of Troops; Hardtack; Malnutrition; Scurvy; Substitutes, for Supplies.

Bibliography

Moore, Jerrold Northrop. *Confederate Commissary General: Lucius Bellinger Northrop and the Subsistence Bureau of the Southern Army.* Shippensburg, PA: White Mane, 1996.

The War of the Rebellion: A Compilation of the Official Records of the Union and Confederate Armies, series 3, vols. 1–5. Washington, DC: Government Printing Office, 1880–1901.

SUBSTITUTES, FOR SUPPLIES

During the Civil War, Southerners employed a variety of substitutes to replace products that they were no longer able to obtain. Before the war, the economy of the South was based mainly on growing cotton. While Southerners did grow other crops and a few cities, such as Richmond, Virginia, had limited manufacturing, the South as a whole relied on imports from the North and England for many basic supplies that Southerners could have produced themselves.

On April 19, 1861, just after the beginning of the Civil War, President Abraham Lincoln called for a Union blockade of the Confederate states. At first the blockade was not very effective and many Southerners foolishly expected that it would remain ineffective. However, by late 1862, bringing in supplies was much more difficult. With the destruction of other materials as a result of military action or bad weather, many parts of the South saw serious shortages, which only increased as the war continued.

Some shortages, such as a lack of luxury fabrics, were merely an annoyance to the wealthy. But others, such as the shortage of quinine, a medical necessity in the malaria-infested South, were quite serious. Medical researchers attempted to find substitutes for quinine and other medicines, trying various herb teas as well as decoctions (boiled extracts) of herbs or barks in whiskey, among other things. None of these remedies had the effect of quinine, although occasionally some proved useful for other ailments. Medical and surgical instruments were also scarce and at times forks, knitting needles, and penknives substituted for more specialized instruments. Because linen was scarce, old sheets and pillowcases were torn up to make bandages. Corncobs sometimes served as corks for medicine bottles. Patients' diets were often restricted by the limited foodstuffs available in the area.

Coffee became scarce in the Confederacy by the fall of 1861, affecting soldiers, civilians, and medical patients alike. Numerous substitutes were attempted, alone or in combination, including various preparations of rye, okra seed, corn, sweet potatoes, chicory, wheat, acorns, dandelion roots, sugar cane, rice, cottonseed, sorghum molasses, English peas, peanuts, and beans. Many types of plant leaves were also used to make teas for both ordinary drinking and medicinal purposes.

Civilian women devised many substitutes for culinary and other products. Some women could be quite creative in their attempts to keep their families fed and clothed with whatever plants and other materials happened to be available locally.

See also: Blockade; Diet, of Hospital Patients; Lincoln, Abraham; Malaria; Quinine; Richmond, Virginia.

Bibliography

Flannery, Michael A. *Civil War Pharmacy: A History of Drugs, Drug Supply and Provision, and Therapeutics for the Union and Confederacy.* New York: Pharmaceutical Products Press, 2004.

Massey, Mary Elizabeth. *Ersatz in the Confederacy: Shortages and Substitutes on the Southern Homefront*. Columbia: University of South Carolina Press, 1952, 1993.

Porcher, Francis Peyre. *Resources of the Southern Fields and Forests, Medical, Economical and Agricultural: Being Also a Medical Botany of the Confederate States; with Practical Information of the Useful Properties of Trees, Plants, and Shrubs*. Charleston, SC: Evans and Cogswell, 1863; reprint, San Francisco: Norman, 1991.

SUPPLY TABLE

Both the Union and the Confederate medical departments had a standard supply table listing the drugs in appropriate quantities that should be on hand in the field medical wagons and in the general hospitals.

The supply tables were based on a selection of what the military medical department believed to be the most useful substances listed in the massive *United States Pharmacopoeia*. A medical reference revised every ten years, the fourth edition of that pharmaceutical bible was adopted in 1860 and published in 1863. This new edition led to May 1863 revisions in the Union standard supply table, which contained about a seventh of the items listed in the *Pharmacopoeia*.

The revised Union table had two parts. The field section listed what should be carried in an army wagon (usually large amounts of the most commonly used items, such as anesthetics, quinine, and opiates) and what should be contained in a medicine wagon (generally smaller amounts of more types of medicines). The hospital section included 127 medicines, as opposed to 79 for the field. The table listed a three-month supply for each substance, arranged according to the approximate size of the hospital (100, 200, 300, 400, 500, or 1,000 beds).

Although early in the war Surgeon General Clement Finley applied the standards very rigidly, his successor, William A. Hammond, treated the list as a general standard that might be adapted to meet the needs of the hospitals or armies. The revised supply table, on Hammond's orders, omitted the popular medicines calomel and tartar emetic, which he believed were being used in quantities detrimental to patient health. The uproar among the members of the medical profession caused by the omission contributed to Hammond's removal from the office of surgeon general.

The Confederate supply table, based on that of the U.S. Army, was likewise revised in 1863, but for a different reason. The Union blockade of Southern ports increasingly restricted the amount of medicines entering the Confederacy. Surgeon General Samuel P. Moore urged the use of indigenous plant medications as a substitute for scarce foreign drugs. Issued on March 1, 1863, the new "Standard Supply Table of the Indigenous Remedies for Field Service and the Sick in General Hospitals" was based on the information in Francis Peyre Porcher's *Resources of the Southern Fields and Forests*. The new table listed each item by its botanical name, its common name, its medical use, the amount of a dose, the form of the dose (powder, fluid extract, etc.), and the amount expected to be a year's supply for 500 men in the field or 100 patients in the hospital. This table was not meant to replace the previous table but to provide supplements and substitutes when necessary.

On both sides, the supply table represented an ideal that often could not be met, due to the strains placed on the medical system by large numbers of sick and wounded soldiers.

See also: Anesthesia; Blockade; Calomel; Finley, Clement Alexander; Hammond, William Alexander; Hospitals, General; Laboratories, Medical; Materia Medica; Medical Purveyors; Moore, Samuel Preston; Opiate Use and Addiction; Porcher, Francis Peyre; *Resources of the Southern Fields and Forests*; Substitutes, for Supplies; Surgeon General.

Bibliography

Flannery, Michael A. *Civil War Pharmacy: A History of Drugs, Drug Supply and Provision, and Therapeutics for the Union and Confederacy.* New York: Pharmaceutical Products Press, 2004.

SURGEON GENERAL

The surgeon general was the highest-ranking military medical official in both the North and the South during the Civil War. In both sections he was given the rank of colonel, the same level held by the surgeon general in the prewar U.S. Army. In an act passed by Congress in April 1862, the Union surgeon general was promoted to brigadier general. Similar changes were proposed and discussed by the Confederate Congress, but never passed.

The surgeon general had overall supervision of the medical department, both field and hospital. He supervised a hierarchy of medical directors and inspectors who in turn supervised the doctors working in the regiments and hospitals. Over time the surgeon general acquired a staff to handle vast amounts of paperwork.

The surgeon general was in charge of seeing that competent doctors were appointed (through examination) and assigned where they could do the most good. He was to issue orders and enforce regulations, to make plans and promote systems to meet the needs of sick and wounded soldiers. He also gave advice and direction to subordinates dealing with particular local issues. In addition, he oversaw a system of paperwork involving numerous reports about supplies, patient statistics, and local problems.

Initially, the surgeon general appointed on each side had to develop a system to care for massive numbers of sick and wounded. Although the Confederates had to begin their program from scratch, it was based on what the military doctors knew from their previous experience in the U.S. army. The Union surgeon general began the war with only a tiny medical department and was little better off than the Confederates. The first two surgeons general, Thomas Lawson (who had already served for twenty-four years and died on May 15, 1861) and Clement A. Finley (who served until April 14, 1862), were unable to grasp the size of the task. Finley tended to be obstructionist and parsimonious about any measures taken to expand and improve patient care, leading to some serious problems after the early battles.

William A. Hammond, who succeeded Finley, was an innovator who worked with his own department and the U.S. Sanitary Commission to improve just about every aspect of the Union medical system. His persistent conflicts with Secretary of War Edwin M. Stanton, however, led to his removal. He was succeeded by Stanton's personal physician and friend, Joseph K. Barnes, first as acting surgeon general from September 3, 1863, to August 22, 1864, and then as surgeon general until his forced retirement on June 30, 1882. Barnes continued many of the reforms begun by Hammond, but with Stanton's blessing.

The Confederates appointed David C. DeLeon as acting surgeon general on May 6, 1861. He was not really competent and resigned in mid-July, when he was replaced for several weeks by Charles H. Smith, another former U.S. army surgeon. Samuel P. Moore began his duties on July 30, 1861, technically in an acting capacity, but made permanent in November 1861 because of his success in the post. The Confederates benefited from having a single surgeon general for most of the war.

On both sides, supervision by competent and innovative surgeons general led to great improvements in soldiers' medical care.

See also: Barnes, Joseph K.; Bull Run (Manassas), First Battle of; DeLeon, David Camden; Examining Boards, Medical; Finley, Clement Alexander; Hammond, William Alexander; Hospital Paperwork; Inspectors, Medical; Lawson, Thomas; Medical Department, Organization of; Moore, Samuel Preston; United States Sanitary Commission.

Bibliography
Cunningham, H.H. *Doctors in Gray: The Confederate Medical Service.* Baton Rouge: Louisiana State University Press, 1958; reprint, Gloucester, MA: Peter Smith, 1970.
(See also sources listed under each individual surgeon general).

SURGEON IN CHARGE

Surgeon in charge was the term used by both Union and Confederate medical departments for the surgeon or, sometimes, assistant surgeon who was in charge of a hospital. This man was usually, but not always, the highest-ranking medical officer at the hospital. In cases where an officer of lower rank was placed in charge because of superior administrative skills, a higher-ranking surgeon, sensitive to his own honor, might complain or even refuse to serve. Although a surgeon in charge would visit wards and prescribe for patients when he could, his post was likely to be primarily administrative in a large, busy hospital. Union hospitals were considered army posts with the surgeon in charge as commander of all the patients and staff. He reported to the medical director of the military department where the hospital was located and through him to the surgeon general and the military commander. In these hospitals the surgeon in charge conducted a formal, ceremonial weekly inspection, usually on Sunday. These inspections inspired a great deal of cleaning on Saturday, a chore that was sometimes neglected earlier in the week. The surgeon in charge was to supervise all the hospital's business and financial dealings with the quartermaster and commissary departments, to be in charge of all patient treatment, and to attend all surgeries performed by his subordinate medical officers.

In the Confederate Army of Tennessee hospitals, the surgeon in charge assigned the patients to their wards, supervised all medical and support staff at the hospital, and hired the cooks, nurses, and laundresses. He made sure that everyone followed hospital regulations. He also requisitioned needed supplies, such as medicine from the medical purveyor, food from the subsistence or commissary department, and wood, bunks, and transportation from the quartermaster department. Whether he could get what he needed depended upon the availability of supplies and the cooperation of the other departments. The surgeon in charge was also responsible for quantities of paperwork: keeping the hospital register, case book, prescription book, and diet book all up to date; corresponding with numerous officials about hospital business; and filling out daily, weekly, and monthly reports of various kinds.

Confederate surgeons in charge of hospitals reported to a post surgeon, if they were in a town with two or more hospitals, or directly to the medical director of hospitals for their army or region.

See also: Cooks; Hospital Paperwork; Hospital Support Staff; Hospitals, General; Laundresses; Medical Directors, of Hospitals; Nurses; Quartermasters; Subsistence Department; Surgeons; Surgeons, Post.

Bibliography

Adams, George Worthington. *Doctors in Blue: The Medical History of the Union Army in the Civil War.* New York: Schuman, 1952; reprint, Dayton, OH: Morningside, 1985.

Greenleaf, Charles R. *A Manual for the Medical Officers of the United States Army.* Philadelphia: J.B. Lippincott, 1864; reprint, San Francisco: Norman, 1992.

Schroeder-Lein, Glenna R. *Confederate Hospitals on the Move: Samuel H. Stout and the Army of Tennessee.* Columbia: University of South Carolina Press, 1994.

SURGEON OF THE DAY *See* Officer of the Day.

SURGEONS

The term *surgeon* referred generally to all physicians (usually called medical officers) employed by commission or contract by the Union and Confederate military.

More than 12,000 surgeons served the Union forces in some capacity, while the Confederates commissioned 3,236 doctors and employed an unknown number temporarily by contract.

More specifically, surgeons were the upper rank of physicians in both the Union and Confederate forces. In general, surgeons had the best qualifications of education and experience. Some had had special training opportunities beyond medical school, such as working at a hospital in New York City or Philadelphia, or had studied in Europe. Some had been medical school professors. Most surgeons had practiced medicine for at least five years, although in a few exceptional instances a recent medical school graduate was commissioned a surgeon. Except for those who were elected medical officers for their regiment in the early part of the war, surgeons had to pass an examination before appointment. During the course of the war, many assistant surgeons passed the examination for promotion to surgeon.

As was true of the lower ranks of medical officers, surgeons served in both the field and the general hospitals. Regimental surgeons usually worked in the field hospitals, somewhat behind the lines, during a battle. These surgeons provided further treatment for the patients initially cared for by the assistant surgeons on the battlefield. Surgeons provided more complex cleaning and dressing of wounds and performed operations, including amputation. Supervisory posts, such as medical director of an army, were also filled by surgeons.

At general hospitals behind the lines, surgeons were likely to have major administrative responsibilities over other doctors and hospital staff members. Some surgeons supervised entire hospitals. They hired cooks, laundresses, and other civilians; made sure that the hospital was properly supplied; and saw that the patients were properly cared for. In the Confederacy a surgeon was also in charge of all the hospitals at a particular location. Any supervisory role meant that the surgeon was responsible for filling out quantities of paperwork, often on standardized forms. A surgeon would also be involved in treating patients with complicated cases, occasionally performing surgery. Although most surgery had already been done in the field, some patients required additional amputations or other surgical intervention to treat bleeding or serious wound infections.

See also: Amputation; Education, Medical; Examining Boards, Medical; Gunshot Wounds, Treatment of; Hospital Paperwork; Hospital Support Staff; Hospitals, Field; Hospitals, General; Medical Directors, Field; Surgeon in Charge; Surgeons, Acting Assistant (Contract); Surgeons, Assistant; Surgeons, Post.

Bibliography
Bollet, Alfred Jay. *Civil War Medicine: Challenges and Triumphs*. Tucson, AZ: Galen, 2002.
Breeden, James O. "Field Medicine at Antietam." *Caduceus* 10 (Spring 1994): 9–22.
Schroeder-Lein, Glenna R. *Confederate Hospitals on the Move: Samuel H. Stout and the Army of Tennessee*. Columbia: University of South Carolina Press, 1994.

SURGEONS, ACTING ASSISTANT (CONTRACT)

Acting assistant surgeon was the term used by both Union and Confederate medical departments to refer to doctors employed on a temporary basis under contract who did not have a military commission. It was often necessary to employ contract surgeons after a battle when the influx of wounded overwhelmed the commissioned medical staff. Acting assistant surgeons might also fill in for commissioned medical officers who were on sick leave or when posts were understaffed.

Several types of persons served as contract surgeons. Some local doctors were willing to help for short periods after a battle, but would not enlist because they had a thriving medical practice and were needed at home. Others were too elderly or otherwise infirm for field service. Yet other acting assistant surgeons had passed the examination for a commission but had not yet been assigned to a regiment or hospital. Some served while waiting for the opportunity to take the examination, and a number, unable to pass the examination, could still perform some medical tasks.

Early in the war, contract surgeons were heavily criticized. After the Battle of Antietam, Northern newspapers complained that many of the doctors who had come to the battlefield were opportunists who performed unnecessary amputations because they wanted the surgical experience, rather than to help the patient. Other contract doctors were alleged to be incompetents, prima donnas who refused to do unpleasant tasks when they were assigned, or members of the medical "sects," such as homeopaths, rather than "regular," properly trained physicians. Some commissioned surgeons looked down on contract surgeons as a class.

Although these criticisms were justified in some cases, most short-term medical workers were competent and did good work. They did not merit the negative stereotype. For example, William Morton (a dentist rather than a surgeon), one of the inventors of anesthesia, volunteered with the Union forces after the Battle of Fredericksburg and administered anesthesia to hundreds of soldiers who were about to undergo surgery. In the Confederacy, several of the doctors who eventually had major responsibilities in the Confederate Army of Tennessee general hospitals began their careers as contract surgeons.

Later in the war, most Union acting assistant surgeons were assigned to hospitals where they changed dressings, prescribed medicine, and helped with administrative matters rather than performed surgery. In the Confederacy, contract surgeons were assigned where they were needed. Altogether, 5,532 contract surgeons served the Union army. The total number of Confederate acting assistant surgeons is not known.

See also: Alternative Medicines; Amputation; Anesthesia; Antietam, Battle of; Hospitals, General; Negligence, by Medical Staff.

Bibliography

Adams, George Worthington. *Doctors in Blue: The Medical History of the Union Army in the Civil War*. New York: Schuman, 1952; reprint, Dayton, OH: Morningside, 1985.

Bollet, Alfred Jay. *Civil War Medicine: Challenges and Triumphs*. Tucson, AZ: Galen, 2002.

Schroeder-Lein, Glenna R. *Confederate Hospitals on the Move: Samuel H. Stout and the Army of Tennessee*. Columbia: University of South Carolina Press, 1994.

SURGEONS, ASSISTANT

Assistant Surgeon was the title given to the entry-level rank of commissioned physicians in the armies of both the North and the South. Men who received this rank normally had a medical degree and had passed an examination, except during the early days of the war when the examination system had not yet been instituted for the volunteer regiments. Usually assistant surgeons were younger and had less medical experience than surgeons; some were recent medical school graduates. Physicians with considerable experience often became surgeons without holding the lower rank. But many assistant surgeons eventually were able to take and pass the examination for promotion to surgeon.

Assistant surgeons served in both the field and the hospitals. Most regiments had a surgeon and an assistant surgeon, the latter in charge of most of the ordinary medical care of the soldiers. The assistant surgeon went into battle with his troops and set up a first aid or triage station just behind the lines. Here he did the initial treatment, such as bandaging wounds, stopping bleeding, splinting broken bones, and administering opiates or whiskey as painkillers, so the patient could be moved to a field hospital or a general hospital for more extensive treatment. Assistant surgeons occupied a dangerous place and many were killed in the line of duty, including several at the Battle of Antietam.

Assistant surgeons in hospitals were usually in charge of one or two wards, with an optimum of seventy patients, although the actual number was often much higher following a battle. They were responsible for patient treatment in their wards, visiting and prescribing for the sick and wounded. Whether in the field or the hospital, assistant surgeons generally did not have supervisory responsibilities, but in certain situations when there were no surgeons, senior assistant surgeons were in charge of entire hospitals for a time.

See also: Alcohol, Medicinal Uses of; Antietam, Battle of; Examining Boards, Medical; Gunshot Wounds, Treatment of; Hospitals, Field; Hospitals, General; Morphine; Opiate Use and Addiction; Surgeons.

Bibliography

Breeden, James O. "Field Medicine at Antietam." *Caduceus* 10 (Spring 1994): 9–22.

Schroeder-Lein, Glenna R. *Confederate Hospitals on the Move: Samuel H. Stout and the Army of Tennessee*. Columbia: University of South Carolina Press, 1994.

SURGEONS, BRIGADE

Brigade surgeons were an upper rank in the Union medical corps, created by an act of Congress on July 22, 1861. The prospective candidate had to apply for and take an examination before a board of medical officers. Once the brigade surgeon passed his test, he was usually placed in a responsible administrative position, such as being in charge of the general hospitals in a large city or serving as the medical director of an army. In these positions, the brigade surgeon had to supervise the performance of his subordinates as they coped with army regulations and paperwork. At times the brigade surgeon provided training in various military medical skills as well.

In the Army of the Potomac, brigade surgeons made sanitary inspections, forwarded statistical reports on the patients, made sure their subordinate doctors had proper medical supplies, trained the musicians and other stretcher-bearers who removed the wounded from the field, and organized field hospitals during combat.

By an act of Congress of July 2, 1862, the rank of brigade surgeon was abolished. Brigade surgeons were to be known thereafter as surgeons of volunteers and were to be more closely attached to the regular army medical staff under the supervision of the surgeon general. Many doctors at the time considered the change to be a demotion.

See also: Brinton, John Hill; Examining Boards, Medical; Hospital Paperwork; Hospitals, General; Medical Directors, Field; Musicians, as Medical Assistants.

Bibliography
Adams, George Worthington. *Doctors in Blue: The Medical History of the Union Army in the Civil War.* New York: Schuman, 1952; reprint, Dayton, OH: Morningside, 1985.
Brinton, John H. *Personal Memoirs of John H. Brinton, Civil War Surgeon, 1861–1865.* New York: Neale, 1914; reprint, Carbondale: Southern Illinois University Press, 1996.

SURGEONS, MORTALITY OF *See* Mortality, of Surgeons.

SURGEONS, POST

Post surgeons were administrative officials, primarily in the Confederacy. When a city or town had several hospitals, one of the best surgeons was assigned to oversee all of them. The official title for this administrator was eventually changed to "surgeon in charge of hospitals," a label that could be confusing because there were surgeons in charge of a single hospital.

The post surgeon supervised all the hospitals and medical officers in his town. He received and transmitted orders from his superiors to the hospitals. Doctors sent hospital reports and other messages to the post surgeon to be relayed to the medical director of hospitals and ultimately to the surgeon general. The post surgeon also negotiated with local citizens for the use of buildings for hospital purposes and tried to solve whatever local problems arose that did not require intervention by a higher medical or military authority. The post surgeon was usually not in charge of any individual hospital himself. Dr. Joseph P. Logan was an important post surgeon for the Army of Tennessee hospitals in Atlanta.

In some cases, Union army hospitals in a particular city might also be supervised by one medical officer who reported to the general commanding the area. But in most instances the surgeons in charge of the individual hospitals reported to the commanders directly and were subject only to reports by U.S. Sanitary Commission and army medical inspectors.

See also: Hospital Paperwork; Inspectors, Medical; Medical Directors, of Hospitals; Surgeon in Charge; United States Sanitary Commission.

Bibliography

Adams, George Worthington. *Doctors in Blue: The Medical History of the Union Army in the Civil War.* New York: Schuman, 1952; reprint, Dayton, OH: Morningside, 1985.

Schroeder-Lein, Glenna R. *Confederate Hospitals on the Move: Samuel H. Stout and the Army of Tennessee.* Columbia: University of South Carolina Press, 1994.

SURGEON'S CALL

Surgeon's call, also known as "sick call," took place early each morning in both the Union and Confederate armies whether the troops were in camp, on the march, or even in prison. Shortly after reveille, the bugler blew the call and an orderly sergeant marched the ailing soldiers from his company to the surgeon's quarters. The assistant surgeon of the regiment generally examined them, while the surgeon might visit those confined to their beds, as well as sick officers. When the assistant surgeon prescribed for a patient, the hospital steward wrote down the prescription and dispensed it if possible.

Surgeon's call was a very important procedure because the assistant surgeon had the power to determine which soldiers would do full duty, do light duty, be excused from duty to remain in their quarters, or be sent to the hospital that day. Most assistant surgeons wanted to be accurate and fair in their judgments, but without modern diagnostic tests, they could only diagnose based on symptoms. In some cases the disease was obvious—measles, for example. However, much of the time the doctor could only make his best guess. Some, realizing their ignorance, were motivated to study their textbooks and improve their skills.

Diagnosis was further complicated by malingerers whose goal was to get out of doing their duty as often as possible and who became adept at imitating various symptoms. One new assistant surgeon realized at his first sick call that he had to get to know the men in his regiment so he would recognize whose ailments were likely to be real. Sometimes a suspected malingerer was actually sick and did not get the treatment he needed, but more often a malingerer would get treatment he did not need.

Some doctors seemed rather cavalier about sick call. One claimed that on the march he ignored any other aspects of disease besides the state of the patient's bowels. If the soldier had diarrhea, this doctor gave him opium, and if the complaint was constipation, the doctor administered calomel (blue mass). According to another officer's report, one regimental doctor had three prescriptions at sick call: calomel, quinine, and wine or brandy. These he dispensed in order as he went down the line so that three men with the same complaint might get three different medicines, depending upon where they were standing. However, even careful, conscientious doctors were sometimes limited in their treatments because of the lack of a variety of medicines.

See also: Alcohol, Medicinal Uses of; Calomel; Diarrhea and Dysentery; Malingerers; Measles; Opiate Use and Addiction; Prisoners of War; Quinine; Surgeons; Surgeons, Assistant.

Bibliography

Bollet, Alfred Jay. *Civil War Medicine: Challenges and Triumphs.* Tucson, AZ: Galen, 2002.

Cunningham, H.H. *Doctors in Gray: The Confederate Medical Service.* Baton Rouge: Louisiana State University Press, 1958; reprint, Gloucester, MA: Peter Smith, 1970.

Wood, Thomas Fanning. *Doctor to the Front: The Recollections of Confederate Surgeon Thomas Fanning Wood, 1861–1865,* ed. Donald B. Koonce. Knoxville: University of Tennessee Press, 2000.

TARTAR EMETIC

Tartar emetic was the name given to a popular medication made with powdered antimony, a poisonous metallic substance that is one of the chemical elements found in the periodic table. Used both to reduce fever and to cause vomiting, tartar emetic was administered to patients with a variety of diseases. Given in small doses every two to three hours, it was considered an important treatment for pneumonia. Tartar emetic was combined with sulphate of magnesia to purge patients with dysentery and also used in combination with cinchona bark (the source of quinine) and powdered opium to treat intermittent fevers.

Correctly concluding that calomel (a mercury-based medicine) and tartar emetic had been overused by medical officers to the detriment of their patients, Union surgeon general William A. Hammond removed the preparations from the supply table by his Circular No. 6 of May 4, 1863. Removal of these medicines caused such uproar among regular physicians that it helped provide an excuse for Hammond's superiors to remove him from his post as surgeon general.

See also: Calomel; Diarrhea and Dysentery; Fevers; Hammond, William Alexander; Malaria; Materia Medica; Medical Purveyors; Pneumonia; Quinine; Supply Table.

Bibliography
Flannery, Michael A. *Civil War Pharmacy: A History of Drugs, Drug Supply and Provision, and Therapeutics for the Union and Confederacy.* New York: Pharmaceutical Products Press, 2004.

TENTS, HOSPITAL

The medical departments of both the North and the South used tents for most field hospitals and to expand the capacity of general hospitals behind the lines during the Civil War. The standard hospital tent was a walled tent, 14 feet long by 15 feet wide and 11 feet high in the center. The side walls were 4½ feet tall and could be raised to increase ventilation. A 21½-foot-by-14-foot fly covered the entire tent but could also be pitched separately to shelter patients during periods of crisis when there was no time to set up tents or tents were not available. One of these tents held about eight patients comfortably, although more could be crowded in by using straw on the ground instead of beds. Two tents could be joined together by opening the ends.

If necessary, the tents could be heated by a rather ingenious system. A fire was kindled in a 2½-foot pit dug outside the tent door. Then a trench was dug through the tent to a chimney outside the other end. The trench was covered with metal plates that radiated heat while the chimney drew the smoke outside.

Sibley tents were also used by hospitals at times, but were much less convenient. Shaped like a teepee, the Sibley tent was 18 feet in diameter at the base and 12 feet high in the center. The center pole obstructed movement for medical personnel and the sides could not be raised, making the tents stifling during the summer. They were most likely to be used for isolating small groups of contagious patients.

Ideally each regiment had three hospital tents and sometimes a Sibley tent. Most field hospitals were located in tents, sometimes even when buildings were available. Hospitals behind the lines frequently used tents to expand hospital capacity, especially during the summer campaigning season. Tents could be transported easily and erected quickly where needed. Confederate Army of Tennessee hospitals in Georgia, the Chimborazo Hospital in Richmond, and Union hospitals in Washington, DC, provide examples of facilities of all types that were expanded by tents.

In many cases, convalescents and patients who were not seriously ill were assigned to tents. Conversely, smallpox patients and those with wound infections, such as erysipelas or hospital gangrene, were isolated in tents to prevent the spread of contagious disease. If necessary, the tents could be burned after use.

Many physicians observed that patients generally recuperated more quickly and with fewer complications in tents than in crowded wards. While they attributed this effect to ventilation, it also helped that tents held fewer patients to spread infections.

See also: Chimborazo Hospital; Convalescents; Erysipelas; Gangrene, Hospital; Hospital Buildings; Hospitals, Field; Hospitals, "Pest" (Smallpox); Infections, of Wounds; Ventilation.

Bibliography

Billings, John D. *Hardtack and Coffee: The Unwritten Story of Army Life.* Boston: George M. Smith, 1887; reprint, Lincoln: University of Nebraska Press, 1993.

Formento, Felix, Jr. *Notes and Observations on Army Surgery.* New Orleans: L.E. Marchand, 1863; reprint, San Francisco: Norman, 1990.

TETANUS

During the Civil War tetanus was fairly unusual, but those soldiers on both sides who contracted it were extremely, painfully ill and usually died.

Tetanus is caused by a bacterium, *Clostridium tetani*, often spread by the dung of large animals, especially horse manure. Although the bacterium does not survive in the open air, it thrives in closed places, such as deep wounds. The disease is commonly known as lockjaw because it usually begins with the jaw muscles freezing, preventing the patient from swallowing and making breathing difficult. Other parts of the body also experience painful, rigid muscle spasms. In the most extreme later stages a patient may have *opisthotonos*, a condition in which the back muscles arch so much that only the back of the patient's head and feet are touching the bed. The disease may prove fatal within a few hours or a few days.

During the Civil War about 505 Union soldiers were diagnosed with tetanus, of whom 89 percent died. Confederate records are missing for the later years of the war, but in 1861–1862 sixty-six cases of tetanus were reported with thirty-one deaths (53 percent), a figure that historians suspect underreports the actual number.

Most of the Union cases occurred in a few locations: in a particular field hospital established after the Battle of Antietam (September 1862) in a stable that was two feet deep in manure; after the Battle of Stone's River (Murfreesboro) in December 1862–January 1863; and after the Battle of the Wilderness in the spring of 1864 among the patients who had had to lie on the floor in a Fredericksburg, Virginia, hospital that had been a stable. There were few or no tetanus cases after the battles of Chancellorsville and Gettysburg or during the Atlanta campaign.

Most Civil War doctors were previously unfamiliar with tetanus. Some who saw the first cases thought the condition had been caused by poisoned bullets. Others blamed the disease on exposure to bad weather, improperly cleaned wounds, pressure on the nerves from bone fragments or bandages, or nerve injuries caused when the doctor treated the wounds.

Doctors tried very hard to save the lives of patients with tetanus, but they could do nothing except treat the symptoms, usually with limited success. Some doctors, recognizing tetanus as a wound infection, treated the disease by amputating the wounded extremity, successfully saving the patient's life in ten of the twenty-nine cases. Others kept the patient under chloroform for a time to relax the muscle spasms, relieving the symptoms for a while. Yet other doctors administered large doses of brandy and opium or provided nutrition through a feeding tube or enemas. Confederate doctors who were members of the Association of Army and Navy Surgeons met in Richmond, Virginia, on January 30, 1864, to discuss the difference between true tetanus and "tetanic spasms."

Although those who contracted tetanus were seriously ill, proportionally there were remarkably few cases. At the time, doctors attributed this low incidence to the fact that so many patients were treated in tents. More recent historians theorize that the most likely reason was that most of the battles were fought on fields that had not been manured.

In the twenty-first century tetanus can be prevented by shots of vaccine, which was first administered during World War I.

See also: Alcohol, Medicinal Uses of; Amputation; Anesthesia; Antietam, Battle of; Association of Army and Navy Surgeons of the Confederate States; Mortality, of Soldiers; Opiate Use and Addiction; Tents, Hospital.

Bibliography

Adams, George Worthington. *Doctors in Blue: The Medical History of the Union Army in the Civil War.* New York: Schuman, 1952; reprint, Dayton, OH: Morningside, 1985.

Bollet, Alfred Jay. *Civil War Medicine: Challenges and Triumphs.* Tucson, AZ: Galen, 2002.

Cunningham, H.H. *Doctors in Gray: The Confederate Medical Service.* Baton Rouge: Louisiana State University Press, 1958; reprint, Gloucester, MA: Peter Smith, 1970.

"Debate on Tetanus." *Confederate States Medical and Surgical Journal* 1 (March 1864): 44–46.

TOMPKINS, SALLY LOUISA (1833–1916)

Sally Louisa Tompkins, a Richmond, Virginia, hospital administrator who was commissioned a captain in the Confederate army, was born at the family plantation, Poplar Grove, in Mathews County, Virginia, on November 9, 1833. She was the daughter of Colonel Christopher Tompkins, a planter and state legislator, and Maria Booth Patterson Tompkins. Sally grew up on the plantation, but, after her father's death, moved to Richmond with her mother shortly before the Civil War.

The First Battle of Bull Run (or Manassas), on July 21, 1861, produced a tremendous number of casualties for which the Confederate medical service was ill prepared. When the government issued a call for Richmond civilians to open their homes to the wounded, Tompkins established a hospital. Judge John Robertson, who had moved his family to the country, offered her the use of his house at Third and Main streets for the purpose. As a result, it was known as Robertson Hospital. Tompkins used some of her own money for appropriate renovations, opening the hospital on August 1, 1861.

The Robertson Hospital was always small, with no more than twenty-five patients. Tompkins ran it with the assistance of a doctor, four female slaves, two disabled veterans, and a number of Richmond society women who provided provisions, supplies, and some nursing care. Tompkins was only about five feet tall, but she was very dignified and determined, a good manager with great physical endurance. She stressed cleanliness, good nursing, and spiritual counsel, holding a prayer service each evening.

Because Tompkins established a good record for healing patients and returning them to duty, the Confederate government made an exception in her case when later in the summer of 1861 it closed small hospitals and consolidated them under government control, requiring that a military officer be in command of each hospital. By order of Confederate president Jefferson Davis, Leroy P. Walker, the secretary of war, issued Tompkins a commission as captain of cavalry on September 9, 1861. Tompkins was the only female Confederate officer and, in fact, probably the only American woman to serve as an officer until the establishment of the Army Nurse Corps in 1901. More important, she was able to continue to run her hospital without government interference and to draw some rations and supplies from the commissary and quartermaster. She refused to accept the pay that went with the commission, however, and purchased many supplies with her own funds.

Over the course of the war at least 1,333 soldiers were treated at the Robertson Hospital, of whom only 73 died. The Robertson had the lowest death rate of any hospital in Richmond, even though many of the most serious cases were sent there. Tompkins continued to run the hospital until it closed in June 1865 after the end of the war.

Remaining in Richmond, Tompkins was involved in charity work, activities related to the Episcopal Church, of which she was a member, and organizations such as the United Confederate Veterans and the Association for the Preservation of Virginia Antiquities. She never married and in 1905, when her health and fortune failed, she moved to the Home for Needy Confederate Women in Richmond, where she died on July 25, 1916. She was buried in Christ Church Cemetery, Mathews County, Virginia.

Several years later, members of the United Confederate Veterans and United Daughters of the Confederacy solicited money for a monument in her honor. Raising $931, they erected an eight-foot-tall monument of white Virginia granite over her grave. The monument was dedicated on June 3, 1925.

See also: Blacks, as Hospital Workers; Bull Run (Manassas), First Battle of; Hospitals, Attitudes Toward; Quartermasters; Richmond, Virginia; Subsistence Department; Women, as Hospital Workers; Women's Hospital Auxiliaries and Relief Societies.

Bibliography

"Capt. Sally Tompkins." *Confederate Veteran* 24 (November 1916): 521, 524.
"Monument to Capt. Sally Tompkins." *Confederate Veteran* 33 (July 1925): 248.
Sabine, David B. "Captain Sally Tompkins." *Civil War Times Illustrated* 4 (November 1965): 36–39.

TRIPLER, CHARLES STUART (1806–1866)

Charles Stuart Tripler, who served for nearly a year as medical director of the Union Army of the Potomac, was born in New York City on January 19, 1806. His father was a successful merchant who suffered serious business reverses when Tripler was young, causing the son to be apprenticed to an apothecary (druggist), Stephen Brown. Brown, who was also a physician, supervised Tripler's education in the evening. Tripler then attended the College of Physicians and Surgeons in New York, graduating in 1827.

Tripler served as a resident at New York's Bellevue Hospital, but wanted very much to be a military physician. Moving to West Point, New York, he assisted

Dr. Walter V. Wheaton with his practice at the post and with his private patients. Tripler also studied mathematics and French with the cadets at the military academy. After passing the medical examination, he was appointed an assistant surgeon in the U.S. Army in October 1830.

Tripler was assigned successively to posts in Maine, Louisiana, Florida, New York, and Michigan. In July 1838, he was promoted to the rank of surgeon. While stationed in Detroit, Michigan, Tripler met Eunice Hunt, whom he married on March 2, 1841. The couple eventually had nine children, but some of them died young. Eunice's recollections, recorded and published in 1910 by her son-in-law, Louis A. Arthur, provide an important source of information about Charles Tripler.

In May 1846, during the Mexican War, Tripler became medical director of a division of the regular army (not volunteers). After the capture of Mexico City, he organized and directed a general hospital there until April 1848. Over the next ten years he served in Detroit, California, and Kentucky, where he wrote *Manual of the Medical Officer of the Army of the United States: Part I Recruiting and the Inspection of Recruits* (1858). Although no other volumes in the projected series ever came out, this one became the standard on the topic. In the winter of 1860–1861, Tripler and George Blackman, professor of surgery at the Medical College of Ohio in Cincinnati, delivered a series of lectures on military surgery at that institution. Published in 1861 as the *Handbook for the Military Surgeon*, the lectures became an important source for training future military physicians. The book contained information on organization of field hospitals, getting supplies, sanitation, and treating gunshot wounds in various parts of the anatomy. Tripler and Blackman cited examples from previous wars and medical theorists.

At the beginning of the Civil War, Tripler was appointed medical director of the Army of the Shenandoah. On August 12, 1861, just after the medical disaster at First Bull Run (Manassas), he succeeded surgeon William S. King as medical director of the Army of the Potomac. The problems he faced were tremendous. The Union army contained many brand-new recruits, largely undisciplined; surgeons who did not know how to prepare military paperwork; and officers who ignored sanitation and health-related orders from surgeons because the physicians were lower-ranking officers. Tripler had difficulty getting information about conditions in the general hospitals, which were largely improvised, poorly organized, and barely supplied. He had no subordinate administrators or inspectors, nor any system to train medical workers.

Tripler immediately moved troops out of a particularly unsanitary area, sent someone to inspect an offensive cavalry camp, and made several other changes, primarily based on advice from U.S. Sanitary Commission observers. He also suggested a plan for an ambulance corps, although it was not actually established while he was medical director.

While Tripler was an excellent medical officer by "old Army" standards, he was too tied to army regulations to meet the need for innovation required by wartime crises. Although he worked hard and made significant administrative and other improvements, he was reluctant to try things that were not provided for in the army regulations. Tripler's efforts were also hampered by a lack of cooperation from other army departments, particularly the quartermaster and subsistence departments, which were responsible for providing transportation and supplies. In addition, surgeons and military officers often failed to cooperate as some officers looked down upon surgeons and were afraid that troops sent to hospitals would never return to the front. Tripler himself tended to provoke opposition by being rather arrogant at times.

During the Peninsula Campaign in the spring of 1862, medical services in the Army of the Potomac were sadly deficient. Filthy transport ships for the wounded were the fault of the quartermaster's department, but most people blamed them on Tripler. On July 4, 1862, Tripler was replaced by Jonathan Letterman. Given his choice of another assignment, Tripler selected the post of chief surgeon of the Department of the Lakes, headquartered first in Detroit, then Columbus, and then Cincinnati, Ohio.

Shortly after the war Tripler developed cancer of the neck and face and died on October 11, 1866.

See also: Ambulance Corps; Bull Run (Manassas), First Battle of; Gunshot Wounds, Treatment of; Hospital Ships; Hospitals, General; Inspectors, Medical; Letterman, Jonathan; Medical Department, Organization of; Quartermasters; Sanitation; Subsistence Department; United States Sanitary Commission.

Bibliography

Adams, George Worthington. *Doctors in Blue: The Medical History of the Union Army in the Civil War.* New York: Schuman, 1952; reprint, Dayton, OH: Morningside, 1985.

Tripler, Charles Stuart, and George Curtis Blackman. *Handbook for the Military Surgeon.* Cincinnati: R. Clarke, 1861; reprint, San Francisco: Norman, 1989.

Tripler, Eunice. *Some Notes of Her Personal Recollections.* New York: Grafton, 1910.

TUBERCULOSIS

Tuberculosis is a serious contagious disease that affected many soldiers and civilians in the North and South during the Civil War. The disease is usually focused in the lungs, although it may also affect other body parts, such as the lymph nodes, an affliction known as scrofula. In the nineteenth century tuberculosis, usually called "consumption" or sometimes "phthisis," was quite common and much dreaded. For a time fiction writers romanticized consumption, recounting the lingering death of a hero or heroine. The illness and death of Eva in *Uncle Tom's Cabin* (1852), by Harriet Beecher Stowe, is a good example of this fictional treatment.

Tuberculosis was most often spread from person to person through coughing, sneezing, or spitting. It could also be spread through the milk of infected cows or by dirty cooking utensils. Consumption tended to be associated with crowded, working-class areas of large cities, conditions that certainly could contribute to its spread. However, persons of any class or location could contract tuberculosis if exposed. Doctors at the time did not realize that consumption was contagious, so they did not isolate sufferers.

People in the early stages of tuberculosis might show few or no symptoms. As a consequence, many men who already had tuberculosis were mustered into the army. The later stages of the disease were more obvious—a serious cough, chest pain, spitting up blood, fever, sweats, weight loss, and weakness. A recruit with tuberculosis symptoms would be rejected by any examining doctor who took his job seriously.

Those who enlisted with tuberculosis sometimes discovered their condition improved by the fresh air and exercise of military life. However, many more found their health worsened by the stress of military maneuvers, bad weather, malnutrition, and other diseases (especially measles). When a soldier was diagnosed and hospitalized with consumption, the standard treatment consisted of nourishing food, alcoholic stimulants, and tonics, such as the decoction of black snakeroot and iodine prescribed by Confederate doctor Francis P. Porcher. Opiates were also given for cough suppression and pain relief.

"Incipient phthisis," or symptoms that suggested that a soldier was getting tuberculosis, sometimes led to a furlough in the hope that he might get better. Tuberculosis was second only to gunshot wounds as a cause of discharge from the army for white Union troops; 20,403 men were released because of the disease. Although a number of soldiers died in the hospital from consumption, many more soldiers died after reaching home and their deaths went unreported. There were fewer new cases of tuberculosis in the Union army after 1862, but more of them terminated fatally.

The bacterial cause of tuberculosis was discovered by 1882, and means were devised to reduce its spread. Since World War II, antibiotics have provided effective treatment for tuberculosis, although it still remains a problem in undeveloped nations.

See also: Alcohol, Medicinal Uses of; Diet, of Hospital Patients; Malnutrition; Measles; Opiate Use and Addiction; Porcher, Francis Peyre.

Bibliography
Bollet, Alfred Jay. *Civil War Medicine: Challenges and Triumphs.* Tucson, AZ: Galen, 2002.
Cunningham, H.H. *Doctors in Gray: The Confederate Medical Service.* Baton Rouge: Louisiana State University Press, 1958; reprint, Gloucester, MA: Peter Smith, 1970.
McNeill, William H. *Plagues and Peoples.* 1976; reprint, New York: History Book Club, 1993.

TURNER'S LANE HOSPITAL

Turner's Lane Hospital, located on Turner's Lane in a suburb of Philadelphia, specialized in the treatment of nerve diseases and injuries (many from gunshot wounds) during the Civil War.

Dr. S. Weir Mitchell (1829–1914), a Philadelphia physician and acting assistant (contract) surgeon at the Filbert Street Hospital, initially developed a special interest in patients with nerve problems because they were so difficult to treat. When the number of patients with nerve injury exceeded the size of his ward, he was able to transfer all of them to Moyamensing Hall, part of the Christian Street Hospital (which opened on May 5, 1862, and closed on October 29, 1864). Here Mitchell recruited a medical school friend to join him in caring for the injured patients. George Read Morehouse (1829–1905), a physician in private practice, also worked as a contract surgeon in the Philadelphia hospitals. The third member of the research and treatment team was William Williams Keen (1837–1932), a regimental assistant surgeon with field experience.

Mitchell proposed building a special hospital for nerve cases, an idea approved by his friend, Surgeon General William A. Hammond. In August 1863 Mitchell rented a country estate, with gardens and plenty of trees, which became Turner's Lane Hospital. He supervised the building of enough single-story pavilion wards to hold 275 to 400 patients (accounts differ on this number). All the patients treated there suffered from nerve diseases or injuries except for those in one ward who were studied and treated by Dr. Jacob M. DaCosta for "soldier's heart," a stress-induced heart syndrome.

Turner's Lane was unusual not only because it was a specialty hospital, but also because it had an administrator, Dr. Charles H. Alden, to manage the hospital while Mitchell, Morehouse, and Keen studied and treated the patients. Keen lived on the hospital grounds. Mitchell and Morehouse, both having private practices, lived in Philadelphia proper. They went out to Turner's Lane about 7:00 each morning to handle any problems, then returned to town to see their private patients. About 3:00 in the afternoon they went back to Turner's Lane and spent four to five hours with Keen examining and treating patients and taking extensive notes. They gathered all the information themselves, not using any clerks or assistants. Two or three times a week they worked until midnight or later, most likely after receiving a number of new patients. Afterward Mitchell and Morehouse walked back to town, discussing the most interesting cases.

Patients at Turner's Lane suffered from a wide variety of problems related to nervous diseases or injuries, including paralysis of various body parts; intense burning pains, usually in the hands and feet (called causalgia); contracted limbs; spasms; palsies; and phantom pain (the sensation of the painful presence of an amputated limb). Epilepsy was also considered a nervous disease. At one point there were eighty epileptics at Turner's Lane. Because of the nature of the problems treated, seizures were common.

The medical team tried many types of treatment. They believed in administering morphine for pain, usually by injection, which was uncommon at the time. Depending on the condition being treated, they also employed wet dressings, poultices, blisters, cold compresses, leeches, counterirritants, bandages and splints for support, hydrotherapy, physical therapy, mild electric shock, massages, and certain kinds of gymnastics. All these treatments were supported by a nourishing diet and good hygiene. The doctors kept careful track of each case, specifying the nature of the wound or illness, symptoms, treatments prescribed, and results. The trio published several articles during the war, but their most important work was the book *Gunshot Wounds and Other Injuries of Nerves* (1864), based on their research.

Because some nerve problems did not stem from an obvious injury, they could be faked. Mitchell and his team made a major effort to root out such malingerers by anesthetizing them, reasoning that malingerers would be unable to continue their charade under anesthesia.

Turner's Lane Hospital closed in June 1865, just after the end of the war.

See also: Amputation; Anesthesia; Convalescents; Cupping and Blistering; Gunshot Wounds, Treatment of; Heart Disease; Malingerers; Medication, Administration of; Mitchell, Silas Weir; Morphine; Surgeons, Acting Assistant (Contract).

Bibliography

Freemon, Frank R. "The First Neurological Research Center: Turner's Lane Hospital During the American Civil War." *Journal of the History of the Neurosciences* (April 1993): 135–142.

Middleton, William S. "Turner's Lane Hospital." *Bulletin of the History of Medicine* 40 (January–February 1966): 14–42.

Mitchell, S. Weir. "Some Personal Recollections of the Civil War." *Transactions of the College of Physicians of Philadelphia*, 3rd series, 27 (1905); reprint, *Journal of Civil War Medicine* 1 (May–June 1997): 5–7.

Mitchell, Silas Weir, George Read Morehouse, and William Williams Keen. *Gunshot Wounds and Other Injuries of Nerves*. Philadelphia: J.B. Lippincott, 1864; reprint, San Francisco: Norman, 1989.

TYPHOID FEVER

Typhoid fever is a serious intestinal disease that afflicted many soldiers North and South during the Civil War, resulting in a high fatality rate. Typhoid is caused by the bacterium *Salmonella typhi*, which is spread through excrement. Food and water could easily be contaminated with the bacteria as a result of poor sanitation, improperly located latrines, unwashed hands, or swarms of flies. Some convalescents and a small number of healthy people who never knew that they had had typhoid were carriers and could spread the disease, especially if they were assigned to cooking duty. The disease tended to be most prevalent in military camps, rather than on the march, and was known as a "camp fever." It struck new recruits especially.

Doctors at the time did not know the cause of typhoid but suspected some type of miasm or vapor in the air. Some doctors also blamed exposure to bad weather, fatigue, improperly prepared food, or the temperament of the patient. Some believed that the disease could begin spontaneously without any contagion at all. Only a tiny minority of medical officers suggested contaminated water as a cause.

Classic typhoid began with a fever accompanied by general fatigue and depression. Diarrhea was often a symptom, although some typhoid patients had constipation. As the disease worsened, the victim suffered headache, back and muscle aches, and loss of appetite. The soldier might also have chills, delirium, a distended abdomen, and bronchitis, possibly leading to pneumonia. Some patients developed rose-colored spots on their chest and abdomen. Severe cases developed "Peyer's patches," enlarged spots on the intestines that could perforate, or cause a hole in the intestine, leading to peritonitis, an inflammation of the abdominal cavity usually resulting in death. Peyer's patches were distinctive to typhoid fever, but could be diagnosed only during an autopsy after the patient's death.

In many cases, without the bacterial tests available in the twenty-first century, it was very difficult to tell whether a patient actually had typhoid fever. Sometimes the disease was so mild that no one thought it was typhoid. Some patients seemed to have mixed symptoms of typhoid and something else, leading to a variety of names used to describe the illnesses, such as typhomalarial fever, typhoid pneumonia, low typhoid, common continued fever, and remittent bilious fever. Some of these patients probably had more than one disease at the same time, since infections spread so easily in camp and hospital. Typhoid was also occasionally confused with typhus. They were often classed together, even though European doctors had determined the differences between the two diseases in the 1830s. Surprisingly, since typhus is now known to be spread by lice, there were not many cases of typhus reported during the Civil War.

Typhoid has a lengthy incubation period and a long recovery time. Even a relatively mild case lasted several weeks, leaving the patient exhausted and requiring several more weeks to regain his strength. Severe cases had a high mortality rate. During the entire war, Union forces reported 79,462 cases of typhoid fever with 29,336 deaths, a fatality rate of 37 percent. During the course of the war the number of typhoid cases decreased, probably because the soldiers developed immunity once they had had typhoid. However, the severity and mortality rate increased for those cases that did occur. Although Confederate statistics are less complete, Confederate surgeon Joseph Jones calculated that typhoid accounted for one-quarter of Southern deaths from all causes between January 1, 1862, and August 1, 1863.

There were no effective or standard treatments for typhoid. Soldiers with typhoid might or might not be isolated in separate wards or tents. To combat the fever, doctors might administer quinine, place cold cloths on the patient's head, and sponge or spray his body with cool water. Diarrhea and pain were treated with opiates. Small doses of turpentine were also given internally. Some doctors prescribed calomel, worsening the diarrhea and possibly adding mercury poisoning to the patient's woes. Some medical officers did their best to provide a nourishing diet, especially when the patient was recovering.

Most typhoid deaths occurred after the fourteenth day of the illness and were caused by such complications as intestinal bleeding, perforated intestines, peritonitis, or pneumonia. Those soldiers who survived typhoid fever developed immunity to it, although they could still carry and spread the disease for months or even years.

Typhoid caused problems not only for individual soldiers but also for regiments and armies, at times rendering large numbers of troops ineffective. The Union Army of the Potomac had many typhoid cases in November 1861 and during the Peninsula Campaign of 1862. In the summer of 1862 the Sixtieth New York Infantry had to be sent away from the front, missing the Second Battle of Bull Run (Manassas), because 767 men had typhoid fever. There were many cases of typhoid at Vicksburg, Mississippi, during the siege in 1863, but fewer at the siege of Petersburg, Virginia (1864–1865) and in the Confederate prison camp at Andersonville, Georgia (1864), because of the greater immunity of veteran troops later in the war. Notable civilians also suffered typhoid fever during the war. Illinois senator and 1860 presidential candidate Stephen A. Douglas died of typhoid in June 1861. President Abraham Lincoln's sons Willie and Tad contracted typhoid fever in February 1862; Willie died on February 20 in the White House.

See also: Andersonville Prison; Bull Run (Manassas), Second Battle of; Calomel; Diarrhea and Dysentery; Fevers; Jones, Joseph; Latrines; Miasms; Mortality, of Soldiers; Opiate Use and Addiction; Peninsula Campaign; Pneumonia; Quinine; Sanitation; Typhomalarial Fever.

Bibliography

Adams, George Worthington. *Doctors in Blue: The Medical History of the Union Army in the Civil War.* New York: Schuman, 1952; reprint, Dayton, OH: Morningside, 1985.

Barnes, Joseph K., ed. *The Medical and Surgical History of the War of the Rebellion (1861–65).* Washington, DC: Government Printing Office, 1870–1888; reprint, Wilmington, NC: Broadfoot, 1990.

Bollet, Alfred Jay. *Civil War Medicine: Challenges and Triumphs.* Tucson, AZ: Galen, 2002.

Cunningham, H.H. *Doctors in Gray: The Confederate Medical Service.* Baton Rouge: Louisiana State University Press, 1958; reprint, Gloucester, MA: Peter Smith, 1970.

Steiner, Paul E. *Disease in the Civil War: Natural Biological Warfare in 1861–1865.* Springfield, IL: C.C. Thomas, 1968.

TYPHOID PNEUMONIA *See* Pneumonia.

TYPHOMALARIAL FEVER

Typhomalarial fever was a diagnostic term introduced by Union surgeon Joseph J. Woodward in July 1862 to replace the term *continued fever*. The new term was never adopted by the Confederates.

Woodward's description of the disease was similar to that of typhoid fever except that it did not include delirium. Many cases of typhomalarial fever probably were mild typhoid fever. In other instances, because typhoid and malaria are both characterized by chills and fever, doctors were unable to tell which disease the patient had. In still other cases, the term may have been accurate because the patient really had both illnesses at the same time.

Union doctors diagnosed 49,871 cases of typhomalarial fever, with a mortality rate of 8.1 percent, lower than that for typhoid fever.

See also: Fevers; Malaria; Typhoid Fever; Woodward, Joseph Janvier.

Bibliography

Bollet, Alfred Jay. *Civil War Medicine: Challenges and Triumphs.* Tucson, AZ: Galen, 2002.

Interior of Ward K at the Armory Square Hospital in Washington, DC, at 6th and B streets SW. The photo was taken in August 1865. (Library of Congress-DIG-cwpb-04246)

The Douglas Hospital, at 2nd and I streets NW in Washington, DC, was photographed from the rear in May 1864. The hospital itself used a pre-existing building, expanded for additional patients by pitching a large number of hospital tents. (Library of Congress-DIG-cwpb-04322)

Contrasting with a neat and clean general hospital ward is the post-battle chaos of a Virginia field hospital, photographed by James F. Gibson on June 30, 1862, three days after the June 27 Battle of Savage's Station, a part of the Peninsula Campaign. (Library of Congress-DIG-cwpb-01063)

An "embalming surgeon" prepares the body of a deceased soldier for shipment home by injecting embalming fluid through a tube. (Library of Congress-DIG-cwpb-01887)

UNITED STATES CHRISTIAN COMMISSION

The United States Christian Commission was a large Northern relief organization during the Civil War. It differed in a number of important ways from its competitor, the United States Sanitary Commission. The Christian Commission was established by members of the Young Men's Christian Association (YMCA) from seven states and Washington, DC, meeting in New York City on November 14, 1861. They intended to minister to soldiers spiritually (through prayer meetings, worship services, and the distribution of tracts, Bibles, and other religious literature) as well as physically (through supplies and nursing). Although local YMCAs had been ministering since the war began, the commission wanted to organize and consolidate the efforts.

The administrative structure of the commission changed over time as needed. The commission originally had twelve members, later forty-eight, and finally fifty. The executive committee, which had authority over all aspects of the commission and its work, started with five members and later expanded to fourteen. There was also a home secretary and a field secretary. Initially the commission had its headquarters in New York City where it was founded, but soon moved to Philadelphia, the home of its chairman, George H. Stuart, a merchant.

The Christian Commission established numerous branches, at least one for each state, as well as women's auxiliaries, with the purpose of arousing public interest, raising funds for the work, recruiting "delegates" to minister to the soldiers, and generally supporting the commission. Ultimately there were 266 women's auxiliaries in seventeen states, preparing supplies for the soldiers and raising almost $200,000. Because the commission had a strong evangelistic goal, most of the participants were members of evangelical Protestant churches and raised their funds through churches. The committees in various locations had the responsibility of raising funds and supplies for particular geographical areas. For example, the New York City branch provided funds for its own local region plus the Union-occupied areas of Virginia, North Carolina, South Carolina, Georgia, and Florida.

To actually minister to the soldiers, the Christian Commission used "delegates," ultimately about 5,000 of them. Delegates were volunteers, unpaid except for their expenses, who spent about six weeks serving where needed. While the delegates were overwhelmingly male and many of them were ordained ministers, a number of women volunteered with the commission, including Annie Wittenmyer, who eventually devised a special diet kitchen for the hospitals. The first official delegate was an Episcopalian minister from Germantown, Pennsylvania, commissioned on May 14, 1862. The delegates reported to agents who supervised the work in a particular army or area. The agents were among the few full-time, paid Christian Commission workers. The Christian Commission was very particular about selecting its workers. Because it was a Protestant organization, it insisted that all its representatives be orthodox Protestant Christians with a recommendation from their pastor.

The goal of the delegates was to minister wherever they were needed. They assisted chaplains with services and conducted them when no chaplains were available. Delegates led prayer meetings, counseled soldiers individually, and comforted the dying. They wrote letters for those who were unable to do so and provided stationery and stamps for soldiers who could write. Delegates distributed supplies when they were needed, as well as Bibles, tracts, and quantities of other religious literature. They were not afraid to perform the very dirtiest tasks in caring for sick and wounded patients, and they dug graves to bury the dead. The delegates served all soldiers, Christian or not, and also ministered to Confederate prisoners of war when they could. The delegates often slept on the ground, had little to eat, and worked very hard. Forty-three of them (including three women) died during or on their way home from their service.

Especially in the early months of the organization, many military doctors opposed the Christian Commission delegates as they opposed most civilian assistance, but eventually the physicians came to appreciate the commission's aid. Their willingness to do the humblest tasks earned commission delegates respect from many soldiers as well.

Nevertheless, the Christian Commission had considerable conflict with the U.S. Sanitary Commission. Because the Sanitary Commission was founded first, its leaders thought that it should control all the Northern relief efforts. Sanitarians bemoaned the diversion of funds and duplication of efforts. Some conflict arose as well because of the religious element in the Christian Commission as opposed to the secular orientation of the Sanitary Commission, although many members of the Sanitary Commission also provided spiritual comfort for the troops.

During the war the U.S. Christian Commission received more than $2.5 million in cash and $3.5 million in goods and publications. It distributed nearly 1.5 million Bibles or New Testaments, 1 million hymnbooks, and over 39 million pages of tracts. Its delegates preached more than 58,000 sermons, held more than 77,000 prayer meetings, wrote over 92,000 letters for soldiers, and performed uncountable nursing services.

See also: Chaplains; Diet, of Hospital Patients; Nurses; United States Sanitary Commission; Western Sanitary Commission; Wittenmyer, Annie Turner; Women's Hospital Auxiliaries and Relief Societies.

Bibliography

Adams, Lois Bryan. *Letter from Washington, 1863–1865*, ed. Evelyn Leasher. Detroit: Wayne State University Press, 1999.

Gordon, Ralph C. "Nashville and the U.S. Christian Commission in the Civil War." *Tennessee Historical Quarterly* 55 (Summer 1996): 99–111.

Henry, James O. "The United States Christian Commission." *Civil War History* 6 (December 1960): 374–388.

Raney, David A. "In the Lord's Army: The United States Christian Commission, Soldiers, and the Union War Effort." In *Union Soldiers and the Northern Home Front: Wartime Experience, Postwar Adjustments*, ed. Paul A. Cimbala and Randall M. Miller, 263–292. New York: Fordham University Press, 2002.

UNITED STATES SANITARY COMMISSION

The United States Sanitary Commission, usually called simply the Sanitary Commission, was a civilian organization initially modeled on one developed in Great Britain during the Crimean War in the mid-1850s. Its goal was to assist the Union army medical department, which was obviously unprepared to meet the needs of the sick and wounded members of an army that had grown tremendously almost overnight.

In April 1861 a number of New York City women, led by several prominent male ministers and doctors, established the Woman's Central Association of Relief to collect supplies and provide other support for the army. After the army medical purveyor in New York turned down offers of supplies because he did not think that the army needed civilian aid, a delegation of a minister and three doctors, representing various aid societies, went to Washington, DC, in mid-May to see what could be done. The four men spent more than a week visiting Winfield Scott (the head of the army), President Abraham Lincoln, Secretary of State William H. Seward, Secretary of War Simon Cameron, second in command of the army medical department Colonel Robert Wood, various members of Congress, and others. Although the delegation received some support, it also experienced delays, discouragement, opposition, and obstruction.

Finally, on June 9, Cameron issued an order to establish the Sanitary Commission, giving it authority to inspect, report, establish guidelines, and provide supplies, in cooperation with the secretary of war and the medical department, in order to improve the health and sanitation of the army. Lincoln signed the order on June 13. Twenty-one commissioners met on June 12. They elected New York Unitarian minister Henry W. Bellows as president. George Templeton Strong became the organization's treasurer. On June 20, the commission offered landscape architect and proven organizer Frederick Law Olmsted the position of executive secretary, essentially manager of operations for the commission. Olmsted immediately began visiting Union camps around Washington, DC, a discouraging process because the camps were filthy and undisciplined while the medical department was unprepared and uncooperative. Olmsted was so critical of the army after the First Battle of Bull Run (Manassas) that his report could not be published as written. Olmsted's other reports demonstrated that the war would be a long one and that the commission needed to develop long-term plans and funding to help the government meet soldiers' needs.

Olmsted set up the operating structure for the commission, with himself at the top and three regional undersecretaries. In addition, twenty sanitary inspectors and other agents were appointed to visit military camps and hospitals, identify problems, and provide instructions for improving care and preventing further difficulties. Women's auxiliaries would collect money and supplies for the commission to distribute. Olmsted was very energetic about traveling, organizing, and gathering support from newspapers and Congressmen for legislation that the Sanitary Commission favored. Bellows, too, gathered statistics, planned, traveled, and met with civilian officials, generals, and other persons to promote the Sanitary Commission's goals. Strong and other commissioners managed the daily business of the commission in their New York office.

Over the course of the war the commission achieved many benefits for U.S. Army troops. It fought vigorously to reorganize the army medical department, including the removal of the recalcitrant Clement A. Finley and the appointment of the progressive William A. Hammond as surgeon general on April 25, 1862. In November 1862 the commission established a directory of hospital patients in Washington, DC, later extended to all Union general hospitals, allowing relatives and friends to find their loved ones. The commission also distributed literature about medical advances to Union surgeons.

The Sanitary Commission is best known, however, for its provision of emergency supplies for the sick and wounded. Especially during and after some of the early battles, the medical department failed to provide medical supplies. At Shiloh (April 1862) and Gettysburg (July 1863), troops were separated from their medical supply trains. After both these battles, as well as after Antietam (September 1862), the Sanitary Commission, able to bypass red tape and provide its own transportation, got supplies to the field before the army did. During the Peninsula Campaign in Virginia (spring and early summer 1862), the commission, under Olmsted's personal leadership, rented boats and fitted them out as hospital transports to take the sick and wounded to hospitals in Washington, Annapolis, New York, and other cities. After the Battle of Fredericksburg (December 1862), the commission provided much-needed blankets and a feeding station for patients on the way from the field hospitals to the general hospitals. Commission agents provided supplies after many smaller engagements as well and equipped field and general hospitals. The Sanitary Commission met emergency needs, not the ordinary resupply functions of the medical department. As the war progressed and the medical department improved its organization and supply process, the commission had fewer desperate crises to meet.

Although the Sanitary Commission paid Olmsted and some agents, most of the labor was voluntary. The funds and supplies came from donations. Many women made hospital clothing, bedding, and food delicacies for the sick and wounded troops. Other supplies were purchased with the funds, which also paid for transportation. Beginning in 1863, women in many parts of the country raised funds by holding often very elaborate "sanitary fairs." They charged admission, gave performances, set up exhibits, sold food, and auctioned off items over the course of several days or weeks.

Although many people supported the work of the Sanitary Commission, others did not. Some even opposed it, and the commission engaged in a number of conflicts as a result. Early in the war the major struggle was with the army medical department, many of whose officers were elderly, infirm, or totally ignorant of the medical needs of a large army. They were rigid, jealous of rank in the medical corps, suspicious of change, and obstructionist. After the departmental reforms of April 1862, conflict arose with Secretary of War Edwin M. Stanton, who opposed the appointment of William A. Hammond, the Sanitary Commission's candidate, as surgeon general. Hammond and the commission generally worked well together, however.

From the beginning, Bellows, the commission's president, wanted to organize and channel civilian donations so supplies could get to the point where they were needed without waste or unnecessary overlap of services. This seemingly sensible goal caused conflict with other relief organizations that resented the centralization and control by New York. The United States Christian Commission, founded in November 1861 in New York but later headquartered in Philadelphia, stressed spiritual service to the soldiers, although it also provided physical aid. The Sanitary Commission was not opposed to religion and, in fact, provided religious literature and comfort. However, the Christian Commission was strictly an evangelical Protestant effort. It objected to Reverend Bellows, a Unitarian, as Sanitary Commission president, as well as to that commission's religiously inclusive practice of distributing Roman Catholic and Jewish materials to members of those faiths.

The U.S. Sanitary Commission also had serious conflicts with the Western Sanitary Commission, which formed in St. Louis in September 1861. The issues were largely territorial. Westerners resented eastern control and did not believe that New Yorkers could understand the needs specific to the West. The easterners, on the other hand, saw the westerners as an example of the kind of factional sentiment that had led to secession and civil war in the first place. In some areas both groups competed for supporters and funds.

Olmsted himself provoked a good deal of conflict within and outside the commission. His feverish work habits, stimulated by the crises that the commission was trying to meet, caused him to suffer from exhaustion and finally to resign on September 1, 1863. The commission continued its work under several successors.

The commission disbanded in July 1865. Some of its agents used remaining funds to assist needy veterans.

See also: Antietam, Battle of; Bellows, Henry Whitney; Bull Run (Manassas), First Battle of; Fredericksburg, Battle of; Finley, Clement Alexander; Gettysburg, Battle of; Hammond, William Alexander; Hospital Ships; Hospitals, Field; Hospitals, General; Inspectors, Medical; Medical Department, Organization of; Olmsted, Frederick Law; Peninsula Campaign; Sanitary Fairs; Sanitation; Shiloh, Battle of; Strong, George Templeton; United States Christian Commission; Western Sanitary Commission; Woman's Central Association of Relief; Women's Hospital Auxiliaries and Relief Societies.

Bibliography

Bender, Robert Patrick. "'This Noble and Philanthropic Enterprise': The Mississippi Valley Sanitary Fair of 1864 and the Practice of Civil War Philanthropy." *Missouri Historical Review* 95 (January 2001): 117–139.

Bremner, Robert H. "The Impact of the Civil War on Philanthropy and Social Welfare." *Civil War History* 12 (December 1966): 293–303.

Maxwell, William Quentin. *Lincoln's Fifth Wheel: The Political History of the United States Sanitary Commission.* New York: Longmans, Green, 1956.

Parrish, William E. "The Western Sanitary Commission." *Civil War History* 36 (March 1990): 17–35.

Rybczynski, Witold. *A Clearing in the Distance: Frederick Law Olmsted and America in the 19th Century.* New York: Scribner, 1999.

USS *RED ROVER*

The USS *Red Rover* was the U.S. Navy's first hospital ship. A side-wheel steamer purchased by the Confederates in November 1861 and turned into an unarmed floating barracks, the *Red Rover* was damaged in the fighting at Island No. 10 in the Mississippi River near New Madrid, Missouri, in April 1862 and captured by Union forces. Towed to St. Louis for repairs, the *Red Rover* was refitted as a hospital boat.

Although other ships on the Mississippi River had been used for temporary treatment and transport of casualties, none had been designed specifically for that purpose. The plan for the *Red Rover* was twofold. It would be a fully equipped and supplied hospital capable of removing the sick and wounded from the ships of the fleet and either caring for them on board or transporting them to a hospital on land. It would also deliver medical supplies and provisions to the ships of the fleet.

Thus, over the course of several renovations, the *Red Rover* was equipped with operating rooms, crew and patient kitchens below deck, some open walls for better air circulation, a steam heating system, an extra steam boiler for laundry, nine bathrooms and water closets, three elevators, cold storage for 300 tons of ice, and enough storage space to hold supplies and provisions for the crew and 200 patients for up to three months. The Western Sanitary Commission provided $3,500 for supplies and recruited two senior surgeons from Boston.

In addition to a substantial crew of whites and contraband blacks (escaped slaves), the *Red Rover* had plenty of medical attendants, including doctors, stewards, nurses (black and white, mostly but not exclusively male), cooks, and laundresses. The nurses included four sisters from the Order of the Holy Cross and several black women who were the first women employed on a U.S. Navy ship.

Beginning its service on June 10, 1862, the *Red Rover* took patients from the warships, which had no room for them, and provided excellent care and good quality food, much of it fresh. The *Red Rover* staff removed and treated wounded from the explosion of the gunboat *Mound City*, the battles for Vicksburg, the Fort Pillow massacre, and the Red River campaign. The staff treated many on board, but transferred long-term cases to hospitals at Mound City, Illinois, and Memphis, Tennessee. When the whole Mississippi River opened to Union traffic with the fall of Vicksburg on July 4, 1863, the *Red Rover* made many trips wherever needed, visiting various ships of the fleet to pick up patients and drop off supplies.

During its naval service, 1,697 patients were admitted to the hospital on the Red Rover, of whom 1,365 were discharged and 157 died on board. The *Red Rover* finished its last supply trip on December 11, 1864, and remained docked as a hospital at Mound City until November 11, 1865, when its last patients were transferred elsewhere. Decommissioned by the navy, it was sold at auction on November 29, 1865, for $4,500.

See also: Blacks, as Hospital Workers; Hospital Ships; Laundresses; Nuns; Nurses; Western Sanitary Commission; Women, as Hospital Workers.

Bibliography

Roca, Steven Louis. "Presence and Precedents: The USS *Red Rover* During the American Civil War, 1861–1865." *Civil War History* 44 (June 1998): 91–110.

VACCINATION, SMALLPOX

Although the English physician Edward Jenner first inoculated against the deadly, disfiguring disease smallpox in 1796, vaccination was not a standard practice at the time of the Civil War. Most army and civilian doctors realized vaccination's importance, especially when smallpox appeared in an army or a city and began to spread rapidly in the crowded conditions. However, orders to vaccinate large numbers of people were difficult to carry out effectively because many were reluctant to be vaccinated, it was difficult to get good vaccine, and the process was unpleasant and often failed.

Procurement of smallpox vaccine that was effective and "pure" was a major challenge throughout the war. The best and safest vaccine was taken from the fluid of cowpox lesions on the udders of cows. Cowpox was similar enough to smallpox to provide immunity from the latter. However, the most approved method of procuring "vaccine matter" in quantity was to vaccinate the arms in multiple places of healthy, previously unvaccinated infants and young children (white or black). On the seventh or eighth day after the vaccination, the resulting lesions could be punctured and the fluid or "lymph" removed with a thin piece of bone or hollow quill. The lymph was allowed to dry and then carefully wrapped. The virus remained active and could be used for vaccination for a week or ten days. The advantage of vaccinating with lymph was that it could be harvested sooner than a scab, an important factor during an epidemic when large numbers of people needed vaccination. However, vaccine could also be procured from a scab removed from the vaccinated arm on the fifteenth day after vaccination. The scab was dried for four or five days and then cut into four to six pieces, which were carefully sealed and, ideally, stored in a cool, dark place until needed.

In the 1860s, doctors did not vaccinate with hypodermic needles. Instead they cut the skin of the upper arm with a knife or other sharp instrument. They then inserted the vaccine. It could be in the form of a paste made from a ground scab mixed with a few drops of water, or a small piece of thread coated with lymph. The doctor could also wipe the dried lymph from a piece of bone or quill inside the cut. The edges of the cut would then be pressed together to keep the vaccine from rubbing off. Some doctors also vaccinated by scraping off the skin and applying the vaccine. However, because this procedure took longer and the vaccine was more likely to rub off, Confederate surgeon general Samuel P. Moore did not recommend it.

A successful vaccination would be obvious when the doctor inspected the vaccinated spot eight days later and saw that a proper lesion had formed. After the scab fell off or was harvested for further vaccinations, a characteristic scar remained.

Not all vaccinations "took" successfully and provided the needed protection. Sometimes the vaccine matter was inert, too old or weak to be effective. The doctor examining the vaccination on the eighth day was able to tell that the immunization had not worked and the person needed to be revaccinated.

Much worse than the failure of the vaccination were the infections that sometimes resulted from contaminated vaccine, unsterile knives, dirty arms, or disease contracted from the person providing the scab. These results were sometimes called "spurious vaccination." In some cases patients developed huge spreading sores, leading to the amputation of the arm or, in the worst cases, death. Sometimes the infection was made worse because the soldier already was weakened by scurvy.

Since vaccination was not a difficult process, a number of soldiers believed that they could do it for themselves. They vaccinated each other using matter from the arm of a comrade or, in at least one instance, a prostitute friend. Ineffective immunization and serious ulcerations almost always resulted. This freelance method of vaccinating frequently spread syphilis as well. In addition, vaccinations made from smallpox patients spread the disease rather than granting protection from it.

By 1863 it was Union army policy to vaccinate every soldier or civilian working with the army who did not have scarring evidence that he had either had smallpox or been effectively vaccinated. The Confederates also made every effort to vaccinate as many soldiers as possible.

See also: Amputation; Hospitals, "Pest" (Smallpox); Infections, of Wounds; Moore, Samuel Preston; Richmond, Virginia; Scurvy; Smallpox; Venereal Disease; Washington, DC.

Bibliography
Bollet, Alfred Jay. *Civil War Medicine: Challenges and Triumphs.* Tucson, AZ: Galen, 2002.
Moore, Samuel P. "Instructions Relative to Vaccination" (July 1, 1863). SC 330, folder 2, Manuscripts Department, Abraham Lincoln Presidential Library, Springfield, IL.

VARIOLOID

Varioloid is a mild form of smallpox, suffered by persons who previously had smallpox or who had been vaccinated. Although varioloid patients might become quite ill, fewer of them died than those who contracted regular smallpox. For example, in the Confederate general hospitals in Virginia, 2,513 men were treated for smallpox between October 1, 1862, and January 31, 1864, and 1,020 of them died. During the same period, 1,196 men suffered from varioloid, but only 39 died.

The most famous varioloid patient during the Civil War was President Abraham Lincoln. On November 19, 1863, he was ill on the train on the way back from delivering his notable speech at the Gettysburg cemetery dedication. He had such a severe headache that he had to lie down with cold cloths on his head. Although he was not officially quarantined at the White House, for the next several weeks few people came to see him. Because he was so often frustrated by office seekers and those who wanted favors that the president could not grant, Lincoln joked during his illness, "Now I have something I can give everybody." The president seems to have been sickest on November 26, when he was confined to his room, and November 27, when his doctor banned all visitors, even cabinet members. Lincoln was still not fully recovered by December 14.

A black man named William H. Johnson had come with Lincoln to Washington from Springfield, Illinois. Johnson had a job in the Treasury Department, but also worked for the president on call as a valet and trusted messenger. He accompanied Lincoln to Gettysburg and then nursed the president during his illness. Unfortunately, Johnson contracted the disease, either from Lincoln or from someone else during the smallpox epidemic in Washington at that time, and died of smallpox in late January 1864. Lincoln paid for Johnson's burial in Arlington Cemetery.

See also: Gettysburg, Battle of; Hospitals, "Pest" (Smallpox); Lincoln, Abraham; Vaccination, Smallpox.

Bibliography

Basler, Roy P. "Did President Lincoln Give the Smallpox to William H. Johnson?" *Huntington Library Quarterly* 35 (May 1972): 279–284.

Miers, Earl Schenck. *Lincoln Day by Day.* 3 vols. Washington, DC: Lincoln Sesquicentennial Commission, 1960.

VENEREAL DISEASE

Venereal diseases were relatively widespread in both the Union and Confederate armies during the Civil War, although their incidence cannot be accurately compared because few Confederate statistical records survive. Gonorrhea ("the clap") and syphilis were the main types of sexually transmitted disease. Other varieties, such as orchitis, were often classified as gonorrhea. Doctors knew that the diseases were spread by sexual contact, although they believed (probably correctly) that particular cases of syphilis had been caused by smallpox vaccinations performed directly from the arm of one soldier to another.

Because urban prostitutes were the source of most venereal disease, it is not surprising that the soldier most likely to become infected was a young recent recruit stationed near a city and not actively involved in combat. Infection rates also rose in veteran troops just returned from furlough because they had had access to cities and often had reenlistment bounties to spend. Among the cities with the worst reputations for prostitution in the Confederacy were Richmond and Petersburg, Virginia, and Dalton, Georgia, while Washington, DC, and Nashville and Memphis, Tennessee, provided much temptation for Union soldiers. Although Union general Joseph Hooker forced prostitutes in Washington to locate in an area nicknamed "Hooker's Division," the slang term *hooker* for prostitute was evidently in use before the Civil War.

After Nashville and Memphis fell to Union control, venereal disease became such a problem that authorities legalized and regulated prostitution after an unsuccessful attempt to ship the prostitutes to Louisville, Kentucky, or Cincinnati, Ohio. Beginning in September 1863, Nashville prostitutes had to pay a fee of fifty cents per week and submit to frequent medical examinations. Those deemed healthy were issued a license. Those found to be diseased were sent to a special hospital, No. 11, a former bishop's home, where they received treatment funded by their weekly fees. Unlicensed prostitutes would be sentenced to thirty days in the workhouse. A similar system was instituted in Memphis in the fall of 1864. These first experiments with legalized prostitution in the United States were quite successful in isolating the women while they were contagious, although they were not actually healed.

Venereal disease cases in the Confederacy were treated in the field unless they were severe, in part to deter soldiers from deliberately contracting venereal disease in order to escape military service. Most patients who required hospitalization behind the lines were treated in general hospitals, but some specialized venereal disease hospitals were established, such as that set up in Kingston, Georgia, in early 1864, for serious cases in the Army of Tennessee. Union forces in occupied Nashville established the "Soldier's Syphilitic Hospital" in the former Hynes High School.

Doctors tried a variety of treatments for venereal diseases, including pokeroots or berries, sarsaparilla, sassafras, jessamine, elder, prickly ash, silkweed root in whiskey, and pine rosin pills. Some tried mercury treatments for syphilis or urethral injections of various substances for gonorrhea. A few tried rest and diet adjustments. Some treatments alleviated the symptoms, while others worsened them, but none actually cured the patient. Because the symptoms disappeared naturally over time, doctors tended to regard the most recent treatment as the "cure." However, the bacterial infections that caused venereal diseases often remained latent and appeared again later, even years later. Confederate general Ambrose Powell Hill had contracted gonorrhea in 1844 while he was a student at West Point. Apparently many of his frequent illnesses during the Civil War were the result of urinary problems caused by the gonorrhea. Some historians believe, although numbers cannot be determined, that many former soldiers eventually infected their wives and as many as one-third of Union and Confederate veterans in veterans' homes in later years died from the effects of venereal disease. The first effective treatment for syphilis, Salvarsan, was not developed until 1910, while penicillin was not used for gonorrhea until 1945.

During the war, white Union troops suffered 73,382 cases of syphilis and 109,397 cases of gonorrhea, roughly 82 cases per 1,000 men per year, of which a total of 136 proved fatal before the war's end. Black Union troops contracted 6,207 cases of syphilis and 8,050 of gonorrhea, about 78 cases per 1,000 men per year, with a total of 32 wartime fatalities.

Confederate statistics are much more fragmentary. For example, in July 1861 in the Army of Northern Virginia, twelve regiments from five states with 11,452 men reported 204 new cases of gonorrhea and 44 of syphilis, while in March 1862 twenty-eight regiments from seven states with 19,942 men reported only fourteen new gonorrhea and ten syphilis cases. In August 1862 only eight of the 312 patients in the Post Hospital in Dalton, Georgia, were admitted for venereal disease. Such sporadic data do not permit any systematic analysis.

A sizable minority of Union and Confederate soldiers contracted venereal disease during the war. Doubtless, the numbers ill from these diseases reduced troop strength and effectiveness on occasion.

See also: Hospitals, General; Mortality, of Soldiers; Richmond, Virginia; Smallpox Vaccinations.

Bibliography

Cunningham, H.H. *Doctors in Gray: The Confederate Medical Service.* Baton Rouge: Louisiana State University Press, 1958; reprint, Gloucester, MA: Peter Smith, 1970.

Jones, James Boyd, Jr. "A Tale of Two Cities: The Hidden Battle Against Venereal Disease in Civil War Nashville and Memphis." *Civil War History* 31 (September 1985): 270–276.

Lowry, Thomas P. *The Story the Soldiers Wouldn't Tell: Sex in the Civil War.* Mechanicsburg, PA: Stackpole, 1994.

Murphy, Lawrence R. "The Enemy Among Us: Venereal Disease Among Union Soldiers in the Far West, 1861–1865." *Civil War History* 31 (September 1985): 257–269.

Welsh, Jack D. *Medical Histories of Confederate Generals.* Kent, OH: Kent State University Press, 1995.

Wiley, Bell Irwin. *The Life of Johnny Reb: The Common Soldier of the Confederacy.* Garden City, NY: Doubleday, 1943, 1971.

VENTILATION

Proper ventilation of hospitals was an important issue for doctors in both the North and the South during the Civil War. The benefits of good ventilation, accompanied by other sanitation measures, had first become evident through the work of Florence Nightingale and her allies during the Crimean War in the mid-1850s.

Doctors were very concerned about "miasms," dangerous, malodorous vapors most often attributed to decaying vegetation, as well as emanations of various sorts from sick persons. Doctors of this era did not know about germs, but believed that noxious smells caused or worsened disease. As a result, they believed that providing plenty of "pure," fresh air would help keep disease from spreading and speed the healing of those already ill.

To this end, the medical departments on both sides tried to adapt buildings converted to hospital use to improve ventilation, with some success. On both sides several doctors also designed pavilion hospitals, with individual buildings for each ward. The designs featured variations on openings along the ridge of the roof, under the eaves, above the windows, and below the windows, which were provided with shutters (sometimes sliding ones) that could be opened or closed to regulate the proper amount of ventilation.

Some doctors and nurses believed that sick and wounded patients recovered best in tent hospitals, which had the greatest fresh air circulation. At least at some seasons this was probably true: because the fresh air did disperse bad odors and there were fewer people in the tent or the pavilion ward to pass germs around, improved ventilation did assist the recovery process of the soldiers.

See also: Hospital Buildings; Hospitals, Pavilion; Miasms; Sanitation; Tents, Hospital.

Bibliography

Bollet, Alfred Jay. *Civil War Medicine: Challenges and Triumphs.* Tucson, AZ: Galen, 2002.

Schroeder-Lein, Glenna R. *Confederate Hospitals on the Move: Samuel H. Stout and the Army of Tennessee.* Columbia: University of South Carolina Press, 1994.

Stout, Samuel H. "On the Best Models and Most Easily Constructed Military Hospital Wards for Temporary Use in War." *Transactions of the International Medical Congress,* 9th session, vol. 2 (1887): 88–91.

VETERAN RESERVE CORPS *See* Invalid Corps.

V.S. *See* Gunshot Wounds.

VULNUS SCLOPETICUM See Gunshot Wounds.

WALKER, MARY EDWARDS (1832–1919)

Mary Edwards Walker served as an acting assistant surgeon in several capacities for the Union forces during the Civil War. Born in Oswego, New York, on November 26, 1832, the daughter of Alvah Walker and Vesta Whitcomb Walker, Mary had four older sisters and a younger brother. She grew up in a freethinking atmosphere where women were considered as capable as men. Her parents also stressed health, exercise, and diet, opposing restrictive clothing, such as corsets, that could damage a woman's health. Her father, a farmer, carpenter, and self-taught medical practitioner, may have influenced Mary's desire to become a physician.

After graduating from Falley Seminary, Mary Walker taught school to earn money for medical studies. In 1855 she graduated from Syracuse Medical College in New York. Syracuse was an "eclectic" rather than a "regular" medical school, meaning that it combined treatments and practices from several medical viewpoints and avoided some of the "heroic" therapies, such as bleeding and purging, for which regular doctors were sometimes notorious.

Later in 1855 Walker married a classmate, Albert Miller, and they established a medical practice together in Rome, New York. Miller, however, was chronically unfaithful and they separated legally in 1861, with a final divorce in 1866.

In addition to practicing medicine, Walker spoke and wrote on dress reform, personally adopting an outfit consisting of a knee-length dress worn over trousers. This practical but unusual attire subjected her to considerable ridicule, opposition, and controversy.

Soon after the Civil War broke out, Walker went to Washington, DC, to apply for a position as a military surgeon for the Union army. She was turned down for a commission because she was a woman, she had graduated from an eclectic medical college (synonymous with "quack" for many regular practitioners), and she dressed in a controversial manner. For about two months, beginning in November 1861, Walker worked as a civilian assistant surgeon volunteer under Dr. J.N. Green in the Indiana Hospital, housed in a part of the U.S. Patent Office. Green, who had worked himself nearly to exhaustion, was glad to have Walker's assistance. Finding her competent, he recommended her for a military commission. When she was still denied such a commission, she returned to New York and from January through March 1862 earned a certificate in hydrotherapy (water cure as well as dietary guidelines) at the Hygeia Therapeutic College. This training would not be acceptable to regular physicians either.

In November 1862 Walker went to General Ambrose Burnside's headquarters in Warrenton, Virginia, and persuaded him to let her treat the sick and wounded as a volunteer. At one point, she was in complete charge of a train full of patients on the way to hospitals in Washington, DC. After the Battle of Fredericksburg in December 1862, she worked at the Lacy House, preparing patients for transportation. Although Walker evidently knew how to perform amputations, she was very much opposed to the surgery in most cases and quietly urged soldiers to resist it.

Doctors in the field and in hospitals were glad for Walker's assistance in emergencies and seemed to have much less trouble accepting a female physician than administrators did. Once an emergency was over, however, Walker was unable to get payment or a commission. As an outspoken, assertive woman in blatantly unconventional clothes, she challenged the male medical establishment too much.

During 1863 Walker was involved in various relief efforts in Washington, DC, particularly as an advocate for sick and wounded soldiers and their families. She opened a residence for women who came to look for or care for their kin but had no place to stay in the crowded city. She also continued to pester authorities for a position as a contract surgeon.

Finally sent to Chattanooga in late 1863, Walker ran afoul of the army's acting medical director, Dr. George E. Cooper, who would only offer her a position as a nurse, which she refused. When General George H. Thomas took her side, however, she received a contract appointment to replace the deceased assistant surgeon of the Fifty-Second Ohio Infantry. Walker had to appear before an examining board made up of her medical enemies, who treated her rudely and proclaimed her completely unqualified because she was a female and an eclectic. Nevertheless, Walker continued to serve with the Fifty-Second Ohio, although, because the troops were relatively healthy, she spent much of her time treating the needy Confederate women and children of northern Georgia. She may also have been a spy for General Thomas. On April 10, 1864, during one of her excursions, Walker was captured by Confederate soldiers and ultimately taken to Richmond, Virginia, where she spent four months as a prisoner of war at Castle Thunder. Exchanged for a Confederate major on August 12, Walker received pay from the federal government for her time with the Fifty-Second Ohio and in prison.

Finally given an official contract, Walker served as the surgeon in charge at the hospital of the Louisville Female Military Prison in Kentucky from October 1864 to March 1865. Despite conflicts with the inmates, she improved the food, discipline, and sanitation of the institution. From April 11 to May 17, 1865, she was stationed at an orphan and refugee home in Clarksville, Tennessee, before her contract ended on June 15.

Walker still wanted a commission in the army to work with the Freedmen's Bureau, even as troops were being mustered out at the close of the war. To this end, she applied to President Andrew Johnson and Secretary of War Edwin M. Stanton, who refused to grant such an appointment. On January 25, 1866, however, she received the Congressional Medal of Honor (to date from November 11, 1865). Walker proudly wore this medal for the rest of her life.

After the war, Walker suffered health problems from her imprisonment and was unable to practice medicine much. She lectured widely but not very remuneratively on dress reform, woman suffrage, and other topics, while becoming increasingly eccentric. She wrote two books, *Hit: Essays on Women's Rights* (1871) and *Unmasked, or the Science of Immorality, To Gentlemen by a Woman Physician* (1878), but never published any account of her military medical experiences. In 1917 Congress deleted her Medal of Honor from the records because it was not combat-related. Angered, Walker refused to return the medal. In that same year Walker, then eighty-five, fell on the Capitol steps in Washington and never fully recovered. She died on February 21, 1919. President Jimmy Carter signed legislation to reinstate Walker's medal on June 10, 1977.

See also: Alternative Medicines; Examining Boards, Medical; Fredericksburg, Battle of; Prisoners of War; Surgeons, Acting Assistant (Contract); Washington, DC; Women, as Doctors.

Bibliography

Graf, Mercedes. *A Woman of Honor: Dr. Mary E. Walker and the Civil War.* Gettysburg, PA: Thomas, 2001.

Leonard, Elizabeth D. *Yankee Women: Gender Battles in the Civil War.* New York: Norton, 1994.

Walker, Dale L. *Mary Edwards Walker: Above and Beyond.* New York: Forge, 2005.

WARD MASTERS

Both Union and Confederate hospitals employed ward masters during the Civil War. These men, one per ward, were under the direct supervision of the hospital steward.

Ward masters had two main duties. First, they were in charge of the patients' belongings. Any valuables, such as watches or money, were given to the surgeon for safekeeping. Otherwise, the soldiers' clothing and equipment were carefully listed in a book, labeled, packaged, and stored on a shelf in the knapsack room. Guns were labeled and stored there as well. Confederate ward masters assigned new patients to their beds and issued hospital clothing. Probably Union ward masters did these tasks also. When a patient returned to his regiment, the ward master restored his property. Soldiers who were discharged from the service received their personal belongings but no government property, such as guns or uniforms. If a patient died while hospitalized, his personal effects remained in the hospital knapsack room until the ward master received instructions about where to send them.

The second major responsibility of the ward master was to receive all furniture, bedding, and cooking utensils for his ward from the steward. The ward master was supposed to record all items and keep them in good condition. Using standardized forms, he listed the contents of each room, including kitchens and offices, associated with his ward. Everything was supposed to be inventoried weekly, and the ward master reported to the steward any property that had been damaged or destroyed.

Confederate ward masters also were responsible for ward cleanliness and for supervising the ward nurses. At least one ward master also functioned as the ward pharmacist, although this job was more commonly the responsibility of the hospital steward. A large hospital might have assistant ward masters. Sometimes acting ward masters were appointed temporarily to fill a vacancy or when battle casualties overwhelmed the hospitals.

See also: Hospital Paperwork; Hospital Support Staff; Sanitation; Stewards, Hospital.

Bibliography

Schroeder-Lein, Glenna R. *Confederate Hospitals on the Move: Samuel H. Stout and the Army of Tennessee.* Columbia: University of South Carolina Press, 1994.

Wood, Thomas Fanning. *Doctor to the Front: The Recollections of Confederate Surgeon Thomas Fanning Wood, 1861–1865,* ed. Donald B. Koonce. Knoxville: University of Tennessee Press, 2000.

Woodward, Joseph Janvier. *The Hospital Steward's Manual: For the Instruction of Hospital Stewards, Ward-Masters, and Attendants in their Several Duties.* Philadelphia: J.B. Lippincott, 1862; reprint, San Francisco: Norman, 1991.

WASHINGTON, DC

Washington, DC, the capital of the United States, was an unusual city when the Civil War began. It contained a number of substantial government buildings, but some of them were incomplete. The Capitol building, for example, had no dome, and the wings for the Senate and the House of Representatives were unfinished. (Construction continued throughout the war.) The Washington Monument was also incomplete, the project having run out of funds at 156 feet. However, visitors to the city could see such interesting sights as the models of inventions in the patent office, as well as the Smithsonian Institution museum, then in a single building.

Washington was really more rural than urban. The government buildings, homes, and other structures tended to be surrounded by a good deal of open space where livestock lived, often unfenced. Most streets were unpaved, covered in choking dust or bottomless mud, depending on the weather. There was a vile, open sewage canal running through part of the city, and slum areas housed prostitutes and crooks of various types.

The 1860 census showed the population of Washington to be 61,122, with another

8,733 in neighboring Georgetown and 5,225 in the surrounding rural area. The population increased dramatically when Congress was in session and subsided when it adjourned. Most of the permanent residents had a Maryland or Virginia heritage, giving a Southern flavor to the city and resulting in many Confederate sympathizers when the war broke out. The population included 11,131 free blacks and 3,185 slaves. Although Washington had "black codes," regulating the conduct and opportunities of free blacks, these had not prevented a number of blacks from prospering as restaurant owners and merchants. Others worked at a variety of trades and service occupations. Most of the slaves were house servants.

Within days of the Confederate attack on Fort Sumter in Charleston harbor, South Carolina, on April 14–15, 1861, troops began to arrive in Washington from Pennsylvania, Massachusetts, and New York. Initially they were quartered wherever space could be found, including the Capitol building and the East Room of the White House. Soon camps were set up on empty land in and near the city. By the fall of 1862 about 250,000 troops were camped in the vicinity. Many camps had serious sanitation problems leading to high disease rates, especially early in the war.

Many other people came to the capital to fill government clerkships, cater to the needs of the soldiers, solicit offices or business opportunities, or prey on the unsuspecting. Thousands of escaped slaves, mostly destitute, unskilled agricultural workers from Virginia, clustered in the city. Slavery was abolished in Washington by act of Congress on April 16, 1862.

Temporary, insubstantial buildings arose all around the city. Housing became crowded and rents increased. Residents opened their extra rooms to boarders. By the fall of 1863 these homeowners were charging twenty to thirty dollars per month for a room, plus four to eight dollars per week for meals. Hotels were much more expensive.

Although women had previously been employed in government offices on occasion, in 1862 Congress officially authorized hiring women clerks. Unfortunately, the pay offered was half of what men earned for doing the same work, often not as well. Nevertheless, many women took jobs as copyists in government offices, freeing some men to join the army.

When the war began, and even as late as the First Battle of Bull Run (Manassas) on July 21, 1861, there was only one hospital in the city. The Washington Infirmary was a three-story brick building on E Street near Judiciary Square. (The infirmary burned down in November 1861.) The army medical department was completely unprepared to provide care for the number of soldiers wounded at Bull Run. As a result, makeshift hospitals were established in the Union Hotel in Georgetown, the Capitol building, the patent office, St. Elizabeth's Insane Asylum, schools, a number of churches, and many private homes.

In November 1861, a smallpox epidemic struck both the army camps around Washington and the civilians. The first smallpox hospital was established in a private home, but soon a specific Hospital for Eruptive Diseases opened on the nearby Kalorama estate. In late 1861, the mayor of Washington ordered smallpox vaccinations for the civilians, including 2,280 poor people who received the vaccinations free. The mayor also took steps to see that smallpox patients were quickly isolated and their contaminated clothing and furniture burned. A second smallpox epidemic struck in December 1863–January 1864, causing people to avoid crowded public gatherings. A senator died of smallpox on January 2, 1864.

During and after the Peninsula Campaign, General George B. McClellan's attempt to reach Richmond, Virginia, in the spring and early summer of 1862, thousands of sick and wounded soldiers were brought to Washington, overwhelming the existing hospitals. Twenty-two new hospitals opened in Washington, thirteen of them in houses of worship, including a Jewish synagogue. In addition, many other hospitals were established in Georgetown, in Alexandria, Virginia, across the Potomac River, and in the rural areas of the District of Columbia. Eighteen of these hospitals opened in July, after the Seven Days battles that concluded the campaign. After the Second Battle of Bull Run (Manassas) in August 1862, 2,000 wounded soldiers occupied the Capitol building.

By this time it was clear that there was only a limited number of buildings in Washington that could be used for hospitals. Pressing them into service temporarily in a crisis did not necessarily provide the best care for sick and wounded soldiers. The medical department began to construct some facilities specifically for patient care. One of the earliest of these was Harewood Hospital, located outside town on the estate of Washington banker William W. Corcoran. Fifteen pavilion wards housed about 2,000 patients. The beautiful grounds included a large vegetable garden that helped to feed the sick and wounded. Other specially constructed pavilion-style hospitals included those known as Armory Square and Judiciary Square.

At times other people joined the regular, often overworked medical personnel in the Washington hospitals. After each battle in Virginia, people came from out of town to look for their wounded relatives, a difficult task because of the inadequate hospital directories. Those who did find a relative often stayed to nurse him. Some unrelated people also worked in the hospitals briefly, as did crusading journalist Jane Grey Swisshelm in May 1863.

Others, who lived and worked in Washington, provided aid on a more consistent basis. The Michigan Soldiers Relief Association included people from Michigan of all classes living in Washington, DC. They met the needs of Michigan troops stationed or hospitalized in the Washington area, visiting those whose relatives could not be with them. Both Mary and Abraham Lincoln visited the hospitals frequently to encourage the soldiers. Mary Lincoln read to the patients, wrote letters for them, and raised funds for Christmas dinner and special treats. Any gifts of liquor sent to the president, she took to the hospitals for the patients. Probably the best known visitor to the Washington hospitals was Walt Whitman, who spent most afternoons and evenings visiting patients, distributing little gifts and treats such as fruit, reading material, and tobacco. In order to raise money for relief agencies, the women of Washington organized a sanitary fair that opened on February 22, 1864, on the third floor of the patent office building.

In addition to the influx of patients after the battles of the spring and summer of 1862, many wounded also came to Washington following the battles of Fredericksburg (December 1862), Chancellorsville (May 1863), and the Wilderness (May 1864). As of May 16, 1864, there were four hospitals in Washington (Douglas, Stanton, Judiciary Square, and Armory Square), five on its northern border (Columbian, Carver, Mount Pleasant, Harewood, and Campbell), one on the east (Finley), two near the Navy Yard (Emory and Lincoln), one in Georgetown (Seminary), and a number in Alexandria. Altogether there were at least twenty-eight hospitals in Washington, six in Georgetown, and five in Alexandria, but the number at any particular time varied. As the war wound down, hospitals were being closed throughout 1865. The Lincoln and Harewood hospitals remained open the longest. They were still in use in 1890.

Washington experienced its worst threat from the Confederates during Jubal Early's raid in July 1864, which cut the city's communication with the North for several days. Clerks and convalescents rushed to the surrounding forts to help militia defend the city until reinforcements from the army arrived.

As the war drew to a close, events such as the fall of Petersburg and then Richmond, quickly followed by the surrender of General Robert E. Lee and the Army of Northern Virginia, led to great celebrations, including the illumination of public and private buildings and the firing of cannon. The excitement came to an abrupt halt when John Wilkes Booth shot President Lincoln at Ford's Theatre on April 14 and the president died the next morning. The city was quickly shrouded in mourning, with most buildings draped in black, as thousands of citizens viewed the body lying in state at the White House and then the Capitol. On April 19 Washington hosted the first of the series of Lincoln funerals that would culminate with his burial in Springfield, Illinois, on May 4. Much of the mourning drapery remained up in Washington until just before the Grand Review, a huge parade by the troops of the eastern armies on May 23 and the western forces on May 24. As the armies disbanded, many hospitals closed, government departments shrank, and the population and overcrowding of Washington also decreased.

See also: Alcohol, Medicinal Uses of; Bull Run (Manassas), First Battle of; Bull Run (Manassas), Second Battle of; Fredericksburg, Battle of; Hospital Buildings; Hospitals, Pavilion; Hospitals, "Pest" (Smallpox); Lincoln, Abraham; Peninsula Campaign; Sanitary Fairs; Smallpox; Vaccination, Smallpox; Whitman, Walt.

Bibliography

Adams, Lois Bryan. *Letter from Washington, 1863–1865,* ed. Evelyn Leasher. Detroit: Wayne State University Press, 1999.

Basler, Roy P. "Did President Lincoln Give the Smallpox to William H. Johnson?" *Huntington Library Quarterly* 35 (May 1972): 279–284.

Brooks, Noah. *Washington, D.C., in Lincoln's Time,* ed. Herbert Mitgang. 1895; reprint, Athens: University of Georgia Press, 1989.

Furgurson, Ernest B. *Freedom Rising: Washington in the Civil War.* New York: Knopf, 2004.

Larsen, Arthur J. *Crusader and Feminist: Letters of Jane Grey Swisshelm, 1858–1865.* St. Paul: Minnesota Historical Society, 1934.

Schultz, Jane E. *Women at the Front: Hospital Workers in Civil War America.* Chapel Hill: University of North Carolina Press, 2004.

Whitman, Walt. *Memoranda During the War.* 1875; reprint, Boston: Applewood, 1990.

WAYSIDE HOSPITALS *See* Hospitals, Wayside.

WESTERN SANITARY COMMISSION

The Western Sanitary Commission (WSC) was an independent Union relief organization founded in St. Louis, Missouri, in September 1861. After the Battle of Wilson's Creek, south of Springfield, Missouri, on August 10, 1861, between 800 and 1,000 wounded soldiers were brought to St. Louis. What small military medical facilities existed were totally unprepared, and the casualties overwhelmed both the military and civilian hospitals.

The Reverend William Greenleaf Eliot, pastor of the Unitarian Church of the Messiah in St. Louis, wanted to establish an organization to coordinate local relief efforts to help the soldiers. His plan was endorsed by Dorothea Dix and by Jessie Benton Frémont, wife of the department commander John C. Frémont. General Frémont established the Western Sanitary Commission by General Orders No. 159 of September 5, 1861. Under the supervision of the departmental medical director and with military cooperation, the commission was to select and prepare suitable buildings for hospital use, provide male and female nurses, improve military camp sanitation, and gather supplies for the troops beyond what the government was able to provide.

The WSC was headed by five commissioners: Eliot; James B. Yeatman, the president, a St. Louis banker and philanthropist; and three other civic leaders in St. Louis. All five were members of Eliot's church. Except for Yeatman, who was from Tennessee, the commissioners were originally from New England and retained connections there that were very useful for commission fund-raising.

The WSC immediately began to have conflicts with the United States Sanitary Commission (USSC), which had been formed in June 1861. Its president, the Reverend Henry W. Bellows, and executive secretary, Frederick Law Olmsted, believed that relief efforts should be centralized for greater efficiency and they were shocked that the WSC refused to submit to their control. They tried to convince Frémont to retract his order. They also attempted to get Secretary of War Simon Cameron and President Abraham Lincoln to force the WSC to become a branch of the USSC, under its control. However, Eliot was able to convince the military and governmental leaders to allow the WSC to remain independent because it was already doing good work. Eliot and his fellow commissioners believed that the situation in Missouri was different from that in the East and that, as a result, one centralized organization could not meet western needs as well as a local association that involved the community in doing its civic duty. Although the WSC remained independent, it did cooperate with the USSC. Nevertheless, there was a great deal of suspicion and friction between the leadership of the two organizations.

The WSC initially worked strictly in Missouri, setting up hospitals for the sick and for convalescents. However, after the fall of Forts Henry and Donelson in February 1862, it expanded its efforts to other areas of the western theater of the war. One of its most important activities in the spring of 1862 was to set up some of the hospital transport boats that served on the Mississippi and other rivers taking sick soldiers and those wounded at the Battle of Shiloh, in the Vicksburg campaign, and in other military operations to general hospitals in St. Louis, Keokuk, Iowa, and other towns. The WSC also established a series of wayside soldiers' "homes," which met the needs of more than 420,000 soldiers in transit to or from their regiments.

In addition to caring for soldiers, the WSC sought to help refugees, white and black, who had fled areas of battle, flooding St. Louis and surrounding regions. The WSC established nine schools for about 3,000 refugee children (white and black) in several towns. The WSC agents who accompanied the armies also sought to help the freedmen by setting up hospitals, providing training opportunities, and improving their camp conditions.

The St. Louis Ladies Union Aid Society, organized in July 1861, was one of the principal groups supplying the WSC. Many other groups also raised funds through benefit concerts, exhibits, and other entertainments. The largest fund-raising effort for the WSC was the Mississippi Valley Sanitary Fair, held in St. Louis from May 17 to June 18, 1864. Similar to other sanitary fairs in featuring exhibits, entertainment, food, and raffles, the St. Louis fair was the third most profitable (behind the fairs held in Philadelphia and New York City), raising $554,591 after expenses.

The WSC did not confine its fund-raising efforts to the western part of the country, however. The commissioners' New England connections brought many contributions from that region, much to the exasperation of the USSC. The WSC leaders explained that because they cared for soldiers who came from all regions of the country, they felt entitled to collect funds outside the west. By the end of the war the WSC had raised $771,000 in cash and $3.5 million in supplies.

The WSC did not disband at the end of the Civil War, but used its leftover funds for philanthropic activities in the St. Louis area. When Eliot died in 1886, the remaining money was given to a nursing school.

See also: Bellows, Henry Whitney; Hospital Ships; Hospitals, General; Hospitals, Wayside; Nurses; Olmsted, Frederick Law; Sanitary Fairs; Sanitation; Shiloh, Battle of; United States Sanitary Commission; Women's Hospital Auxiliaries and Relief Societies.

Bibliography
Binder, Robert Patrick. "'This Noble and Philanthropic Enterprise': The Mississippi Valley Sanitary Fair of 1864 and the Practice of Civil War Philanthropy." *Missouri Historical Review* 95 (January 2001): 117–139.

Parrish, William E. "The Western Sanitary Commission." *Civil War History* 36 (March 1990): 17–35.

WHISKEY *See* Alcohol, Medicinal Uses of.

WHITMAN, WALT (1819–1892)

Poet Walt Whitman, visitor at and observer of Union hospitals during the Civil War, was born May 31, 1819, on Long Island, New York, the second of the nine children of Walter and Louisa Van Velsor Whitman. Young Walt grew up in Brooklyn and attended a charity school due to the poverty of his family (and possible alcoholism of his father). He left school at age eleven and worked as an office boy for several attorneys before getting a job in a printing office. He taught school from 1836 to 1841, but printing, journalism, and writing essays and poetry would be his main occupations thereafter.

Although Whitman wrote both poetry and prose earlier, the first surviving examples of his work date from 1838. Throughout his career many of his writings were not signed, leading to debates among Whitman scholars over some pieces that he *might* have written. Whitman published the first edition of his most famous work, the poetry collection *Leaves of Grass*, in 1855, setting the type himself. The poems, which created controversy and offended many (at the time and since) because of their sexuality and their lack of rhyme, have also been considered by critics to be a watershed in American poetry. The collection went through six American editions during the author's lifetime (the last in 1881), to each of which Whitman added more poems. Recent biographers have made much of Whitman's alleged homosexuality as displayed in his poetry, but hardly any of his nineteenth-century contemporaries noticed this, nor were there any scandals about his relationships with men. Close male friendships were viewed from an entirely different perspective during the period.

When the Civil War began, Whitman was unemployed, suffering from personal depression, and hanging out with New York carriage drivers or with a group of bohemian authors and artists in Pfaff's beer cellar. He did not enlist in the military nor did he work with any of the voluntary associations such as the U.S. Sanitary Commission or the Christian Commission. After his brother, First Lieutenant George Washington Whitman of the Fifty-First New York Infantry, was wounded at Fredericksburg in December 1862, Walt Whitman went in search of him. George was only slightly wounded, but what Walt saw of the troops and the hospitals gave him a sense of mission. Supported by his wages for part-time clerical work in Washington, the income from occasional published articles and poems, and by donations from friends in Brooklyn and elsewhere, Whitman became a regular visitor at many of the hospitals in Washington. He was neither a nurse nor a missionary. Instead, his goal was to bring comfort and cheer by his presence and through small gifts. The items he distributed included paper, envelopes, stamps, pencils, fruit, cookies, pickles, horehound candy, books, jelly, handkerchiefs, underwear, socks, combs, toothbrushes, soap, towels, brandy, ice cream, magazines, fruit syrups, tobacco, and small amounts of money (usually five to fifty cents). He tried to meet special requests, in one case bringing a patient a rice pudding.

Whitman estimated that between the end of 1862 and the end of the war in 1865 he made 600 visits, ministering in some way to between 80,000 and 100,000 sick and wounded troops. These visits might last from an hour to staying all night by the bedside of a restless or dying patient. Whitman cared for anyone in need of his help, whether Union soldiers, hospitalized Confederates, or blacks in nearby contraband camps ("contraband" was a nickname for escaped slaves). Whitman usually visited hospitals in the afternoon and the evening as well as on Sunday. Most patients were glad to see him and hospital staff members welcomed his visits.

During the war Whitman took copious notes on his experiences, some of which were published as *Memoranda During the War* (1875) and in *Specimen Days* (1882). He also wrote a number of poems that were published in *Drum-Taps* (1865).

After the war was over, Whitman continued to visit the hospitals in Washington until the last one closed. Even then he stayed on in Washington, working as a government clerk until he suffered a stroke in January 1873 and moved to Camden, New Jersey, where his brother George lived. Whitman continued to write and publish both poetry and prose. He had certain faithful supporters, but his work still excited controversy. Whitman died in Camden on March 26, 1892, of bronchial pneumonia. Apparently this was a complication of tuberculosis, which he had contracted during the war.

See also: Fredericksburg, Battle of; Hospital Buildings; Hospital Support Staff; Hospitals, General; Tuberculosis; United States Christian Commission; United States Sanitary Commission; Washington, DC.

Bibliography

Loving, Jerome. *Walt Whitman: The Song of Himself.* Berkeley: University of California Press, 1999.

Morris, Roy, Jr. *The Better Angel: Walt Whitman in the Civil War.* New York: Oxford University Press, 2000.

Whitman, Walt. *Memoranda During the War.* 1875; reprint, Boston: Applewood, 1990.

WITTENMYER, ANNIE TURNER (1827–1900)

Annie Turner Wittenmyer, a Union relief worker, was born on August 26, 1827, in Sandy Springs, Ohio, one of at least six children of John G. and Elizabeth Smith Turner. She was well educated for her era. In 1847 she married William Wittenmyer, a wealthy merchant some years her senior. The couple moved from Ohio to

Keokuk, Iowa, in 1850. They had four or five children, but only one son survived infancy. William Wittenmyer died sometime in the 1850s, leaving his widow and son in comfortable circumstances.

Even before the Civil War began, Wittenmyer was involved with service to the needy. She began and taught at a free school for Keokuk children whose families were unable to afford the cost of education. She also started a Sunday school that grew into the Chatham Square Methodist Episcopal Church in Keokuk.

When the Civil War began, Keokuk was a convenient point from which to send Iowa soldiers to the front, but it also became a place to which sick and wounded soldiers returned for hospitalization. Wittenmyer and other local women, realizing that their individual efforts were inadequate, organized the Keokuk Ladies' Soldiers' Aid Society on May 31, 1861, to pool their resources. Wittenmyer became corresponding secretary for the group. Besides providing for soldiers in local hospitals, the aid society also supplied other Iowa soldiers further afield, so it sent Wittenmyer on a fact-finding trip. Leaving her son in Keokuk with her mother and sister, Wittenmyer made numerous trips, taking clothing, bedding, medicine, and food to the hospitalized soldiers and reporting back to Keokuk what further supplies were necessary.

Other women's relief groups that formed in Iowa began sending their supplies to the front through Keokuk and Wittenmyer. Iowa governor Samuel J. Kirkwood formed the Iowa Army Sanitary Commission on October 13, 1861. He appointed thirteen prominent men as leaders, completely ignoring the work that the women had been doing. The women's groups were then ordered to report and send their funds to the new organization. The Keokuk ladies and their supporters refused to do so, leading to several years of conflict and confusion between the competing relief groups. Wittenmyer also suffered much personal opposition from the new group.

Meanwhile, as an appointed state relief agent, Wittenmyer traveled extensively, taking supplies wherever they were needed. She did not hesitate to visit field hospitals under fire and to report bad conditions to generals who could have hospitals moved. She nursed soldiers, saw that they were properly fed, and provided spiritual encouragement as well. In October 1863, Wittenmyer proposed a plan for an asylum for Iowa soldiers' orphans, which was soon established in Farmington.

In December 1863, Wittenmyer had the idea of developing special diet kitchens in the hospitals. The following May, she resigned as Iowa sanitary agent and became diet kitchen supervisor under the auspices of the Christian Commission. Based on the argument that for most patients proper diet was more important than medicine, the special diet kitchens were designed to prepare the food appropriate for the very sick and severely wounded. Wittenmyer compiled a cookbook for use in these kitchens. Under the command of the surgeon in charge of the hospital, each diet kitchen was to have two female managers to supervise the cooks. In a large hospital, the women would supervise twenty to thirty men, usually convalescents or partly disabled soldiers, cooking and serving food for up to 1,800 patients, three times a day. Although some surgeons objected to women being anything more than cooks or servants, the diet kitchens were mostly successful. More than 100 were established by the end of the war and credited with saving the lives of thousands of soldiers. After the war ended, the diet kitchens were closed by August 15, 1865.

For several years after the war, Wittenmyer managed a second orphan's home, established in Davenport, Iowa. Then, in 1870, she moved to Philadelphia, where, for eleven years, she published *Christian Woman*, a periodical devoted to temperance and moral living. She became even more involved in the temperance movement when she served as the first president of the Women's Christian Temperance Union (1874–1879). She was one of the first to join the Grand Army of the Republic's auxiliary, the Woman's Relief Corps, when it was organized in 1883, and became its president in 1889. Wittenmyer was instrumental in persuading Congress to pass a bill on August 5, 1892, granting pensions to Civil War nurses. Any woman who could document having served for at least six months could receive a pension of twelve dollars per month. By this time, Wittenmyer was herself in some need, and Congress passed a special bill in 1898 granting her a pension of twenty-five dollars a month.

In 1895 Wittenmyer published an account of her wartime experiences called *Under the Guns*. She died at her home in Saratoga, Pennsylvania, on February 2, 1900.

See also: Convalescents; Cooks; Diet, of Hospital Patients; United States Christian Commission; Women, as Hospital Workers; Women's Hospital Auxiliaries and Relief Societies.

Bibliography
Brunk, Quincelea Ann. "Forgotten by Time: An Historical Analysis of the Unsung Lady Nurses of the Civil War." PhD dissertation, University of Texas at Austin, 1992.

Leonard, Elizabeth D. *Yankee Women: Gender Battles in the Civil War.* New York: Norton, 1994.

Wittenmyer, Annie. *Under the Guns: A Woman's Reminiscences of the Civil War.* Boston: E.B. Stillings, 1895.

WOMAN'S CENTRAL ASSOCIATION OF RELIEF

The Woman's Central Association of Relief was instrumental in originating and supplying the U.S. Sanitary Commission during the Civil War. The association began in New York City in April 1861, just after the Civil War broke out. Dr. Henry W. Bellows, a Unitarian minister in New York; Dr. Elisha Harris, the superintendent of the quarantine hospital on Staten Island; and Dr. Elizabeth Blackwell, the first woman to receive a medical degree, were important organizers of the association. These three met with about fifty locally prominent women at the New York

Infirmary for Women in late April in order to discuss how they might be able to aid the troops. They issued a call for a larger meeting.

The next meeting, held at the Cooper Institute (or Cooper Union) on April 29, attracted between 3,000 and 4,000 women. As was customary at the time, men led the meeting, even though the purpose was to create a women's organization. Dr. Bellows prepared the constitution and ninety-two women signed it. In addition to choosing a name, the women approved a three-part purpose: to act as an auxiliary to the army and hospital medical staff, to gather supplies for the troops at a central depot, and to train women nurses for hospital work. To carry out their plan, the association appointed an executive committee, a registration committee, and a finance committee, all of which had both male and female members.

Shortly after the meeting, Bellows and Harris, with several other men, went to Washington, DC, to examine the medical situation. Because medical care and camp sanitation were so poor, the group developed a plan to organize the U.S. Sanitary Commission and persuaded President Abraham Lincoln to establish it in June 1861. Most historical accounts that mention the Woman's Central Association stop after giving it credit for originating the Sanitary Commission.

In fact, the Woman's Central Association of Relief continued to operate throughout the war as one of the largest suppliers of the Sanitary Commission. The association soon expanded by forming auxiliaries outside New York City, establishing a network that collected supplies in eastern and central New York, Connecticut, Rhode Island, northern New Jersey, Massachusetts, and Vermont, as well as Canada and Europe.

The registration committee was supposed to select the most qualified female applicants for special nurses' training, oversee that training in the hospitals of New York City, outfit the women with supplies, and get them to the places where they were most needed. Dr. Blackwell was in charge of this committee. The original idea was that after a few weeks of training, the women selected, largely from the upper class, would be prepared to instruct and supervise the male soldier nurses. However, in practice, these women tended to be poorly treated in the military medical system. The association did send thirty-two nurses to military hospitals through November 1861, but ceased the training program after that.

The Woman's Central Association of Relief had its office at No. 10 Cooper Union, where Louisa Lee Schuyler served as executive secretary. At the office, volunteers unpacked the supplies that had arrived, sorted them into categories, and repacked them in boxes containing a single type of item. The women carefully kept a series of books recording what supplies had been received, what boxes they had been repacked in, and how many of each type of item were available to send to the Sanitary Commission for distribution.

Throughout the war the women of the association devised various ways to keep supplies coming in. For example, they urged each local association to send a box a month to the headquarters, labeled for distribution to whoever needed it most, rather than to the soldiers of any particular location or state.

In addition, the association published a pamphlet and sent out speakers to encourage contributions.

Ironically, the sanitary fairs, which became popular fund-raisers for the Sanitary Commission later in the war, actually slowed down the process of getting supplies because preparing for the fairs occupied the women's time and energy. Nevertheless, the Woman's Central Association of Relief accomplished a prodigious amount of work. Between May 1, 1861, and July 7, 1865, it collected and sent 291,475 shirts to the field, as well as numerous other supplies. In all, the women shipped nearly 19,000 boxes to the Sanitary Commission. The Woman's Central Association of Relief disbanded on July 7, 1865.

See also: Bellows, Henry Whitney; Dix, Dorothea Lynde; Nurses; Sanitary Fairs; United States Sanitary Commission; Women's Hospital Auxiliaries and Relief Societies; Woolsey Sisters.

Bibliography

Curtis, Julia B. "Woman's Central Association of Relief." In *Women's Work in the Civil War: A Record of Heroism, Patriotism, and Patience*, ed. L.P. Brockett and Mary C. Vaughan, 527–539. Philadelphia: Zeigler, McCurdy, 1867.

WOMEN, AS DOCTORS

Only a tiny group of women served as doctors during the Civil War. Cultural sensibilities of the period saw women, at least white women of the middle and upper classes, as delicate, fragile creatures who needed to be protected from the horrors of war, including the sad and gruesome scenes in hospitals. In addition, it was considered inappropriate for women to deal with the intimate bodily needs of men to whom they were not related. Women who wanted to aid their cause, North or South, by caring for sick and wounded soldiers had enough difficulty getting positions as nurses, though eventually nursing was accepted as a natural, nurturing activity for women, an outgrowth of the duties in their traditional sphere. But female doctors stretched, and even went beyond, the boundaries of cultural acceptability. At the time of the Civil War, there were only about 200 women doctors in the United States, most of whom had earned their degrees from sectarian (such as homeopathic or eclectic) medical schools, which were more likely to admit female students than the "regular" schools. Elizabeth Blackwell, the first female medical graduate, had earned her degree in 1849, only twelve years before the war. People were not yet accustomed to female doctors, most of whom confined their practice to treating women and children.

Another issue confronting women doctors was the matter of control. The male medical establishment felt threatened by competent women. Military medical men were even more threatened than civilian doctors because women doctors would have rank and command over men. The military blocked most female doctors' attempts to serve, sometimes by rejecting their non-"regular" medical credentials.

Mary Edwards Walker persistently and aggressively sought a military medical commission in the Union army, beginning in the fall of 1861. After serving in several unpaid volunteer capacities but refusing to work as a nurse, Walker finally received a succession of contract assistant surgeon posts, beginning in 1864, though only one involved service with troops in the field. She was the only woman hired as a doctor by the military during the Civil War, although she did not receive a commission.

In addition to Walker, seven women doctors are known to have served the Union army and two the Confederate, mostly working as nurses or volunteers. Sarah Chadwick Clapp was an assistant surgeon to the Seventh Illinois Cavalry for nine or ten months, some of them spent in the hospitals of Cairo, Illinois. However, because she was a woman, the state medical examining board refused to give her an examination, so she was neither commissioned nor paid.

Next to Walker, Esther Hill Hawks is the woman doctor about whom most is known because her diary has been published. A graduate of the New England Female Medical College (1857), she followed her husband, John Milton Hawks, a regimental doctor with the U.S. Colored Troops, to the South Carolina Sea Islands and Florida, where she cared for the wounded after the attack on Fort Wagner (South Carolina) and the Battle of Olustee (or Ocean Pond, Florida), as well as the freedmen living on the Sea Islands. She spent most of her time, however, as a teacher.

Chloe Annette Buckel, a graduate of the Women's Medical College of Pennsylvania, practiced at hospitals for women and children in New York and Chicago before the war. During the war she worked as a nurse with the Indiana Sanitary Commission, recruiting and supervising nurses, setting up field hospitals, and finally serving as chief nurse at the Jefferson General Hospital in Jeffersonville, Indiana. Mary Frame Thomas Myers also worked as a nurse for the Indiana Sanitary Commission.

Susan Edson, an 1854 graduate of the Cleveland Homeopathic College, and Caroline Brown Winslow, who graduated from the Western College of Homeopathy in 1856, worked as nurses in Washington, DC, hospitals (and practiced medicine there after the war). Hettie K. Painter of New Jersey nursed in several hospitals and was reputed to be a Union spy.

Orianna (Orie) Russell Moon, an 1857 graduate of the Female Medical College of Pennsylvania, nursed for the Confederates at the General Hospital in Charlottesville, Virginia. The other Confederate doctor who nursed during the Civil War was Ella Cooper. Although Cooper completed the course at the Medical College of Cincinnati, the school authorities refused to grant her a degree because she was a woman.

Despite almost universal discouragement of women doctors, at least six Civil War nurses found their calling and studied medicine after the Civil War.

See also: Alternative Medicines; Hawks, Esther Hill; Nurses; United States Sanitary Commission; Walker, Mary Edwards; Western Sanitary Commission.

Bibliography

Graf, Mercedes. *A Woman of Honor: Dr. Mary E. Walker and the Civil War.* Gettysburg, PA: Thomas, 2001.

Schultz, Jane E. *Women at the Front: Hospital Workers in Civil War America.* Chapel Hill: University of North Carolina Press, 2004.

Schwartz, Gerald, ed. *A Woman Doctor's Civil War: Esther Hill Hawks' Diary.* Columbia: University of South Carolina Press, 1984, 1989.

Walker, Dale L. *Mary Edwards Walker: Above and Beyond.* New York: Forge, 2005.

WOMEN, AS HOSPITAL WORKERS

Women worked in a variety of roles in the hospitals of both the North and the South. There were essentially four types of women hospital workers: short-term volunteers, often local women who cared for the wounded after a battle; long-term volunteers, often elite women who refused pay and sometimes bought supplies with their own funds; paid employees; and Roman Catholic nuns.

Women's jobs in hospitals clustered around "domestic" tasks that women would perform at home—cooking, cleaning, washing, nursing, and supervising others who were doing domestic work. Who did what jobs mostly depended on a hierarchy of race and class. Women of the upper class tended to be volunteers, working with hospital auxiliaries and relief associations to solicit and provide supplies, and visiting hospitals to dispense treats and necessities. The fairly small number of elite women who went to work in the hospitals usually occupied supervisory positions (called matrons in the South) or served as nurses. They usually refused to accept pay. Many of them, during or after the war, wrote accounts of their wartime work.

Middle-class women might accept pay or volunteer, work in hospitals in supervisory or nursing positions, or participate in relief associations, much as elite women did. Working-class women, a number of them immigrants, did not have the option of volunteering for more than short periods of time because they needed to earn money. Some of these women followed their husbands to the field, serving as laundresses officially, but often nursing sick soldiers in the men's tents or the field hospitals. When these women worked in the general hospitals, they might nurse, but more often they did the cleaning, cooking, or laundry (hospital laundresses were frequently called matrons in the North).

Black women, slave or free, worked in many hospitals. Free black women usually sought jobs voluntarily, although they could be more or less forced into employment in the South. Certain urban slaves were permitted to find jobs on their own and pay a portion of their wages to their master; others, urban and rural, were hired out by their masters or were impressed. Regardless of their possible higher qualifications, black women usually were assigned to cleaning, cooking, and washing jobs. Many of them, however, also nursed soldiers during crisis periods after battles, although they rarely received the title of nurse for doing so.

Women came to hospital work in a number of ways. In the North a sizable minority of women were hired under the auspices of Dorothea Dix, the official superintendent of nurses. Some others came under the sponsorship of local or national relief agencies. In both the North and the South, many women went to hospitals to care for a sick or wounded husband, son, or brother and stayed on to care for others when their patient either got well or died. Some women, hearing of the need through "help wanted" notices, word of mouth, or news of a large number of wounded arriving after a battle, simply turned up at hospitals.

Many surgeons and other male hospital workers did not welcome women to the hospitals. Typically, Victorian women, at least of the upper and middle classes, were considered too delicate for the nasty sights, sounds, and smells of a hospital. Caring for the intimate needs of men (except for male relatives) was regarded as immodest. While many women had nursed sick relatives at home, most had no grasp of the discipline and regulations of an army hospital. Many surgeons resented giving women any authority. Power struggles ensued, as when Phoebe Pember, matron of the second division of Chimborazo Hospital in Richmond, Virginia, took control of the keys to the storeroom where the whiskey barrel was kept.

However, other surgeons welcomed women from the very beginning because they kept the wards clean, provided good food, and improved patient morale with homelike cheer and comfort. Some surgeons who initially rejected women workers came to appreciate the benefits they provided. Others at least appreciated the nuns, who were used to discipline because of their experience in religious communities and were less likely to complain, make demands, or give commands.

Although Southern women were discouraged from working in hospitals throughout the war, such participation by Northern women became more acceptable after 1862. This attitude received a boost from the publication of *Hospital Sketches* by Louisa May Alcott in 1863.

Although the exact number of women who served in Civil War hospitals cannot be known because many Confederate records were destroyed and only limited records were kept for Union volunteers, more than 21,000 Northern women are known to have worked in hospitals in a paid capacity during the Civil War. Many soldiers on both sides owed their lives to the care of women hospital workers.

See also: Alcohol, Medicinal Uses of; Alcott, Louisa May; Blacks, as Hospital Workers; Chimborazo Hospital; Cooks; Dix, Dorothea Lynde; Hospital Support Staff; Laundresses; Matrons; Nuns; Nurses; Pember, Phoebe Yates Levy; Women, as Doctors; Women's Hospital Auxiliaries and Relief Societies. (See also names of individual women.)

Bibliography

Leonard, Elizabeth D. *Yankee Women: Gender Battles in the Civil War.* New York: Norton, 1994.

Schultz, Jane E. *Women at the Front: Hospital Workers in Civil War America.* Chapel Hill: University of North Carolina Press, 2004.

(See also books by and about individual women).

WOMEN'S HOSPITAL AUXILIARIES AND RELIEF SOCIETIES

Women all over the North and South began to form hospital auxiliaries and relief agencies as soon as the Civil War broke out. The earliest known was established in Bridgeport, Connecticut, on April 15, 1861. Some groups were organized with officers and constitutions while others were loose networks of women sending supplies to contacts when a special need arose. Although the exact number of relief societies cannot be known, there were undoubtedly thousands.

While many men and women of the era thought it inappropriate for women to work in hospitals, most saw the task of making or collecting supplies to feed, clothe, and heal soldiers as consistent with women's domestic role. Shirts, underdrawers, sheets, blankets, bandages, wines, jellies, preserved fruits, lemons, and other types of food were among the items women prepared to send to hospitals. In the North most local societies channeled their supplies to a larger agency such as the Woman's Central Association of Relief (New York), the U.S. Sanitary Commission, the Western Sanitary Commission, or the U.S. Christian Commission. These supplies usually traveled a considerable distance from the donors to the recipients.

Although providing relief supplies was considered appropriate "women's work," managing relief agencies was not. Men who did not believe that women were capable of management often interfered with women's leadership. A number of women's organizations had at least some male officers who were often figureheads while the women did the work. In Iowa, where women were managing their relief society with great success, jealous men tried to undercut their work by founding a rival association, causing duplication of effort and confusion.

An important conflict for many women's relief societies concerned the destination of their supplies. Many donors, both North and South, preferred contributing supplies to regiments of local boys or at least to soldiers from the donors' own state. But agencies such as the U.S. Sanitary Commission and some hospitals in the South urged people to send their donations for general use by whatever soldiers needed them most, rather than allowing better care for the soldiers of some states than for others.

While the main purpose of relief organizations was to provide supplies for the troops, women also set up hospital auxiliaries that established and ran hospitals. These organizations were more common in the South, nearer to the battlefields where private homes and other buildings often had to be commandeered and turned into hospitals on very short notice. In addition to providing supplies, the women hired laundresses, nurses, and local doctors to prescribe for the patients. In at least some places, such as the Gordon Hospital in Nashville, Tennessee, female managers came into conflict with military surgeons because of a lack of military discipline, organization, and proper record keeping by the women.

A number of women's auxiliaries functioned quite successfully along main travel routes, especially in the South, where they established wayside hospitals to give short-term rest and refreshment to sick, wounded, and convalescent soldiers traveling to and from furloughs.

See also: Hospital Buildings; Hospitals, Wayside; United States Christian Commission; United States Sanitary Commission; Western Sanitary Commission; Wittenmyer, Annie Turner; Women, as Hospital Workers; Woman's Central Association of Relief; Woolsey Sisters.

Bibliography
Adams, Lois Bryan. *Letter from Washington, 1863–1865*, ed. Evelyn Leasher. Detroit: Wayne State University Press, 1999.

Leonard, Elizabeth D. *Yankee Women: Gender Battles in the Civil War.* New York: Norton, 1994.

Schroeder-Lein, Glenna R. *Confederate Hospitals on the Move: Samuel H. Stout and the Army of Tennessee.* Columbia: University of South Carolina Press, 1994.

Woolsey, Jane Stuart. *Hospital Days: Reminiscence of a Civil War Nurse.* 1868; reprint, Roseville, MN: Edinborough, 1996, 2001.

WOODWARD, JOSEPH JANVIER (1833–1884)

A Union assistant surgeon and author of medical manuals and reports, Joseph Janvier Woodward was the son of Joseph Janvier Woodward Sr. and his wife, Elizabeth Graham Cox Woodward. The younger Joseph was born on October 30, 1833, in Philadelphia. He graduated from Central High School with a Bachelor of Arts degree in 1850. After studying medicine privately with George B. Wood, a professor at the University of Pennsylvania medical school, Woodward enrolled there and received his medical degree in 1853. Because he was still too young to practice medicine (younger than twenty-one), Woodward returned to Central High School, where he received a Master of Arts and graduated as valedictorian in 1855.

By that time, Woodward was practicing medicine in Philadelphia, as well as conducting study classes for medical students and teaching them how to use a microscope to study pathological (diseased) anatomy. Woodward was one of the first researchers to use photomicrography (taking photographs through a microscope). In the late 1850s he wrote and delivered a number of papers on cancer as a result of his research.

When the Civil War began, Woodward enlisted as an assistant surgeon on August 5, 1861. He served with an artillery regiment in the Army of the Potomac until May 1862, when he was assigned to the surgeon general's office. Also in that month, Surgeon General William A. Hammond established the Army Medical Museum to collect medical and surgical specimens and to prepare *The Medical and Surgical History of the War of the Rebellion*. In Circular No. 5 of June 9, 1862, he appointed Woodward to prepare the medical part of that history.

In addition, Woodward wrote two helpful manuals. The first, *The Hospital Steward's Manual*, published in late 1862, gave instructions in all aspects of the duties of hospital stewards, ward masters, nurses, and other attendants. It even included a selection of recipes for hospital cooking developed during the Crimean War by chef Alexis Soyer. Woodward's other book, *Outlines of the Chief Camp Diseases of the United States Armies: As Observed During the Present War* (1863), was based on his own experiences and the statistics gathered through June 30, 1862, by the surgeon general's office. Besides discussing the causes of disease, Woodward analyzed the various camp fevers, diarrhea, measles, catarrh, and pneumonia.

Woodward was one of the two doctors who performed the postmortem examination on President Abraham Lincoln after he was assassinated in April 1865. Once the war was over, Woodward continued preparing reports and, eventually, the first two volumes of *The Medical and Surgical History*, published in 1870 and 1879. The volumes were well illustrated with lithographs and engravings, some based on Woodward's photomicrography. He also planned the exhibit for the army medical department and museum for the 1876 centennial exposition in Philadelphia.

By 1860 Woodward had married his first wife, Eva, by whom he had a son and a daughter. Eva evidently died during the 1860s, for by 1870 he was married to Blanche Wendell of Washington, DC. They had two sons and a daughter.

Woodward continued his research and writing, but by 1875 he began to have serious health problems, causing him to take some months of leave in order to recover. After President James A. Garfield was shot and wounded on July 2, 1881, Woodward provided medical care until the president died on September 19. Following Garfield's death, there was much controversy about Woodward's treatment, leading to a further decline in Woodward's own health, this time mental as well as physical.

In 1883 Woodward was in such a severe state of chronic depression that he was confined in a mental institution in Pennsylvania. There, on August 17, 1884, he committed suicide by jumping off a balcony.

See also: Army Medical Museum; Brinton, John Hill; Catarrh; Diarrhea and Dysentery; Diet, of Hospital Patients; Fevers; Hammond, William Alexander; Lincoln, Abraham; *The Medical and Surgical History of the War of the Rebellion*; Stewards, Hospital; Surgeon General; Ward Masters.

Bibliography

Henry, Robert S. *The Armed Forces Institute of Pathology: Its First Century, 1862–1962.* Washington, DC: Government Printing Office, 1964.

Woodward, Joseph Janvier. *The Hospital Steward's Manual: For the Instruction of Hospital Stewards, Ward-Masters, and Attendants, in Their Several Duties.* Philadelphia: J.B. Lippincott, 1862; reprint, San Francisco: Norman, 1991.

———. *Outlines of the Chief Camp Diseases of the United States Armies, as Observed During the Present War.* Philadelphia: J.B. Lippincott, 1863; reprint, San Francisco: Norman, 1992.

WOOLSEY SISTERS

The Woolsey sisters, members of a wealthy, close-knit New York family, served as nurses and hospital administrators during and after the Civil War. Charles William Woolsey (1802–1840) married Jane Eliza Newton (1801–1874) in 1827. They had seven daughters and a son: Abby (1828–1893), Jane (1830–1891), Mary (1832–1864), Georgeanna (1833–1906), Eliza (1835–1917), Harriet (1837–1878), Caroline (1838–1914), and Charles (1840–1907). Charles Woolsey Sr. died in a steamer accident just before the birth of his son, when his oldest daughter was only eleven. His wife was a very resourceful woman who raised the children, aided by relatives. All the children were well educated; participated in the musical, literary, and religious life of New York City; and had strong political, abolitionist, and Unionist views.

The family had participated in philanthropic activities before the Civil War, so it was quite natural for the sisters to become involved with the Woman's Central Association of Relief, a predecessor of the U.S. Sanitary Commission, organized in New York City in April 1861. The Woolsey women made bandages and hospital clothes and collected other supplies at their home for the Sanitary Commission to send to the field. Abby, who had a talent for organization, worked hard to provide and ship supplies throughout the war.

Georgeanna was one of the first women to be accepted for basic nurses training in New York City hospitals in May 1861. She and Eliza went to Washington, DC, where they worked in a camp tent hospital, delivered supplies to other hospitals, and nursed patients in the storeroom of the U.S. Patent Office among the models of various patented devices. The two sisters inspected area hospitals for the Woman's Central Association and helped new nurses get properly oriented. They also served on the *Daniel Webster*, the first hospital transport in the eastern theater. Georgeanna worked on other transport ships as well for about six months in 1862. After Eliza's husband, Joseph Howland, was wounded at Gaines's Mill on June 27, 1862, Eliza went home with him to New York, ending her nursing career.

Jane, after initially working to gather relief supplies, first became involved with nursing soldiers brought to hospitals in New York City. Beginning in January 1863, Jane and Georgeanna served for some months at a hospital in Newport, Rhode Island. Georgeanna and her mother cared for patients at Gettysburg during the summer of 1863. Georgeanna wrote about their experiences in a small book called

Three Weeks at Gettysburg, which was sold at the New York sanitary fair to raise funds for the Sanitary Commission.

Georgeanna and Jane nursed at Point Lookout Hospital in Maryland before the area became a prisoner of war camp. Then, in the fall of 1863, they became superintendents of nursing at the hospital in Fairfax Theological Seminary near Alexandria, Virginia. Jane remained there, managing the nursing staff and the special diet kitchen, until the hospital closed in August 1865. After the war, she published an account of these experiences called *Hospital Days* (1868). In 1864 Georgeanna moved from the Fairfax hospital to work with the wounded from the battles around Spotsylvania Courthouse in Virginia and then at a hospital in Beverly, New Jersey.

Even the youngest Woolsey sisters participated in nursing efforts. Harriet and Caroline both worked in New York City hospitals on occasion. In the spring of 1862 Harriet and her mother worked for about three months in Washington, DC, hospitals. In 1864 Caroline worked with Georgeanna at the hospital in New Jersey. Only Mary, among the Woolsey sisters, seems not to have been directly involved with nursing. She was married with several young children and died suddenly in 1864.

After the war Abby, Jane, and Georgeanna were able to put their nursing and administrative experience to good use. Abby helped to found the Bellevue Training School for Nurses, attached to Bellevue Hospital in New York City. She served on numerous boards and committees and was the librarian of the school for twelve years. After four years of teaching at a freedmen's school, Jane was the resident director (manager) of Presbyterian Hospital of New York City, from 1872 to 1876. However, she became a semi-invalid as a result of a bout with rheumatic fever. Georgeanna and her husband, Dr. Frank Bacon, were instrumental in establishing and nurturing the growth of the Connecticut Training School for Nurses at New Haven Hospital.

The Woolsey women had a remarkable record as nurses and hospital administrators during the Civil War and in developing nursing as a profession for women in the postwar period.

See also: Cooks; Diet, of Hospital Patients; Hospital Ships; Hospital Support Staff; Nurses; Sanitary Fairs; United States Sanitary Commission; Woman's Central Association of Relief; Women, as Hospital Workers.

Bibliography

Austin, Anne L. *The Woolsey Sisters of New York: A Family's Involvement in the Civil War and a New Profession (1860–1900)*. Philadelphia: American Philosophical Society, 1971.

Bacon, Georgeanna Woolsey, and Eliza Woolsey Howland. *My Heart Toward Home: Letters of a Family During the Civil War*. 1898; reprint, ed. Daniel John Hoisington. Roseville, MN: Edinborough, 2001.

Woolsey, Jane Stuart. *Hospital Days: Reminiscence of a Civil War Nurse*. 1868; reprint, Roseville, MN: Edinborough, 1996, 2001.

 CHRONOLOGY

1842		Dr. Crawford Long uses ether as anesthetic during surgery in Georgia
1846	October 16	First public use of ether as anesthetic, by Dr. William T.G. Morton in Boston
1847		Dr. James Young Simpson introduces chloroform
1853–1856		Crimean War waged by Russia against Turkey, Britain, and France
1854, fall– 1856, July		Florence Nightingale works as nurse and administrator in the Crimea
1855–1857		Alexis Benoit Soyer perfects hospital cooking recipes
1859	February	Daniel E. Sickles shoots and kills his wife's lover, Philip Barton Key
	April 26	Sickles acquitted of murder using a temporary insanity defense
	December	Florence Nightingale's *Notes on Nursing* is published
1860	November 6	Abraham Lincoln elected president of the United States
	December 20	South Carolina secedes from the United States
1861	January 9	Mississippi secedes from the United States
	January 10	Florida secedes from the United States
	January 11	Alabama secedes from the United States
	January 19	Georgia secedes from the United States
	January 26	Louisiana secedes from the United States
	February 1	Texas secedes from the United States
	February 4	Convention of seceded states meets in Montgomery, Alabama

1861	February 9	Jefferson Davis elected provisional president of the Confederate States of America (CSA)
	February 18	Davis inaugurated as president of CSA
	February 26	CSA Congress passes act establishing army medical department
	March 4	Abraham Lincoln inaugurated as president of United States
	April 12–14	CSA attacks Fort Sumter in Charleston harbor, beginning the Civil War; CSA uses barge as hospital ship there
	April 14	One soldier killed and several wounded by gunpowder explosion when firing salute during evacuation of Fort Sumter
	April 15	Earliest known women's relief society established in Bridgeport, Connecticut
	April 17	Virginia secedes from the United States
	April 19	President Abraham Lincoln announces blockade of CSA; citizens of Baltimore attack troops on way to Washington, DC: twelve civilians and four soldiers die, thirty soldiers wounded; Clara Barton, in Washington, nurses soldiers wounded in Baltimore; Dorothea Dix volunteers herself and other women to nurse soldiers
	April 25	Preliminary meeting in New York City about organizing to provide supplies for soldiers
	April 29	Woman's Central Association of Relief organized in New York City
	May 6	David C. DeLeon appointed acting CSA surgeon general; Arkansas and Tennessee secede from the United States
	May 15	U.S. surgeon general Thomas Lawson dies
	May 20	CSA Congress votes to make Richmond, Virginia, the national capital; North Carolina secedes from the United States
	May 21	CSA Congress passes act that prisoners of war should receive same rations as private soldiers
	May 24	Col. Elmer Ellsworth shot and killed after lowering a CSA flag in Alexandria, Virginia; his body is embalmed
	May 31	Women in Iowa organize Keokuk Ladies' Soldiers' Aid Society
	June 1	Richard S. Ewell is first CSA officer wounded, in skirmish at Fairfax Court House, Virginia
	June 3	Illinois senator and 1860 Democratic presidential candidate Stephen A. Douglas dies of typhoid fever in Chicago

1861	June 9	Mary Ann "Mother" Bickerdyke arrives in Cairo, Illinois, and begins hospital cleanup; Secretary of War Simon Cameron issues order establishing U.S. Sanitary Commission
	June 10	Dorothea Dix appointed U.S. superintendent of women nurses
	June 12	Sanitary Commission organizational meeting in New York City
	June 13	President Abraham Lincoln approves order establishing Sanitary Commission
	June 20	Frederick Law Olmsted offered position of executive secretary for Sanitary Commission
	July	St. Louis Ladies Aid Society formed
	July	J. Julian Chisolm publishes *A Manual of Military Surgery for the Use of Surgeons in the Confederate Army*
	July 12	CSA acting surgeon general David C. DeLeon resigns
	July 21	First Battle of Bull Run (Manassas), Virginia
	July 22	U.S. Congress creates rank of brigade surgeon
	July 30	Samuel P. Moore appointed CSA acting surgeon general
	August 1	Sally Tompkins opens Robertson Hospital in Richmond
	August 3	U.S. Congress approves establishing corps of medical cadets
	August 10	Battle of Wilson's Creek, Missouri
	August 12	Charles S. Tripler becomes medical director for Army of the Potomac
	September	Ambulance train cars first used by Union army in Missouri
	September	George Gibson, original commissary-general of U.S. Army, dies
	September 5	Gen. John C. Frémont establishes Western Sanitary Commission
	September 9	Sally Tompkins commissioned CSA captain so she can remain in charge of Robertson Hospital
	October	Northwestern Sanitary Commission (branch of U.S. Sanitary Commission) founded in Chicago
	October	Chimborazo Hospital established outside Richmond
	November	Smallpox epidemic among troops and civilians in Washington
	November	First U.S. medical cadets selected
	November 14	Meeting of Young Men's Christian Association delegates in New York City organizes U.S. Christian Commission

1861	Late November	Samuel P. Moore appointed permanent CSA surgeon general
	December	Juliet O. Hopkins establishes two hospitals for Alabama troops in Richmond
	December 23– January 1862	Gen. George B. McClellan ill with typhoid fever
1862	January	James M. Sanderson publishes cookbook for soldiers
	January 11	Simon Cameron resigns as U.S. secretary of war
	January 15	Edwin M. Stanton confirmed as U.S. secretary of war
	February 6	CSA's Fort Henry, in Tennessee, surrenders
	February 7	*City of Memphis* becomes first U.S. hospital transport ship on western rivers
	February 16	CSA's Fort Donelson, in Tennessee, surrenders
	February 20	William Wallace "Willie" Lincoln dies in White House of typhoid fever
	February 22	Inauguration of CSA president Jefferson Davis
	February 25	U.S. troops occupy Nashville, Tennessee
	March	Jane C. Hoge and Mary A. Livermore visit hospitals in Cairo and Mound City, Illinois, and St. Louis, Missouri
	March	Prototype U.S. medicine wagon constructed, design by Jonathan Letterman
	March 3	John Bell Hood promoted to brigadier general and given command of "Hood's Texas Brigade"
	March 7–8	Battle of Pea Ridge (Elkhorn Tavern), Arkansas
	March 9	Battle of ironclads *Monitor* and *Merrimack* at Hampton Roads, Virginia
	March 17	First Army of the Potomac troops leave for Fortress Monroe, Virginia, beginning Peninsula Campaign
	April	Juliet O. Hopkins establishes third hospital for Alabama troops in Richmond
	April 4	Army of the Potomac begins moving up peninsula toward Richmond
	April 5–May 3	Siege of Yorktown, Virginia
	April 6–7	Battle of Shiloh, Tennessee
	April 6	CSA Gen. Albert S. Johnston bleeds to death from wound at Shiloh
	April 14	U.S. surgeon general Clement A. Finley forced to retire

1862	April 16	Law abolishes slavery in Washington; U.S. Congress passes bill reforming army medical department
	April 25	William A. Hammond appointed U.S. surgeon general
	May	CSA Gen. Thomas J. "Stonewall" Jackson and medical director Hunter H. McGuire negotiate exchange of captured U.S. surgeons
	May 4–5	Battle of Williamsburg, Virginia
	May 6	Samuel H. Stout authorized to impress free blacks as cooks and nurses for Chattanooga hospitals
	May 14	Rev. George Bringhurst commissioned first delegate of U.S. Christian Commission
	May 20	President Abraham Lincoln signs Homestead Act
	May 21	U.S. surgeon general William A. Hammond issues Circular No. 2 establishing Army Medical Museum
	May 22–mid-June	Gen. George B. McClellan ill with dysentery
	May 24	CSA cavalry capture 1,500 cases of chloroform from U.S. supply train near Winchester, Virginia
	May 29	CSA forces evacuate Corinth, Mississippi, without a fight
	May 31–June 1	Battle of Seven Pines (Fair Oaks), Virginia
	May 31	CSA Gen. Joseph E. Johnston wounded in Battle of Seven Pines; CSA hospital administrator Juliet O. Hopkins wounded at Battle of Seven Pines
	June 1	Gen. Robert E. Lee replaces Gen. Joseph E. Johnston as commander of Army of Northern Virginia
	June 9	U.S. surgeon general William A. Hammond issues Circular No. 5 assigning Joseph J. Woodward and John H. Brinton to work on *The Medical and Surgical History of the War of the Rebellion*
	June 10	Gen. George B. McClellan proposes to Gen. Robert E. Lee that captured physicians not be treated as prisoners of war; USS *Red Rover* begins service as hospital ship on western rivers
	June 12–15	CSA cavalry under Gen. J.E.B. Stuart ride around the Army of the Potomac
	June 17	Gen. Robert E. Lee agrees that captured physicians should not become prisoners of war
	June 19	Gen. George B. McClellan releases all CSA surgeons held as prisoners; President Abraham Lincoln signs bill prohibiting slavery in U.S. territories

1862	June 25–July 1	Seven Days battles in Virginia
	June 26	Gen. Robert E. Lee releases all captured U.S. surgeons; Battle of Mechanicsville (part of Seven Days)
	June 27	Lafayette Guild becomes medical director for Army of Northern Virginia; Battle of Gaines's Mill (part of Seven Days)
	June 30	Battle of Glendale (Frayser's Farm) (part of Seven Days)
	July 1	Battle of Malvern Hill (part of Seven Days)
	July 2	U.S. Congress abolishes rank of brigade surgeon
	July 4	Jonathan Letterman replaces Charles S. Tripler as medical director for Army of the Potomac
	July 11	President Abraham Lincoln names Gen. Henry W. Halleck as general-in-chief of all U.S. armies
	July 16	U.S. Congress passes act providing soldier amputees with allowance of $50 for artificial arm and $75 for leg
	July 22	U.S. and CSA leaders sign cartel for exchange of prisoners of war
	August 1	John H. Brinton becomes first curator of Army Medical Museum
	August 2	Gen. George B. McClellan orders establishment of ambulance corps for Army of the Potomac
	August 13	Clara Barton arrives on battlefield of Cedar Mountain, Virginia, with supplies
	August 22	Gen. Braxton Bragg makes Samuel H. Stout medical director of all Army of Tennessee (CSA) general hospitals
	August 28	CSA Gen. Richard S. Ewell wounded in left kneecap at Groveton, Virginia
	August 29	Dr. Hunter H. McGuire amputates Ewell's left leg
	August 29–30	Second Battle of Bull Run (Manassas), Virginia
	ca. September	U.S. army establishes convalescent camp at Alexandria, Virginia
	September 7	U.S. surgeon general William A. Hammond's proposal of an ambulance corps for each U.S. army is rejected by Secretary of War Edwin M. Stanton
	September 14	Battle of South Mountain, Maryland; Clara Barton arrives at battlefield with supplies
	September 17	Battle of Antietam, Maryland, bloodiest single day in American history; U.S. medical department uses ambulance corps for first time; Clara Barton brings supplies and nurses patients at Poffenberger farm

1862	September 19	Alexander Gardner and James Gibson photograph Antietam battlefield
	September 20	U.S. army medical department supplies finally begin to arrive at Antietam
	September 22	President Abraham Lincoln issues preliminary Emancipation Proclamation
	October 8	Battle of Perryville, Kentucky
	October 30	Medical director Jonathan Letterman orders Army of the Potomac field hospitals organized by divisions rather than regiments
	November	Women's council of the U.S. Sanitary Commission meets in Washington
	November	U.S. Sanitary Commission establishes patient directory for Washington hospitals
	November–February 1863	Smallpox epidemic in Richmond
	November 7	Gen. George B. McClellan replaced in command of Army of the Potomac by Gen. Ambrose E. Burnside
	November 12	U.S. surgeon general William A. Hammond proposes establishing army medical laboratories based on naval model
	November 25	CSA system of hospital matrons established
	December	A.J. Foard becomes medical director for Department of the West (CSA)
	December	U.S. Congress establishes office of medical inspector general for army
	December 8	Mary Livermore and Jane Hoge become associate managers of Chicago branch of U.S. Sanitary Commission
	December 13	Battle of Fredericksburg, Virginia; Clara Barton works in hospital in Fredericksburg during battle; Louisa May Alcott begins work as nurse at Union Hotel Hospital, Georgetown, DC
	December 18	Phoebe Pember becomes matron of second division of Chimborazo Hospital in Richmond
	December 31 and January 2, 1863	Battle of Murfreesboro (Stone's River), Tennessee
1863	January	Dr. E.A. Flewellen succeeds A.J. Foard as medical director of Army of Tennessee (CSA)

1863	January 1	Curator John H. Brinton issues first catalog of Army Medical Museum specimens; Emancipation Proclamation goes into effect
	January 12	U.S. surgeon general William A. Hammond orders suitable buildings to be found in New York City and Philadelphia to serve as medical laboratories
	January 20	Hannah Ropes, Louisa May Alcott's supervisor, dies of typhoid fever at Union Hotel Hospital in Georgetown
	January 25	Gen. Joseph Hooker replaces Gen. Ambrose Burnside as commander of Army of the Potomac
	February 9	U.S. Congress promotes commissary-general to rank of brigadier general
	March 1	CSA medical department issues supplementary supply table of indigenous remedies
	March 12	CSA establishes post of medical director of hospitals
	March 13	Explosion at CSA ordnance lab in Richmond kills thirty-five workers, mostly women and girls
	March 30	Gen. Ulysses S. Grant orders establishment of ambulance corps in Army of the Tennessee (U.S.)
	April	Gen. Robert E. Lee has an illness from which he never fully recovers
	April	Invalid Corps organized for U.S. army
	April 2	Hungry women in Richmond riot for bread
	April, late	Army medical laboratory opens in Philadelphia
	May 1–4	Battle of Chancellorsville, Virginia
	May 1	CSA Congress orders establishment of wayside hospitals
	May 2	CSA Gen. Thomas J. "Stonewall" Jackson wounded by his own men after reconnaissance at Chancellorsville and has left arm amputated
	May 4	U.S. surgeon general William A. Hammond issues Circular No. 6, removing calomel and tartar emetic from supply table
	May 10	CSA Gen. Thomas J. "Stonewall" Jackson dies of pneumonia
	May 18	U.S. forces begin siege of Vicksburg, Mississippi
	May 22	*The Commonwealth* begins serial publication of Louisa May Alcott's "Hospital Sketches"
	June 27	Gen. Joseph Hooker replaced as commander of U.S. Army of the Potomac by Gen. George G. Meade
	July 1–3	Battle of Gettysburg, Pennsylvania

1863	July 1	U.S. Gen. John F. Reynolds killed by CSA sharpshooter
	July 2	CSA Gen. John Bell Hood wounded in left arm; U.S. Gen. Daniel E. Sickles wounded in right leg, which is amputated
	July 4	Fall of Vicksburg to U.S. forces
	July 18	Fifty-fourth Massachusetts Infantry (black) loses colonel and 25 percent of troops in attack on Fort Wagner near Charleston, South Carolina
	July 22	Camp Letterman tent hospital opens just outside Gettysburg
	August	Louisa May Alcott's *Hospital Sketches* published in book form
	August	Confederate hospitals evacuate Chattanooga
	August	Turner's Lane Hospital for nerve injuries and diseases opens outside Philadelphia
	August, late	Association of Army and Navy Surgeons of the Confederate States founded in Richmond
	September 1	Frederick Law Olmsted resigns as executive secretary of U.S. Sanitary Commission
	September 3	Joseph K. Barnes appointed acting U.S. surgeon general
	September 19–20	Battle of Chickamauga, Georgia
	September 20	CSA Gen. John Bell Hood wounded in right thigh and has leg amputated
	October	Acting U.S. surgeon general Joseph K. Barnes permits women to bypass Dorothea Dix when applying for nursing positions
	October 27– November 7	First sanitary fair held, in Chicago
	November	E.A. Flewellen resigns as medical director of Army of Tennessee (CSA)
	November 19	President Abraham Lincoln delivers Gettysburg Address
	November 19– mid-December	President Abraham Lincoln suffers from varioloid (mild smallpox)
	November 20	Camp Letterman tent hospital at Gettysburg closes
	November 23–25	Battle of Chattanooga, Tennessee
	December– January 1864	Smallpox epidemic in Washington
	December	Annie T. Wittenmyer proposes special diet kitchens for U.S. army hospitals

1863	December 14–21	Sanitary fair in Boston
	December 21 –January 9, 1864	Sanitary fair in Cincinnati
1864		Annie T. Wittenmyer publishes *A Collection of Recipes for the Use of Special Diet Kitchens in Military Hospitals*
	January	Women's council of U.S. Sanitary Commission meets in Washington
	January	Richmond residents organize Association for the Relief of Maimed Soldiers to provide artificial limbs for amputees
	January	*Confederate States Medical and Surgical Journal* begins publication
	January 2	Lemuel J. Bowden, Republican senator from Virginia, dies of smallpox in Washington
	January 10	Construction of Andersonville prison in Georgia begins
	January 19	U.S. surgeon general William A. Hammond is court-martialed
	February	A.J. Foard resumes post of medical director for Army of Tennessee (CSA)
	February 17	CSA Congress establishes Invalid Corps
	February 22 –March 11	Sanitary fair in Brooklyn, New York
	February 22	Sanitary fair opens in Washington
	February 23	Army of Tennessee (CSA) sets up reserve surgical corps
	February 27	First U.S. prisoners of war arrive at Andersonville
	March	Capt. Henry Wirz appointed commandant at Andersonville prison
	March	Orders issued to establish officers' hospital in every U.S. military department
	March 11	U.S. Congress officially establishes ambulance corps for every army
	March 15	CSA surgeon general Samuel P. Moore orders each army to set up reserve surgical corps
	March 18	U.S. army Invalid Corps reorganized as Veteran Reserve Corps; President Abraham Lincoln attends sanitary fair in Washington
	April 4–23	Sanitary fair in New York City, most profitable of the fairs

1864	April 10	Dr. Mary E. Walker captured by CSA and held as prisoner of war
	April 18	President Abraham Lincoln attends sanitary fair in Baltimore
	May 5–7	Battle of the Wilderness, Virginia
	May 7	Gen. William T. Sherman's forces begin moving toward Atlanta
	May 11	CSA cavalryman Gen. J.E.B. Stuart mortally wounded at Battle of Yellow Tavern, Virginia
	May 17–June 18	Mississippi Valley Sanitary Fair in St. Louis
	May 22	Prisoner of war patients at Andersonville move to new hospital
	June 1–3	Battle of Cold Harbor, Virginia
	June 1	U.S. commissary-general of prisoners Col. William Hoffman orders 20 percent reduction in prisoner of war rations
	June 7–28	Great Central Sanitary Fair in Philadelphia
	June 14	CSA Gen. Leonidas Polk, Louisiana Episcopal bishop, killed by cannon ball at Pine Mountain, Georgia
	June 16	President Abraham Lincoln attends sanitary fair in Philadelphia
	June 18	U.S. Col. Joshua L. Chamberlain severely wounded during attack on Rives's Salient at Petersburg, Virginia; Gen. Ulysses S. Grant begins siege of Petersburg
	June 27	Battle of Kennesaw Mountain, Georgia
	June 29	Joseph P. Taylor, U.S. commissary-general, dies
	July	First CSA prisoners of war arrive at Elmira, New York
	July 11–12	CSA Gen. Jubal Early leads raid on Washington area
	July 17	Gen. John Bell Hood succeeds Gen. Joseph E. Johnston in command of CSA Army of Tennessee
	July 18	CSA assistant surgeon Frank M. Dennis dies in ambulance train accident in Georgia
	August 10	Col. William Hoffman, U.S. commissary-general of prisoners, prohibits prisoners of war from purchasing food from sutlers or receiving food packages
	August 18	U.S. surgeon general William A. Hammond dismissed from service after court-martial finds him guilty on trumped-up charges
	August 22	Joseph K. Barnes becomes surgeon general

1864	September	John H. Brinton removed as curator of Army Medical Museum
	September	Dr. Joseph Jones, CSA medical researcher, visits Andersonville prison
	September 2	U.S. forces occupy Atlanta, Georgia
	October 3	Dr. George A. Otis becomes curator of Army Medical Museum
	November 8	Abraham Lincoln reelected president of United States
	November 16	Gen. William T. Sherman's troops begin March to the Sea through Georgia
	November 21	CSA Army of Tennessee begins march toward Tennessee
	November 30	Battle of Franklin, Tennessee, in which five CSA generals are killed and one mortally wounded
	December 15–16	Battle of Nashville, Tennessee
	December 21	U.S. troops occupy Savannah, Georgia
1865	January 15	Fort Fisher, North Carolina, falls to U.S. forces, closing Wilmington, last port open to blockade runners
	February 13	Fire burns army medical laboratory at Astoria, New York
	February 15	Lucius B. Northrop removed as CSA commissary-general
	February 16	Isaac M. St. John appointed CSA commissary-general
	February 25	Joseph E. Johnston replaces John Bell Hood as commander of remnants of CSA Army of Tennessee
	March 4	Second inauguration of President Abraham Lincoln
	March 18	U.S. prisoners of war begin to be shipped from Andersonville, Georgia, for exchange
	March 27	Louisiana Hospital in Richmond selected for use as mental hospital
	March 29	U.S. Gen. Joshua L. Chamberlain wounded in attack on Quaker Road, Virginia
	April 2	Petersburg, Virginia, falls to U.S. forces; CSA government evacuates Richmond; many CSA medical records and March 1865 issue of *Confederate States Medical and Surgical Journal* burn in fires that destroy parts of Richmond
	April 3	U.S. troops occupy Richmond
	April 5	U.S. secretary of state William H. Seward fractures jaw in carriage accident

1865	April 9	Gen. Robert E. Lee surrenders Army of Northern Virginia at Appomattox Court House, Virginia
	April 14	Actor John Wilkes Booth shoots President Abraham Lincoln in the head at Ford's Theatre in Washington; Booth breaks leg while escaping
	April 15	Booth's broken leg set by Dr. Samuel A. Mudd near Bryantown, Maryland; Lincoln dies at 7:22 a.m.; his body autopsied by Dr. Joseph J. Woodward and Edward Curtis, then embalmed
	April 19	Washington funeral service for President Abraham Lincoln
	April 26	Booth shot and killed in tobacco barn in Virginia; Gen. Joseph E. Johnston surrenders Army of Tennessee to Gen. William T. Sherman near Durham Station, North Carolina
	May 4	Abraham Lincoln buried in receiving vault at Oak Ridge Cemetery, Springfield, Illinois; Andersonville prison closes
	May 9– June 30	Eight Lincoln assassination conspirators, including Samuel A. Mudd, tried by military commission in Washington; four sentenced to hang, Mudd and three others sentenced to imprisonment at Fort Jefferson in the Dry Tortugas
	May 10	Jefferson Davis captured near Irwinville, Georgia
	May 23–24	Grand review of U.S. armies in Washington
	July	U.S. Sanitary Commission disbands
	July 7	Woman's Central Association of Relief disbands; four Lincoln assassination conspirators hanged in Washington
	July 11	Last CSA prisoners of war leave prison at Elmira, New York
	July–August	Clara Barton, Dorence Atwater, and others mark prisoner of war graves at Andersonville
	August 23	Trial of Capt. Henry Wirz, commander at Andersonville prison, begins in Washington
	November 10	Andersonville commander Henry Wirz is hanged
1866		U.S. Congress provides free transportation to artificial limb fittings for veteran amputees
	January 25	Dr. Mary E. Walker receives Congressional Medal of Honor for war services
	February 15	North Carolina is first state to provide funds for artificial legs for CSA amputees
	July	U.S. medical cadet corps ends
	December 22	Army Medical Museum moves to new quarters in Ford's Theatre

1867		Dr. Joseph Lister publishes information on antiseptics
1868	June 8	U.S. Congress grants appropriation for publication of 5,000 copies of *The Medical and Surgical History of the War of the Rebellion*
1869	February 8	President Andrew Johnson pardons Dr. Samuel A. Mudd
1870		U.S. Congress provides U.S. veteran amputees with replacement artificial limbs every five years; first volume of *The Medical and Surgical History of the War of the Rebellion* published
1874	May 20–21	Association of Medical Officers of the Army and Navy of the Confederacy founded in Atlanta, Georgia
1879	August	William A. Hammond's court-martial conviction overturned
1892	August 5	Congress passes bill granting pensions to women who served as Civil War nurses
1898	July 20	Association of Medical Officers of the Army and Navy of the Confederacy refounded in Atlanta
1900–1917		*Southern Practitioner* publishes articles on CSA medicine
1917		Congress retracts Dr. Mary E. Walker's Medal of Honor
1977	June 10	President Jimmy Carter signs legislation to reinstate Dr. Mary E. Walker's Medal of Honor
2002		Legal efforts by descendants to have Dr. Samuel A. Mudd declared innocent fail

❧ BIBLIOGRAPHY ❧

Abel, E. Lawrence. "Rattle, Toot, Tweet." *Civil War Times Illustrated* 40 (October 2001): 52–59.

Adams, George Worthington. "Confederate Medicine." *Journal of Southern History* 7 (May 1940): 151–166.

———. *Doctors in Blue: The Medical History of the Union Army in the Civil War.* New York: Schuman, 1952; reprint, Dayton, OH: Morningside, 1985.

Adams, Lois Bryan. *Letter from Washington, 1863–1865,* ed. Evelyn Leasher. Detroit: Wayne State University Press, 1999.

Alcott, Louisa May. *Hospital Sketches.* 1863; reprint, Boston: Applewood, 1986.

Armstrong, Warren B. *For Courageous Fighting and Confident Dying: Union Chaplains in the Civil War.* Lawrence: University Press of Kansas, 1998.

"Artificial Limbs—How to Make Them." *Confederate States Medical and Surgical Journal* 1 (April 1864): 59.

"Association of Army and Navy Surgeons." *Confederate States Medical and Surgical Journal* 1 (January 1864): 13–16.

"Association to Purchase Artificial Limbs for Maimed Soldiers." *Confederate States Medical and Surgical Journal* 1 (March 1864): 44.

Attie, Jeanie. *Patriotic Toil: Northern Women and the American Civil War.* Ithaca, NY: Cornell University Press, 1998.

Austin, Anne L. *The Woolsey Sisters of New York: A Family's Involvement in the Civil War and a New Profession (1860–1900).* Philadelphia: American Philosophical Society, 1971.

Bacon, Georgeanna Woolsey, and Eliza Woolsey Howland. *My Heart Toward Home: Letters of a Family During the Civil War.* 1898; reprint, ed. Daniel John Hoisington. Roseville, MN: Edinborough, 2001.

Baker, Nina Brown. *Cyclone in Calico: The Story of Mary Ann Bickerdyke.* Boston: Little, Brown, 1952.

Barnes, Joseph K., ed. *The Medical and Surgical History of the War of the Rebellion (1861–65).* Washington, DC: Government Printing Office, 1870–1888; reprint, Wilmington, NC: Broadfoot, 1990.

Basler, Roy P., ed. *The Collected Works of Abraham Lincoln.* 10 vols. New Brunswick, NJ: Rutgers University Press, 1953.

———. "Did President Lincoln Give the Smallpox to William H. Johnson?" *Huntington Library Quarterly* 35 (May 1972): 279–284.

Baxter, Colin F. "Dr. James Baxter Bean, Civil War Dentist: An East Tennessean's Victorian Tragedy." *Journal of East Tennessee History* 67 (1995): 34–57.

Beers, Fannie A. *Memories: A Recollection of Personal Experiences During Four Years of War.* Philadelphia: J.B. Lippincott, 1888; reprint, Alexandria, VA: Time-Life, 1985.

Bender, Robert Patrick. "'This Noble and Philanthropic Enterprise': The Mississippi Valley Sanitary Fair of 1864 and the Practice of Civil War Philanthropy." *Missouri Historical Review* 95 (January 2001): 117–139.

Berlin, Jean V., ed. *A Confederate Nurse: The Diary of Ada W. Bacot, 1860–1863.* Columbia: University of South Carolina Press, 1994.

Berman, Gary E. "Civil War Embalming: A Short History." *Journal of Civil War Medicine* 1 (July–August 1997): 3–4.

Billings, John D. *Hardtack and Coffee: The Unwritten Story of Army Life.* Boston: George M. Smith, 1887; reprint, Lincoln: University of Nebraska Press, 1993.

Blustein, Bonnie Ellen. *Preserve Your Love for Science: Life of William A. Hammond, American Neurologist.* Cambridge: Cambridge University Press, 1991.

Boatner, Mark Mayo, III. *The Civil War Dictionary.* New York: David McKay, 1959.

Bollet, Alfred Jay. *Civil War Medicine: Challenges and Triumphs.* Tucson, AZ: Galen, 2002.

Breeden, James O. *Joseph Jones, M.D.: Scientist of the Old South.* Lexington: University Press of Kentucky, 1975.

Bremner, Robert H. "The Impact of the Civil War on Philanthropy and Social Welfare." *Civil War History* 12 (December 1966): 293–303.

Brinton, John H. *Personal Memoirs of John H. Brinton, Civil War Surgeon, 1861–1865.* New York: Neale, 1914; reprint, Carbondale: Southern Illinois University Press, 1996.

Brockett, L.P., and Mary C. Vaughan. *Women's Work in the Civil War: A Record of Heroism, Patriotism, and Patience.* Philadelphia: Zeigler, McCurdy, 1867.

Brooks, Noah. *Washington, D.C., in Lincoln's Time*, ed. Herbert Mitgang. 1895; reprint, Athens: University of Georgia Press, 1989.

Brown, Thomas J. *Dorothea Dix: New England Reformer.* Cambridge, MA: Harvard University Press, 1998.

Brumgardt, John R., ed. *Civil War Nurse: The Diary and Letters of Hannah Ropes.* Knoxville: University of Tennessee Press, 1980.

Brunk, Quincealea Ann. "Forgotten by Time: An Historical Analysis of the Unsung Lady Nurses of the Civil War." PhD dissertation: University of Texas at Austin, 1992.

Calcutt, Rebecca Barbour. *Richmond's Wartime Hospitals.* Gretna, LA: Pelican, 2005.

Calhoun, J. Theodore. "Rough Notes of an Army Surgeon's Experience During the Great Rebellion." *Medical and Surgical Reporter*, whole series No. 316; new series vol. 9, no. 6 (November 8, 1862): 149–150; reprint, *Journal of Civil War Medicine* 9 (January–March 2005): 17–18.

"Capt. Sallie Tompkins." *Confederate Veteran* 24 (November 1916): 521, 524.

Carter, Samuel, III. *The Riddle of Dr. Mudd.* New York: Putnam, 1974.

Castel, Albert. "Dead on Arrival: The Life and Sudden Death of General Albert Sidney Johnston." *Civil War Times* (March 1997): 30–37.

Cawood, Hobart G. *The Medical Service at Chickamauga.* Fort Oglethorpe, GA: Chickamauga and Chattanooga National Military Park, 1964.

Chambers, S.R. "On the Treatment of Camp Itch." *Confederate States Medical and Surgical Journal* 2 (January 1865): 10.

Chisolm, John Julian. *A Manual of Military Surgery.* Richmond, VA: West & Johnston, 1861; reprint, San Francisco: Norman, 1989.

Claiborne, John H. "On the Use of Phytolacca Decandra in Camp Itch." *Confederate States Medical and Surgical Journal* 1 (March 1864): 39.

Coco, Gregory A. *A Vast Sea of Misery: A History and Guide to the Union and Confederate Field Hospitals at Gettysburg, July 1–November 20, 1863.* Gettysburg, PA: Thomas, 1988.

Confederate States Medical and Surgical Journal. January 1864–February 1865; reprint, Metuchen, NJ: Scarecrow, 1976; reprint, San Francisco: Norman, 1992.

Cooper, William J., Jr. *Jefferson Davis, American.* New York: Knopf, 2000.

Courtwright, David T. "Opiate Addiction as a Consequence of the Civil War." *Civil War History* 24 (June 1978): 101–111.

Cowen, David L. "Materia Medica and Pharmacology." In *The Education of American Physicians: Historical Essays,* ed. Ronald L. Numbers, 95–121. Berkeley: University of California Press, 1980.

Cozzens, Peter. *This Terrible Sound: The Battle of Chickamauga.* Urbana: University of Illinois Press, 1992.

Cumming, Kate. *Kate: The Journal of a Confederate Nurse, 1862–1865,* ed. Richard Barksdale Harwell. Baton Rouge: Louisiana State University Press, 1959, 1987; reprint, Savannah, GA: Beehive, 1975. Originally published as *A Journal of Hospital Life in the Confederate Army of Tennessee from the Battle of Shiloh to the End of the War: With Sketches of Life and Character, and Brief Notices of Current Events During That Period.* Louisville, KY: John P. Morton, 1866.

Cunningham, H.H. *Doctors in Gray: The Confederate Medical Service.* Baton Rouge: Louisiana State University Press, 1958; reprint, Gloucester, MA: Peter Smith, 1970.

Curtis, Julia B. "Woman's Central Association of Relief." In *Women's Work in the Civil War: A Record of Heroism, Patriotism, and Patience,* ed. L.P. Brockett and Mary C. Vaughan, 527–539. Philadelphia: Zeigler, McCurdy, 1867.

Dammann, Gordon E. "Jonathan A. Letterman, Surgeon for the Soldiers." *Caduceus* 10 (Spring 1994): 23–34.

Daniel, Larry J. *Shiloh: The Battle That Changed the Civil War.* New York: Simon and Schuster, 1997.

Davis, James A. "More Work Than Play: Insights from the Letters of J. Herbert George, Civil War Musician." *Journal of American Culture* 26 (December 2003): 464–473.

Davis, William C. *Battle at Bull Run: A History of the First Major Campaign of the Civil War.* Baton Rouge: Louisiana State University Press, 1977.

———. *Jefferson Davis: The Man and His Hour.* New York: HarperCollins, 1991.

———. *A Taste for War: The Culinary History of the Blue and Gray.* Mechanicsburg, PA: Stackpole, 2003.

Dean, Eric T., Jr. *Shook Over Hell: Post–Traumatic Stress, Vietnam, and the Civil War.* Cambridge, MA: Harvard University Press, 1997.

"Death of Dr. Hunter McGuire." *Southern Practitioner* 22 (October 1900): 466–468.

"Debate on Tetanus." *Confederate States Medical and Surgical Journal* 1 (March 1864): 44–46.

DeLeon, Thomas Cooper. *Four Years in Rebel Capitals.* Mobile, AL: Gossip Printing, 1890; reprint, Alexandria, VA: Time-Life, 1983.

Donald, David Herbert. *Lincoln.* New York: Simon and Schuster, 1995.

Downs, Alan. "'The Responsibility Is Great': Joseph E. Johnston and the War in Virginia." In *Civil War Generals in Defeat,* ed. Steven E. Woodworth, 29–70. Lawrence: University Press of Kansas, 1999.

Duffy, John. *From Humors to Medical Science: A History of American Medicine.* 2nd ed. Urbana: University of Illinois Press, 1993.

Duncan, Louis C. *The Medical Department of the United States Army in the Civil War.* Washington, DC: Author, 1914; reprint, Gaithersburg, MD: Butternut, 1985.

"E.A. Flewellen, M.D." *Southern Practitioner* 24 (April 1902): 207, 209.

Edwards, C.J. "Pneumonia in the Confederate Army." *Southern Practitioner* 33 (September 1911): 478–480.

Engle, Stephen D. "'Thank God, He Has Rescued His Character': Albert Sidney Johnston,

Southern Hamlet of the Confederacy." In *Leaders of the Lost Cause: New Perspectives on the Confederate High Command,* ed. Gary W. Gallagher and Joseph T. Glatthaar, 133–163. Mechanicsburg, PA: Stackpole, 2004.

Fahey, John H. "The Fighting Doctor: Bernard John Dowling Irwin in the Civil War." *North and South* 9 (March 2006): 36–50.

Farr, Warner Dahlgren. "Samuel Preston Moore: Confederate Surgeon General." *Civil War History* 41 (March 1995): 41–56.

Faust, Drew Gilpin. "The Civil War Soldier and the Art of Dying." *Journal of Southern History* 67 (February 2001): 3–38.

———. "'Numbers on Top of Numbers': Counting the Civil War Dead." *Journal of Military History* 70 (2006): 995–1009.

Faust, Patricia L., ed. *Historical Times Illustrated Encyclopedia of the Civil War.* New York: Harper and Row, 1986.

Figg, Laurann, and Jane Farrell-Beck. "Amputation in the Civil War: Physical and Social Dimensions." *Journal of the History of Medicine and Allied Sciences* 48 (October 1993): 454–475.

Fitzpatrick, Michael F. "The Mercy Brigade: Roman Catholic Nuns in the Civil War." *Civil War Times Illustrated* 36 (October 1997): 34–40.

Flannery, Michael A. "Another House Divided: Union Medical Service and Sectarians During the Civil War." *Journal of the History of Medicine* 54 (October 1999): 478–510.

———. *Civil War Pharmacy: A History of Drugs, Drug Supply and Provision, and Therapeutics for the Union and Confederacy.* New York: Pharmaceutical Products Press, 2004.

———. "The Life of a Hospital Steward: The Civil War Journal of Spencer Bonsall." *Pharmacy in History* 42, no. 3–4 (2000): 87–98.

"The Florence Nightingale of the South." *Confederate Veteran* 27 (February 1919): 46.

Foard, Andrew Jackson, file. Personal Papers of Medical Officers and Physicians. Adjutant General's Office. RG 94, National Archives, Washington, DC.

Formento, Felix, Jr. *Notes and Observations on Army Surgery.* New Orleans: L.E. Marchand, 1863; reprint, San Francisco: Norman, 1990.

Forsyth, Henry H., et al. *In Memorium* [Jane C. Hoge]. Chicago: Illinois Printing and Binding, [ca. 1890].

Freemon, Frank R. "The First Neurological Research Center: Turner's Lane Hospital During the American Civil War." *Journal of the History of the Neurosciences* (April 1993): 135–142.

———. *Gangrene and Glory: Medical Care during the American Civil War.* Madison, NJ: Fairleigh Dickinson University Press, 1998; reprint, Urbana: University of Illinois Press, 2001.

———. "Lincoln Finds a Surgeon General: William A. Hammond and the Transformation of the Union Army Medical Bureau." *Civil War History* 33 (March 1987): 5–21.

———. *Microbes and Minié Balls: An Annotated Bibliography of Civil War Medicine.* Rutherford, NJ: Fairleigh Dickinson University Press, 1993.

Furgurson, Ernest B. *Ashes of Glory: Richmond at War.* New York: Knopf, 1996.

———. *Freedom Rising: Washington in the Civil War.* New York: Knopf, 2004.

Gaillard, Edwin S. *The Medical and Surgical Lessons of the Late War.* Louisville, KY: Louisville Journal Job Print, 1868.

Gallagher, Gary W., and Joseph T. Glatthaar, eds. *Leaders of the Lost Cause: New Perspectives on the Confederate High Command.* Mechanicsburg, PA: Stackpole, 2004.

Garraty, John A., and Mark C. Carnes, eds. *American National Biography.* 24 vols. New York: Oxford University Press, 1999.

Gill, Gillian. *Nightingales: The Extraordinary Upbringing and Curious Life of Miss Florence Nightingale.* New York: Ballantine, 2004.

Gillett, Mary C. "Thomas Lawson, Second Surgeon General of the U.S. Army: A Character Sketch." *Prologue* 14 (Spring 1982): 15–24.

Glatthaar, Joseph T. "The Costliness of Discrimination: Medical Care for Black Troops in the Civil War." In *Inside the Confederate Nation: Essays in Honor of Emory M. Thomas,* ed. Lesley J. Gordon and John C. Inscoe, 251–271. Baton Rouge: Louisiana State University Press, 2005.

Gordon, Paul, and Rita Gordon. *Frederick County, Maryland: A Playground of the Civil War.* Frederick, MD: Heritage Partnership, 1994.

Gordon, Ralph C. "Nashville and the U.S. Christian Commission in the Civil War." *Tennessee Historical Quarterly* 55 (Summer 1996): 99–111.

Graf, LeRoy P., Ralph W. Haskins, and Paul H. Bergeron, eds. *The Papers of Andrew Johnson,* vols. 8–15. Knoxville: University of Tennessee Press, 1967–2000.

Graf, Mercedes. *A Woman of Honor: Dr. Mary E. Walker and the Civil War.* Gettysburg, PA: Thomas, 2001.

Gray, Michael P. "Elmira, a City on a Prison-Camp Contract." *Civil War History* 45 (December 1999): 322–338.

Green, Carol C. *Chimborazo: The Confederacy's Largest Hospital.* Knoxville: University of Tennessee Press, 2004.

Greenleaf, Charles R. *A Manual for the Medical Officers of the United States Army.* Philadelphia: J.B. Lippincott, 1864; reprint, San Francisco: Norman, 1992.

Griffith, Lucille. "Mrs. Juliet Opie Hopkins and Alabama Military Hospitals." *Alabama Review* 6, no. 2 (1953): 99–120.

Guild, Pattie. "Journey to and from Appomattox." *Confederate Veteran* 6 (1898): 11–12.

Haller, John S., Jr. *Farmcarts to Fords: A History of the Military Ambulance, 1790–1925.* Carbondale: Southern Illinois University Press, 1992.

———. *Medical Protestants: The Eclectics in American Medicine, 1825–1939.* Carbondale: Southern Illinois University Press, 1994.

Hambrecht, F. Terry. Biographical data on Confederate physicians who died during the American Civil War. Unpublished research in progress from May 20, 2006 update.

Hamilton, Frank Hastings. *A Practical Treatise on Fractures and Dislocations.* Philadelphia: Blanchard & Lea, 1860; reprint, San Francisco: Norman, 1991.

Harmon, William J. "The Lion of the Union: The Pelvic Wound of Joshua Lawrence Chamberlain." *Journal of Civil War Medicine* 6 (April–June 2002): 30–33.

Hasegawa, Guy R. "The Civil War's Medical Cadets: Medical Students Serving the Union." *Journal of the American College of Surgeons* 193 (July 2001): 81–89.

Hasegawa, Guy R., and F. Terry Hambrecht. "The Confederate Medical Laboratories." *Southern Medical Journal* 96 (December 2003): 1221–1230.

Hawk, Alan. "An Ambulating Hospital: or, How the Hospital Train Transformed Army Medicine." *Civil War History* 48 (September 2002): 197–219.

Heitman, Francis B. *Historical Register and Dictionary of the United States Army, From Its Organization, September 29, 1789, to March 2, 1903.* Washington, DC: Government Printing Office, 1903.

Hennessy, John J. *Return to Bull Run: The Campaign and Battle of Second Manassas.* New York: Simon and Schuster, 1993.

Henry, James O. "The United States Christian Commission." *Civil War History* 6 (December 1960): 374–388.

Henry, Robert S. *The Armed Forces Institute of Pathology: Its First Century, 1862–1962.* Washington, DC: Government Printing Office, 1964.

Hoge, Mrs. A.H. *The Boys in Blue; or, Heroes of the "Rank and File."* New York: E.B. Treat, 1867; Chicago: C.W. Lilley, 1867.

Holland, Mary Gardner. *Our Army Nurses: Stories from Women in the Civil War.* 1895, 1897; reprint, Roseville, MN: Edinborough, 1998.

Horigan, Michael. *Elmira: Death Camp of the North.* Mechanicsburg, PA: Stackpole, 2002.

Johns, Frank S., and Anne Page Johns. "Chimborazo Hospital and J.B. McCaw, Surgeon in Chief." *Virginia Magazine of History and Biography* 62, no. 2 (1954): 190–200.

Johnson, Edward C., and Gail R. Johnson, eds. "A Civil War Embalming Surgeon: The Story of Dr. Daniel H. Prunk." *The Director* [National Funeral Directors Association] (January 1970); reprint, *Museum News* [Illinois Funeral Service Foundation] (June 1970): 2–4.

Jones, James Boyd, Jr. "A Tale of Two Cities: The Hidden Battle Against Venereal Disease in Civil War Nashville and Memphis." *Civil War History* 31 (September 1985): 270–276.

Josyph, Peter, ed. *The Wounded River: The Civil War Letters of John Vance Lauderdale, M.D.* East Lansing: Michigan State University Press, 1993.

Kauffman, Michael W. *American Brutus: John Wilkes Booth and the Lincoln Conspiracies.* New York: Random House, 2004.

Kaufman, Martin. "American Medical Education." In *The Education of American Physicians: Historical Essays,* ed. Ronald L. Numbers, 7–28. Berkeley: University of California Press, 1980.

Keneally, Thomas. *American Scoundrel: The Life of the Notorious Civil War General Dan Sickles.* New York: Nan A. Talese/Doubleday, 2002.

Kohl, Rhonda M. "'This Godforsaken Town': Death and Disease at Helena, Arkansas, 1862–63." *Civil War History* 50 (March 2004): 109–144.

Krick, Robert K. "'Snarl and Sneer and Quarrel': General Joseph E. Johnston and an Obsession with Rank." In *Leaders of the Lost Cause: New Perspectives on the Confederate High Command,* ed. Gary W. Gallagher and Joseph T. Glatthaar, 165–203. Mechanicsburg, PA: Stackpole, 2004.

Kunhardt, Dorothy Meserve, and Philip B. Kunhardt Jr. *Twenty Days.* New York: Castle Books, 1965.

Kuz, Julian E., and Bradley P. Bengtson. *Orthopaedic Injuries of the Civil War: An Atlas of Orthopaedic Injuries and Treatments During the Civil War.* Kennesaw, GA: Kennesaw Mountain, 1996.

Larsen, Arthur J. *Crusader and Feminist: Letters of Jane Grey Swisshelm, 1858–1865.* St. Paul: Minnesota Historical Society, 1934.

"The Late Dr. A.J. Foard." *Nashville (TN) Republican Banner,* May 16, 1868.

Lattimer, John K. *Kennedy and Lincoln: Medical and Ballistic Comparisons of Their Assassinations.* New York: Harcourt Brace Jovanovich, 1980.

Leale, Charles A. *Lincoln's Last Hours: Address Delivered Before the Commandery of the State of New York Military Order of the Loyal Legion of the United States.* New York: privately printed, 1909.

Leonard, Elizabeth D. *Yankee Women: Gender Battles in the Civil War.* New York: Norton, 1994.

Lewis, Samuel E. "The Florence Nightingale of the South." *Southern Practitioner* 30 (September 1908): 420–424.

———. "Samuel Preston Moore, M.D., Surgeon General of the Confederate States." *Southern Practitioner* 23 (August 1901): 381–386.

Livermore, Mary A. *My Story of the War.* Hartford, CT, 1887; reprint, New York: Da Capo, 1995.

Long, E.B., and Barbara Long. *The Civil War Day by Day: An Almanac, 1861–1865.* New York: Doubleday, 1971; reprint, New York: Da Capo, 1985.

Loving, Jerome. *Walt Whitman: The Song of Himself.* Berkeley: University of California Press, 1999.

Lowry, Thomas P. *The Story the Soldiers Wouldn't Tell: Sex in the Civil War.* Mechanicsburg, PA: Stackpole, 1994.

Lowry, Thomas P., and Jack D. Welsh. *Tarnished Scalpels: The Court-Martials of Fifty Union Surgeons.* Mechanicsburg, PA: Stackpole, 2000.

Lyon, A.A. "Malingerers." *Southern Practitioner* 26 (September 1904): 558–564.

Maher, Sister Mary Denis. *To Bind Up the Wounds: Catholic Sister Nurses in the U.S. Civil War.* Westport, CT: Greenwood, 1989.

Manlove, Anna Gaut. "Mrs. Ella King Newsom Trader." *Confederate Veteran* 21 (July 1913): 343–344.

Marvel, William. *Andersonville: The Last Depot.* Chapel Hill: University of North Carolina Press, 1994.

Massey, Mary Elizabeth. *Ersatz in the Confederacy: Shortages and Substitutes on the Southern Homefront.* Columbia: University of South Carolina Press, 1952, 1993.

Masson, Ann, and Bryce Reveley. "When Life's Brief Sun Was Set: Portraits of Southern Women in Mourning, 1830–1860." *Southern Quarterly* 27 (Fall 1988): 33–56.

Maust, Roland R. *Grappling with Death: The Union Second Corps Hospital at Gettysburg.* Dayton, OH: Morningside, 2001.

Maxwell, William Quentin. *Lincoln's Fifth Wheel: The Political History of the United States Sanitary Commission.* New York: Longmans, Green, 1956.

McAdams, Benton. *Rebels at Rock Island: The Story of a Civil War Prison.* DeKalb: Northern Illinois University Press, 2000.

McMurry, Richard M. *John Bell Hood and the War for Southern Independence.* Lexington: University Press of Kentucky, 1982.

McNeill, William H. *Plagues and Peoples.* 1976; reprint, New York: History Book Club, 1993.

McPherson, James M. *Battle Cry of Freedom: The Civil War Era.* New York: Oxford University Press, 1988; reprint, New York: Ballantine, 1989.

———. *Crossroads of Freedom: Antietam: The Battle That Changed the Course of the Civil War.* New York: Oxford University Press, 2002.

———. *For Cause and Comrades: Why Men Fought in the Civil War.* New York: Oxford University Press, 1997.

———. *Ordeal by Fire: The Civil War and Reconstruction.* New York: Knopf, 1982.

Middleton, William S. "Turner's Lane Hospital." *Bulletin of the History of Medicine* 40 (January–February 1966): 14–42.

Miers, Earl Schenck. *Lincoln Day by Day.* Washington, DC: Lincoln Sesquicentennial Commission, 1960.

Miller, William J., comp. "The Grand Campaign: A Journal of Operations in the Peninsula Campaign, March 17–August 26, 1862." In *The Peninsula Campaign of 1862: Yorktown to the Seven Days,* vol. 1, ed. William J. Miller, 177–205. Campbell, CA: Savas Woodbury, 1993.

Mitchell, Silas Weir. "Some Personal Recollections of the Civil War." *Transactions of the College of Physicians of Philadelphia,* 3rd series, 27 (1905); reprint, *Journal of Civil War Medicine* 1 (May–June 1997): 5–7.

Mitchell, Silas Weir, George Read Morehouse, and William Williams Keen. *Gunshot Wounds and Other Injuries of Nerves.* Philadelphia: Lippincott, 1864; reprint, San Francisco: Norman, 1989.

Mohr, Clarence L. "The Atlanta Campaign and the African American Experience in Civil War Georgia." In *Inside the Confederate Nation: Essays in Honor of Emory M. Thomas,* ed. Lesley J. Gordon and John C. Inscoe, 272–294. Baton Rouge: Louisiana State University Press, 2005.

"Monument to Capt. Sally Tompkins." *Confederate Veteran* 33 (July 1925): 248.

Moone, Debby. "Artifact Under Exam: Wooden Stretcher Bed." *Surgeon's Call* 3 (March 1998): 2, 10.

Moore, Jerrold Northrop. *Confederate Commissary General: Lucius Bellinger Northrop and the Subsistence Bureau of the Southern Army.* Shippensburg, PA: White Mane, 1996.

Moore, Samuel P. "Instructions Relative to Vaccination." (July 1, 1863). SC 330, folder 2. Manuscripts Department, Abraham Lincoln Presidential Library, Springfield, Illinois.

Morris, Roy, Jr. *The Better Angel: Walt Whitman in the Civil War.* New York: Oxford University Press, 2000.

Murphy, Lawrence R. "The Enemy Among Us: Venereal Disease among Union Soldiers in the Far West, 1861–1865." *Civil War History* 31 (September 1985): 257–269.

Myers, Robert Manson, ed. *Children of Pride: A True Story of Georgia and the Civil War.* New Haven, CT: Yale University Press, 1972.

Nightingale, Florence. *Notes on Nursing: What It Is and What It Is Not.* New York: D. Appleton, 1860; reprint, Mineola, NY: Dover, 1969.

Numbers, Ronald L., ed. *The Education of American Physicians: Historical Essays.* Berkeley: University of California Press, 1980.

Oates, Stephen B. *A Woman of Valor: Clara Barton and the Civil War.* New York: Free Press, 1994.

Obituary, "Deering J. Roberts." *Confederate Veteran* 33 (June 1925): 228.

Obituary, "Dr. E.A. Flewellen." *Confederate Veteran* 20 (January 1912): 33.

Olson, Kenneth E. *Music and Musket: Bands and Bandsmen of the American Civil War.* Westport, CT: Greenwood, 1991.

Parrish, William E. "The Western Sanitary Commission." *Civil War History* 36 (March 1990): 17–35.

Pember, Phoebe Yates. *A Southern Woman's Story: Life in Confederate Richmond.* 1879; reprint, ed. Bell Irvin Wiley. Jackson, TN: McCowat-Mercer, 1959; reprint, Covington, GA: Mockingbird, 1974.

Pfanz, Donald C. *Richard S. Ewell: A Soldier's Life.* Chapel Hill: University of North Carolina Press, 1998.

Phalen, James M. "Clement Alexander Finley." *Army Medical Bulletin* 52 (April 1940): 38–41.

———. "Joseph K. Barnes." *Army Medical Bulletin* 52 (April 1940): 47–51.

———. "Thomas Lawson." *Army Medical Bulletin* 52 (April 1940): 33–37.

Porcher, Francis Peyre. *Resources of the Southern Fields and Forests, Medical, Economical and Agricultural: Being Also a Medical Botany of the Confederate States; with Practical Information of the Useful Properties of Trees, Plants, and Shrubs.* Charleston, SC: Evans and Cogswell, 1863; reprint, San Francisco: Norman, 1991.

Pryor, Elizabeth Brown. *Clara Barton, Professional Angel.* Philadelphia: University of Pennsylvania Press, 1987.

Quintard, Charles Todd. *Doctor Quintard, Chaplain C.S.A. and Second Bishop of Tennessee: The Memoir and Civil War Diary of Charles Todd Quintard.* Sewanee, TN: University Press of Sewanee, 1905; reprint, ed. Sam Davis Elliott. Baton Rouge: Louisiana State University Press, 2003.

Rable, George C. *Fredericksburg! Fredericksburg!* Chapel Hill: University of North Carolina Press, 2002.

Raney, David A. "In the Lord's Army: The United States Christian Commission, Soldiers, and the Union War Effort." In *Union Soldiers and the Northern Home Front: Wartime Experiences, Postwar Adjustments,* ed. Paul A. Cimbala and Randall M. Miller, 263–292. New York: Fordham University Press, 2002.

Reed, Harry. "A Hand to Hold While Dying: Dr. Charles A. Leale at Lincoln's Side." *Lincoln Herald* 79 (Spring 1977): 21–26.

Regulations for the Army of the Confederate States, 1862. Richmond, VA: J.W. Randolph, 1862; reprint, San Francisco: Norman, 1992.

Regulations for the Medical Department of the Confederate States Army. Richmond: Richie and Dunnavant, 1863.

Reilly, Philip R. *Abraham Lincoln's DNA and Other Adventures in Genetics.* Cold Spring Harbor, NY: Cold Spring Harbor Laboratory Press, 2000.

Riley, Harris D., Jr. "Jefferson Davis and His Health, Part I: June, 1808–December, 1860." *Mississippi History* 49 (August 1987): 179–202.

———. "Jefferson Davis and His Health, Part II: January, 1861–December, 1889." *Mississippi History* 49 (November 1987): 261–287.

Robertson, James I. "The Scourge of Elmira." *Civil War History* 8, no. 2 (1962): 80–97; reprint, *Civil War Prisons,* ed. William B. Hesseltine. Kent, OH: Kent State University Press, 1972.

———. *Soldiers Blue and Gray.* Columbia: University of South Carolina Press, 1988.

———. *Stonewall Jackson: The Man, the Soldier, the Legend.* New York: Macmillan, 1997.

Roca, Steven Louis. "Presence and Precedents: The USS *Red Rover* During the American Civil War, 1861–1865." *Civil War History* 44 (June 1998): 91–110.

Rokicki, Ryan. "Artifact Under Exam: Adhesive Plaster: The Sticky Bandage." *Surgeon's Call* 8 (Spring 2003): 15.

Roper, John Herbert, ed. *Repairing the "March of Mars": The Civil War Diaries of John Samuel Apperson, Hospital Steward in the Stonewall Brigade, 1861–1865.* Macon, GA: Mercer University Press, 2001.

Rosenberg, Charles E. *The Care of Strangers: The Rise of America's Hospital System.* New York: Basic Books, 1987.

Rutkow, Ira M. *Bleeding Blue and Gray: Civil War Surgery and the Evolution of American Medicine.* New York: Random, 2005.

Rybczynski, Witold. *A Clearing in the Distance: Frederick Law Olmsted and America in the 19th Century.* New York: Scribner, 1999.

Sabine, David B. "Captain Sally Tompkins." *Civil War Times Illustrated* 4 (November 1965): 36–39.

Sanders, Charles W., Jr. *While in the Hands of the Enemy: Military Prisons of the Civil War.* Baton Rouge: Louisiana State University Press, 2005.

Savitt, Todd L. *Medicine and Slavery: The Diseases and Health Care of Blacks in Antebellum Virginia.* Urbana: University of Illinois Press, 1978.

Schroeder, Glenna R. "The Civil War Diary of Chaplain Stephen C. Bowers." *Indiana Magazine of History* 79 (June 1983): 167–185.

Schroeder-Lein, Glenna R. *Confederate Hospitals on the Move: Samuel H. Stout and the Army of Tennessee.* Columbia: University of South Carolina Press, 1994.

———. "'While the Participants Are Yet Alive': The Association of Medical Officers of the Army and Navy of the Confederacy." In *Inside the Confederate Nation: Essays in Honor of Emory M. Thomas,* ed. Lesley J. Gordon and John C. Inscoe, 335–348. Baton Rouge: Louisiana State University Press, 2005.

Schroeder-Lein, Glenna R., and Richard Zuczek. *Andrew Johnson: A Biographical Companion.* Santa Barbara, CA: ABC-Clio, 2001.

Schultz, Jane E. "Between Scylla and Charybdis: Clara Barton's Wartime Odyssey." *Minerva: Quarterly Report on Women and the Military* 14 (Fall–Winter 1996): 45–68.

———. *Women at the Front: Hospital Workers in Civil War America.* Chapel Hill: University of North Carolina Press, 2004.

Schwartz, Gerald, ed. *A Woman Doctor's Civil War: Esther Hill Hawks' Diary.* Columbia: University of South Carolina Press, 1984, 1989.

Sears, Stephen W. *Landscape Turned Red: The Battle of Antietam.* New Haven, CT: Ticknor and Fields, 1983.

Shaw, Maurice F. *Stonewall Jackson's Surgeon Hunter Holmes McGuire: A Biography.* Lynchburg, VA: H.E. Howard, 1993.

Sheldon, George. *When the Smoke Cleared at Gettysburg: The Tragic Aftermath of the Bloodiest Battle of the Civil War.* Nashville, TN: Cumberland House, 2003.

Shenk, Joshua Wolf. *Lincoln's Melancholy: How Depression Challenged a President and Fueled His Greatness.* Boston: Houghton Mifflin, 2005.

Shutes, Milton H. *Lincoln and the Doctors: A Medical Narrative of the Life of Abraham Lincoln.* New York: Pioneer, 1933.

Slawson, Robert G. *Prologue to Change: African Americans in Medicine in the Civil War Era.* Frederick, MD: NMCWM Press, 2006.

Smith, George Winston. *Medicines for the Union Army: The United States Army Laboratories During the Civil War*. Madison, WI: American Institute for the History of Pharmacy, 1962; reprint, New York: Pharmaceutical Products Press, 2001.

Smith, Jennifer Lund. "The Reconstruction of 'Home': The Civil War and the Marriage of Lawrence and Fannie Chamberlain." In *Intimate Strategies of the Civil War: Military Commanders and Their Wives*, ed. Carol K. Bleser and Lesley J. Gordon, 157–177. New York: Oxford University Press, 2001.

Smith, Mrs. S.E.D. *The Soldier's Friend: Being a Thrilling Narrative of Grandma Smith's Four Years Experience and Observations, as Matron, in the Hospitals of the South . . .* Memphis, TN: Bulletin Publishing, 1867.

Smith, Timothy B. *The Untold Story of Shiloh: The Battle and the Battlefield*. Knoxville: University of Tennessee Press, 2006.

Southern Practitioner 22–39 (1900–1917).

Spielman, Andrew, and Michael D'Antonio. *Mosquito: The Story of Man's Deadliest Foe*. New York: Hyperion, 2001.

Steiner, Paul E. *Disease in the Civil War: Natural Biological Warfare in 1861–1865*. Springfield, IL: C.C. Thomas, 1968.

Stern, Madeline B. *Louisa May Alcott: A Biography*. Norman: University of Oklahoma Press, 1950, 1978; reprint, New York: Random, 1996.

Stout, Samuel H. "On the Best Models and Most Easily Constructed Military Hospital Wards for Temporary Use in War." *Transactions of the International Medical Congress*, 9th session, vol. 2 (1887): 88–91.

Street, James, Jr. "Under the Influence: Did Civil War Soldiers Depend on Drugs and Alcohol?" *Civil War Times Illustrated* 27 (May 1988): 30–35.

Strong, George Templeton. *Diary of the Civil War, 1860–1865*, ed. Allan Nevins. New York: Macmillan, 1962.

"Study Traces Gene Defect in Abe's Family." *Springfield (IL) State Journal-Register*, November 2, 1994, 10.

Swanberg, W.A. *Sickles the Incredible*. New York: Scribners', 1956.

Taylor, Lenette S. *"The Supply for Tomorrow Must Not Fail": The Civil War of Captain Simon Perkins Jr., a Union Quartermaster*. Kent, OH: Kent State University Press, 2004.

Taylor, William. "Conservatism in Army Surgery: Some Field Reminiscences." *Southern Practitioner* 27 (November 1905): 625–628.

Temple, Wayne C. "Jane Currie Blaikie Hoge." In *Notable American Women, 1607–1950: A Biographical Dictionary*, ed. Edward T. James et al. Cambridge, MA: Belknap Press of Harvard University Press, 1971.

Thomas, Emory M. *The Confederate State of Richmond: A Biography of the Capital*. Austin: University of Texas Press, 1971.

———. *Robert E. Lee: A Biography*. New York: Norton, 1995.

Thompson, William T. "Sanitary Fairs of the Civil War." *Civil War History* 4 (March 1958): 51–67.

Tombstone, Edward A. Flewellen, Glenwood Cemetery, Thomaston, Georgia.

Tripler, Charles Stuart and George Curtis Blackman. *Handbook for the Military Surgeon*. Cincinnati: R. Clarke, 1861; reprint, San Francisco: Norman, 1989.

Tripler, Eunice. *Some Notes of Her Personal Recollections*. New York: Grafton, 1910.

Trulock, Alice Rains. *In the Hands of Providence: Joshua L. Chamberlain and the American Civil War*. Chapel Hill: University of North Carolina Press, 1992.

United States Census, 1850, Alabama, Mobile, Mobile, 653.

United States Census, 1860, District of Columbia, Washington, 1st Ward, 209.

United States Census, 1870, New Mexico, Santa Fe, Santa Fe, 3rd Precinct, 349.

United States Census, 1880, Pennsylvania, Philadelphia, Philadelphia, 448C.

Venet, Wendy Hamand. "The Emergence of a Suffragist: Mary Livermore, Civil War Activism, and the Moral Power of Women." *Civil War History* 48 (June 2002): 143–164.

Waddell, Ronald. "Ships of War—Ships of Hope: The Women and Their Hospital Ships in the Mississippi Valley Campaigns of the Civil War." *Journal of Women's Civil War History* 2 (2002): 86–119.

Waitt, Robert W., Jr. *Confederate Military Hospitals in Richmond.* Richmond, VA: Richmond Civil War Centennial Committee, 1964.

Walker, Dale L. *Mary Edwards Walker: Above and Beyond.* New York: Forge, 2005.

The War of the Rebellion: A Compilation of the Official Records of the Union and Confederate Armies. Washington, DC: Government Printing Office, 1880–1901.

Wegner, Ansley Herring. *Phantom Pain: North Carolina's Artificial Limbs Program for Confederate Veterans.* Raleigh: Office of Archives and History, North Carolina Department of Cultural Resources, 2004.

Weigley, Russell F. *Quartermaster General of the Union Army: A Biography of M.C. Meigs.* New York: Columbia University Press, 1959.

Weisberg, Barbara. *Talking to the Dead: Kate and Maggie Fox and the Rise of Spiritualism.* San Francisco: HarperSanFrancisco, 2004.

Welsh, Jack D. *Medical Histories of Confederate Generals.* Kent, OH: Kent State University Press, 1995.

———. *Medical Histories of Union Generals.* Kent, OH: Kent State University Press, 1996.

———. *Two Confederate Hospitals and Their Patients, Atlanta to Opelika.* Macon, GA: Mercer University Press, 2005.

Welsh, Jack D., and Thomas P. Lowry. "Chronic Diarrhea During and After the Civil War: Post-Gastroenteritis Chronic Diarrhea." *Journal of Civil War Medicine* 6 (October–December 2002): 118–120.

Whitman, Walt. *Memoranda During the War.* 1875; reprint, Boston: Applewood, 1990.

Who Was Who in America: Historical Volume, 1607–1896. Chicago: Marquis, 1963.

Widney, John A. Unpublished diaries, 1862–1865. SC 1653. Manuscripts Department, Abraham Lincoln Presidential Library, Springfield, IL.

Wiley, Bell Irvin. *The Life of Billy Yank: The Common Soldier of the Union.* Garden City, NY: Doubleday, 1952, 1971.

———. *The Life of Johnny Reb: The Common Soldier of the Confederacy.* Garden City, NY: Doubleday, 1943, 1971.

Wilson, Harold S. *Confederate Industry: Manufacturers and Quartermasters in the Civil War.* Jackson: University Press of Mississippi, 2002.

Winters, William. *The Musick of the Mocking Birds, the Roar of the Cannon: The Civil War Diary and Letters of William Winters,* ed. Steven E. Woodworth. Lincoln: University of Nebraska Press, 1998.

Wise, Stephen R. *Lifeline of the Confederacy: Blockade Running During the Civil War.* Columbia: University of South Carolina Press, 1988.

Wittenmyer, Annie. *Under the Guns: A Woman's Reminiscences of the Civil War.* Boston: E.B. Stillings, 1895.

Wood, Thomas Fanning. *Doctor to the Front: The Recollections of Confederate Surgeon Thomas Fanning Wood, 1861–1865,* ed. Donald B. Koonce. Knoxville: University of Tennessee Press, 2000.

Woodward, C. Vann, ed. *Mary Chesnut's Civil War.* New Haven, CT: Yale University Press, 1981.

Woodward, Joseph Janvier. *The Hospital Steward's Manual: for the Instruction of Hospital Stewards, Ward-Masters, and Attendants, in Their Several Duties.* Philadelphia: J.B. Lippincott, 1862; reprint, San Francisco: Norman, 1991.

———. *Outlines of the Chief Camp Diseases of the United States Armies, As Observed During the Present War.* Philadelphia: J.B. Lippincott, 1863; reprint, San Francisco: Norman, 1992.

Woodworth, Steven E., ed. *Civil War Generals in Defeat.* Lawrence, KS: University Press of Kansas, 1999.

———. "When Merit Was Not Enough: Albert Sidney Johnston and Confederate Defeat in the West, 1862." In *Civil War Generals in Defeat,* ed. Steven E. Woodworth, 9–27. Lawrence: University Press of Kansas, 1999.

———. *While God Is Marching On: The Religious World of Civil War Soldiers.* Lawrence: University Press of Kansas, 2001.

Woolsey, Jane Stuart. *Hospital Days: Reminiscence of a Civil War Nurse.* 1868; reprint, Roseville, MN: Edinborough, 1996, 2001.

❦ INDEX ❧

O

Rain, 274, 288
Randolph, Mrs. George W., 242
Rank, of army officers, 227
    of medical officers, 292, 317
Rapier, John, 47
Rappahannock River, 113–14
Rash, 200–1
Rations, 203, 304
    cooked, 90, 194, 262
    lack of variety in, 89, 119
    monetary value of, 140–41
    not eaten, 140
    of alcohol, 3, 5
    poor quality of, 89–90, 119, 125
    reduced, 90
    shortages of, 89
    standard amounts of, 89–90, 125, 140
    three-days, 194
Rats, stewed, 89
Rebels at Rock Island (McAdams), 133
Receipts, 255–56
Recipes, for special diets, 74, 88, 346
Recollections of a Rebel Surgeon (Daniel), 130
Records, British medical, 141
    Confederate, destruction of, 24, 143–45, 176
    errors in, 219, 288
    medical, 124, 141–43, 147, 153, 227, 282, 284, 309
        poorly kept, 345
        sale of, 284
    of hospital property, 329
    of supplies, 210, 255, 282
"Records, Recollections, and Reminiscences," of Confederate physicians, 280
Recruits, 305, 309, 322
    rejection of, 265, 307
Red River Campaign, 319
Red Rover (ship), 145–46, **318–19**
    statistics, 319
Red tape, 255, 316
Reeder, Andrew H., 124
Reflux esophagitis, 166
Reforms, medical, 38, 43, 124, 238
    resistance to, 54
Refugees, 242, 267, 327, 334
Register, of patients, 293
Regulations
    hospital, 282, 293, 297
    medical, 291

Regulations *(continued)*
    military, 227, 270, 291, 297, 305–6
    of Confederate medical department, 70, 88
Regulations for the Medical Department of the Confederate States Army, 88
Relief efforts
    by civilians, 37–38, 54, 269–70, 313–16
    by women, 37–39, 88, 134, 229, 231, 269–70, 273, 313, 315–16
Relief workers, independent, 37–38
Religious counsel, 64, 233, 313–14, 317
Religious literature, 313–14, 317
Repairing the "March of Mars" (Roper), 131–32
Reports, 210, 237, 315–16
    daily, 293
    erroneous, 246
    inspection, 163
    medical, 141–43, 147, 291, 298
    monthly, 142, 202, 210, 293
    morning, 142, 172
    statistical, 201, 210, 297
    weekly, 293
Reprints, of Civil War books, 131
Republican convention (1860), 190
Republican Party, 187
Requisitions, for supplies, 18
Resaca, GA, 66, 226
Researchers, 123, 173, 215, 248–49
Resection, 17, 112, 121, 214, **261–62**, 280
    mortality from, 261
Reserve surgical corps, **262–63**
Resignation, 228
Resorts, as hospitals, 139
Resources of the Southern Fields and Forests (Porcher), 129, 208, 217, 249, **263–64**, 290
Respiratory illnesses, 48
Rest, 323
Rest facilities, for soldiers in transit, 159
Restlessness, 240, 250, 279
Retaliation, 98
Revaccination, 278, 321
Reveille, 298
Revivals, 81
Revolutionary War, 63, 170
Reynolds, John F., 116
Rheumatic fever, 128, 264–65, 348
    treatment of, 128

Strong, Ellen Ruggles, 286

Strong, George Templeton, 238, **286–87**, 315–16

Stuart, George H., 313

Stuart, James Ewell Brown (Jeb), 244

Stuart, John T., 187

Stump, of amputated limb, 16–17, 24, 30, 102–3, 136, 280

Subsistence department, 227, 254, **287–88**, 293, 304, 306

  statistics, 288

Substitutes

  for coffee, 91, 289

  for supplies, 129, **289**, 291

    botanical, 9, 50, 258, 289

Sudley Church, 53

Sugar, 90

Sugar cane, 289

Sugar of lead, 100

Suicide, 221, 250

Sulfa drugs, 248

Sulphate of iron, 27

Sulphate of lime, 26–27

Sulphate of magnesia, 300

Sulphur, 59–60

Sulphuric acid, 26

Sunday school, for slaves, 166

Sunken road (Fredericksburg), 113

Superintendents, women as, 88, 138

Supervision, medical, 291

  of hospitals, 207, 217, 292–94, 297–98

  of physicians, 291, 297

Supervisors, women, as, 196–97, 233, 235, 348

Supplies, 255, 297, 306

  abandonment of, 245–46

  barter for, 88, 150, 255

  capture of, 176, 218, 240, 274

  contracts for, 254

  damage to, 255

  delayed shipment of, 18–19, 24, 256, 284

  destruction of, 171, 245, 288–89

  distributed by civilians, 37–38, 44, 46, 313

  distributed by quartermasters, 254

  for Alabama soldiers, 137–38

  furnished by U.S. Christian Commission, 314

  furnished by U.S. Sanitary Commission, 315–17

  gathered by civilians, 259, 333

Supplies (*continued*)

  gathered by women, 74, 88, 114, 127, 134–35, 138, 148, 150, 190, 229, 303, 313, 315–17, 334, 337, 339–40, 342, 344, 347

  impressment of, 255

  medical, 32–33, 50, 262–63

    acquisition of, 210, 258

    as contraband of war, 50, 188–89, 217

    distribution of, 210–11

    guarding of, 211

    importation of, 210, 257

    manufacture of, 210

    purchase of, 210

    shortages of, 211

    storage of, 210–11

    transportation of, 211

  procurement of, 147, 153, 254–55, 293–94, 305, 317

  purchase of, 231, 254–55, 304, 317

  refill of, 205, 211, 316

  shortages of, 18–19, 24, 34, 38, 42–43, 45, 53, 56, 66–67, 72, 88–89, 117, 134, 137, 144, 150, 162, 185, 211, 227, 231, 245, 254, 256, 267, 284, 289, 316

    due to blockade, 49–50, 129, 249, 264, 288–89

    in hospitals, 141, 305

    in prisoner of war camps, 252

  stored, 38, 114, 138, 211, 255

  theft of, 228, 283

  transportation of, 254–56, 272–73

Supply table, 10, 58, 124, 175, 210, **290–91**, 300

Supply trains, 33, 117

  capture of, 56, 125

Surgeon general, xiv, 43, 83–84, 142, 163, 204, 206–8, 210, 216, 278, 290, **291–92**, 293, 297–98, 300, 346

  acting, 36, 84, 124, 216, 292

  Confederate, 83–84, 216–17, 283, 292

  duties of, 291

  to rank as brigadier general, 36, 204, 291

  Union, 35–36, 108, 123–24, 181, 184–85, 201, 204, 206, 208, 215, 291–92

Surgeon in charge, 112, 140–42, 152–53, 155, 158, 163, 180, 197, 204, 207, **292–93**, 294, 337

  duties of, 292–93

Surgeon in charge of hospitals, 297

Surgeon on call, 237

❧ ABOUT THE AUTHOR ❧

Glenna R. Schroeder-Lein, a California native, graduated from the University of Georgia with a PhD in history. She has taught as an adjunct at four colleges and universities. Formerly an assistant editor of *The Papers of Andrew Johnson,* she is presently manuscripts librarian at the Abraham Lincoln Presidential Library in Springfield, Illinois. Her published work includes *Confederate Hospitals on the Move: Samuel H. Stout and the Army of Tennessee* (1994); *Andrew Johnson: A Biographical Companion* (coauthor, 2001); and numerous journal articles and book reviews.